E-Business and E-Commerce Management

Strategy, Implementation and Practice

DAVE CHAFFEY

An imprint of Pearson Education
Harlow, England • London • New York • Boston • San Francisco • Toronto • Sydney • Singapore • Hong Kong
Tokyo • Seoul • Taipei • New Delhi • Cape Town • Madrid • Mexico City • Amsterdam • Munich • Paris • Milan

Pearson Education Limited
Edinburgh Gate
Harlow
Essex CM20 2JE
England

and Associated Companies throughout the world

Visit us on the World Wide Web at:
www.pearsoneduc.com

First published 2002

ISBN 0273 65188 9

British Library Cataloguing-in-Publication Data
A catalogue record for this book is available from the British Library

Library of Congress Cataloging-in-Publication Data
Chaffey, Dave, 1963–
E-business and e-commerce management: strategy, management, and applications/
Dave Chaffey.
p. cm.
Includes bibliographical references and index.
ISBN 0–273–65188–9 (pbk.)
1. Electronic commerce. 2. Business enterprises–Computer networks. I. Title: Ebusiness and ecommerce management. II. Title.

HF5548.32.C472 2002
658'.05–dc21

2001033041

10 9 8 7 6 5 4 3 2
06 05 04 03 02

Typeset in Great Britain by 3
Printed by Ashford Colour Press Ltd., Gosport

Brief contents

Contents

Preface

In 1849 a group of settlers travelling west towards the Promised Land, California, entered a then unnamed valley. The valley presented a harsh environment with a barrier of mountains to the west making the way forward unclear. Some of the settlers lost their lives as they sought to find a route west before eventually reaching California and what was to become one of the most prosperous places on Earth. As the group left the valley, one of the women in the group turned and said 'Goodbye Death Valley' and hence the valley got its name.

The route to e-business success is also not straightforward and similarly fraught with difficulties of selecting the correct strategic direction and surviving in an increasingly harsh competitive environment. Not all who follow the route survive. However, the competitive drivers to follow this route, such as demand from customers and adoption by competitors make this journey essential. The rewards are evident from those early adopters who identified the opportunity early and steered their companies in the right direction.

This book is intended to equip current and future managers with some of the knowledge and practical skills to help them navigate their organizations towards e-business.

A primary aim of this book is to identify and review the key management decisions required by organizations moving to e-business and consider the process by which these decisions can be taken. Key questions are: What approach to e-business strategy do we follow? How much do we need to invest in e-business? Which processes should be our e-business priorities? Should we adopt new business and revenue models? What are the main changes that need to be made to the organization to facilitate e-business?

Given the broad scope of e-business, this book takes an integrative approach drawing on new and existing approaches and models from many disciplines including information systems, strategy, marketing, supply and value chain management, operations and human resources management.

What is e-business management?

As we will see in Chapter 1, **electronic business (e-business)** is aimed at enhancing the competitiveness of an organization by deploying innovative information and communications technology throughout an organization and beyond, through links to partners and customers. It does not simply involve using technology to automate existing processes, but should also involve using technology to help change these processes. To be successful in managing e-business, a breadth of knowledge is needed of different business processes and activities from across the value chain such as marketing and sales, through new product development, manufacturing and inbound and outbound logistics. Organizations also need to manage the change required by new processes and technology through what have traditionally been support activities such as human resources management.

Electronic business (e-business)

All electronically mediated information exchanges, both within an organization and with external stakeholders supporting the range of business processes.

From this definition, it is apparent that e-business involves looking at how electronic communications can be used to enhance all aspects of an organization's **supply chain management**. It also involves optimizing an organization's **value chain**, a related concept that describes the different value-adding activities that connect a company's supply side with its demand side. The e-business era also involves management of a network of interrelated value chains or **value networks**.

Supply chain management
The coordination of all supply activities of an organization from its suppliers and partners to its customers.

Value chain
A model for analysis of how supply chain activities can add value to products and services delivered to the customer.

Value networks
The links between an organization and its strategic and non-strategic partners that form its external value chain.

Electronic commerce (e-commerce)
All electronically mediated information exchanges between an organization and its external stakeholders.

Sell-side e-commerce
E-commerce transactions between an organization and its customers.

Buy-side e-commerce
E-commerce transactions between an organization and its suppliers and other partners.

What is e-commerce management?

To this point we have exclusively used the term 'e-business', but what of 'e-commerce'? Both these terms are applied in a variety of ways; to some they mean the same, to others they are quite different. As explained in Chapter 1, what is most important is that they are applied consistently within organizations so that employees and external stakeholders are clear about how the organization can exploit electronic communications. The distinction made in this book is to use **electronic commerce (e-commerce)** to refer to all types of electronic transactions between organizations and stakeholders whether they are financial transactions or exchanges of information or other services. These e-commerce transactions are either **buy-side e-commerce** or **sell-side e-commerce** and the management issues involved with each aspect are considered separately in Part 2 of the book. E-business is applied as a broader term encompassing e-commerce but also including all electronic transactions within an organization.

Management of e-commerce involves prioritizing buy-side and sell-side activities and putting in place the plans and resources to deliver the identified benefits. These plans need to focus on management of the many risks to success, some of which you may have experienced when using e-commerce sites; from technical problems such as transactions that fail, sites that are difficult to use or are too slow, through to problems with customer service or fulfilment, which also indicate failure of management.

How is this book structured?

The overall structure of the book shown in *Figure P.1* follows a logical sequence: introducing e-business terms, concepts and history of development in Part 1; reviewing alternative strategic approaches and applications of e-business in Part 2 and how strategy can be implemented in Part 3. Within this overall structure, differences in how electronic communications are used to support different business processes are considered separately. This is achieved by distinguishing between how electronic communications are used, from buy-side e-commerce aspects of supply chain management in Chapters 6 and 7, to the marketing perspective of sell-side e-commerce in Chapters 8 and 9. Figure P.1 shows the emphasis of perspective for the particular chapters.

Part 1: Introduction (Chapters 1–4)

Part 1 introduces e-business and e-commerce. It seeks to clarify basic terms and concepts by looking at different interpretations of terms and applications through case studies.

- *Chapter 1: Introduction to e-business and e-commerce.* Definition of the meaning and scope of e-business and e-commerce. Introduction to business use of the

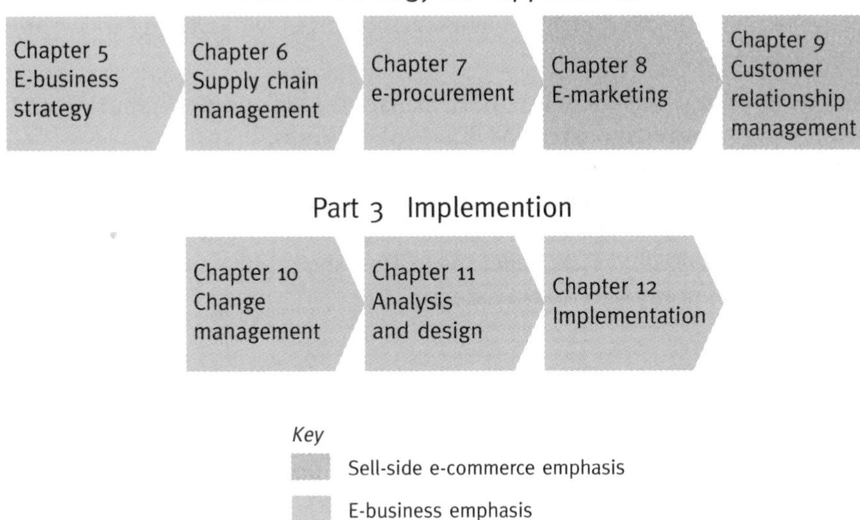

Figure P.1 Structure of the book

Internet – what are the benefits and barriers to adoption and how widely used is it?

- *Chapter 2: E-commerce fundamentals.* Introduction to new business models and marketplace structures enabled by electronic communications.
- *Chapter 3: E-business infrastructure.* Background on the hardware, software and telecommunications that need to be managed to achieve e-business.
- *Chapter 4: E-environment.* Describes the macro-environment of an organization that presents opportunities and constraints on strategy and implementation.

Part 2: Strategy and applications (Chapters 5–9)

In Part 2 of the book approaches to developing e-business strategy and applications are reviewed for the organization as a whole (Chapter 5) and with an emphasis on buy-side e-commerce (Chapters 6 and 7) and sell-side e-commerce (Chapters 7 and 8).

- *Chapter 5: E-business strategy.* Approaches to developing e-business strategy. Differences from traditional strategic approaches. Relation to IS strategy.
- *Chapter 6: Supply chain management.* A supply chain perspective on strategy with examples of how technology can be applied to increase supply chain and value chain efficiency.
- *Chapter 7: E-procurement.* Evaluation of the benefits and practical issues of adopting e-procurement.

- *Chapter 8: E-marketing.* A sell-side e-commerce perspective to e-business, reviewing differences in marketing required through digital media. Structured around developing an e-marketing plan.
- *Chapter 9: Customer relationship management.* Reviews marketing techniques that apply e-commerce for acquiring and retaining customers.

Part 3: Implementation (Chapters 10–12)

Management of e-business implementation is described in Part 3 of the book in which we examine practical management issues involved with creating and maintaining e-business solutions.

- *Chapter 10: Change management.* How to manage the organizational, human and technology changes required in the move to e-business.
- *Chapter 11: Analysis and design.* We discuss the main issues of analysis and design raised by e-commerce systems that need to be discussed by managers and solutions providers.
- *Chapter 12: Implementation and maintenance.* How should e-commerce systems be managed and monitored once they are live?

Who should use this book?

Students

This book has been created as the main student text for undergraduate and postgraduate students taking specialist marketing courses or modules which cover e-business, e-commerce or e-marketing. The book is relevant to students who are:

- *undergraduates on business programmes* which include modules on the use of the Internet and e-commerce. This includes specialist degrees such as electronic business, electronic commerce, Internet marketing and marketing or general business degrees such as business studies and business administration and business management;
- *undergraduate project students* who select this topic for final year projects / dissertations – this book is an excellent source of resources for these students;
- *undergraduates completing work placement* involved with different aspects of e-business such as managing the intranet or company web site;
- *postgraduates students on specialist masters degrees in electronic commerce, electronic business or e-marketing and generic MBA, Certificate in Management, Diploma in Management Studies* which involve modules or electives for electronic commerce and digital marketing.

What does the book offer to lecturers teaching these courses?

The book is intended to be a comprehensive guide to all aspects of deploying e-business and e-commerce within an organization. The book builds on existing theories and concepts and questions the validity of these models in the light of the differences between the Internet and other media. The book references the emerging body of literature specific to e-business, e-commerce and e-marketing. As such, it can be used across several modules. Lecturers will find the book has a good range of case studies, activities and exercises to support their teaching. These activities assist in using the book for student-centred learning as part of directed study. Web links given in the text and at the end of each chapter highlight key information sources for particular topics.

Practitioners

There is also much of relevance in this book for the industry professional including:

- *Senior managers and directors* seeking to apply the right e-business and e-commerce approaches to benefit their organization.
- *Information systems managers* who are developing and implementing e-business and e-commerce strategies.
- *Marketing managers* responsible for defining an e-marketing strategy and implementing and maintaining the company web site.
- *Supply chain, logistics and procurement managers* wanting to see examples of best practice in using e-commerce for supply chain management.
- *Technical project managers or web masters* who may understand the technical details of building a site, but have a limited knowledge of business or marketing fundamentals.

Student learning features

A range of features have been incorporated into this book to help the reader get the most out of it. They have been designed to assist understanding, reinforce learning and help readers find information easily. The features are described in the order you will encounter them.

At the start of each chapter

- *Learning objectives*: a list describing what readers can learn through reading the chapter and completing the activities.
- *Management issues*: a summary of main issues or decisions faced by managers related to the Chapter topic area.
- *Chapter at a glance*: a list of main topics, focus on topics and case studies.
- *Links to other chapters*: a summary of related topics in other chapters.
- *Introductions*: succinct summaries of the relevance of the topic to marketing students and practitioners together with content and structure.

In each chapter:

- *Activities*: Short activities in the main text that develop concepts and understanding often by relating to student experience or through reference to web sites. Model answers are provided to activities at the end of the chapter where applicable.
- *Case studies*: real-world examples of issues facing companies that implement e-business. Questions at the end of the case study highlight the main learning points from each case study.
- *Running case studies*: The B2B Company and The B2C Company. These two cases are used throughout the book in activities to encourage students to think about solutions to commonly faced management decisions related to a

Guided tour

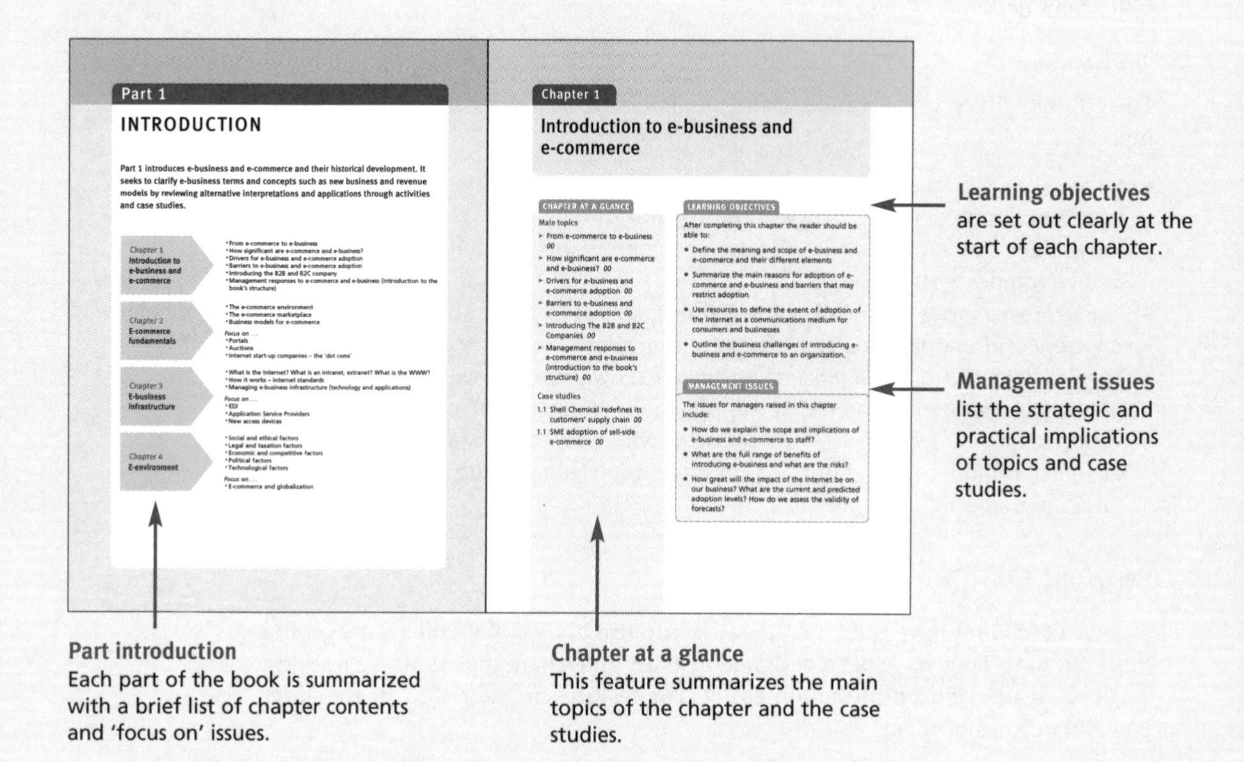

Part 1
INTRODUCTION
Part 1 introduces e-business and e-commerce and their historical development. It seeks to clarify e-business terms and concepts such as new business and revenue models by reviewing alternative interpretations and applications through activities and case studies.
Chapter 1 Introduction to e-business and e-commerce
• From e-commerce to e-business
• How significant are e-commerce and e-business?
• Drivers for e-business and e-commerce adoption
• Barriers to e-business and e-commerce adoption
• Introducing the B2B and B2C company
• Management responses to e-commerce and e-business (introduction to the book's structure)
Chapter 2 E-commerce fundamentals
• The e-commerce environment
• The e-commerce marketplace
• Business models for e-commerce
Focus on ...
• Portals
• Auctions
• Internet start-up companies – the 'dot coms'
Chapter 3 E-business infrastructure
• What is the Internet? What is an intranet, extranet? What is the WWW?
• How it works – Internet standards
• Managing e-business infrastructure (technology and applications)
Focus on ...
• EDI
• Application Service Providers
• New access devices
Chapter 4 E-environment
• Social and ethical factors
• Legal and taxation factors
• Economic and competitive factors
• Political factors
• Technological factors
Focus on ...
• E-commerce and globalization
Chapter 1
Introduction to e-business and e-commerce
CHAPTER AT A GLANCE
Main topics
➤ From e-commerce to e-business 00
➤ How significant are e-commerce and e-business? 00
➤ Drivers for e-business and e-commerce adoption 00
➤ Barriers to e-business and e-commerce adoption 00
➤ Introducing The B2B and B2C Companies 00
➤ Management responses to e-commerce and e-business (introduction to the book's structure) 00
Case studies
1.1 Shell Chemical redefines its customers' supply chain 00
1.1 SME adoption of sell-side e-commerce 00
LEARNING OBJECTIVES
After completing this chapter the reader should be able to:
• Define the meaning and scope of e-business and e-commerce and their different elements
• Summarize the main reasons for adoption of e-commerce and e-business and barriers that may restrict adoption
• Use resources to define the extent of adoption of the Internet as a communications medium for consumers and businesses
• Outline the business challenges of introducing e-business and e-commerce to an organization.
MANAGEMENT ISSUES
The issues for managers raised in this chapter include:
• How do we explain the scope and implications of e-business and e-commerce to staff?
• What are the full range of benefits of introducing e-business and what are the risks?
• How great will the impact of the Internet be on our business? What are the current and predicted adoption levels? How do we assess the validity of forecasts?

Learning objectives are set out clearly at the start of each chapter.

Management issues list the strategic and practical implications of topics and case studies.

Part introduction
Each part of the book is summarized with a brief list of chapter contents and 'focus on' issues.

Chapter at a glance
This feature summarizes the main topics of the chapter and the case studies.

Links to other chapters
This drag and drop style feature highlights the connections between chapters.

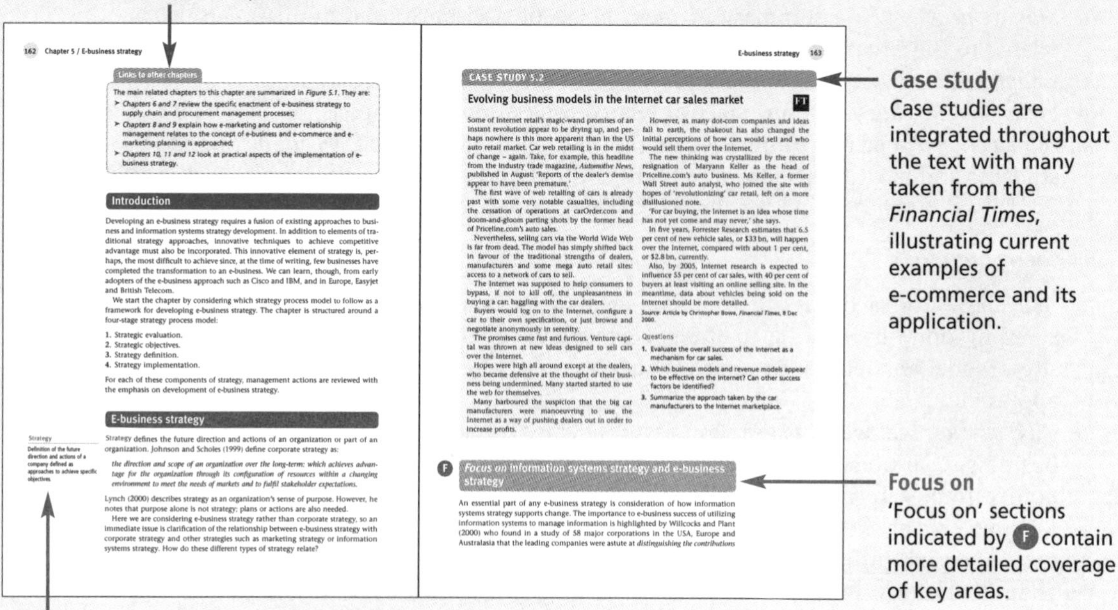

162 Chapter 5 / E-business strategy
Links to other chapters
The main related chapters to this chapter are summarized in Figure 5.1. They are:
➤ Chapters 6 and 7 review the specific enactment of e-business strategy to supply chain and procurement management processes;
➤ Chapters 8 and 9 explain how e-marketing and customer relationship management relates to the concept of e-business and e-commerce and e-marketing planning is approached;
➤ Chapters 10, 11 and 12 look at practical aspects of the implementation of e-business strategy.
Introduction
E-business strategy
Strategy
E-business strategy 163
CASE STUDY 5.2
Evolving business models in the Internet car sales market
Questions
1. Evaluate the overall success of the Internet as a mechanism for car sales.
2. Which business models and revenue models appear to be effective on the Internet? Can other success factors be identified?
3. Summarize the approach taken by the car manufacturers to the Internet marketplace.
Focus on information systems strategy and e-business strategy

Case study
Case studies are integrated throughout the text with many taken from the *Financial Times*, illustrating current examples of e-commerce and its application.

Focus on
'Focus on' sections indicated by (F) contain more detailed coverage of key areas.

Key terms
are explained through the text in a margin glossary.

Exercises
At the end of each chapter, self-assessment, essay and discussion and examination questions test students' knowledge.

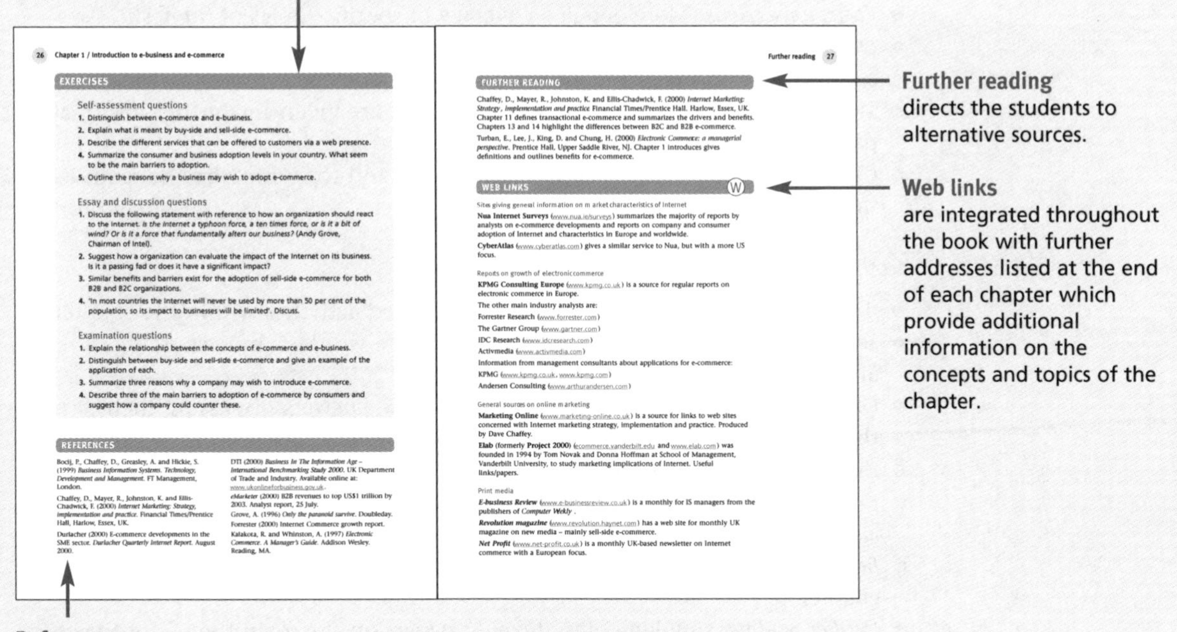

26 Chapter 1 / Introduction to e-business and e-commerce

EXERCISES

Self-assessment questions

1. Distinguish between e-commerce and e-business.
2. Explain what is meant by buy-side and sell-side e-commerce.
3. Describe the different services that can be offered to customers via a web presence.
4. Summarize the consumer and business adoption levels in your country. What seem to be the main barriers to adoption.
5. Outline the reasons why a business may wish to adopt e-commerce.

Essay and discussion questions

1. Discuss the following statement with reference to how an organization should react to the Internet. *Is the Internet a typhoon force, a ten times force, or is it a bit of wind? Or is it a force that fundamentally alters our business?* (Andy Grove, Chairman of Intel).
2. Suggest how a organization can evaluate the impact of the Internet on its business. Is it a passing fad or does it have a significant impact?
3. Similar benefits and barriers exist for the adoption of sell-side e-commerce for both B2B and B2C organizations.
4. 'In most countries the Internet will never be used by more than 50 per cent of the population, so its impact to businesses will be limited'. Discuss.

Examination questions

1. Explain the relationship between the concepts of e-commerce and e-business.
2. Distinguish between buy-side and sell-side e-commerce and give an example of the application of each.
3. Summarize three reasons why a company may wish to introduce e-commerce.
4. Describe three of the main barriers to adoption of e-commerce by consumers and suggest how a company could counter these.

REFERENCES

Bocij, P., Chaffey, D., Greasley, A. and Hickie, S. (1999) *Business Information Systems. Technology, Development and Management.* FT Management, London.

Chaffey, D., Mayer, R., Johnston, K. and Ellis-Chadwick, F. (2000) *Internet Marketing: Strategy, implementation and practice.* Financial Times/Prentice Hall, Harlow, Essex, UK.

Durlacher (2000) E-commerce developments in the SME sector. *Durlacher Quarterly Internet Report.* August 2000.

DTI (2000) *Business In The Information Age – International Benchmarking Study 2000.* UK Department of Trade and Industry. Available online at: www.ukonlineforbusiness.gov.uk.

eMarketer (2000) B2B revenues to top US$1 trillion by 2003. Analyst report, 25 July.

Grove, A. (1996) *Only the paranoid survive.* Doubleday.

Forrester (2000) Internet Commerce growth report.

Kalakota, R. and Whinston, A. (1997) *Electronic Commerce. A Manager's Guide.* Addison Wesley. Reading, MA.

Further reading 27

FURTHER READING

Chaffey, D., Mayer, R., Johnston, K. and Ellis-Chadwick, F. (2000) *Internet Marketing: Strategy, implementation and practice* Financial Times/Prentice Hall. Harlow, Essex, UK. Chapter 11 defines transactional e-commerce and summarizes the drivers and benefits. Chapters 13 and 14 highlight the differences between B2C and B2B e-commerce.

Turban, E., Lee, J., King, D. and Chung, H. (2000) *Electronic Commerce: a managerial perspective*. Prentice Hall, Upper Saddle River, NJ. Chapter 1 introduces gives definitions and outlines benefits for e-commerce.

WEB LINKS (W)

Sites giving general information on market characteristics of Internet

Nua Internet Surveys (www.nua.ie/surveys) summarizes the majority of reports by analysts on e-commerce developments and reports on company and consumer adoption of Internet and characteristics in Europe and worldwide.

CyberAtlas (www.cyberatlas.com) gives a similar service to Nua, but with a more US focus.

Reports on growth of electronic commerce

KPMG Consulting Europe (www.kpmg.co.uk) is a source for regular reports on electronic commerce in Europe.

The other main industry analysts are:

Forrester Research (www.forrester.com)

The Gartner Group (www.gartner.com)

IDC Research (www.idcresearch.com)

Activmedia (www.activmedia.com)

Information from management consultants about applications for e-commerce:

KPMG (www.kpmg.co.uk, www.kpmg.com)

Andersen Consulting (www.arthurandersen.com)

General sources on online marketing

Marketing Online (www.marketing-online.co.uk) is a source for links to web sites concerned with Internet marketing strategy, implementation and practice. Produced by Dave Chaffey.

Elab (formerly **Project 2000**) (ecommerce.vanderbilt.edu and www.elab.com) was founded in 1994 by Tom Novak and Donna Hoffman at School of Management, Vanderbilt University, to study marketing implications of Internet. Useful links/papers.

Print media

E-business Review (www.e-businessreview.co.uk) is a monthly for IS managers from the publishers of *Computer Wekly* .

Revolution magazine (www.revolution.haynet.com) has a web site for monthly UK magazine on new media – mainly sell-side e-commerce.

Net Profit (www.net-profit.co.uk) is a monthly UK-based newsletter on Internet commerce with a European focus.

Further reading
directs the students to alternative sources.

Web links
are integrated throughout the book with further addresses listed at the end of each chapter which provide additional information on the concepts and topics of the chapter.

References
An extensive set of references is included in every chapter.

The Companion Web Site

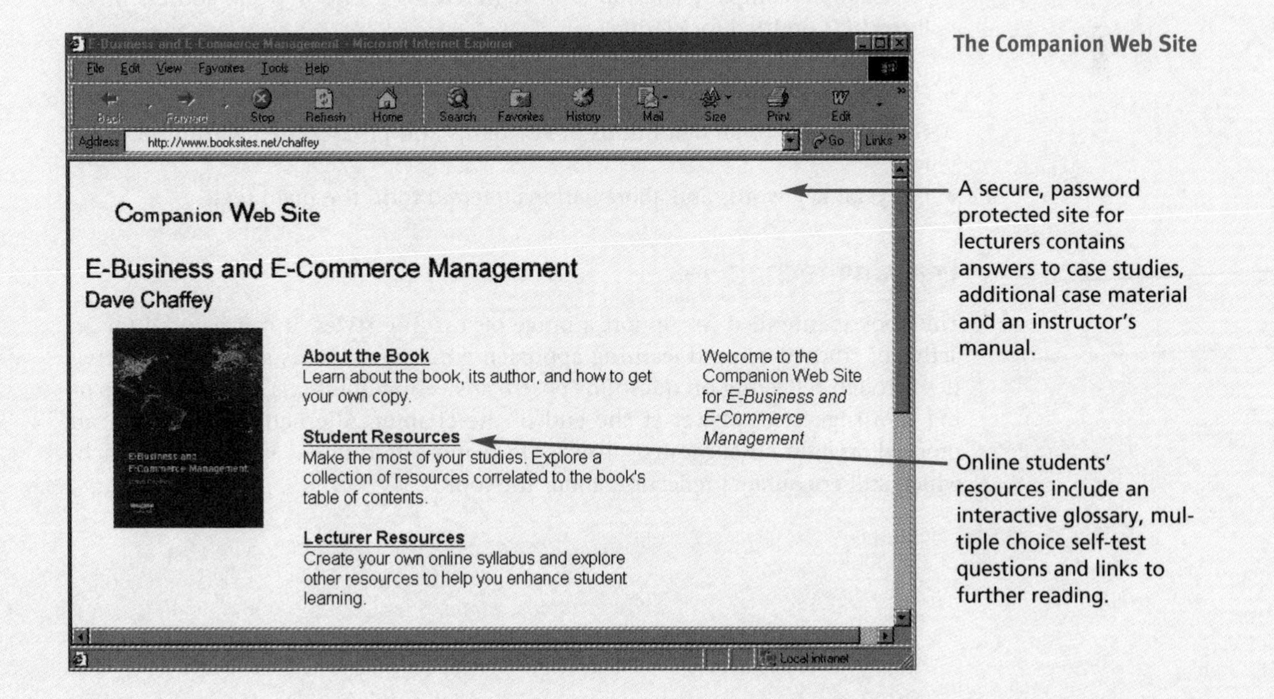

A secure, password protected site for lecturers contains answers to case studies, additional case material and an instructor's manual.

Online students' resources include an interactive glossary, multiple choice self-test questions and links to further reading.

particular topic. Managers can substitute their own organization to reflect on how they are approaching an issue. The two companies are introduced in *Chapter 1, p. 18.*

- *Focus on sections*: More detailed coverage of specific topics of interest.
- *Definitions*: when significant terms are first introduced the main text contains succinct definitions in the margin for easy reference.
- *Web links*: where appropriate, web addresses are given for further information particularly those to update information.
- *Chapter summaries*: intended as revision aids and to summarize the main learning points from the chapter.

At the end of each chapter

- *Answers to activities*: model answers for selected activities within the chapter.
- *Self-assessment exercises*: short questions which will test understanding of terms and concepts described in the chapter.
- *Discussion questions*: require longer essay-style answers discussing themes from the chapter, and can be used for essays or as debate questions in seminars.
- *Essay questions*: conventional essay questions.
- *Examination questions*: typical short answer questions found in exams and can also be used for revision.
- *References*: these are references to books, articles or papers referred to within the chapter.
- *Further reading*: supplementary texts or papers on the main themes of the chapter. Where appropriate a brief commentary is provided on recommended supplementary reading on the main themes of the chapters.
- *Web Links*: these are significant sites that provide further information on the concepts and topics of the chapter. All web site references within the chapter, for example company sites, are not repeated here. The web site address prefix 'http://' is omitted for clarity.

At the end of the book

- *Glossary*: a list of all definitions of key terms and phrases used within the main text.
- *Index*: all key words and abbreviations referred to in the main text.

Learning techniques

The book is intended to support a range of learning styles. It can be used for an active or student-centred learning approach whereby students attempt the activities through reflecting on questions posed, answering questions and then comparing to a suggested answer at the end of the chapter. Alternatively students can proceed straight to suggested answers in a more traditional learning approach, which still encourages reflection about the topic.

Companion Web Site

Free supplementary materials are available via the Pearson Education Companion Web Site at www.booksites.net to support all users of the book. This regularly updated Web Site contains advice, comments, support materials and hyperlinks to sites mentioned in the text. There is a password-protected area for lecturers giving suggested answers to case studies and exercises, additional cases and Microsoft Powerpoint presentation masters.

A Companion Web Site accompanies *E-Business and E-Commerce Management,* by Dave Chaffey

Visit the *E-Business and E-Commerce Management* Companion Web Site at www.booksites.net/chaffey to find valuable teaching and learning material including:

For Students and Lecturers:

- Study material designed to help you improve your results
- Interactive glossary and search function
- Feedback facility
- For each chapter:
  - Learning objectives and management issues
  - Introduction, summary and further reading
  - Multiple choice questions to test your learning
  - Links to relevant sites on the World Wide Web

For Lecturers:

- A secure, password protected site with teaching material
- A Lecturer's Guide to each chapter
- Case studies from textbook in downloadable format
- Answers to case studies
- Additional case studies from textbook in downloadable format
- Powerpoint slides of all diagrams in the book

The author's timeline

	1960	
1963	Born	Black and white television
	1970	
1976		Colour television
	1980	
1982 1985	BSc, Imperial College, London	First used computer-programmed mainframe using punch cards.
1988	PhD, University of Leeds	Wrote PhD on mainframe
1989	Project Manager in software house developing GIS for marketing planning.	First used PC
	1990	
1991	Software Engineering Manager for company producing packaged and bespoke engineering software	Sent first e-mail
1994	Project Manager for customer-facing financial services systems	Started using World Wide Web
1995	Senior Lecturer, Business Information Systems, Derbyshire Business School, University of Derby	First ordered book online
1997	Delivering CIM Internet Marketing seminars	Built first web site
1998	*Groupware, Workflow and Intranets* published	Mobile phone
1999	*Business Information Systems* published	
	2000	
2000	*Internet Marketing* published	Interactive digital TV
2000	MSc E-commerce course launched at Derby	WAP phone
2001	CIM E-marketing award launched at Derby	

This timeline supports *activity 3.2* (p. 71). This considers the diffusion of technological innovation at home and in the workplace. The author first started using a computer regularly when he was 18, yet his 4 year old daughter is already an Internet user. Readers can compare their own adoption of computer technology at home and at work. How do you think the use of the Internet and its successors for e-commerce and e-entertainment will change as successive generations become increasingly computer literate?

Acknowledgements

The author would like to thank the team at Pearson Education in Harlow for their help in the creation of this book. Many thanks also to the reviewers who have greatly assisted in developing the book:

Fintan Clear, Brunel University; Neil Doherty, Loughborough University; Jean-Noel Ezingeard, Henley Management College; Dr. Felicia Fai, University of Bath; Lisa Harris, Brunel University; Sue Hartland, Gloucestershire Business School at Cheltenham and Gloucester College of Higher Education; Mike Healy, University of Westminster; Eric van Heck, Rotterdam School of Management, The Netherlands; Dipak Khakhar, Lund University, Sweden; Robert Proops, University of Westminster; Professor Michael Quayle, University of Glamorgan; Richard Riley, University of Central England; Gurmak Singh, University of Wolverhampton; John Twomey, Brunel University; Gerry Urwin, Coventry University.

We are grateful to the following for permission to reproduce copyright material:

Figure 1.4 from Internet Commerce Growth Report, Forrester Research, April 2000; Figure 1.5 from B2B revenues to top US$1 trillion by 2003. Analyst report, 25 July, eMarketer 2001; Figure 1.6 from www.cooksons.com, Cooksons Tools web site; Figure 1.7 from www.mondus.com, Mondus web site; Figure 2.5 from www.vauxhall.co.uk, Vauxhall e-commerce site; Table 2.7 from *Management Today*, published by Haymarket Business Publications (M.T. Bain); Figure 2.8 from www.uk.kelkoo.com; Figure 2.10 from www.priceline.com, Priceline Europe web site; Figure 2.12 from www.verticalneteurope.com; Figures 3.9 and 3.10 from www.webpeft.net, © Zeus Technology Ltd 2001; Figures 3.11, 3.12, 3.16, 4.6, 4.7, 5.6, 6.7, 6.8, 6.9, 9.5, 9.6 and 12.7 from *Business in the Information Age – International Benchmarking Study 2000.* UK Department of Trade and Industry, 2000; Figures 4.1 and 9.4 from National Statistics Omnibus Survey, October 2000 © Crown Copyright 2000; Figure 4.5 from www.netpoll.net; Figure 4.8 from www.truste.org; Figure 5.18 from www.dabs.com; Figure 6.11 and Figure 11.16 from www.sainsburystoyou.co.uk, Sainsbury's web site; Figures 7.2, 7.4, 7.5 and 7.8 from Tranmit plc; Figure 8.14 from www.jungle.com; Figure 8.15 from Truffles intranet; Table 9.4 from Nielsen/NetRatings, April 2000; Figure 9.10 from www.silicon.com; Figure 10.7 from www.oticon.com; Figure 10.10 from www.knowledgespace.com; Figure 11.13 from www.netpoll.net; Figure 11.14 from www.egg.com; Figure 12.12 from www.mineit.com © MINEit Software 2001; Figure 12.16 from www.skyescottage.co.uk; Box in chapter 4 'Psychographic segmentation from Netpoll' from www.netpoll.net; Case Study 7.2 from *Computer Weekly*, 6 July 2000; Case Study 8.1 based on three *Revolution* articles available on archive at www.revolution.haynet.com; Case Study 10.3 from Computer Weekly, 27 July 2000; Case Study 12.1 from *Computing*, 7 July 2000.

Case Study 1.2 from 'SMEs can punch above their weight' by Nuala Moran, *Financial Times* Information Technology Supplement © *Financial Times* 3 May 2000; Case Study 2.1 from 'Dynamic pricing' by Anne Queree, *Financial Times* Information Technology Supplement © *Financial Times* 1 March 2000; Case Study 2.2 from an article in *Financial Times* Information Technology Supplement © *Financial Times* 3 May 2000; Case Study 3.1 from 'Selecting a service' by Philip Manchester, © *Financial Times* 2 August 2000; Case Study 4.1 from 'Early start on the web pays off' by Rahul Jacob © *Financial Times*, 6 September 2000; Case Study 4.2 from 'E-Government action plan: Singapore has set aside US$1.5bn to implement its highly advanced e-government strategy' © *Financial Times*, 6 December 2000; Case Study 4.3 from 'Electronic Newspapers' by Rob Newing, *Financial Times* Information Technology Supplement © *Financial Times* 7 June 2000; Case Study 5.1 from 'Bold strategy for the internet dimension' based on an interview with Hermann-Josef Lamberti of Deutsche Bank, written by Andrew Fisher, © *Financial Times* 5 April 2000; Case Study 5.2 from 'Web retailing' by Christopher Bowe, © *Financial Times* 8 December 2000; Case Study 5.3 from 'IT expertise of directors' by Alison Maitland © *Financial Times* 17 November 2000; Case Study 6.1 from an article by Geoffrey Nairn © *Financial Times* 3 May 2000; Case Study 9.1 from 'Behaviour is key to web retailing strategy' by Eric Clemens and Michael Row © *Financial Times* 13 November 2000; Case Study 9.2 from 'Integration: Scramble to cope with the demands of e-commerce' by Philip Manchester © *Financial Times* 2 February 2000; Case Study 11.1 from 'Data Integration' by Geoffrey Nairn, © *Financial Times*, 5 July 2000; Case Study 11. 2 from an article by Christopher Field © *Financial Times*, 3 May 2000.

Whilst every effort has been made to trace the owners of copyright material, in a few cases this has proved impossible and we take this opportunity to offer our apologies to any copyright holders whose rights we may have unwittingly infringed.

Part 1

INTRODUCTION

Part 1 introduces e-business and e-commerce and their historical development. It seeks to clarify e-business terms and concepts such as new business and revenue models by reviewing alternative interpretations and applications through activities and case studies.

Chapter 1
Introduction to e-business and e-commerce

- From e-commerce to e-business
- How significant are e-commerce and e-business?
- Drivers for e-business and e-commerce adoption
- Barriers to e-business and e-commerce adoption
- Introducing the B2B and B2C Companies
- Management responses to e-commerce and e-business (introduction to the book's structure)

Chapter 2
E-commerce fundamentals

- The e-commerce environment
- The e-commerce marketplace
- Business models for e-commerce

Focus on . . .
- Portals
- Auctions
- Internet start-up companies – the 'dot coms'

Chapter 3
E-business infrastructure

- What is the Internet? What is an intranet, extranet? What is the WWW?
- How it works – Internet standards
- Managing e-business infrastructure (technology and applications)

Focus on . . .
- EDI
- Application Service Providers
- New access devices

Chapter 4
E-environment

- Social factors
- Legal factors
- Economic and competitive factors
- Political factors
- Technological innovation and technology assessment

Focus on . . .
- E-commerce and globalization

Chapter 1

Introduction to e-business and e-commerce

CHAPTER AT A GLANCE

Main topics

Case studies

LEARNING OBJECTIVES

After completing this chapter the reader should be able to:

- Define the meaning and scope of e-business and e-commerce and their different elements
- Summarize the main reasons for adoption of e-commerce and e-business and barriers that may restrict adoption
- Use resources to define the extent of adoption of the Internet as a communications medium for consumers and businesses
- Outline the business challenges of introducing e-business and e-commerce to an organization.

MANAGEMENT ISSUES

The issues for managers raised in this chapter include:

- How do we explain the scope and implications of e-business and e-commerce to staff?
- What are the full range of benefits of introducing e-business and what are the risks?
- How great will the impact of the Internet be on our business? What are the current and predicted adoption levels? How do we assess the validity of forecasts?

Links to other chapters

The main related chapters are:

- *Chapter 2* examines the principal e-commerce business and marketplace models in more detail;
- *Chapter 3* introduces the technical infrastructure of software and hardware that companies must incorporate to achieve e-commerce;
- *Chapter 5* describes approaches to e-business strategy introduced in *Chapter 1*.

Introduction

We live in an era of 'e-everything'. Managers are in danger of being swept away by the deluge of information exhorting them to adopt everything from e-commerce, e-crm, e-procurement, e-logistics to e-business. Industry analysts, media, suppliers and governments are all inciting managers to embrace these concepts in their organizations pointing to stratospheric projections of e-commerce revenue, exponential increases in the number of adopters and the threat of the 'do-nothing' option.

Andy Grove, Chairman of Intel, one of the early adopters of e-commerce, has made a metereological analogy with the Internet. He says:

> *Is the Internet a typhoon force, a ten times force, or is it a bit of wind? Or is it a force that fundamentally alters our business?* (Grove, 1996)

This statement seems to encapsulate how managers must respond to digital technologies; the impact will vary through time from minor for some companies to significant for others, and an appropriate response is required. This book will explore the strategies and practical techniques managers can use to assess the impact and leverage of the technology and at the same time minimize risks. The strategies and tactics described will be based on models developed by academics, industry analysts and solutions providers and will be illustrated by considering case studies of organizations from around the world.

Yet the start of the millennium reminded us that business success cannot be assured by investment in digital technology. The bubble has burst with sharp devaluations in 'dot-coms' stocks, the failure of some of the fêted start-up companies such as Boo.com and Boxman. These events indicate that there are many hazards on the road to success and managers must devise strategies and implementation techniques that do not over-expose their companies to risk, yet innovate in a highly competitive, dynamic marketplace.

The emphasis of this book is on how established organizations can learn lessons from early adopters and the successes and failures of the dot-coms (*Chapter 2, p. 53*). Success stories from traditional companies well suited to exploiting the new medium show great potential that is undiminished by the dot-com failure. Networking specialist Cisco (www.cisco.com) and European airline EasyJet (www.easyjet.com) both now derive over 80 per cent of their revenue through the electronic medium.

In this chapter we start by considering the proliferation of 'e-terms' and why it is essential for managers to be clear about the scope of opportunities offered by e-business and e-commerce. We then consider the reasons for business interest in e-commerce and e-business; risks to adoption and how we can overcome them through defining strategies and introducing new processes, technologies and structures to successfully introduce these changes.

From e-commerce to e-business

The rapid advancement of technology and its application by business seems to be accompanied by similar rapid changes in terminology. The use of the term 'electronic commerce' has been supplemented by additional terms such as e-business, e-marketing, i-commerce and more specialist terms such as e-crm, e-tail and e-procurement. Do we need to be concerned about the terminology? The short answer is no; Mougayer (1998) notes that it is understanding the services that can be offered to customers, and the business benefits that are obtainable through e-business that are important. However, labels are convenient in defining the *scope* of the changes we are looking to make within an organization through using electronic communications. Managers need to communicate the extent of changes they are proposing through introducing digital technologies to employees, customers and partners. Complete activity 1.1 to start unravelling these different terms.

Understanding e-commerce and e-business

Activity 1.1

Purpose

To encourage discussion of what is understood by 'e-commerce' and 'e-business' and their significance to managers.

Questions

1. Make a list of terms prefixed by 'e-' you have encountered in the media that describe the impact electronic communications technology is making on different business processes or functional parts of organization.
2. Explain how these terms relate to each other in a typical business.
3. What is the value of these terms? Do they represent a substantial shift in managerial thinking and practice, or are they the latest management fad promoted by the analysts and marketers from the solutions providers?

For answer see p. 23.

E-commerce defined

Electronic commerce (e-commerce) is often thought to simply refer to buying and selling using the Internet; people immediately think of consumer retail purchases from companies such as Amazon. But e-commerce involves much more than electronically mediated financial transactions between organizations and customers. Many commentators refer to e-commerce as *all* electronically mediated transactions between an organization and any third party it deals with. By this definition,

Electronic commerce (e-commerce)
All electronically mediated information exchanges between an organization and its external stakeholders.

non-financial transactions such as customer requests for further information would also be considered to be part of e-commerce. Kalakota and Whinston (1997) refer to a range of different perspectives for e-commerce:

1. *A communications perspective* – the delivery of information, products/services or payment by electronic means.
2. *A business process perspective* – the application of technology towards the automation of business transactions and workflows.
3. *A service perspective* – enabling cost cutting at the same time as increasing the speed and quality of service delivery.
4. *An online perspective* – the buying and selling of products and information online.

Zwass (1998) uses a broad definition of e-commerce. He refers to it as:

the sharing of business information, maintaining business relationships, and conducting business transactions by means of telecommunications networks.

The UK government also uses a broad definition:

E-commerce is the exchange of information across electronic networks , at any stage in the supply chain, whether within an organization, between businesses, between businesses and consumers, or between the public and private sector, whether paid or unpaid. (E-commerce@its.best.uk,1999)

All these definitions imply that electronic commerce is not solely restricted to the actual buying and selling of products, but also pre-sale and post-sales activities across the supply chain.

When evaluating the impact of e-commerce on an organization, it is instructive to identify opportunities for buy-side and sell-side e-commerce transactions as depicted in *Figure 1.1*, since systems with different functionality will need to be created in an organization to accommodate transactions with buyers and suppliers. **Buy-side e-commerce** refers to transactions to procure resources needed by an organization from its suppliers. Read *case study 1.1* for a review of how Shell has developed a new system that enables buy-side e-commerce for its customers. **Sell-side e-commerce** refers to transactions involved with selling products to an organization's customers. *Case study 1.2* illustrates the potential for sell-side e-commerce amongst SMEs. Remember that, as illustrated by case study 1.1, an e-commerce transaction can be considered from two perspectives: sell-side from the perspective of the selling organization and buy-side from the perspective of the buying organization. Marketers from RS Components (www.rswww.com) promote its sell-side e-commerce system by hosting seminars for buyers within the purchasing department of its customers that explain the cost savings available through e-commerce.

Buy-side e-commerce
E-commerce transactions between a purchasing organization and its suppliers.

Sell-side e-commerce
E-commerce transactions between a supplier organization and its customers.

When distinguishing between buy-side and sell-side e-commerce we are looking at different aspects of managing an organization's supply chain. **Supply chain management** (SCM) is the coordination of all supply activities of an organization from its suppliers and delivery of products to its customers. The opportunities for using e-commerce to streamline and restructure the supply chain are described in more detail in *Chapter 6* and highlighted by *case study 1.1*. The **value chain** is a related concept that describes the different value-adding activities that connect a

Supply chain management
The coordination of all supply activities of an organization from its suppliers and partners to its customers.

Value chain
A model for analysis of how supply chain activities can add value to products and services delivered to the customer.

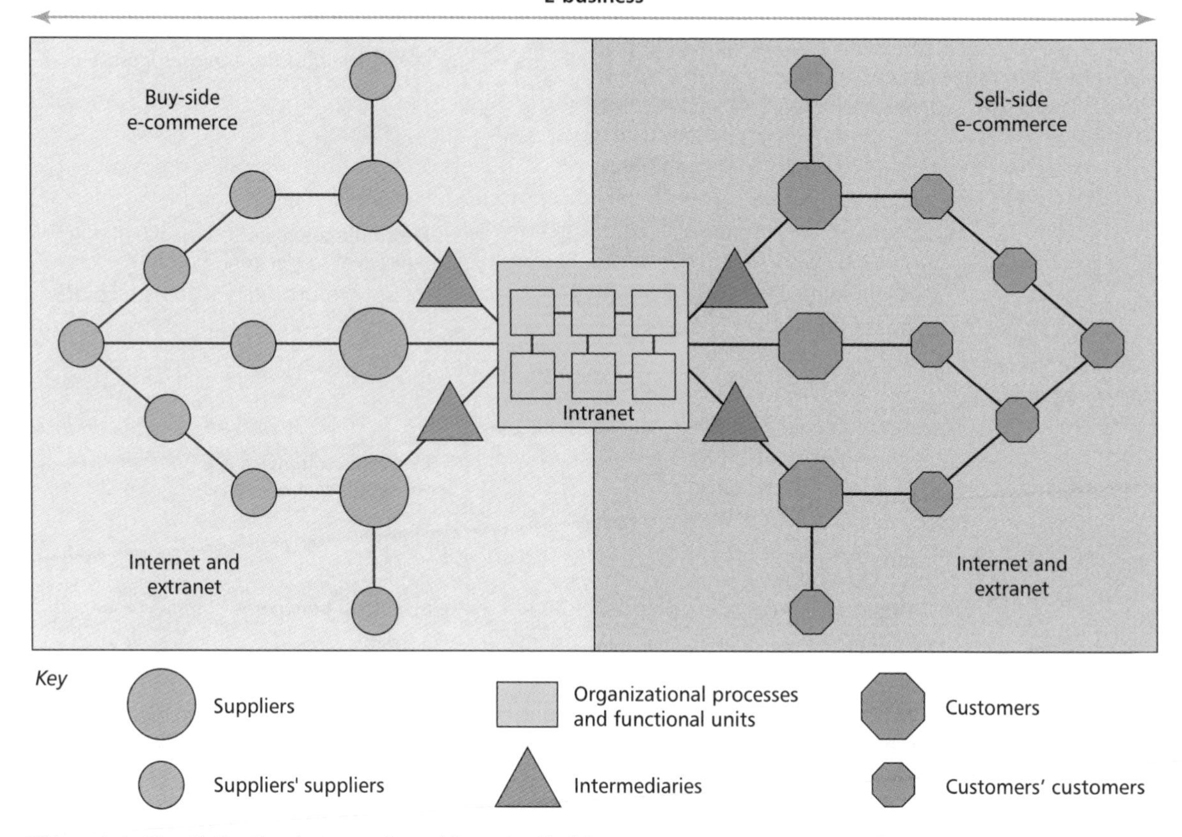

Figure 1.1 The distinction between buy-side and sell-side e-commerce

company's supply side with its demand side. We can identify an *internal* value chain within the boundaries of an organization and an *external* value chain where these activities are performed by partners. Note that in the era of e-business a company will manage many interrelated value chains, so in *Chapter 6* we also consider the concept of a **value network**.

Value network
The links between an organization and its strategic and non-strategic partners that form its external value chain.

E-business defined

Given that *Figure 1.1* depicts different types of e-commerce, what then is e-business? Let us start from the definition by IBM (www.ibm.com/e-business), who were one of the first suppliers to coin the term:

> *e-business (e' biz' nis) – the transformation of key business processes through the use of Internet technologies.*

Referring back to *Figure 1.1*, the key business processes referred to in the IBM definition are the organizational processes or units in the centre of Figure 1.1. They include research and development, marketing, manufacturing and inbound and outbound logistics The buy-side e-commerce transactions with suppliers and the sell-side e-commerce transactions with customers can also be considered to be key businesses processes.

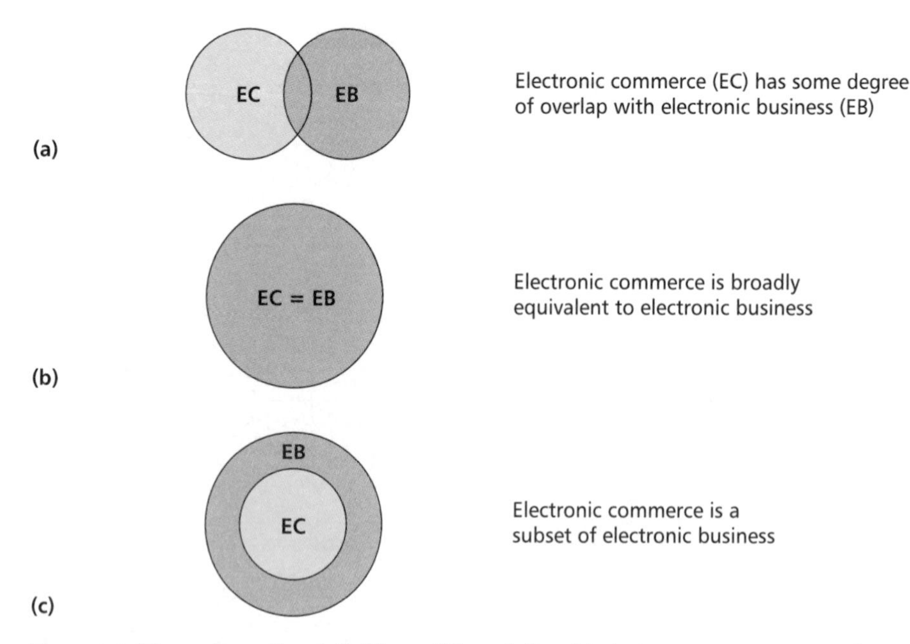
EC
EB
Electronic commerce (EC) has some degree of overlap with electronic business (EB)
(a)
EC = EB
Electronic commerce is broadly equivalent to electronic business
(b)
EB
EC
Electronic commerce is a subset of electronic business
(c)

Figure 1.2 Three alternative definitions of the relationship between e-commerce and e-business

Figure 1.2 presents some alternative viewpoints of the relationship between e-business and e-commerce. In Figure 1.2 (a) there is a relatively small overlap between e-commerce and e-business. From Figure 1.1 we can reject Figure 1.2(a) since the overlap between buy-side and sell-side e-commerce is significant. Figure 1.2(b) seems to be more realistic, and indeed many commentators seem to consider e-business and e-commerce to be synonymous. It can be argued, however, that Figure 1.2(c) is most realistic since e-commerce does not refer to many of the transactions *within* a business, such as processing a purchasing order, that are part of e-business. In an international benchmarking study analysing the adoption of e-business in SMEs the Department of Trade and Industry emphasizes the application of technology in the full range of business processes, but also emphasizes how it involves innovation. The DTI describes e-business as:

> *when a business has fully integrated information and communications technologies (ICTs) into its operations, potentially redesigning its business processes around ICT or completely reinventing its business model ... e-business, is understood to be the integration of all these activities with the internal processes of a business through ICT.* (DTI, 2000)

Electronic business (e-business)
All electronically mediated information exchanges, both within an organization and with external stakeholders supporting the range of business processes.

So e-commerce can best be conceived as a subset of **e-business** and this is the perspective we will use in this book. Since the interpretation in Figure 1.2(b) is equally valid, what is important within any given company, is that managers involved with the implementation of e-commerce/e-business are agreed on the scope of what they are trying to achieve!

In *Chapter 8* we go on to consider how e-marketing, a concept now used by many marketing professionals relates to the concepts of e-business and e-commerce. To summarize this section and for further perspectives on e-business and e-commerce complete *activity 1.2*.

What is e-commerce? What is e-business?

Activity 1.2

Purpose of activity

To illustrate different interpretations of e-commerce from different types of organization.

Activity

Visit the web sites of suppliers and government organizations listed below and then attempt to produce definitions for electronic commerce and electronic business that would explain the concept to a manager thinking of investing in new technology.

Accenture (www.accenture.com)

IBM (www.ibm.com/e-business)

UK government (www.dti.gov.uk/infoage, www.isi.gov.uk)

European Union (www.europa.eu.int/comm/internal_market/en/media/eleccomm)

OECD (www.oecd.org/dsti/sti/it/ec/prod/online.htm)

US government (www.ecommerce.gov)

For answer see p. 23

CASE STUDY 1.1

Shell Chemical redefines its customers' supply chain

Shell Chemical manufactures the chemicals used by other manufacturers of many industrial and consumer products. Shell's customers use detergents, solvents, plastics, elastomers and epoxy resins to produce everything from automotive paints and aircraft structures to diapers and plastic bottles.

Within such an organization, supply chain management has a dramatic impact on the bottom line. The managers of Shell's SIMON – Shell Inventory Managed Order Network – believe that supply chain management refers to both the upstream and downstream relationships that affect our business.

Shell used SIMON to turn around their downstream supply chain processes – the ones dedicated to getting

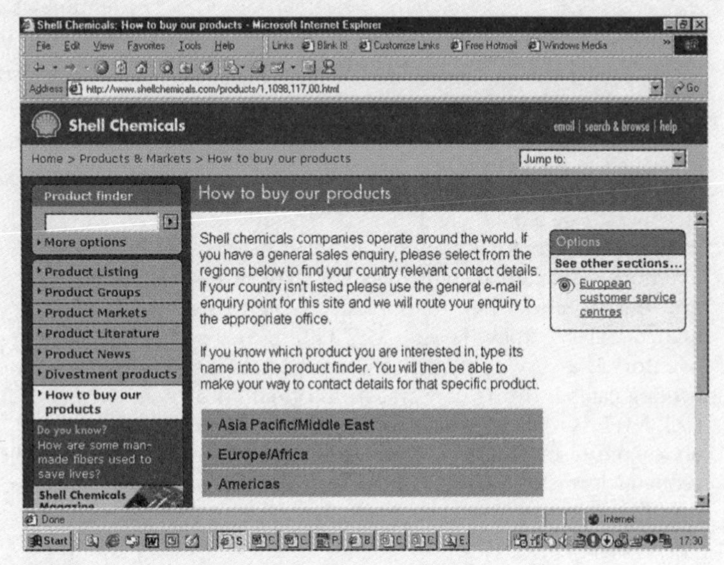

Figure 1.3 **Shell Chemical product support site** (www.shellchemicals.com)

▶ CASE STUDY *continued*

goods to their customers. Since SIMON, a Lotus Notes e-business application, was successful in the downstream process it was then applied to its upstream processes – acquiring raw materials from suppliers.

The managers of the system state that: 'SIMON enables the transfer of responsibility for inventory management from customer to supplier. There is no need for a Shell Chemical customer to place an order. Through SIMON, we're able to proactively keep vital inventory on their shelves, so to speak. Customers pay only for what they consume. We are their sole-source supplier. It's a cutting-edge supplier/customer business model – one that's built on a relationship of mutual trust and a belief that there are significant benefits to be realized on both sides.'

Traditional operations model

Before the introduction of SIMON, there was a danger that Shell's customers might run out of an essential chemical, so plant time and then revenues are lost. To avoid this, companies tend to maintain 'safety stock' levels. Re-ordering then occurs when inventory gets too close to these safety stock levels. The difficulty is that a typical re-supply order takes about two weeks from the time the order is placed. This delay occurs since chemicals must be weighed at the plant, loaded onto railcars and then sent to the customer, who then weighs the materials at the other end before moving them into inventory. Miscalculations tend to lead to rush orders. Rush orders are more expensive and quite common. Billing was inefficient: an invoice was sent out for every single railcar load of product that was sent from Shell to their customer.

New operational model

The new arrangement is known as supplier-managed inventory (SMI). Since companies are wary of running out of stock they traditionally tend to use inflated safety stock levels. Maintaining excess inventory is a very costly process since it eats into working capital. In the new system information on stock levels is replicated back to the Shell customer service centre in Houston, Texas, where Shell can reconcile it with their SAP MRP system. A Shell account service rep is automatically presented with a re-supply plan. If the plan indicates that stocking levels at the customer site are low, the rep fills out an electronic purchase order and initiates a new shipment to the customer. Previously, the customer would have had to explicitly initiate each new order. Now, once a month (not once per railcar load!), an invoice is generated. The invoice is based on consumption figures, not shipments.

Using the new SIMON application that the customer accesses from a Notes client, the customer can find out:

- the amount of product consumed in the past 24 hours
- the amount of new product that arrived and was unloaded in the same period
- current and anticipated production schedules, and known changes to those schedules
- status of these orders and shipments
- estimated dates of arrival and shipment weights
- receipt and unloading dates
- current stock and consumption levels
- a comparison of metered and calculated consumption from a 'Reconciliation' tab,
- the mutually agreed-upon plan for management of inventory from a 'Site level agreements' tab.

Through access to this information Shell customers receive the following benefits. The use of SIMON:

- Eliminates expensive excess inventory, which means an increase in working capital.
- Facilitates timely, low-cost 're-synching' of supply chain.
- Ensures product is on site whenever needed.
- Ensures quicker response times to changing conditions.
- Reduces transaction costs (e.g. invoices and data entry).
- Eliminates erratic order patterns.
- Reduces order processing overhead.
- Streamlines financial statements and reconciliation processes.

SIMON was first introduced to 23 of Shell's largest, most strategic customer accounts during Summer 1996 and now supports over 50 accounts. Within 12 months, Shell experienced a $20 million increase in additional product sales, and Shell stated that its customers were reporting increased flexibility in its ▶

▶ CASE STUDY *continued*

acquisition and delivery processes. Shell also stated that there were more sole supplier accounts as a result of this system, suggesting it is giving rise to some lock-in. In the second phase, Shell extended SIMON to its suppliers, enabling suppliers to manage the inventories of items they provided to Shell so that Shell could achieve similar benefits to its customers.

Implementation

SIMON is described by Shell as a Notes-based corporate extranet acting as a customer inventory management system. This represents a change from the industry standard practice of using electronic data interchange (EDI) forms, telephone orders, and paper invoices to communicate with customers. However, EDI didn't give Shell the flexibility it needed to accommodate data on exceptions and processes. The company invested roughly $200,000 and two months to set up the Shell Inventory Management Order Network at the first site. A server in the customer's purchasing department replicates changes to Shell's internal SIMON server. Those changes are available to Shell account representatives via a token ring network.

Source: Adapted from the IBM e-business web site case study (www.ibm.com/ebusiness).

Questions

1. The SIMON system supports both 'upstream and downstream' business relationships. Explain how this relates to *Figure 1.1* and whether you would consider it an e-commerce system or e-business system.
2. Draw a table summarizing the before and after implementation roles for Shell and their customers (downstream side).
3. This description of SIMON is explained from the Shell perspective. Using your answer to question 2, state whether you think the customer truly benefits, or is Shell transferring some of its workload to the customer?
4. Visit the Shell web site (*Figure 1.3*). Are these facilities available online? Try to explain the services provided.

How significant are e-commerce and e-business?

As managers, we need to assess the impact of e-commerce and e-business on our marketplace and organizations. How should we respond? How much do we need to invest? What are our priorities and how quickly do we need to act? Answering these questions is an essential part of formulating an e-business and e-marketing strategy and is considered in more detail in *Part 2*. To answer these questions marketing research will need to be conducted to determine the current levels of adoption of the Internet for trading amongst customers and competitors in our market sector and in other sectors. *Activity 1.3* illustrates some sources of information. More detail on levels of adoption are presented at the start of *Chapter 4*.

E-commerce adoption by consumers and businesses

Activity 1.3

Purpose

To examine estimates of the current and future size of e-commerce trade and critically review the validity of these estimates.

Activity

Nua and Cyberatlas are two content aggregator sites that compile estimates from different industry analysts of e-commerce activity in different sectors and in different geographic markets.

Visit Nua (www.nua.ie/surveys) and Cyberatlas (www.cyberatlas.com).

1. Consumer demand
   (a) Summarize the demand for access to the Internet in your country in millions of users and use historical data to show how this has varied through time. How does access vary between home and work? What are the implications for the retail company?
   (b) What are the future projections for total B2C demand? To answer this, it may help to visit the web site of one of the major industry analysts such as Forrester (www.forrester.com) or IDC (www.idcresearch.com).

For answer see p. 24

2. Business demand
   (a) Summarize the business demand for access to the Internet in your country as a proportion of all businesses and calculate the annual percentage growth and show how this has varied between years.
   (b) What are the future projections for total B2B demand?

Now complete *activity 1.4* to gain an appreciation of the overall impact of e-commerce on trading.

Activity 1.4 Global variations in e-commerce adoption

Purpose

To explore the importance of e-commerce in comparison with traditional channels on a global basis.

Activity

1. Comment on the overall percentage of sales for e-commerce predicted for 2004 across all markets.

2. Comment on the variation in percentage of sales for e-commerce predicted for 2004 in different markets.

3. Comment on the growth rates indicated over the four years of predictions.

4. Compare the prediction for the current year in comparison with that made in 2000.

For answers see p. 24

One of the difficulties for companies wishing to invest in e-commerce is in predicting the impact of technology in the future. While we can base growth on industry forecasts such as *Figure 1.4*, great care must be taken on the basis of these figures. *Activity 1.5* explores the difficulties in making use of analyst forecasts.

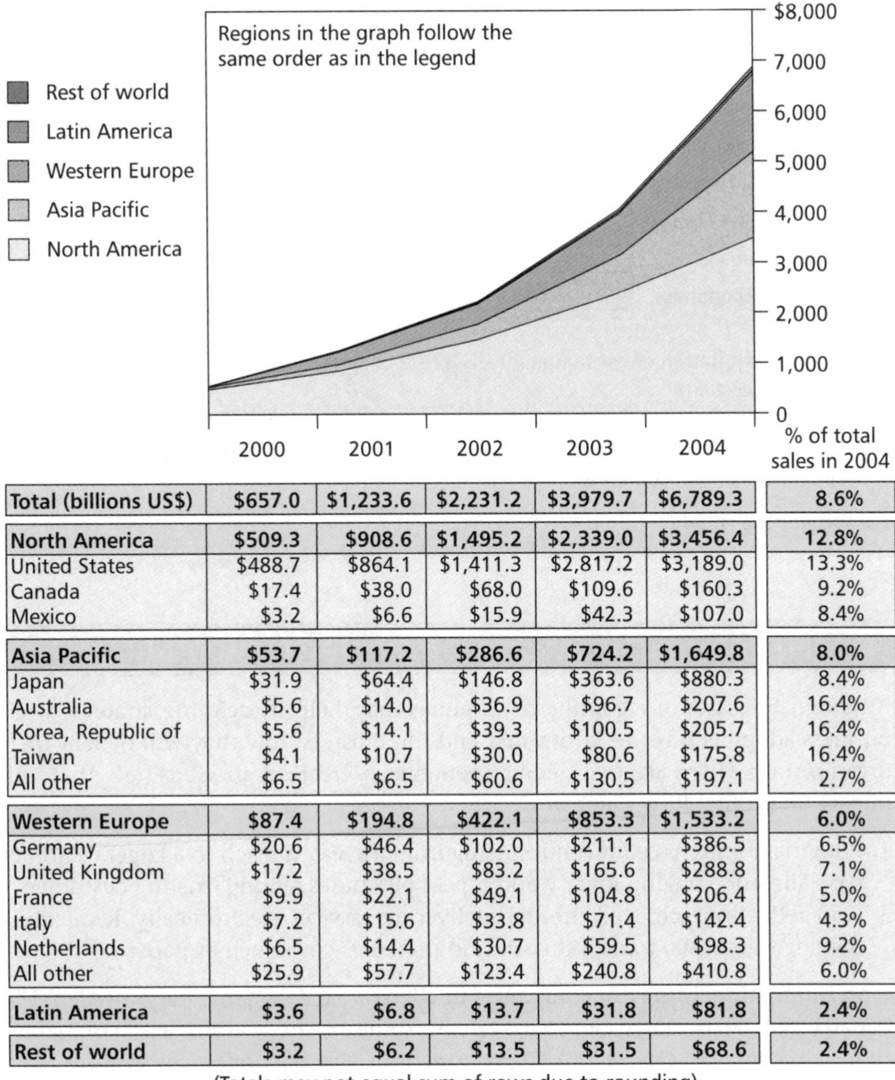

	2000	2001	2002	2003	2004	% of total sales in 2004
Total (billions US$)	**$657.0**	**$1,233.6**	**$2,231.2**	**$3,979.7**	**$6,789.3**	**8.6%**
North America	**$509.3**	**$908.6**	**$1,495.2**	**$2,339.0**	**$3,456.4**	**12.8%**
United States	$488.7	$864.1	$1,411.3	$2,817.2	$3,189.0	13.3%
Canada	$17.4	$38.0	$68.0	$109.6	$160.3	9.2%
Mexico	$3.2	$6.6	$15.9	$42.3	$107.0	8.4%
Asia Pacific	**$53.7**	**$117.2**	**$286.6**	**$724.2**	**$1,649.8**	**8.0%**
Japan	$31.9	$64.4	$146.8	$363.6	$880.3	8.4%
Australia	$5.6	$14.0	$36.9	$96.7	$207.6	16.4%
Korea, Republic of	$5.6	$14.1	$39.3	$100.5	$205.7	16.4%
Taiwan	$4.1	$10.7	$30.0	$80.6	$175.8	16.4%
All other	$6.5	$6.5	$60.6	$130.5	$197.1	2.7%
Western Europe	**$87.4**	**$194.8**	**$422.1**	**$853.3**	**$1,533.2**	**6.0%**
Germany	$20.6	$46.4	$102.0	$211.1	$386.5	6.5%
United Kingdom	$17.2	$38.5	$83.2	$165.6	$288.8	7.1%
France	$9.9	$22.1	$49.1	$104.8	$206.4	5.0%
Italy	$7.2	$15.6	$33.8	$71.4	$142.4	4.3%
Netherlands	$6.5	$14.4	$30.7	$59.5	$98.3	9.2%
All other	$25.9	$57.7	$123.4	$240.8	$410.8	6.0%
Latin America	**$3.6**	**$6.8**	**$13.7**	**$31.8**	**$81.8**	**2.4%**
Rest of world	**$3.2**	**$6.2**	**$13.5**	**$31.5**	**$68.6**	**2.4%**

(Totals may not equal sum of rows due to rounding)

Figure 1.4 Estimates of combined B2B and B2C e-commerce growth.
Source: Forrester Research (April 2000)

How accurate are forecasts of e-commerce growth?

Activity 1.5

Purpose

To consider the validity of industry estimates of e-commerce growth and implications for decision making.

Activity

1. Review *Figure 1.5* and explain some of the reasons for the discrepancies in forecasts.

▶

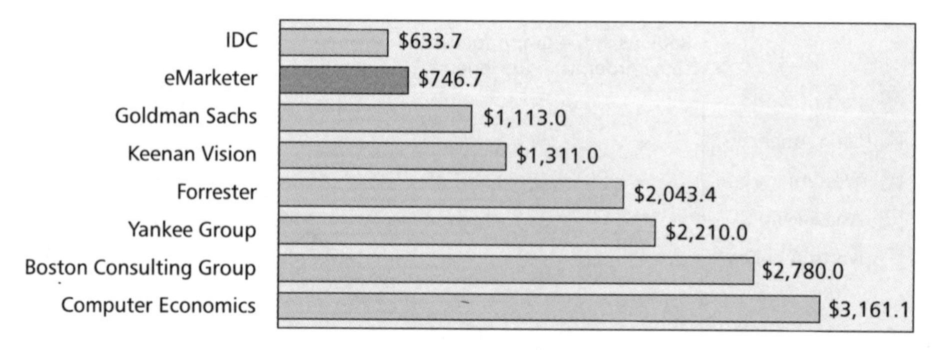

Figure 1.5 Compilation of estimates for US B2B e-commerce revenue ($ billion) in 2003.
Source: eMarketer (2001)

2. What are the implications of these discrepancies for managers assessing the importance of e-commerce?

For answer see p. 24

Drivers for e-business and e-commerce adoption

Although forecasts of e-commerce revenues may help in defining strategy, what business adopters want to know, first and foremost, is how they will benefit their organization. There are two general benefits to creating an e-business that will impact on profitability. These are

1. Potential for increased revenue arising from increased reach to a larger customer base and encouraging loyalty and repeat purchases among existing customers.
2. Cost reduction achieved through delivering services electronically. Reductions include staff costs, transport costs and materials costs such as paper.

An international study of companies in UK, France, Germany, Italy, Sweden, US, Canada and Japan has sought to evaluate some of the reasons why companies adopt e-commerce (DTI, 2000). Drivers identified in previous surveys were rated out of 4 by e-commerce adopters where 4 = very important and 1 = unimportant. The different drivers were rated as follows:

Cost/efficiency drivers

1. Increasing speed with which supplies can be obtained (2.76)
2. Increasing speed with which goods can be despatched (2.63)
3. Reduced sales and purchasing costs (2.65)
4. Reduced operating costs (2.73)

Competitiveness drivers

5. Customer demand (2.86)
6. Improving the range and quality of services offered (2.83)
7. Avoid losing market share to businesses already using e-commerce (2.7)

This survey suggests that the cost/efficiency drivers and competitiveness drivers are of similar importance. The survey also reports on score for non-adopters and unsurprisingly all these benefits are rated significantly lower.

Together these benefits may contribute to increased profitability. Many of these benefits are referred to in *case study 1.2*. However, it is well known that the majority of dot-coms are not profitable since the significant investment needed to create, market and maintain e-commerce and e-business services may be greater than revenues. A similar situation occurs for existing companies investing in e-business; it may be several years before break-even on an e-commerce or e-business initiative.

When reviewing potential benefits, it is useful to identify both tangible benefits (for which monetary savings or revenues can be identified) and intangible benefits (for which it is more difficult to calculate cost savings). The types of potential benefits are summarized in *Table 1.1*.

Table 1.1 Tangible and intangible benefits from e-commerce and e-business

Tangible benefits	*Intangible benefits*
● Increased sales from new sales leads giving rise to increased revenue from: – new customers, new markets – existing customers (repeat-selling) – existing customers (cross-selling). ● Marketing cost reductions from: – reduced time in customer service – online sales – reduced printing and distribution costs of marketing communications. ● Supply-chain cost reductions from: – reduced levels of inventory – increased competition from suppliers – shorter cycle time in ordering. ● Administrative cost reductions from more efficient routine business processes such as recruitment, invoice payment and holiday authorization.	● Corporate image communication ● Enhance brand ● More rapid, more responsive marketing communications including PR ● Faster product development lifecycle enabling faster response to market needs ● Improved customer service ● Learning for the future ● Meeting customer expectations to have a web site ● Identify new partners, support existing partners better ● Better management of marketing information and customer information ● Feedback from customers on products

CASE STUDY 1.2

SME adoption of sell-side e-commerce

FT

The Internet has given small companies the same reach to global marketplaces as larger rivals which have invested millions in building an international presence.

Eighteen months ago, Cooksons Tools, a builders' merchants in Cheshire, north-west England, was contemplating joining the ranks of small companies that have given in to the muscle of the DIY multiples, and shutting up shop for good.

'We were battling hard just to hold our own, rather than being able to grow the business,' says

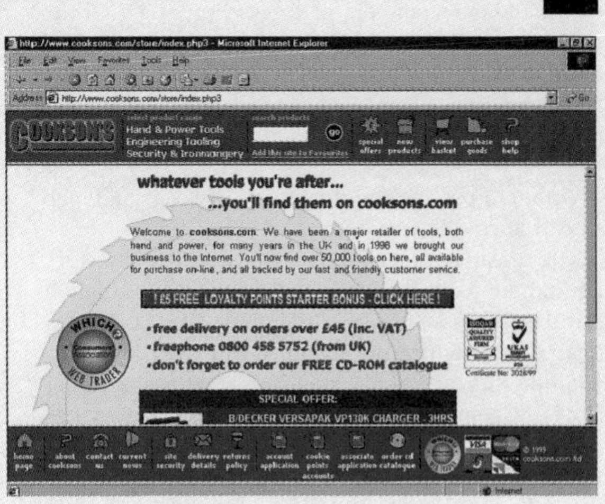

Figure 1.6 Cooksons Tools web site (www.cooksons.com)

▶ CASE STUDY *continued*

Stuart Armstrong, managing director. 'To stay in business, we had to change the way we operated.'

Then the company decided to try selling via the Internet (*Figure 1.6*), and since then it has gone from serving customers in a seven-mile radius of its depot in Stockport, to serving customers worldwide. Cooksons.com has even sold Korean tools back to customers in Korea.

Turnover from the traditional business, established more than 40 years ago, now stands at £1m a year. The web site, which went live in March 1999, rapidly attracted orders worth £1600 a day. Turnover doubled every 2.5 months in the first year of operation.

Cooksons managed to do this without cannibalizing its existing business – less than 1 per cent of orders on the web site come from existing customers.

Mr Armstrong says that the margin on Internet sales is lower, but because sales volume is higher and the costs of selling are lower, the company can afford to sell goods 15 per cent cheaper.

Such is the power of the Internet to deliver world markets to parochial businesses. And the evidence is that small companies do recognize that electronic channels can vastly extend their range.

Research carried out by the market research organization MORI shows that more than 50 per cent of SMEs would like to sell more online, and are looking for a simple way to do it. However, SMEs are lagging behind larger competitors in their use of the Internet, according to a survey of 2500 SMEs across Europe by IDC, the IT research organization.

Overall, 66 per cent had access to the Internet, compared to 76 per cent of larger companies. Of the 66 per cent, far fewer were using the Internet to generate sales, with 30 per cent of retailers and wholesalers, but only 17 per cent of manufacturers and 9.2 per cent of business services SMEs were selling via the net.

Only 6.6 per cent of the SMEs surveyed had web sites that could carry out online transactions.

The research, carried out on behalf of the network equipment company Cisco Systems, identified a number of 'fast tracker' SMEs that, like Cooksons, have used the Internet to transform their business. Examples include Sarl Noraude, a French mail order clothing company with 30 employees, which has rapidly expanded sales of made-to-measure shirts with a web site that allows customers to input measurements, select the style and fabric, and purchase made-to-measure shirts online.

Another is Paper One, a Swedish producer of fine papers, which has gone from start-up to £3.8m turnover in two years by enabling customers to order via the web site at any time, 365 days a year.

These examples show how the Internet has changed the rules that have governed business for centuries, according to Robert Lloyd, vice-president of Enterprise and Small-Medium lines of business at Cisco. He says: 'A four-fold increase in turnover, for example, can now be accommodated through technology in a matter of days, if not hours, instead of having to wait weeks or months to recruit and train staff, increase production, and so on.'

And it is not just existing small companies that have seized the opportunity to compete outside their traditional range. Large, established multinationals are probably more discomfited by the rise of a brand new breed of SMEs, the dot-coms. These companies may be small in terms of physical assets, but they are becoming the giants of the Internet, expanding their customer bases rapidly, and taking significant market share from traditional businesses.

The early focus of e-commerce development in SMEs has been in using the Internet to target new retail customers, but now a range of business-to-business e-commerce services is developing. The MORI research was commissioned by Mondus.com, a recently established electronic marketplace dedicated to the needs of SMEs (*Figure 1.7*).

Rouzbeh Pirouz, founder and chief executive, says: 'We set up this business because research shows that to date services have been oriented to bigger businesses and the benefits of e-procurement have passed over SMEs.'

Mondus allows SMEs to get multiple quotes for goods and services via the Internet, rather than having to ring round or write to suppliers. 'SMEs get access to suppliers outside their immediate geography. From June, we will have a global database of suppliers.'

The site, which includes foreign language translation and credit checking services, began operating in October 1999. After six months there were 50,000 SMEs on the system, 90 per cent of them buyers. 'We have gone from two quotes per order posted on the system to five quotes per order,' says Mr Pirouz. 'It is unlikely that companies would gather more than that using traditional methods.'

▶

There is no charge for signing up to the site but Mondus takes a small percentage on each deal concluded.

Another example of an e-commerce site dedicated to SMEs is B2B.com, set up by Barclays Bank. As well as providing online banking, this site is a portal for a range of products and services used by SMEs and provides secure purchase-to-payment procurement.

Chris Lendrum, chief executive of Barclays corporate banking, says the site will cover all essential services, 'from the purchase of stationery and raw materials through to the administration of human resources.'

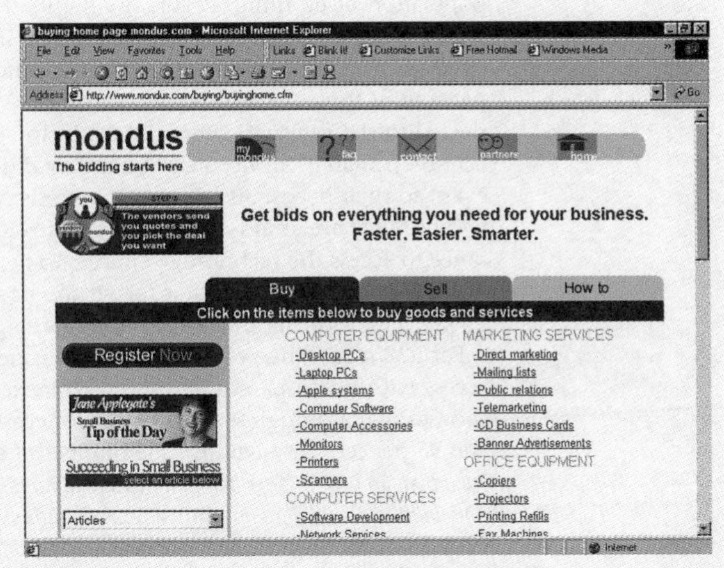

Figure 1.7 Mondus web site (www.mondus.com)

This site is targeted at companies with a turnover between £5m and £250m. However, Barclays has 450,000 SME customers with a lower turnover, which are serviced by its retail banking operations. It has set up a 40:60 joint venture company with the Internet provider FreeServe to provide e-commerce services for these customers.

The point is that the Internet makes it cheaper to market and sell to SMEs, spurring the development of e-services dedicated to this sector. A good example of this is the way in which Application Service Providers, which deliver and maintain software applications via the web, are targeting SMEs.

Western Europe has 16 million companies that are classified as SMEs. While they already represent a significant chunk of the economy, the Internet is giving them the ability to punch beyond their weight. 'Nowhere has the effect of the Internet been felt so much as in its ability to give SMEs the strength to compete and beat multinational companies,' says Mr Lloyd.

Source: 'SMEs can punch above their weight' by Nuala Moran, *Financial Times*, 3 May 2000, Information Technology supplement (www.ft.com/ftit)

Questions

1. Explain how Cooksons Tools used the Internet to support their business.
2. Explain the differences in margin for Internet sales.
3. Visit the Cooksons Tools web site and assess the range of services it offers in relation to Table 1.1.
4. What is Mondus? How does it facilitate trade among SMEs?

Barriers to e-commerce and e-business adoption

While it can be seen that there are many tangible and intangible benefits from developing e-commerce and e-business services, there are many difficulties inherent in achieving e-business success. The most significant of these barriers are those that stifle demand for e-commerce services. We saw in *activity 1.3* that levels of Internet access are one barrier, but for those with access there may be further barriers to spending. An insight into the factors affecting Internet adoption is provided by the *Which* magazine 2000 Internet survey of UK users (*Which*, 2000).

A large proportion of current non-Internet users (51 per cent) say they will never get connected to the Internet. This amounts to 15 million adults out of a total population of 60 million. This highlights the barriers to adoption with cost and poor understanding of the benefits of the Internet being the reasons most often cited for not using the service. The reluctance to go online increases with age, 85 per cent of those over 55 saying in the 1999 survey saying they will never be connected to the Internet. When asked, in the 1999 survey, why they would remain non-users, half of all non-users said they did not believe that the Internet was relevant to their needs; 30 per cent have resisted because of the cost and 16 per cent because they are afraid of or do not understand the technology. Part of the reluctance to access the technology appears to be based on ignorance, with 25 per cent not knowing that a computer (or set top box) is necessary to get online and only 37 per cent knowing that a telephone line is necessary.

For B2B companies, although many businesses now have access to the Internet, access within companies is uneven. For example, a survey of UK SMEs in 2000 showed that although 90 per cent have access to the Internet (87 per cent in small and 95 per cent in medium), the number of employees with access to the Internet was only 41 per cent for medium business and 46 per cent in small business (Durlacher, 2000). In an individual business, this could mean that although the R&D or marketing team may have access, those involved in purchasing may not. Further data on access levels is presented in *Figure 4.6*.

The DTI (2000) study also evaluated some of the barriers to B2B e-commerce (DTI, 2000). Barriers were rated out of 5 by e-commerce adopters where 1 = strongly disagree and 5 = strongly agree. The different barriers were rated as follows by non-adopters:

- No tangible benefits (3.51)
- E-commerce is not relevant to the business (3.6)
- The technology costs are too high (3.5)
- Concern about fraud (3.11)
- Concern about confidentiality (3.22)

The non-adopters seem to believe strongly that investment in e-commerce is not worthwhile. Note that security is not the main barrier, as expected perhaps; it is lack of imperative.

Introducing The B2B and B2C Companies

The significance of e-commerce and e-business will vary between every business and organization in terms of adoption by customers in its marketplace and the timing and amount of investment needed. In particular, as we have seen, adoption is likely to vary between businesses and consumers. For this reason it has become conventional to consider **business-to-business (B2B)** e-commerce and **business-to-consumer (B2C)** e-commerce separately. Differences between these e-commerce models and C2C and C2B approaches are described in more detail in *activity 2.2*.

Business-to-business (B2B)
Commercial transactions are between an organization and other organizations.

Business-to-consumer (B2C)
Commercial transactions are between an organization and consumers.

Due to differences in B2B and B2C e-commerce, throughout the book we shall distinguish between B2B and B2C e-commerce. To prompt readers to think about the differences between e-commerce management decisions required for B2B and B2C e-commerce and to give a common theme through the book we shall also consider two typical companies. These generic companies will be referred to as 'The B2B Company', a medium-to-large company selling paints and chemicals used for coating products manufactured by other companies, and 'The B2C Company', a smaller company selling kitchenware to consumers. *Activity 1.6* introduces these companies as the basis for activities later in the book.

Introducing The B2B Company and The B2C Company

Activity 1.6

Purpose

To introduce the running case companies used for activities throughout the book.

The B2B Company

The B2B Company is an international company employing 600 people worldwide including 300 at its head office. Its annual turnover is approximately £100 million and it was established in 1955.

Products

There are two different types of products:

1. *Composites* – sold to other businesses to be incorporated in their products. For example, products are used in the mouldings and coatings for boats, trains, planes and cars. There are about 200 top customers who are responsible for the majority of revenue in this area. These orders are usually delivered by tanker load, with some customers receiving several loads each week. There are about 800 smaller customers who purchase in quantities measured in drums. There are over 100 product variants of composites for different applications.
2. *Speciality polymers* – the polymer technology is incorporated into graphic arts for use in paper and board applications (such as overprint varnishes on cereal packets and glossy magazines). There are about 10 key speciality polymer customers. These are also ordered in bulk.

Products are sold through independent distributors in over 90 countries worldwide. The company grew during the 1990s through joint ventures or acquisitions of manufacturing facilities in France, the Middle East, South Africa, USA, Scandinavia and the Czech Republic.

Distribution

Products are sold through independent distributors in over 90 countries worldwide. The company grew during the 1990s through joint ventures or acquisitions of manufacturing facilities in France, the Middle East, South Africa, USA, Scandinavia and the Czech republic.

Competitors

There are two major European competitors who have not adopted e-commerce and a single US competitor who recently introduced an e-commerce system.

Existing information systems

The company currently use the ERP system PRISM (http://www.marcam.com/products/prism) to manage information on customers, orders, inventory and logistics. This will need to be integrated with the e-commerce solution.

The B2C Company

The B2C Company is a small company that was established in 1984 and has 80 staff. Approximately half the staff are in production and the other half are divided

▶

Activity 1.6 *continued*

between management, administration and retail. It manufactures kitchenware and sells these products and similar items from other manufacturers through its network of shops.

Products

The B2C Company manufactures and sells plastic kitchenware such as storage containers, plates, bags and kitchen implements.

Distribution

It opened its first shop on the trading estate where it manufactures its products and has since opened three other shops in towns in the north of the country. It also sells its products through traditional outlets such as department stores, supermarkets and small specialist retailers. Finally it has sold its products by mail order for about ten years. No products are currently sold abroad.

Competitors

The B2C Company or 'It'/'The Company' has three major national competitors, two of which have adopted e-commerce, and a major European competitor which also has an e-commerce system.

Existing information systems

The company uses Sage for its accounts together with specialist manufacturing and catalogue software.

Questions

1. For each of the two companies summarize the business benefits of e-commerce and e-business using the simple mnemonic of the 6Cs (Bocij *et al.*, 1999), that is cost reduction, new capability, communication, control, customer service and competitive advantage. You should mark each benefit as to whether it is an advantage arising from buy- or sell-side e-commerce or enhancement of e-business processes. Alternatively, you may wish to consider a not-for-profit organization such as a charity, local government or the health service that can be considered to be B2C.
2. Discuss the differences in benefits between the B2B and B2C organizations.

For answers see p. 25

Management responses to e-commerce and e-business

A primary aim of this book is to consider the management issues when businesses look to take advantage of the opportunities afforded by e-commerce and e-business. How should an e-business strategy be developed? To what extent can we use existing business and IS strategy models? What are the main changes that need to be made to the organization as part of implementing the strategy? These issues are explored in more detail in *Part 2*. Before we can develop e-business strategy a foundation is needed. This is provided in *Part 1* of the book.

Part 1: Introduction

Part 1 describes the background to e-business as follows:

- *Chapter 1: Introduction to e-business and e-commerce*. Definition of the meaning and scope of e-business and e-commerce. Introduction to business use of the Internet – what are the benefits and barriers to adoption and how widely used is it?

- *Chapter 2: E-commerce fundamentals*. Introduction to new business models and marketplace structures enabled by electronic communications.
- *Chapter 3: E-business infrastructure*. Background on the hardware, software and telecommunications that need to be managed to achieve e-business.
- *Chapter 4: E-environment*. Describes the macro-environment of an organization that presents opportunities and constraints on strategy and implementation.

Part 2: Strategy and applications

In Part 2 of the book approaches to developing e-business strategy are covered by reviewing how e-business strategy and applications should be developed for the organization as a whole (*Chapter 5*) and with an emphasis on the buy-side (*Chapters 6 and 7*) and the sell-side (*Chapters 7 and 8*).

- *Chapter 5: E-business strategy*. Approaches to developing e-business strategy. Differences from traditional strategic approaches. Relation to IS strategy.
- *Chapter 6: Supply chain management*. A supply chain perspective on strategy with examples of how technology can be applied to increase supply chain and value chain efficiency.
- *Chapter 7: E-procurement*. Evaluation of the benefits of adopting e-procurement.
- *Chapter 8: E-marketing*. A sell-side e-commerce perspective to e-business reviewing differences in marketing required through digital media.
- *Chapter 9: Customer relationship management*. Using e-commerce as part of acquiring, retaining and extending customers.

Here we introduce some of the strategy issues involved with e-business using the classic McKinsey 7S strategy instrument. This is summarized in *Figure 1.8* to

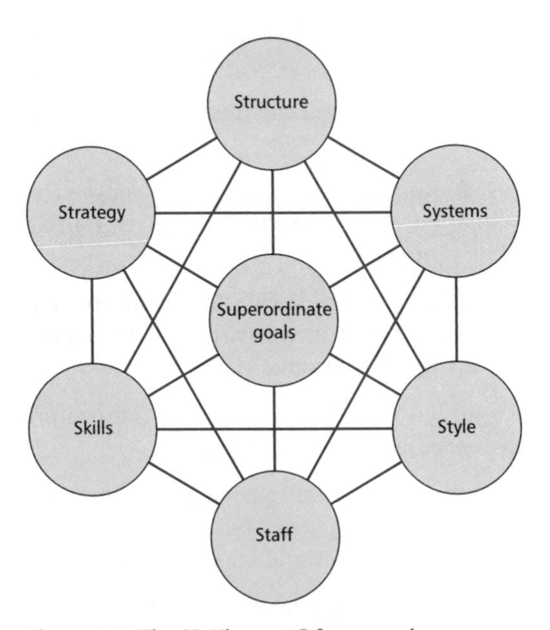

Figure 1.8 The McKinsey 7S framework

highlight some aspects that need to be managed when developing a business strategy (*activity 1.7*).

Activity 1.7 **Applying the 7S framework to e-business initiatives**

Purpose

To illustrate some of the key strategy issues of implementing e-business.

Question

Take either The B2B or B2C Company and consider organizational changes that may be required for each of the 7Ss. Which factors do you feel are ignored by the 7Ss?

For answer see p. 25

Part 3: Implementation

E-commerce management is described in *Part 3* of the book in which we examine practical management issues involved with creating and implementing e-business solutions.

- *Chapter 10: Change management.* How to manage the organizational, human and technology change required in the move to e-business.
- *Chapter 11: Analysis and design.* We discuss the main issues of analysis and design raised by e-commerce systems that need to be discussed by managers and solutions providers.
- *Chapter 12: Implementation and maintenance.* How should e-commerce systems be managed and monitored once they are live?

Summary

1. Electronic commerce traditionally refers to electronically mediated buying and selling.
2. Sell-side e-commerce involves all electronic business transactions between an organization and its customers, while buy-side e-commerce involves transactions between an organization and its suppliers.
3. Electronic business is a broader term referring to how technology can benefit all internal business processes and interactions with third parties. This includes buy-side and sell-side e-commerce and the internal value chain.
4. The monetary value of e-commerce for business-to-business (B2B) transactions greatly exceeds that for business-to-consumer transactions (B2C).
5. The main business drivers for introducing e-commerce and e-business are opportunities for increased revenues and reducing costs, but many other benefits can be identified that improve customer service and corporate image.
6. Adoption of the Internet is limited by lack of imperative, cost of access and security fears.

7. Introducing new technology is not all that is required for success in introducing e-commerce and business. Clearly defined objectives, creating the right culture for change, mix of skills, partnerships and organizational structure are arguably more important.

ACTIVITY ANSWERS

1.1 Understanding e-commerce and e-business

1. The terms you may have listed include e-commerce, e-business, e-marketing, e-procurement, e-logistics, e-tailer or e-retailer, e-finance, e-recruitment, e-service, e-crm (customer relationship management), e-procurement and e-strategy. For a fuller definition of the main terms see the section *E-commerce defined*.
2. You will have noted that the terms tend to describe a range of business activities within an organization. They typically refer to business processes that form part of the value chain from inbound logistics and purchasing (e-procurement) to outbound logistics (e-fulfilment) and managing the customer relationship through e-marketing and e-crm. Note that they do not apply to support departments such as e-HRM or e-accounting. See the section *E-commerce and the value chain.*

   As explained in the section *E-commerce defined* you may have noted that e-business and e-commerce are generally taken to have a broad meaning, and these are made up of different aspects such as e-procurement and e-crm.

   The significance of the terms will vary according to their relevance to departmental managers; this is perhaps a difficulty since the big picture may be lost.
3. This discussion point is raised since managers should and will naturally question new management concepts and technologies. These terms are initially communicated by word-of-mouth between customer and consultant and suppliers. For widespread adoption they will be promulgated by adverts and features in specialist media such as trade publications for computing or purchasing professionals and then the general media such as newspapers and television. This may also be in response to government and technology supplier organizations wishing to increase adoption.

   To answer whether this is a passing fad we can review typical adoption patterns of technology through time for new management concepts and technology and then look at specific adoption of technology. This is done in the section *Adoption of e-commerce and e-business.*

(W) 1.2 What is e-commerce? What is e-business?

A typical definition from the European Union site follows. This is a useful definition for managers since it explains the range of business activities that occur through e-commerce.

> *Electronic commerce refers to any activity which involves enterprises interacting and doing business with customers, with each other or with administrations by electronic means.*
>
> *It includes electronic ordering of goods and services which are delivered using traditional channels such as post or couriers (indirect electronic commerce), on-line ordering, payment and delivery of intangible goods and services such as software, electronic magazines, entertainment services and information services (direct electronic commerce), electronic fund transfers, electronic share trading, electronic bills of lading, commercial auctions, collaborative design and engineering, on-line sourcing, public procurement, direct consumer marketing and after-sales service.* (Electronic Commerce: Commission presents framework for future action, 16 April 1997. (www.europa.eu.int/comm/eurostat)

Notice that at the IBM site, there is no reference to e-commerce, their focus is e-business, while the reverse is true at the Andersen Consulting site!

(W) 1.3 E-commerce adoption by consumers and businesses

Nua (www.nua.ie/surveys/how_many_online/index.html) reported over 400 million users worldwide at January 2001, with 83 million European users including 15 million in the UK.

Data from Fletcher Research, now part of Forrester Research (www.fletch.co.uk), based on 50,000 UK households published in December 1999 included the following predictions for UK Internet penetration for adult users (millions). Compare these to the actual figures for the year you read this!

1998 – 10.6m (23% of population with access)
1999 – 15.7m (33% of population with access)
2000 – 18.8m (40% of population with access)
2001 – 21.6m (46% of population with access)
2002 – 23.7m (50% of population with access)
2003 – 24.5m (52% of population with access)

Location of internet access, total adult users (millions)

1998 – Home 5.4m	Work 5.5m	Academia 1.5m
1999 – Home 10.4m	Work 6.5m	Academia 1.5m
2000 – Home 13m	Work 7.4m	Academia 1.6m
2001 – Home 15.3m	Work 8.7m	Academia 1.7m
2002 – Home 17.3m	Work 9.6m	Academia 1.7m
2003 – Home 18.3m	Work 10.1m	Academia 1.7m

1.4 Global variations in e-commerce adoption

1. The figure of 8.4% is relatively small compared with other channels (even though it is based on rapid growth forecasts). This suggests that despite the hype about e-commerce it is only suited to certain products such as books, CDs, travel and catalogue B2B sales.
2. The figure for N. America (12.8%) is significantly higher than for Asia/Pacific (8.0%) and Western Europe (6.0%), which in turn is much higher than that for Latin America and the Rest of the World (2.4%). The regions which gain early experience of e-commerce are clearly in a better position to exploit it in the future. It does not appear as if global disparities in trade are likely to be reduced by e-commerce, at least in the short term; indeed it may accentuate them.
3. Overall, there is a predicted increase by a factor of 10 between 2000 ($657 billion) and 2004 ($6789 billion). It is difficult to imagine that organizations and consumers will be dynamic enough that this number will purchase online.
4. Not applicable, but in all likelihood the growth will have been overestimated.

1.5 How accurate are forecasts of e-commerce growth?

1. Possible reasons for the discrepancies include:
   - Differences in what is meant by B2B (which market sectors are included and excluded?).
   - Differences in what is meant by e-commerce (e.g. does it include EDI, does it only refer to completely automated online transactions?).
   - Difficulties in extrapolating from a relatively small number of current online purchasers when a rapid increase is forecast (see *Figure 1.4*).

- Variations in assumptions of adoption of Internet access and whether it is acceptable to purchase online.

2. Clearly great care has to be taken in using these analyst figures. Managers' own estimates of revenues within their companies need to specify a worst case and best case scenario for e-commerce revenues – others in the company need to be educated about the difficulties of forecasting. Estimates for a particular industry should be used rather than industry-wide averages. It can also be argued that even if there are large discrepancies, all estimates still mark a major change on traditional marketplaces.

1.6 Introducing The B2B Company and The B2C Company

1. Benefits for The B2B Company:
   - Cost reduction – cost of sales and promotion may be reduced and lower prices passed onto customers.
   - Capability – may be able to increase penetration in countries that do not have a significant share. May help reduce the amount of goods stored. Composites could be sold to 800 customers via e-commerce system – can potentially increase number of smaller customers.
   - Communication – system can improve communications with customers and distributors through updates of product and technical information.
   - Control – the web site can be used to monitor interest in product from customers.
   - Customer service – customers can use e-commerce system to track delivery and manage inventory better through reducing time for ordering.
   - Competitive advantage –will be dependent on the use of e-commerce by competitors – may gain customers over two European competitors and necessary to compete in the US market.

   Benefits for The B2C Company:
   - Cost reduction – as above.
   - Capability – opportunity for mail order e-commerce – should be relatively easy since based on existing trading model. May be potential for overseas market.
   - Communication – to customers.
   - Control – again, monitoring of interest in products.
   - Customer service – enquiries about products can be detailed on the web site – more room than in print catalogue. Opening times and special offers can be promoted. This may reduce the number of phone enquiries.
   - Competitive advantage – since the majority of its competitors have, or are developing, an e-commerce system, the introduction of a new system is essential for long-term competitive advantage.
2. It is evident that there are many similarities between the B2B and B2C cases. It is difficult to generalize the differences, but the following are apparent here:
   - For The B2C Company there is arguably a larger market potential for national and overseas sales; for The B2B Company, it is a major manufacturer who is already well known around the world.
   - For The B2C Company it is easier to sell direct to customers since there are number of people involved in the buying decision for The B2B Company.
   - The purchasing process is more complex for The B2B Company since chemicals have to be dispatched by tanker and many have to be manufactured on demand.

1.7 Applying the 7S framework to e-commerce initiatives

- Structure – how will be the e-business change be managed? Is a separate division required or can the change be matrix managed (*Chapter 10*)?

- Systems – do new operating procedures or business processes need to be introduced? Can existing IS be used to implement change or will new systems be required?
- Style – is the current, possibly conservative, style of the company consistent with the way the company wants to project its image? Will decisions be made fast enough? Will risks be taken to trial new business models and new technology?
- Staff – is the appropriate mix of staff available?
- Skills – are the correct skills available internally? What training is required? Do we need to outsource some services?
- Superordinate goals – this refers to the higher goals of the company that may be encapsulated in the mission statement. In modern parlance, do the senior managers 'get' the significance of the Internet and will they act?

A possible criticism of the 7S model is that it is internally focused. How well the company forms and leverages partnerships with suppliers and customers is now seen as a key element of strategy. Related to this is how well the company responds to the industry restructuring that has occurred as part of e-commerce. Can it take advantage of disintermediation and reintermediation within the industry (*Chapter 2*)?

EXERCISES

Self-assessment questions

1. Distinguish between e-commerce and e-business.
2. Explain what is meant by buy-side and sell-side e-commerce.
3. Describe the different services that can be offered to customers via a web presence.
4. Summarize the consumer and business adoption levels in your country. What seem to be the main barriers to adoption?
5. Outline the reasons why a business may wish to adopt e-commerce.
6. What are the main differences between business-to-business and business-to-consumer e-commerce?
7. Summarize the impact of the introduction of e-business on different aspects of an organization.
8. What is the relevance of intermediary sites such as Mondus (www.mondus.com) to the B2B company?

Essay and discussion questions

1. Discuss the following question with reference to how an organization should react to the Internet. *Is the Internet a typhoon force, a ten times force, or is it a bit of wind? Or is it a force that fundamentally alters our business?* (Andy Grove, Chairman of Intel).
2. Suggest how a organization can evaluate the impact of the Internet on its business. Is it a passing fad or does it have a significant impact?
3. Similar benefits and barriers exist for the adoption of sell-side e-commerce for both B2B and B2C organizations.

4. 'In most countries the Internet will never be used by more than 50 per cent of the population, so its impact to businesses will be limited'. Discuss.
5. 'Confusion over the meaning of terms e-commerce and e-business will limit the adoption of e-business in many businesses'. Discuss.
6. Analyze *Figure 1.4* commenting on:
   - the overall percentage of sales for e-commerce predicted for 2004 across all markets;
   - the variation in percentage of sales for e-commerce predicted for 2004 in different markets;
   - the growth rates indicated over the four years of predictions;
   - the implications for the developing world.

Examination questions

1. Explain the relationship between the concepts of e-commerce and e-business.
2. Distinguish between buy-side and sell-side e-commerce and give an example of the application of each.
3. Summarize three reasons why a company may wish to introduce e-commerce.
4. Describe three of the main barriers to adoption of e-commerce by consumers and suggest how a company could counter these.
5. Outline the internal changes a company may need to make when introducing e-business.
6. Summarize the differences between adoption of Internet access for consumers and businesses and give reasons for these differences.
7. Name three risks to a company that introduces buy-side e-commerce.
8. Name three risks to a company that introduces sell-side e-commerce.

REFERENCES

Bocij, P., Chaffey, D., Greasley, A. and Hickie, S. (1999) *Business Information Systems. Technology, Development and Management*. FT Management, London.

Chaffey, D., Mayer, R., Johnston, K. and Ellis-Chadwick, F. (2000) *Internet Marketing: Strategy, implementation and practice*. Financial Times Prentice Hall, Harlow, UK.

Durlacher (2000) E-commerce developments in the SME sector. *Durlacher Quarterly Internet Report*. August 2000.

DTI (2000) *Business In The Information Age – International Benchmarking Study 2000*. UK Department of Trade and Industry. Available online at: www.ukonlineforbusiness.gov.uk.

eMarketer (2001) B2B revenues to top US$1 trillion by 2003. Analyst report, 25 July.

Grove, A. (1996) *Only the paranoid survive*. Doubleday.

Forrester (2000) Internet Commerce growth report. Available online at www.forrester.com.

Kalakota, R. and Whinston, A. (1997) *Electronic Commerce. A Manager's Guide*. Addison Wesley. Reading, MA.

Mougayer, M. (1998) E-commerce? E-business? Who E-cares? Computer World web site (www.computerworld.com), 2 November.

Quelch, J. and Klein, L. (1996) The Internet and international marketing. *Sloan Management Review*, Spring, 61–75.

(1980) McKinsey Quarterly

Which (2000) Annual Internet User survey www.which.net/whatsnew/pr/jul00/general/survey.html, 7 November.

Zwass, V. (1998) Structure and macro-level impacts of electronic commerce: from technological infrastructure to electronic marketplaces. In *Emerging Information Technologies*, ed. K. Kendall, Sage publications, Thousand Oaks, CA.

FURTHER READING

Chaffey, D., Mayer, R., Johnston, K. and Ellis-Chadwick, F. (2000) *Internet Marketing: Strategy, implementation and practice*. Financial Times Prentice Hall. Harlow, Essex, UK. Chapter 11 defines transactional e-commerce and summarizes the drivers and benefits. Chapters 13 and 14 highlight the differences between B2C and B2B e-commerce.

Turban, E., Lee, J., King, D. and Chung, H. (2000) *Electronic Commerce: a managerial perspective*. Prentice Hall, Upper Saddle River, NJ. Chapter 1 introduces, gives definitions and outlines benefits for e-commerce.

WEB LINKS

Sites giving general information on market characteristics of Internet

Nua Internet Surveys (www.nua.ie/surveys) summarizes the majority of reports by analysts on e-commerce developments and reports on company and consumer adoption of Internet and characteristics in Europe and worldwide.

CyberAtlas (www.cyberatlas.com) gives a similar service to Nua, but with a more US focus.

Reports on growth of electronic commerce

KPMG Consulting Europe (www.kpmg.co.uk) is a source for regular reports on electronic commerce in Europe.

The other main industry analysts are:

Forrester Research (www.forrester.com)

The Gartner Group (www.gartner.com)

IDC Research (www.idcresearch.com)

Activmedia (www.activmedia.com)

Information from management consultants about applications for e-commerce:

KPMG (www.kpmg.co.uk, www.kpmg.com)

Arthur Andersen (www.arthurandersen.com)

Ernst and Young (www.ey.com – US, www.eyi.com – global, www.eyuk.com – UK)

Accenture (www.accenture.com)

PricewaterhouseCoopers (www.pwcglobal.com, www.pwcglobal.com/uk)

IBM (www.ibm.com, www.uk.ibm.com, www.ibm.com/e-business)

Deloitte and Touche (www.dttus.com – US site, www.dc.com – Deloitte Consulting)

General sources on online marketing

Marketing Online (www.marketing-online.co.uk) is a source for links to web sites concerned with Internet marketing strategy, implementation and practice. Produced by Dave Chaffey.

Elab (formerly **Project 2000**) (ecommerce.vanderbilt.edu and www.elab.com) was founded in 1994 by Tom Novak and Donna Hoffman at School of Management,

Vanderbilt University, to study marketing implications of Internet. Useful links/papers.

Print media

E-business Review (www.e-businessreview.co.uk) is a monthly for IS managers from the publishers of *Computer Weekly*.

Revolution magazine (www.revolution.haynet.com) has a web site for monthly UK magazine on new media – mainly sell-side e-commerce.

Net Profit (www.net-profit.co.uk) is a monthly UK-based newsletter on Internet commerce with a European focus.

Chapter 2

E-commerce fundamentals

CHAPTER AT A GLANCE

Main topics

Focus on . . .

Case study

LEARNING OBJECTIVES

After completing this chapter the reader should be able to:

- Evaluate changes in trading patterns and marketplace models enabled by e-commerce
- Identify the main business models of electronic trading
- Describe different revenue models and transaction mechanisms available through hosting an e-commerce site.

MANAGEMENT ISSUES

The fundamentals of e-commerce imply these questions for managers:

- What are the implications of changes in marketplace structures for how we trade with customers and other partners?
- Which business models and revenue models should we consider to exploit the Internet?
- What will be the importance of online marketplace hubs or exchanges to our business?

Links to other chapters

The main related chapters are:

- *Chapter 3* explains the hardware and software infrastructure enabling these new business models;
- *Chapters 4 and 5* consider appropriate strategic responses to these new models and paradigms;
- *Chapter 6* explores new models of the value chain in more detail;
- *Chapter 7* explores the effect of new intermediaries and marketplaces on procurement.

Introduction

Disruptive technologies
New technologies that prompt businesses to reappraise their strategic approaches.

Electronic communications are **disruptive technologies** that have already caused major changes in industry structure, marketplace structure and business models. Consider a B2B organization such as 'The B2B Company'. Traditionally it has sold its products through a network of distributors. With the advent of e-commerce it now has the opportunity to bypass distributors and trade directly with customers via a web site, and it also has the opportunity to reach customers through new B2B marketplaces. Knowledge of the opportunities and threats presented by these changes is essential to those involved in defining business, marketing and information systems strategy. In this chapter we introduce a number of frameworks that will be applied throughout the remainder of the book when considering the e-commerce and e-business strategies that companies should adopt in response to the Internet. To conclude the chapter, we evaluate the Internet start-ups – the dot-coms launched in response to the opportunities provided by new business models, and see what lessons can be learnt from the dot-com failures.

The chapter starts by considering the different participants and constraints in the e-commerce environment. We then look at how electronic communications have facilitated restructuring of the relationships between members of the electronic marketplace – a key feature of e-commerce. Electronic communications have also given rise to many exciting new business models and we investigate the potential of these also.

Throughout this chapter we mainly consider the sell-side elements of e-commerce rather than the e-business as a whole. This approach has been chosen since the focus is mainly on how an organization can restructure relationships on the downstream side of its supply chain. A review of the entire supply chain is completed in *Chapter 6*.

The e-commerce environment

All organizations operate within an environment that influences the way in which they conduct business. Strategy development is strongly influenced by considering the environment the business operates in. *Figure 2.1* illustrates some of the elements that may influence the way in which an organization operates.

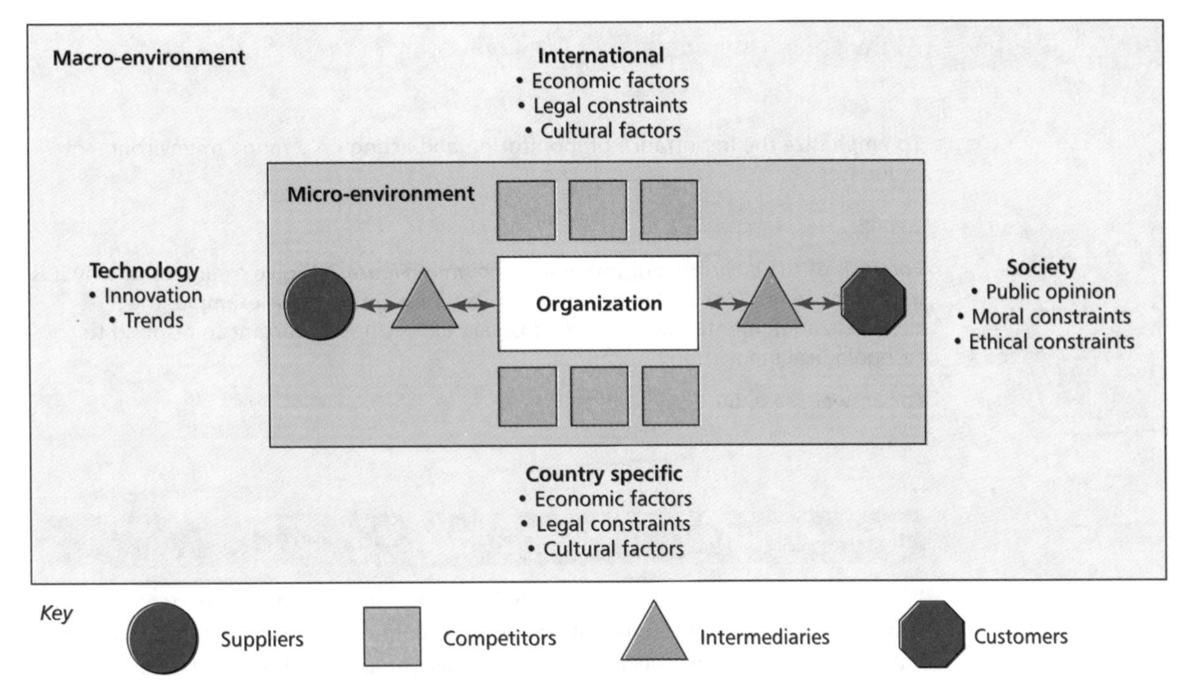

Figure 2.1 The environment in which e-business services are provided

For e-commerce strategy, the most significant influences are those of the immediate marketplace that is shaped by the needs of customers and how services are provided to them through competitors, intermediaries and via upstream suppliers. Wider influences are provided by local and international economic conditions and legislation together with what business practices are acceptable to society. Finally, technological innovations are vital in providing opportunities to provide superior services to competitors or through changing the shape of the marketplace. For example, a web site with *personalization facilities* (*Chapter 9, p. 355*) can provide information tailored for a customer that offers advantages beyond a competitor's offerings. What are the implications of these environmental influences for a company? If you look at the top 100 companies from 50 years ago in your country you will probably find that less than a quarter of them remain in the top 100; many may have even have ceased to exist. There are many reasons why this may be the case, but a key issue will be failure to monitor and respond to these environmental influences. Given that these influences vary rapidly and will have a major impact on the success of a company, it is important that the current environment is monitored and future environment trends are anticipated. This is an important role of *knowledge management* (*Chapter 10, p. 403*). Not only must employees be charged with monitoring these environmental factors, but it must be possible to disseminate this information so that decision makers can take appropriate action. In a later chapter we examine some of the issues of *the e-commerce environment* (*Chapter 4, p. 122*) in more detail using the SLEPT framework to examine Social, Legal, Political, Economic and Technological issues. Now complete *activity 2.1* to review the importance of these environmental influences.

Activity 2.1 **Why are environment influences important?**

Purpose

To emphasize the importance of monitoring and acting on a range of environment influences.

Activity

For each of the environment influences shown in *Figure 2.1*, give examples of why it is important to monitor and respond in an e-business context. For example, the personalization mentioned in the text is part of why it is important to respond to technological innovation.

For answer see p. 60

The e-commerce marketplace

In this section we look at how electronic communications have changed relationships between the different participants of commercial transactions. Since the nature of these changes according to whether the transaction is between business and consumer or between businesses (inter-organizational), we start by reviewing differences between these type of transactions. We then look at how the channel structures of organizations have been changed through the process of disintermediation and reintermediation. Locations for trading and mechanisms of commercial exchange in the electronic marketplace are then reviewed. Management teams have difficult decisions to take about which of these new models of trading is relevant to them, so we take a questioning approach looking at some examples that have worked, and some that haven't.

Restructuring of the supply chain and value chain is not discussed in this chapter since it is covered later (*Chapter 6, p. 215*).

Business or consumer model

It is commonplace to identify e-business opportunities in terms of whether an organization is transacting with consumers (**business-to-consumer (B2C)**) or other businesses (**business-to-business (B2B)**). *Activity 2.2* shows why studies of e-commerce often distinguish between B2B and B2C – the characteristics of trading in each environment are quite different in terms of devising strategy and marketing techniques.

Business-to-consumer (B2C)
Commercial transactions are between an organization and consumers.

Business-to-consumer (B2B)
Commercial transactions are between an organization and other organizations.

Business-to-business transactions predominate over the Internet, in terms of value, if not frequency. For example, a report by analyst *eMarketer* (www.emarketer.com) predicted that by the end of 2000 B2B e-commerce would account for 79 per cent of total e-commerce, 82 per cent by end 2001, 85 per cent by 2002 and 87 per cent by 2003. *Figure 2.2* helps explain why this is the case. It shows that there are many more opportunities for B2B transactions than B2C, both between an organization and its suppliers, together with intermediaries, and through distributors such as agents and wholesalers with customers.

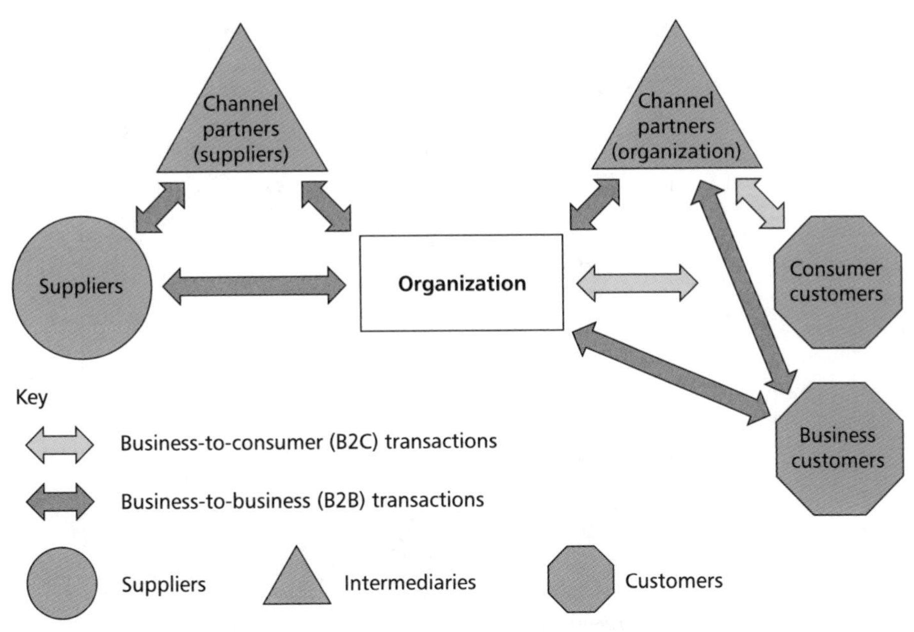

Figure 2.2 B2B and B2C interactions between an organization, its suppliers and its customers

Why distinguish between B2B and B2C?

Activity 2.2

Purpose

To introduce the differences between B2B and B2C e-commerce that must be taken into consideration when devising strategy and tactics

Activity

Consider how you think the characteristics summarized in the first column below differ for B2C and B2B. Refer to *Figure 2.2* when completing your answer.

Table 2.1 Differences in characteristics between B2B and B2C e-commerce

Characteristic	*B2C*	*B2B*
Proportion of adopters with access Complexity of buying decisions Channel Purchasing characteristics Product characteristic		

For answer see p. 60

Figure 2.3 gives examples of different companies operating in the business-to-consumer (B2C) and business-to-business (B2B) sphere. *Figure 2.3* also presents two additional types of transaction, that where consumers transact directly with consumers (C2C) and where initiate trading with companies (C2B). Note that the C2C and C2B monikers are less widely used (e.g. *The Economist*, 2000), but they do highlight significant differences between Internet-based commerce and earlier forms of commerce. Consumer-to-consumer interactions were relatively rare, but as the

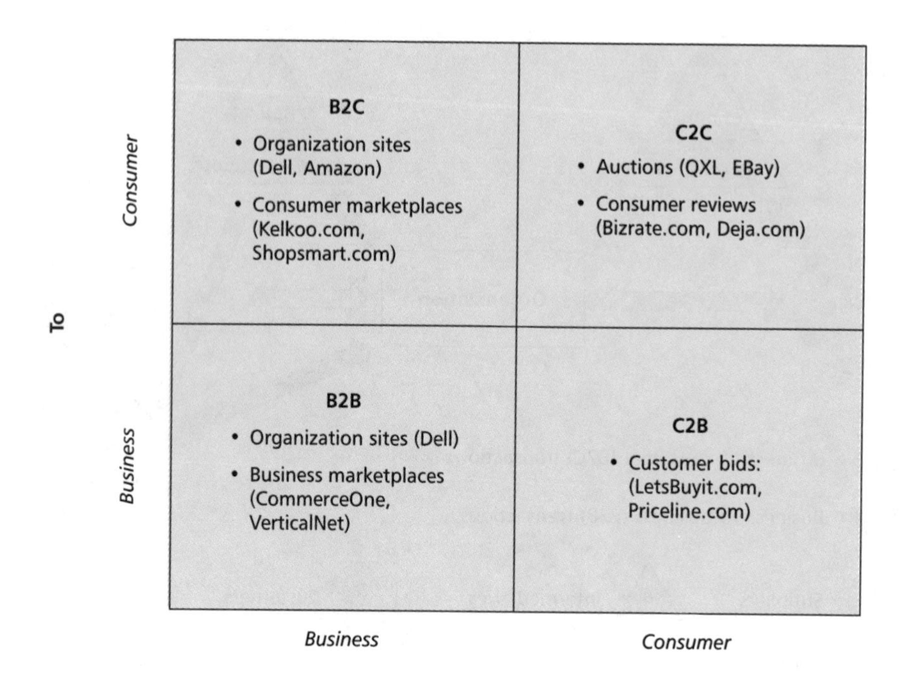

Figure 2.3 Summary of transaction alternatives between businesses and consumers

example shows are now very common in the form of *online auctions* (*Chapter 2, p. 46*) and the *community* (*Chapter 9, p. 359*) components of sites. Indeed, Hoffman and Novak (1996) suggest that C2C interactions are a key characteristic of the Internet that is important for companies to take into account C2C interactions as is shown by *activity 2.3*. It should be noted before we leave C2C and C2B interactions that although it is useful to identify these separately, both types of site are set up by intermediary *businesses*, so they can be considered to be part of B2C.

As well as the models shown in *Figure 2.3*, it has been suggested that employees should be considered as a separate type of consumer through the use of intranets; this is referred to as employee-to-employee or E2E.

Activity 2.3 Why C2C interactions at Bizrate matter for retailers

Purpose

To highlight the relevance of C2C sites to B2C companies.

Questions

1. Visit the Bizrate site (www.bizrate.com). Visit this site and explain the actions a company should take if it is not listed on this site.
2. The Country Bookshop (www.countrybookshop.co.uk) is relatively unusual as a European e-tailer on this site. Visit the comments for this site and explain the benefits to this company.

For answers see p. 61

Marketplace channel structures

Channel structures describe the way a manufacturer or selling organization delivers products and services to their customers. The distribution channel will consist of one or more intermediaries such as wholesalers and retailers. For example, a music company is unlikely to distribute its CDs directly to retailers, but will use wholesalers who have a large warehouse of titles which are then distributed to individual branches according to demand. A company selling business products may have a longer distribution channel involving more intermediaries.

The relationship between a company and its channel partners shown in *Figure 2.2* can be dramatically altered by the opportunities afforded by the Internet. This occurs because the Internet offers a means of bypassing some of the channel partners. This process is known as **disintermediation** or 'cutting out the middleman'.

Disintermediation
The removal of intermediaries such as distributors or brokers that formerly linked a company to its customers.

Figure 2.4 illustrates disintermediation in a graphical form for a simplified retail channel. Further intermediaries such as additional distributors may occur in a business-to-business market. Figure 2.4(a) shows the former position where a company markets and sells it products by 'pushing' them through a sales channel. *Figure 2.4*(b) and (c) show two different type of disintermediation in which the wholesaler (b) or the wholesaler and retailer (c) are bypassed allowing the producer to sell and promote direct to the consumer. The benefits of disintermediation to the producer are clear – it is able to remove the sales and infrastructure cost of selling selling through the channel. Benjamin and Weigand (1995) calculate that, using the sale of quality shirts as an example, it is possible to make cost savings of 28 per cent in the case of (b) and 62 per cent for case (c). Some of these cost savings can be passed on to the customer in the form of cost reductions.

At the start of business hype about the Internet in the mid-1990s there was much speculation that widespread disintermediation would see the failure of many intermediary companies as direct selling occurred. While many companies have taken advantage of disintermediation, the results have sometimes been less than spectacular. Vauxhall (www.vauxhall.co.uk; see *Figure 2.5*), the UK part of General Motors, started selling its cars direct to customers in the mid-1990s, but despite a major advertising campaign, only several hundred cars were sold direct over the Internet in the first year. In fact, although disintermediation has occurred, the

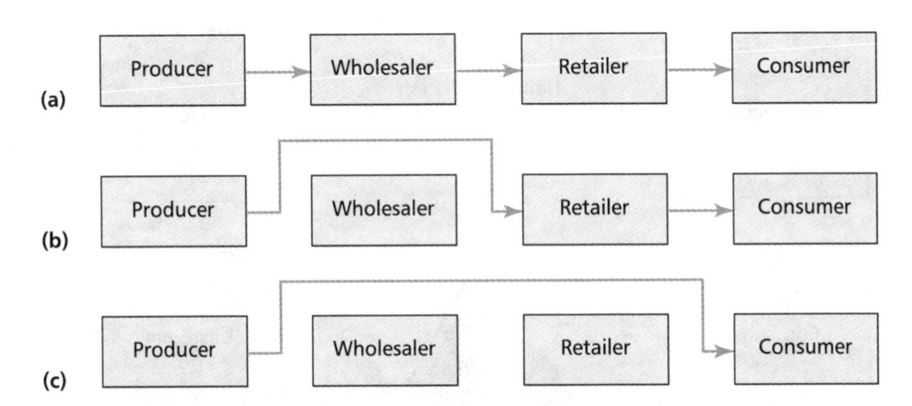

Figure 2.4 Disintermediation of a consumer distribution channel showing (a) the original situation, (b) disintermediation omitting the wholesaler, and (c) disintermediation omitting both wholesaler and retailer

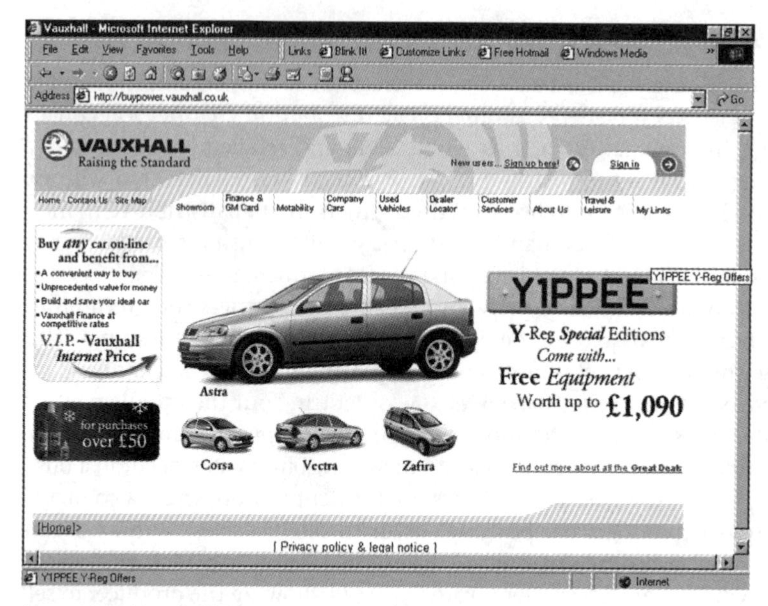

Figure 2.5 **Vauxhall e-commerce site (www.vauxhall.co.uk)**

pattern illustrated in *Figure 2.6* has occurred. Let's take the example of car insurance in the UK market. In *Figure 2.6*(a) we commence with the traditional situation in which many sales were through brokers such as the Automobile Association (www.theaa.co.uk). With disintermediation (*Fig 2.6*(b)) there was the opportunity to sell direct, initially via call-centres as with Direct Line (www.directline.co.uk) and then complemented by a transactional web site as was the case for Eagle

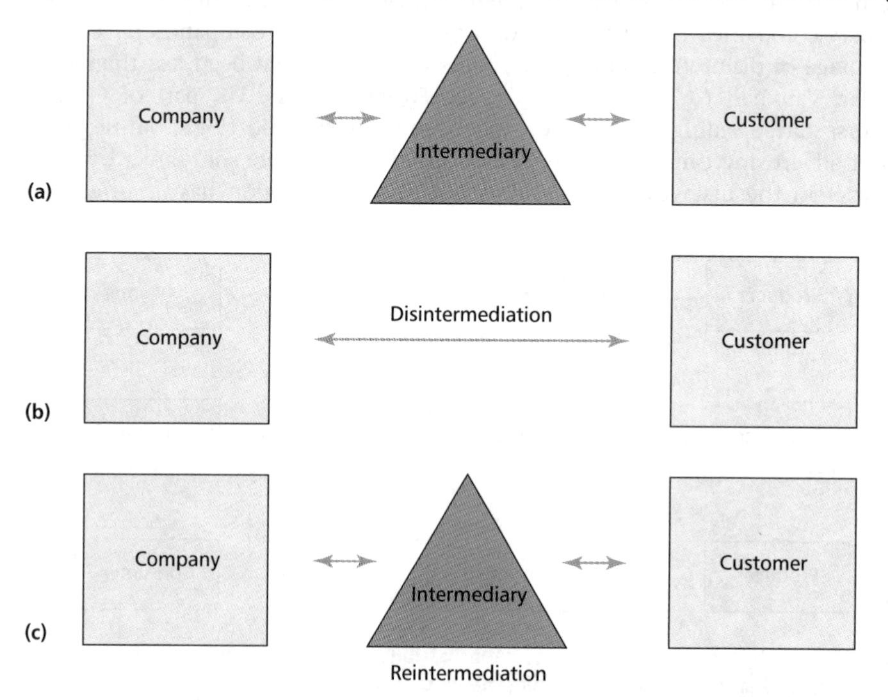

Figure 2.6 **From original situation (a) to disintermediation (b) and reintermediation (c)**

Star (www.eaglestar.co.uk). Purchasers of products still needed assistance in the selection of products and this led to the creation of new intermediaries, a process referred to as **reintermediation** (Fig 2.6(c)). In the UK Screentrade (www.screentrade.co.uk) was established as a broker to enable different companies to sell direct.

Reintermediation
The creation of new intermediaries between customers and suppliers providing services such as supplier search and product evaluation.

Figure 2.7 shows the operation of reintermediation in a graphical form. Following disintermediation where the customer goes direct to different suppliers to select a product, this becomes inefficient for the consumer. Taking again the example of someone buying insurance, to decide on the best price and offer, they would have to visit, say, five different insurers and then return to the one they decide to purchase from. Reintermediation removes this inefficiency by placing an intermediary between the purchaser and seller. This intermediary performs the price evaluation stage of fulfilment since its database has links updated from prices contained within the databases of different suppliers.

What are the implications of reintermediation for the e-commerce manager? First, it is necessary to make sure that your company, as a supplier, is represented with the new intermediaries operating within your chosen market sector. This implies the need to integrate, using the Internet, databases containing price information with that of different intermediaries. Second, it is important to monitor the prices of other suppliers within this sector (possibly by using the intermediary web site for this purpose). Third, it may be appropriate to create your own intermediary, for example DIY chain B&Q has set up its own intermediary to help budding

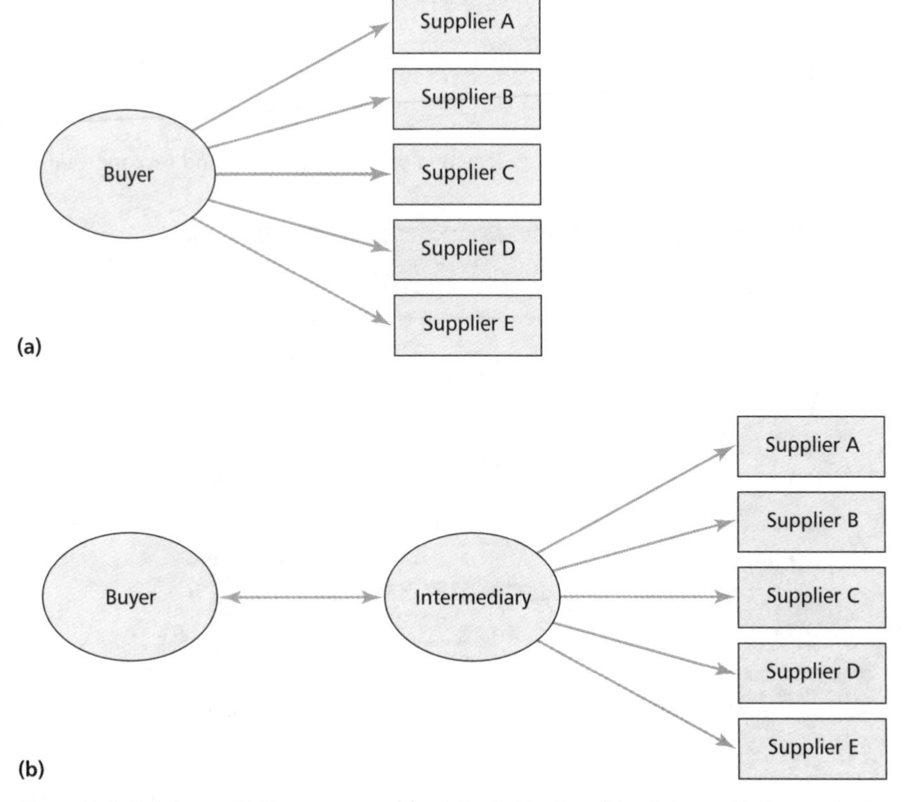

Figure 2.7 Reintermediation process: (a) original situation (b) reintermediation contacts

DIYers, but is positioned separately from its owners. Such tactics to counter or take advantage of reintermediation are sometimes known as **countermediation**.

Countermediation
Creation of a new intermediary by an established company.

There are many different types of intermediary in addition to the broker intermediaries such as Screen trade that simplify the purchase and sale of goods. Bizrate (see *Figure 2.3*) is a further type of intermediary, in this case bringing consumers together.

Sarkar *et al.* (1996) identify many different types of new intermediaries (mainly from a B2C perspective) whom they refer to as cybermediaries. Others have referred to the intermediaries since they are essentially information brokers. Hagel and Rayport (1997) use **infomediary** specifically to refer to sale of customer information. This term is not widely used today, since it is inconsistent with the concept of *permission marketing* (*Chapter 9, p. 332*).

Infomediary
A business whose main source of revenue derives from capturing consumer information and developing detailed profiles of individual customers for use by third parties.

Some of the main new intermediaries identified by Sarkar *et al.* (1996) are:

- Directories (such as Yahoo, Excite).
- Search engines (Altavista, Infoseek).
- Malls (BarclaySquare, Buckingham Gate).
- Virtual resellers (Owns inventory and sells direct, e.g. Amazon, CDNow).
- Financial intermediaries (offering digital cash and cheque payment services such as Digicash).
- Forums, fan clubs and user groups (referred to collectively as virtual communities).
- Evaluators (sites which act as reviewers or comparison of services)

Activity 2.4 highlights the alternative revenue models available to these new intermediaries, in this case an evaluator, and speculates on their future.

Activity 2.4 Kelkoo.com, an example of revenue models for new intermediaries

Purpose

To provide an example of the services provided by cybermediaries and explore their viability as businesses.

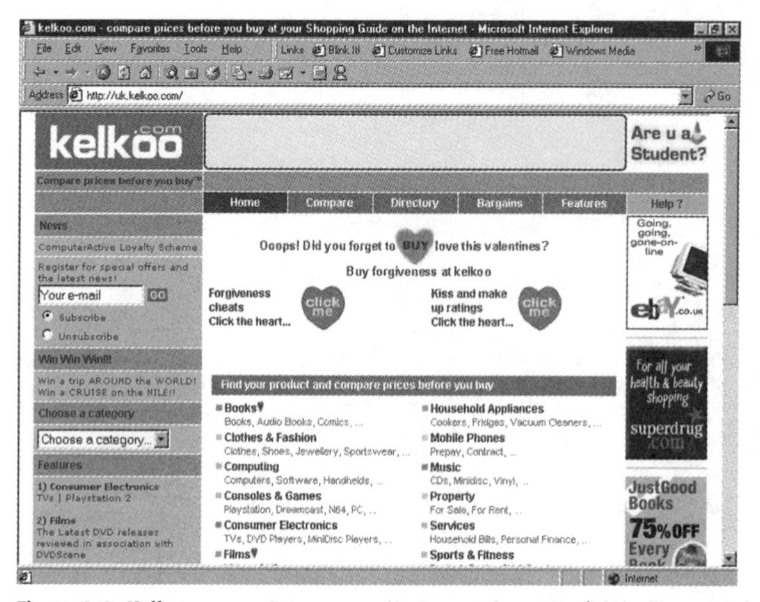

Figure 2.8 Kelkoo.com, a European price comparison site (uk.kelkoo.com)

Questions

1. Visit the Kelkoo web site (www.kelkoo.com) and search for this book, a CD or anything else you fancy. Explain the service that is being offered to customers.
2. Write down the different revenue opportunities for this site (some may be evident from the site, but others may not; write down your ideas also).
3. Given that there are other competing sites in this intermediary category such as Shopsmart (www.shopsmart.com), assess the future of this online business using press releases and comments from other sites such as Moreover (www.moreover.com).

For answers see p. 61

A further type of intermediary is the *virtual marketplace* or virtual trading community. These are of vital importance in the B2B marketplace. From the supplier's or manufacturer's perspective they provide a new channel for selling their products. If the marketplace is set up by major players in an industry such as the Covisint marketplace created by Ford, GM and DaimlerChrysler (www.covisint.com) it will probably be essential to trade with key customers via this method, since this will be a prerequisite for trading with the customer. From the viewpoint of the B2B customer procuring supplies, the virtual marketplace offers the opportunity for lower prices as pricing becomes more transparent, giving rise to greater price competition. The form of these marketplaces is considered in more detail in *Focus on electronic marketplaces* (*Chapter 7, p. 272*).

Focus on portals

At the time that Sarkar *et al.* (1996) described the different types of cybermediaries listed above, there were many separate web sites offering these types of services. For example, Altavista (www.altavista.com) offered **search engine** facilities and Yahoo! (www.yahoo.com) offered a **directory** of different web sites. Since this time, such sites have diversified the services offered. Altavista now also offers a directory obtained from the Open Directory service (www.dmoz.org). Yahoo! now offers a search engine using the Google service (www.google.com). It is apparent that diversification has occurred through the introduction of new intermediaries that provide services to other intermediaries and also through acquisition and merger.

Search engines, spiders and robots
Automatic tools known as spiders or robots index registered sites. Users search this by typing keywords and are presented with a list of pages.

Directories or catalogues
Structured listing of registered sites in different categories.

Portal
A web site that acts as a gateway to information and services available on the Internet by providing search engines, directories and other services such as personalized news or free e-mail.

The concept of the **portal** has evolved to reflect the range of services offered by some cybermediaries. The term 'portal' originated with reference to sites that were the default home pages of users. In other words, when users started their web browser, the first page they saw was their personal home page. When users use a newly installed browser it will be set up so that the home page is that of the company who produces it. In the case of Microsoft this is usually www.msn.com (The Microsoft Network) or www.microsoft.com, and for Netscape it is home.netscape.com.

Portals are significant since they are the prime real estate of the Internet.

Inspection of the most visited sites in Europe (*Table 2.2*) shows that the top ten in the UK are all portals.

Table 2.2 Jupiter MMXI – top 10 domains in the UK (June 2000 measurement period, at home panel) (www.mediametrix.com)

Rank	*Top 10 domains*	*Unique visitors (000)*	*Reach in %*
1	MSN.com	3 863	36.4
2	Yahoo.com	3 676	34.6
3	Freeserve.com	3 543	33.4
4	Microsoft.com	3 040	28.6
5	MSN.co.uk	2 468	23.3
6	Passport.com	2 134	20.1
7	Yahoo.co.uk	2 123	20.0
8	Lycos.com	2 122	20.0
9	BBC.co.uk	1 730	16.3
10	Demon.net	1 564	14.7
	Total Digital Media	**10 613**	**100**

Portals are important to companies looking to use banner advertising or sponsorship to promote their products (*Chapter 9*). Owing to their importance, companies owning web sites have attracted significant investment that has increased, or some would say, over-inflated their stock prices. The reach and future potential of portals is such that traditional media companies have been active in acquiring these companies, for example Infoseek has been acquired by Disney as part of the new Go portal (www.go.com).

Activity 2.5 **Portal services and revenue models**

Purpose

To illustrate the range and depth of services available at leading portals and how this contributes to revenue models.

Question

Visit the Yahoo! site relevant to your country (from www.yahoo.com) or a similar portal of your choice and identify the range of services offered. Which are pure services, and which are basically providing information from other sources?

For answer see p. 61

Types of portals

Portals vary in scope and the services they offer, so naturally terms have evolved to describe the different types of portals. It is useful, in particular for marketers, to understand these terms since they act as a checklist that companies are represented on the different types of portals. *Table 2.3* shows different types of portals. It is apparent that there is overlap between the different types of portal. Yahoo!, for instance, is a horizontal portal since it offers a range of services, but it has also been developed as a geographical portal for different countries and, in the US, even for different cities.

Table 2.3 Portal characteristics

Type of portal	*Characteristics*	*Example*
Access portal	Associated with ISP	Freeserve (www.freeserve.net)
Horizontal or functional portal	Range of services: search engines, directories, news recruitment, personal information management, shopping, etc.	Yahoo! (www.yahoo.com) Excite (www.excite.com) Lycos (www.lycos.com)
Vertical	May cover a single function e.g.: – news – and industry sector	Moreover (www.moreover.com) Chemdex (www.chemdex.com)
Geographical (region, country, local area)	May be: – horizontal – vertical	Yahoo! country versions Countyweb (www.countyweb.com)
Marketplace	May be: – horizontal – vertical – geographical	Marketsite (www.marketsite.net) PlasticsNet (www.plastics.net)
Media type	Voice portal Streaming media portal	

Location of trading in marketplace

While traditional marketplaces have a physical location, Internet-based markets have no physical presence – it is a virtual marketplace. Rayport and Sviokla (1996) use this distinction to coin a new term **electronic marketspace**. This has implications for the way in which the relationships between the different actors in the marketplace occur.

Electronic marketspace
A virtual marketplace such as the Internet in which no direct contact occurs between buyers and sellers.

The new electronic marketspace has many alternative virtual locations where an organization needs to position itself to communicate and sell to its customers. Thus one tactical marketing question is: 'what representation do we have on the Internet?' One aspect of representation that needs to be considered is the different types of marketplace location. Berryman *et al.* (1998) have identified a useful framework for this (*Table 2.4*).

Seller-controlled sites are the main home page of the company and are e-commerce enabled. Buyer-controlled sites are intermediaries which have been set up such that it is the buyer who initiates the market-making. This can occur through procurement posting where a purchaser specifies what they wish to

Table 2.4 Different types of marketplace identified

Marketplace	Examples of marketplace sites
Sell-side (seller controlled)	Vendor sites i.e. home site of company with e-commerce facilities. Intermediaries controlled by sellers.
Buy-side (buyer controlled)	Intermediaries controlled by buyers. Web site procurement posting e.g. www.zygonet.com, www.respond.com; purchasing agents and aggregators e.g. www.powerbuy.com, www.letsbuyit.com.
Marketplace (neutral)	Intermediaries not controlled by buyers. Industry (e.g. www.industry.net); product-specific search engines (e.g. CNET www.computer.com); information marts; business malls (www.barclaysquare.com); auction space (www.ubid.com).

Source: Adapted from Berryman *et al.*, 1998

purchase, it is sent by e-mail to suppliers registered on the system and then offers are awaited. Aggregators involve a group of purchasers combining to purchase a multiple order thus reducing the purchase cost. Neutral sites are independent evaluator intermediaries that enable price and product comparison.

As shown by *Figure 1.1*, the location of e-commerce transactions can be categorized as buy-side, sell-side or a neutral marketplace, hub or exchange intermediary based. See for example Turban *et al.* (2000) and Robinson (2000). It is also useful to consider the scale of e-commerce when evaluating the long-term potential of an e-commerce site and in particular *business-to-business marketplaces or exchanges* (*Chapter 7, p. 272*). Has the facility been set up by a single supplier or multiple suppliers? Can it support many customers or is it available to a limited number of customers? Such questions need to be asked by companies developing an e-business strategy since it will govern who it is best to partner with both for procurement and sales. Such questions are answered from a strategic perspective in later chapters. *Figure 2.9* shows five alternatives across the continuum of trading for trading within the electronic marketspace. The options can be summarized as follows:

- Sell-side @ supplier's site (typically one supplier to many customers). Examples: Most e-tailers such as Amazon (www.amazon.com) or Dell (www.dell.com).
- Sell-side @ distribution portal (some suppliers to many customers).
- Buy-side @ buyer's site (many (or some) suppliers to a single customer).

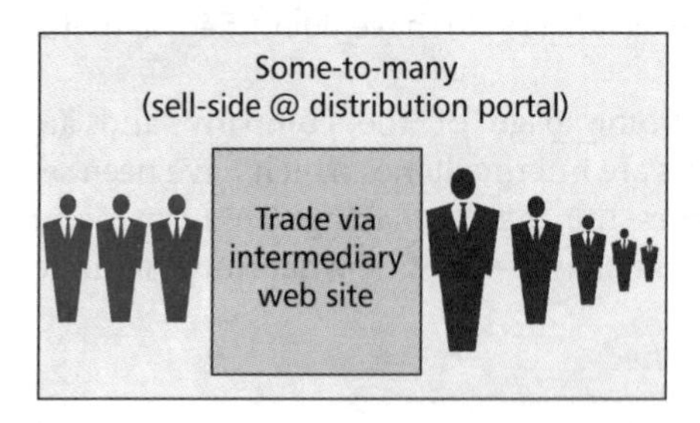

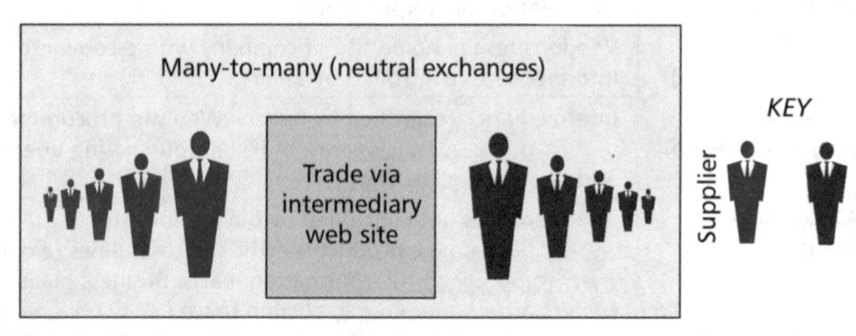

Figure 2.9 Variations in the location and scale of trading on e-commerce sites

Examples: General Electric Trading Post Network was the first to set up this type of arrangement (tpn.geis.com).

- Buy-side @ procurement portal (many suppliers to selected customers).
- Neutral exchanges, marketplaces or hubs (many suppliers to many customers). Examples: Vertical Net (www.vertical.net) and CommerceOne Marketsite (www.marketsite.net).

Commercial arrangements for transactions

Markets can also be considered from another perspective – that of the type of commercial arrangement that is used to agree a sale and price between the buyer and supplier. The main types of commercial arrangements are shown in *Table 2.5*.

It can be seen from Table 2.5 that each of these commercial arrangements is similar to traditional arrangements. Although the mechanism cannot be considered to have changed, the relative importance of these different options has changed with the Internet. Owing to the ability to publish rapidly new offers and prices, auction has become an important means of selling on the Internet. eBay has achieved a turnover of several billion dollars from consumers offering items from cars to antiques. Many airlines have successfully trialled auctions to sell seats remaining on an aircraft just before a flight, and this has led to the site www.lastminute.com that can broker or link to such offers.

An example of a completely new commercial mechanism that has been made possible through the web is provided by priceline.com europe Ltd (www.priceline.co.uk) (*Figure 2.10*), a licensee of priceline.com Incorporated. This travel site is characterized by its unique and proprietary 'Name Your Own Price™' buying

Table 2.5 Commercial mechanisms and online transactions

Commercial (trading) mechanism	*Online transaction mechanism of Nunes* et al. *(2000)*
1. Negotiated deal Example: can use similar mechanism to auction as on Commerce One (www.commerceone.net)	Negotiation – bargaining between single seller and buyer Continuous replenishment – ongoing fulfilment of orders under pre-set terms
2. Brokered deal Example: intermediaries such as Screentrade (www.screentrade.co.uk)	Achieved through online intermediaries offering auction and pure markets online
3. Auction Examples: C2C: E-bay (www.ebay.com) B2B: Industry to Industry (www.itoi.com)	Seller auction – buyers' bids determine final price of sellers' offerings Buyer auction – buyers request prices from multiple sellers Reverse – buyers post desired price for seller acceptance
4. Fixed price sale Example: All e-tailers	Static call – online catalogue with fixed prices Dynamic call – online catalogue with continuously updated prices and features
5. Pure markets Example: Electronic share dealing	Spot – buyers' and sellers' bids clear instantly
6. Barter Example: www.bartertrust.com	Barter – buyers and sellers exchange goods

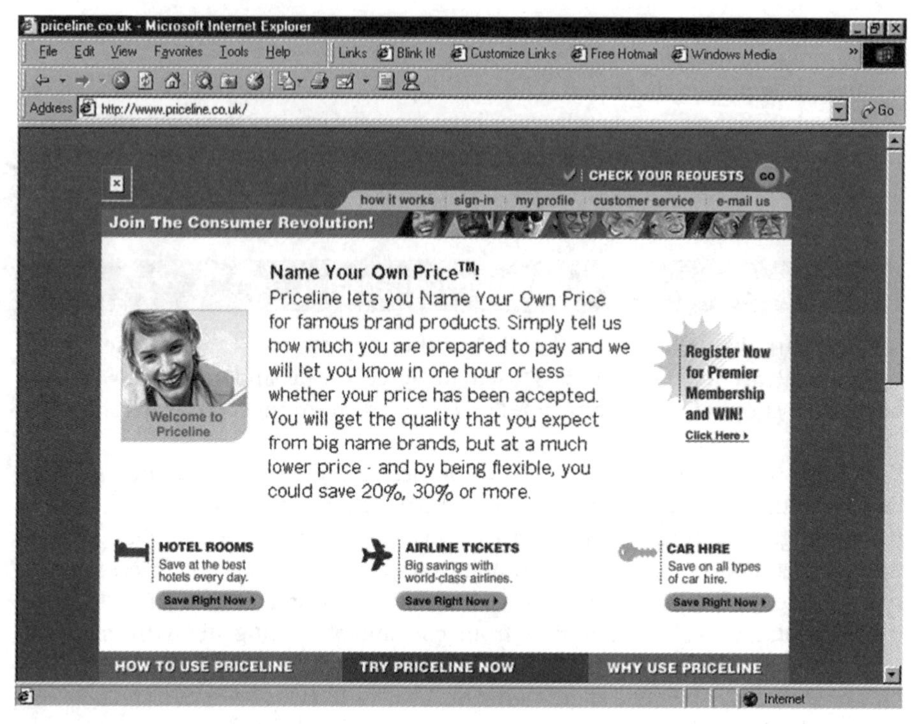

Figure 2.10 Priceline Europe* (www.priceline.co.uk)

service. Here, users enter the price they wish to pay for airline tickets, hotel rooms or car hire together with their credit card details. If priceline can match the user's price and other terms with inventory available from its participating suppliers, the deal will go ahead. This business model has been successful in the US where priceline.com Incorporated, a NASDAQ listed company (PCLN), had a user base in 2000 of more than 5 million. In the UK, priceline europe has three core services: airline tickets, hotels and car hire.

F *Focus on* auctions

With the success of e-bay (www.ebay.com), auctions have been highlighted as one of the new business models for the Internet. But how do auctions work, what infrastructure is required and what is the potential for B2B auctions? In this section we will address some of these issues.

Auctions involve determination of the basis for product or service exchange between a buyer and seller according to particular trading rules that help select the best match between the buyer and seller from a number of participants.

Klein (1997) identifies different roles for auction:

1. *Price discovery* – an example of price discovery is in the traditional consumer auction involving bidding for antiques. Antiques do not have standardized prices,

* Currently US site

but the auction can help establish a realistic market price through a gathering of buyers.

2. *Efficient allocation mechanism* – the sale of items that are difficult to distribute through traditional channels falls into this category. Examples include 'damaged inventory' that has a limited shelf life or is only available at a particular time such as aircraft flight or theatre tickets. Lastminute.com (www.lastminute.com) has specialized in disposal of this type of inventory in Europe, not always by means of auctions.
3. *Distribution mechanism* – as a means of attracting particular audiences.
4. *Coordination mechanism* – here the auction is used to coordinate the sale of a product to a number of interested parties; an example is the broadband spectrum licences for 3G telecoms in the UK (www.spectrumauctions.gov.uk).

To understand auctions it is important to distinguish between offers and bids. An **offer** is a commitment for a trader to sell under certain conditions such as a minimum price. A **bid** is made by a trader to buy under the conditions of the bid such as a commitment to purchase at a particular price.

Offer
A commitment by a trader to *sell* under certain conditions.

Bid
A commitment by a trader to *purchase* under certain conditions.

There are many potential combinations of the sequence of bids and offers and these have been stated by Reck (1997). Despite the combinations, certain common types of auction trading patterns can be identified. For example, Commerce One (www.commerceone.net) offers auctions as one method of exchange. There are two main types of auction that are offered by Commerce One, but there are a lot of permutations on these basic models.

1. *Forward, upward or English auction (initiated by seller).* These are the type of auctions available on consumer sites such as e-Bay. Increasing bids are placed within a certain time limit and the highest bid will succeed provided the reserve (minimum) price is exceeded. According to Commerce One, companies may use online forward auctions to sell slow-moving, excess or obsolete inventory items. The forward auction can also potentially be used to perform price discovery in a market.
2. *Reverse or downward auction (initiated by buyer).* These are more common on business-to-business sites such as Commerce One. Here, the buyer places a request for tender or quotation (RFQ) and many suppliers compete, decreasing the price with the supplier with the lowest price getting the contract. According to Commerce One, companies may use reverse auctions to:
   - rationalize suppliers in a particular spending category;
   - source new components in an area they are unfamiliar with.

Commerce One also offers a basic Exchange where buyers and sellers can offer and bid, but without the constraints of an auction. *Case study 2.1* shows how auctions can be used in a B2B context.

CASE STUDY 2.1

Dynamic pricing at SmithKline Beecham

FT

When the healthcare company SmithKline Beecham bought supplies of a basic solvent recently, the price was 15 per cent lower than the day's spot price in the commodity market. On other purchases also of highly specified solvents and chemicals, SmithKline Beecham is regularly beating its own historic pricing by between 7 and 25 per cent.

The reason is that SmithKline Beecham is using

▶ CASE STUDY *continued*

the Internet to hold downward or 'reverse' auctions in which suppliers bid against each other for pre-specified contracts. FreeMarkets, the company that manages the SmithKline Beecham auctions, quotes examples of savings achieved by other clients in these virtual marketplaces: 42 per cent on orders for printed circuit boards, 41 per cent on labels, 24 per cent on commercial machinings and so on.

As well as production items, the process also works well for many services, such as car hire contracts.

This pricing free-for-all sounds a little shocking at first. After all, successful companies are supposed to buy on quality, nurture critical supplier relationships, and think strategically. And, of course, they still do.

Guy Allen, director of purchasing at SmithKline Beecham emphasises that the auction itself is a new part of a still rigorous buying process. 'It's just one tool in our toolbox,' he says. 'The process only works if you put good purchasing management up front.' This includes issuing a particularly detailed request for proposals (RFP) to which hopeful suppliers respond as usual, but without quoting a price.

Based on the RFPs, selected suppliers are invited to take part in the auction.

Training in using the software is available. Once the bidding starts, the participants see every bid, but not the names of the bidders. In the final stages of the auction, each last bid extends the bidding time by one more minute. One auction scheduled for two hours ran for four hours and 20 minutes and attracted more than 700 bids.

A buyer need not necessarily accept the lowest bid, but may still prefer to use a tried and tested supplier at a slightly higher price. But the reverse auction offers buyers a number of benefits: it shortens the time spent negotiating separately with each supplier, the inclusion of non-incumbent suppliers can help to bring pricing down and, according to Mr Allen, 'It makes the process a little more transparent, since everyone can see the lowest price on offer. In general, non-incumbent suppliers like the process, though some incumbent suppliers are a little less happy.'

SmithKline Beecham is using private online auctions for global procurement of highly specified items at a spend that is attractive to the market. In contrast, Andrew Biggs, managing director of Bidbusiness.co.uk, is providing public reverse auction facilities for what he describes as 'low touch' products – construction bricks and sand and gravel, for example – as well as haulage services and builders' skips. Buyers can post their tenders on his specialist sites and sellers can bid for the work using a pseudonym.

Mirroring the need for liquidity in successful financial markets, auctions need a competitive environment and public auction sites seek to attract more buyers and sellers through features such as Category Watch from OpenSite, the company that supplies software for Bidbusiness. This feature will notify registered users by e-mail when an item of interest to them is posted.

Now companies that provide auction facilities are looking to factor other variables into their software as well, to let buyers and sellers take account of differences in transport costs, lead times, duration of warranty periods and so on.

The strength of the auction is that it allows prices to fluctuate according to demand and factors in the value of opportunity. But, arguably, its weakness is the fixed nature of the event. The auction format demands the simultaneous attention of everyone interested in that particular contract or item.

Airlines try to match availability to demand and reward early bookers by creating fare classes where some seats on a particular flight cost more than others. The problem is that fare classes are determined in advance and fare differentials can be rigid, creating a blunt tool, according to Sharookh Cambata, president of Greaves Travel USA, an airline ticket wholesaler.

Greaves has teamed up with Equant to develop a dynamic pricing engine to automatically adjust the price of airline tickets according to demand. First, the airline needs to be able to track all bookings into one point, so the pricing engine can view the current request against other demands. The pricing engine must then work rapidly. Customers booking through a web site, for example, are not going to wait minutes for lengthy number crunching; they want an instant price.

Greaves will soon start trials of the new system, called 'Web-fares', but Mr Cambata believes it also has potential for other pre-booked travel services, such as hotel accommodation. Using the system, a web site user would quickly get the price for the flight or service they wanted, but could also be directed to a cheaper alternative at a different time.

Online auctions are no longer just for surplus

goods or unwanted gifts, and the advent of 'd-commerce' is more than marketing hype. The concept of dynamic pricing is gathering interest very quickly. For example, Transco, the UK provider of gas piping infrastructure, has recently introduced web-based auctions to sell capacity in its pipelines, since demand for gas fluctuates according to weather and other conditions.

Dynamic pricing is a convincing example of the way in which the internet will fundamentally change the way we do business.

Source: Anne Queree, *Financial Times* Technology supplement, 1 March 2000.

Questions

1. Explain how SmithKline Beecham is achieving lower prices than traditionally through e-commerce.
2. To what extent do you think this approach would work for companies smaller than SmithKline Beecham?
3. What are the implications for a dynamic pricing engine referred to a supplier and its customers?

Business models for e-commerce

Business model
A summary of how a company will generate revenue identifying its product offering, value-added services, revenue sources and target customers.

A consideration of the different **business models** made available through e-commerce is of particular importance to both existing and start-up companies. Venkatram (2000) points out that existing businesses need to use the Internet to build on current business models, while at the same time experimenting with new business models. New business models may be important to gain a competitive advantage over existing competitors, while at the same time heading off similar business models created by new entrants. For start-ups or dot-coms the viability of a business model will be crucial to funding from venture capitalists. But what is a business model? Timmers (1999) defines a 'business model' as:

> *An architecture for product, service and information flows, including a description of the various business actors and their roles; and a description of the potential benefits for the various business actors; and a description of the sources of revenue.*

It can be suggested that a business model for e-commerce requires consideration of the marketplace from several different perspectives:

- Does the company operate in the B2B or B2C arena, or a combination?
- How is the company positioned in the value chain between customers and suppliers?
- What is its value proposition and for which target customers?
- What are the specific revenue models that will generate different income streams?
- What is its representation in the physical and virtual world, e.g. high street presence, online only, intermediary, mixture?

Timmers (1999) identifies no less than 11 different types of business model that can be facilitated by the web as follows:

1. *E-shop* – marketing of a company or shop via web;
2. *E-procurement* – electronic tendering and procurement of goods and services;
3. *E-malls* – a collection of e-shops such as Indigo Square (www.indigosquare.com);
4. *E-auctions* – these can be for B2C e.g. Ebay (www.ebay.com) or B2C e.g. QXL (www.qxl.com);

5. *Virtual communities* – these can be B2C communities such as Xoom (www.xoom.com) or B2B communities such as Vertical Net (www.vertical.net); these are important for their potential in e-marketing and are described in the section on virtual communities, Chapter 9;
6. *Collaboration platforms* – these enable collaboration between businesses or individuals e.g. E-groups (www.egroups.com), now part of Yahoo! (www.yahoo.com) services;
7. *Third-party marketplaces* – marketplaces are described in *Focus on electronic B2B marketplaces* in Chapter 7;
8. *Value chain integrators* – offer a range of services across the value chain;
9. *Value chain service providers* – specialize in providing functions for a specific part of the value chain such as the logistics company UPS (www.ups.com);
10. *Information brokerage* – provide information for consumers and businesses, often to assist in making the buying decision or for business operations or leisure;
11. *Trust and other services* – examples of trust services include Which Web Trader (www.which.net/webtrader) or Truste (www.truste.org) which authenticate the quality of service provided by companies trading on the web.

Pant and Ravichandran (2001) have also produced a similar list of business models.

Now complete *activity 2.6* to assess whether it is possible to simplify these business models and read *case study 2.1* to see examples of new revenue models that can be used by a forward-looking retailer.

Activity 2.6 Exploring business models

Purpose

To explore the different types of business model available on the web and suggest a structure for evaluating business models.

Question

Identify overlap between the different business models identified by Timmers (1999). Can you group the different business model into different types of services? Do you think these businesses models operate in isolation?

For answer see p. 62

Figure 2.11 suggests a different perspective for reviewing alternative business models. There are three different perspectives from which a business model can be viewed. Any individual organization can operate in different categories, as the examples below show, but most will focus on a single category for each perspective. Such a categorization of business models can be used as a tool for *formulating e-business strategy* (*Chapter 5, p. 191*). The three perspectives, with examples are:

1. *Marketplace position perspective*. The book publisher here is the manufacturer, Amazon is a retailer and Yahoo! is both a retailer and a marketplace intermediary.
2. *Revenue model perspective (p. 52)*. The book publisher can use the web to sell direct and Yahoo! and Amazon can take commission-based sales. Yahoo! also has advertising as a revenue model.
3. *Commercial arrangement perspective (p. 45)*. All three companies offer fixed price sales, but in its place as a marketplace intermediary, Yahoo! also offers other alternatives.

1. Marketplace position

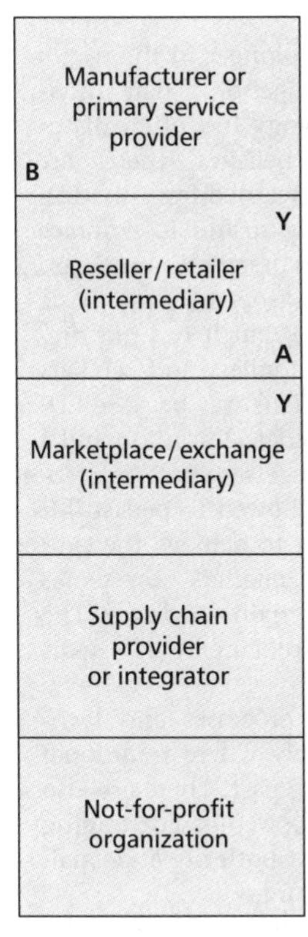

2. Revenue model

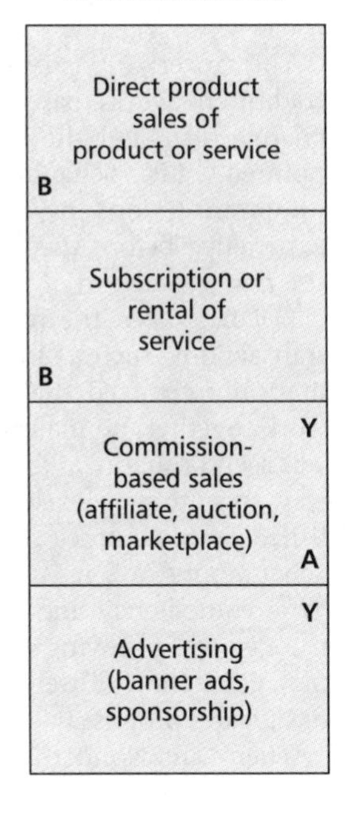

3. Commercial model

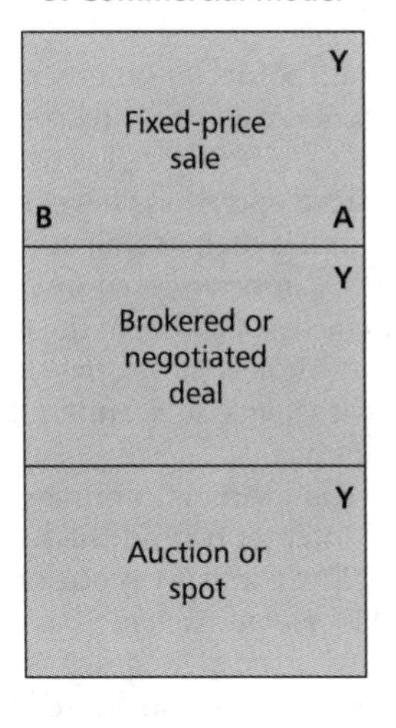

Key

Y = Yahoo!

A = Amazon

B = Book publisher

Figure 2.11 Alternative perspectives on business models

CASE STUDY 2.2

Ahold explore new ways to reach customers

Food retailing is a mature business and growth-hungry retailers have traditionally opened new stores or hit the acquisition trail. The Internet now offers a new way to grow revenues through online sales and also a powerful tool to boost margins through streamlined supply chains.

Ahold, a leading Dutch retailer, is employing all these strategies in an attempt to become one of the world's leading retailers. It has expanded aggressively outside its domestic market and today has 4000 stores in Europe, the US and Latin America. Its latest acquisition is US Foodservice, a $7 bn food services business with 40 distribution centres in the US.

Alongside this traditional expansion, the Dutch food giant is also expanding its online sales, which in 1999 generated sales of E60 m.

'We believe it is the right moment to expand our e-commerce activities,' says Cees Van der Hoeven, president and chief executive. He predicts Internet sales will grow rapidly to more than E200 m in 2000 and double that figure in 2001.

Looking ahead, Ahold is exploring new ways to reach customers and use distribution networks. It wants to become a 'multi-channel food provider' capable of serving millions of customers at any one time, not just at home but in locations as diverse as sports stadiums, petrol stations and hospitals. The acquisition of US Foodservice is a step in this direction.

By 2010, Ahold aims to have a wider variety of store formats ranging from large centres with food, restaurants and freshly made take-out meals, to convenience stores close to residential areas. The stores ▶

▶ CASE STUDY *continued*

will also function as pick-up points for other services ordered by phone or electronically from its specialized distribution centres.

Ultimately, it sees its store operations developing into sales and service channels that, as well as catering for 'walk-in' shoppers, can be accessed by internet, smart phones or interactive TV. One of the more futuristic ideas is to link Ahold's stores to 'smart' refrigerators equipped with barcode scanners that order groceries automatically.

As well as growing revenue through online sales, Ahold is keen to use the Internet behind the scenes to improve procurement. The company is one of the founders of the WorldWide Retail Exchange, a web-based business-to-business exchange designed to simplify trading between retailers and more than 100,000 suppliers and distributors. The exchange should start operating by mid-year.

E-commerce provides a golden opportunity to lower costs and enhance supply chain performance, according to Tom Schaumburg, vice-president of supply chain initiatives at Ahold USA.

'The grocery business has traditionally had a rather complex trading structure and manual processes have dominated. This has given food retailers a very poor performance when compared with other channels,' he says.

In the case of non-perishable foods, it is not uncommon to have 100 days of inventory in the supply chain. The new generation of big 'category killer' retailers has shown food retailers a better way to manage their supply chains. 'Other channels have much more robust and efficient supply chain practices,' says Mr Schaumburg.

The grocery industry was a pioneer in the use of trading networks based on electronic data interchange (EDI) but the technology has often disappointed. Mr Schaumburg believes there are important lessons that can be learned from the EDI experience before the industry rushes to embrace the new generation of Internet-based e-commerce.

EDI has taken the paperwork out of a few basic transactions, such as invoicing, but it has not dramatically changed the way suppliers and retailers work together, he maintains. This was because EDI was seen primarily as a technological solution and a way to automate existing processes. But if established business processes are allowed to persist, Mr Schaumburg says it is difficult to achieve the new 'core competency' model that retailers now see as the key to improving supply chain efficiency. The new generation of web-based procurement systems has greater promise.

'There are wonderful new processes and technologies to work collaboratively where traditional EDI has not worked well in the past. There are also interesting discussions about web-based trading communities which can benefit both big and small player alike,' says Mr Schaumburg.

'But we must have a shared vision of what a core competency looks like and we must address the existing barriers highlighted by the EDI experience.'

Source: *Financial Times* IT in Retailing supplement, 3 May 2000.

Question

Summarize how the Internet is integrated into new business models mentioned in the article.

Revenue models

Revenue models
Describe methods of generating income for an organization.

Revenue models specifically describe different techniques for generation of income. For existing companies, revenue models have revolved largely around the income from sales of products or services. This may be either for selling direct from the manufacturer or supplier of the service or through an intermediary who will take a cut of the selling price. Both of these revenue models are, of course, still crucial in online trading. There may, however, be options for other methods of generating revenue; perhaps a manufacturer may be able to sell advertising space or sell digital services that were not previously possible. *Activity 2.7* explores some of the revenue models that are possible.

Revenue models at Vertical Net Europe 

Activity 2.7

Purpose

To illustrate the range of revenue-generating opportunities for a company operating as an Internet pureplay.

Figure 2.12 Vertical Net web site showing range of specialist B2B marketplaces

Vertical Net (www.vertical.net) is a business-to-business intermediary that has operated in the US since 1995. It has expanded through acquisition and now includes over 50 industry-specific or vertical portals to facilitate trade between suppliers and their customers. All operate under a similar format with similar revenue models under the Vertical Net banner. In early 2000, it launched in Europe.

Question

Visit the Paints and Coatings site and explore the different facilities on the site for revenue generation.

For answer see p. 62

Focus on Internet start-up companies – the 'dot-coms'

F

To conclude the chapter, we evaluate the new Internet start-ups – the dot-coms launched in response to the availability of new business and revenue models. We also consider what lessons can be learnt from the dot-com failures. The emphasis of e-business and e-commerce management is deliberately placed on how electronic communications will impact on existing organizations. But, much of the media coverage of e-commerce in this new medium is on how start-ups are faring. In this section, we consider some of the core attributes of start-up companies. We also reflect on the impact of the 'dot-com' phenomenon on existing organizations.

Dot-coms
Businesses whose main trading presence is on the Internet.

Internet start-ups started to be referred to as '**dot-coms**' in the late 1990s since their business model is firmly based on the Internet medium and their web address typically ends in 'dot-com'. The best-known example is probably Amazon.com (www.amazon.com); others include Yahoo! (www.yahoo.com) and CDNow (www.cdnow.com). Note that the extent to which their business presence and operations are on the Internet is dependent on the type of services offered. For Yahoo!, the majority of its services are offered online, although promotion of the services is necessary in the 'real world', since most of its audience spend more time in the real world than the virtual world – this is the most effective medium for communicating its services. For dot-com e-tailers such as Amazon that sell physical products that have to be distributed to customers, their offline operations are very important to delivering customer satisfaction. As will be seen in the section on *logistics* (*Chapter 6, p. 240*) a major factor affecting Amazon's profitability is how its products are distributed from different warehouses. Furthermore, Amazon has opened some physical retail units also to compete with existing book retailers.

From 'bricks and mortar' to 'clicks and mortar'

Bricks and mortar
A traditional organization with limited online presence.

'Clicks and Mortar'
A business combining an online and offline presence.

Clicks only or Internet pureplay
An organization principally with an online presence.

These expressions were used in 1999/2000 to refer to traditional '**bricks and mortar**' enterprises with a physical presence, but limited Internet presence. In the UK, an example of a 'bricks and mortar' store would be the bookseller Waterstones (www.waterstones.co.uk), that when it ventured online would become '**clicks and mortar**'. As mentioned above, some virtual merchants such as Amazon that need to operate warehouses and shops to sustain growth have also become 'clicks and mortar' companies. An Internet pureplay which only has an online representation is referred to as '**clicks only**'. In reality these are rare – most companies need inbound and outbound phone connections.

Assessing dot-com businesses

Dot-com companies are often perceived as dynamic and successful owing to the rapid increase in visitors to sites, or sales, or due to initial valuations on stock markets. In reality, it is difficult to assess the success of these companies since despite positive indications in terms of sales or audience, the companies are often not profitable.

Burn rate
The speed at which dot-coms spend investors' money.

Boo.com is an interesting case of the potential and pitfalls of an e-commerce start-up and criteria for success, or one could say 'how not to do it'. The boo.com site was launched in November 1999 following two significant delays in launching and in January 2000 it was reported that 100 of its 400 employees had been made redundant due to disappointing initial revenues of about £60,000 in the Christmas period. Boo faced a high '**burn rate**' because of the imbalance between promotion and site development costs and revenues. As a consequence, it appeared to change its strategy by offering discounts of up to 40 per cent on fashions from the previous season. Closure followed in mid 2000 and the boo.com brand was purchased by an American entrepreneur and can still continue.

Boo.com sold upmarket clothing brands such as North Face, Paul Smith and Helly Hansen. Its founders were all under 30 and include Kajsa Leander, an ex-model. Investors provided a reported £74 million in capital. This enthusiasm is partly based on the experience of two of the founders in creating bokus.com, a relatively successful online bookseller.

As with all new companies, it is difficult for investors to assess the long-term sustainability of start-ups. There are a number of approaches that can be used to assess the success and sustainability of these companies. There have been many examples where it has been suggested that dot-com companies have been overvalued by investors who are keen to make a fast return from their investments. There have been some clear anomalies if traditional companies are compared to dot-coms. *Table 2.6* gives an example from the travel industry.

Table 2.6 Comparison between a traditional company and a dot-com, June 2000

	Thomson Travel	*lastminute.com*
Formed	1965	1998
Turnover	£3 billion	£2.6 million
Profit/loss	£77 million	– £6 million
Market capitalization	£980 million	£700 million

Valuing dot-coms

Desmet *et al.* (2000) apply traditional discounted cash flow techniques to assess the potential value of dot-coms. They point out that that traditional techniques do not work well when profitability is negative, but revenues are growing rapidly. They suggest that for new companies the critical factors to model when considering the future success of a company are:

1. The cost of acquiring a customer through marketing.
2. The contribution margin per customer (before acquisition cost).
3. The average annual revenues per year from customers and other revenues such as banner advertising and affiliate revenues.
4. The total number of customers.
5. The customer **churn rate**.

Churn rate
The proportion of customers (typically subscribers) that no longer purchase a company's products in a time period.

As would be expected intuitively, modelling using these variables indicates that for companies with a similar revenue per customer, contribution margin and advertising costs, it is the churn rate that will govern their long-term success. To look at this another way, given the high costs of customer acquisition for a new company, it is the ability to retain customers for repeat purchases which governs the long-term success of companies. This then forces dot-com retailers to compete on low prices with low margins to retain customers.

A structured evaluation of the success and sustainability of UK Internet start-ups has been undertaken by UK management consultancy Bain and Company in conjunction with *Management Today* magazine and was described in Gwyther (1999). Their aim was to identify 25 of the most successful UK Internet companies described as the Management Today/Bain e25 and indicated in *Table 2.7*. Six criteria were used to assess the companies as follows:

1. Concept

This describes the strength of business model. It includes:

- potential to generate revenue including the size of the market targeted;
- 'superior customer value', in other words how well is the proposition of the service differentiated from competitors;
- first-mover advantage.

2. Innovation

This criterion looks at another aspect of the business concept, which is the extent to which the business model merely imitates existing real-world or online models. Note that imitation is not necessarily a problem if it is applied to a different market or audience. For example UK auction company qxl.com (www.qxl.com) has applied the existing model of US companies such as eBay (www.ebay.com) and Ubid (www.ubid.com) to the UK and European market with a focus on white-label consumer goods. Qxl was started by Tim Jackson, a former journalist, who is a multimillionaire on paper following the valuation of qxl.com at £280 million on its first day of trading. Companies that continue to innovate will clearly gain competitive advantage and this is also assessed.

3. Execution

A good business model does not, of course, guarantee success. If there are problems with aspects of the implementation of the idea, then the start-up will fail. Aspects of execution that can be seen to have failed for some companies are:

- promotion – online or offline techniques are insufficient to attract sufficient visitors to the site;
- performance, availability and security – some sites have been victims of their own success and have not been able to deliver fast access to the sites or the technical problems have meant that the service is unavailable or insecure. Some sites have been unavailable despite large-scale advertising campaigns due to delays in creating the web site and its supporting infrastructure;
- fulfilment – the site itself may be effective, but customer service and consequently brand image will be adversely affected if products are not dispatched correctly or promptly.

4. Traffic

This criterion is measured in terms of page impressions and online revenues. Page impressions or visits are not necessarily an indication of success dependent on the business model. After the viability of the business model, how it will be promoted is arguably the most important aspect for a start-up. A critical volume of revenue-generating users of a service is required to repay the investment in these companies. Promotion from zero-base is difficult and costly if there is a need to reach a wide audience. An important decision is the investment in promotion and how it is split between online and offline techniques. Perhaps surprisingly, to reach the mass market, traditional advertising seems to be required to get the message about the service across clearly to the numbers required. Observation of the companies in *Table 2.7* shows that traditional media exposure is necessary for companies such as boo.com that are aiming to reach the mass market. Boo has had major TV and newspaper campaigns. Online promotion through banner ads may also be included in the campaign. Some of the other companies such as lastminute.com and qxl.com have been able to grow without the initial investment in advertising. These have grown more organically, helped by favourable word of mouth and mentions in newspaper features supported by some traditional advertising. Promotion for all these companies seem to indicate that the Internet medium is simply adding an additional dimension to the communications mix and traditional advertising is still required.

5. *Financing*

This describes the ability of the company to attract venture capital or other funding to help execute the idea. This is particularly important given the cost of promoting these new concepts.

6. *Profile*

This is the ability of the company to generate favourable publicity and to create awareness within its target market.

Table 2.7 ***Management Today*****/Bain e25 (adapted from www.clickmt.com/e25/index)**

Ranking	*Company*	*Product*
1	nCipher	Encryption
2	orchestream	Data software
3	ingenta	Research infomediary
= 4	WSGN	Fashion infomediary
= 4	QXL.com	Auctions
= 6	Sportal	Sports portal
= 6	Affinity Internet	Business ISP
= 6	sportingbet.com	Gambling
9	Gameplay	Games
= 10	Mediasurface	Content management
= 10	lastminute.com	Late bookings
12	silicon.com	IT news
= 13	365 Corporation	Sports portal
= 13	virtual internet	Web hosting
15	netstore	Data backup
= 16	Internet Exchange	Net cafés
= 16	netbenefit	e-solutions
18	peoplesound.com	Music
19	iOra	Mobile internet
= 20	mondus	Online tenders
= 20	Adeptra	Multi-channel content
22	Zygon	e-commerce support
23	Shopsmart.com	Comparison shopping
24	iii	Personal finance portal
25	Schoolsnet	Education portal

CASE STUDY 2.3

A short history of lastminute.com

Lastminute.com was a European innovation, since at launch, no equivalent site existed in the US. Its business model is based on commission from selling 'distressed inventories' which will have no value if they are not sold immediately. This includes hotel rooms, airline and theatre tickets. It has 1000

▶ CASE STUDY *continued*

suppliers including British Airways, Bass Hotels and Virgin. In February 2000 it claimed over 800,000 registered users, growing at about 30 per cent per month and about 5 million page impressions each month. The preferences of users for the type of service required are held on database and then matched against the offers of suppliers to the site. The choice of suppliers is one of the key differences between an intermediary site such as this and one hosted by a single supplier or travel agency.

The company was founded by Brent Hoberman, 31, and Martha Lane-Fox, 27, both Oxford graduates. Hoberman suggested the idea in 1996 while working at Spectrum, a company specializing in new media strategies. At the time, Lane-Fox said that the idea was too complex and would need thousands of suppliers to be effective. Hoberman and Lane-Fox raised £600,000 to get the company going and achieved many high profile backers such as France Telecom, Deutsche Telecom, Sony Music Entertainment, the British Airports Authority and Intel and venture capital company Arts Alliance Advisers. One problem was the domain name which had been registered by a Sardinian businessman. Both founders were adamant that their site had to be called this and the Sardinian was happy to sell it for several hundred thousand pounds. This can be compared to the owner of Jungle.com, a Californian who sold it for £235,000 to the site's founder.

The company hoped to use the money from flotation to increase access to the service by offering access to its service by WAP mobile and has signed deals with BT Cellnet and Orange to help achieve this. Other site improvements will also be made – Lane-Fox has been quoted as saying 'We've spent a lot of money improving the back-end, but we want to do more with the front-end'. The improvements to the 'back-end' have been necessary to avoid problems with customer service. Writing in *Computer Weekly*, 2 March 2000, Anne Hyland reported that several customers had money deducted from their account without purchasing any products from the site. For example, Charlotte Brett, a London customer has had £50 deducted from her account on three occasions in January and February 2000. The money was recredited to her account, but Ms Brett was quoted as saying 'I am a very angry customer; in my experience they have failed on the three key areas of technology, customer service and Internet capability'. Brent Hoberman said the problems were caused by its third-party credit-authority firm.

What of the future threats and opportunities for the company? In a *Guardian* interview with Jamie Doward on 27 February 2000 Lane-Fox was asked about the threat of a major ticket site setting up its own site. Lane Fox dismissed this possibility: 'Companies can't do it on their own web site because they fear cannibalization', and she says of first-mover advantage: 'you still have to set the company up and we're starting to get critical mass in Europe'. Lastminute.com have opened offices in London, Paris, Munich and Stockholm to help achieve this and is looking to move into the US market through an alliance with bargain travel retailer priceline.com.

Questions

1. Visit the lastminute.com site and research news sites such as Moreover (another dot-com, www.moreover.com) to establish the current success of lastminute.com in terms of the measures listed above and site registrants and page impressions.
2. Explain the business and revenue model for lastminute.com and assess the potential for profitability.
3. Explain the relative success of lastminute.com and Thomson Travel using the six criteria listed above and used to assess the *Management/Today* Bain e25.
4. What action do you consider the founders of the company should take to ensure the future success of www.lastminute.com?

The end of the affair

The media have played a key role in the dot-com story. Initially the media helped produce stratospheric prices for dot-coms by tempting investors with instant gains when companies went through IPOs (Independendent Public Offerings). The media could then also report on the newsworthy spectacle of the failure of many of these businesses. As failure of more and more dot-coms was reported this also impacted the share prices of the more successful dot-coms such as Yahoo! and even other technology stocks. Popular analogies for the dot-com collapse are the bursting of the South Sea Company's bubble in 1720 and the wilting of the fortunes invested in tulips in the 17th century.

The impact of the dot-com phenomenon on traditional organizations

The failure of so many dot-coms has accounted for much adverse publicity in the media and e-commerce and e-business are perhaps perceived by some as a fad. However, for every story about dot-com failure there is perhaps an untold story of e-business success. The two examples introduced in Chapter 1 illustrate how existing companies such as Cisco and EasyJet have been able to transform their businesses to achieve competitive advantage through enacting over 80 per cent online. In the background, traditional companies have continued to adopt new technologies. The changes made by existing business are aptly summed up by David Weymouth, Barclays Bank chief information officer (Simons, 2000) who says:

> *There is no merit in becoming a dot-com business. Within five years successful businesses will have embraced and deployed at real-scale across the whole enterprise the processes and technologies that we now know as dot-com.*

What then is the legacy of the dot-com phenomenon? What can we learn from the dot-com successes and failures? The following guidelines can be suggested for managers developing e-commerce strategy for their own companies:

1. Explore new business and revenue models.
2. Perform continuous scanning of the marketplace and respond rapidly.
3. Set up partner networks to leverage the expertise and reputation of specialists.
4. The real world is still important for product promotion and fulfilment.
5. Examine the payback and return on investment of new approaches carefully.

Summary

1. The constantly changing e-business environment should be monitored by all organizations in order to be able to respond to changes in social, legal, economic, political and technological factors together with changes in the immediate marketplace that occur through changes in customer requirements and competitor and intermediaries' offerings.
2. The e-business marketplace involves transactions between organizations and consumers (B2C) and other businesses (B2B). Consumer to consumer (C2C) and consumer to business categories (C2B) can also be identified.
3. The Internet can cause *disintermediation* within the marketplace as an organization's channel partners such as wholesalers or retailers are bypassed. Alternatively the Internet can cause *reintermediation* as new intermediaries with a different purpose are formed to help bring buyers and sellers together in a *virtual marketplace* or marketspace. Evaluation of the implications of these changes are important to strategy.
4. Trading in the marketplace can be sell-side (seller controlled), buy-side (buyer controlled) or at a neutral marketplace.

5. A business model is a summary of how a company will generate revenue identifying its product offering, value-added services, revenue sources and target customers. Exploiting the range of business models made available through the Internet is important to both existing companies and start-ups.
6. The Internet may also offer opportunities for new revenue models such as commission on affiliate referrals to other sites or banner advertising.
7. The opportunity for new commercial arrangements for transactions include negotiated deals, brokered deals, auctions, fixed price sales and pure spot markets and barters should also be considered.
8. The success of dot-com or Internet start-up companies is critically dependent on their business and revenue models and traditional management practice.

ACTIVITY ANSWERS

2.1 Why are environment influences important?

Immediate environment

- Customers – which services are they offering via their web site that your organization could support them in?
- Competitors – need to be benchmarked as described in *Chapter 5* in order to review the online services they are offering – do they have a competitive advantage?
- Intermediaries – are new or existing intermediaries offering products or services from your competitors while you are not represented?
- Suppliers – are suppliers offering different methods of procurement to competitors that give them a competitive advantage?

Macro-environment

- Society – what is the ethical and moral consensus on holding personal information?
- Country specific, international legal – what are the local and global legal constraints for example on holding personal information, or taxation rules on sale of goods?
- Country specific, international economic – what are the economic constraints of operating within a country or global constraints?
- Technology – what new technologies are emerging by which to deliver online services such as interactive digital TV and mobile phone-based access?

2.2 Why distinguish between B2B and B2C?

Table 2.8 Differences in characteristics of B2C and B2B trading

Characteristic	*B2C*	*B2B*
Proportion of adopters with access	Low to medium	High to very high
Complexity of buying decisions	Relatively simple – individual and influencers	More complex – buying process involves users, specifiers, buyers, etc.
Channel	Relatively simple – direct or from retailer	More complex, direct or via wholesaler, agent or distributor
Purchasing characteristics	Low value, high volume or high value, low volume. May be high involvement	Similar volume/value. May be high involvement. Repeat orders (rebuys) more common
Product characteristic	Often standardized items	Standardized items or bespoke for sale

2.3 Why C2C interactions at Bizrate matter for retailers

1. The actions taken by a company should depend on the reach of the site. There may be many of these intermediary sites and it may not be practical to partner with all of them – only the ones with the largest audience. Bizrate has been operational since 1996, so it is well established and has a large range of retailers. The company should review the criteria for assessing quality and be sure it will perform relatively well on the site. It should then seek listing and carefully monitor the comments received and those about its competitors – this is a relatively inexpensive form of marketing research and a good driver for improving the quality of e-commerce service.
2. Representation on this site gives a great opportunity for new business by promoting the service in international markets. It also gives competitive advantage in existing markets where rivals are not represented.

2.4 Kelkoo.com, an example of revenue models for new intermediaries

1. Kelkoo provides a *price-comparison* service. The desired product is typed in and a database is searched for suppliers who have this product. Different prices and other extras such as delivery and guarantees are then listed. Typically the consumer will pick the supplier with the lowest price.
2. The main revenue will come from commission for products bought. Kelkoo will be an affiliate of each of the e-tailers it is linked to and will be paid a small percentage of product purchase price by the e-tailer from which the product is purchased. Other revenue models include general banner advertising on the site, together with advertisements from the manufacturers of products (such as book publishers) or from the retailers (a small banner ad may be placed by the retailer to establish its credibility).
3. A problem with the business model of such intermediaries is that only a small percentage is paid by the retailer, so many transactions must be purchased. This is also a problem for the similar service from lastminute.com (www.lastminute.com). It is forecast that the next stage will be a shake-out as many of the cybermediaries and B2B marketplaces fail leaving room for a handful of key players in each sector. As a consequence intermediaries such as Kelkoo are spending a large proportion of their funding capital on advertising to build their marketshare.

2.5 Portal services and revenue models

The answer is provided in Table 2.3 for the international site (www.yahoo.com).

Table 2.9 Range of services available from Yahoo!

Name	*Revenue source*
Directory and search engine facilities	General and keyword related banner ads. Affiliate revenue from other sites e.g. Amazon
Connect: e-mail, Chat, Messenger, mobile	Banner ads. Mainly added by acquisition
Media: News, general and specific e.g. sports, finance	Banner ads, sponsorship. Provided by partners
Personal tools – address book, calendar, tasks, links	Banner ads. Mainly added by acquisition
Shopping for cars, property and jobs	Commission on sales, banner adverts
Auctions	Commission on sales, revenue generator
Classifieds	Free apart from banner ads

2.6 Exploring business models

An immediate distinction can be made between the operation of individual companies (*e-shop*) using the web to sell direct to the customer and deal with suppliers (*e-procurement*) and intermediary services such as *e-auctions* and *third-party marketplaces* which make up most of the remaining services. For some business models such as *virtual communities* and *e-auctions* it could be argued that these services could be provided by intermediaries or businesses, but are often best provided by neutral intermediaries.

Overlap can be identified between e-auctions, e-malls, third-party marketplaces and business communities since they all facilitate the exchange of products between sellers and buyers. It can be argued that the business model is similar, but the mechanism for exchange is different. It can be argued that some of the business models referred to are simply instances of the mechanism of exchange, for example e-auctions as distinct from fixed price sales (e-shop). Auctions could potentially occur for the e-shop, third-party marketplace as well as e-auction.

2.7 Revenue models at Vertical Net Europe

The following revenue generating activities can be identified:

- Banner advertising
- Fees for hosting an e-commerce shop-front
- Commission on sales occurring at the site (from sellers)
- Commission on auctions
- Commission on affiliate referrals to other sites

Note that there is a careful balance for this business type of generating revenue and not discouraging potential suppliers or buyers. For this reason the service is free to buyers and sellers can list minimum services. A challenge for intermediaries is that although the site may achieve a high turnover, the revenue to the company can be small if it is based on commission on sales.

Revenue models will use a combination of techniques as follows:

- Online commerce – sale of products (direct or indirect)
- Online commerce – sale of digital services (can be on subscription basis or pay per view)
- Ad revenue through banner advertising or sponsorship of content/services

EXERCISES

Self-assessment questions

1. Outline the main options for trading between businesses and consumers.
2. Explain the concept of disintermediation and reintermediation with reference to a particular industry; what are the implications for a company operating in this industry?
3. Describe the three main alternative locations for trading within the electronic marketplace.
4. What are the main types of commercial transactions that can occur through the Internet or in traditional commerce?
5. E-business involves re-evaluating value chain activities. What types of changes can be introduced to the value chain through e-business?
6. List the different business models identified by Timmers (2000).

7. Describe some alternative revenue models for a web site from a magazine publisher.
8. Draw a diagram summarizing the different types of online marketplace.

Essay and discussion questions

1. Disintermediation and reintermediation occur simultaneously within any given market. Discuss.
2. For an organization you are familiar with, examine the alternative business and revenue models afforded by the Internet and assess the options for the type and location of e-commerce transitions.
3. For a manufacturer or retailer of your choice, analyze the balance between partnering with portals or providing equivalent services from your web site.
4. Contrast the market potential for B2B and B2C auctions.
5. Select an intermediary site and assess how well it makes use of the range of business models and revenue models available to it through the Internet.

Examination questions

1. Explain disintermediation and reintermediation using examples.
2. Describe three different revenue models for a portal such as Yahoo!
3. What is meant by buy-side, sell-side and marketplace-based e-commerce?
4. What are the different mechanisms for online auctions?
5. Describe two alternative approaches for using e-business to change a company's value chain.
6. Explain what a business model is and relate it to an Internet pureplay of your choice.
7. Outline the elements of the e-business environment for an organization and explain its relevance to the organization.
8. Give three different transaction types that an industry marketplace could offer to facilitate trade between buyers and suppliers.

REFERENCES

Benjamin, R. and Weigand, R. (1995) Electronic markets and virtual value-chains on the information superhighway. *Sloan Management Review*, Winter, 62–72.

Berryman, .K., Harrington, L., Layton-Rodin, D. and Rerolle, V. (1998) Electronic commerce: three emerging strategies. *The Mckinsey Quarterly,* no. 1, 152–9.

Desmet, D., Francis, T., Hu, A., Koller, M. and Riedel, G. (2000) Valuing dot coms. *The McKinsey Quarterly*, no. 1. Available online at www.mckinseyquarterly.com.

Economist (2000) E-commerce survey. Define and sell. Supplement, 26 February, 6–12.

eMarketer (2000) B2B revenues to top US$1 trillion by 2003. Analyst report, 25 July.

Gwyther, M. (1999) Jewels in the web. *Management Today*, November, 63–9.

Hagel, J. and Rayport, J. (1997) The new informediaries. *The McKinsey Quarterly*, no. 4, 54–70.

van Heck, E. and Ribbers, P. (1997) Experiences with

electronic auctions in the Dutch flower industry. *International Journal of Electronic Markets*, 4(7), 29–34.

Hoffman, D.L., and Novak, T.P. (1996) Marketing in hypermedia computer-mediated environments: conceptual foundations. *Journal of Marketing*, 60 (July), 50–68.

Kalakota, R. and Robinson, M. (2000) *e-business. Roadmap for Success*. Addison-Wesley, Reading, MA.

Klein, S. (1997) Introduction to electronic auctions. *International Journal of Electronic Markets*, 4(7), 3–6.

Net Profit (1999) *Opportunity and Threat Varies Sector by Sector as Internet Business Develops*. Staff report, October www.netprofit.co.uk.

Nunes, P., Kambil, A. and Wilson, D. (2000). The all-in-one market. *Harvard Business Review*, May–June, 2–3.

Pant, S. and Ravichandran, T. (2001) A framework for information systems planning for e-business. *Logistics Information Mangement*, 14(1), 85–98.

Porter, M.E. (1980) *Competitive Strategy*. Free Press, New York.

Rayport, J. and Sviokla, J. (1996) Exploiting the virtual value-chain. *The McKinsey Quarterly*, no. 1, 20–37.

Reck, M. (1997) Trading characteristics of electronic auctions. *International Journal of Electronic Markets*, 4(7), 17–23.

Robinson, E. (2000) Battle to the bitter end. *Business 2.0*, July, 134–44.

Sarkar, M., Butler, B. and Steinfield, C. (1996) Intermediaries and cybermediaries. A continuing role for mediating players in the electronic marketplace. *Journal of Computer Mediated Communication*, 1(3). Online-only journal, no page numbers.

Simons, M. (2000) Setting the banks alight, *Computer Weekly*, 20 July, 6.

Timmers, P. (1999) *Electronic Commerce Strategies and Models for Business-to-Business Trading*. Series on information systems, John Wiley and Sons, Chichester, England.

Turban, E. (1997) Auctions and bidding on the Internet: an assessment. *International Journal of Electronic Markets*, 4(7), 7–11.

Turban, E., Lee, J., King, D. and Chung, H. (2000) *Electronic Commerce: a Managerial Perspective*. Prentice Hall, Upper Saddle River, NJ.

Venkatram, N. (2000) Five steps to a dot-com strategy: how to find your footing on the web. *Sloan Management Review*, Spring 2000, 15–28.

FURTHER READING

Deise, M., Nowikow, C., King, P. and Wright, A. (2000) *Executive's Guide to E-business. From Tactics to Strategy*. John Wiley and Sons, New York, NY. Introductory chapters consider buy- and sell-side options and later chapters look at value chain transformation.

Fingar, P., Kumar, H. and Sharma, T. (2000) *Enterprise E-commerce*. Meghan-Kiffler, Press, Tampa, FL. These authors present a model of the different actors in the e-marketplace that is the theme throughout this book.

Timmers, P. (1999) *Electronic Commerce Strategies and Models for Business-to-Business Trading*. Series on information systems. John Wiley and Sons, Chichester, England. Provides coverage of value-chain analysis and business model architectures in Chapter 3.

Turban, E., Lee, J., King, D. and Chung, H. (2000) *Electronic Commerce: a Managerial Perspective*. Prentice Hall, Upper Saddle River, NJ. Chapter 1 introduces industry structures and models for e-commerce.

Varianini, V. and Vaturi, D. (2000) Marketing lessons from e-failures. *The McKinsey Quarterly*, no. 4, 86–97.

WEB LINKS

Silicon.com (www.silicon.com) has commentary on new business models and interview with companies involved with change.

Computer Weekly e-business review (www.computerweekly.co.uk) has case studies and features of new business models.

Business 2.0 (www.business2.com) has regular features on the business model of the new economy.

International Journal of Electronic Markets (www.electronicmarkets.org) is published by Institute for Media and Communications Management, University of St Gallen, Switzerland.

Journal of Computer-Mediated Communication (www.ascusc.org/jcmc or http://jcmc.huji.ac.il) on the web quarterly since June 1995. JCMC is a joint project of the Annenberg School for Communication at the University of Southern California and the Information Systems Division of School of Business Administration, Hebrew University of Jerusalem.

Management Today e25 (www.clickmt.com/e25/index.cfm) contains top 25 UK Internet start-ups and criteria.

International Journal of Electronic Commerce (www.cba.bgsu.edu/ijec) is a refereed quarterly devoted to advancing the understanding and practice of electronic commerce. Edited by Vladimir Zwass. Hosted at Bowling Green State University.

For other online e-commerce-related journals see University of Ulster ecom (http://ecom.infm.ulst.ac.uk/Journals.html)

Chapter 3

E-business infrastructure

CHAPTER AT A GLANCE

LEARNING OBJECTIVES

After completing this chapter the reader should be able to:

- Outline the hardware and software technologies used to build an e-business infrastructure within an organization and with its partners
- Outline the hardware and software requirements necessary to enable employee access to the Internet and hosting of e-commerce services.

MANAGEMENT ISSUES

The issues for managers raised in this chapter include:

- What are the practical risks to the organization of failure to manage the e-commerce infrastructure adequately?
- How should staff access to the Internet be managed?

Links to other chapters

This chapter is an introduction to Internet hardware and software technologies. It gives the technical background to *Chapters 1 and 2* and to *Parts 2 and 3*. Its focus is on understanding the technology used but it also gives an introduction to how it needs to be managed. The main chapters that cover management of the e-business infrastructure are:

- *Chapter 10, Change management,*
- *Chapter 11, Analysis and design* (including architecture design) and
- *Chapter 12, Implementation and maintenance.*

Introduction

E-business infrastructure
The hardware and software architecture necessary to achieve electronic communications within a business and with its partners.

Defining an adequate **e-business infrastructure** is vital to all companies adopting e-business. Infrastructure refers to the combination of hardware such as servers and client PCs in an organization, the network used to link this hardware and the software applications used to deliver services to workers within the e-business and also to its partners and customers. Infrastructure also includes the architecture of the networks, hardware and software and where it is located. Remember that today, much infrastructure management is located outside the company through third-party managed servers and networks.

We start our coverage of e-business infrastructure by considering the technical infrastructure for the Internet, extranets, intranets and the World Wide Web. We then look at how these facilities work by reviewing the standards that are used to enable electronic communications, including communications standards such as TCP/IP and EDI and publishing standards such as HTML and XML. Some management issues of hosting e-business services are then reviewed, specifically management of services by external parties and how to manage staff access to the Internet. Finally, we focus on how new access technologies such as mobile phones and interactive digital TV will change the way the Internet is used in the future.

We refer above to an *adequate* infrastructure, but what does this mean? For the manager in the e-business, this is the a key question. While it is important to be able to understand some of the technical jargon and concepts when talking to third-party suppliers of hardware and software, what is of crucial importance is to be aware of some of the limitations (and also the business potential) of the hardware and software solutions. Through being aware of these problems, managers of an organization can work with their partners to ensure a good level of service is delivered to everyone, internal and external, who is using the e-business infrastructure. To highlight some of the problems that may occur if the infrastructure is not managed correctly, complete *activity 3.1*.

Activity 3.1 **Infrastructure risk assessment for The B2C Company**

Purpose

To indicate potential problems to customers, partners and staff of the e-business if technical infrastructure is not managed adequately.

Note, a fuller version of this assessment of levels of risk for all types of service problems that may be experienced on a web site is given in *activity 12.1* (*Chapter 12, p. 470*).

Activity

Make a list of the potential problems for different users of e-business services that could be created by The B2C Company. You should consider problems faced by users of e-business applications who are both internal and external to the organization. Base your answer on problems you have experienced on a web site that can be related to network, hardware and software failures.

For answer see p. 114

You should think about solutions to these risks, and when you have completed reading this chapter you should be able to identify solutions to these problems.

What is the Internet?

The **Internet** enables communication between millions of connected computers worldwide. Information is transmitted from client PCs whose users request services to server computers that hold information and host business applications that deliver the services in response to requests. As such, the Internet is a large-scale **client/server** system. By the end of 2000, Nua compilations estimated that worldwide there were over 400 million users of clients accessing over 23 million web sites hosted on servers (web update: www.nua.ie/surveys, www.iconomap.com). See Bocij *et al.* (1999) for a more detailed description of the client/server architecture. The client PCs within homes and businesses are connected to the Internet via local **Internet Service Providers** (ISPs) which, in turn, are linked to larger ISPs with connection to the major national and international infrastructure or **backbones** (*Figure 3.1*). In the UK, at the London Internet Exchange which is the Docklands area of East London, a facility exists to connect multiple backbones of the major ISPs within the UK onto a single high-speed link out of the UK into Europe and through to the US. These high-speed links can be thought of as the motorways on the 'information superhighway', while the links provided from ISPs to consumers are equivalent to slow country roads.

The Internet

The Internet refers to the physical network that links computers across the globe. It consists of the infrastructure of network servers and communication links between them that are used to hold and transport information between the client PCs and web servers.

Client/server

The client/server architecture consists of *client* computers, such as PCs, sharing resources such as a database stored on a more powerful *server* computer.

Internet Service Provider (ISP)

A provider providing home or business users with a connection to access the Internet. They can also host web-based applications.

Backbones

High-speed communications links used to enable Internet communications across a country and internationally.

The Internet timeline

The Internet is only the latest of a series of developments in the way that the human race has used technology to disseminate information. Kampas (2000) identifies ten stages that are part of five 'megawaves' of change. The first six stages are summarized in *Table 3.1*. It is evident that many of the major advances in the use of information have happened within the last one hundred years. This indicates that the difficulty of managing technological change is likely to continue. Kampas goes on to speculate on the impact of access to lower cost, higher bandwidth technologies.

The history and origin of the Internet as a business tool is surprising since it has taken a relatively long time to become an essential part of business. It started life

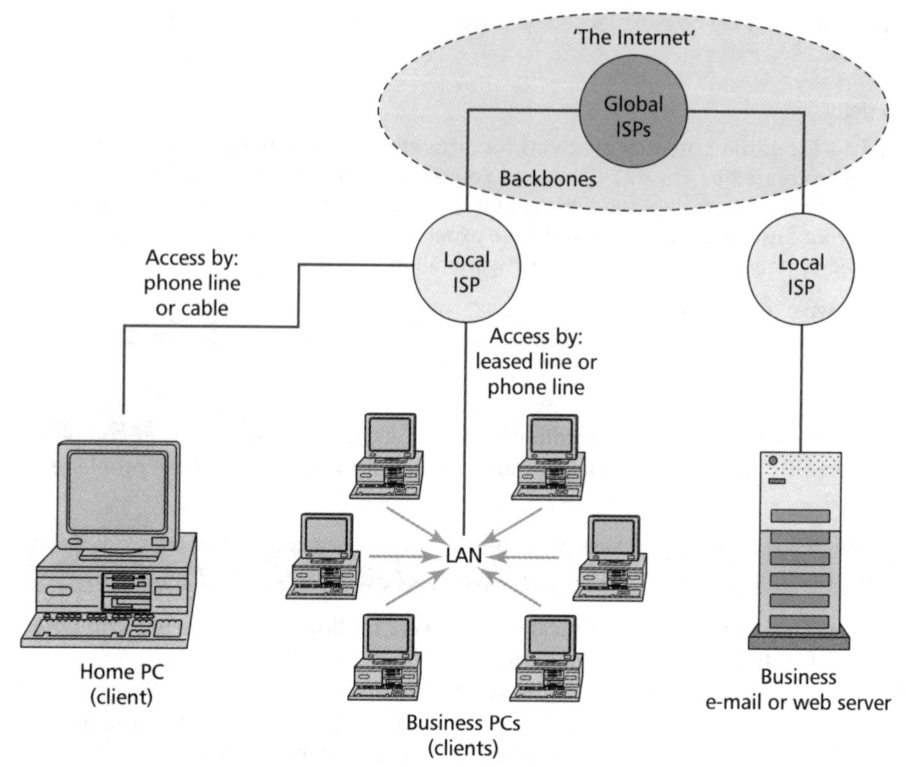

Figure 3.1 Infrastructure components of the Internet

Table 3.1 Six stages of advances in the dissemination of information

Stage	*Enabling technology*	*Killer applications and impact*
1. Documentation 3,500 BC to 1452	Written language and the development of clay tablets in Mesopotamia	Taxes, laws and accounting giving rise to the development of civilization and commerce
2. Mass publication 1452 to 1946	The Gutenburg press of movable metal type	Demand for religious and scientific texts resulting in scientific advances and ideological conflicts
3. Automation 1946 to 1978	Electric power and switching technologies (vacuum tubes and transistors)	Code breaking and scientific calculations. Start of information age
4. Mass interaction 1978 to 1985	Microprocessor and personal computer	Spreadsheets and word processing
5. Infrastructuralization 1985 to 1993	Local and wide area networks, graphical user interfaces	E-mail and enterprise resource planning
6. 1993 to c.2005 Mass communication	Internet, World Wide Web, Java	Mass information access for communications and purchasing

Source: (adapted from Kampas, 2000)

at the end of the 1960s as the ARPAnet research and defence network in the US that linked servers used by key military and academic collaborators. It was established as a network that would be reliable even if some of the links were broken. This was achieved since data and messages sent between users were broken up into smaller packets and could follow different routes. Read Gillies and Cailliau (2000) for a detailed description of the history of the Internet.

Although the Internet was subsequently extended worldwide and was used extensively by academic and defence communities, it has only recently been catapulted into mainstream business and consumer use. What is the reason for this relatively slow development? *Activity 3.2* explains this.

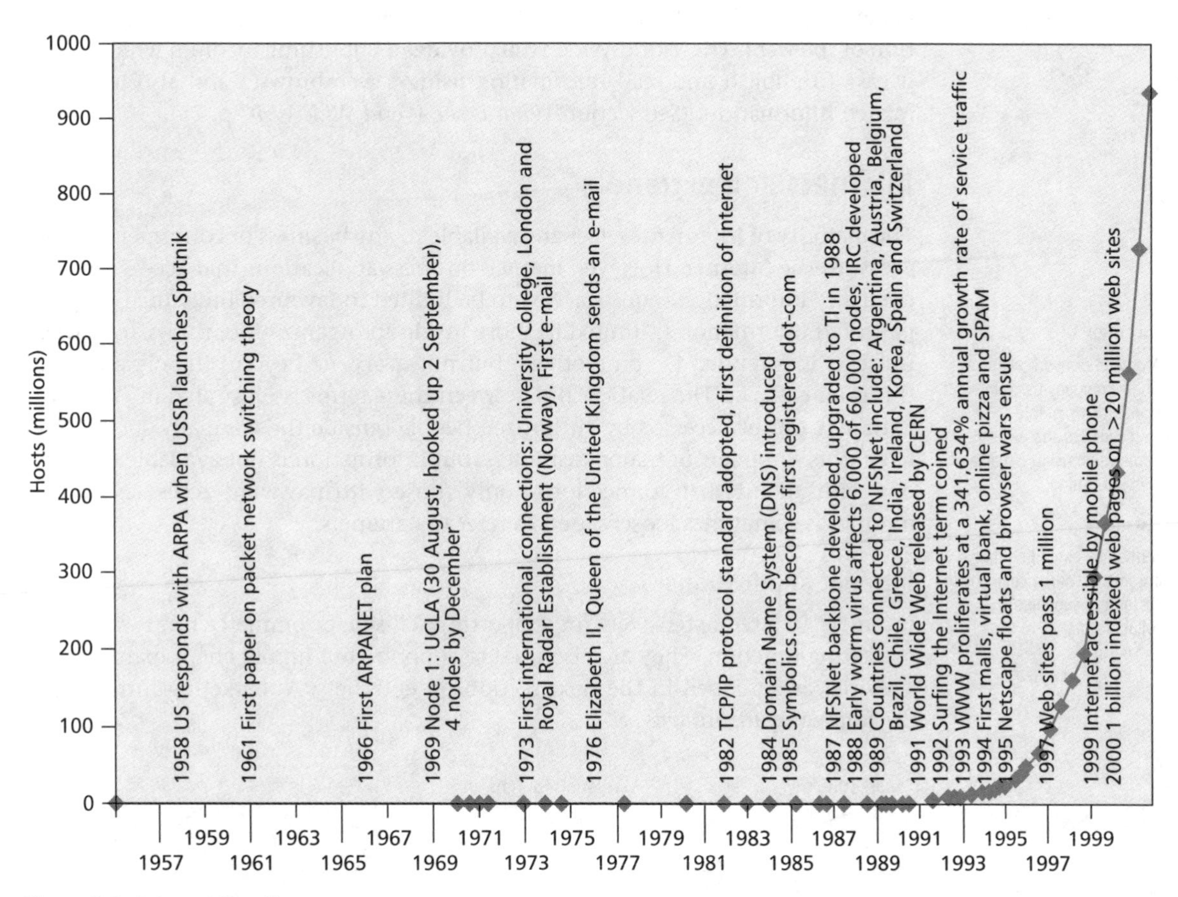

Figure 3.2 Internet timeline

The development of the Internet

Activity 3.2

Purpose

To highlight reasons for the development of the Internet as a vital enabler for business.

Questions

Referring to *Figure 3.2:*

1. Give reasons why the Internet took a long time to develop into today's essential business tool.
2. Develop your own timeline of significant events on the Internet. A key source is the Hobbes Internet timeline (www.isoc.org/guest/zakon/Internet/History/HIT.html) or

that of Gillies and Cailliau (2000). See the author's timeline (p. xxii). See also the *Focus on new access devices* section (p. 106). You may want to speculate on how timelines will differ for future generations.

For answer see p. 115

It is the advent of the World Wide Web that was invented by Tim Berners Lee of CERN to help share research easily that is responsible for the massive growth in business use of the Internet. (See Berners-Lee (1999) for a description of the invention of the web). The World Wide Web provides a publishing medium which makes it easy to publish and read information using a web browser and also to link to related information. (See section *What is the World Wide Web?* p. 75).

Intranets and extranets

The majority of Internet services are available to any business or consumer who has access to the Internet. However, many e-business applications that access sensitive company information require access to be limited to favoured individuals or third parties. If information is limited to those inside an organization, this is an **intranet**. If access is extended to some others, but not everyone beyond the organization, this is an **extranet**. The relationship between these terms is illustrated in *Figure 3.3*. Extranets can be accessed by authorized people outside the company such as collaborators, suppliers or major customers, but information is not available to everyone with an Internet connection – only those with password access. Note that intranet is sometimes loosely used to refer to extranets.

Intranet
A private network within a single company using Internet standards to enable employees to share information using e-mail and web publishing.

Extranet
Formed by extending the intranet beyond a company to customers, suppliers and collaborators.

Intranet applications

Intranets are used extensively for supporting sell-side e-commerce from within the marketing function. They are also used to support core supply chain management activities as described in the next section on extranets. A marketing intranet has the following advantages:

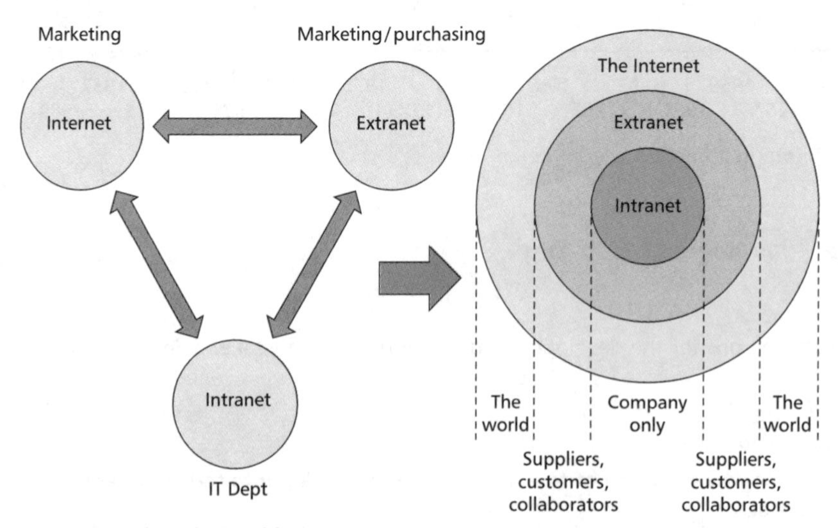

Figure 3.3 The relationship between intranets, extranets and the Internet

- Reduced product lifecycles – as information on product development and marketing campaigns is rationalized can get products to markets faster.
- Reduced costs through higher productivity, and savings on hard copy.
- Better customer service – responsive and personalized support with staff accessing customer over the web.
- Distribution of information through remote offices nationally or globally.

Intranets are also used for internal marketing communications since they can include the following types of information:

- Staff phone directories
- Staff procedures or quality manuals
- Information for agents such as product specifications; current list and discounted prices; competitor information; factory schedules; and stocking levels which normally has to be updated frequently and can be costly
- Staff bulletin or newsletter
- Training courses

Activity 12.4 (p. 492) looks at the type of content and maintenance issues for an intranet for The B2B Company.

Extranet applications

It will be seen in *Chapter 6* that extranets are used extensively to support supply chain management as resources are ordered from suppliers and transformed into products and services delivered to customers. At Marshall Industries, for example, when a new customer order is received across the extranet it automatically triggers a scheduling order for the warehouse (transferred by intranet), an order acknowledgement for the customer and a shipping status when the order ships (Mougayer, 1998). To enable different applications within a company such as a sales ordering system and an inventory control system interoperate with each other and databases in other companies, requires an internal company intranet to be created that can then communicate across an extranet with applications on another company intranet. To enable different applications on the intranet to communicate, **middleware** is used by systems integrators.

Middleware
Software used to facilitate communications between business applications including data transfer and control.

This middleware technology that is used to connect together different business applications and their underlying databases across extranets is now also referred to as **enterprise application integration (EAI)** (*Internet World*, 1999). Such applications include a sales-order processing system and a warehousing system. It now also includes software programs from different organizations.

Enterprise application integration (EAI)
Software used to facilitate communications between business applications including data transfer and control.

Internet World (1999) reported on an example of EAI implementations in which computer distributor Ingram Micro Inc. and build-to-order PC manufacturer Solectron Corp. have integrated their respective applications so that Ingram can check availability of parts with Solectron before placing an order to build a computer. This EAI project, the result of a strategic relationship between Ingram and Solectron since last year, integrates several applications in each company. Previously, Ingram had to place orders without knowing whether Solectron had the inventory to build systems, making it difficult to promise a delivery date to its customers. The new system helps Ingram give a guaranteed two-day delivery on orders. The data integration has been achieved using XML data exchange (p. 85) from XML Server software (www.extricity.com), which translates data from applications on each end of the connection.

A further example of the use of an extranet on a global basis is that of Mecalux (www.mecalux.com). Mecalux, based in Barcelona, Spain, is involved in the design, manufacture and assembly of storage systems, from simple slotted angle rack to sophisticated self-supporting warehouses. Since it was formed in 1996, the company has expanded and has offices in Argentina, Germany, England, France, Portugal, Singapore and Mexico. One of the challenges of this expansion was to improve communications between its representatives around the world and to supply them with the information needed to improve customer service. The management team decided they wanted to create a paperless company where information flows freely in all locations around the world. This makes it easier for the engineers to have the information necessary to respond to any customer's requirements. The extranet created to solve this problem has, for example, enabled representatives in Singapore to tap into data held on the server in Spain to check the availability of the product and get the specifications (such as measurements and price) to a local customer in the shortest possible timeframe. The solution also permits technicians and engineers to collaborate on ideas and work together on future designs from anywhere in the world.

Firewalls

Firewalls are necessary when creating an intranet or extranet to ensure that outside access to the confidential information does not occur. Firewalls are usually created as software mounted on a separate server at the point the company is connected to the Internet. Firewall software can then be configured to only accept links from trusted domains representing other offices in the company. A firewall has implication for e-marketing since staff accessing a web site from work may not be able to access some content such as graphics plug-ins.

Firewall
A specialized software application mounted on a server at the point the company is connected to the Internet. Its purpose to prevent unauthorized access into the company from outsiders.

The use of firewalls within the infrastructure of a company is illustrated in *Figure 3.4*. It is evident that multiple firewalls are used to protect information on the company. The information made available to third parties over the Internet and extranet is partitioned by another firewall using what is referred to as the demilitarized zone (DMZ). Corporate data on the intranet is then mounted on other servers inside the company.

The design of security measures for e-business is reviewed in the *Focus on security design* (*Chapter 11, p. 453*).

To summarize this section on intranets and extranets complete *activity 3.3*.

Activity 3.3 Business benefits of intranets and extranets for The B2B Company

Purpose

To illustrate reasons why companies may want to create intranets and extranets.

Activity

Suggest why The B2B Company, or a company of your choice, may want to set up an intranet or extranet. Think about the types of information the company may want to share with some companies only or which value-added services can be offered for key customers.

For answer see p. 115

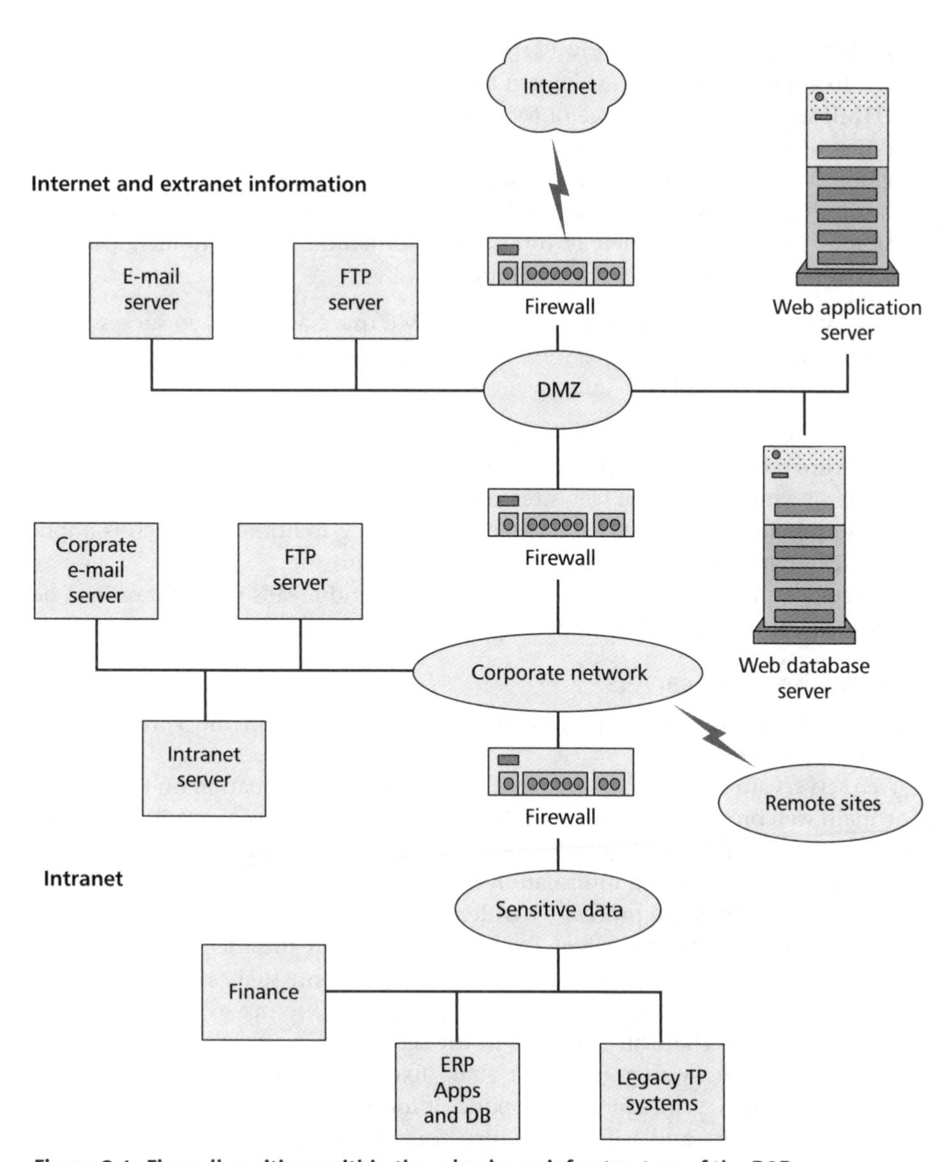

Figure 3.4 Firewall positions within the e-business infrastructure of the B2B company

What is the World Wide Web?

The **World Wide Web**, or 'web' for short, provides a standard method for exchanging and publishing information on the Internet. If we take the analogy of television, then the Internet would be equivalent to the broadcasting equipment such as masts and transmitters, and the World Wide Web is equivalent to the content of different TV programmes. The medium is based on standard document formats such as (HTML (Hypertext Markup Language), p. 84) that can be thought of as similar to a word-processing format such as that used for Microsoft Word documents. This standard has been widely adopted since:

World Wide Web (WWW)
The most common technique for publishing information on the Internet. It is accessed through web browsers which display web pages of embedded graphics and HTML/XML encoded text.

Hyperlink
A method of moving between one web site page and another, indicated to the user by an image or text highlighted by underlining and/or a different colour.

- it offers **hyperlinks** which allow users to readily move from one document or web site to another – the process known as 'surfing';
- HTML supports a wide range of formatting making documents easy to read on different access devices;
- graphics and animations can be integrated into web pages;
- interaction is possible through HTML-based forms that enable customers to supply their personal details for more information on a product, perform searches, ask questions or make comments.

It is the combination of web browsers and HTML that has proved so successful in establishing widespread business use of the Internet. The use of these tools provides a range of benefits including:

- easy to use since navigation between documents is enabled by clicking on hyperlinks or images. This soon becomes a very intuitive way of navigation which is similar across all web sites and applications;
- it can provide a graphical environment supporting multimedia which is popular with users and gives a visual medium for advertising;
- the standardization of tools and growth in demand means information can be exchanged with many businesses and consumers.

Web browsers and servers

Web browsers
Browsers such as Microsoft Internet Explorer provide an easy method of accessing and viewing information stored as web documents on different servers.

Web servers
Store and present the web pages accessed by web browsers.

Web browsers are software used to access the information on the WWW that is stored on **web servers.**

Web servers are used to store, manage and supply the information on the WWW. The main web browsers are Microsoft Internet Explorer and Netscape Navigator or Communicator. Browsers display the text and graphics accessed from web sites and provide tools for managing information from web sites.

Figure 3.5 indicates the process by which web browsers communicate with web servers. A request from the client PC is executed when the user types in a web address, clicks on a hyperlink or fills in an online form such as a search. This request is then sent to the ISP and routed across the Internet to the destination server using the mechanism described in the section on *protocols*. The server then returns the requested web page if it is a **static** (fixed) page, or if it requires reference to a database, such as a request for product information it will pass the query on to a database server and will then return this to the customer as a **dynamically created web page**. Information on all page requests is stored in a **transaction log file** which records the page requested, time it was made and the source of the enquiry. This information can be analysed to assess the success of the web site as explained in *Chapter 12, p. 507*.

Static web page
A page on the web server that is invariant.

Dynamic web page
A page that is created in real-time, often with reference to a database query, in response to a user request.

Transaction log files
A web server file that records all page requests

Internet access software applications

Over its lifetime, many tools have been developed to help find, send and receive information across the Internet. Web browsers used to access the World Wide Web are the latest of these applications. These tools are summarized in *Table 3.2*. In this section we will briefly discuss the relevance of some of the more commonly used tools to the modern organization. The other tools have either been superseded by the use of the World Wide Web or are of less relevance from a business perspective.

The application of the Internet for marketing in this book concentrates on the use of e-mail and the World Wide Web since these tools are now most commonly

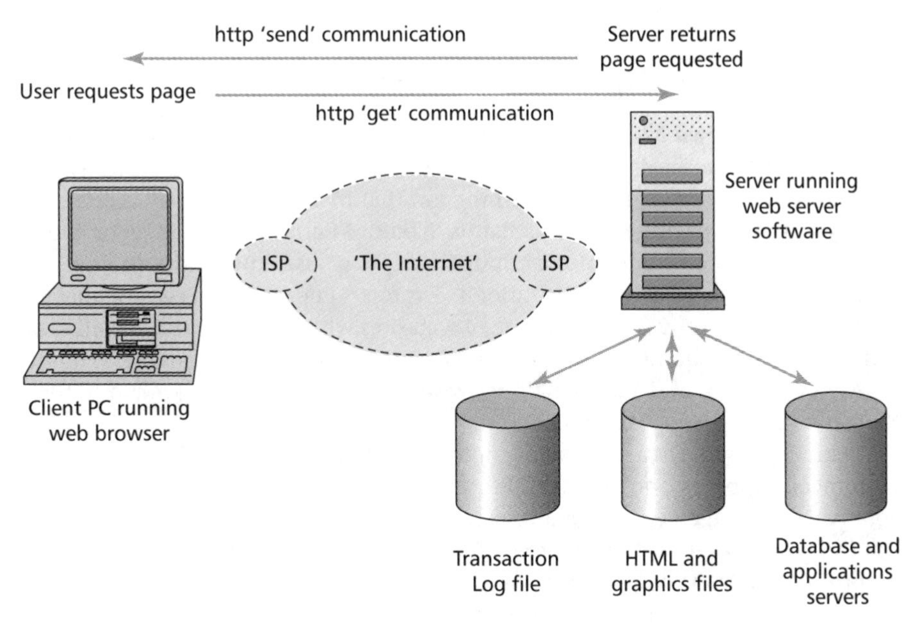

Figure 3.5 Information exchange between a web browser and web server

Table 3.2 Applications of different Internet tools

Internet tool	*Summary*
Electronic mail or e-mail	Sending messages or documents, such as news about a new product or sales promotion between individuals. A primitive form of 'push' channel.
Internet Relay Chat (IRC)	This is a synchronous communications tool which allows a text-based 'chat' between different users who are logged on at the same time. Of limited use for marketing purposes.
Usenet newsgroups	A widely used electronic bulletin board used to discuss a particular topic such as a sport, hobby or business area. Traditionally accessed by special newsreader software, can now be accessed via a web browser from www.deja.com.
FTP file transfer	The File Transfer Protocol is used as a standard for moving files across the Internet. FTP is available as a feature of web browsers that is used for marketing applications such as downloading files such as product price lists or specifications. Also used to update HTML files on web pages.
Gophers, Archie and WAIS	These tools were important before the advent of the web for storing and searching documents on the Internet. They have largely been superseded by the web which provides better searching and more sophisticated document publishing.
Telnet	This allows remote access to computer systems. For example a retailer could check to see whether an item was in stock in a warehouse using a telnet application.
Push channel	Information is broadcast over the Internet or an intranet and received using a web browser or special program for which a subscription to this channel has been set up. This technique is still used for automated software distribution, but has not proved popular as a method for accessing web content by users.
World Wide Web	Widely used for publishing information and running business applications over the Internet.

used by businesses for digital marketing. Many of the other tools such as e-mail, IRC and newsgroups, that formerly needed special software to access them, are now available from the WWW.

Electronic mail or e-mail

E-mail is well known as a method of sending and receiving electronic messages. It has been available across the Internet for over 20 years. E-mails are typically written and read in a special mail reader program that in a large company is often part of a groupware package such as Lotus Notes, Microsoft Exchange or Novell Groupwise. Smaller companies or individuals may use lower cost or free mail programs such as Microsoft Outlook Express, Eudora or Pegasus mail. A relatively recent innovation is the use of web sites which provide free e-mail facilities and do not require any special software other than a web browser. Hotmail (www.hotmail.com) and Yahoo mail (www.yahoo.com) are the best known of these. Kennedy (2001) gives a practical description of Internet based e-mail.

E-mail is now vital as a method of communicating internally and externally with customers, suppliers and partners. Since many e-mails are received and sent by companies, management of e-mail is a major management issue for the e-business. For example ZDNet (2000) reported that Dell receives 50,000 e-mail messages a month and 100,000 order-status-requests a month from customers. It is thought that globally four billion e-mail messages are sent daily with 300 million SMS messages. For Dutch Electronics Company Philips International, 110,000 users within the firm create seven million e-mails and 700 Gb of data a week. A large company with an average of 8000 corporate e-mail users spends more £1 million a year as users try to find and retrieve old e-mail messages, often from archives.

Inbound e-mail
E-mail received from outside the organization such as customer and supplier enquiries.

Outbound e-mail
E-mail sent from the company to other organizations.

E-mail management involves developing procedures and using systems to ensure that inbound and outbound e-mail is processed efficiently. **Inbound e-mail** should be routed to the correct person. E-mails may be sent from a customer to a company requesting information such as product specifications or quotations. Autoresponders or mail-bots are used to notify customers that their response is being dealt with. For example, an e-mail sent to products@company_name.com could automatically dispatch a summary of a company's products. **Outbound e-mail** may be used on an ad hoc basis or as part of a standardized method of keeping customers informed as through a regular e-mail newsletter. Managing inbound and outbound e-mail is an important issue for customer service delivery (*Chapter 9, p. 361*).

Internet relay chat (IRC)

Internet relay chat (IRC) is a low-cost Internet tool giving real-time communication between individuals. As a user in one location types in a comment, it is simultaneously available to those around the world who are 'tuned in' to a particular channel and can then type in a reply. As with other tools mentioned in this section, IRC formerly required a special tool, but has migrated to the web and now has millions of users. IRC seems to be used more for recreational than business use. In a marketing context, it is often inconvenient for a company and its customers to communicate simultaneously (synchronously) since the relevant people may not be available. Asynchronous delivery systems such as e-mail or discussion forums are more practical. For a company wishing to provide a customer support facility to view questions from other customers, discussion groups are more practical.

Usenet newsgroups

There are over 25,000 Usenet newsgroups and they may be updated by up to three million messages each day. These can be thought of as an electronic bulletin board that is read by a closed community. Questions or statements are posted by one person who is looking for further information and the others will reply and lists of related questions will be held together in what is known as a 'thread'. Usenet is mainly used by special interest groups such as people discussing their favourite pastime, like fishing or archery. They are not used that much by businesses, unless as a means of studying consumer behaviour. There are some newsgroups for announcing the introduction of new products or staff vacancies. Newsgroups tend not to be used extensively by business people, since they have to be aware of them and have the technical know-how to set them up. Setup can be difficult because a special piece of software known as a newsreader used to be required to read and contribute to newsgroups. Today, it is much easier to read and contribute to newsgroups since specialist web sites such as Deja (www.deja.com) enable this.

Newsgroups are named in a particular format, broken down into several parts, the first part usually indicating the type of information or country it refers to and the last part the specific topic:

- alt – for 'alternative', e.g. alt.comedy.british or alt.music.kylie-minogue
- rec – recreation includes the largest number of groups, e.g. rec.climbing or uk.rec.climbing
- talk – discussions, e.g. talk.politics.tibet
- biz – business, a surprisingly small number of these, e.g. biz.marketplace.investors is used to offer new investment products
- comp – computer queries solved, e.g. comp.virus
- sci – range of scientific discussions and opinions, e.g. sci.med.cardiology or documents
- soc –social issues, e.g. soc.geneaology.misc

FTP (file transfer protocol)

In a business context **file transfer protocol (FTP)** programs are used to upload or transfer HTML web pages and graphics to a web site when a site is created or modified. Such facilities are now incorporated into many web site authoring programs such as Microsoft Frontpage or Allaire Cold Fusion.

File transfer protocol (FTP)
Standard used for uploading and downloading files to and from web servers.

How does it work? Internet standards

We have introduced the general terms and concepts that describe the operation of the Internet and World Wide Web. In this section we look in more detail at the standards that have been adopted to enable transfer of information. Knowledge of these terms is essential for anyone involved in the management of e-commerce since discussion with suppliers may involve them.

Networking standards

The importance of Internet standards is indicated since they are at the heart of definitions of the Internet. According to Leiner *et al.* (2000) on 24 October 1995 the Federal Networking Council unanimously passed a resolution defining the term Internet.

> *'Internet' refers to the global information system that – (i) is logically linked together by a globally unique address space based on the Internet Protocol (IP) or its subsequent extensions/follow-ons; (ii) is able to support communications using the Transmission Control Protocol/Internet Protocol (TCP/IP) suite or its subsequent extensions/follow-ons, and/or other IP-compatible protocols; and (iii) provides, uses or makes accessible, either publicly or privately, high level services layered on the communications and related infrastructure described herein.*

TCP/IP

TCP/IP
The Transmission Control Protocol is a transport layer protocol that moves data between applications. The Internet protocol is a network layer protocol that moves data between host computers.

TCP/IP development was led by Robert Kahn and Vince Cerf in the late 1960s and early 1970s and, according to Leiner *et al.* (2000), four ground rules controlled Kahn's early work on this protocol. These four ground rules highlight the operation of the TCP/IP protocol:

1. Distinct networks would be able to communicate seamlessly with other networks.
2. Communications would be on a best effort basis, that is, if a data packet didn't reach the final destination, it would be retransmitted from the source until successful receipt.
3. Black boxes would be used to connect the networks; these are now known as the gateways and routers produced by companies such as Cisco and 3Com. There would be no information retained by the gateways in order to keep them simple.
4. There would be no global control of transmissions, these would be governed by the requester and sender of information.

It can be seen that simplicity, speed and independence from control were at the heart of the development of the TCP/IP standards.

The data transmissions standards of the Internet such as TCP/IP are part of a larger set of standards known as the Open Systems Interconnection (OSI) model. This defines a layered model that enables servers to communicate with other servers and clients. When implemented in software, the combined layers are referred to as a protocol stack. The seven layers of the OSI model are:

- *Application*. The program such as a web browser that creates and receives messages.
- *Presentation*. These protocols are usually part of the operating system.
- *Session*. This includes data transfer protocols such as SMTP, HTTP and FTP.
- *Transport*. This layer ensures the integrity of data transmitted. Examples include the Internet Transmission Control Protocol and Novell SPX.
- *Network*. Defines protocols for opening and maintaining links between servers. The best known are the Internet IP protocol and Novell IPX.
- *Data-link*. Defines the rules for sending and receiving information.
- *Physical*. Low level description of physical transmission methods.

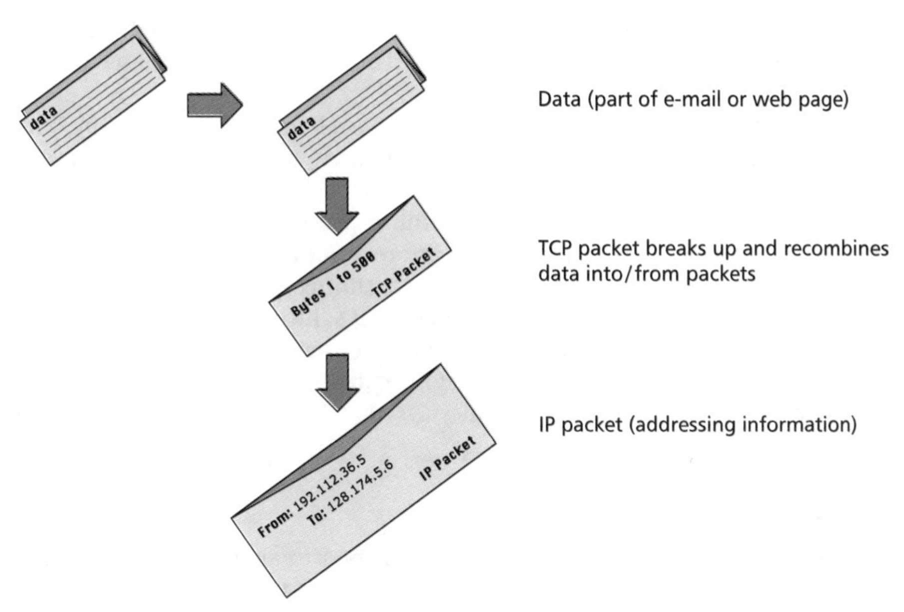

Figure 3.6 The TCP/IP protocol

The postal service is a good analogy for the transmission of data around the Internet using the TCP/IP protocol. Before we send mail, we always need to add a destination address. Likewise, the IP protocol acts as an addressed envelope that is used to address a message to the appropriate IP address of the receiver (*Figure 3.6*).

The Internet is a packet-switched network that uses TCP/IP as its protocol. This means that, as messages or packets are sent, there is no part of the network that is dedicated to them. This is the same as when your letters and parcels are sent by post they are mixed with letters and parcels from other people. The alternative type of network is the circuit-switched network such as phone systems where the line is dedicated to the user for the duration of the call. Taking the analogy further, the transmission media of the Internet such as telephone lines, satellite links and optical cables are the equivalent of the vans, trains and planes that are used to carry post. Transmission media for the Internet include analogue media such as phone lines and faster, digital media such as Integrated Service Digital Network technology (ISDN) and more recently Asynchronous Digital Subscriber Line (ADSL).

In addition to the transmission media, components of the network are also required to direct or route the packets or messages via the most efficient route. On the Internet these are referred to as routers or hubs, and are manufactured by companies such as Cisco and 3 Com. The routers are the equivalent of postal sorting offices which decide the best route for mail to take. They do not plan the entire route of the message, but rather they direct it to the next router that seems most appropriate given the destination and current network traffic.

Some addressing information goes at the beginning of your message; this information gives the network enough information to deliver the packet of data. The **IP address** of a receiving server is usually in the form 207.68.156.58 which is a numerical representation of a better known form such as www.microsoft.com. Each IP address is unique to a given organization, server or client, in a similar way to postal

IP address
The unique numerical address of a computer.

codes referring to a small number of houses. The first number refers to the top level domain in the network, in this case .com. The remaining numbers are used to refer to a particular organization.

Once the Internet message is addressed, the postal analogy is not so apt since related information is not sent across the Internet in one large message. For reasons of efficiency, information sent across IP networks is broken up into separate parts called **packets**. The information within a packet is usually between 1 and 1500 characters long. This helps to route information most efficiently and fairly with different packets sent by different people gaining equal priority. The transmission control protocol TCP performs the task of splitting up the original message into packets on dispatch and re-assembling it on receipt. Combining TCP and IP, you can think of an addressed IP envelope containing a TCP envelope which in turn contains part of the original message that has been split into a packet (*Figure 3.6*).

Packet
Each Internet message such as an e-mail or http request is broken down into smaller parts for ease of transmission.

The HTTP protocol

HTTP (hypertext transfer protocol)
HTTP or hypertext transfer protocol is a standard which defines the way information is transmitted across the Internet between web browsers and web servers.

HTTP, the hypertext transfer protocol is a standard used to allow web browsers and servers to transfer requests for delivery of web pages and their embedded graphics. When you click on a link while viewing a web site, the web browser you are using will request information from the server computer hosting the web site using the http protocol. Since this protocol is important for delivering the web pages, the letters http:// are used to prefix all web addresses. HTTP messages are divided into HTTP 'get' messages for requesting and web page and HTTP 'send' message as shown in *Figure 3.5*. The web pages and graphics transferred in this way are transferred as packets, which is why web pages do not usually download gradually but in jumps as different groups of packets arrive.

The inventor of http, Tim Berners-Lee, describes its purpose as follows (Berners-Lee, 1999):

> *HTTP rules define things like which computer speaks first, and how they speak in turn. When two computers agree they can talk, they have to find a common way to represent their data so they can share it.*

Uniform resource locators (URL)

Uniform (universal) resource locators (URL)
A web address used to locate a web page on a web server.

Web addresses refer to particular pages on a web server which is hosted by a company or organization. The technical name for web addresses is **uniform or universal resource locators (URLs)**. URLs can be thought of as a standard method of addressing similar to postal or ZIP codes, that makes it straightforward to find the name of a site.

Web addresses are usually prefixed by 'http://' to denote the http protocol that is explained above. Web addresses always start with 'http://', so references to web sites in this book and in most promotional material from companies omit this part of the URL. Indeed, when using modern versions of web browsers, it is not necessary to type this in as part of the web page location since it is added automatically by the web browser. Although the vast majority of sites start with 'www', this is not universal, so it is necessary to specify this.

Web addresses are structured in a standard way as follows:

http://www.domain-name.extension/filename.html

Domain names

The domain name refers to the name of the web server and is usually selected to be the same as the name of the company, and the extension will indicate its type. The extension is known as the global top level domain (gTLD). There are also some 250 country code top level domains (ccTLD).

Common gTLDs are:

- **.com** represents an international or American company such as www.travelagency.com
- **.co.uk** represents a company based in the UK such as www.thomascook.co.uk
- **.ac.uk** a UK-based university (e.g. www.derby.ac.uk)
- **.org.uk** or **.org** are not-for-profit organizations (e.g. www.greenpeace.org)
- **.net** a network provider such as www.virgin.net

The 'filename.html' part of the web address refers to an individual web page, for example 'products.html' for a web page summarizing a company's products. When a web address is typed in without a filename, for example www.bt.com, the browser automatically assumes the user is looking for the home page, that by convention is referred to as index.html. When creating sites, it is therefore vital to name the home page index.html. The file index.html can also be placed in sub-directories to ease access to information. For example, to access a support page a customer would type www.bt.com/support.

Note that gTLDs are continuously under review and in 2000 ICANN, the Internet Corporation for Assigned Names and Numbers (www.icann.org), granted seven new gTLDs. Available from June 2001 are .biz for business, .name to be used by individuals, .museum, .pro for professionals, .aero for aviation, .coop for co-operatives and .info. Some of the proposed gTLDs refused included '.sex', '.shoes', '.kids' and '.xxx'. The introduction of these names, while increasing choice where .com names have already been assigned, may make finding the URL of a company more difficult – it may no longer be sufficient to take the name of the company and add '.com'. According to another view, existing companies such as Amazon will attempt to register with the new domain such as '.biz' which will not help to increase the availability of gTLD names.

ICANN is also involved in domain name arbitration. Its first case involved an individual who offered the name WorldWrestlingFederation.com to the World Wrestling Federation. The WWF won since it was considered the individual was 'cybersquatting'. In another case, Penguin Books stated that it had a claim to www.penguin.org which had been registered by an individual. But in this Penguin lost since the respondent argued convincingly that he was known as Penguin and his wife as Mrs Penguin!

The long-term solution for the difficulty of users for matching company and brand names with URLs seem to be lookup systems. One such system is RealNames (www.realnames.com) which has been integrated into search engines such as Altavista.com. RealNames was established in 1998. Centraal, the company that operates RealNames, will register company names and brands for $100 and it offers a searching service to consumers where the consumer types a company or product they are looking for and its search engine will then list matches. In March 1999 there were 15,000 registered companies or brands registered with RealNames and three million other companies.

Another approach to identify companies online is from OneName (www.onename.com). This company is promoting the eXtensible Name Service (XNS) as a new way to exchange information automatically between agents instead of manually via people. A person and business can use XNS, which is based on XML, to privately exchange information from contact data to credit cards, all under a legally binding privacy contract for every single transaction. It remains to be seen whether this service creates a sufficient critical mass to be successful. A similar approach is being proposed by the DOI (www.doi.org).

Domain name registration

If a company wants to establish a web presence it needs to register a domain name that is unique to it. Domain names can be registered via an ISP or at more favourable rates direct from the domain name services:

1. InterNIC – www.internic.net: registration and information about sites in the .com, .org and .net domains.
2. Nomination – www.nomination.uk.com: is an alternative registration service for the UK, allowing you to register in the (uk.com) pseudo-domain (also AlterNIC).
3. Nominet – www.nominet.org.uk: main co.uk site

Web page standards

Content
The design, text and graphical information which forms a web page. Good content is the key to attracting customers to a web site and retaining their interest or achieving repeat visits.

The information, graphics and interactive elements that make up the web pages of a site are collectively referred to as **content**. Different standards exist for text, graphics and multimedia. The saying 'content is king' is often applied to the World Wide Web, since the content will determine the experience of the customer and whether he or she will return to a web site in future.

Text information – HTML (Hypertext Markup Language)

HTML (Hypertext Markup Language)
A standard format used to define the text and layout of web pages. HTML files usually have the extension .HTML or .HTM.

Web page text has many of the formatting options available in a word processor. These include applying fonts, emphasis (bold, italic, underline) and placing information in tables. Formatting is possible since the web browser applies these formats according to instructions that are contained in the file that makes up the web page. This is usually written in **HTML** or **Hypertext Markup Language**. HTML is an international standard established by the World Wide Web Consortium (and published at www.w3.org) intended to ensure that any web page authored according to the definitions in the standard will appear the same in any web browser. HTML files can be authored in an ordinary text editor such as the Notepad program available with Microsoft Windows. Modern word processors also have an option to save formatted information in the HTML format. Alternatively, many software utilities are available to simplify writing HTML.

A brief example of HTML is given for a simplified home page for The B2B Company in *Figure 3.7*. The HTML code used to construct pages has codes or instruction tags such as <TITLE> to indicate to the browser what is displayed. The <TITLE> tag indicates what appears at the top of the web browser window. Each starting tag has a corresponding end tag usually marked by a '/', for example <B>plastics</B> to embolden plastics.

The simplicity of HTML compared to traditional programming languages makes it possible for simple web pages to be developed by non-specialists such as mar-

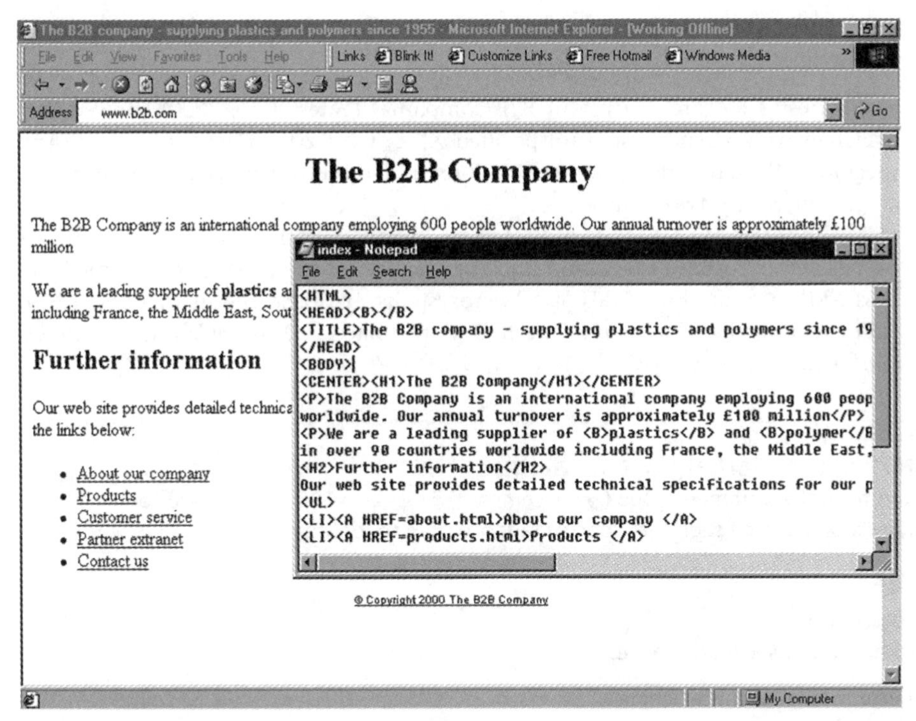

Figure 3.7 Home page index.html for The B2B Company in a web browser showing HTML source in text editor

keting assistants, particularly if templates for more complex parts of the page are provided. Interactive forms and brochures and online sales are more complex and usually require some programming expertise, although tools are available to simplify these. See detailed information on creating HTML pages (*Chapter 12, p. 474*).

Text information and data – XML (eXtensible Markup Language)

When the early version of HTML was designed by Tim Berners-Lee at CERN, he based it on the existing standard for representation of documents. This standard was SGML, the Standard Generalized Markup Language that was ratified by the ISO in 1986. SGML uses tags to identify the different elements of a documents such as title and chapters. HTML used a similar approach, for example the tag for title is <TITLE>. While HTML proved powerful in providing a standard method of displaying information that was easy to learn, it was purely presentational. It lacked the ability to describe the data on web pages. These weaknesses have been acknowledged and, in an effort coordinated by the World Wide Web consortium, the first **XML** or **eXtensible Markup Language** was produced in February 1998. This is also based on SGML. The key word describing XML is 'extensible'. This means that new markup tags can be created that facilitate the searching and exchange of information. For example, product information on a web page could use the XML tags <NAME>, <DESCRIPTION>, <COLOUR> and <PRICE>. The tags can effectively act as a standard set of database field descriptions so that data can be exchanged through B2B exchanges.

XML or eXtensible Markup Language
A standard for transferring structured data, unlike HTML which is purely presentational.

XML information comprises:

- Extensible Style Sheet (XSL)
- Document Type Definition (DTD)

A Forrester Research survey of B2B companies (Yates *et al.*, 2000) showed that over half were already using unspecified XML, with 20 per cent using industry-specific XML standards; 49 per cent still used EDI, but this was expected to fall to 4 per cent within two years.

The importance of XML is indicated by its incorporation by Microsoft into its BizTalk server forB2B integration and the creation of the ebXML (electronic business XML) standard by rivals Sun Microsystems. It is also the main standard for data exchange for Commerce One B2B Marketplace (see *Example XML for Online Marketplace catalogue* box).

Example XML for Online Marketplace catalogue

This example is taken from the Commerce One (www.commerceone.net) xCBL 3.0 standard for publishing catalogue data. It can be seen that specific tags are used to identify:

- Product ID
- Manufacturer
- Long and short description
- Attributes of product and associated picture.

There is no pricing information in this example.

```
<CatalogData>
<Product>
<Action Value="Delete"/>
<ProductID>118003-008</ProductID>
</Product>
<Product Type="Good" SchemaCategoryRef="C43171801">
<ProductID>140141-002</ProductID>
<UOM><UOMCoded>EA</UOMCoded></UOM>
<Manufacturer>Compaq</Manufacturer>
<LeadTime>2</LeadTime>
<CountryOfOrigin>
<Country><CountryCoded>US</CountryCoded></Country>
</CountryOfOrigin>
<ShortDescription xml:lang="en">Armada M700 PIII 500
12GB</ShortDescription>
<LongDescription xml:lang="en">
This light, thin powerhouse delivers no-compromise performance in a sub-five pound form
factor. Size and Weight(HxWxD): 12.4 X 9.8 X 1.1 in 4.3 - 4.9 lbs (depending on
configuration) Processor: 500-MHZ Intel Pentium III Processor with 256K integrated
cache Memory: 128MB of RAM, expandable to 576MB Hard Drive: 12.0GB Removable
SMART Hard Drive Display Graphics: 14.1-inch color TFT with 1024 x 768 resolution
(up to 16M colors internal) Communication: Mini-PCI V.90 Modem/Nic Combo Operating
System: Dual Installation of Microsoft Windows 95 &amp; Microsoft Windows 98
</LongDescription>
<ProductAttachment>
<AttachmentURL>file:\5931.jpg</AttachmentURL>
```

```
<AttachmentPurpose>PicName</AttachmentPurpose>
<AttachmentMIMEType>jpg</AttachmentMIMEType>
</ProductAttachment>
<ObjectAttribute>
<AttributeID> Processor Speed</AttributeID>
<AttributeValue>500MHZ</AttributeValue>
</ObjectAttribute>
<ObjectAttribute>
<AttributeID>Battery Life</AttributeID>
<AttributeValue>6 hours</AttributeValue>
</ObjectAttribute>
</Product>
```

Source: www.commerceone.com/download/xCBL3ForContent.pdf

Graphical images (GIF and JPEG file)

Graphics produced by graphic designers or captured using digital cameras can be readily incorporated into web pages as images. **GIF (Graphics Interchange Format)** and **JPEG (Joint Photographics Experts Group)** refer to two standard file formats most commonly used to present images on web pages. GIF files are limited to 256 colours and are best used for small simple graphics such as banner adverts, while JPEG are best used for larger images where image quality is important such as photographs. Both formats use image compression technology to minimize the size of downloaded files.

GIF (Graphics Interchange Format)
A graphics format and compression algorithm best used for simple graphics.

JPEG (Joint Photographics Experts Group)
A graphics format and compression algorithm best used for photographs.

Animated graphical information (GIFs and plug-ins)

GIF files can also be used for interactive banner adverts. **Plug-ins** are additional programs, sometimes referred to as helper applications, that work in association with the web browser to provide features not present in the basic web browser. The best known plug-ins are probably the one for Adobe Acrobat that is used to display documents in .pdf format (www.adobe.com) and the Macromedia Flash and Shockwave products for producing interactive graphics (www.macromedia.com).

Plug-ins
An add-on program to a web browser providing extra functionality such as animation.

Audio and video standards

Traditionally sound and video or rich media have been stored as the Microsoft standards .WAV and .AVI. A newer sound format for music is MP3. These formats are used on some web sites, but they are not appropriate for sites such as the BBC (www.bbc.co.uk), since the user would have to wait until the whole clip downloads before hearing or viewing it. Streaming media are now used for many multimedia sites since they enable video or audio to start playing within a few seconds – it is not necessary for the whole file to be downloaded before it can be played. Formats for **streaming media** have been established by Real Networks (www.realnetworks.com).

Streaming media
Sound and video that can be experienced within a web browser before the whole clip is downloaded.

Managing e-business infrastructure

The management of e-business infrastructure is informed by reviewing two different perspectives of the infrastucture. These are:

1. *Technology infrastructure*. This refers mainly to the hardware infrastructure referred to in the previous sections. This includes the provision of servers, clients, networks and also systems software such as operating systems and browsers (Layers II, III and IV in *Figure 3.8*).
2. *Applications infrastructure*. This refers mainly to the software provision of the infrastructure. This is the applications software used to deliver services to employees, customers and other partners (Layer I in *Figure 3.8*).

Each of these elements of infrastructure present separate management issues. At this point the management issues are introduced, while more detailed discussion of management solutions is presented in *Chapters 10, 11 and 12*.

Alternative models of the infrastructure of an organization have been proposed by Zwass (1998) and Kampas (2000). Zwass (1998) describes a framework for the Internet consisting of three main levels which are:

1. *Infrastructure*. The hardware, software, databases and telecommunications.
2. *Services*. Software-based services such as search-engines, digital money and security systems.
3. *Products and services*. The web sites of individual companies and marketplaces.

Kampas (1998) describes a five-level model of what he refers to as the information system function chain:

1. *Storage/physical*. Memory and disk hardware components.
2. *Processing*. Computation and logic provided by the processor.
3. *Infrastructure*. This refers to the human and external interfaces and also the network, referred to as extrastructure.

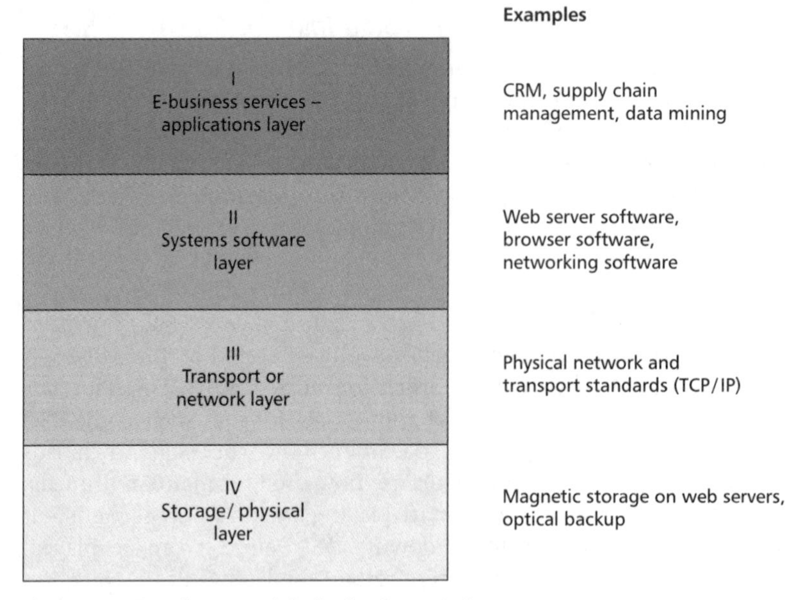

Figure 3.8 Four-layer model of e-business infrastructure

4. *Application/content*. This is the data processed by the application into information.
5. *Intelligence*. Additional computer-based logic that transforms information to knowledge.

This five-layer model is similar to *Figure 3.8*. Each of these elements of infrastructure present separate management issues which we will consider separately. At this point the management issues are introduced, while more detailed discussion of management solutions is presented in *Chapters 10, 11 and 12*.

Managing technology infrastructure

Management of the technology infrastructure requires decisions on layers II, III and IV in *Figure 3.8*. What management decisions have to be taken at each level?

Layer II – Systems software

The key management issue is standardization throughout the organization. Standardization leads to reduced numbers of contacts for support and maintenance and can reduce purchase prices through multi-user licences. Systems software choices occur for the client, server and network. On the client computers, the decision will be which browser software to standardize on, for example Microsoft Explorer, Netscape Communicator or more specialized software such as the Lotus Notes client or the Opera browser. Standardized plug-ins should be installed across the organization. The systems software for the client will also be decided on; this will probably be a variant of Microsoft Windows, but alternatives such as Sun Microsystems' Solaris may also be considered. For the server, there may be many servers in the global organization, both for the Internet and intranets. Using a standardized web server software such as Apache will help maintenance. Networking software will also be decided on; this could be Microsoft sourced or from other suppliers such as Sun Microsystems or Novell.

Layer III – Transport or network

Decisions on the network will be based on the internal company network, which for the e-business will be an intranet and the external network, either an extranet or VPN (p. 102) or links to the public Internet. The main management decision is whether internal or external network management will be performed by the company or outsourced to a third party. Outsourcing of network management is common. Standardized hardware is also needed to connect clients to the Internet, for example, a modem card or external modem in home PCs or a network interface card (NIC) to connect to the company network (LAN) for business computers.

Layer IV – Storage

The decision on storage is similar to that for the transport layer. Storage can be managed internally or externally. This is not an either/or choice. For example, intranet and extranet are commonly managed internally while Internet storage such as the corporate web site is commonly managed externally or at an application service provider (p. 105).

We will now consider decisions involving third-party service providers of the technology infrastructure.

Internet Service Providers

Internet Service Provider (ISP)
Companies that provide home or business users with a connection to access the Internet and hosting of web sites.

Service providers are usually referred to as **ISPs** or **Internet Service Providers**. Providers who also provide some specialized web content to users such as America Online or Compuserve are sometimes distinguished as OSPs or online service providers. ISPs are telecommunications companies which provide access to the Internet for home and business users. ISPs have two main functions. First, they can provide a link to a company or individual which enables them to access the World Wide Web and send Internet e-mail. Second, they can host web sites or provide a link from a company's web servers to enable other companies and consumers access to a corporate web site. Note that as well as these basic services many ISPs have extended their services to become applications service providers (*ASPs, p. 105*).

For many years, service providers such as Compuserve charged according to the number of hours a user was connected to the Internet. This was additional to the charge of the user making the connection to the ISP via a phone call. In recent years the cost of these services has been greatly reduced, now only amounting to the cost of a local telephone call – see the mini-case study on free access to the Internet for further details. With increased competition, lower flat-rate charges were introduced. In 1998 free services such as Freeserve from Dixons (www.freeserve.net), followed by, in 1999, Virgin (www.virgin.net), Tesco supermarkets (www.tesco.net) and BT (www.btclickfree.co.uk), changed the pricing model dramatically. With Freeserve signing up over one million customers in its first year it was thought that Internet access would remain free. The business model of free ISPs now appears untenable since they cannot generate sufficient revenue from advertising or affiliates to remain profitable. In 2000 Freeserve was sold to a French company and Breath, the fourth-largest ISP in the UK, closed with losses of over £50 m.

Figure 3.1 shows the way in which companies or home users connect to the Internet. The diagram is greatly simplified in that there are several tiers of ISPs. A user may connect to one ISP which will then transfer the request to another ISP which is connected to the main Internet backbone.

Issues in managing ISPs

The primary issue in managing ISPs is to ensure a satisfactory service quality at a reasonable price. Organizations hosting events have to have web sites with the capacity to deal with large increases in traffic volume. The official site of the Wimbledon tennis tournament (www.wimbledon.org) in 2000 received 2.3 billion hits in a fortnight compared to 942 million hits the previous year, with the site busiest during the fifth set of the semi-final between André Agassi and Pat Rafter, registering 963,948 hits a minute. The official Euro 2000 web site (www.euro2000.org), recorded around one billion hits during the tournament. For these large sites, a single server is not used – the Euro 2000 site was hosted in 10 locations with traffic balanced so that each user went to the closest and fastest location. We will now examine the elements of service quality – speed, availability and security.

Speed of access

Speed of access of a customer, employee or partner to services on an e-business server is determined by both the speed of server and the speed of the network connection to the server. The speed of the site governs how quick the response is to a request for information from the end user. This will be dependent on the speed of the server machine on which the web site is hosted and how quickly the server processes the information. If there are only a small number of users accessing information on the server, then there will not be a noticeable delay on requests for pages. If, however, there are thousands of users requesting information at the same time then there may be a delay and it is important that the combination of web server software and hardware can cope. Web server software will not greatly affect the speed at which requests are answered. The speed of the server is mainly controlled by the amount of primary storage (for example, 1024 Mb RAM memory is faster than 512 Mb RAM) and the speed of the magnetic storage (hard disk). Many of the search engine web sites now store all their index data in RAM since this is faster than reading data from the hard disk. Companies will pay ISPs according to the capabilities of the server. An important point is whether the server is **dedicated** or shared. Clearly if content on a server is shared with other sites hosted on the same server then performance will be affected by demand loads on these other sites. For high traffic sites servers may be located across several computers with many processors to spread the demand load. Such arrangements are sometimes referred to as 'web farms'. New methods of hosting content summarized by Spinrad (1999) have been introduced to improve the speed of serving web pages. These methods involve distributing content on servers around the globe. Two rival schemes emerging are Akamai Freeflow (www.akamaitech.net) and Sandpiper Networks Footprint (www.sandpiper.com). These are used by companies such as Yahoo, Apple and other 'hot spot' sites likely to receive many hits.

Dedicated server
Server only contains content and applications for a single company.

The speed is also governed by the speed of the network connection, commonly referred to as the network **bandwidth**. The bandwidth of a web site's connection to the Internet and the bandwidth of the customer's connection to the Internet will affect the speed with which web pages and associated graphics load onto the customer's PC. The term is so-called because of the width of range of electromagnetic frequencies an analogue or digital signal occupies for a given transmission medium.

Bandwidth
Indicates the speed at which data is transferred using a particular network media. It is measured in bits-per-second (bps).

Bandwidth gives an indication of the speed at which data can be transferred from a web server along a particular medium such as a network cable or phone line. In simple terms bandwidth can be thought of as the size of a pipe along which information flows. The higher the bandwidth, the greater the diameter of the pipe, and the faster information is delivered to the user.

The bandwidth required for acceptable quality of service is proportional to the complexity of the data. For example, more bandwidth is required to download a graphical image in one second compared to downloading a page of text in one second.

Bandwidth measures are in bits per second where one character or digit, such as the number '1', would be equivalent to 8 bits. So a modem operating at 57,600 bits per second (57.6 kbps) will transfer information at 7200 characters per second (57,600/8). When selecting an ISP it is important to consider the bandwidth of the connection between the ISP and the Internet. Choices may be:

- ISDN – 56 kbps up to 128 kbps
- Frame relay – 56 kbps up to T1 (1.55 Mbps)
- Dedicated point-to-point – 56 kbps up to T3 (45 Mbps): connected to the Internet backbone.

Bandwidth measures

Kbps (one kilobit per second or 1,000 bps (a modem operates at up to 56.6 kbps)

Mbps (one megabit per second or 1,000,000 bps, company networks operate at 10 or more Mbps)

Gbps (one gigabit per second or 1,000,000,000 bps, fibre-optic or satellite links operate at Gbps)

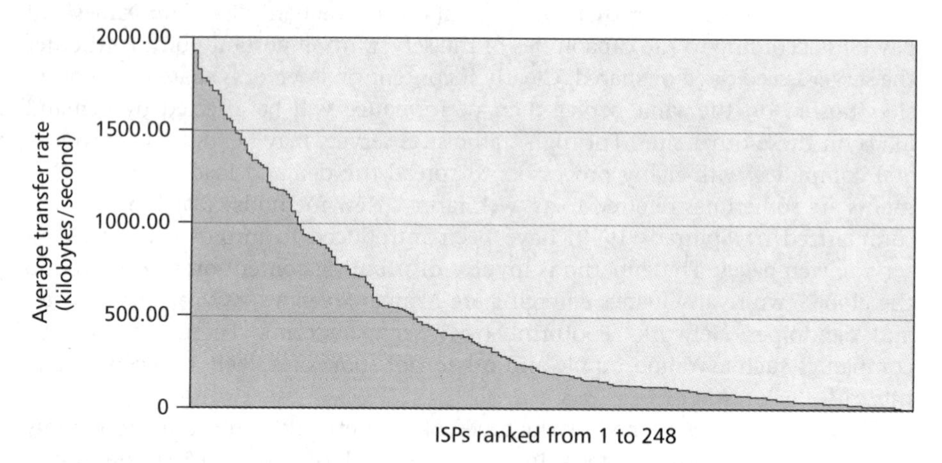

Figure 3.9 Variation in average transfer rate of data from a web server, compilation of UK ISPS from Zeus (http://www.zeus.com)
Source: www.webperf.net, © Zeus Technology Ltd 2001.

A medium to large business connects to an ISP using a high speed phone line such as T1 line. A T1 line can handle approximately 1.5 million bits per second, while a smaller business will use a normal phone line using a modem that can usually handle a maximum of 56,600 bits per second, or ISDN which is up to twice as fast.

Some ISPs are not connected directly to the Internet backbone and are linked to it via other providers. Their service will be slower than those directly connected to the main Internet backbone since information has to 'jump' several different network links.

Figure 3.9 shows that there is a large variation in speed of service delivery by ISPs, so it is important that managers monitor their sites' performance in comparison to industry standards.

Availability

Availability refers to the amount of time that a web site is available to customers. For a company offering 24 × 7 services, it should be 100 per cent. However, inspection of *Table 3.3* and *Figure 3.10* shows that this is often not the case. For an e-commerce site, such as travel site E-bookers, a large amount of revenue could be lost if availability drops below 100 per cent. Of course, this will not only be revenue lost from customers unable to complete their transactions, but also revenue lost from potential or current customer who are unlikely to use the site in the future because of the disruption they have faced.

Table 3.3 Variation in download and availability of top UK sites, November 2000

Download (secs)	*Availability (%)*
Yahoo 1.09	100.00
Autobytel 2.61	100.00
BBC 3.09	99.57
Ebookers 3.49	96.54
Worst 85.85	77.49

Source: Keynote (www.keynote.com)

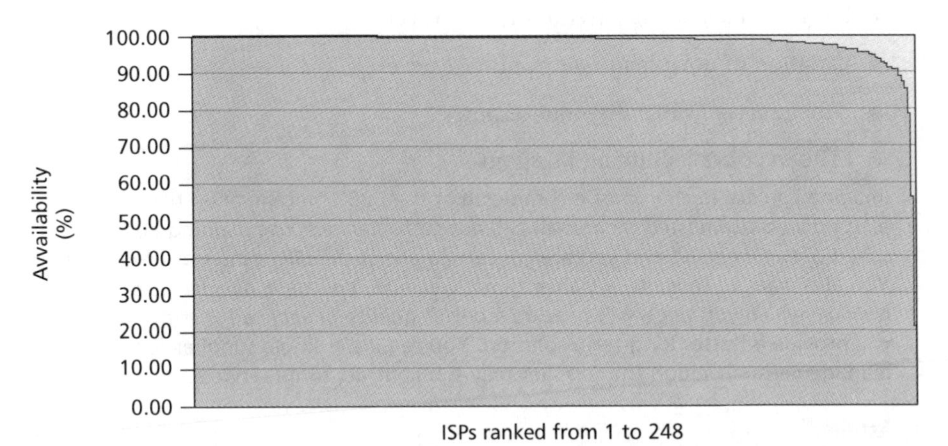

Figure 3.10 Variation in web server availability, compilation of UK ISPS from Zeus (http://www.zeus.com)

Source: www.webperf.net, © Zeus Technology Ltd 2001.

Service level agreements

To ensure the best speed and availability a company should check the **service level agreements (SLAs)** carefully when outsourcing web site hosting services. The SLA will define confirmed standards of availability and performance measured in terms of the *latency* or network delay when information is passed from one point to the next (measured as London to New York). The SLA also includes notification to the customer detailing when the web service becomes unavailable with reasons why and estimates of when the service will be restored. Further information on SLAs is available at www.uk.uu.net/support/sla/. *Activity 3.4* gives sources where individuals or companies can monitor the performance of their ISP and *case study 3.1* summarizes some of the management issues involved with hosting.

Service level agreements
A contractual specification of service standards a contractor must meet.

Security

Security is another important issue in service quality. How to control security was referred to in the earlier section on firewalls and is considered in detail in the *Focus on security design* (*Chapter 11, p. 453*).

Activity 3.4 Assessing ISP performance

Purpose

To highlight management issues in monitoring and controlling ISP performance.

Activity

1. Several UK Internet magazines such as *Internet Works* (www.iwks.com) or *Internet Magazine* (www.internet-magazine.com) provide monthly performance assessments of different ISPs. Services for companies to assess their performance are also provided by Keynote (www.keynote.com), Zeus (www.zeus.co.uk and http://webperf.net) and Mercury Interactive (www.mercuryinteractive.com).

   Visit the site of these suppliers and review the variation of the ISPs in term of different factors. Which is the fastest, which is the slowest. How does your ISP fare?

   - Long-term availability trend for web server.
   - Variation of download rate from web server.
   - E-mail server availability and response.
   - FTP server availability and response.

2. Imagine you are in charge of e-commerce at the B2B Company. You have an existing web site hosted by a small ISP, but customers are complaining about the speed of the web site and you are concerned about the ISP going out of business. You also want to move to a transactional web site. You have decided to select a new ISP which you hope will provide a better quality of service for customers and will provide a better long-term solution. You require a single supplier for ease of management, although the supplier may sub-contract some services.

Questions

1. List the services you would require.
2. What are the key factors on which you will judge the ISP?

For answers see p. 115

CASE STUDY 3.1

Selecting a supplier for hosting web site services

Although the 2000 Olympic Games took place in Sydney, the web-based results service was administered from the other side of the world – at Bristol in the UK.

High-speed telecommunications and standard web access software makes such remote operation not only possible, but also desirable: 'Only a couple of years ago, everyone wanted their web site in their office. But now organizations are beginning to see the advantages of getting someone else to shoulder the technology burden and take advantage of the economies of scale,' says Dominic Brodrick, business development manager at Hewlett Packard's (HP) global e-services group, the organization responsible for the Olympic Games results service.

The physical location of a web site, he says, is becoming largely irrelevant: 'We tried the results system out originally for the 1998 World Cup soccer tournament and registered a record number of hits on the site. In both cases, the location of the web server is really not important – only the availability and scalability of the site.'

Some IT applications naturally fall into the category of 'non-core' activities. Companies have, for example, been quite happy to buy in payroll services on the basis that it is an application dictated by external forces and offers no competitive edge.

On the surface, third-party hosting of web sites appears to fall into the same category. Like payroll, the processes and technology are standard – communications and presentation in this case being defined by the Internet standards such as Transmission Control Protocol/Internet Protocol (TCP/IP) and Hypertext Mark-up Language (HTML).

Unlike payroll applications, however, company web sites are in the marketing front line. The degree to which they can be put in the hands of a third party depends on how closely the web site is linked with legacy databases and other internal IT systems. The new wave of e-business applications that require web sites to process financial transactions are inevitably more complex than simple 'information' sites.

'There are several different levels of outsourcing – from a simple shared web server to a full-blown e-commerce system. The level a company chooses will depend on the number of sites, the nature of the web site traffic and the demand for bandwidth,' says Mike Gordon, commercial director at Virtual Internet, a specialist web-hosting company.

'Whatever level they come in at, the drivers are the same – the need to cut IT costs, the economies of scale and the need for reliable systems – available 24 hours a day. With outsourcing they can start thinking in terms of a fixed cost and predictable service. It lets a company become more productive without worrying about the technology,' he continues.

Virtual Internet concentrates on straightforward web-hosting – either by providing space on a large server system or managing dedicated servers for individual companies. This is especially appealing to small and medium-sized enterprises (SMEs) because it offers a level of service they could not possibly afford from their own resources, he says.

'The great thing about external web-hosting for SMEs is that it gives them the same facilities that larger companies enjoy – but at a reasonable fixed cost,' he adds.

Nick Bryan, chief technology officer at software consultant CWB, says the costs involved in do-it-yourself web sites can quickly escalate. He sees this as the main incentive to hire a third party to provide the service: 'If you start to add up the cost of the hardware and software (typically £4,000) – plus the telecommunications bandwidth (£12,000 a year) – and then add in the cost of managing the site once it is working, you are talking about a lot of money – typically more than £100,000. This is obviously beyond the resources of small companies or new start-ups,' he says.

Mr Bryan recommends a cautious approach to hiring web-hosting services – with special attention to the relationship between companies and service suppliers.

'The website is becoming one of the most important IT assets for any company so it is essential that it is secure and available. But, given the speed with which new companies expand, you also need reassurances about scalability. You need to find a hosting partner that can support the options you want both now and in the future.'

Mr Brodrick of HP agrees that security and scalability are two priorities when selecting a hosting service. But he also sees it as important that the web-host supplier is in a strong position to continue developing the technology: 'If you are running a basic site then obviously you don't need to worry about the more complex operations such as high-level security and financial transaction processing. We specialise in offering a premium service – a full turnkey operation for larger enterprises and we have a large development budget to update the service continuously.'

He describes some of the innovations currently under development. 'Web sites offer lots of opportunity to personalize – so we are working with Broadvision, for example, to give different views of the same site. We are also working on video streaming for Jordan Formula One and Music3W in addition to developing access through WAP (Wireless Application Protocol) phones and digital television.'

Mr Brodrick stresses that all these developments continue the same process of working with accepted standards – tailoring them to meet specific requirements: 'Standards are an essential part of developing web-hosting services – you need to work with standard components that can be customized easily.'

Source: Article by Philip Manchester, *Financial Times*, 2 August 2000.

▶ CASE STUDY *continued*

Questions

1. Do you believe web site hosting is a non-core activity? Justify your answer.
2. What are the arguments for outsourcing web site hosting?
3. What factors should be considered when evaluating a web-hosting supplier?

Managing employee access to the Internet

A further issue with setting up access to the Internet through an ISP is the level of staff access. Governments incite employers to empower employees by widening access in order to increase competitiveness. However, is it practical to give all employees access or should it be limited? An extreme example of the type of problem that can arise is highlighted by the case of Lois Franxhi, a 28-year-old IT manager who was sacked in July 1998 for making nearly 150 searches over four days in office hours for a holiday. As with many unfair dismissals, the case was not clearcut, with Mrs Franxhi claiming the company sacked her because of sex discrimination – she was pregnant at the time of the dismissal. The tribunal dismissed these claims finding that the employee has lied about the use of the Internet, saying she had only used it for one lunchtime when, in fact records showed she had used it over four days. More recently hundreds of employees have been sacked for access to and distribution of material interpreted as 'lewd' by their employers. Complete *activity 3.5* for a discussion of actions a company can take to deal with these problems of employee access.

Activity 3.5 Controlling employee access to the Internet

Purpose

To consider the issues involved with granting access employees access to the Internet and personal e-mail addresses.
(Web update: www.ukonlineforbusiness.gov.uk)

Activity

In this scenario, you are a senior manager at The B2B Company who has just read the latest International Benchmarking study commissioned by the DTI (DTI, 2000) that presents data from across Europe and North America and Japan on access levels (*Figures 3.9* and *3.10*). Employee access to the Internet for your company is limited. You want to remain competitive, but are concerned about the issues of staff time wasting indicated by an article you read in the *Guardian* and the cost and possible problems with employee relations of monitoring staff access.

Questions

Referring to *Figures 3.11* and *3.12*:

1. Prepare a list of advantages and disadvantages of enabling widespread employee access.
2. Make another list of actions you will need to take when you proceed with granting wider access.

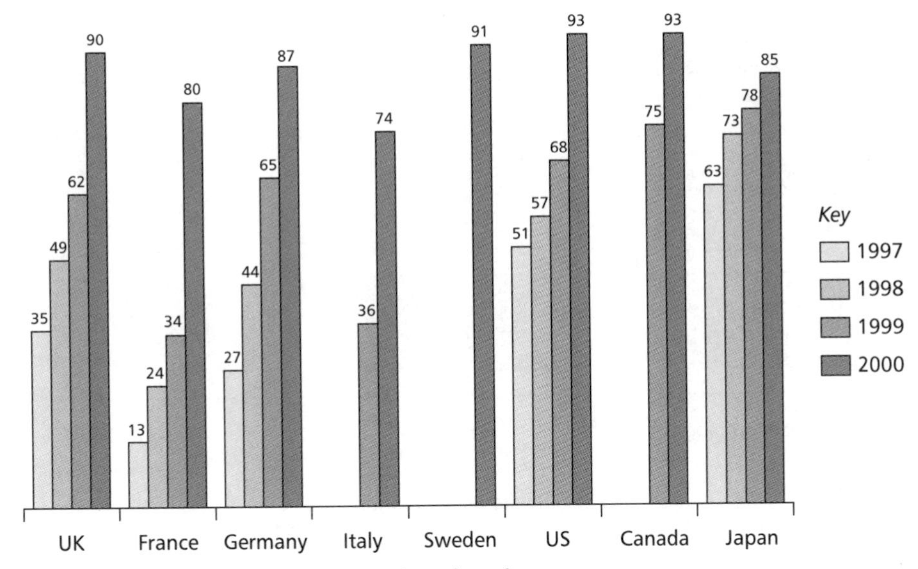

Base: All respondents weighted by number of employees

Figure 3.11 Business access to the Internet between 1997 and 2000.
Source: DTI (2000)

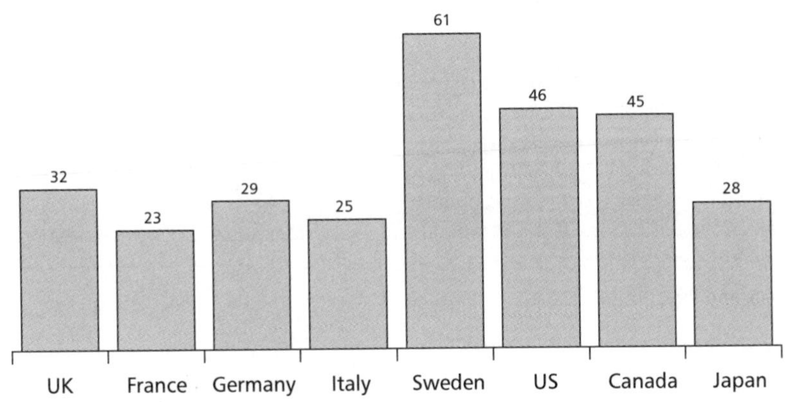

Base: All respondents weighted by number of employees
Note: In a typical Internet-using business in the UK on average 32% of employees use the Internet at least monthly

Figure 3.12 Percentage of employees accessing the Internet each month.
Source: DTI (2000)

A supplementary question is to consider the data in *Figures 3.9* and *3.10* from a marketing perspective. What does this data suggest about the use of the Internet as a business-to-business marketing tool?

For answers see p. 116

Managing applications infrastructure

E-business applications infrastructure
Applications that provide access to services and information inside and beyond an organization.

Management of the **e-business applications infrastructure** concerns delivering the right applications to all users of e-business services. The issue involved is one that

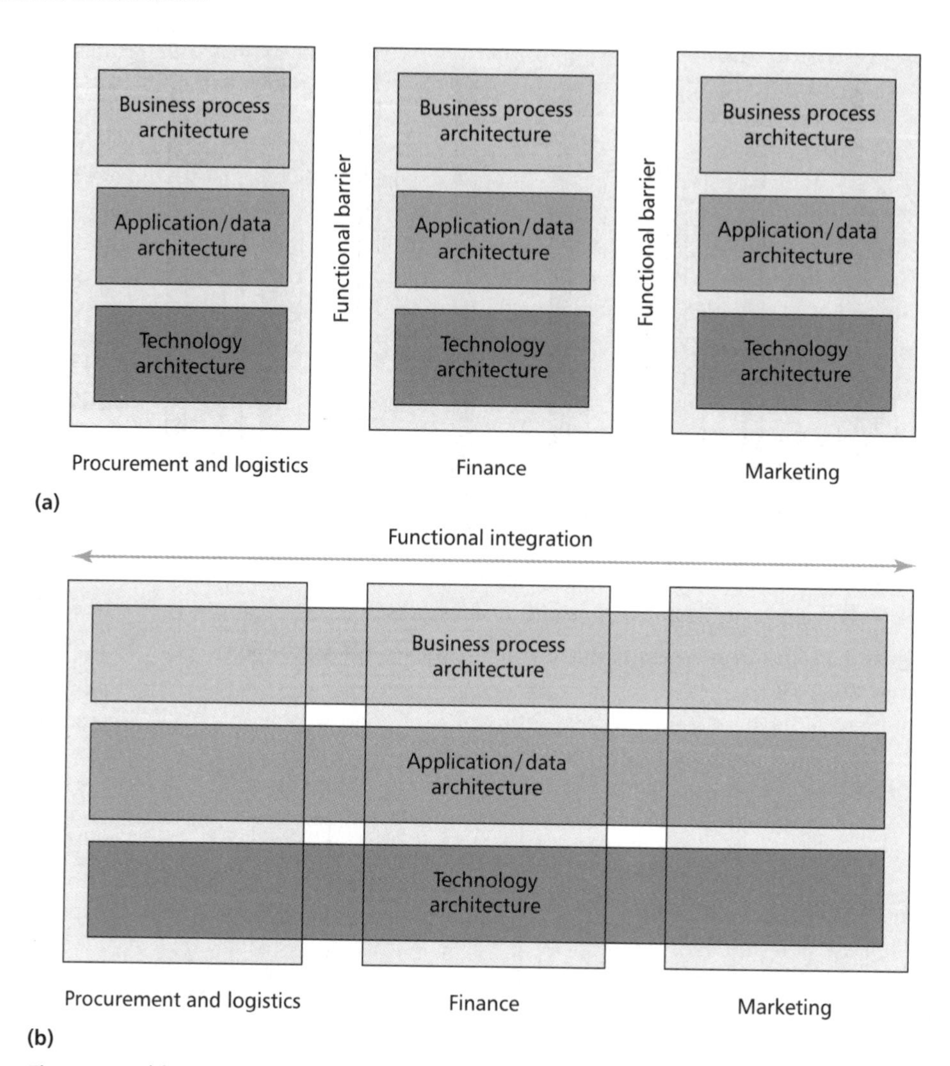

Figure 3.13 (a) Fragmented applications infrastructure (b) integrated applications infrastructure.

Source: adapted from Hasselbring (2000)

has long been a concern of IS managers, namely to deliver access to integrated applications and data that are available across the whole company. Traditionally businesses have developed applications silos or islands of information as depicted in *Figure 3.13(a)*. This shows that these silos may develop at three different levels: (1) there may be different technology architectures used in different functional areas giving the problems discussed in the previous section (2) there will also be different applications and separate databases in different areas (3) process or activities followed in the different functional areas may also be different.

These applications silos are often a result of decentralization or poorly controlled investment in information systems, with different departmental managers selecting different systems from different vendors. This is inefficient in that it will often cost more to purchase applications from separate vendors, and also will be more costly to support and upgrade. Even worse is that such a fragmented approach stifles decision making and leads to isolation between functional units. An operational example of the problems this may cause is if a customer phones a B2B company for the status of a bespoke item they have ordered, where the person in customer support may have access to their personal details but not the status of their job, which is stored on a separate information system in the manufacturing unit. Problems can also occur at a tactical and strategic level. For example, if a company is trying to analyse the financial contribution of customers, perhaps to calculate lifetime values, some information about customers' purchases may be stored in a marketing information system, while the payments data will be stored in a separate system within the finance department. It may prove difficult or impossible to reconcile these different data sets.

To avoid the problems of a fragmented applications infrastructure, companies attempted throughout the 1990s to achieve the more integrated position shown in Figure 3.13(b). Here the technology architecture, applications and data architecture and process architecture are uniform and integrated across the organization. To achieve this many companies turned to **Enterprise Resource Planning (ERP)** vendors such as SAP, Baan, PeopleSoft and Oracle.

Enterprise Resource Planning applications (ERP)
Software providing integrated functions for major business functions such as production, distribution, sales, finance and human resources management.

The approach of integrating different applications is entirely consistent with the principle of e-business, since applications services must be must provide to integrate the whole *supply chain and value chain* (*Chapter 7, p. 216*). It is noteworthy that many of the ERP vendors such as SAP have repositioned themselves as suppliers of e-business solutions! The difficulty for those managing e-business infrastructure is that there is not, and probably never can be, a single solution of components from a single supplier. For example, to gain competitive edge, companies may need to turn to solutions from innovators who, for example, support new channels such as WAP, provide knowledge management solutions or sales management solutions. If these are not available from their favoured current supplier, do they wait until these components become available or do they attempt to integrate new software into the application? Thus managers are faced with a precarious balancing act between standardization or core product and integrating innovative systems where applicable. *Figure 3.14* illustrates this dilemma. It shows how different types of applications tend to have strengths in different areas. ERP systems were originally focused on achieving integration at the operational level of

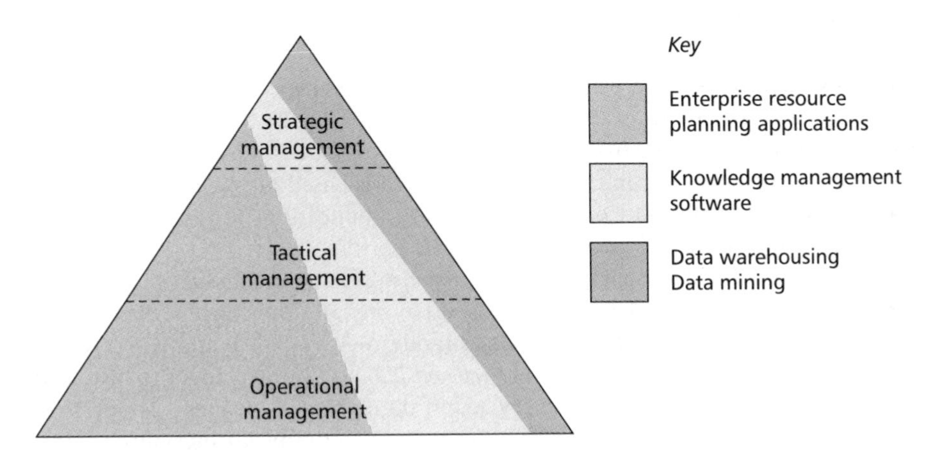

Figure 3. 14 Differing use of applications at levels of management within companies

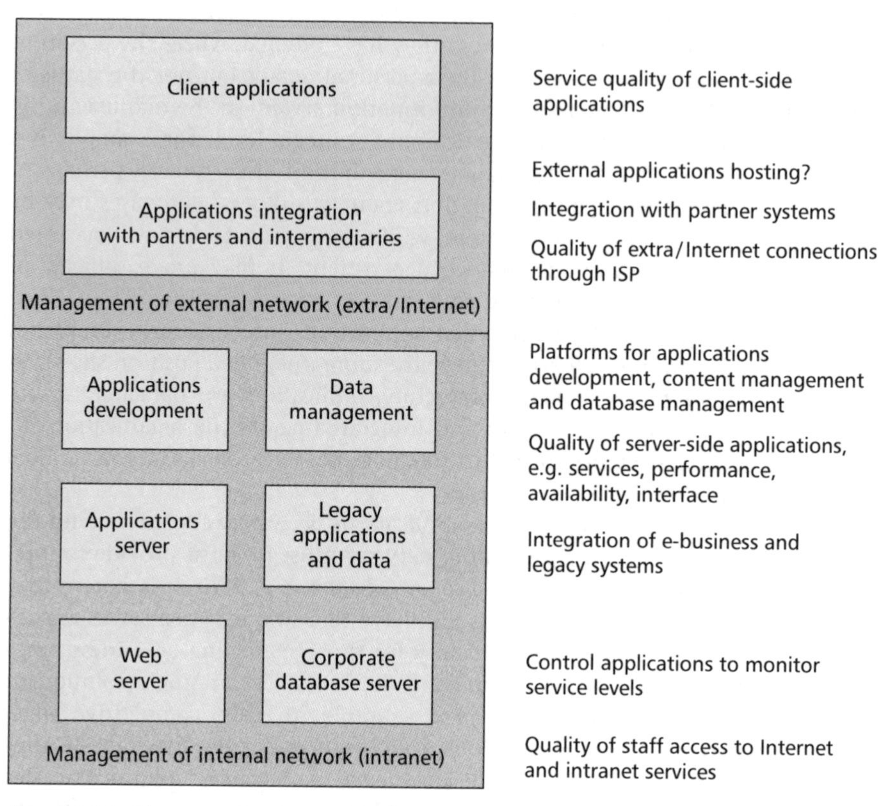

Figure 3.15 Elements of e-business infrastructure that require management

an organization. Solutions for other applications such as business intelligence in the form of data warehousing and data mining tended to focus on tactical decision making based on accessing the operational data from within ERP systems. Knowledge management software also tends to cut across different levels of management. *Figure 3.14* only shows some types of applications, but it shows the trial of strength between the monolithic ERP applications and more specialist applications looking to provide the same functionality.

In this section we have introduced some of the issues of managing e-business infrastructure. These are examined in more detail later in the book. *Figure 3.15* summarizes some of these management issues and *Table 3.4* references where these topics are dealt with later in the book. *Figure 3.15* is based on the layered architecture introduced at the start of this section with applications infrastructure at the top and technology infrastructure towards the bottom.

In the final parts of this chapter we review three contrasting issues in e-business infrastructure. Electronic data interchange (EDI) predates the concept of electronic commerce, yet it shares the same goals as modern e-commerce and is receiving a new lease of life as Internet EDI. The *Focus on EDI* section explains the history of this approach and how it has been revised in the light of e-business. Applications service providers (ASP) represent a significant change in how business applications are delivered. The *Focus on ASPs* section indicates the increasing importance of

Table 3.4 Key management issues of e-business infrastructure

Main issue	*Detail*	*Where covered?*
Which type of e-business applications do we develop?	For example supply chain management, e-procurement, secure online ordering, customer relationship management	*Chapter 4* sections on e-business services and staged models. *Chapters 7,8 and 9* on specific e-business applications
Which technologies do we use?	For example, e-mail, web-based ordering vs EDI	Focus on EDI section in this chapter
How do we achieve quality of service in applications?	Requirements are: business fit, security, speed, availability and errors	*Chapter 11* on design, *Chapter 12* on implementation
Where do we host applications?	Internal or external sourcing and hosting?	Focus on ASPs section in this chapter. Managing partnerships section in *Chapter 9* on SCM
Application integration	Integration of e-business solutions with: – legacy systems – partner systems – B2B exchanges and intermediaries	Section on integrating information systems into supply chain management in *Chapter 6*
Which access platforms do we support? Which development technologies and standards do we use?	Mobile access, interactive digital TV e.g. CGI, Perl, Cold Fusion, ActiveX etc	Focus on access devices in this section *Chapter 12*

ASPs as an e-business solution. Finally, e-business managers have to grapple with the increasing range of technology platforms they need to support. The *Focus on access devices* section addresses this issue.

Focus on EDI

Transactional e-commerce predates PCs and the World Wide Web by some margin. In the 1960s, **Electronic Data Interchange (EDI)** **Financial EDI** and **Electronic Funds Transfer (EFT)** over secure private networks became established modes of intra- and inter-company transaction. The idea of standardized document exchange can be traced back to the 1948 Berlin Airlift, where a standard form was required for efficient management of items flown to Berlin from many locations. This was followed by electronic transmission in the 1960s in the US transport industries. The EDIFACT (Electronic Data Interchange for Administration, Commerce and Transport) standard was later produced by a joint United Nations/European committee to enable international trading. There is also a similar X12 EDI standard developed by the ANSI Accredited Standards Committee.

Electronic Data Interchange (EDI)
The exchange, using digital media, of structured business information, particularly for sales transactions such as purchase orders and invoices between buyers and sellers.

Financial EDI
Aspect of electronic payment mechanism involving transfer of funds from the bank of a buyer to a seller.

Electronic Funds Transfer (EFT)
Automated digital transmission of money between organizations and banks.

Clark (1998) considers that EDI is best understood as the replacement of paper-based purchase orders with electronic equivalents, but its applications are wider than this. The types of documents exchanged by EDI include business transactions such as orders, invoices, delivery advice and payment instructions as part of EFT. There may also be pure information transactions such as a product specification, for example engineering drawings or price lists. Clark (1998) defines EDI as:

the exchange of documents in standardised electronic form, between organisations, in an automated manner, directly from a computer application in one organisation to an application in another.

DTI (2000) describes EDI as follows:

Electronic data interchange (EDI) is the computer-to-computer exchange of structured data, sent in a form that allows for automatic processing with no manual intervention. This is usually carried out over specialist EDI networks.

It is apparent from these definitions that EDI is one form, or a subset of, electronic commerce. A key point is that direct communication occurs between applications (rather than between computers). This requires information systems to achieve the data processing and data management associated with EDI and integration with associated information systems such as sales order processing and inventory control systems.

According to IDC (1999), revenues for EDI network services were already at $1.1 billion in 1999 and are forecast to reach over $2 billion by 2003. EDI is developing through new standards and integration with Internet technologies to achieve **Internet EDI**. IDC (1999) predicts that Internet EDI's share of EDI revenues will climb from 12 per cent to 41 per cent over the same period. The international benchmarking survey (*Figure 3.16*) suggests that EDI is increasing in most countries. Such data should be treated with caution since respondents may not be clear on the strict meaning of EDI.

Internet EDI
Use of EDI data standards delivered across non-proprietary IP networks.

Internet EDI enables EDI to be implemented at lower costs since rather than using proprietary, so-called **value added networks (VANs)** it uses the same EDI standard documents such as that for a purchase order illustrated below, but using lower cost transmission techniques through **virtual private networks (VPNs)** or the public Internet. Reported cost savings are up to 90 per cent (EDI Insider, 1996). EDI Insider estimated that this cost differential would cause an increase from the 80,000 companies in the United States using EDI in 1996 to hundreds of thousands. Internet EDI also includes EDI structured documents being exchanged by e-mail or in a more automated form using FTP.

Value added network (VAN)
A secure wide area network that uses proprietary rather than Internet technology.

Virtual private networks (VPN)
A secure, encrypted (tunnelled) connection between two points using the Internet, typically created by ISPs for organizations wanting to conduct secure Internet trading.

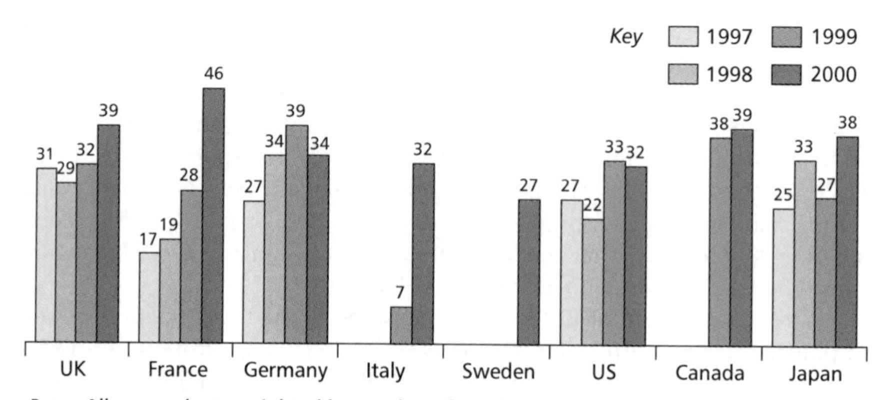

Base: All respondents weighted by number of employees

Figure 3.16 Businesses that use EDI (%)
Source: DTI (2000)

Benefits and limitations of EDI

The benefits of EDI are the same as those for Internet-based electronic commerce between organizations. The benefits of using EDI to streamline business processes include:

- More rapid fulfilment of orders. Reduced lead times are achieved through reduced times in placing and receiving order, reduced times of information in transit and through integration with other processes.
- Fewer errors in data entry and less time spent by the buyer and supplier on exception handling.
- Reduced costs resulting from reduced staff time, material savings such as paper and forms and improved inventory control.

Flymo, the largest lawnmower manufacturer in the UK, is typical of how many companies have moved from EDI to Internet EDI. Traditionally, it has used EDI for linking to the largest retailers, such as the DIY superstore where the trading volume and the potential cost savings required it. Smaller retailers, however, could not order electronically, because they could not afford the cost of setting up dedicated links to Flymo. This meant that Flymo had the expense of processing and rekeying paper and fax-based documents. With the advent of the Internet-based e-commerce, Flymo could create an Internet EDI system that solved its administrative overheads, but was also affordable for the smaller retailer. Supplier IBM created what is known as the 'Internet for dealers network'. This gives the retailers two facilities. The first is a CD-ROM for offline ordering, which can be used to enter orders offline. They then open up a transmit form screen and the data is transmitted in a similar format to the traditional EDI links. The dealers can also log onto the extranet with their user name and password and place an order, check the status of previous orders, make invoice inquiries, and view their full account history.

Early EDI solutions were expensive to implement. Despite efforts to create national and international standards for document formats, they were based on proprietary technologies which tended to lock a company into that supplier since each EDI link tended to be set up specifically for a single supplier and buyer. This made it difficult to switch the connection to another supplier. If a company was multi-sourcing rather than single sourcing then separate EDI standards might be needed for each supplier. Internet EDI tends to reduce these disadvantages.

Although EDI was established before Internet-based e-commerce became widespread, it appears to have a future. The volume of Internet EDI is increasing rapidly and revision of EDI standards to be compatible with XML (XML/EDI standards proposed by the XML EDI group (www.xmledi.com)) should guarantee its continued use. The use of XML by B2B exchanges such as Commerce One and Microsoft Biznet is essentially an extension of EDI.

How does EDI work?

EDI is based on standard specifications based on traditional paper or fax-based documents or forms for transactions such as purchase orders and invoices. EDI standards can be integrated into a range of software from purchasing systems to sales order processing systems or ERP. Transmission of the EDI documents can be achieved through a VAN, Internet EDI, FTP or even e-mail. To gain an appreciation of the way EDI specifications work see the box 'Example EDI Specification for a purchase order'. This shows that for each type of transaction, in this case a purchase order, different codes are used to denote different items such as item, required delivery date and location.

Example EDI specification for a purchase order

This definition of a purchase order is based on the international standard: ASC X12 850 Purchase Order. Each standard such as this one is based on its own specific syntax. It is broken down into *segments* or blocks of information made up of different *data elements* that have their own code. The specification includes data elements such as the currency (CUR), delivery location (N1-4), shipment dates and times (DTM) and line item product details (PO1).

Purchase order specification

1. ISA – Interchange Control Header
2. GS – Functional Group Header (for Combination set)
3. ST – Indicates the start of a transaction set
4. BEG – Beginning of Purchase Order
5. NTE – Note Segment
6. CUR – Currency
7. REF – Reference Numbers
8. FOB – FOB Related Instructions (shipment payer)
9. SSS – Special Services
10. CSH – Header Sale Condition
11. DTM – Date/Time Reference
12. PWK – Paperwork
13. TD5 – Carrier Details
14. N1 – Name Information
15. N2 – Additional Name Information
16. N3 – Address Information
17. N4 – Geographic Location
18. PO1 – Baseline Item Data
19. PWK – Paperwork
20. PKG – Marking, Packaging, Loading
21. REF – Reference Numbers
22. IT8 – Conditions of Sale
23. SDQ – Destination Quantity
24. DTM – Date/Time Reference
25. SCH – Line Item Schedule
26. N1 – Name Information
27. N2 – Additional Name Information
28. N3 – Address Information
29. N4 – Geographic Location
30. REF – Reference Numbers
31. FOB – FOB Related Instructions
32. TD5 – Carrier Details
33. CTT – Transaction Totals

▶

34. SE – Transaction Set Trailer
35. GE – Functional Group Trailer
36. IEA – Interchange Control Trailer

Purchase order example based on the specification above

```
ISA*00* *00*
*01*007061617*01*00507479*930906*2018*U*00303*000007023*0*P**^
GS*BS*007061617*005070479*930906*2025*1225*X*003030^
ST*850*121653^
BEG*00*NE*MOG009364501**950910*CSW11095^
NTE*GEN*FOR ILLUSTRATION PURPOSES ONLY^
CUR*BY*USA^
REF*PR*1234567890^
FOB*PC^
SSS*C*ZZ*ID^
CSH*SC^
DTM*071*950915*1100*CD*19^
TD5**2*YFSY*M*ROUTING*****CD*2^
N1*ST**92*H98111A1^
N3*DEPARTMENT MI5*6565 WELLS AVENUE^
N4*STE GENEVIEVE*MO*636951465*USA^
PO1*1*3*EA***BP*K6200^
CTT*1*3^
SE*16*121653^
GE*1*1225^
IEA*1*000007023^
```

Source: e-business solution provider MISG (www.misg.com/products/edi_guidelines/edi_guidelineS.html)

Focus on applications service providers

Application server

An application server provides a business application on a server remote from the user.

Applications service providers (ASPs) offer great potential for reducing the cost of administering information systems. An application server can be considered to be a relatively new application of three-tier client-server approach (see Bocij *et al.* (1999), Chapter 12 for a description) consisting of a graphical user interface server, an application or business logic server, and a database or transaction server. Links to legacy application databases and transaction management applications are part of this final tier.

Traditionally, companies have employed their own information systems support staff to manage different types of business applications such as e-mail. An applications service provider offers an alternative where the e-mail application is hosted remotely or off-site on a server operated by an ASP. For example, *ITWeek* (2000), reported that Opus group, a marketing agency with 60 staff, outsourced management of its Microsoft Exchange (e-mail and groupware) package to ASP NetStore (www.netstore.com). The quoted price was £19.95 in 2000. Other application services include Microsoft Office or accounting packages. On a larger scale, Pizza Hut, KFC and Taco Bell signed a $50 million dollar contract to provide operational systems to all 6545 restaurants in over 100 countries. The operational systems include labour, inventory management, supplier ordering and performance reporting. The investment enables standardization of back-office systems across the company and also cost reductions since no back-office server is required in each outlet. The A-services venture (www.cwas.net) from Cable and Wireless, Microsoft and Compaq offers services such as Office for £175 per user per year, but also includes a low specification PC, and network connection, plus 24-hour support. This is effectively outsourcing of IS infrastructure using a new model enabled by the Internet.

A further example of an ASP is that described in *Chapter 12*, where Red Sheriff (www.redsheriff.com) provide a service to companies to monitor the customer activity on their web site. Customers log into the Red Sheriff web server in Australia to access reports on their web site.

Activity 3.6 illustrates the decision making process involved with using the ASP approach.

Activity 3.6

Opportunities for using ASPs by the B2B company

Purpose

To highlight the advantages and disadvantages of the ASP approach.

Question

Develop a balanced case for the managing director explaining the ASP approach and summarizing its advantages and disadvantages.

For answer see p. 116

Focus on new access devices

The advent of new technologies for customers to access content across the Internet such as mobile commerce or interactive digital TV poses a difficult dilemma for organizations hosting e-commerce since, to be competitive, the investment decision must be made before the extent of its impact is apparent. These issues apply, in particular, to business-to-consumer companies since the content made available for new access devices has mainly been targeted at consumers. Imagine you are the e-commerce manager at the B2C company: what would be the benefits and drawbacks of updating your e-commerce systems to support these new platforms? The benefits of deciding to invest could include:

- Early mover advantage
- Learning about the technology
- Customer acquisition
- Customer retention
- Improve corporate or brand image

However, it will be difficult to estimate the number of new customers who may be acquired and the profitability of the project may be sacrificed to achieve the other benefits above. As new technologies become available, companies need to assess the technology, understand the services that may be relevant to their customers and work out a strategy and implementation plan. It also becomes necessary to support development across multiple platforms, for example retailers such as WH Smith Online use a database to generate book catalogue content for display on web, mobile or interactive digital TV platforms.

Although it may appear there is a divergence in access devices from PC to phone to TV, in the long term most commentators expect **technology convergence** to occur.

Technology convergence
A trend in which different hardware devices such as TVs, computers and phones merge and have similar functions.

Mougayer (1998) identifies different types of convergence:

- *Infrastructure convergence* – this is the increase in the number of delivery media channels for the Internet such as phone-lines, microwave (mobile phones), cable and satellite. These are now often being used in combination.
- *Information appliance (technology) convergence* – the use of different hardware devices to access and deliver the content of the Internet.
- *Supplier convergence* – the overlap between suppliers such as Internet Service Providers, Online Access Providers and more traditional media suppliers such as the telcos and cable companies.

Mobile access devices

Mobile technologies are not new; it has been possible for many years to access the Internet for e-mail using a laptop connected via a modem. The need for a large device to access the Internet was overcome with the development of personal digital assistants (PDAs) such as the Palm Computing Palm VII or Psion that accessed the Internet via a wireless connection.

The characteristics that mobile or wireless connections offer to their users can be summarized by the supposedly idyllic image used in many adverts of a user accessing the Internet via a laptop or phone from a field, riverbank or mountaintop. They provide ubiquity (can be accessed from anywhere); reachability (their users can be reached when not in their normal location) and convenience (it is not necessary to have access to a power supply or fixed-line connection). In addition to these obvious benefits, there are additional benefits that are less obvious: they provide security – each user can be authenticated since each wireless device has a unique identification code; their location can be used to tailor content and they provide a degree of privacy compared with a desktop PC – looking for jobs on a wireless device might be better than under the gaze of a boss. An additional advantage that will shortly be available is that of instant access or 'always on'; here there is no need to dial-up a wireless connection.

In addition to offering voice calls, mobile phones have increasingly been used for e-mail and Short Message Service (SMS). SMS is effectively a simple form of e-mail that enables messages to be transferred between mobile phones. In early 2000, it was estimated that there were over 2 billion SMS messages exchanged each month. These consist of voice mail notifications, alerts about news or messages direct between phone users.

In 1999 the first of a new generation of mobile phones such as the Nokia 7110 were introduced that offered the opportunity to access the Internet. These are known as **Wireless Application Protocol** or WAP phones, or in more common parlance web-enabled or Internet phones. What these phones offer is the facility to

Wireless Application Protocol (WAP)
WAP is a technical standard for transferring information to wireless devices, such as mobile phones.

access information on web sites that has been specially tailored for display on the small screens of mobile phones. There is a tremendous amount of hype about these phones since they provide all the benefits that have been provided by the World Wide Web, but in a mobile form.

How does WAP work?

Figure 3.17 summarizes the hardware requirements for a WAP system. A user needs a WAP-enabled handset that is used to type in WAP web addresses. WAP pages are then accessed using wireless techniques from a WAP gateway that is connected to a traditional web server where the WAP pages are hosted. Portals from the mobile phone companies or new phone portals will be used to configure the services on the phone such as setting up Short Message Service.

As *Figure 3.18* shows, the different parts of the standard are consistent with those for the Internet. For example, there are layers for security and starting and finishing a transaction. The equivalent of the HTML authoring layer is the 'Wireless Application Environment'. Development of applications for this environment uses **Wireless Markup Language (WML)**. This is similar to HTML in that it is a markup language, but introduces new concepts in accordance with the media. To speed access, each WML file is referred to a 'deck' and consists of several cards that can be displayed sequentially without reconnecting. For more information on the technology see www.anywhereyougo.com; more information on the standards is available at www.wapforum.org. To see how WAP phones work, visit the emulators at: www.gelon.net, www.phone.com, www.anywhereyougo.com.

Wireless Markup Language (WML)
Standard for displaying mobile pages transferred by WAP.

Demand for services

In the UK in early 2000, WAP mobiles such as the Nokia 7110 were available from suppliers such as BT Cellnet, Orange and Vodafone. Virgin was planning an emulation service for existing phones. Demand for the services appear to be high with many consumers reporting they were unable to purchase in early 2000. Durlacher Research reported that demand for WAP as a percentage of all mobiles is likely to climb from 9 per cent at the end of 2000 to 22 per cent in 2001 to 85 per cent in 2003.

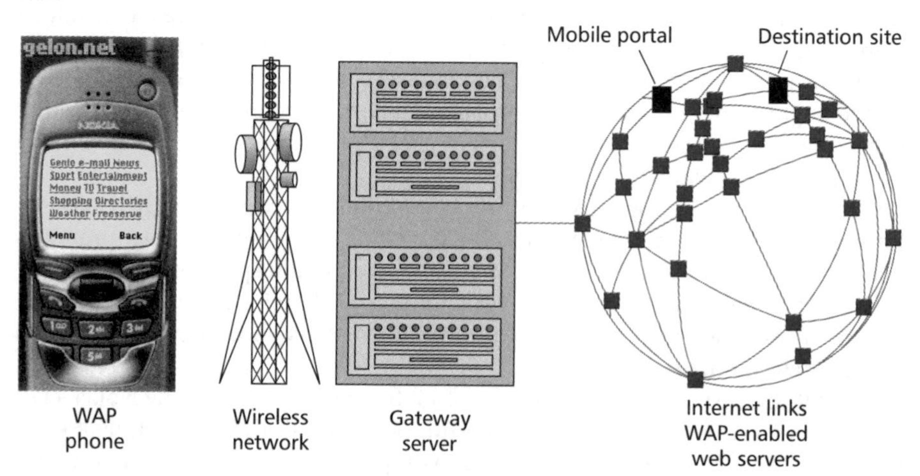

Figure 3.17 Hardware and software infrastructure for WAP system

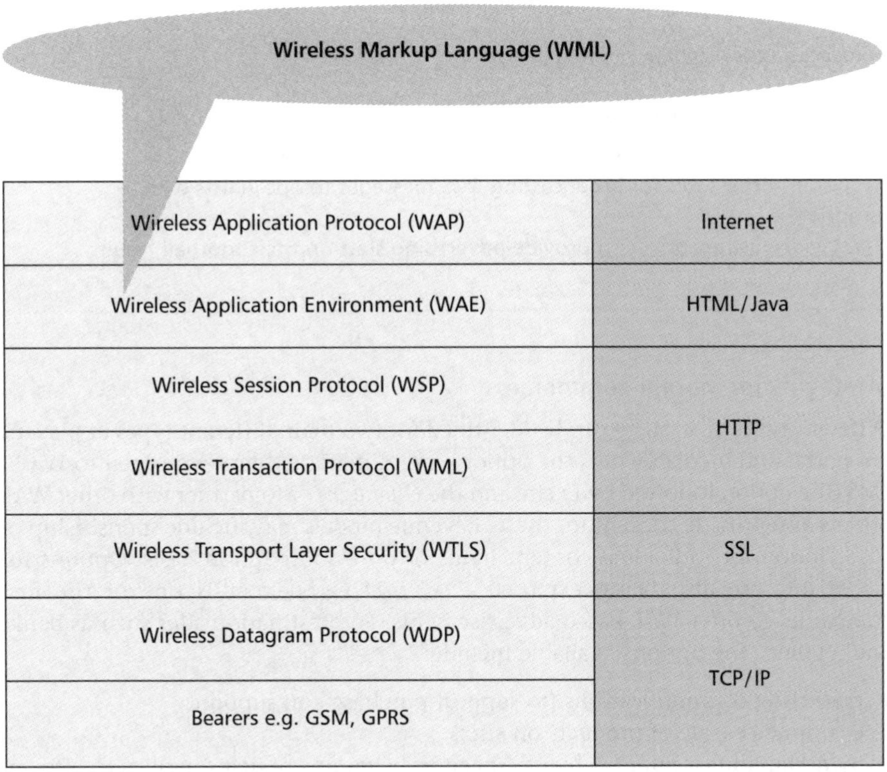

Wireless Markup Language (WML)

Wireless Application Protocol (WAP)	Internet
Wireless Application Environment (WAE)	HTML/Java
Wireless Session Protocol (WSP)	HTTP
Wireless Transaction Protocol (WML)	
Wireless Transport Layer Security (WTLS)	SSL
Wireless Datagram Protocol (WDP)	TCP/IP
Bearers e.g. GSM, GPRS	

Figure 3.18 Different layers of the WAP standard

The services delivered for consumers, to date, have been mainly transactional rather than informational. This is expected given the limited viewing area of the WAP phone. Consumer applications to date include retail (WH Smith Online books, the Carphone Warehouse), ticketing (lastminute.com), broking, banking (the Woolwich), gambling (Ladbrokes), bill payment and job searching. Some informational services based on personalization such as that of Excite UK have also been launched. This includes information such as stock prices, news, cinemas, weather, horoscopes and reminders.

Services for businesses delivered by WAP are currently less developed, but are forecast by Durlacher to centre on supply-chain integration where there will be facilities to place orders, check stock availability, notification of dispatch and to track orders.

How successful is WAP and SMS?

Penetration

- Only 220,000 WAP handsets in circulation of 30 million mobile users (<1 per cent), but ...
- 60 per cent of mobile users intend to upgrade to WAP in next 12 months, awareness at 90 per cent.
- Mobile Internet users forecast to reach 18 million by 2002, 44.5 million subscribers by December 2005, accounting for approximately 80.3 per cent of total mobile subscriptions.

Allegra Strategies ProjectIcon report (www.allegra.co.uk).

Examples of use of SMS marketing techniques

- 50 million SMS messages are sent in Europe each day (1.5 billion per month).
- Skim com (www.skim.com) offer tools for broadcasting SMS messages to opt-in lists with advertising as appropriate.
- Give Us the Score (www.giveusthescore.com) provide advertising slots on their football results new services.

Strategies for mobile-commerce

Different types of strategy can be identified for two main different types of players. For portal and media owners the options are to migrate their own portal to WAP / SMS (the option followed by Excite and the *Guardian*) or to partner with other WAP portals and provide content for these. Revenue models may include sponsorship or subscription for individual content items or on a subscription basis. Options for advertising are also being explored – www.247europe.com is one of the first companies to offer WAP-based advertisements. For destination sites such as banks and retailers, the options available include:

- marketing communications (to support purchase and support),
- e-commerce (sale of products on site),
- brand building – improve brand image by being one of first suppliers to offer an innovative service.

One of the best methods for marketing WAP-based services is currently via banner adverts on a company's existing web site. There have been no examples of companies specifically promoting WAP services in offline media other than the Telecoms companies. As for web sites, a method of building traffic is to register with all the fledgling WAP portals. Media companies seem to have been working hard to establish partnerships.

Future mobile services

In 2001 new services will become available on GPRS (General Packet Radio Service). These offer a faster connection than GSM on which they are based. Later, in 2002 or 2003 a completely new generation (3G) of services will become available by UMTS; with this, delivery of sound and images should be possible with instant access or 'always on'. In the UK auctions for the licence to operate on this frequency have exceeded £20 billion, such is the perceived importance of these services by the telecommunications companies. Many commentators now believe it will be difficult for the telcos to recoup this money and this has resulted in large falls in their share prices.

Figure 3.19 summarizes these new standards for accessing the mobile Internet. For each new technology there is an envelope between the lowest and highest possible transmission speeds. Very often the hype is based on the upper limit, but when implemented only the lower limit is achieved.

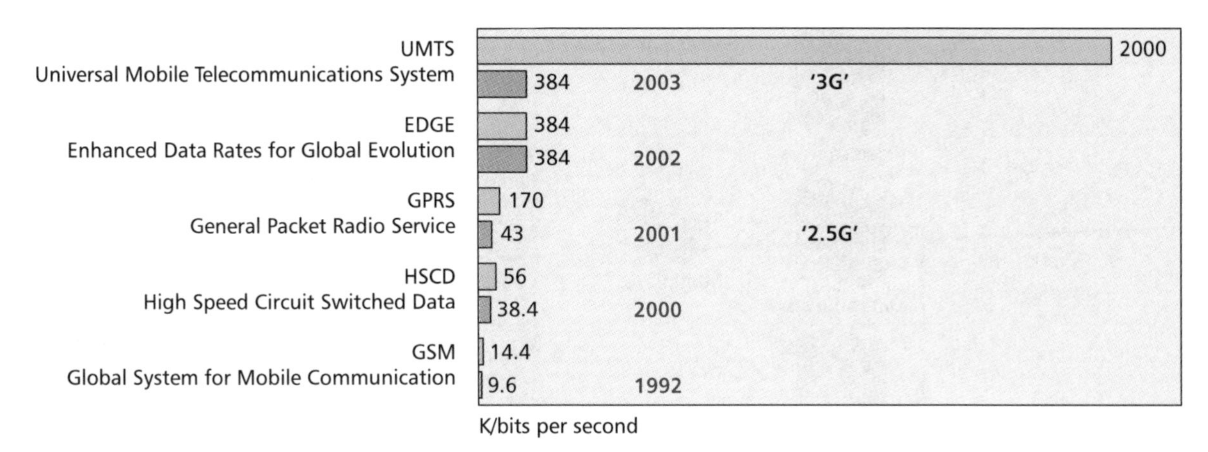

Figure 3.19 Mobile access technologies

Interactive digital television

Interactive digital television (iDTV) has now been used in Europe for several years to deliver broadcasting to homes and offer new interactive services. In France, Canal Plus launched iDTV in 1996 and the Television par satellite was launched in 1997, while Spain, Italy and Germany have had these facilities since 1996 or 1997. It offers similar e-commerce facilities to the Internet, but is provided with a simpler interface that can be operated from a remote control. IDTV has a limited number of suppliers compared to the Internet since start-up costs are higher. The amount of information available from providers is lower because of limited bandwidth on site.

In the UK, there are several providers. The figures show that the number of users is less than those with Internet access, but often these may be complementary services for people who do not want full Internet access.

1. **Sky Digital's** Open service can be viewed by three million subscribers and has content from HSBC, Woolwich, Woolworths, Dixons, Carphone Warehouse, Somerfield, BA, Going Places and Next. This is known as a 'Walled Garden service' since it is not open access like the Internet. Retailers have to pay Open a fixed rent, and a proportion of all sales. Although there are few reported figures of the overall use of these services, individual examples indicate some early success: HSBC registered 80,000 customers within three weeks of whom 20,000 were new. Domino Pizza had 10,000 requests in the first 10 days, and expects 5 per cent of sales to come from this source by 2001.
2. **ON Digital** launched a text service summer 2000 and e-mail in March 2000 with the promise of web access by year-end. Coverage is via existing aerials, but this is restricted in some areas. This gives 600,000 subscribers in total.
3. **ntl:** launched Internet TV in March 99 and from Quarter2 2000 will offer iDTV following the acquisition of this service from Cable and Wireless. These services have approximately one million subscribers.
4. **Telewest**, a cable provider in the Midlands, offers access to about 1.5 million subscribers.

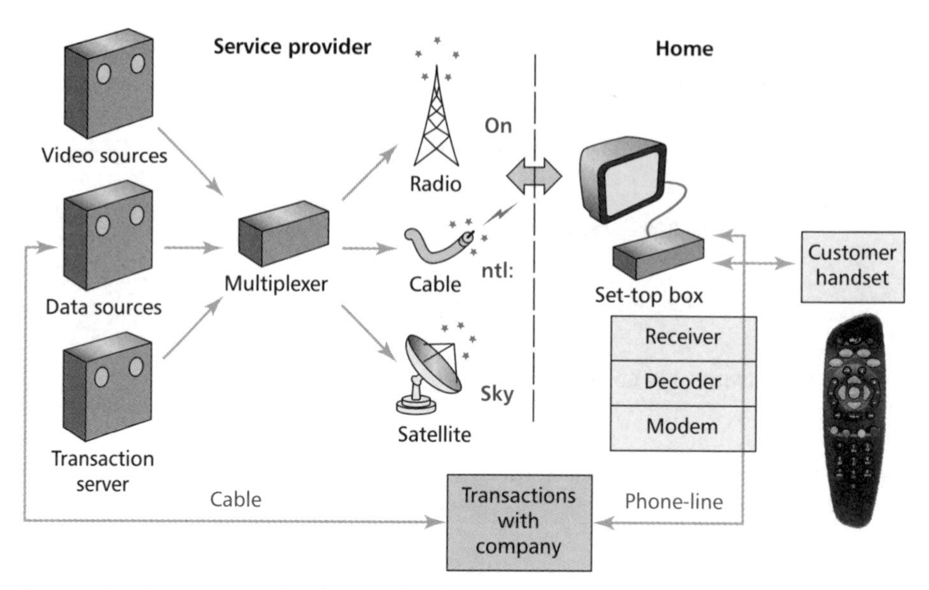

Figure 3.20 Components of an interactive digital TV system

How does interactive digital TV work?

Figure 3.20 shows that a set-top box is an important component of the interactive digital TV system. This is used to receive and decode the message from a satellite dish or cable that is then displayed on a conventional TV. The set-top box also includes a modem that is used to pass back selections made on the interactive shopping channel to the company across the Internet.

Services include:

- Interactive advertising where users can request more information or sign up for a promotion giving direct feedback on the success of an advert. One of the first in Spring 2000 was for 'Chicken Tonite'. Direct sales are not permitted. There is a problem with viewers losing attention in subsequent ads, so interactive adverts are always last.
- Enhanced TV: this includes home shopping, banking, travel bookings and e-mail with video on demand.

When a company decides how to respond to iDTV several levels of commitment can be identified:

- *Promotion* – using interactive ads
- *Content* – repurpose web site
- *Content* – new interactive services
- *E-commerce* – perhaps for a limited range of products

There is also the issue of which platform(s) to support in different countries.

Future digital access technologies

It is too early to say what the long-term prospects for the new access devices are, but an early indication of the relative importance of the different platforms is provided by Loot, the classified ads service. In March 2000, the figures for page impressions were:

- 62,356, WAP
- 1.71 million, interactive digital TV
- 12.21 million, web site

Looking further ahead, Forrester Research reported on 7 September 2000 that mobile phones, iDTV and PDAs will achieve just 19 per cent of total online retail for Europe by 2005 with mobile phones making up 3 per cent of online retail and iDTV 16 per cent. Furthermore the 2000 *Which* survey (www.which.net) on 11 July 2000 suggested that 15 million will not access the Internet using any device. New access locations such as Internet cafés could be important. For example, in Europe the Internet café market is forecast to grow at 24.5 per cent per year to 630 outlets and 15,400 Internet terminals by 2002. The number of Internet café visitors is expected to rise from 21.8 million visitors per year to 42.2 million visitors by 2002.

Other new digital access devices may affect the future infrastructure requirements. These include Digital home storage. Its promoters are describing this as 'The biggest change in conventional broadcasting since the industry began'. Variously referred to as personal video recorders, home media servers or content refrigerators, they all involve recording a TV programme direct to a magnetic disk which gives 20 hours of recording time. Examples are TiVo and ReplayTV. These offer the opportunity to pause a programme while a programme is transmitted, record it and return to it later. It may also be possible to filter out adverts.

The future of the Internet infrastructure

For many first time and regular users, the Internet is seen as frustrating because of its speed. Of course, the poor performance is, to an extent, a consequence of the success of the Internet in attracting over half a billion users. Action to improve this situation takes the form of projects by government departments such as education and defence together with business initiatives. The Internet 2 project is coordinated by the University Corporation for Advanced Internet Development (UCAID), an association formed by 34 international universities in 1996. UCAID's Internet 2 project is directed at software aspects of the infrastructure. These include the concept of 'teleimmersion' where different people can occupy virtual space from different locations. The development of broadband access will also enable improved use of multimedia. On a more fundamental level, UCAID is reviewing how improvements in the standards of the Internet such as Ipv6 can be used in Internet 2. IPv6 is a revision of the IP protocol that is intended to give better performance and increase the number of addresses available. This could enable, for example, walking through a prototype building to discuss its merits. Other initiatives from the United States include new high speed network backbones such as Abilene, the National Science Foundation's Very High Speed Backbone Network Service (VBNS) and new defence networks to link military organizations.

Summary

1. The Internet is a global communications network that is used to transmit the information published on the World Wide Web (WWW) in a standard format based on hypertext markup language (HTML) using different standard protocols such as HTTP and TCP/IP.

2. Companies deliver e-business services to employees and partners through web servers which are often hosted at third party companies known as Internet Service Providers (ISP). Web servers will be linked to applications servers, database servers and legacy applications to deliver these services.

3. Consumers and business users access these e-business services using web browser software, with connections to the Internet also managed by an ISP through which they can access web servers.

4. Intranets are private networks used inside companies to share information. Internet-based tools such as e-mail, FTP and the World Wide Web are all used as methods of sharing this information. Not all Internet users can access intranets since access is restricted by firewalls and password controls. Extranets are similar to intranets, but they are extended beyond the company to third parties such as suppliers, distributors or selected customers.

7. Standards to enable delivery of information include:
   - Communications standards such as TCP/IP and HTTP.
   - Text information standards such as HTML, XML and WML.
   - Graphical information standards such as GIF and JPEG.
   - Multimedia standards such as Shockwave, Flash and streaming audio and video.

8. Managing staff access to Internet involves taking decisions about the number of staff with access and how much time can be permitted and the nature of monitoring used for e-mails and web pages.

9. Managers need to decide on internal or external management of the technology and applications infrastructure of an organization.

10. Electronic data interchange (EDI) involves the structured transfer of information, particularly for online B2B purchasing transactions. It can now occur over the Internet as Internet EDI.

11. Applications Service Providers are increasingly important as businesses look to reduce infrastructure costs and improve e-business service delivery through external hosting of applications and data outside an organization.

12. Managers of e-commerce services need to monitor the adoption of new access devices for the Internet including mobile phones and interactive digital TV. An e-commerce infrastructure should be designed to readily enable new access media to be supported as they develop.

ACTIVITY ANSWERS

3.1 Infrastructure risk assessment for The B2C Company

Some of the possible problems you may have identified are:

1. Web site communications too slow.
2. Web site not available.
3. Bugs on site through pages being unavailable or information typed in forms not being executed.
4. Ordered products not delivered on time.

5. E-mails not replied to.
6. Customers' privacy or trust is broken through security problems such as credit cards being stolen or addresses sold to other companies.

It will be apparent that although most of these problems are technical, they arise because humans have not managed the infrastructure adequately. They have not invested enough to solve these issues or have not tested solutions adequately to check for deficiencies. Additionally, in the case of some problems such as e-mails not being responded to, this may be entirely a problem in the process created (or not created) by managers to deal with inbound e-mails.

3.2 The development of the Internet

Possible reasons for the slow development of the Internet include:

- The cost of specialized leased line connection to the Internet was only affordable for the largest companies. Access via phone lines did not happen until the 1980s.
- The limited deployment of desktop computers in organizations. The PC was not invented until the early 1980s.
- The potential of the Internet to reduce costs as a business tool was not widely recognized at company or government levels, so there was no momentum to achieve the benefits. It was positioned as an academic and military tool.
- Difficulties in use of early tools of the Internet. As will be seen below, the development of the World Wide Web was critical in providing ease-of-use.

3.3 Business benefits of intranets and extranets for The B2B Company

Both intranets and extranets are set up whenever information or services need to be shared, but if the information is sensitive it should not be shared with everyone who can access the Internet. For The B2B Company such information would include:

- company performance or sales figures (intranet);
- product pricing which may be different for different countries or customers (extranet);
- technical product information for customers or agents (extranet);
- sales transactions (extranet);
- customer support where it is not desirable for competitors or media to find out about problems with products (extranet).

In addition to providing information, extranets are a marketing aid in that they indicate preferential treatment or an added-value service for key customers or distributors. This may help increase the loyalty of these third parties. Most e-commerce transactions involve the user selecting a username and password in order to access their account or track their product.

3.4 Assessing ISP performance

1. List of services:
   - Ensuring domain name registration is kept updated
   - Hosting web site
   - Hosting web catalogue (application service provider)
   - Hosting secure payment service
   - Hosting e-mail server
2. Key factors on which ISP will be judged:

   Technical factors
   - Speed of link to Internet (bandwidth)
   - Speed at which pages are delivered dependent on bandwidth and server performance

- Availability of server (how reliable is the server?)
- Scalability – how will the server respond to peaks of traffic or a long-term growth?
- Ease of updating web site or catalogue, are any tools provided to help this?
- Successful transmission of e-mails
- Security of site to prevent others updating or where secure transactions are required

Commercial factors:

- Cost of services (initial payment, regular subscription payment and any one-off fees such as those involved with a complete update of the web site)
- Support provided – how responsive is the company when a problem is notified?

Size and profitability of company (will it survive in the long term?)

3.5 Controlling employee access to the Internet

1. *Advantages:*
   - Better understanding of marketplace for marketing, sales and engineers in the new product development team, e.g. monitor competitor and customer use of the web and product and event announcements.
   - Research tool to obtain best prices for buyers in procurement group
   - Access to customer information on intranet for remote workers (sales reps)
   - Increase employee job satisfaction?

   Disadvantages:
   - Cost of setting up software and paying for additional traffic to ISP
   - Cost of lost staff time and disruption when accessing net for personal purposes
   - Transfer of company information outside company via e-mail (legal risk)
   - Staff use of the web and e-mail for job-hunting
   - Problem of staff using the web to access unsavoury material
2. List of actions
   - Consult staff for views?
   - Prepare cost/benefit
   - Prepare plan and communicate to staff
   - Prioritize or limit staff access (e.g. one per group). Run pilot?
   - Prepare amendments to contract about what staff can access and when, e.g. half hour per day for personal use or unlimited after 6pm
   - Select software for monitoring staff access (e.g. keyword snooping, monitoring images, remote viewing of terminals) and inform staff about this

3.6 Opportunities for using ASPs by The B2B Company

Advantages:

- Quick time to deploy new applications
- No in-house staff or capital costs
- Predictable cost

Disadvantages:

- Performance
- Security outages
- Security fears
- Transfer of data and ownership of applications if the ASP relationship fails.

EXERCISES

Self-assessment questions

1. What is the difference between the Internet and the World Wide Web?
2. Describe the two main functions of an Internet Service Provider (ISP). How do they differ from Applications Service Providers?
3. Distinguish between intranets, extranets and the Internet.
4. Describe the standards involved when a web page is served from a web server to a user's web browser.
5. What are the management issues involved with enabling staff access to a web site?
6. Explain the following terms:
   - HTML
   - HTTP
   - XML
   - FTP
7. What is the difference between static web content written in HTML and dynamic content developed using a scripting language such as Javascript?
8. What software and hardware is required to access the Internet from home?

Essay and discussion questions

1. 'Without the development of the World Wide Web by Tim Berners-Lee, the Internet is unlikely to have become a commercial medium.' Discuss.
2. 'In the future the distinction between intranets, extranets and the intranet for marketing purposes is likely to disappear.' Discuss.
3. Discuss the merits and disadvantages of locating company e-business services inside a company, in comparison with outsourcing to an ISP or ASP.
4. You are consultant to a small retailer interested in setting up a transactional e-commerce site. Create a summary guide for the company about the stages that are necessary in the creation of a web site and the management issues involved.

Examination questions

1. You have been tasked with arranging Internet access for other employees in your company. Summarize the hardware and software needed.
2. How would you explain to a friend what they need to purchase to access the World Wide Web using the Internet? Explain the hardware and software needed.
3. Explain the term electronic data interchange. Is it still relevant to companies?
4. Describe how the following tools would be used by a company hosting a web site:
   - HTML
   - FTP
   - CGI

▶

5. The existence of standards such as HTML and the HTTP protocol has been vital to the success and increased use of the World Wide Web. Explain why.
6. What benefits to a business-to-business company does the XML standard offer over HTML?
7. Explain why the e-business coordinator of a company might investigate the use of applications service providers.
8. Explain the differences between intranet, extranet and the Internet from an e-business perspective.

REFERENCES

Berners-Lee, T. (1999) *Weaving the Web. The Past, Present and Future of the World Wide Web by its Inventor*. Orion Publishing, London, UK.

Bickerton, P., Bickerton, M. and Simpson-Holey, K. (1998) *Cyberstrategy*. Butterworth Heinemann, Oxford. Chartered Institute of Marketing series.

Bocij, P., Chaffey, D., Greasley, A. and Hickie, S. (1999) *Business Information Systems. Technology, Development and Management*. FT Management, London.

Burdman, J. (1999) *Collaborative Web Development: Strategies and best Practices for Web Teams*. Addison Wesley, Reading, MA.

Chaffey, D. (1998) *Groupware, Workflow and Intranets – Reengineering the Enterprise with Collaborative Software*. Digital Press, Woburn, MA.

Clark, R. (1998) *Electronic Data Interchange (EDI): An Introduction*. www.anu.edu.au/people/Roger.Clarke/EC/EDIIntro.html

DTI (2000) *Business In The Information Age – International Benchmarking Study 2000*. UK Department of Trade and Industry. Available online at: www.ukonlineforbusiness.gov.uk.

EDI Insider (1996) Internet EDI: separating hope from hype. *EDI Insider*, 1(1). Washington Publishing Company. www.wpc-edi.com/Insider/Articles/V1/I-1B.html

Freedman, A., Glossbrenner, A. and Glossbrenner, E. (1998) *The Internet Glossary and Quick Reference*. AMACOM, New York.

Gillies, J. and Cailliau, R. (2000) *How the Web was Born*. Oxford University Press, New York.

Hasselbring, W. (2000) Information system integration. *Communications of the ACM*, 43(6), 33–8.

IDC (1999) *Reinventing EDI: Electronic Data Interchange Services Market Review and Forecast, 1998–2003*. International Data Corporation.

Internet World (1999) Enterprise application integration – middleware apps scale firewalls. *Internet World*, 17 May.

IT Week (2000) Why small firms still shun ASPs. *IT Week*, 13 November, p. 74.

Kampas, P. (2000) Road map to the e-revolution. *Information Systems Management Journal*, Spring, 8–22.

Kennedy, A. (2001) *The Internet. The Rough Guide*. Rough Guides, London.

Leiner, B., Cerf, V., Clark, D., Kahn, R., Kleinrock, L., Lynch, D., Postel, J., Roberts, J. and Wolff, S. (2000) *A Brief History of the Internet*. Published by the Internet Society. www.isoc.org/internet-history/brief.html. Continuously updated document.

Mougayer, W. (1998) *Opening Digital Markets – Battle Plans and Strategies for Internet Commerce*, 2nd edn. CommerceNet Press, McGraw-Hill, NY.

Spinrad, P. (1999). The new cool. Akamai overcomes the Internet's hotspot problem. *Wired*. 7 August 152–4.

Yates, S., Rutstein, C. and Voce, C. (2000) *Demystifying B2B Integration*. Forrester Research Report, September.

ZDNet (2000) www.zdnet.co.uk/itweek/specials/2000/ecommerce2/

Zwass, V. (1998) Structure and macro-level impacts of electronic commerce: from technological infrastructure to electronic marketplaces. In *Emerging Information Technologies*, ed. K. Kendall, Sage Publications, Thousand Oaks, CA.

FURTHER READING

Berners-Lee, T. (1999) *Weaving the Web. The Past, Present and Future of the World Wide Web by its Inventor*. Orion Publishing, London, UK. A fascinating, readable description of how the concept of the web was developed by the author with his thoughts on its future development.

Gillies, J. and Cailliau, R. (2000) *How the Web was Born*. Oxford University Press, New York. Another readable book, this time, despite the title, on the whole history of the Internet.

WEB LINKS

A brief history of the Internet (www.isoc.org/internet-history/brief.html) Updated history by key players in its design – Barry M. Leiner, Vinton G. Cerf, David D. Clark.

IT Toolbox (www.ittoolbox.com): guidelines, articles on e-business, ERP, CRM and data warehousing.

RosettaNet (www.rosettanet.org): organization promoting exchange of B2B data.

Howstuffworks (www.howstuffworks.com): good explanations with diagrams of many Internet technologies.

Whatis.com (www.whatis.com): succinct explanations of technical terms.

XMLEDI (www.xmledi.com/.net): organization promoting use of XML to support EDI.

XML.com (www.xml.com) XML resources.

Virgin Biznet (www.virginbiz.net): portal to enable SMEs to move online. Explains stages and tools involved in plain language.

UK Online For Business (www.ukonlineforbusiness.gov.uk): Government portal.

Chapter 4

E-environment

CHAPTER AT A GLANCE

Main topics

Focus on . . .

Case studies

LEARNING OBJECTIVES

After completing this chapter the reader should be able to:

- Identify the different elements of the e-environment that impact on an organization's e-business and e-marketing strategy
- Assess the impact of legal, moral and ethical constraints or opportunities on a company and devise solutions to accommodate them
- Assess the role of macro-economic factors such as economics, taxation and legal constraints

MANAGEMENT ISSUES

The issues for managers raised in this chapter include:

- What are the constraints placed on developing and implementing an e-business strategy by the e-environment?
- What factors influence the adoption of new digital media and how can we estimate future demand for online services?
- How can trust and privacy be assured for the customer while seeking to achieve marketing objectives of customer acquisition and retention?

Links to other chapters

The main related chapters are:

- *Chapter 2 E-commerce fundamentals* – introduces the different elements of the e-environment.
- The strategic approaches outlined in *Part 2* (*Chapters 5, 6 and 8*) require consideration of the constraints placed on strategy by the e-environment.

Introduction

In *Chapter 2* we introduced the importance of monitoring changes in the environment and how they impact an organization. In *Figure 2.1* (*Chapter 2, p. 33*) we presented the main environment factors as those immediate to the company – the marketplace or macro-environment. These are presented in *Table 4.1* as the macro- and micro-environment factors.

Table 4.1 Factors in the macro- and micro-environment of an organization

Macro-environment	*Micro-environment (e-marketplace)*
Social	The organization
Legal, ethical and taxation	Its customers
Economic	Its suppliers
Political	Its competitors
Technological	Intermediaries
Competitive	The public at large

In this chapter we concentrate on the role of the macro-environment forces. These are sometimes referred to as the SLEPT factors used to structure this chapter. SLEPT stands for Social, Legal, Economic, Political and Technological factors. Aspects of the micro-environment or e-marketplace such as competitors, suppliers and intermediaries are considered in other chapters. Now complete *activity 4.1* to reflect on some of the macro-environmental factors that have to be considered by the e-business manager.

Activity 4.1 **Introduction to social, legal and ethical issues**

List all the social, legal and ethical issues that the manager of a sell-side e-commerce web site needs to consider to avoid annoying the users of his or her site or which may leave the company facing prosecution. You can base your answer on what may concern you, your friends or family when you access a web site.

For answers see p. 153

The issues identified in *activity 4.1* and others such as economic and competitive pressures tend to change rapidly, particularly dynamic factors associated with advances in technology. Organizations that either do not monitor these environmental factors, or those that do respond to them adequately, will not remain competitive and may fail. The process of monitoring the environment is usually referred to as **environmental scanning**. This often occurs as an ad hoc process in which many employees and managers will monitor the environment and will,

Environmental scanning and analysis
The process of continuously monitoring the environment and events and responding accordingly.

perhaps, respond appropriately. The problem with the ad hoc approach is that if there is not a reporting mechanism then some major changes may not be apparent to managers. Environmental analysis is required to evaluate different information and respond accordingly.

This chapter is structured according to the macro-environment factors listed in *Table 4.1*. For each factor we look at new issues raised for managers responsible for e-commerce trading. For those actively involved in the implementation of e-business, and in particular sell-side e-commerce, factors associated with buyer behaviour are also important when implementing e-commerce. These are covered separately in the section *Focus on buyer behaviour* (*Chapter 9, p. 342*).

Social factors

In this section we look at the social and cultural impacts of the Internet. These are important from a marketing perspective since they govern demand for Internet services and propensity to purchase online. Further aspects of social reaction to the Internet are considered from an e-marketing context in *Focus on buyer behaviour* and *virtual communities* (*Chapter 9, p. 342 and p. 359*). Complete *activity 4.2* to start to review some of the social issues associated with the Internet.

Understanding enablers and barriers to consumer adoption

Activity 4.2

Purpose

To identify reasons why consumers may be encouraged online or may resist.

Activity

Access a recent survey in your country of attitudes to the Internet. In particular, you should concentrate on reasons why customers have used the Internet or have not used the Internet at all. In the UK, *Which*? surveys are available at www.which.net. *Figure 4.1* highlights different uses of the Internet in the UK.

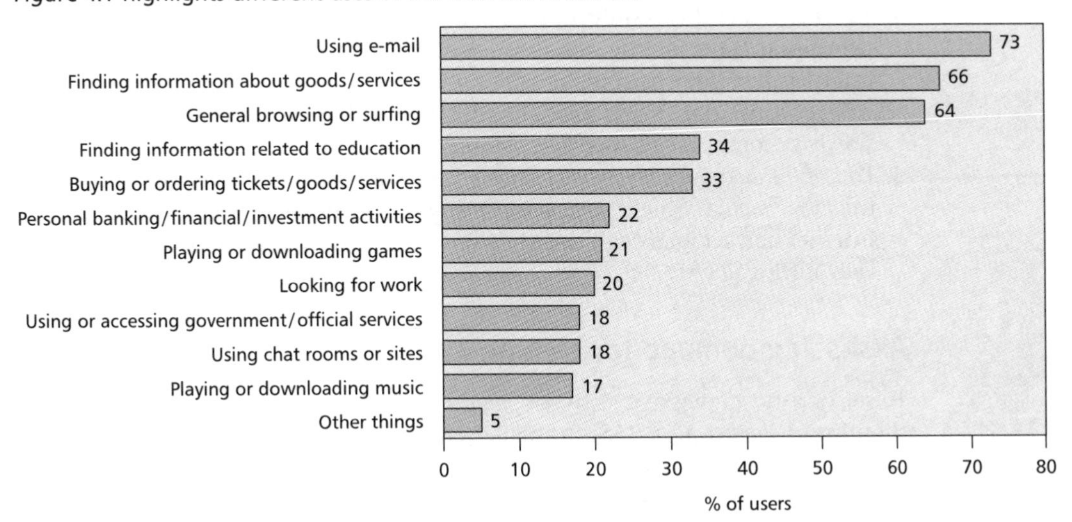

Figure 4.1 Popular online activities in the UK.
Source: (ONS, 2000)

1. Summarize the levels of usage of the medium for access, purchasing and other activities for different age groups.
2. Summarize and explain the reasons why access and shopping levels are not 100 per cent.
3. What actions could or should companies take to reduce these barriers?

Alternatively, devize an ad hoc survey to investigate attitudes to and use of the Internet using friends, family or classmates as respondents. Example questions might include: what have you bought online, if not why not? How many hours do you spend online each month? How many e-mails do you receive or send? What stops you using the Internet more? What aspects of the Internet are you concerned about?

Factors governing Internet adoption

It is useful for e-business managers to understand the different factors that affect how many people actively use the Internet. If these are understood for customers in a target market, action can be taken to overcome some of these barriers. For example, marketing communications can be used to reduce fears about the value proposition, ease of use and security (*Chapter 9, p. 335*). Chaffey *et al.* (2000) suggest that the following factors are important in governing adoption:

1. *Cost of access.* This is certainly a barrier for those who do not already own a home computer: a major expenditure for many households. The other main costs are the cost of using an ISP to connect to the Internet and the cost of using the media to connect (telephone or cable charges). Free access will certainly increase adoption and usage.
2. *Value proposition.* Customers need to perceive a need to be online – what can the Internet offer that other media cannot? Examples of value proposition include access to more supplier information and possibly lower prices. In 2000, company advertisements started to refer to 'Internet prices'.
3. *Ease of use.* This includes the ease of first connecting to the Internet using the ISP and the ease of using the web once connected.
4. *Security.* While this is only, in reality, a problem for those who shop online, the perception generated by news stories may be that if you are connected to the Internet then your personal details and credit card details may not be secure. It will probably take many years for this fear to diminish as using the Internet slowly becomes established as a standard way of purchasing goods.
5. *Fear of the unknown.* Many will simply have a general fear of the technology and the new media which is not surprising since much of the news about the Internet non-adopters will have heard will concern pornography, fraud and privacy infringements.

Assessing demand for e-commerce services

To set realistic strategic objectives (*Chapter 5, p. 182*) such as online revenue contributions (*Chapter 5, p. 185*) for digital channels, e-commerce managers need to understand the level of customer access and activity in each marketplace. What is the key customer profile information that managers must collect using market research? For each customer segment and for each digital channel such as Internet, interactive digital TV or mobile we need to know the proportion of customers who:

1. Have access to the channel.
2. Are influenced by using the channel.
3. Purchase using the channel.

This information can be gathered as secondary research by the researcher by accessing many online data sources. Primary research can be used to better understand these characteristics in the target market. We will now review each of these three factors which affect demand for e-commerce services. We start by reviewing these factors for consumers in the B2C marketplace.

Internet access

E-commerce provides a global marketplace, and this means we must review access and usage of the Internet channel at many different geographic levels: worldwide, between continents and countries.

On a worldwide basis, a relatively small proportion of the population has access to the Internet. *Figure 4.2* shows that despite rapid growth from the mid-1990s to about 400 million users by the end of 2000 this only represents less than 10 per cent of the population. The level of access will be determined by the five factors listed in the previous section, but clearly cost will be the major factor explaining the overall proportion of access. So, in terms of SLEPT environment factors, this is also an *economic factor* (p. 140).

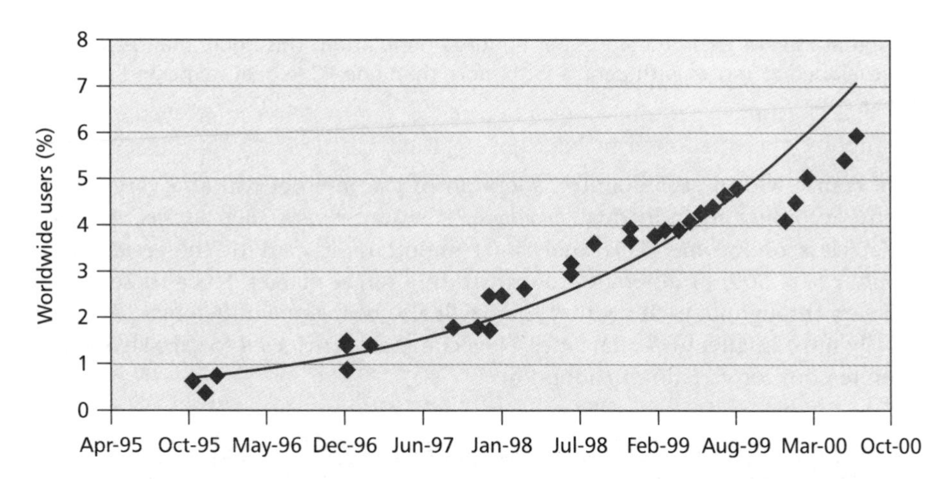

Figure 4.2 Percentage of global population with Internet access (adapted from Nua compilations at www.nua.ie/surveys)

To look at the scale of variation between different continents complete *activity 4.3*.

Global variation in Internet provision

Activity 4.3

Visit the web site of the International Telecommunications Union (ITU) (www.itu.int/ti/industryoverview/index.htm). Choose Internet indicators. This presents data on Internet and PC penetration in over 200 countries. A summary of the indicators for different continents is presented in *Figure 4.3*.

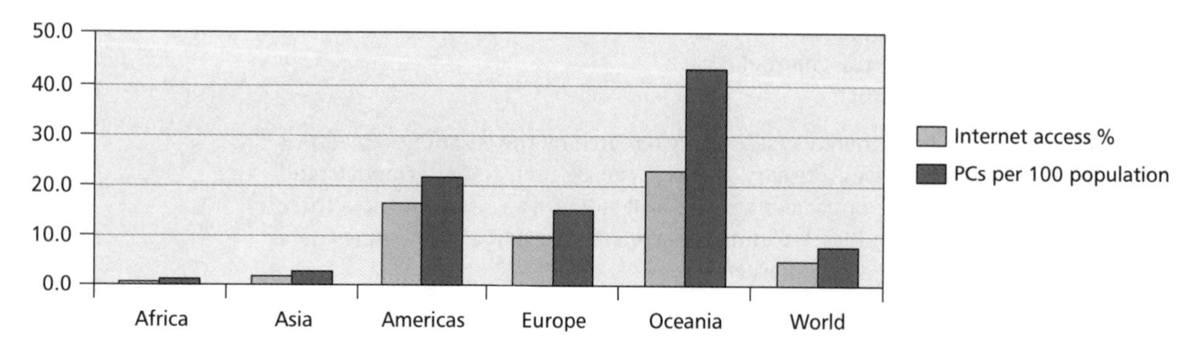

Figure 4.3 Global variation in number of PCs per hundred population and percentage Internet access

Questions

1. Find your country and compare the number of PCs per hundred population and per cent Internet access compared with other countries in your region and on a global basis.
2. Now attempt to explain reasons for the disparity between your country and other countries.
3. Can you see your country equalling or exceeding the US in terms of these indicators?

Note that PCs are recorded as PCs per hundred population. This figure may be skewed in developed countries with people with more than one PC (e.g. at home and at work).

Demographic characteristics
Variations in attributes of the populations such as age, sex and social class.

Of course within each country, adoption of the Internet will also vary significantly according to individual **demographic characteristics** such as sex, age and social class or income. This analysis is important as part of the *segmentation* *(Chapter 8, p. 304)* of different groups within a target market. Since these factors will vary throughout each country there will also be regional differences. Access is usually much higher in capital cities. Now complete *activity 4.4* to gain an appreciation reasons for variation in adoption.

Activity 4.4 Adoption of the Internet according to demographic characteristics

Purpose

To highlight variation in Internet access according to individual consumer characteristics.
Web update: see www.emori.co.uk/tracker.htm for up-to-date data on demographics in the UK.

Activity

1. Refer to *Figure 4.4* and summarize variation between the overall UK population and Internet users according to:
   - sex
   - age
   - social group.

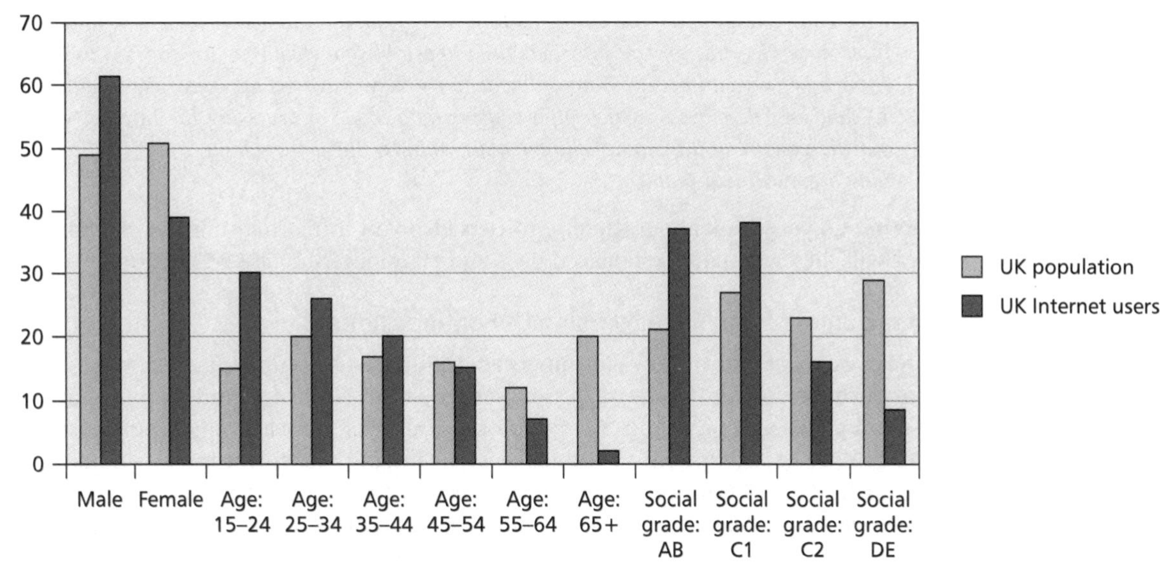

Figure 4.4 Variation in demographic characteristics of UK Internet users (based on Durlacher (1999a); survey of 4000 households)

2. Attempt to explain this variation and suggest how it may change in the future.

For answer see p. 153

From the activity it can be seen that the stereotype of the typical Internet user as male, around thirty years of age and with high disposable income no longer holds true. Many females and more senior 'silver surfers' are also active.

To fully understand online customer access we also need to consider the users' access location, access device and 'webographics', all of which are significant for segmentation and constraints on *site design* (*Chapter 11, p. 446*). Webographics is a term coined by Grossnickle and Raskin (2001). According to these authors webographics includes:

- Usage location (in most countries, many users access either from home or work, with home being the most popular choice)
- Access device (browser and computer platform; remember that interactive TV and mobile access are becoming more important)
- Connection speed
- ISP
- Experience level
- Usage type
- Usage level

Finally, we musn't forget the non-users who comprise more than half of the adult population in many countries. Paul Kitchen, Head of Which? Online, comments in the Which.net July 2000 user survey (www.which.net):

> *For the third year running, the annual Which? Online survey has highlighted that a large proportion of the population is refusing to get online and saying that they never*

will. These 'never-users' are telling us that they think the Internet is irrelevant to them. Internet service and content providers need to establish a clear message for non-users to show how they can benefit from online activity. New methods of access like interactive TV and mobile phones, which offer consumers a mode of accessing the Internet without the expense of a PC, may change many minds. But if they don't, the digital divide may become a real problem.

What do you think about these non-users? Do you think their minds will change, or will they gradually be replaced by a more computer-literate generation?

Consumers influenced by using the online channel

Psychographic segmentation
A breakdown of customers according to different characteristics.

Next we must look at how consumers are influenced by online media, a key aspect of buyer behaviour (*Chapter 9, p. 342*). As we saw in *Figure 4.1*, finding information about goods and services is a popular online activity, but each organization needs to capture data about online influence in the buying process for their own market. To help them better understand their customers, marketers develop **pyschographic segmentations**. Specialized psychodemographic profiles have been developed for web users, for example see Bickerton *et al.* (2000). See the box *Psychographic segmentation from Netpoll* for an example of this type of segmentation. Which profile do you fit? Each characterization can refer to males or females.

Psychographic segmentation from Netpoll

Gameboy – 15,
netsavvy

Cyberlad – 23,
'loaded man online'

Cybersec– 31,
work user

Hit and runner – 38,
directed

Infojunky – 40,
addicted

Cybermum– 42,
busy

Figure 4.5 Psychographic segmentation for web users
Source: Netpoll (www.netpoll.net).

The GameBoy Aged 15 – still at school and living at home – accesses the Internet mainly at home (or at his mates') – or sometimes at school/college or at a Cybercafé. Into playing online games and getting into role-playing (in MUDs – multiple user dungeons) – thinks he is pretty net savvy and pretty hip. Other interests include football (could have a 'chelsea.co.uk' email address).

The CyberLad Aged 23 – basically 'loaded man' online – accesses at work and at home. Bit of a Jack the lad and thinks he knows it all as far as the Net is concerned. He certainly doesn't want anyone telling him how he should use it. Interests include sex and sport, and sport and sex – spends a lot of time online searching for smut and then emailing it to his mates. Probably not the sort of bloke you'd want to run into after closing time on a Friday night.

The CyberSec Aged 31 – works as a PA to the boss of a small firm – super-competent and well turned out, but also very much 'one of the girls.' Only accesses the Internet at the office – first got online in order to do research for the boss (on clients, industry news, etc.) and to make arrangements for him (plane tickets, accommodation). 'Not really into computers and that' – but has started to explore on her own a bit. Perks up at any mention of shopping.

The InfoJunky Aged 40 (could either be male or female) – married with two children – possibly a middle-rank civil servant or a partner at a small firm of solicitors. Probably inclined to wear tweed jackets and hush puppies. Likes the feeling of being in touch and in control that the Internet gives him. He is under the impression that the time he spends online is a big benefit to his job, but given that he gets sidetracked so much, this is very debatable. Reads too many newspapers and magazines.

The Hit n' Runner Aged 38 (could either be male or female) – successful professional or a high flying marketing exec. Both seriously career-minded, she and her partner aren't sure if they're going to get round to having kids. Accesses the Internet at work and certainly doesn't see the Net as any form of entertainment but as a way of accessing information. Very impatient if she can't find what she wants or if the site is slow to download. She banks online and manages her portfolio, and is also researching that holiday she never gets the time to take.

The CyberMum Aged 42 – married with three kids, aged 17, 14 and 8, and works in a 'caring' profession. Slightly overweight and can't keep to her diet – but other things are more important to her. Her husband thought it would be a good idea if they got online when he started spending one week in four at company HQ in Holland, so that they could exchange e-mail messages. She really likes e-mail and uses it to keep in touch with her sister in Australia. The kids seem to spend so much time on the Internet, but she can't see what all the fuss is about – she'd rather read a magazine, if she ever got the time. Having said that, she would like to be able to shop online – if only she knew how it worked.

Purchased online

Customers will only purchase products online that meet the criteria of the *Electronic Shopping Test* (*Chapter 8, p. 301*). Recent research (NOP, 2000) suggests that an increasing proportion of people are prepared to buy online, with a sizeable proportion of online users having purchased within the last month. The survey stated that:

> *a quarter of those who had used the Internet in the last four weeks had shopped online, with the total number of online shoppers having more than doubled since this time last year. Half (51%) of those who had shopped online had bought something from a website they had bought from before. Over nine out of ten online shoppers (94%) say that they intend to shop online in the future, a claim reinforced by the fact that the overall level of dissatisfaction with the experience of online shopping to date is only 3%. 75% of online shoppers expect to be spending more money on online shopping by the summer of 2001.*

Additionally Windham (2001) found that contrary to received wisdom, online shoppers tend to enjoy shopping in any environment. She found that only 1 per cent of people who were web shoppers said that they hated going to the shops, while 10 per cent of traditional purchasers said they hated going to the stores.

Despite this upbeat portrayal of online shopping, in most countries online purchases are well below online access and, as we have said above, marketing communications need to encourage users to purchase online or provide alternative methods for purchase such as phone, i.e to allow for *mixed-mode buying* (*Chapter 9, p. 343*).

Online demand for business services

We now turn our attention to how we profile online access for business users. The B2B market is more complex than B2C in that variation in demand will occur according to different types of organization and people within the buying unit in the organization. This analysis is also important as part of the *segmentation* (*Chapter 8, p. 304*) of different groups within a B2B target market. We need to profile business demand according to:

1. *Variation in organization characteristics*
   - Size of company (employees or turnover)
   - Industry sector and products
   - Organization type (private, public, government, not for profit)
   - Division
   - Country and region
2. *Individual role*
   - Role and responsibility from job title, function or number of staff managed
   - Role in buying decision (purchasing influence)
   - Department
   - Product interest
   - Demographics: age, sex and possibly social group

B2B profiles

We can profile business users of the Internet in a similar way to consumers by assessing:

1. *The percentage of companies with access*
   In most developed countries more than three quarters of businesses have Internet access, regardless of size, suggesting the Internet is very effective in terms of reaching companies (see *Figure 4.6*).

   Although the Internet seems to be used by many companies we also need to ask whether it reaches the right people in the buying unit. Access is not necessarily available to all employees. Although over three quarters of businesses have access, the DTI (2000) data also shows that access is usually available to less than 50 per cent of employees. For example, restricting access to a single PC in a department is common practice.
2. *Influenced online*
   Figure 4.7 indicates that for many companies the Internet is important in identifying online suppliers with the majority, especially the larger companies, identifying some suppliers online.

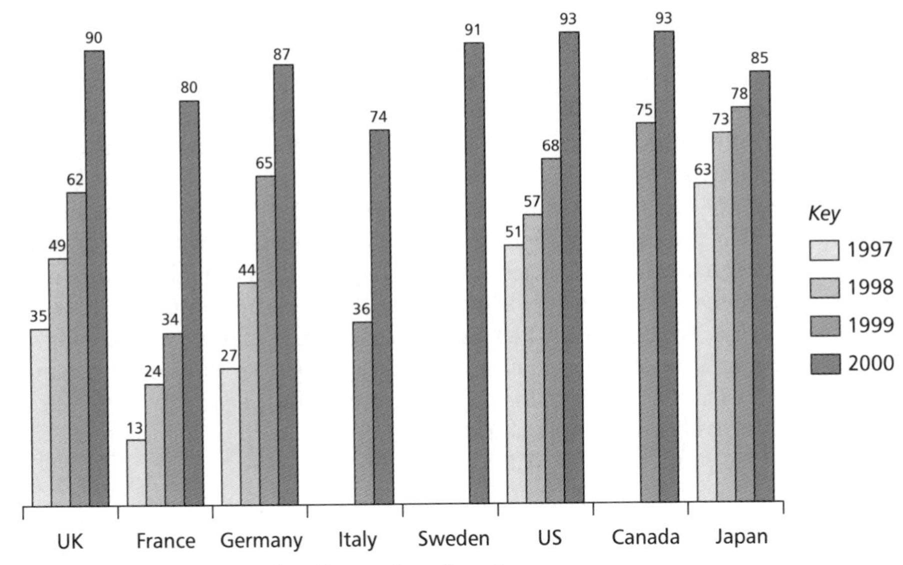

Base: All respondents weighted by number of employees

Figure 4.6 Percentage of businesses with Internet access.
Source: DTI (2000).

3. *Purchase online*
   In terms of access device and purchase method, e-mail and the web are widely used for online purchases, with extranets and EDI less important since these are the preserve of larger companies.

In summary, to estimate online revenue contribution to determine the amount of investment in e-business we need to research the number of connected customers, the percentage whose offline purchase is influenced online and number who buy online.

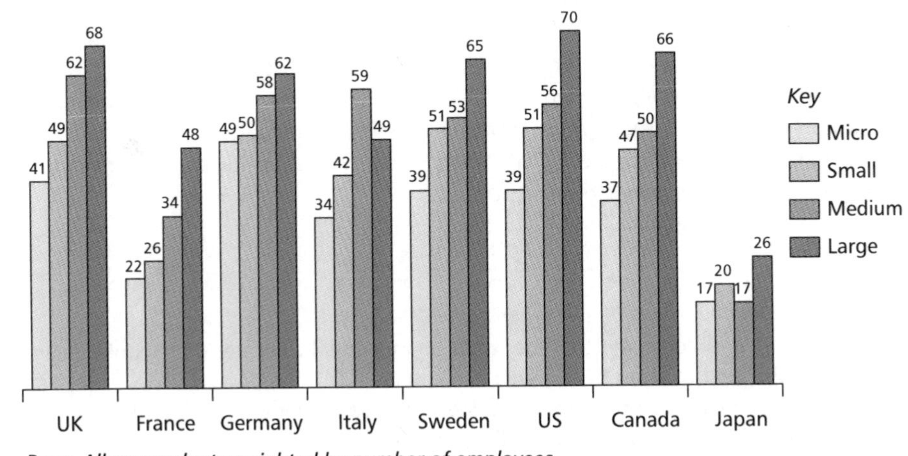

Base: All respondents weighted by number of employees

Figure 4.7 Percentage of businesses that identify suppliers online by business size.
Source: DTI (2000).

Ethical issues of sell-side e-commerce

Ethical issues involved with the Internet are closely associated with adoption levels and buyer behaviour. It will be shown in this section that a company that has a poor grasp of the ethics of e-commerce is likely to haemorrhage online customers. Effective e-commerce requires a delicate balance to be struck between the benefits the individual (or companies) will gain from personalization and the amount of information that they are prepared for companies to hold about them. For business-to-business marketing the benefits to both parties of sharing information may be more apparent since this typically involves stronger relationships between buyers and sellers. For example, when a supermarket chain makes its demand forecasts available to a supplier, it will clearly benefit both parties since more revenue will accrue to each. For business-to-consumer marketing the synergy is less clear and the privacy issue is more of a barrier to the development of the Internet. It is on this aspect of privacy that we will concentrate.

Privacy and trust

According to Chaffey *et al.* (2000) privacy of consumers on the Internet covers three related issues:

1. *Collecting and holding personal information.*

One of the difficulties of using the Internet for one-to-one marketing is that it is not easy to identify the end-user in order to target them with specific promotional information. To do this, it is necessary to invade the user's privacy by planting **cookies** or electronic tags on the end-user's computer. Alternatively customers can be made to log-in to an extranet with a user name and password which is a less subversive method of personalization. It is also necessary to ask customers about their personal details such as name, address, job and services required in order to match the cookie or log-in with the preferences of the person. By doing this it is possible to identify a user's preferences and behaviour since each time they visit a site, the cookie on the PC will be read to confirm the identity of the user (see the box 'What are cookies?' for more information).

Cookies
Cookies are small text files stored on an end-user's computer to enable web sites to identify them.

It is possible to block cookies if the user finds out how to block them, but this is not straightforward and many customers do not know that their privacy is being infringed. Cookies have a bad reputation since it is believed that they could be used to capture credit-card information or other personal information. In reality, this is unlikely to occur since cookies usually only contain an identification number that does not give away any personal secrets.

What are cookies?

A 'cookie' is a data file placed on your computer that identifies an individual computer. The cookie is placed on the computer via the web browser by the web site you visit. This is a powerful technique from a marketing point of view since it is used to identify a particular customer and tailor the web session accordingly – a key goal of personalization.

Note that without the use of cookies it is not possible to uniquely identify an individual since the log files mentioned in *Chapter 12* simply record an IP address which may differ between different sessions if connecting using an ISP. Cookie derives from a Unix term 'magic cookie' that meant something passed between routines or programs that enables the receiver to perform some operation. Eric Raymond in the New Hacker's Bible makes the analogy with a check for redeeming dry cleaning.

Cookies are stored as individual text files in the directory \windows\cookies on a personal computer. There is usually one file per company. For example: dave_chaffey@british-airways.txt. This file contains encoded information as follows:

FLT_VIS IK:bapzRnGdxBYUUID:Jul-25-1999I british-airways.com/ 0 425259904 29357426 1170747936 29284034 *

The information in the cookie file is essentially just an identification number and a date of the last visit although other information can be stored.

Cookies are specific to a particular browser and computer, so if a user connects from a different computer such as at work or starts using a different browser, the web site will not identify him or her as a similar user.

Some examples of cookie use

- Cookies can be used to deliver personalized content when linked with preferences expressed using collaborative filtering. Cookies are used to identify users and retrieve their preferences from a database.
- DoubleClick (www.doubleclick.net) uses cookies to track the number of times a particular computer has been shown a particular banner advertisement. When advertisers register with DoubleClick they create one or more target audience profiles. When a user visits a registered site a banner dynamically matches them to the target user profile. For any future visits by that user the DoubleClick server retrieves the ID number from the cookie and stores information about the visit.
- 'Shopping carts' in e-commerce sites use cookies to store what the user wishes to order at a site prior to finalizing a purchase. When the user is ready to check out the server reads the cookie file and initiates a transaction based on what is in the shopping cart.
- Log-file analysis software such as Webtrends (www.webtrend.com) relies on cookies to find the proportion of repeat visitors to a web site.
- 'Amazon customizes itself to each individual visiting its pages. You enter your name, address and credit card details once and thereafter can buy any book just by clicking a single icon on the screen (on subsequent visits to the site, credit card details can be retrieved from a secure database using the identification number in the cookie). The computer system watches what you buy and judges your tastes and then starts offering titles it thinks may appeal to your taste ... It creates a learning relationship that gets smarter and smarter the more you use it ... The reason this is a compelling model is that it makes the customer more loyal to you. I buy books from Amazon and, in all probability, I could get them cheaper somewhere else. But why would I bother? I know Amazon, it's easy to use and to buy somewhere else I would have to go through the business of entering my address and credit card details again.' Don Peppers, *Sunday Times* 13 June 1999.

Privacy concerns about cookies

Antagonism exists towards the cookie due to a lack of disclosure – the cookies are passed surreptitiously and thus give the feeling that the user's privacy has been invaded. Scare stories have been spread that cookies contain personal and credit card details, but this is not the case unless an error has been made by the webmaster. Normally they only contain an identification code which is used to retrieve these details from a database.

A study of almost 60,000 Internet users at the University of Michigan for the Hermes project (www.personal.umich.edu/~sgupta/hermes) indicated that over 81 per cent felt that cookies were undesirable.

Despite these concerns, the cookie is becoming ubiquitous at major commercial sites as a means of tracking users.

For additional information about cookies visit:
www.netscape.com/newsref/std/cookie_spec.html
www.cookiecentral.com.

In the future, user awareness of cookies will increase, and an increasing number of users may block cookies which may reduce the effectiveness of one-to-one marketing. Complete *activity 4.5* to assess people's perceptions of them.

Activity 4.5 What do you think about cookies?

Purpose

To investigate the nature of cookies and to gain an appreciation of people's perception of cookies.

Activity

1. First, look at how many cookies you receive. For Microsoft Internet Explorer users, access the Windows/Cookies directory. What proportion of sites that you have visited use cookies? How do you feel about this?
2. Now look at how you can stop cookies being planted on your PC.

   On the **Tools** menu in Internet Explorer, click **Internet Options**.
   - Click the **Security** tab.
   - Click the **Custom Level** button.
   - You can see that by default cookies are permanently enabled. You also have the option just to enable cookies for an individual session and they are removed afterwards.

   For Netscape:
   - Select the **Edit** and then **Preferences**.
   - In the **Category**: column, select **Advanced**.
   - In the Cookies section, Netscape gives four choices – to accept all cookies, to accept only the cookies that get sent back to the originating server (and thus do not stay on your hard drive), to disable all cookies, or to warn you every time you are being asked to accept a cookie.

   For the next few days try the options of prompting for cookie or even disabling cookies. Do you think the web can work without cookies?
3. What do you think about cookies being enabled by default? Does this invade your personal space? To look at the practical reasons why cookies are enabled by default choose the option to prompt when cookies are placed – and then try to access sites; you will see this is annoying.
4. To get a feeling for the strength of feeling of others about cookies perform a search on cookies and personal privacy.

5. Finally visit the privacy statement with information on cookies at Etoys (www.etoys.com) and RS Components (www.rswww.com). Do you feel better about cookies now you understand them better as explained by a site owner?

An indication of users' opinion about privacy is indicated by the Pew Internet and American Life Project (Pew, 2000). The report found that 86 per cent of the 1017 Internet users surveyed favoured an 'opt-in' privacy policy. However, 27 per cent of users said they would never submit personal information and 24 per cent provided a false name or information. Fifteen per cent of Internet users just got online in the last six months. New users are most likely to be concerned about privacy and web site security.

With regard to cookies, 54 per cent of users think tracking is harmful because it invades privacy, but 56 per cent of Internet users are unaware that the 'cookie' is the primary online tracking tool. Ten per cent of users have set their browsers to reject cookies while 9 per cent used encryption to scramble their email and 5 per cent use anonymizing software, which hides the computer identity from websites.

Another study (Cyber Dialogue, 2000) presents a different perspective, finding that consumers are not concerned with giving their personal details online; rather, they are concerned with how this personal information is used by companies. In the study of 1500 Internet users, 80 per cent said they are willing to give their name, details of education, age and hobbies in exchange for customized or personalized content. Forty-nine per cent believed that a site which shares their personal information with another site is violating their privacy.

There are several initiatives that are being taken by industry groups to reassure web users about threats to their personal information. The first of these is TRUSTe (www.truste.org) (*Figure 4.8*), sponsored by IBM, Netscape with sites validated by

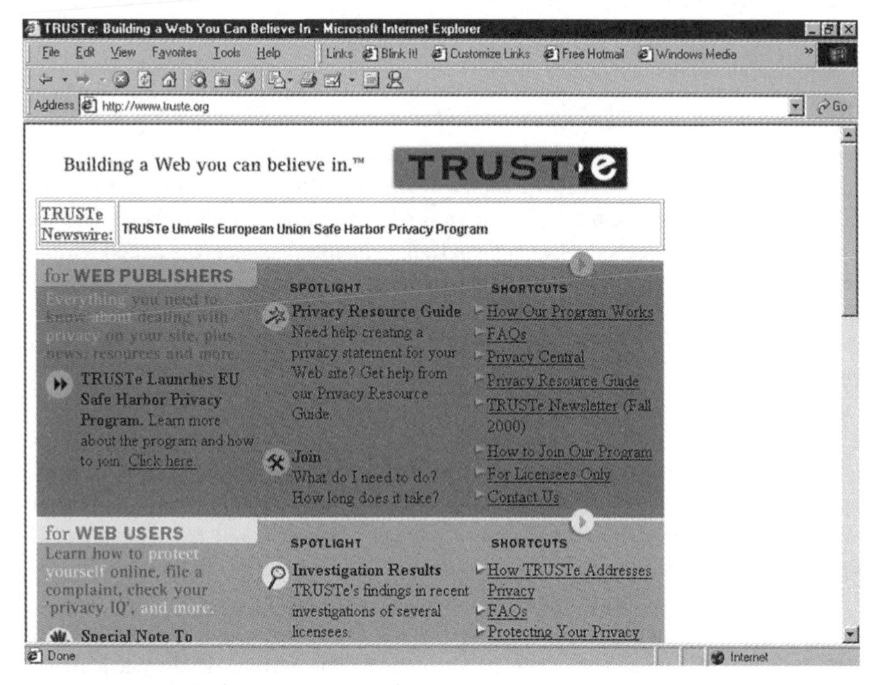

Figure 4.8 TRUSTe (www.truste.org)

PricewaterhouseCoopers and KPMG . The validators will audit each site, checking the site's privacy statement to see whether it is valid. For example, a privacy statement will describe:

- how a site collects information;
- how the information is used;
- who the information is shared with;
- how users can access and correct information;
- how users can decide to deactivate themselves from the site or withhold information from third parties.

A recent UK initiative is the Consumer Association/Which Web trader (www.which.net/webtrader/) which aims to 'ensure consumers get a fair deal and to provide them with protection if things go wrong'. E-tailers who have signed up to this include Barclaysquare, Blackwells, The Carphone Warehouse and EasyJet.

Government initiatives will also define best practice in this area and may introduce laws to ensure guidelines are followed. In the UK, the data protection act covers some of these issues and the 1999 European data protection act also has draft laws to help maintain personal privacy on the Internet.

2. Disclosing personal information to third parties

Customers may be quite happy to give personal information to a company that they have formed a relationship with. They are likely to be less than happy if this company then sells this information on to another company and they are subsequently bombarded with promotional material either online or offline. For this reason the TRUSTe mentioned in the previous section also sets down best practice for disclosing information to third parties. The other risk in this category is that of hackers accessing information held about a customer on servers within a company. For example, the infamous hacker Kevin Mitnick was known for accessing over 20,000 credit card numbers on a company server.

3. Sending unsolicited e-mails to consumers

Spamming
Bulk e-mailing of unsolicited mail.

Spamming, the sending of unsolicited mail or messages to large numbers of Internet users, is nothing new. A well known incident in the mid-1990s was when Canter and Siegel, the infamous 'Green Card Lawyers', spammed thousands of Usenet news groups with a message offering to help immigrants get US green cards. Bourne (1996) observed that 'To say the least, traditional users of the net were dumbfounded and shocked. They fought back the only way they could. They flamed Carter and Siegel with thousands of messages, temporarily shutting down their service provider.'

Opt-in
A customer proactively agrees to receive further information.

Opt-out
A customer declines the offer to receive further information.

Privacy issues that marketers should consider when conducting e-mail marketing are well covered by the Which Web Trader code (www.which.net/trader). Perhaps the most important facilities on an e-commerce site to provide for legal and ethical reasons are the principles of '**opt-in**' and '**opt-out**'. The concept of opt-in is that communications are only sent to customers if they have agreed to receive information, for example, by filling in an online form and ticking a box to say they are happy to receive further communications. The principle of opt-out is that the customers will not be contacted in future if they have asked not to be. For example, if customers are on an e-mail list, they will no longer be sent it, if they ask to be opted-out or removed from the list.

The revised 1998 Data Protection Act in the UK that includes local enactment of European legislation is typical of what has evolved in many countries to help protect personal information. Under the new act, companies must:

1. Inform the user, before asking for information:
   - who the company is
   - what personal data is collected, processed and stored
   - purpose of collection
2. Ask for consent for collecting sensitive personal data and good practice to ask before collecting any type of data.
3. Provide a statement of privacy policy. 'A privacy statement helps individuals to decide whether or not to visit a site and, when they do visit, whether or not to provide any personal information to the data controller.'
4. Always let individuals know when 'cookies' or other covert software are being used to collect information about them.
5. Never collect or retain personal data unless it is strictly necessary for the organization's purposes. For example, a person's name and full address should not be required to provide an online quotation. If extra information is required for marketing purposes this should be made clear and the provision of such information should be optional.
6. Amend incorrect data when informed and tell others. Enable correction on-site.
7. Only use data for marketing (by the company, or third parties) when a user has been informed this is the case and has agreed to this (this is opt-in).
8. Provide the option for customers to stop receiving information (this is opt-out).
9. Use technology to protect the customer information on your site.

This summary of the implications of the act is based on information at the UK data protection web site (www.dataprotection.gov.uk/dprhome.htm).

To summarize this section we can suggest that e-commerce managers need to take these actions to overcome ethical issues such as privacy to achieve reassurance, gain trust and build loyalty:

1. Provide clear and effective privacy statements.
2. Follow privacy and consumer protection guidelines in all local markets.
3. Make security of customer data a priority.
4. Use independent certification bodies.
5. Emphasize the excellence of service quality in all marketing communications.

Legal factors

Knowledge of legal issues is, of course, also vital to e-commerce managers, since when they seek to exploit new marketplaces they will be subject to local legal constraints. For example, Germany has specific laws that prohibit explicit comparisons between products and Belgium has a law that discount sales may only occur in January and July. Governments looking to foster e-commerce develop guidelines to help companies adhere to laws in countries in which they are seeking to operate. In the UK guidelines are published at www.itcompliance.com; these show that to trade in the UK there are 40 different laws that a company may be subject to!

Some of the main e-commerce related legal issues on which companies need to seek specific legal advice are:

1. *Domain name registrations and trademarking of new Internet brands*. There have been many disputes about ownership of company domains (URLs).
2. *Advertising standards*. Most countries have specific laws to avoid misrepresentation to the consumer and uncompetitive practices.
3. *Defamation and libel*. Information published on a site critical of another company's people or products could represent libel.
4. *Copyright and intellectual property rights (IPR)*. Permissions must be sought for information or images sourced elsewhere in the same way as for any other media.
5. *Data protection act and privacy law*. Sites must protect data held on consumers according to the local law.
6. *Taxation on electronic commerce*. For companies involved in e-commerce, sales tax must be collected from consumers.

Taxation

How to change tax laws to reflect globalization through the Internet is a problem that many governments are grappling with. The fear is that the Internet may cause significant reductions in tax revenues to national or local governments if existing laws do not cover changes in purchasing patterns. In Europe, the use of online betting in lower tax areas such as Gibraltar has resulted in lower revenues to governments in the countries where consumers would have formerly paid gaming tax to the government via a betting shop. Large UK bookmakers such as William Hill and Victor Chandler are offering Internet-based betting from 'offshore' locations such as Gibraltar. The lower duties in these countries offer the companies the opportunity to make betting significantly cheaper than if they were operating under a higher tax regime. This trend has been dubbed as LOCI or Location Optimized Commerce on the Internet by Mougayer (1998). Meanwhile the government of the country from which a person places the bet will face a drop in its tax revenues. In the UK the government has sought to reduce the revenue shortfall by reducing the differential between UK and overseas costs.

The extent of the taxation problem for governments is illustrated by the US ABC News (2000), which reported that between $300 million and $3.8 billion of potential tax revenue was lost by authorities in 2000 in the US as more consumers purchased online. The revenue shortfall occurs because online retailers need to impose sales or use tax only when goods are being sent to a consumer who lives in a state (or country) where the retailer has a bricks-and-mortar store. Buyers are supposed to pay voluntarily the appropriate sales taxes when buying online but this rarely happens in practice. This makes the Internet a largely tax-free area in the US.

Since the Internet supports the global marketplace it could be argued that it makes little sense to introduce tariffs on goods and services delivered over the Internet. Such instruments would, in any case, be impossible to apply over products delivered electronically. This position is currently that of the US. In the document 'A Framework for Global Electronic Commerce', the president stated that:

> *The United States will advocate in the World Trade Organization (WTO) and other appropriate international fora that the Internet be declared a tariff-free zone.*

Tax jurisdiction

Tax jurisdiction determines which country gets tax income from a transaction. Under the current system of international tax treaties, the right to tax is divided between the country where the enterprise that receives the income is resident ('residence' country) and that from where the enterprise derives that income ('source' country). Laws on taxation are rapidly evolving and vary dramatically between countries. A proposed EU directive intends to deal with these issues by defining the place of establishment of a merchant as being where they pursue an economic activity from a fixed physical location. At the time of writing the general principle that is being applied is that tax rules are similar to a conventional mail-order sale; for the UK, the tax principles are as follows:

- if the supplier (residence) and the customer (source) are both in the UK, VAT will be chargeable;
- exports to private customers in the EU will either attract UK VAT or local VAT;
- exports outside the EU will be zero-rated (but tax may be levied on import);
- imports into the UK from the EU or beyond will attract local VAT, or UK import tax when received through customs;
- services attract VAT according to where the supplier is located. This is different from products and causes anomalies if online services are created. For example, a betting service located in Gibraltar enables UK customers to gamble at a lower tax rate than with the same company in the UK.

Freedom restrictive legislation

Although governments enact legislation in order to protect consumer privacy on the Internet as described in the previous section, it is also worth noting that some individuals and organizations believe that legislation may also be too restrictive. In the UK, a new Telecommunications Act and Regulation of Investigatory Powers act (RIP) took several years to enact since companies were concerned to ensure security and to give security forces the ability to monitor all communications passing through ISPs. This was fiercely contested due to cost burdens placed on infrastructure providers and in particular the Internet Service Providers (ISPs) and of course many citizens and employees may not be happy about being monitored either!

The Freedom House (www.freedomhouse.org) is a human rights organization created to reduce censorship since it believes government censorship laws may be too restrictive. It notes in a report (Freedom House, 2000) that governments in many countries, both developed and developing, are increasingly censoring online content. Only 69 of the countries studied have a completely free media, while 51 have a partly free media and 66 countries suffer heavy government censorship. Censorship methods include implementing licensing and regulation laws, applying existing print and broadcast restrictions to the Internet, filtering content and direct censoring after dissemination. In Asia and the Middle East, governments frequently cite protection of morality and local values as reasons for censorship. Countries where Internet access is mostly or totally controlled by the authorities include Azerbaijan, Belarus, Burma, China, Cuba, Iran, Iraq, Kazakhstan, Kyrgyzstan, Libya, North Korea, Saudi Arabia, Sierra Leone, Sudan, Syria, Tajikistan, Tunisia, Turkmenistan, Uzbekistan and Vietnam. Even the US government tried to control access to certain Internet sites with the Communications Decency Act in 1996, but this was unsuccessful. Refer to *activity 4.6* to discuss these issues.

Activity 4.6 Government and company monitoring of electronic communications

Purpose

To examine the degree to which governments and organizations should monitor electronic communications.

Activity

Write down the arguments for and against each of these statements, debate individually or a group to come to a consensus:

1. *'This house believes that organizations have no right to monitor employees' use of e-mail or the web.'*

   Use Moreover (www.moreover.com) to research action taken by the government of your country to monitor and control Internet communications.

2. *'This house believes that governments have no right to monitor all Internet-based communications passing through ISPs.'*

   Use Moreover (www.moreover.com) to research recent cases where employees have been dismissed for accessing or sending e-mails or web content that is deemed unsuitable. Is this just used as an excuse for dismissing staff?

What action do you think managers in a company should take with regard to monitoring employee access? Should laws be set at national or should action be taken by individual companies?

Economic and competitive factors

The economic health and competitive environment in different countries will determine the e-commerce potential of each. Managers developing e-commerce strategies will target the countries that are most developed in the use of the technology. Knowledge of different economic conditions is also part of budgeting for revenue from different countries. For example, Fisher (2000) notes that the Asian market for e-commerce is predicted to triple within three years. However, within this marketplace there are large variations. Relative to income, the cost of a PC is still high in many parts of Asia for people on low incomes. Fisher (2000) suggests that there will be a division between information 'haves' and 'have-nots' and as we will see in the section on *Political factors* this is dependent on government factors. In China there is regulation on foreign ownership of Internet portals and ISPs which could hamper development. User access to certain content is also restricted. Despite this access in China is doubling every six months and at this rate China could have the largest user base within 10 years!

The trend towards globalization can arguably insulate a company to some extent from fluctuations in regional markets, but is of course no protection from a global recession. Managers can also study e-commerce in these leading countries to help predict future e-commerce trends in their own country.

Inspection of *Figures 4.3 and 4.4* shows that there are wide variations in the level of use of the Internet in different continents and countries, particularly for consumer use. According to Roussel (2000) economic, regulatory and cultural issues are among the factors affecting use of the Internet for commercial transactions. The relative importance of these means e-commerce will develop differently in every country. Roussel (2000) rated different countries according to their readiness to use the Internet for business. This was based on two factors – propensity for e-commerce and Internet penetration. To calculate the propensity of a country for e-commerce transactions, the business environment was evaluated using the Economic Intelligence Unit (www.eiu.com) rating of countries according to 70 different indicators, such as the strength of the economy, political stability, the regulatory climate, taxation policies and openness toward trade and investment. Cultural factors were also considered, including language and the attitude toward online purchasing as opposed to browsing. The two graphed factors do not correspond in all countries, for example Scandinavian users frequently use the Internet to gain information, helped by widespread English usage, but they are less keen to purchase online due to concerns about security. Internet penetration varies widely and is surprisingly low in some countries, for example in France, which was earlier a leader in e-commerce through its Minitel system, and in Japan (*Figure 4.9*).

Now review *case study 4.1* to see how global variations in propensity to adopt new technology can affect the success of an online venture.

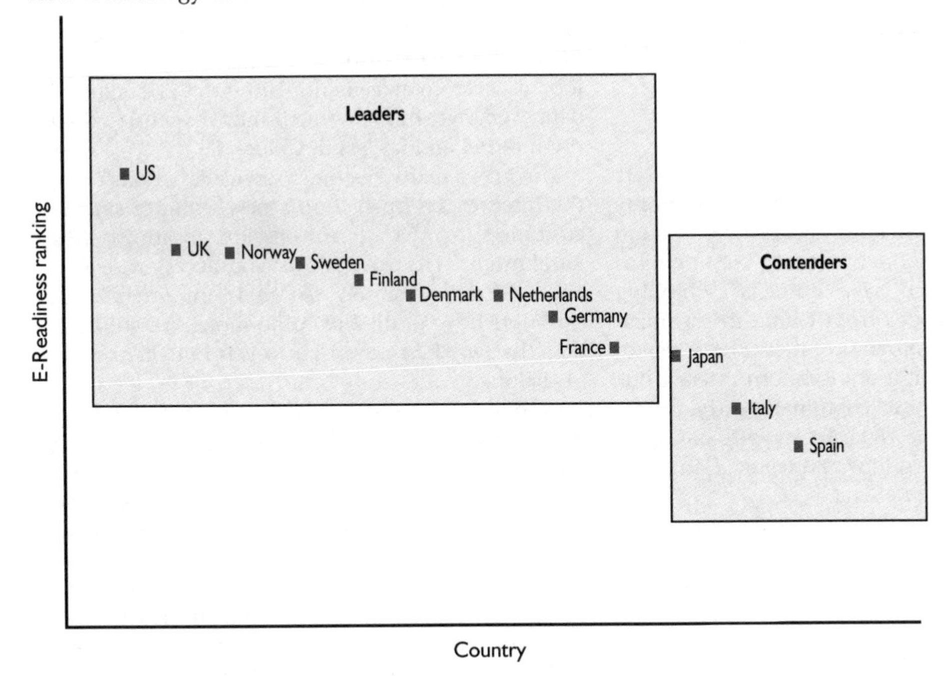

Figure 4.9 Leaders and contenders in e-commerce

Source: adapted from The Economist Intelligence Unit/Pyramid Research e-readiness ranking (www.eiu.com)

CASE STUDY 4.1

Variations in take-up of online services for Orient Overseas Container Line (OOCL)

No one could accuse Orient Overseas Container Line (OOCL) of faddishness towards the Internet. The Hong Kong-based shipping group made its first moves on to the web in the mid-1990s, long before the current daily addiction to the movements of Nasdaq took hold. By 1995, when only a fraction of global companies even had a web site, OOCL allowed customers online access to basic ship schedule information, much like the flight schedules airlines make available on the Internet or by phone.

'This was not a public relations issue,' says Niels Kim Balling, OOCL's general manager, corporate marketing. 'It had to be something our customers would find useful. From the start, we wanted an interactive, real-time exchange of information.'

It was a small step but the payback, in terms of new business from all the attention the company garnered, was almost immediate. The initial investment was $250,000 and Mr Balling estimates the new business that came in as a result of the innovation more than covered the cost in three months.

Challenge

At first glance, few industries would seem less likely Internet converts than the decidedly old-economy shipping industry. Yet the business revolves around a continual flow of information across continents as a customer in Chicago, say, contracts a shipping company to move goods from China to Australia. The need to track the progress of movements makes the Internet a powerful tool to smooth interactions with the customer. Just coordinating the information flow among the 160 offices OOCL has in 47 countries around the world would seem a Herculean challenge in a pre-Internet era.

Harnessing the Internet to do just that has given OOCL an early lead in moving the shipping business online, analysts say. For the more than 50-year-old Hong Kong shipping company, founded by C.Y. Tung in 1947 in a bid to create the first international Chinese merchant fleet, OOCL's quick move online could provide a competitive advantage. Even if it does not have the flashy style of an Aristotle Onassis at its helm, the company is something of a local celebrity in Hong Kong; it is owned by the family of the city's chief executive, Tung Chee-hwa.

In his role as leader of Hong Kong since 1997, Mr Tung has ambitions to make the city an IT hub for Asia, but most companies in the territory are decidedly low-tech and many are still figuring out how to get their e-mail systems right. OOCL, by contrast, could prove a role model with the launch of its IRIS-2 system. Salomon Smith Barney analyst Charles de Trenck says that at the peak of its rollout last summer, OOCL employed over 100 programmers and web designers in Silicon Valley. The company has moved away from a reliance on mainframes and the IBM ES 9000 has been shut down to move main IT functions onto the Internet, deploying five HP 9000 super servers for the backbone and 350 additional servers globally.

What this hardware adds up to is an ability to deepen the relationships between OOCL and customers' back offices, allowing two-way data exchanges and mass customization of service agreements. It also allows the shipping line to do a better job of yield management. Hitherto, EDI allowed data exchange, but it is much more expensive than the Internet and far less flexible.

Moving so many customer service functions on to the Internet has opened up a new world of smaller customers for OOCL in obscure locations, like Kazakhstan. 'The web allows you access to everybody. Some remotely located importers and exporters have pushed us to do more. We got business that we didn't even know was out there,' says Mr Balling.

Despite reaching out to an even more far-flung customer base, the move by existing customers to access services through the company's web site has been relatively slow. As often happens in the brave new world of the Internet, customer service innovations, such as allowing online access to post-order services like cargo tracking or the bill of lading (the contract to the goods), do not immediately win over the entire customer base, many of whom seem complacently happy with the way things were. 'This is not a technology issue. It is a business process issue,' says Mr Balling.

The initial switch was also possibly slowed by Y2K

concerns. By April 2000, however, the switch of customers to accessing the full complement of online services really began to take off. In Singapore, 40 per cent of all business with OOCL is conducted through the web site, while in North America it is about one third.

Beyond that, the growth in online interaction has been mixed; Germany has been 'explosive' but France has been a bit of a 'sleeper', reports Mr Balling. On a global basis, nearly 10 per cent of all business is being conducted through the company's web site.

Mr de Trenck at Salomon Smith Barney estimates that OOCL can deliver an additional $10 m to the bottom line in 2000 as a result of savings from the Internet portion of its total revenues. The early start by OOCL is already delivering results.

Source: Article by Rahul Jacob in *Financial Times*, 6 September 2000.

Question

Discuss reasons for differing take-up of Internet services offered by OOCL.

Focus on e-commerce and globalization

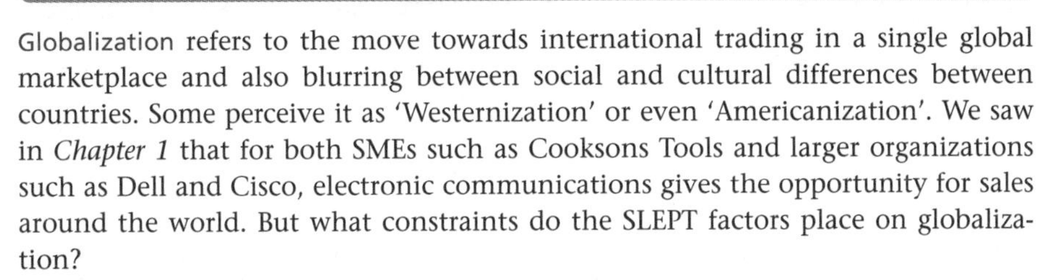

Globalization refers to the move towards international trading in a single global marketplace and also blurring between social and cultural differences between countries. Some perceive it as 'Westernization' or even 'Americanization'. We saw in *Chapter 1* that for both SMEs such as Cooksons Tools and larger organizations such as Dell and Cisco, electronic communications gives the opportunity for sales around the world. But what constraints do the SLEPT factors place on globalization?

Globalization
The increase of international trading and shared social and cultural values.

Quelch and Klein (1996) point out some of the consequences for organizations that wish to compete in the global marketplace; they say a company must have:

- *a 24 hour order taking and customer service response capability;*
- *regulatory and customs-handling experience to ship internationally;*
- *in-depth understanding of foreign marketing environments to assess the advantages of its own products and services.*

Language and cultural understanding may also present a problem and a smaller or medium company is unlikely to possess the resources to develop a multi-language version of its site or employ staff with language skills. On the other hand, Quelch and Klein (1996) note that the growth of the use of the Internet for business will accelerate the trend of English becoming the lingua franca of commerce.

Hamill and Gregory (1997) highlight the strategic implications of e-commerce for business-to-business exchanges conducted internationally. They note that there will be increasing standardization of prices across borders as businesses become more aware of price differentials. Secondly, they predict that the importance of traditional intermediaries such as agents and distributors will be reduced by Internet-enabled direct marketing and sales.

Larger organizations typically already compete in the global marketplace, or have the financial resources to achieve this. But what about the smaller organization? Most governments are looking to encourage SMEs to use electronic commerce to tap into the international market. Advice from governments must reassure SMEs wishing to export overseas. Hamill and Gregory (1997) identify the barriers to SME internationalization shown in *Table 4.2*. Complete *activity 4.7* to look at the actions that can be taken to overcome these barriers.

Activity 4.7 Overcoming SME resistance to e-commerce

Purpose

To highlight barriers to exporting amongst SMEs and suggest measures by which they may be overcome by governments.

Activity

For each of the four barriers to internationalization given in *Table 4.2* suggest the management reasons why the barriers may exist and actions that governments can take to overcome these barriers. Evaluate how well the government in your country communicates the benefits of e-commerce through education and training.

Table 4.2 Issues in SME resistance to exporting

Barrier	*Management issues*	*How can barrier be overcome?*
1. Psychological **2.** Operational **3.** Organizational **4.** Product/market		

Source: barriers from Hamill and Gregory (1997) and Poon and Jevons (1997)

For answer see p. 153

Political factors

The political environment is shaped by the interplay of government agencies, public opinion, consumer pressure groups such as CAUCE (the coalition against unsolicited e-mail), www.cauce.org, and industry-backed organizations such as TRUSTe (www.truste.org) that promote best practice amongst companies. The political environment is one of the drivers for establishing the laws to ensure privacy and to achieve taxation as described in previous sections.

Political action enacted through government agencies to control the adoption of the Internet can include:

- promoting the benefits of adopting the Internet for consumers and business to improve a country's economic prosperity;
- sponsoring research leading to dissemination of best practice amongst companies, for example the UK's Code of Best Practice for E-business (www.itcompliance.com);
- enacting legislation to protect privacy or control taxation;
- setting up international bodies to coordinate the Internet such as ICANN (The Internet Corporation for Assigned Names and Numbers, www.icann.com) who will introduce new top-level domains such as .firm and .store.

Some examples of the role of government organizations in promoting and regulating e-commerce are given by these examples from the European Commission:

- In 1998 new data protection guidelines were enacted as is described in the section on privacy to help protect consumers and increase the adoption of e-commerce by reducing security fears.

- The eEurope Action Plan was launched in May 2000 with objectives of 'a cheaper, faster, more secure Internet; investing in people's skills and access; and stimulating the use of the Internet'. The commission intends to increase Internet access relative to the US, in order to make Europe more competitive.
- Also in May 2000, the EC announced that it wanted the supply of local loops, that is the copper cables that link homes to telephone exchanges, to be unbundled so that newer companies can compete with traditional telecommunications suppliers. The objective here, the provision of widespread broadband services, is a major aim of the EU.

The types of initiative launched by governments are highlighted by the launch in the UK, in September of 1999, a new 'UK online' campaign (www.ukonline.gov.uk), a raft of initiatives and investment aimed at moving people, business and government itself online. An e-envoy and e-minister have also been appointed. The Prime Minister said:

> *There is a revolution going on in our economy. A fundamental change, not a dot-com fad, but a real transformation towards a knowledge economy. So, today, I am announcing a new campaign. Its goal is to get the UK online. To meet the three stretching targets we have set: for Britain to be the best place in the world for e-commerce, with universal access to the Internet and all government services on the net. In short, the UK online campaign aims to get business, people and government online.*

Specific targets have been set for the proportion of people and businesses who have access, including public access points for those who cannot currently afford the technology. Managers who are aware of these initiatives can tap into sources of funding for development or free training to support their online initiatives. Read *case study 4.2* for one example of how a government has taken decisive action to use the Internet for **e-government** and relate this to your country.

E-government
The use of Internet technologies to provide government services to citizens.

CASE STUDY 4.2

Singapore government creates 'intelligent island'

Do you need a certified replacement copy of your birth certificate? In most countries, residents would not know where to begin looking. And for those that do, the fear of long queues in bureaucratic government departments might lead them to put off searching altogether.

However, an attempt in Singapore to build a comprehensive electronic government means residents need only head to the government web site (gov.sg). The front page offers the eCitizen centre, which lists subheadings ranging from Employment to Family, where the section on birth can be found. Electronic signboards direct users to the birth extract application section, which details the cost, various ways to pay for the copy, and when to expect it in the mail.

Other government services are just as easy to access. Singapore has set a goal to remain relevant and responsive in the new digital economy. To achieve that aim, it has drawn up an outline of ways to develop Singapore into what it calls a top 'infocomm' capital with a thriving Internet economy by 2010. To this end, it brought forward by two years the full liberalization of the telecoms sector to 1 April 2000 to make the domestic market globally competitive.

'Governments all over the world have a major role to play in realizing the socio-economic potential and benefits of the Internet economy for their industries and their citizens,' says Tony Tan Keng Yam, deputy prime minister and minister for defence. 'The Singapore government embarked on

▶ CASE STUDY *continued*

a massive computerization programme as early as the 1980s. By the 1990s, we had gone online. Now we are going a step further. We have begun the process of transforming ourselves into an e-government, one that members of the public and businesses can reach, communicate and interact with virtually.'

There are five strategic thrusts in the e-government action plan: delivering integrated electronic services; using infocomm technologies to build new capability and capacity; innovating with infocomm technologies; being proactive and responsive; and reinventing government in the digital economy.

The first thrust – delivering integrated electronic services – has led the government to make those key public services that can be delivered electronically available by the end of 2001. Already, about 130 public services, including provisions for filing police reports and applying for telephone lines, are delivered electronically. And the public is using them – about 500,000 electronic returns were filed to the Inland Revenue Authority this year.

The second thrust – using infocomm technologies to build new capability and capacity – goes beyond computerizing society to develop a nation of people equipped to use the new technologies on offer. The government's master plan for information technology in education, for example, trains teachers to bring IT into schools to prepare future generations for the digital economy.

'We will equip our public servants with the necessary skills, tools, systems and infrastructure to make them effective workers in the digital economy,' said Mr Tan.

The third thrust – innovating with infocomm technologies – calls on the government to experiment with new technologies, such as interactive broadband multimedia and wireless technologies, to keep pace with the private sector. This is already happening: the Land Transport Authority, Meteorological Services and Ministry of Defence offer some services through WAP technology.

The fourth thrust – being proactive and responsive – requires government staff to be fluent in the new technologies on offer so they can stay abreast of international developments. 'Systems and services must be delivered at Internet speed and continuously fine-tuned to respond to customer needs and feedback,' Mr Tan said.

The fifth thrust – reinventing government in the digital economy – calls for funding to be allocated to prepare public servants to use infocomm technologies. 'There is a need to sensitize public servants to the impact of infocomm technologies on the economic and social landscape so that they can continue to make meaningful policy decisions,' he added.

The government has set aside S$1.5 bn to make the e-government action plan a reality during the next three years. 'But more important than funding for the action plan is the mindset change that is needed to propel Singapore forward in the new economy,' Mr Tan said. To be a leader in this field, 'Singapore is prepared to do things differently'.

It is also doing its best to ensure the public is equipped to take advantage of the changes. 'The Singapore government recognized the vast economic potential of the Internet economy several years ago,' says Yeo Cheow Tong, minister for communications and IT. 'Together with the private sector, we have invested heavily in Internet infrastructure to give Singapore the first mover advantage in the region.'

Singapore has established Singapore ONE, a broadband infrastructure now accessible by more than 99 per cent of homes, all schools and many public libraries and community centres. It has also put in place a secure infrastructure to support e-commerce. The government provided S$150 m in 2000 to stimulate the demand for and supply of interactive broadband multimedia content and services.

To prevent a digital divide, the government has created specific programmes to enable senior citizens, union leaders, homemakers and the youth to go online. It is equipping low-income families with used computers together with free Internet access, in addition to basic training.

'Singapore is undoubtedly one of the most advanced nations in propagating e-business and e-government,' said Jinn Sin Lin, IBM Global Services' vice president of public sector services in the Asia-Pacific region. IBM has been working with the government in technology development since the 1980s.

'Major government applications are deployed and actively used on the Internet by both businesses, citizens and economic partners around the world,' Mr Lin said. 'The e-business and e-government success of Singapore is a demonstration of the strong commitment and excellence in execution of a solid partnership between Singapore's government, businesses, citizens and major IT industry players.'

Source: Article by Sheila McNulty, *Financial Times*, 6 December 2000.

Questions

1. Compare the action taken by the Singaporean government (the five thrusts) to that taken in your own country.
2. Do you think such investment in e-government is desirable or cost-effective?

Internet governance

Internet governance describes the control put in place to manage the growth of the Internet and its usage. Governance is traditionally undertaken by government, but the global nature of the Internet makes it less practical for a government to control cyberspace. Dyson (1998) says:

Internet governance
Control of the operation and use of the Internet.

> *Now, with the advent of the Net, we are privatizing government in a new way – not only in the traditional sense of selling things off to the private sector, but by allowing organizations independent of traditional governments to take on certain 'government' regulatory roles. These new international regulatory agencies will perform former government functions in counterpoint to increasingly global large companies and also to individuals and smaller private organizations who can operate globally over the Net.*

The US approach to governance, formalized in the Framework for Global Electronic Commerce in 1997, is to avoid any single country taking control.

Dyson (1998) describes different layers of jurisdiction. These are:

1. Physical space comprising each individual country where its own laws such as those governing taxation, privacy and trading and advertising standards hold.
2. ISPs – the connection between the physical world and virtual world.
3. Domain name control (www.icann.net) and communities.
4. Agencies such as TRUSTe (www.truste.org).

Technological innovation and technology assessment

One of the great challenges of managing e-commerce is the need to be able to assess which new technological innovations can be applied to give competitive advantage. For example, personalization technology is intended to enhance the customers' online experience and increase their loyalty. However, a technique such as personalization requires a large investment in software and hardware technology such as Broadvision or Engage to be able to implement it effectively. How does the manager decide whether to proceed and which solution to adopt? The manager may have read several articles in the trade and general press which have highlighted the issue and then faces a difficult decision as to whether to:

- ignore the use of the technique, perhaps because it is felt to be too expensive, untried, or the manager simply doesn't believe the benefits will outweigh the costs;
- enthusiastically adopt the technique without a detailed evaluation since the hype alone convinces the manager that the technique should be adopted;

- evaluate the technique and then take a decision whether to adopt it according to the evaluation.

Depending on the attitude of the manager, this behaviour can be summarized as:

1. Cautious, 'wait and see' approach.
2. Risk-taking, early adopter approach.
3. Intermediate approach.

This diffusion-adoption process (represented by the bell-curve in *Figure 4.10*) was identified by Rogers (1983) who classified those trialling new products as innovators, **early adopters**, early majority, late majority, to laggards.

Early adopters
Companies or departments that invest in new technologies and techniques.

Figure 4.10 can be used in two main ways as an analytical tool to help managers. First it can be used to understand the stage at which customers are in adoption of a technology, or any product. For example, the Internet is now a well-established tool and in many developed countries we are into the late majority phase of adoption with larger numbers of users of services. This suggests it is essential to use this medium for marketing purposes. But if we look at WAP technology (*Chapter 3, p. 107*) it can be seen that we are in the innovator phase, so investment now may be wasted since it is not clear how many will adopt the product. Secondly, managers can look at adoption of a new technique by other businesses – from an organizational perspective. For example, an online supermarket could look at how many other e-tailers have adopted personalization to evaluate whether it is worthwhile adopting the technique.

Trott (1998) looks at this organizational perspective to technology adoption. He identifies different requirements that are necessary within an organization to be able to respond effectively to technological change or innovation. These are:

- Growth orientation – a long-term rather than short-term vision
- Vigilance – the capability of environment scanning
- Commitment to technology – willingness to invest in technology
- Acceptance of risk – willingness to take managed risks
- Cross-functional cooperation – capability for collaboration across functional areas
- Receptivity – the ability to respond to externally developed technology

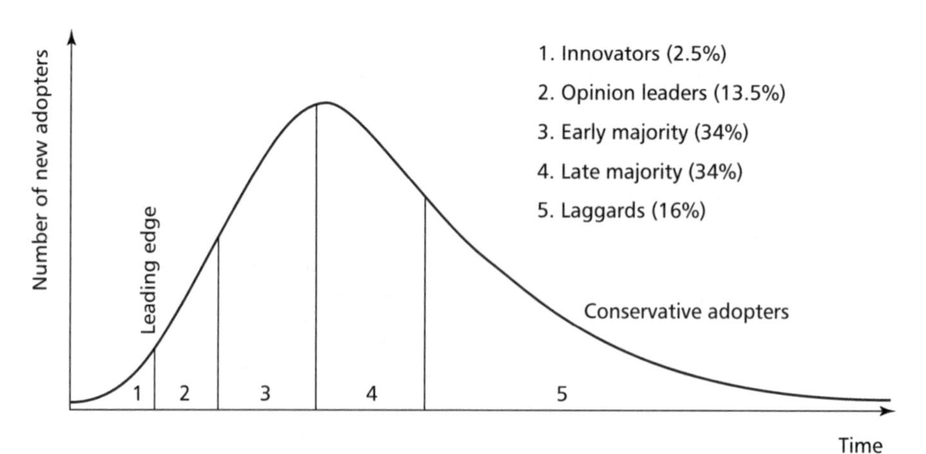

Figure 4.10 Diffusion-adoption curve

- Slack – allowing time to investigate new technological opportunities
- Adaptability – a readiness to accept change
- Diverse range of skills – technical and business skills and experience

The problem with being an early adopter (as an organization) is that being at the leading edge of using new technologies is often also referred to as the 'bleeding edge' due to the risk of failure. New technologies will have bugs, may integrate poorly with the existing systems or the marketing benefits may simply not live up to their promise. Of course, the reason for risk taking is that the rewards are high – if you are using a technique that your competitors are not, then you will gain an edge on your rivals. For example, RS Components (www.rswww.com) was one of the first UK suppliers of industrial components to adopt personalization as part of its e-commerce system (*Figure 4.11*). They have learnt the strengths and weaknesses of the product and now know how to position it to appeal to customers. It offers facilities such as customized pages, access to previous order history and the facility to place repeat orders or modified re-buys. This has enabled them to build up a customer base that is familiar with using the RS Components online services; these customers are then less likely to swap to rival services in the future.

It may also be useful to identify how rapidly a new concept is being adopted. When a product or service is adopted rapidly this is known as rapid diffusion. The access to the Internet is an example of this. In developed countries the use of the Internet has become widespread more rapidly than the use of TV, for example. It seems that in relation to interactive digital TV and Internet-enabled mobile phones are relatively slow-diffusion products!

So, what action should e-commerce managers take when confronted by new

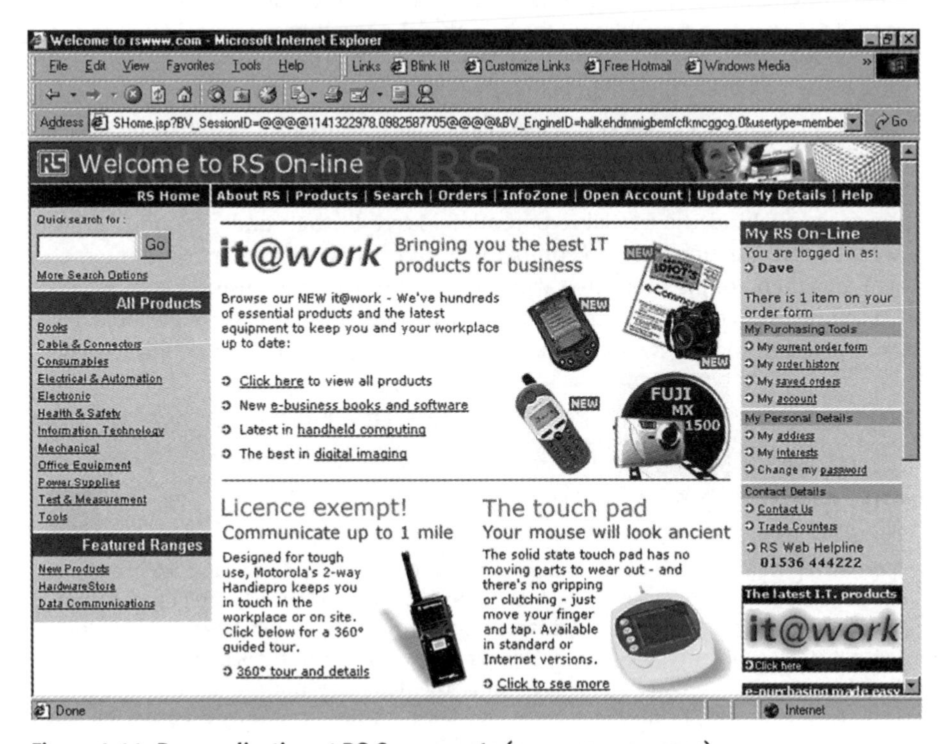

Figure 4.11 Personalization at RS Components (www.rswww.com)

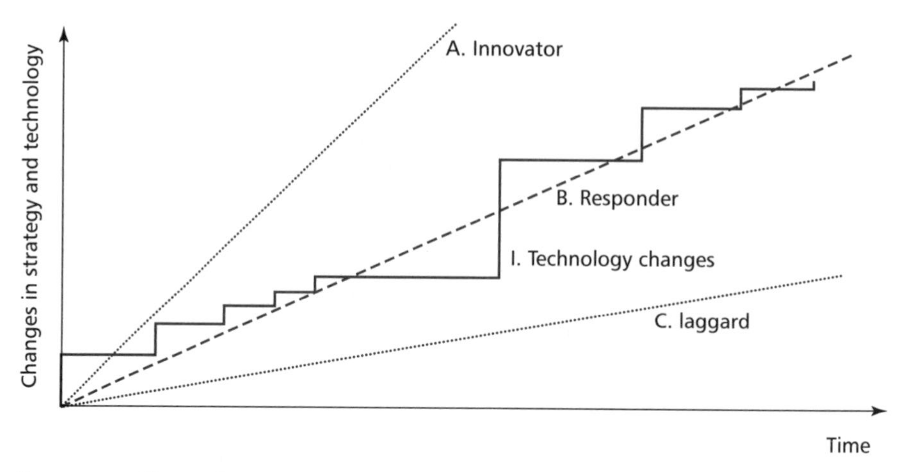

Figure 4.12 Alternative responses to changes in technology

techniques and technologies? There is no straightforward rule of thumb, other than that a balanced approach must be taken. It would be easy to dismiss many new techniques as fads, or classify them as 'not relevant to my market'. However, competitors will probably be reviewing new techniques and incorporating some, so a careful review of new techniques is required. This indicates that benchmarking of 'best of breed' sites within sectors and in different sectors is essential as part of environmental scanning. However, by waiting for others to innovate and review the results on their web site, a company may have already lost six to 12 months. *Figure 4.12* summarizes the choices. The stepped curve I shows the variations in technology through time. Some changes may be small incremental changes such as a new operating system, others such as the introduction of personalization technology are more significant in delivering value to customers and so improving business performance. Line A is a company that is using innovative business techniques, that adopts technology early, or is even in advance of what the technology can currently deliver. Curve C shows the conservative adopter whose use of technology lags behind the available potential. Curve B, the middle ground, is probably the ideal situation where a company monitors new ideas as early adopters trial them and then adopts those that will positively impact the business.

As a conclusion to this chapter we look in *case study 4.3* at the use of portable books as a new technology. How does a manager in the media industry respond to this?

CASE STUDY 4.3

Is there a future for print?

As computers become pervasive, newsprint looks ripe for replacement. But attempts to create electronic newspapers must overcome huge social and technical challenges before they ever replace newsprint versions on a large scale.

Based on crushed trees and recycled paper, printed papers can be costly to deliver, and information soon becomes dated. In contrast, screen-based bulletins can have an instant global reach, with low-cost delivery – and they can be personalized to give readers only the data they want.

However, these facilities certainly do not spell the

end of print media. Consider, for example, the role of respected business papers which aim not only to inform, but also to educate, entertain and often act as a 'paper of record'.

In an age of information overload, business readers, for example, often trust editors – with all the benefits of computer-assisted journalism – to select the reports that really matter, along with authoritative analysis, all packaged in a handy newsprint format.

In contrast, new media demand various types of costly devices for Internet connection. Online advertising revenues are still small, compared with print. Papers also have a longer 'shelf-life', especially when filed for handy reference – a useful point for readers and advertisers alike.

Assuming that screen-based readers have easy access to electronic filtering, then this can be helpful in finding highly focused information. Although online reports can be 'personalized', reading them can become a boring routine, with all the physical limitations of screen-size and battery-life for mobile devices.

In contrast, browsing a broad selection of newspaper headlines can, in just a few moments, attract the reader's attention to new and unexpected topics which can just as easily be put aside and read later. This is sometimes referred to as 'serendipity' – the ability to make 'happy chance finds'.

These discoveries – generally more easily made via a well-edited printed page – can entertain and inform readers, keeping them in touch with what is going on in their region and the wider world. New forms of digital printing, with personalization facilities and special editions for niche markets, are also on the horizon.

In comparing print and screen-based services, 'we are talking about two philosophically different media,' says Albert Scardino, the Pulitzer Prize-winning journalist. 'One is a mass-medium that exposes large numbers of people to the same information. The other is a customized medium that reflects the pluralistic nature of the Internet. The two cultures haven't melded yet.'

TheStreet.com, an electronic news service, tries to give prominent placement on its home page to unexpected features that go beyond 'hard news'. 'There is definitely a reader interest in the surprise element,' says Dave Kansas, its editor-in-chief and chief strategic officer. 'We find people are more receptive to this approach at the weekend and in non-market hours.

'Initially, they want customization, but they instinctively understand that that is not the whole picture. They need context and perspective, so we use weekend bulletins as a guide to that week's interesting information.'

Analysts at the Gartner Group have researched the newspaper and magazine reading habits of Internet users and found that only 11 per cent had decreased the time spent reading. However, the detailed findings suggest that this is because they have less time available – not that traditional print is being displaced.

'The real threat to newsprint will come when we get cheap, unmetered broadband access, so people will be able to spend more time on the Internet,' says Mike Welch, vice president for electronic business at Gartner Group. 'This facility will decrease the time available for other activities, including the reading of newspapers,' he suggests.

Mr Scardino points out that, with computers, productivity is highest in repetitive tasks, whereas searching for information on a news web site is always a bespoke task, so productivity can be extremely low.

From a technology viewpoint, 'it is pretty difficult to improve on paper,' explains Oscar Koenders, senior manager for product development at Toshiba Europe. 'It has an "endless battery life", a very high contrast ratio, plus it's very light in weight – and extremely cheap.' However, Toshiba is concerned about the amount of paper being used and, as well as reusable paper with removable ink, it is looking at replacement technology.

For electronic news delivery, a notebook computer is too heavy and a mobile phone is too small, as research shows that people want a minimum of 15-inch diagonal display.

Toshiba is researching flexible screens made from light-emitting polymer that can be rolled up. Instead of batteries, it will be powered by fuel cells that produce their own energy.

Xerox Corporation is working with 3M on a similar concept and IBM has produced two prototype devices it calls an 'electronic newspaper', which consist of up to eight double-sided screens, joined vertically, similar to a newspaper. The system allows each section of a 'newspaper' to be displayed at the same time.

With a normal screen, viewers are forced to read sequentially, one page after another, says Robert Steinbugler, manager of strategic design at IBM. 'When you talk to people about the pleasures they get out of a newspaper, the whole idea is to discover things you didn't know you wanted to know about.

▶

▶ CASE STUDY *continued*

'The new concept shows multiple pages with lots of articles that you can browse until something catches your eye. It is a random, enjoyable experience, which is what we tried to capture.'

The approach these companies are taking seems like trying to digitize 'legacy thinking', but their point is to try and repeat the convenience and serendipity of newsprint. It remains to be seen whether users will be prepared to pay enough for the device to make it economically feasible.

'These devices work well under artificial light, but if you take them outside they are difficult to read,' warns Ren Schuster, chief executive officer for consumer industrial markets at KPMG Management Consulting. 'Everybody wants the system to be as thin as a sheet of paper, but it could be as thick as a quarter of an inch, which is bulky and not very attractive.'

Until – and unless – electronic newspapers can learn to entertain and inform on the scale of the print media, the future may well be a hybrid approach, with an electronic news service with, for example, real-time share prices and statistics. It would be complemented by printed in-depth analysis.

Mr Kansas points out that if newspapers could survive the radio and television ages, the Internet age will not destroy them either. Today, the number of newspapers and magazines titles in circulation around the world is at record levels.

Source: Article by Rod Newing, *Financial Times*, Information Technology supplement, 7 June 2000.

Questions

1. Based on the article, list the reasons why it is unlikely newsprint will be replaced.
2. List the benefits of media accessed online.
3. Do you see a future for print? Remember that this article was published both online and in a traditional newspaper by a journalist who may have a vested interest!
4. You are publishing director for a traditional publisher. You already have a web site, but how do you respond to the advent of e-books?

Summary

1. Environmental scanning and analysis are necessary in order that a company can respond to environmental changes and acts on legal and ethical constraints on its activities.
2. Environmental constraints are related to the micro-environment variables reviewed in *Chapter 5* and the macro-environment variables in this chapter using the SLEPT mnemonic.
3. Social factors that must be understood include buyer behaviour characteristics such as access to the Internet and perceptions about it as a purchasing tool.
4. Ethical issues include the need to safeguard consumer privacy and security of details. Privacy issues include collection and dissemination of customer information, cookies and the use of direct e-mail.
5. Legal factors to be considered by e-commerce managers include: domain name registration, copyright and data protection.
6. Economic factors considered in the chapter are the regional differences in the use of the Internet for trade. Different economic conditions in different markets are considered in developing e-commerce budgets.
7. Political factors involve the role of governments in promoting e-commerce, but also trying to restrict it.
8. Rapid variation in technology requires constant monitoring of adoption of the technology by customers and competitors and appropriate responses.

ACTIVITY ANSWERS

4.1 Introduction to social, legal and ethical issues

The following answers are a small selection of what may be suggested. The following are covered in more detail later in the chapter:

- Cookies
- Are we limiting access to information from certain sections of society (social exclusion)?
- Privacy of personal information entered on a web site
- Sending unsolicited e-mail
- Replying promptly to e-mail
- Copyright
- Site content and promotional offers/adverts are in keeping with the different laws in different countries
- Providing text, graphics and personality in keeping with social mores of different countries

4.4 Adoption of the Internet according to demographic characteristics

- Gender – men may suggest this is due to higher levels of technophobia amongst women, women may suggest it is because men like gadgets and obsess about information such as football team history. Despite this, the male/female ratio is converging fast.
- Age – older age groups are under-represented on the Internet; this is likely to remain the case until the younger generation become old. There is the phenomenon of the 'silver surfer' that suggests the proposition of the web for those in the 55+ sector will become clearer and adoption will increase.
- Social group – ABC1 adoption is higher. This is likely to remain the case due to cost of purchase of PCs. Adoption amongst C2DEs will increase as lower-cost Internet access becomes available through more general access devices such as interactive TV and mobile phones.

4.7 Overcoming SME resistance to e-commerce

Table 4.3 Issues in SME resistance to exporting (barriers from Hamill and Gregory (1997) and Poon and Jevons (1997))

Barrier	*Management issues*	*How can barrier be overcome?*
1. Psychological	Will the investment be recouped? Do we have the human resources?	Success stories of companies who have become exporters can show the contribution to revenue possible and the expenditure necessary
2. Operational	Do we need to translate web content for language and cultural differences? How do we deal with country specific laws and taxation? How do we build e-services? How do we make transactions secure?	Highlight availability and cost of specialists for legal advice, export documentation and translation Publicity about the range of low-cost, off-the-shelf solutions for implementing e-commerce
3. Organizational	Do we have the right structure and responsibilities? Do we need to open new overseas sales offices?	Provide training on best practice for organizational structure and employee development
4. Product/market	Which market do we target? Do products or packaging require modification for overseas markets?	Benchmarking from other countries can help address these issues

EXERCISES

Self-assessment questions

1. Why is environmental scanning necessary?
2. Give an example how each of the macro-environment factors may directly drive the content and services provided by a web site.
3. Summarize the social factors that govern consumer access to the Internet. How can companies overcome these influences once people venture online?
4. What actions can e-commerce managers take to safeguard consumer privacy and security?
5. What are the general legal constraints that a company acts under in any country?
6. How do governments attempt to control the use of the Internet?
7. Summarize adoption patterns across the continents.
8. How should innovation be managed?

Essay and discussion questions

1. You recently started a job as e-commerce manager for a bank. Produce a checklist of all the different legal and ethical issues that you need to check for compliance on the existing web site of the bank.
2. How should the e-commerce manager monitor and respond to technological innovation?
3. Benchmark different approaches to achieving and reassuring customers about their privacy and security using three or four examples for a retail sector such as travel, books, toys or clothing.
4. 'Internet access levels will never exceed 50% in most countries.' Discuss.
5. Select a new Internet access technology (such as phone, kiosks or TV) that has been introduced in the last two years and assess whether it will become a significant method of access.

Examination questions

1. Explain the concept of a 'virtual community'. What are the benefits to the organization that hosts it?
2. Explain the different layers of governance of the Internet.
3. Summarize the macro-environment variables a company needs to monitor.
4. Explain the purpose of environmental scanning.
5. Give three examples of how web sites can use techniques to protect the user's privacy.
6. What are the three key factors which affect consumer adoption of the Internet?
7. Explain the significance of the diffusion-adoption concept to the adoption of new technologies to:
   (a) Consumers purchasing technological innovations.
   (b) Businesses deploying technological innovations.

8. What action should an e-commerce manager take to ensure compliance with ethical and legal standards of their site?

REFERENCES

ABC News (2000) *Ecommerce Causes Tax Shortfall in US*. News story on ABC.com, 27 July. http://abcnews.go.com/sections/business/DailyNews/internettaxes000725.html

Berthon, B., Pitt, L. and Watson, R. (1998) The World Wide Web as an industrial marketing communication tool: models for the identification and assessment of opportunities. *Journal of Marketing Management*, 14, 691–704.

Bettman, J. (1979) *An Information Processing Theory of Consumer Choice*. Addison Wesley, Reading, MA.

Bickerton, P., Bickerton, M. and Pardesi, U. (2000) *CyberMarketing*, 2nd edn. Butterworth Heinemann, Oxford. Chartered Institute of Marketing series.

Bourne, S. (1996) Business vs. the Internet culture. *InfoNation*, http://www.infonation.com/culture.html

Breitenbach, C. and van Doren, D. (1998) Value-added marketing in the digital domain: enhancing the utility of the Internet. *Journal of Consumer Marketing*, 15(6), 559–75.

Chaffey, D., Mayer, R., Johnston, K. and Ellis-Chadwick, F. (2000) *Internet Marketing: Strategy, Implementation and Practice*. Financial Times Prentice Hall, Harlow, UK.

Cyber Dialogue (2000) Privacy report 25 April, published online at: http://www.cyberdialogue.com/resource/press/releases/2000/04-19-cd-privacy.html

DTI (2000) *Business In The Information Age – International Benchmarking Study 2000*. UK Department of Trade and Industry. Based on 6000 phone interviews across businesses of all sizes in eight countries. Statistics update: available online at: www.ukonlineforbusiness.gov.uk.

Durlacher (1999a) UK online community. *Durlacher Quarterly Internet Report*. Q3 1999, pp. 7–11, London, UK.

Durlacher (1999b) UK residential analysis. *Durlacher Quarterly Internet Report*. Q4 1999, London, UK.

Dyson, E. (1998) *Release 2.1. A Design for Living in the Digital Age*. Penguin Books, London, UK.

Fisher, A. (2000) Gap widens between the 'haves' and 'have-nots'. *Financial Times*, 5 December.

Freedom House (2000) *Censoring dot-gov report*. 17 April. http://www.freedomhouse.org/news/pr041700.html New York, NY.

Grossnickle, J. and Raskin, O. (2001) *The Handbook of Online Marketing Research, Knowing Your Customer Using the Net*. McGrawHill, New York, NY.

Hagel, J. (1997) *Net Gain: Expanding Markets through Virtual Communities*. Harvard Business School Press, Boston, MA.

Hamill, J. and Gregory, K. (1997) Internet marketing in the internationalisation of UK SMEs. *Journal of Marketing Management*, 13, 9–28.

Lewis, H. and Lewis, R. (1997) Give your customers what they want. *Selling on the Net. Executive Book Summaries*, 19(3), March.

Mougayer, W. (1998) *Opening Digital Markets – Battle Plans and Strategies for Internet Commerce*, 2nd edn. CommerceNet Press, McGraw-Hill, NY.

NOP (2000) *NOP Internet User Profile Survey* (11 September 2000 for June–July). NOP, London. www.nopres.co.uk

ONS (2000) National Statistics Omnibus Survey – October 2000. http://www.statistics.gov.uk/press_release/Archive.asp

Pew (2000) Pew Internet and American Life Project. http://pewinternet.org/reports. Reported by Nua (www.nua.ie) 22 August.

Poon, S. and Jevons, C. (1997) Internet-enabled international marketing: a small business network perspective. *Journal of Marketing Management*, 13, 29–41.

Quelch, J. and Klein, L. (1996) The Internet and international marketing. *Sloan Management Review*, Spring, 61–75.

Rogers, E. (1983) *Diffusion of innovations*, 3rd edn. Free Press, New York.

Roussel, A. (2000) Leaders and laggards in B2C commerce. Gartner Group report, 4 August. SPA-11-5334 www.gartner.com

Trott, P. (1998) *Innovation Management and New Product Development*. Financial Times Prentice Hall, Harlow, UK.

Windham, L. (2001) *The Soul of the New Consumer. The Attitudes, Behaviours and Preferences of e-customers*. Allworth Press, New York, NY.

FURTHER READING

Chaffey, D., Mayer, R., Johnston, K. and Ellis-Chadwick, F. (2000) *Internet Marketing: Strategy, Implementation and Practice*. Financial Times Prentice Hall, Harlow, UK. Chapter 2 summarizes buyer behaviour, Chapters 10 and 15 consider ethical and legal issues involved with relationship marketing.

Dibb, S., Simkin, L., Pride, W. and Ferrell, O. (2000) *Marketing. Concepts and Strategies*. Houghton Mifflin, Boston, MA. 4th edn. In Chapter 2, the authors introduce the different elements of the marketplace from a marketing perspective.

Dyson, E. (1998) *Release 2.1. A Design for Living in the Digital Age*. Penguin Books, London, UK. Chapters 5 (Governance), 8, (Privacy), 9 (Anonymity) and 10 (Security) are of particular relevance.

Garfinkel, S. (2000) *Database Nation*. O'Reilly, UK. This book is subtitled 'the death of privacy in the 21st century' and this is the issue on which it focuses (includes Internet and non-Internet related privacy).

Slevin, J. (2000) *The Internet and Society*. Polity Press. A book about the Internet that combines social theory, communications analysis and case studies from both an academic and applied perspective.

WEB LINKS

Nua (www.nua.ie/surveys) and **Cyberatlas** (www.cyberatlas.com) have specific links on demographics, privacy and censorship that were used to source many of the examples from this chapter.

eMarketer web stats (www.emarketer.com/estats): similar to Cyberatlas survey.

http://www.nua.ie/surveys/how_many_online/index.html: update on number of users worldwide.

(www.oecd.org/eco/wp/onlinewp.htm#2000): OECD global development of e-commerce working papers. No. 252 is e-commerce paper.

Internet Indicators (www.internetindicators.com): produced by University of Texas e-commerce Centre, sponsored by Cisco.

FT Life on the Net (specials.ft.com/lifeonthenet.index.html): articles on a range of social issues from health to education.

The Industry Standard (www.thestandard.com/research/metrics): metrics section on usage of Internet.

Site reach figures – Media Metrix, Nielsen and Netvalue MR

European operation of **Media Metrix** at http://www.mmxieurope.com has figures from European panel of the reach of particular sites. As does **Nielsen** http://www.eratings.com and www.netvalue.com.

User characteristics

http://www.gvu.gatech.edu/user_surveys/: The 11th survey has not been scheduled, but previous surveys are of value.

E-mori (www.e-mori.co.uk): UK-specific profiles of web users.

NOP (www.nopres.co.uk): UK-specific surveys of web usage.

Privacy

IT Compliance – e-business best practice guidelines (www.itcompliance.com): the Code of Best Practice, published by The Stationery Office and developed by Compaq with legal approval by Baker & McKenzie, is offered free of charge.

Part 2

STRATEGY AND APPLICATIONS

In Part 2 of the book approaches to developing e-business strategy and applications are reviewed for the organization as a whole (Chapter 5), with an emphasis on buy-side e-commerce (Chapters 6 and 7) and sell-side e-commerce (Chapters 8 and 9).

Chapter 5
E-business strategy

- E-business strategy
- Strategic situation analysis
- Strategic objectives
- Strategy definition
- Strategy implementation

Focus on ...
- Information systems strategy and e-business strategy

Chapter 6
Supply chain management

- What is supply chain management?
- Options for restructuring the value chain
- Using information systems to restructure the supply chain
- Supply chain management

Focus on ...
- The value chain

Chapter 7
E-procurement

- What is e-procurement?
- Drivers of e-procurement
- Risks and impacts of e-procurement
- Implementing e-procurement
- Automated e-purchasing – the future of purchasing

Focus on ...
- Estimating e-procurement costs savings
- Electronic B2B marketplaces

Chapter 8
E-marketing

- What is e-marketing?
- E-marketing planning
- Situation analysis
- Strategic objectives
- Strategy
- Tactics
- Action and control

Focus on ...
- Characteristics of new media marketing communications
- Online branding

Chapter 9
Customer relationship management

- Customer acquisition management
- Customer retention management
- Excelling in e-commerce service quality
- Customer extension
- Technology solutions for CRM

Focus on ...
- Marketing communications for customer acquisition
- Online buyer behaviour
- Excelling in e-commerce service quality

Chapter 5

E-business strategy

CHAPTER AT A GLANCE

Main topics

Focus on ...

Case studies

LEARNING OBJECTIVES

After completing this chapter the reader should be able to:

- Follow an appropriate strategy process model for e-business
- Apply tools to generate and select e-business strategies
- Outline alternative strategic approaches to achieve e-business.

MANAGEMENT ISSUES

Consideration of e-business strategy raises these issues for management:

- How does e-business strategy differ from traditional business strategy?
- How should we integrate e-business strategy with existing business and IS strategy?
- How should we evaluate our investment priorities and returns from e-business?

Links to other chapters

The main related chapters to this chapter are summarized in *Figure 5.1*. They are:

- *Chapters 6 and 7* review the specific enactment of e-business strategy to supply chain and procurement management processes;
- *Chapters 8 and 9* explain how e-marketing and customer relationship management relate to the concept of e-business, and e-commerce and e-marketing planning are approached;
- *Chapters 10, 11 and 12* look at practical aspects of the implementation of e-business strategy.

Introduction

Developing an e-business strategy requires a fusion of existing approaches to business and information systems strategy development. In addition to elements of traditional strategy approaches, innovative techniques to achieve competitive advantage must also be incorporated. This innovative element of strategy is, perhaps, the most difficult to achieve since, at the time of writing, few businesses have completed the transformation to an e-business. We can learn, though, from early adopters of the e-business approach such as Cisco and IBM, and in Europe, Easyjet and British Telecom.

We start the chapter by considering which strategy process model to follow as a framework for developing e-business strategy. The chapter is structured around a four-stage strategy process model:

1. Strategic evaluation.
2. Strategic objectives.
3. Strategy definition.
4. Strategy implementation.

For each of these components of strategy, management actions are reviewed with the emphasis on development of e-business strategy.

E-business strategy

Strategy
Definition of the future direction and actions of a company defined as approaches to achieve specific objectives.

Strategy defines the future direction and actions of an organization or part of an organization. Johnson and Scholes (1999) define corporate strategy as:

> *the direction and scope of an organization over the long-term: which achieves advantage for the organization through its configuration of resources within a changing environment to meet the needs of markets and to fulfil stakeholder expectations.*

Lynch (2000) describes strategy as an organization's sense of purpose. However, he notes that purpose alone is not strategy; plans or actions are also needed.

Here we are considering e-business strategy rather than corporate strategy, so an immediate issue is clarification of the relationship between e-business strategy with corporate strategy and other strategies such as marketing strategy or information systems strategy. How do these different types of strategy relate?

Johnson and Scholes (1999) note that there are different levels of strategy within all organizations. They identify *corporate strategy* which is concerned with the overall purpose and scope of the organization; *business unit strategy* which defines how to compete successfully in a particular market and *operational strategies* that are concerned with achieving corporate and business unit strategies. Additionally there are what can be described as *functional strategies* that describe how the corporate and business unit strategies will be operationalized in different functional areas or business processes. Functional or process strategies refer to marketing, supply chain management, human resources, finance and information systems strategies.

E-business strategy should support corporate strategy objectives and it should also support functional marketing and supply chain management strategies. *Figure 5.1* shows one interpretation of the relationship between e-business and other strategies. These are the main strategies reviewed in Part 2 of this book. Other strategies such as human resources are not shown although this is an important issue in *change management* (*Chapter 10, p. 381*). The relationships between strategies are shown as double-ended arrows since different strategies will *inform or impact* each other – they should be tightly integrated. For example, e-business strategy will be based on corporate objectives such as which markets to target and targets for revenue generation from electronic channels. However these corporate objectives will be based on opportunities and threats identified from environment analysis and objectives defined in the e-business strategy. So it can be said that e-business strategy does not only support corporate strategy, but should also influence or impact it. There are many alternative forms of *Figure 5.1* which are appropriate for different organizations according to a management team's perception of

E-business strategy
Definition of the approach by which applications of internal and external electronic communications can support and influence corporate strategy.

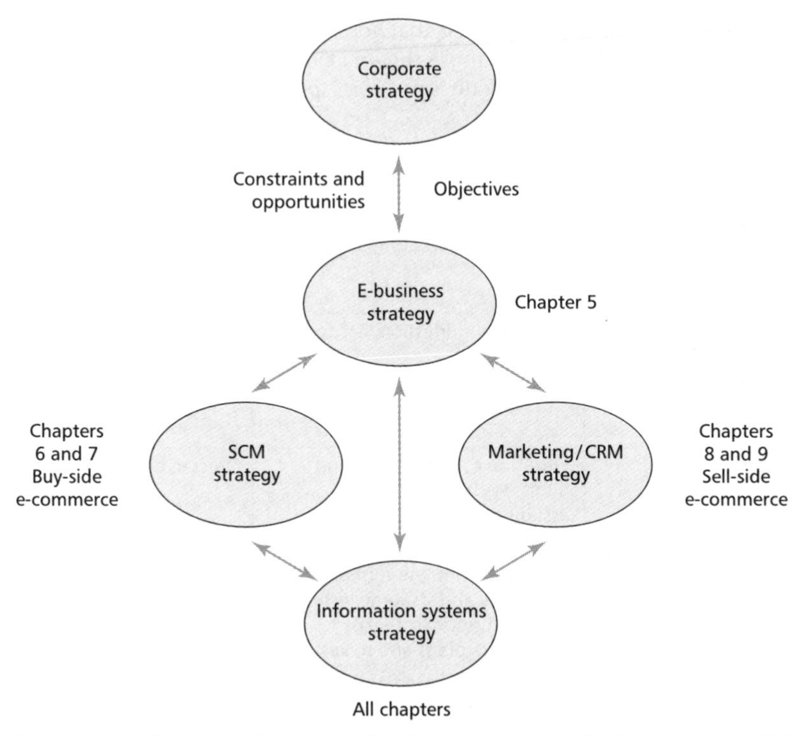

Figure 5.1 Relationship between e-business strategy and other strategies (SCM = supply chain management, CRM = customer relationship management)

e-business. For a company that achieves most of its business in the physical world the marketing and SCM strategies will be more important than e-business strategy. For a services company such as a software publisher or a media owner where the nature of the product lends itself to using electronic communications to streamline the *value chain* (*Chapter 6, p. 228*), *Figure 5.1* will be appropriate.

Strategy process models for e-business

Strategy process model
A framework for approaching strategy development.

Before developing any type of strategy, a management team needs to agree the process they will follow for generating and then implementing the strategy. A **strategy process model** provides a framework that gives a logical sequence to follow to ensure inclusion of all key activities of e-business strategy development. It also ensures that e-business strategy can be evolved as part of a process of continuous improvement.

Before the advent of e-business, many strategy process models had been developed for each of the strategies described above. To what extent can management teams apply these models to e-business strategy development? Although strategy process models differ in the emphasis and terminology, they all have common elements. Complete *activity 5.1* to discuss what these common elements are.

Activity 5.1 Selecting an e-business strategy process model

Purpose

To identify the applicability of existing strategy process models to e-business.

Activity

Review three or four strategy process models that you have encountered in other modules. These could be models such as those shown in *Table 5.1*. Note that columns in this table are independent – each row does not correspond across models.

Table 5.1 Alternative strategy process models

Lynch (2000) Sequential corporate strategy model	*Johnson and Scholes (1999)* Parallel corporate strategy model	*McDonald (1999)* Sequential marketing strategy model	*Smith (1999) SOSTAC™* Sequential marketing strategy model *See Chapter 8*
Environment analysis (e.g. marketplace, customers, competitors) Resource analysis (e.g. human, financial and operational)	Strategic analysis (environment, resources, expectations, objectives and culture)	Goal setting (mission, corporate objectives)	Situation analysis
Vision, mission and objectives	Strategic choice (generation of options, evaluation of options, selection of strategy)	Situation review (marketing audit, SWOT analysis, assumptions)	Objective setting
Strategy development	Strategic implementation (resource planning, people and systems, organization structure)	Strategy formulation (marketing objectives and strategy, estimate expected results, identify alternative plans and mixes)	Strategy
Strategy implementation		Resource allocation and monitoring (budget, first-year implementation plan)	Tactics Actions Control

Questions

1. What are the strengths and weaknesses of each model?
2. What common features do the models share? List the key elements of an appropriate strategy process model.

For answer see p. 209

Through considering alternative strategy process models such as those of *Table 5.1*, common elements are apparent:

1. Internal and external environment scanning or analysis are needed. Scanning occurs both during strategy development and as a continuous process in order to respond to competitors.
2. Clear statement of vision and objectives required. Clarity is required to communicate the strategic intention both to employees and the marketplace. Objectives are also vital to act as a check as to whether the strategy is successful!
3. Strategy development can be broken down into strategy option generation, evaluation and selection. An effective strategy will usually be based on reviewing a range of alternatives and selecting the best on its merits.
4. After strategy development, enactment of the strategy occurs as strategy implementation
5. Control is required to monitor operational and strategy effectiveness problems and adjust the operations or strategy accordingly.

Additionally, the models suggest that these elements, although generally sequential, are also iterative and require reference back to previous stages. In reality there is overlap between these stages.

To what extent, then, can this traditional strategy approach be applied to e-business? We will now review some suggestions for how e-business strategy should be approached.

Hackbarth and Kettinger (2000) suggest a four stage 'strategic e-breakout' model with stages of:

1. Initiation
2. Diagnosis of the industry environment
3. Breakout to establish a strategic target
4. Transition or plotting a migration path

This model emphasizes the need to innovate away from traditional strategic approaches by using the term 'breakout' to show the need for new *marketplace structures* (*Chapter 2, p. 37*) and *business/revenue models* (*Chapter 2, p. 49*). A weakness of this approach is that it does not emphasize objective setting and control. However, Hackbarth and Kettinger's paper is valuable in detailing specific e-business strategy development activities. For example, the authors suggest that company analysis and diagnosis should review the firm's capabilities with respect to the customers, suppliers, business partnerships and technologies.

The UK Institute of Directors (2000) suggest the following differences between traditional business strategy and e-business strategy.

1. *Planning horizon*. Traditional business strategy is based on predictability, assuming it is possible to forecast the future and to then develop business plans in one-, three-, five- or ten-year spans while e-business strategy focuses on adaptability and responsiveness with implementation time of three months or less and limited predictability.
2. *Planning cycles*. From one-time development effort to iterative strategic development since competitive advantage is very fleeting and the pace of technological change is rapid.
3. *Power base*. From positional power or strength in the marketplace to informational power where success is based on access, control and manipulation of critical information.
4. *Core focus*. From factory and production goods to customer focus.

Chaston (2000) presents a marketing-oriented approach to 'selecting e-strategies and constructing an e-plan'. This approach can, however, be applied to e-business since it relates to electronic commerce resources, market position and financial performance. His ten step e-marketing plan is:

1. A situation review
2. A SWOT analysis
3. A summary of key issues
4. A statement of future objectives
5. A strategy to achieve future objectives
6. A marketing mix for delivering strategy
7. An action plan
8. Financial forecasts
9. Control systems
10. Contingency plans

Deise *et al.* (2000) present a novel approach to developing e-business strategy. Their approach is based on work conducted for clients of management consultants PricewaterhouseCoopers. They suggest that the focus of e-business strategy will vary according to the evolutionary stage of e-business. Initially the focus will involve the enhancement of the selling channels (sell-side e-commerce); this then tends to be followed by value-chain integration (buy-side e-commerce), and creation of a value network. We will return to this issue of emphasis in the section on strategy definition (p. 188).

Venkatraman (2000) suggests a five-stage strategy process for what he describes as a 'dot-com strategy', for existing businesses looking to make use of new digital media. The five stages are presented as five questions for a management team:

1. *What is your strategic vision*? This concludes consideration of business models and how to achieve differentiation.
2. *How do you govern dot-com operations*? Governance is divided into operational decisions (production, sourcing, logistics, marketing and human resources) and the trade-off with financial decisions (investment logic, funding sources and performance criteria, i.e. objectives).
3. *How do you allocate key resources for the dot-com operations*? To operationalize the e-business, which techniques are used for resourcing: commit internal resources, form strategic alliances or outsource?

4. *What is your operating infrastructure for the dot-com operations?* Venkatraman emphasizes the importance of the infrastructure in adding value to the customer through functionality, personalization and ensuring privacy.
5. *Is your management team aligned for the dot-com agenda?* This considers the responsibilities and structures used for executing the other aspects of the strategy such as vision, resourcing and infrastructure.

It could be argued that questions 2 to 5 are more about strategy implementation than definition. The importance of resourcing and structuring for the move to e-business is a characteristic of e-business strategy. Venkatraman (2000) also highlights the need to continuously scan the environment and so revise the strategy; he says

> *We need to abandon calendar-driven models of strategy perfected under the predictable conditions of the Industrial Age. We should embrace the philosophy of experimentation since the shape of future business models is not obvious.*

The speed at which change may occur in e-business is indicated by the speed at which new access technologies are adopted. *Figure 5.2* shows how for the UK, the time which it takes for new technologies to reach a million adopters is rapidly declining. Retailers who cannot adapt to make use of the new technologies described in the *Focus on new access devices* section (*Chapter 3, p. 106*) will lose market share to more nimble competitors and may never recover.

Plant (2000), following examination of 40 US and European organizations, suggests that the e-commerce strategy (buy-side and sell-side) should devise approaches for seven dimensions made up of four positional factors (technology, service, market, brand) and three bonding (internal) factors (leadership, infrastructure, organizational learning).

Bringing together the ideas of these pioneering authors on e-business we can note that it does appear that existing strategy elements such as environment analysis,

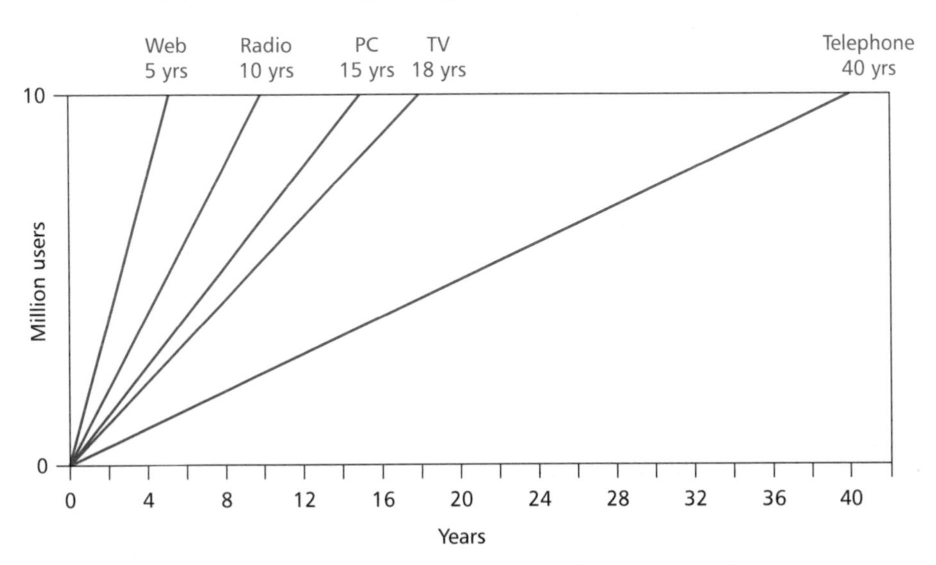

Figure 5.2 Time taken for different technologies to reach one million adopters in the UK.
Source: Online Research Agency

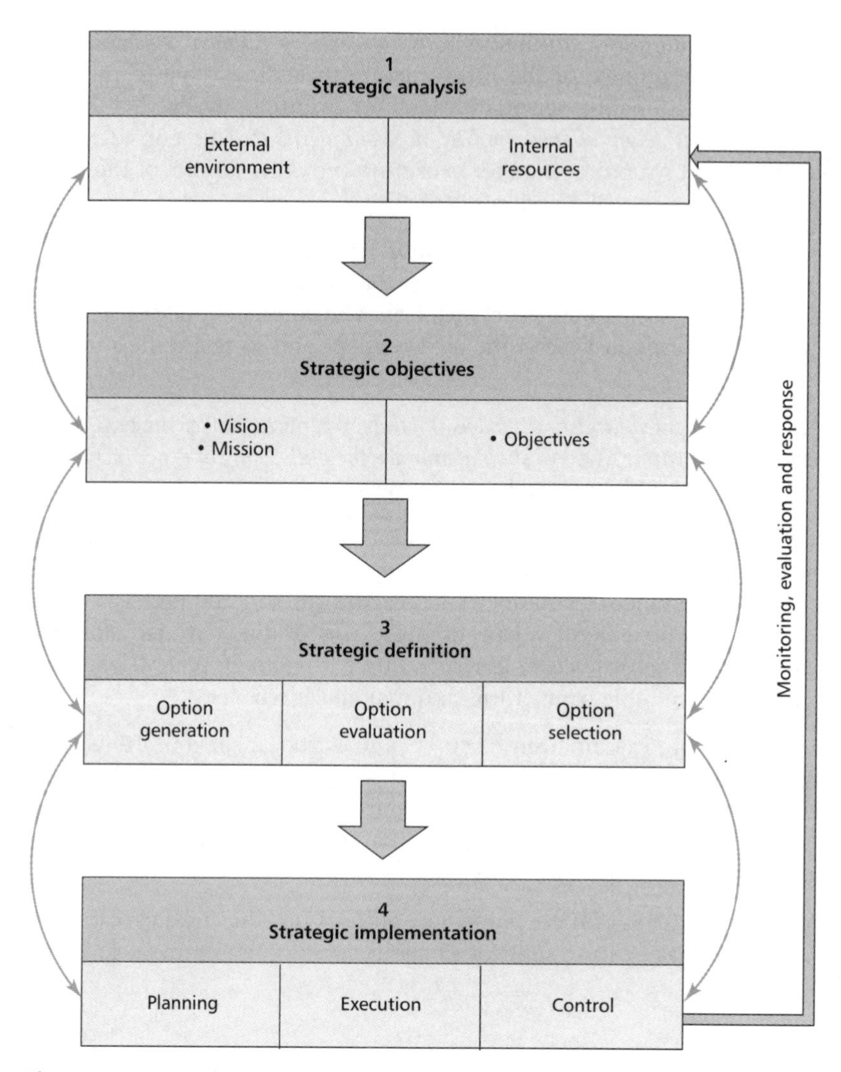

Figure 5.3 A generic strategy process model

objective setting and strategy definition are naturally still required. However there is greater emphasis on restructuring and resourcing through using new technology to build an infrastructure and supporting knowledge management (*Chapter 10, p. 403*) to achieve quality customer service. Based on existing models and a review of newer models, this chapter is structured according to a generic four-stage strategy process model depicted in *Figure 5.3*.

Prescriptive strategy
The three core areas of strategic analysis, strategic development and strategy implementation are linked together sequentially.

Note the use of two-way arrows in Figure 5.3 to indicate that each stage is not discrete, but rather it involves referring backwards or forwards to other strategy elements. Each strategy element will have several iterations. The arrows in Figure 5.3 highlight an important distinction in the way in which strategy process models are applied. Referring to the work of Mintzberg and Quinn (1991), Lynch (2000) distinguishes between prescriptive and emergent strategy approaches. In the **prescriptive strategy** approach he identifies three elements of strategy – strategic analy-

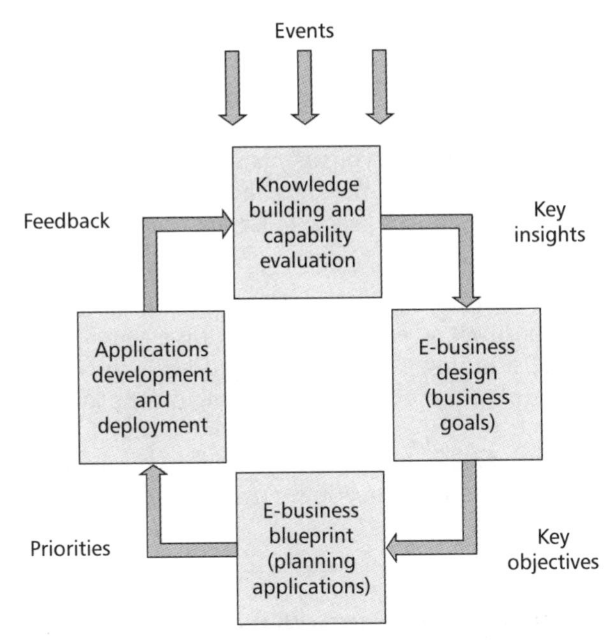

Figure 5.4 Dynamic e-business strategy model

Source: Adapted from description in Kalakota and Robinson (2000)

sis, strategic development and strategy implementation, and these are linked together sequentially. Strategic analysis is used to develop a strategy, and it is then implemented. In other words, the strategy is prescribed in advance. Alternatively, the distinction between the three elements of strategy may be less clear. This is the **emergent strategy** approach where strategic analysis, strategic development and strategy implementation are interrelated. Lynch (2000) does point out, however, that strategic analysis can be regarded as distinctive and usually occurs before strategy development and implementation. Johnson and Scholes (1999) seek to highlight the emergent strategy approach. It can be suggested that the emergent strategy approach is an essential part of any e-business strategy to enable response in a highly dynamic environment.

Emergent strategy
Strategic analysis, strategic development and strategy implementation are interrelated and are developed together.

Kalakota and Robinson (2000) recommend a dynamic, emergent strategy process specific to e-business. The elements of this strategy approach are shown in *Figure 5.4*. It essentially shares similar features to *Figure 5.3*, but with an emphasis on responsiveness with continuous review and prioritization of investment in new applications.

We will now examine each of the main strategy elements of *Figure 5.3* in more detail.

Strategic analysis

Strategic analysis
Collection and review of information about an organization's internal processes and resources and external marketplace factors in order to inform strategy definition.

Strategic analysis or situation analysis involves review of

- the internal resources and processes of the company and a review of its activity in the marketplace;
- the immediate competitive environment (micro-environment) including cus-

tomer demand and behaviour, competitor activity, marketplace structure and relationships with suppliers and partners.
- the wider environment (macro-environment) in which a company operates; this includes economic development and regulation by governments in the forms of law and taxes together with social and ethical constraints such as the demand for privacy. These macro-environment factors, including the social, legal, economic and political factors, were reviewed in *Chapter 4* and are not considered further in this chapter.

The elements of situation analysis for the e-business are summarized in *Figure 5.5*. For the effective, responsive e-business, as explained earlier, it is essential that situation analysis or environmental scanning is a continuous process with clearly identified responsibilities for performing the scanning and acting on the knowledge acquired.

In this chapter we start with the internal perspective of how a company currently uses technology and then we then review the competitive environment.

Resource and process analysis

Resource analysis
Review of the technological, financial and human resources of an organization and how they are utilized in business processes.

Resource analysis for e-business is primarily concerned with the degree to which a company has in place the appropriate *technological and applications infrastructure* (*Chapter 3, p. 88*) and financial and human resources to support it. These resources must be harnessed to together give efficient *business processes* (*Chapter 11, p. 422*). We start by looking at current resources for e-business by looking at the stage of e-business development.

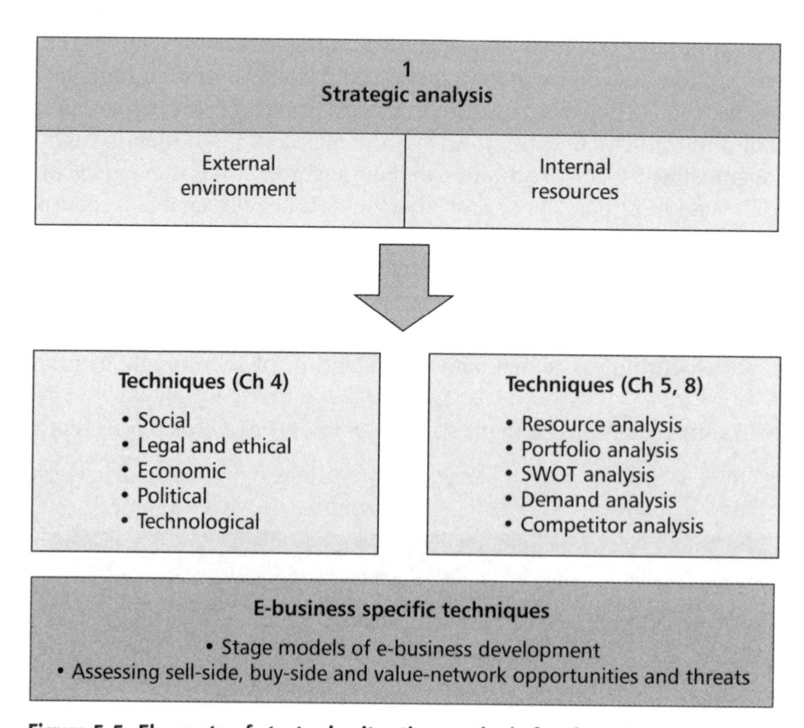

Figure 5.5 Elements of strategic situation analysis for the e-business

Stage models of e-business development

Stage models are helpful in reviewing how advanced a company is in its use of information and communications technology (ICT) to support its processes. Stage models have traditionally been popular in the analysis of the current application of business information systems (BIS) within an organization. For example, the six-stage model of Nolan (1979) refers to the development of use of information systems within an organization from initiation with simple data processing through to a mature adoption of BIS with controlled, integrated systems.

When assessing the current use of ICT within a company it is instructive to analyse the extent to which an organization has implemented the technological infrastructure and support structure to achieve e-business. In an early model focusing on sell-side web site development, Quelch and Klein (1996) developed a five-stage model referring to the development of sell-side e-commerce. For existing companies the stages are:

1. Image and product information
2. Information collection
3. Customer support and service
4. Internal support and service
5. Transactions.

Considering sell-side e-commerce, Chaffey *et al.* (2000) suggest there are six choices for a company deciding on which *marketing services* to offer via an online presence:

- *Level 0. No web site or presence on web.*
- *Level 1. Basic web presence.* Company places an entry in a web site listing company names such as www.yell.co.uk to make people searching the web aware of the existence of a company or its products. There is no web site at this stage.
- *Level 2. Simple static informational web site.* Contains basic company and product information sometimes referred to as brochureware.
- *Level 3. Simple interactive site.* Users are able to search the site and make queries to retrieve information such as product availability and pricing. Queries by e-mail may also be supported.
- *Level 4. Interactive site supporting transactions with users.* The functions offered will vary according to company. They will be usually limited to online buying. Other functions might include an interactive customer service helpdesk which is linked into direct marketing objectives.
- *Level 5. Fully interactive site supporting the whole buying process.* Provides relationship marketing with individual customers and facilitating the full range of marketing exchanges.

Similar stage models have been developed for e-business by Hackbarth and Kettinger (2000) and Willcocks and Sauer (2000). In these, the sell-side e-commerce perspective of Quelch and Klein (1996) occupies the early stages, but with greater organizational transformation and involvement of the upstream supply chain at later stages. Considering buy-side e-commerce, the corresponding levels of *product sourcing applications* can be identified:

- *Level I.* No use of the web for product sourcing and no electronic integration with suppliers.
- *Level II.* Review and selection from competing suppliers using intermediary web

sites, B2B exchanges and supplier web sites. Orders placed by conventional means.

- *Level III*. Orders placed electronically through EDI, via intermediary sites, exchanges or supplier sites. No integration between organization's systems and supplier's systems. Rekeying of orders necessary into procurement or accounting systems.
- *Level IV*. Orders placed electronically with integration of company's procurement systems.
- *Level V*. Orders placed electronically with full integration of company's procurement, manufacturing requirements planning and stock control systems.

A staged model which focuses on these buy-side applications of e-commerce based on the results of an international benchmarking study (DTI, 2000) is shown in *Figure 5.6*. They liken the process of adoption as similar to moving up the steps of a ladder. Companies start off using e-mail to communicate internally and with suppliers (step 1) before moving to offering product information and availability checking (step 2); online ordering (step 3); online payment (step 4); online progress tracking (step 5) and finally, when the e-business is achieved, all stages are integrated (step 6).

Note that typical stage models of web site development such as those described above are most appropriate to companies whose products can be sold online through transactional e-commerce. In fact stage models could be developed for a range of different types of online presence and business models (*Chapter 2, p. 49*) each with different objectives. Four of the major different types of online presence are:

1. *Transactional e-commerce site*. Stage models as described above. Examples: a car manufacturer such as Vauxhall (www.buypower.vauxhall.co.uk) or retailers such as Tesco (www.tesco.com).

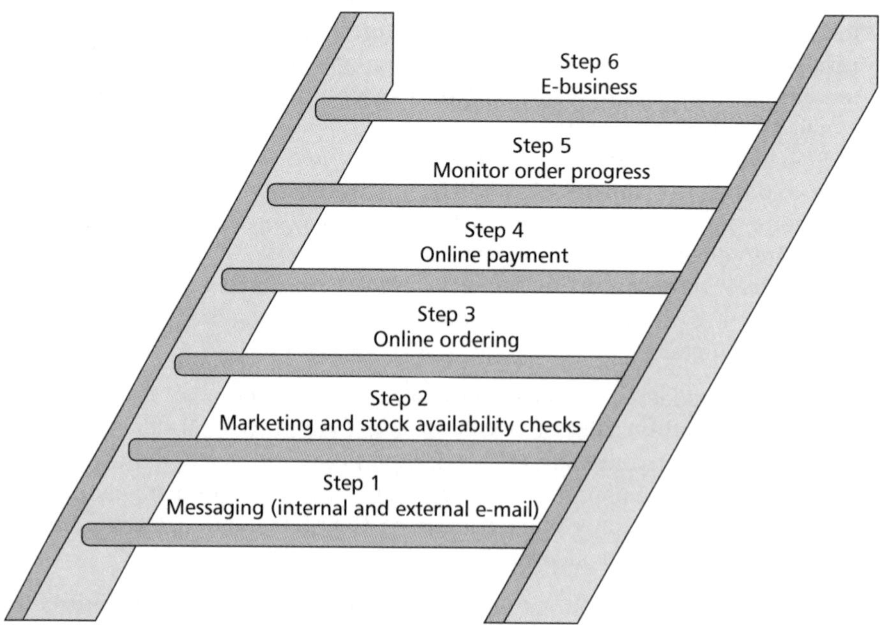

Figure 5.6 Adoption steps of e-business services
Source: DTI (2000)

2. *Services-oriented relationship building web site*. For companies such as professional services companies, online transactions are inappropriate. Through time these sites will develop increasing information depth and question and answer facilities. Examples: PricewaterhouseCooper (www.pwcglobal.com), Accenture (www.accenture.com) and Arthur Andersen KnowledgeSpace (www.knowledge space.com).
3. *Brand building site*. These are intended to support the offline brand by developing an online experience of the brand. They are typical for low-value, high volume Fast Moving Consumer Goods (FMCG brands). Examples: Tango (www.tango.com), Guinness (www.guinness.com).
4. *Portal site*. Information delivery as described in *Chapter 2*. Examples: Yahoo! (www.yahoo.com) and Vertical Net (www.verticalnet.com).

As a summary to this section *Table 5.2* presents a synthesis of stage models for e-business development. Organizations can assess their position on the continuum between stage 1 to 4 for the different aspects of e-business development shown in the column on the left.

Table 5.2 A stage model for e-business development

	1. Web presence	*2. E-commerce*	*3. Integrated e-commerce*	*4. E-business*
Services available	Brochureware or interaction with product catalogues and customer service	Transactional e-commerce on buy-side or sell-side	Buy- and sell-side integrated with ERP or legacy systems Personalization of services	Full integration between all internal organizational processes and elements of the value network
Organizational scope	Isolated departments, e.g.marketing department	Cross-organizational	Cross-organizational	Across the enterprise and beyond (extraprise)
Transformation	Technological infrastructure	Technology and new responsibilities identifiedfor e-commerce	Internal business processes and company structure	Change to e-business culture, linking of business processes with partners
Strategy	Limited	Sell-side e-commerce strategy, not well integrated with business strategy	E-commerce strategy integrated with business strategy using a value-chain approach	E-business strategy incorporated as part of business strategy

When companies devise the strategies and tactics to achieve their objectives they may return to the stage models to specify which level of innovation they are looking to achieve in the future.

Applications portfolio analysis

Analysis of the current portfolio of business applications within a business is used to assess current information systems capability and also to inform future strategies. A widely applied framework is that of McFarlan and McKenney (1993) with the modifications of Ward and Griffiths (1996). *Figure 5.7* illustrates the results of a portfolio analysis for The B2B Company applied within an e-business context. It can be seen that current applications such as human resources, financial management and production line management systems will continue to support the

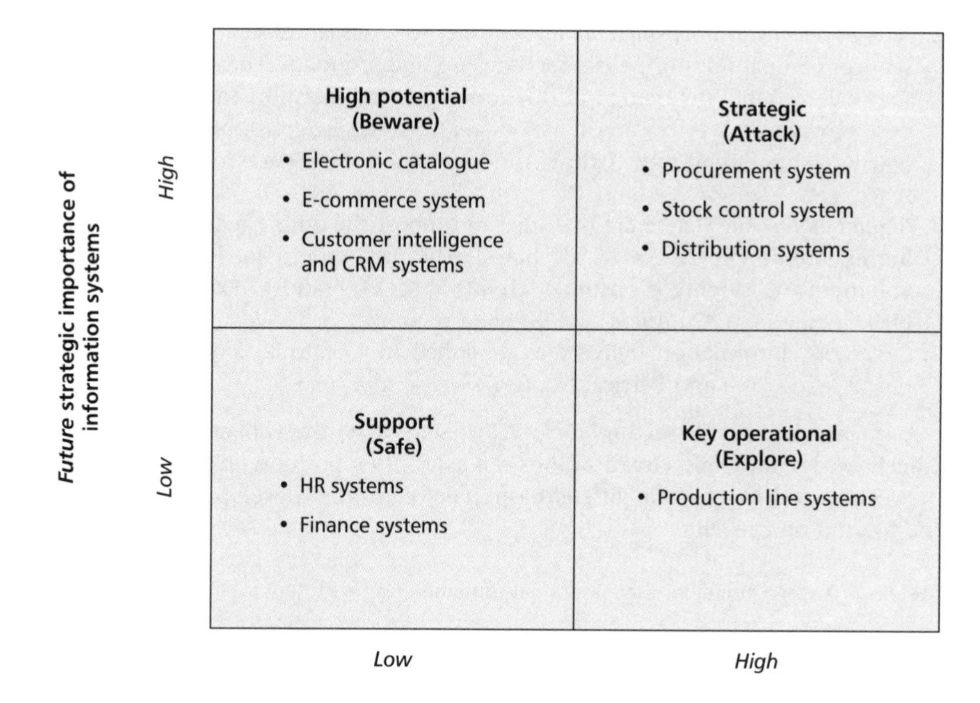

Figure 5.7 Summary applications portfolio analysis for The B2B Company

operations of the business and will not be a priority for future investment. In contrast, to achieve competitive advantage, applications for maintaining a dynamic customer catalogue online, online sales and collecting marketing intelligence about customer buying behaviour will become more important. Applications such as procurement and logistics will continue to be of importance in an e-business context. Of course the analysis will differ greatly according to the type of company; for a professional services company or a software company, its staff will be an important resource hence systems that facilitate the acquisition and retention of quality staff will be strategic applications.

A weakness of the portfolio analysis approach is that today applications are delivered by a single e-business software or *enterprise resource planning* (*Chapter 3, p. 99*) application. Given this, it is perhaps more appropriate to define the *services* that will be delivered to external and internal customers through deploying information systems.

In addition to portfolio analysis, organizations should also review the capability of their *technology infrastructure* (*Chapter 3, p. 88*) such as hardware and networking facilities to deliver these applications.

Organizational and IS SWOT analysis

SWOT analysis
Strengths, weaknesses, opportunities and threats.

SWOT analysis is a relatively simple yet powerful tool that can help organizations analyse their internal resources in terms of strengths and weaknesses and match them against the external environment in terms of opportunities and threats. In

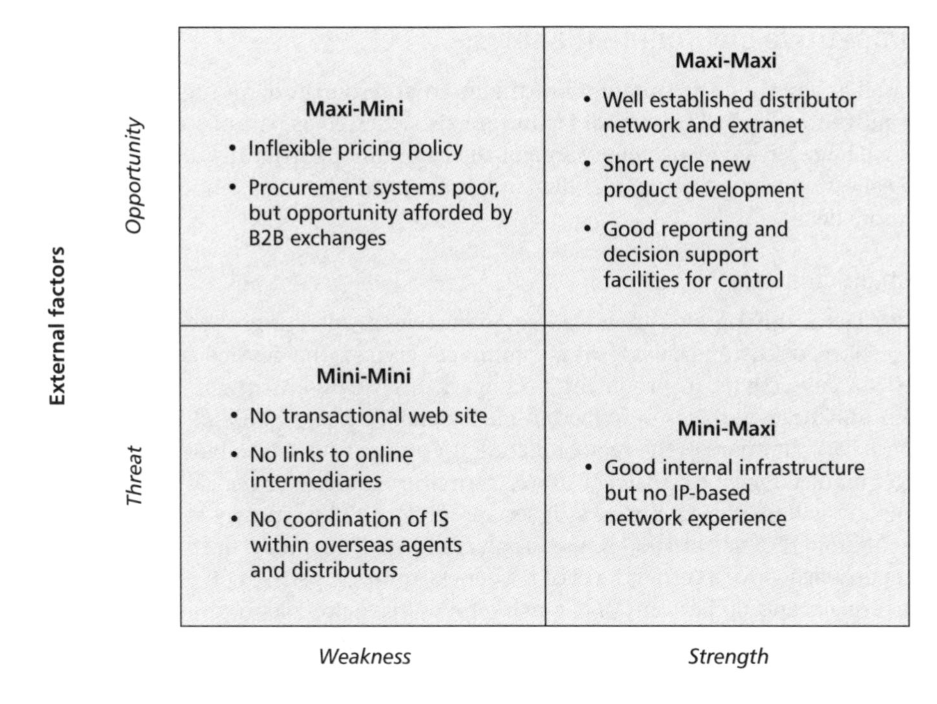

Figure 5.8 SWOT analysis for The B2B Company

an e-business context, SWOT analysis can combine corporate, marketing, supply chain and information systems issues, or a separate SWOT can be performed for each. SWOT analysis is of greatest value when it is used not only to analyse the current situation, but also as a tool to formulate strategies. To achieve this it is useful once the strengths, weaknesses, opportunities and threats have been listed to combine them as shown in *Figure 5.8*, which shows an example SWOT analysis for The B2B Company. The approaches such as mini-maxi are read in order of approach to external factors and then approach to internal factors. So mini-maxi means minimize external factors, maximize internal factors. It can be suggested that the mini-mini and mini-maxi sectors should be paid greatest attention since these are the key deficiencies of the company.

Human and financial resources

Resource analysis will also consider these two factors:

1. *Human resources*. To take advantage of the opportunities identified in strategic analysis the right resources must be available to deliver e-business solutions. The importance of having a human resources approach that enables the recruitment and retention of staff is examined in *Chapter 10, Change management*. The need for new structures and cultures to achieve e-business is also covered.
2. *Financial resources*. Assessing financial resources for information systems is usually conducted as part of investment appraisal (*p. 206*) and budgeting for enhancements to new systems.

Competitive environment analysis

As well as assessing the suitability of the internal resources of an organization for the move to e-business, external factors are also assessed as part of strategic analysis. We have already considered some of the external opportunities and threats for a business, but here we consider demand analysis and look at competitive threats in more detail.

Demand analysis

Demand analysis for e-business
Assessment of the demand for e-commerce services amongst existing and potential customer segments.

A key factor driving e-business strategy objectives is the current level and future projections of customer usage of e-commerce services, the **demand analysis**. Since this is a key activity in producing an e-marketing plan which will feed into the e-business strategy this is described in more detail in *Chapter 8 (p. 290)*.

Figure 5.9 summarizes the type of picture the strategist needs to build up for each target market. *Figure 8.4* (p. 292) shows a specific example for the car market. Any company will operate in a market it serves: for The B2B Company there may be a potential market size of 1000 B2B customers in a given country. In this market the company may have a certain level of awareness amongst perhaps 80 per cent of the marketplace and 60 per cent of the market may have purchased products at some point and current market share (by customers) may be 30 per cent. This demand for products then needs to be considered relative to the number of companies who have Internet access and are actively using the web site of the company. Access to the web may be high at a company level, but will be lower for individuals who are involved with making the buying decision. As mentioned in *Chapter 4*, to collect useful research we need to know levels of access amongst the different members of the buying unit such as users, influencers, approvers and buyers.

For buy-side e-commerce a company also needs to consider the e-commerce services its suppliers offer: how many offer services for e-commerce and where they

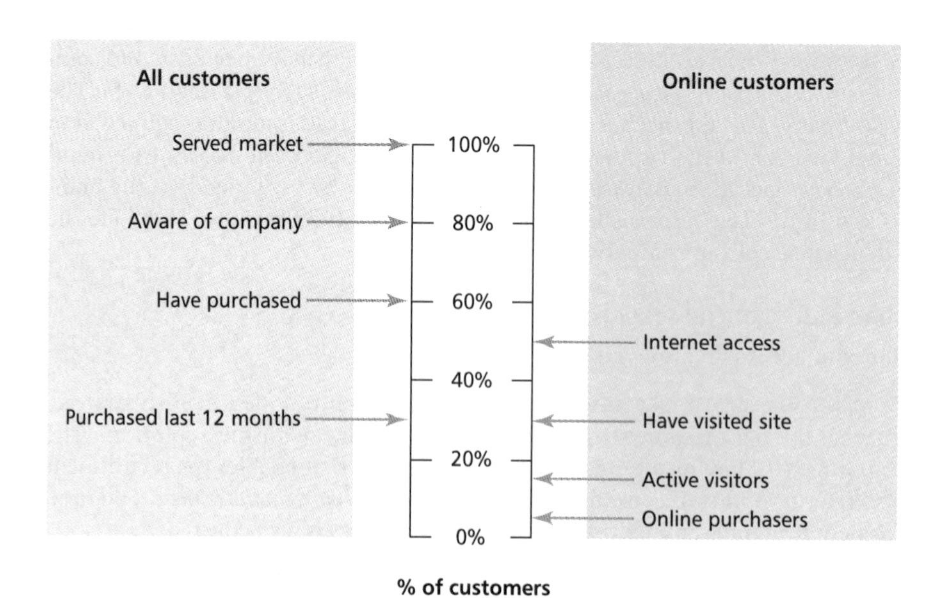

Figure 5.9 Customer demand for e-marketing services for The B2B Company

are located (e.g. direct with suppliers, in customer solutions or marketplaces (*Chapter 7, p. 272*).

Assessing competitive threats

Michael Porter's classic 1980 model of the five main competitive forces that impact a company still provides a valid framework for reviewing threats arising in the e-business era. *Figure 5.10* shows the main threats updated to place emphasis on the competitive threats to the e-business. Threats have been grouped into buy-side (upstream supply chain), sell-side (downstream supply chain) and competitive threats. The main differences from the five forces model of Porter (1980) are the distinction between competitive threats from intermediaries (or partners) on the buy-side and sell-side. We will now review these e-business threats in more detail.

Competitive threats

1. Threat of new e-commerce entrants

For traditional 'bricks and mortar' companies (*Chapter 2, p. 54*) this has been a common threat for retailers selling products such as books and financial services. For example, in Europe, traditional banks have been threatened by the entry of completely new start-up competitors such as First-e (www.first-e.com) or traditional companies from a different geographic market who use the Internet to facilitate their entry into an overseas market. Citibank (www.citibank.com) have used this approach. These new entrants have been able to succeed in a short time since they do not have the cost of developing and maintaining a distribution network to sell their products and these products do not require a manufacturing base. In other words, the *barriers to entry* are low. However to succeed, new entrants need to be market leaders in executing marketing and customer service. The costs of achieving these will be high. These could perhaps be described as *barriers to success* rather than barriers to entry. This competitive threat is less common in vertical business-to-business markets involving manufacture and process industries such as the chemical or oil industry since the investment barriers to entry are much higher.

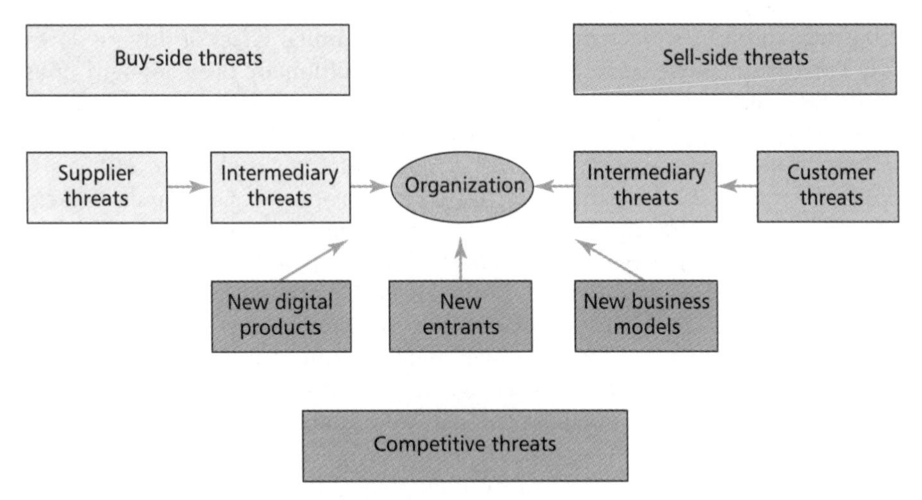

Figure 5.10 Competitive threats acting on the e-business

2. Threat of new digital products

This threat can occur from established or new companies. The Internet is particularly good as a means of providing information-based services at a lower cost. The greatest threats are likely to occur where product fulfilment can occur over the Internet as is the case with delivering share prices, industry-specific news or software. This may not affect many business sectors, but is vital in some such as newspaper, magazine and book publishing, music and software distribution. In photography, Kodak have responded to a major threat of reduced demand for traditional film by increasing its range of digital cameras to enhance this revenue stream and by providing online services for customers to print and share digital photographs. The extent of this threat can be gauged by review of product in the context of *Figure 5.10*.

3. Threat of new business models

This threat can also occur from established or new companies. This threat is related to competitive threat 2 in that it concerns new methods of service delivery. The threats from existing competitors will continue, with the Internet perhaps increasing rivalry since price comparison is more readily possible and the rival e-businesses can innovate and undertake new product development and introduce alternative business and revenue models with shorter cycle times than previously. This again emphasizes the need for continual environment scanning. See the section on business and revenue models, p. 191 for examples of strategies that can be adopted in response to this threat.

Sell-side threats

1. Customer power and knowledge

This is perhaps the single biggest threat posed by electronic trading. The bargaining power of customers is greatly increased when they are using the Internet to evaluate products and compare prices. This is particularly true for standardized products for which offers can be compared for different suppliers through price comparison engines provided by intermediaries such as Easyshop (www.easyshop.com) or MySimon (www.mysimon.com). For commodities, auctions on business-to-business exchanges can also have a similar effect of driving down price. Purchase of some products that have not traditionally been thought of as commodities may become more price sensitive. This process is knwon as **commoditization**. Examples of goods that are becoming commoditized include electrical goods and cars. The issue of online pricing is discussed in *Chapter 8* (*p. 313*).

Commoditization
The process whereby product selection becomes more dependent on price than differentiating features, benefits and value-added services.

In the business-to-business arena too, the bargaining power of customers is likely to be increased since the customers will become aware of alternative products and services that they may previously have been unaware of, and customers will then use this knowledge to negotiate. A further issue is that the ease of use of the Internet channel makes it easier for customers to swap between suppliers. With a specific EDI link that has to be set up between one company and another, there may be reluctance to change this arrangement. With the Internet, which offers a more standard method for purchase through web browsers, the barriers to swapping to another supplier will be lower. It should be noted, however, that there are still barriers to swapping since once a customer invests time in understanding how to use a web site to select and purchase products, they may not want to learn another service. This is the reason why it is a competitive advantage for a company to offer a web-based service before its competitors.

2. Power of intermediaries

A significant downstream channel threat is the potential loss of partners or distributors if there is a channel conflict resulting from *disintermediation* (*Chapter 2, p. 37*). For example, a car distributor could switch to an alternative manufacturer if its profitability was threatened by direct sales from the manufacturer. *The Economist* (2000) reported that to avoid this type of conflict, Ford US are now using dealerships as part of the e-commerce solution and are still paying commission when sales are achieved online. This also helps protect their revenue from the lucrative parts and services market.

An additional downstream threat is the growth in number of intermediaries (another form of partners) to link buyers and sellers. These include consumer portals such as Which (www.which.net) and business-to-business exchanges such as Commerce One (www.commerceone.net). This threat links to the rivalry between competitors. If a company's competitors are represented on a portal while the company is absent or, worse still, are in an exclusive arrangement with a competitor, then this can potentially exclude a substantial proportion of the market. For example, in the billion dollar market involved in the verification of consumer products and business shipments such as oil, chemicals and grain, Integrated Testing Services (www.itsgroup.com) found that its main rival, the Swiss SGS Group (Société Generale de Surveillance, www.sgsgroup.com) had signed an exclusive arrangement for verification of cars on the Carbuster site. Despite its vintage, SGS has proved adaptable to the new trading environment and has set up its own verification portal (SGS Online certification, www.sgsonline.com) which offers a Gold Seal 'kitemark' that is indicative of 'an extremely good likelihood that sellers so rated would satisfy their buyers' requirements on pre-defined aspects of quality, quantity or delivery'. This is an example of countering new intermediaries, sometimes referred to as a countermediation strategy. Through seizing opportunities SGS has pre-empted threats from existing competitors such as ITS and start-ups such as Oxford, UK-based Clicksure.

Buy-side threats

1. Power of suppliers

This can be considered as an opportunity rather than a threat. Companies can insist, for reasons of reducing cost and increasing supply chain efficiency, that their suppliers use electronic links such as EDI or Internet EDI (*Chapter 3, p. 101*) to process orders. Additionally, the Internet tends to reduce the power of suppliers since barriers to migrating to a different supplier are reduced, particularly with the advent of *business-to-business exchanges* (*Chapter 7, p. 272*). However, if suppliers insist on proprietary technology to link companies, then this creates soft lock-in due to the cost or complexity of changing suppppliers.

2. Power of intermediaries

Threats from buy-side intermediaries such as business-to-business exchanges are arguably less than those from sell-side intermediaries, but risks arising from using these services should be considered. These include the cost of integration with these intermediaries, particularly if different standards of integration are required for each. They may pose a threat from increasing commission once established.

From the review above, it should be apparent that the extent of the threats will be dependent on the particular market a company operates in. Generally the threats seem to be greatest for companies who currently sell through retail distributors and have products that can be readily delivered to customers across the Internet or via parcel courier. *Case study 5.1* highlights how one company has analysed its competitive threats and developed an appropriate strategy.

CASE STUDY 5.1

E-commerce strategy at Deutsche Bank

FT

Online competition is forcing banks to rethink drastically how they can best serve their customers.

In a disused factory building at the edge of Frankfurt, executives and managers of Germany's biggest bank are hard at work learning about the immense changes that the Internet will wreak on their business.

It is an incongruous setting for an induction into e-commerce and all that it implies for the traditional world of banking – especially in Germany, where change tends to be gradual and there are more banks per head of population than in most countries.

But Deutsche Bank is determined to ram the message home to managers and employees that the Internet will change the banking world – and thus their bank – out of all recognition. It also chose the old factory hall as the venue to announce its e-commerce strategy, Global E, to the press.

The high-tech presentation included a dizzy array of Internet partnerships, initiatives and projects aimed at transforming Deutsche Bank from an old economy institution to a financial concern more in tune with the new web-based economy.

It is an ambitious undertaking which goes beyond the plans of some rival banks in the Internet age. But Hermann-Josef Lamberti, the director who heads the bank's IT operations and is masterminding the e-commerce thrust, says Global E had to be launched as an entire programme rather than as a series of piecemeal projects. Previously, the bank had about 200 separate e-commerce projects.

'We want to bring the capital markets of this world and the customers together,' says Mr Lamberti, former head of IBM in Germany who joined the bank in December 1998. 'We believe that the possibilities of the Internet will catapult us into a completely new form of business model.'

Mr Lamberti and his fellow directors – notably Rolf Breuer, the chairman – wanted to make this clear inside as well as outside the bank. 'The whole management team and employees have to be included in this transformation process,' adds Mr Lamberti. 'It can't work if these new technologies are separated from the real world.'

Managing its own internal change will be just as hard, if not harder, than meeting the challenge of the Internet, believes Mr Lamberti. 'We have analysed how the internet affects our individual business sectors – and we had to accept that none of them could be excluded.'

Hence the wide scope of the Global E programme. It covers all types of customers – institutional, corporate and individual – and includes a host of partnerships with Internet and industry names such as SAP, America Online, Yahoo!, Nokia, Lycos and La Caixa.

'It would not have been enough to talk of individual projects, to say "let's do retail brokerage here and maybe business customers can do foreign exchange tomorrow over the Internet and then we can discuss ECNs (electronic communications networks or quasi-securities exchange systems)."

'Those are all product elements – they are important in themselves but do not lead to transformation.' The bank wanted to show how new technology could be used to bring customers and markets together online. Thus it was keen to announce the full range of its e-commerce strategy at once, under the branding of Global E 'as the unifying element'.

The news of the merger with Dresdner Bank followed shortly after the e-commerce presentation, putting Global E rather in the shade. Analysts were generally impressed with the scope and style of the e-commerce launch, but wonder whether Deutsche Bank has taken on too much. Also, they note that other banks are also rapidly moving into e-commerce, especially the business-to-business market.

Mr Lamberti insists that the merger will not distract Deutsche's attention from its Internet strategy. He says the deal 'will increase the importance of the e-commerce strategy even further'.

While Dresdner has announced e-commerce plans, these are by no means as advanced as Deutsche Bank's. 'We will extend our strategy to Dresdner's operations and work together,' he says. This could be especially important in the arena of electronic marketplaces, where companies carry out business transactions online. 'The merger should give us even more clout in the corporate market.'

With planned e-commerce investments of some E1bn a year – a figure unlikely to change much after the merger – Deutsche Bank is betting heavily on its Internet strategy. Mr Lamberti is adamant that the surge of Internet competition leaves it no choice. Globalization will anyway lead to a further concentration on the investment banking scene, where the German bank intends to remain a leading operator in such areas as debt capital markets, derivatives and clearing.

'There will be fewer players in the top leagues in the US, Europe and Japan. We don't see anyone else in Germany, France or the UK as big rivals, but we see the Americans.' Among noteworthy US competitors, he names Citibank, Chase Manhattan, Merrill Lynch and Morgan Stanley Dean Witter.

But perhaps the most threatening source of competition comes from the rapidly evolving Internet scene – from niche providers who can target the most promising markets.

'These are the retail brokers, the Charles Schwabs, the ConSors [the German online broker], the E*Trades, the E-Loans, the e-mortgage providers – the e-whatever you want.'

Such niche operators must not be underestimated, believes Mr Lamberti. 'They will be in a position to act very quickly and play a role through alliances, unburdened by the legacy systems which a traditional bank carries.'

On the retail side, where Deutsche Bank will concentrate on more affluent clients, he foresees a further challenge as the Internet makes it easier for banks to tackle foreign markets without having to open expensive branch networks. Similar retail banking models will develop in the US and Europe. 'Five or 10 years ago, we would have said this is absurd – there are completely different market conditions, consumer behaviour and regulatory conditions.'

But now, the banking market is set to change direction. For US banks, especially, freed from the restraints imposed by the Glass-Steagall Act – which separated commercial and investment banking and has just been repealed after 66 years – this opens up new horizons. 'For the first time, they see an opportunity to break through Fortress Europe, including the retail market.'

'Through the removal of the Glass-Steagall Act, the US has created for itself the regulatory conditions to reorder its banking structure. This newly structured banking sector will use the possibilities of the Internet to include other continents in its strategy.'

Mr Lamberti expects this to happen on two levels. Firstly, US banks, brokerages or other financial providers will link up with portals, Internet service providers (ISPs), application service providers (ASPs) or telephone companies. This will link their services with a large potential customer base.

Secondly, they could target specific customer segments with tailored products and services – such as access to online IPOs (initial public offerings) – using the ISP location as the base.

Thus Mr Lamberti foresees the rise of 'the global retail customer' as the Internet breaks down regional barriers. Citibank has aimed its services at the worldwide market, but other banks have so far tended to shy away from such a strategy – 'the dimensions are just enormous'.

Source: Article by Andrew Fisher based on an interview with Hermann-Josef Lamberti of Deutsche Bank, *Financial Times*, 5 April 2000.

Questions

1. Summarize the analysis of the bank's competitive environment in the second part of the article.
2. Referring to *Figure 5.6* or Porter's Five Forces analysis summarize the typical competitive threats for a bank such as the Deutsche Bank and the strategy they can take to counter these threats.

Competitor analysis

Competitor analysis for e-business
Review of e-business services offered by existing and new competitors and adoption by their customers.

Competitor analysis is also a key aspect of e-business situation analysis, but since it is also a key activity in producing an e-marketing plan which will feed into the e-business strategy this is also described in more detail in *Chapter 8 (p. 293)*.

Resource-advantage mapping

Core competencies
Resources, including skills or technologies that provide a particular benefit to customers.

Customer value
Dependent on product quality, service quality, price and fulfilment time.

Once the external opportunities and internal resources have been reviewed, it is useful to map the internal resource strengths against external opportunities, to identify, for example, where competitors are weak and can be attacked. To identify internal strengths, definition of **core competencies** is one approach. Lynch (2000) explains that core competencies are the resources, including knowledge, skills or technologies that provide a particular benefit to customers, or increase **customer value** relative to competitors. Customer value is defined by Deise *et al.* (2000) as dependent on product quality, service quality, price and fulfilment time. So, to understand core competencies we need to understand how the organization is differentiated from competitors in these areas. Benchmarking e-commerce services of competitors as described in *Chapter 8, p. 293* is important here. The cost-base of a company relative to its competitors is also important since lower production costs will lead to lower prices. Lynch (2000) argues that core competencies should be emphasized in objective setting and strategy definition.

Strategic objectives

Strategic objectives
Statement and communication of an organization's mission, vision and objectives.

Defining and communicating an organization's **strategic objectives** is a key element of any strategy process model since (1) the strategy definition and implementation elements of strategy must be directed at how best to achieve the objectives and (2) the overall success of e-business strategy will be assessed by comparing actual results against objectives and taking action to improve strategy. Note that objective setting typically takes place in parallel with strategic analysis and strategy definition as part of an iterative process.

Figure 5.11 highlights some of the key aspects of strategic objective setting that will be covered in this section.

Defining vision and mission

Corporate vision is defined in Lynch (2000) as 'a mental image of the possible and desirable future state of the organization'. It provides a backdrop for the development of purpose and strategy of the organization.

The Institute of Directors (2000) suggest that a coherent vision is a critical part of developing an e-business strategy. They suggest the following elements as part of this vision:

- *Relevance* – the company must understand the potential of new technology to impact the business.
- *Change* – the company must be prepared to revise its business model more frequently in the light of the changing business environment.
- *Value* – the timeframe for returns must be determined so that stakeholder value can be protected and increased.

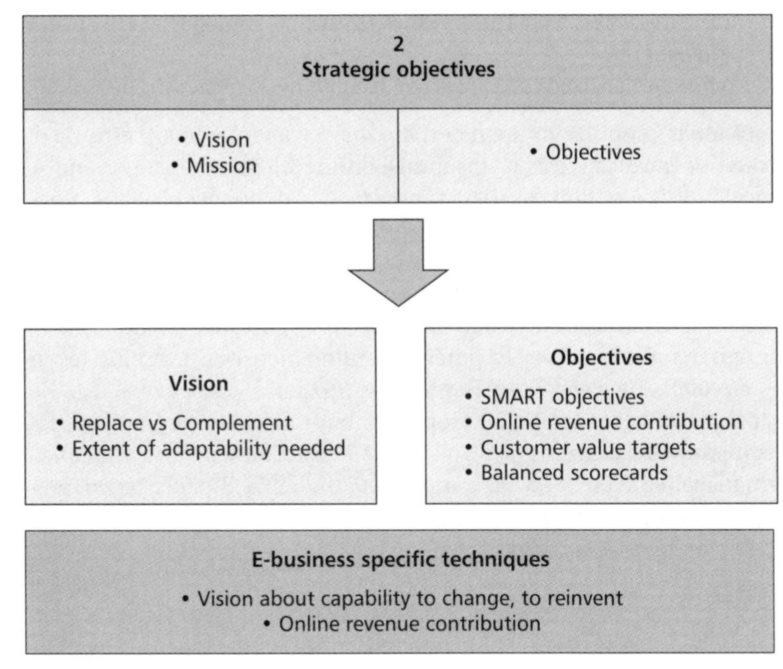

Figure 5.11 Elements of strategic objective setting for the e-business

- *People* – competencies must be acquired and developed to help achieve the vision.

Simons (2000a), in referring to the vision of Barclays Bank, illustrates the change in thinking required for e-business vision. He reports that to execute the vision of the bank 'a high tolerance of uncertainty' must be introduced. The group CEO of Barclays (Matt Barrett) said:

> *our objective is to use technology to develop entirely new business models ... while transforming our internal structure to make us more efficient and effective. Any strategy that does not achieve both is fundamentally flawed.*

From a sell-side e-commerce perspective, a key objective is whether the Internet will primarily *complement* the company's other channels or whether it will *replace* other channels. Vision also encompasses the timeframe or the rate of change of replacement; will replacement happen over a period of two years or ten years? Whether the vision is to complement or replace it is important to communicate this to staff and other stakeholders such as customers, suppliers and shareholders. The clarity of such vision, backed up by realistic plans and actions has been shown to have a major impact on the stock market value of companies.

Clearly, if it is believed that e-commerce will primarily replace other channels, then it is important to invest in the technical, human and organizational resources to achieve this. Kumar (1999) suggests that replacement is most likely to happen when:

1. customer access to the Internet is high;
2. the Internet can offer a better value proposition than other media (i.e. propensity to purchase online is high);

3. the product can be delivered over the Internet (it can be argued that this is not essential for replacement);
4. the product can be standardized (user does not usually need to view to purchase).

If at least two of Kumar's conditions are met there may be a replacement effect. For example, purchase of travel services or insurance online fulfils criteria 1, 2 and 4. As a consequence, physical outlets for these products may no longer be viable since the service can be provided in a cheaper, more convenient form online. The closure of British Airways travel retail units and AA shops is indicative of this change with the business being delivered completely by phone or online sales channel. The extent to which these conditions are met will vary through time, for example as access to the Internet and propensity to purchase online increases. A similar test is de Kare-Silver's *Electronic Shopping Test* (*Chapter 8, p. 301*).

A similar vision of the future can be developed for buy-side activities such as procurement. A company can have a vision for how e-procurement and e-enabled supply chain management (SCM) will complement or replace paper-based procurement and SCM over a future time period.

Objective setting

The relationship between objectives, strategies and performance measures is illustrated by the e-business strategic plan for The B2B Company in *Table 5.3*. Each of the performance indicators should also have a timeframe in which to achieve these objectives. Despite the dynamism of e-business, some of the goals that require processes to be re-engineered cannot be achieved immediately. Prioritization of objectives, in this case from 1 to 6, can help in communicating the e-business vision to staff and also when allocating resources to achieve the strategy. Objectives should be *SMART* (*Chapter 12, p. 509*). A more general objective is timescales for achieving the different levels of e-business shown in *Table 5.2 p. 173*.

Table 5.3 Objectives, strategies and performance indicators for The B2B Company (in order of priority)

Objectives	*Strategies to achieve goals*	*Key performance indicators (critical success factors)*
1. Develop revenue from new geographical markets	1. Create e-commerce facility for standard products and assign agents to these markets	1. Achieve combined revenue of £1m by year end Online revenue contribution of 70%
2. Increase revenue from smaller-scale purchases from retailers	2. Create e-commerce facility for standard products	2. Increase sales through retailers from 15% to 25% of total by year 2 Online revenue contribution of 30%
3. Ensure retention of key account customers	3. Soft lock-in by developing extranet facilities Continued support from sales reps	3. Retain five key account customers Online revenue contribution of 100% from these 5
4. Improve efficiency of sourcing raw materials	4. Develop e-procurement system	4. Reduce cost of procurement by 5% by year end, 10% by year 2 Achieve 80% of purchasing online
5. Reduce time to market and costs for new product development	5. Use collaboration and project management tools	5. Reduce cost and time to market by average of 10% by year 3
6. Protect and increase efficiency of distributor and partner network	6. Create partner extranet and aim for paperless support	6. Reduce cost of sales in each of 5 main geographical markets by 30%

Organizations must consider the relative importance of objectives for revenue generation and improving internal process or supply chain efficiency. Think about what Oleson (2000) says:

IDC places most weight in identifying sources of income in the areas of organizational impact and greater process efficiency, believing that too much emphasis has been placed on being first to market in the assessment of income resulting from gaining a competitive advantage.

The online revenue contribution

By considering the demand analysis, competitor analysis and factors such as those defined by Kumar (1999) an Internet or **online revenue contribution** objective can be set. This key e-business objective states the percentage of company revenue *directly* generated through online transactions. However, for some companies such as B2B service companies, it is unrealistic to expect a high direct online contribution. In this case, an *indirect* online contribution can be stated; this is where the sale is influenced by the online presence but purchase occurs using conventional channels, for example a customer selecting a product on a web site and then phoning to place the order. Online revenue contribution objectives can be specified for different types of products, customer segments and geographic markets. They can also be set for different digital channels such as web, mobile or interactive digital TV.

Online or Internet revenue contribution
An assessment of the direct or indirect contribution of the Internet to sales, usually expressed as a percentage of overall sales revenue.

Figure 5.12 shows how these objectives can be presented and measured for a company. Here the data is an average across 441 fast-growth US companies with revenues from $1million to $50 million surveyed by PricewaterhouseCoopers (2000). Owing to the importance of online revenue contributions, this topic is also covered in *Chapter 8, p. 296* and *Figure 8.5* shows how online revenue contributions have to be estimated for the future in order to resource e-business appropriately.

An example of objective setting within a particular company is provided by Goodwin (2000) who reports that UK retail group Kingfisher, owners of Woolworth, B&Q, Superdrug and many less well-known brands, has set the objective of growing its e-commerce sales from £40 million in 2000 to £1.5 billion by 2004, this representing 10 per cent of group sales. To achieve this it has created a separate e-business division known as e-Kingfisher. Company sites such as DIY retailer B&Q have moved up the technology adoption ladder from an informational site to a transactional site. The company has also set objectives for using IT further up its supply chain. Woolworths is installing a SAP system to link its web site and interactive TV channels with its financial and stock management systems and B&Q is using a similar approach.

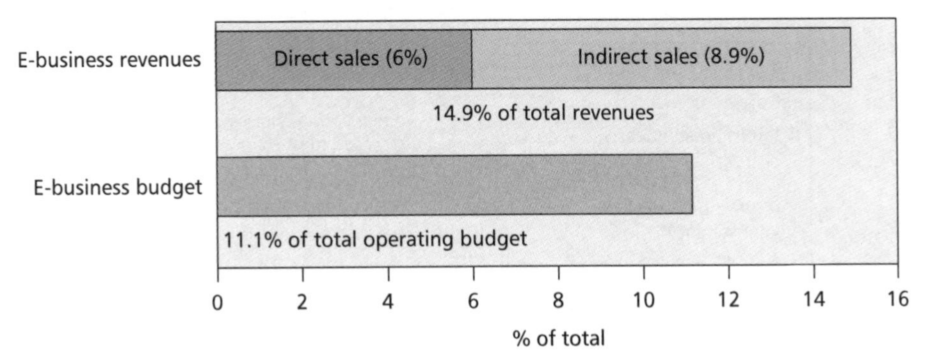

Figure 5.12 Direct and indirect Internet contributions for fast growth companies in the US.
Source: PricewaterhouseCoopers (2000)

Activity 5.2 Assessing the significance of digital channels

Purpose

To illustrate the issues involved with assessing the suitability of the Internet for e-commerce.

Table 5.4 Vision of online revenue contribution for The B2B Company

Products/services	*Now*	*2 years*	*5 years*	*10 years*
Example: Cars, US Direct online sales Indirect online sales	 5% 50%	 10% 70%	 25% 90%	 50% 95%
Financial services Direct online sales Indirect online sales				
Clothing Direct online sales Indirect online sales				
Business office supplies Direct online sales Indirect online sales				

Activity

For each of the following products assess the suitability of the Internet for delivery of the product or service and position it on the grid in *Figure 5.13* with justification and make estimates in Table 5.4 for the direct and indirect online revenue contribution in five and ten years' time for different products in your country. Choose specific products within each category.

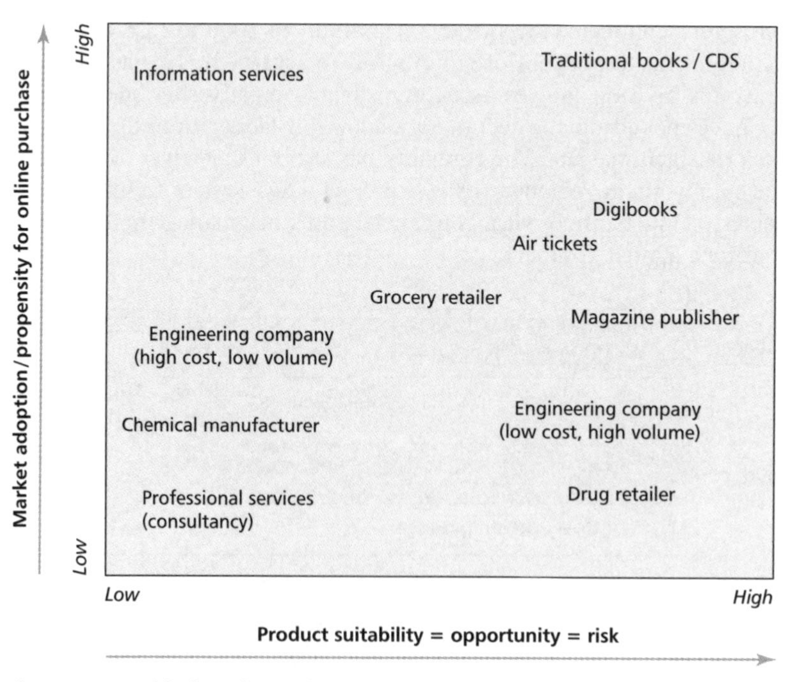

Figure 5.13 Grid of product suitability against market adoption for transactional e-commerce (online purchases)

An equivalent buy-side measure to the online revenue contribution is the proportion of procurement that is achieved online. This can be broken down into the proportion of electronic transactions for ordering, invoicing, delivery and payment as described in *Chapter 7*. Deise *et al.* (2000) note that the three business objectives for procuring materials and services should be improving supplier performance, reducing cycle time and cost for indirect procurement and reducing total acquisition costs. Metrics can be developed for each of these.

The balanced scorecard approach to objective setting

Integrated metrics such as the **balanced scorecard** have become widely used as a means of translating organizational strategies into objectives and then providing metrics to monitor the execution of the strategy. The balanced scorecard, popularized in a *Harvard Business Review* article by Kaplan and Norton (1993), can be used to translate vision and strategy into objectives. In part, it was a response to overreliance on financial metrics such as turnover and profitability and a tendency for these measures to be retrospective rather than looking at future potential as indicated by innovation, customer satisfaction and employee development. In addition to financial data, the balanced scorecard uses operational measures such as customer satisfaction, efficiency of internal processes and also the organization's innovation and improvement activities including staff development.

Balanced scorecard
A framework for setting and monitoring business performance. Metrics are structured according to customer issues, internal efficiency measures, financial measures and innovation.

The main areas of the balanced scorecard are:

1. *Customer concerns*. These include time (lead time, time to quote etc.), quality, performance, service and cost. Example measures from Halifax bank from Olve *et al.* (1999): satisfaction of mystery shoppers visiting branches and from branch customer surveys.
2. *Internal measures*. Internal measures should be based on the business processes that have the greatest impact on customer satisfaction: cycle time, quality, employee skills, productivity. Companies should also identify critical core competencies and try to guarantee market leadership. Example measures from Halifax bank: ATM availability (%), conversion rates on mortgage applications (%), arrears on mortgage (%).
3. *Financial measures*. Traditional measures such as turnover, costs, profitability and return on capital employed. For publicly quoted companies this measure is key to shareholder value. Example measures from Halifax bank: gross receipts (£), mortgage offers (£), loans (£).
4. *Learning and growth: innovation and staff development*. Innovation can be measured by change in value through time (employee value, shareholder value, percentage and value of sales from new products). Examples: management performance, training performance, new product development.

For each of these four areas management teams will define objectives, specific measures, targets and initiatives to achieve these targets. For some companies, such as Skandia Life, the balanced scorecard becomes much more than a performance measurement system and provides a framework for the entire business strategy process. Olve *et al.* (1999) make the point that a further benefit of the scorecard is that it does not solely focus on outcomes, but also considers measures that are performance drivers that should positively affect the outcomes. For example investment in technology or employee training are performance drivers.

More recently, as the scorecard has been widely used, it has been suggested that it provides a useful tool for aligning business and IS strategy, see for example Der Zee and De Jong (1999).

Table 5.5 outlines how the balanced scorecard could be deployed in The B2B Company to support its e-business strategy. More detailed examples of balanced scorecards for a range of European countries are provided in Olve *et al.* (1999).

Table 5.5 An example of the balanced scorecard for The B2B Company

Scorecard component	*Objective metric*
Customer perspective	Customer satisfaction index Customer acquisition rate Customer retention rate (churn)
Process	Average time for new product development (months) Procurement lead times Sales cycle lead time
Financial	Revenue Margin
Innovation and employee development	Number of new product releases per year Training hours attended per employee. Target 30 hours/year

Strategy definition

Strategy definition
Formulation, review and selection of strategies to achieve strategic objectives.

The **definition of strategy** is driven by the objectives and vision referred to in the previous sections. As strategy is formulated based on vision and objectives it is necessary to frequently revisit and revise them.

In this section the key strategic decisions faced by a management team developing e-business strategy are reviewed. For each of the areas of strategy definition that we cover managers will generate different options, review them and select them as shown in *Figure 5.14*. As you read through the six key decisions think about how

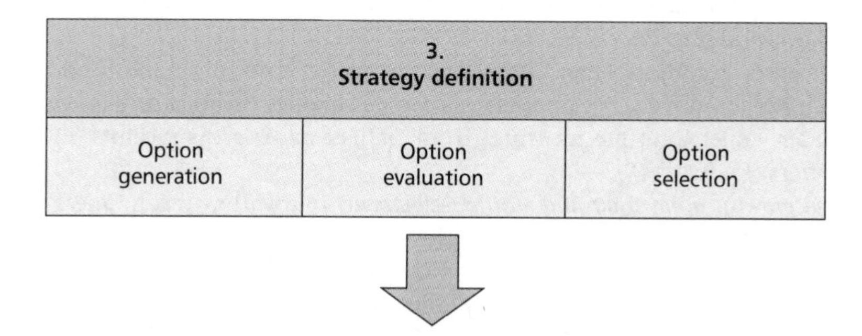

Figure 5.14 Elements of strategy definition for the e-business

these decisions are going to vary according to the many different organizational characteristics: B2C, B2B, physical products or intangible services or mixed, size of organization, stage in product lifecycle, market penetration, not-for-profit. What strategy decisions would be taken for organizations you are familiar with?

Decision 1: E-business priorities

The e-business strategy must be directed according to the priority of different strategic objectives such as those in *Table 5.3*. If the priorities are on the sell-side as are objectives 1 to 3 in *Table 5.3*, then the strategy must be to direct resources at these objectives. For a B2B company that is well known in its marketplace worldwide and cannot offer products to new markets, an emphasis on *buy-side* e-commerce and the value chain may be more appropriate.

E-business strategy priorities can be summarized as Gulati and Garino (2000) have put it: *'Getting the right mix of bricks and clicks'* (*Chapter 2, p. 54*). This expression usually refers to sell-side e-commerce. The general options for the mix of 'bricks and clicks' are shown in *Figure 5.15*. A similar figure was produced by de Kare-Silver (2000) who suggests that strategic e-commerce alternatives for companies should be selected according to the percentage of the target market using the channel and the commitment of the company. The idea is that the commitment should mirror the readiness of consumers to use the new medium. If the objective is to achieve a high online revenue contribution of more than 70 per cent then this will require fundamental change for the company to transform to a 'bricks and clicks' or 'clicks only' company.

In the terminology of de Kare Silver (2000) the strategic alternatives given in

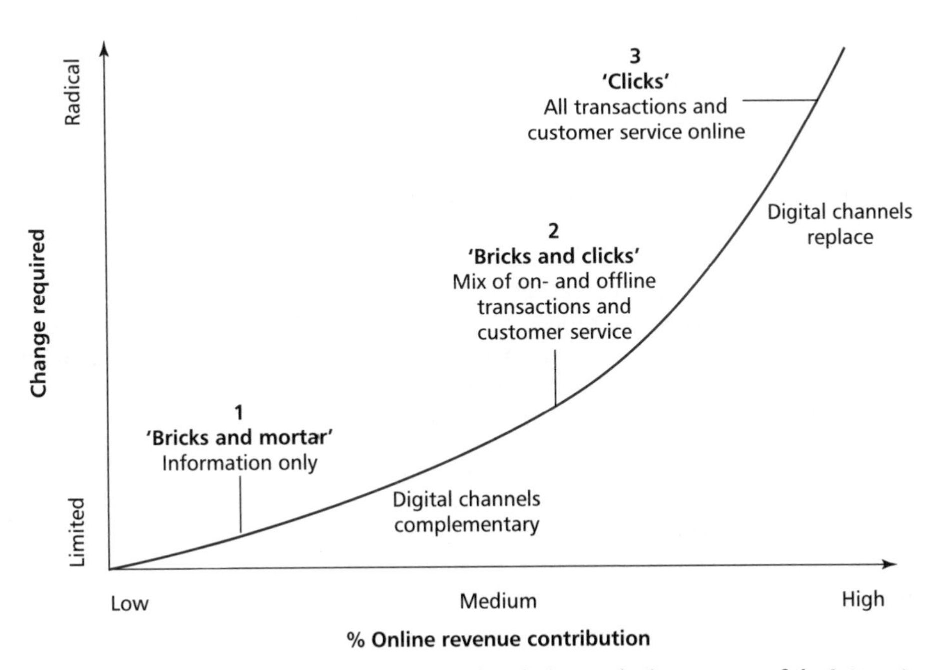

Figure 5.15 Strategic options for a company in relation to the importance of the Internet as a channel

Figure 5.15 range from those where there is a limited response to the medium such as 'information only' or 'subsume' in business through to spinning-off the electronic commerce part of a company into a 'separate business' or even 'switching fully' to an Internet-based business. Internet-only businesses, particularly start-ups, are sometimes referred to as **Internet pureplays**. Although the 'switch-fully' alternative may seem unlikely for many businesses, it is already happening. In the UK, the Automobile Association and British Airways have closed the majority of their retail outlets since orders are predominately placed via the Internet or by phone. However the transition to a service that is entirely clicks-only is unlikely for the majority of companies. Both of these examples require the phone channel, indeed dot-coms such as lastminute.com have set up a call centre because this is what customers require and others such as Amazon have developed a limited high-street presence.

Internet pureplays
A company trading online that has limited or no physical presence such as retail units.

Decision 2: Restructuring

Closely related to Decision 1 is whether the company should restructure in order to achieve the priorities set for e-business. Gulati and Garino (2000) identify a continuum of approaches from integration to separation. The choices are:

1. *In-house division (integration)*. For example, the RS Components Internet Trading Channel (www.rswww.com)
2. *Joint venture (mixed)*. The company creates an online presence in association with another player.
3. *Strategic partnership (mixed)*. This may also be achieved through purchase of existing dot-coms, for example, in the UK Great Universal Stores acquired e-tailer Jungle.com for its strength in selling technology products and strong brand while John Lewis purchased Buy.com's UK operations.
4. *Spin-off (separation)*. For example, Egg bank is a spin-off from the Prudential financial services company.

Referring back to *Figure 5.15*, the in-house division or joint venture will be typical for the clicks-and-mortar approach while the strategic partnership or spin-off are more likely to be used to create a clicks-only operation.

Gulati and Garino (2000) give the advantages of the integration approach as being able to leverage existing brands, to be able to share information and achieve economies of scale (e.g. purchasing and distribution efficiencies). They say the spin-off approach gives better focus, more flexibility for innovation and the possibility of funding through flotation. For example Egg has been able to create a brand distinct from Prudential and has developed new revenue models such as retail sales commission. They say that separation is preferable in situations where:

- a different customer segment or product mix will be offered online
- differential pricing is required between online and offline
- there is a major channel conflict
- the Internet threatens the current business model
- additional funding or specialist staff need to be attracted

Additionally, from a technology viewpoint it may be quicker to develop a new infrastructure rather than integrating with an existing one, but again economies of scale are lost.

An example of the integration approach is provided by Barclays Bank. Simons (2000b) reported that Barclays wants to double its profits in three years through a radical transformation of its business processes. It has created an 'e-enablement task force' and their plan involves revising IS strategy, significant outsourcing and investments in customer relationship management systems. The impetus for this strategy is the threat of new rivals such as Egg, Cahoot, Smile and Intelligent Finance. The group CIO of Barclays (David Weymouth) said

> *the transformation requires a fundamental shift in operating model internally ... [Benchmarking had shown] a dramatic gap between our potential opportunities in this area and our actions thus far.*

It is seen that changes in organization structure range from setting up a new department, through setting up a new strategic business unit to creating autonomous companies. Simons (2000b) reports that Barclays Bank considered four different e-business structures which are similar to those of Gulati and Garino (2000):

1. Integrated operation with the e-business contained within existing line of business, for example American Express or Charles Schwab.
2. Separate standalone line of business, a model chosen by firms such as Citibank and Sears and Roebuck.
3. Spin-off with the the e-business established as a separate entity, a model chosen by firms such as Procter and Gamble and Bank One.
4. Portfolio/incubator, a model where the e-business is managed as an investment. This approach has been adopted by Dupont and UPS.

Barclays selected the integrated model; they felt that this would 'allow stand-alone e-activities in each line of business, while ensuring coordination and integration'. However this model still requires fundamental restructuring of Barclays operations and IT infrastructure with substantial outsourcing.

Goodwin (2000) reports that Kingfisher have used the second approach and have set up e-kingfisher, a new business unit. The hope is that Kingfisher will be able to enjoy the best of both the dot-com and bricks-and-mortar approaches. By pooling their resources the Kingfisher brands will be able to move with all the speed and agility of an Internet start-up, but unlike Internet start-ups their brands will be sufficiently well known to attract customers without the need for enormous investment. Paul Worthington, the Chief Technical Officer at Kingfisher, is reported as stating that 'everything has to be done at e-speed, but everything has to be done well. That's a real tension'. Approaches for restructuring organizations in response to e-ebusiness transformation are an important issue in *change management* (*Chapter 10, p. 381*).

Within a business there are also many options for internal restucturing such as the creation of an inhouse division referred to above.. These options are considered as part of *change management* (*Chapter 10, p. 395*).

Decision 3: Business and revenue models

Another aspect of e-business strategy formulation is review of opportunities from new *business and revenue models* (*Chapter 2, p. 49*). Evaluating new models is important since if companies do not innovate then competitors and new entrants will and companies will find it difficult to regain the initiative. Equally, if inappropriate business or distribution models are chosen, then companies may make substantial losses.

Early (first) mover advantage
An early entrant into the marketplace.

One example of how companies can review and revise their business model is provided by Dell Computer. Dell gained **early mover advantage** in the mid 1990s when it became one of the first companies to offer PCs for sale online. Its sales of PCs and peripherals grew from the mid 1990s with online sales of $1 million per day to 2000 sales of $50 million per day. Based on this success it has looked at new business models it can use in combination with its powerful brand to provide new services to its existing customer base and also to generate revenue through new customers. In September 2000, Dell announced plans to become a supplier of IT consulting services through linking with enterprise resource planning specialists such as software suppliers, systems integrators and business consulting firms. This venture will enable the facility of Dell's Premier Pages to be integrated into the procurement component of ERP systems such as SAP and Baan, thus avoiding the need for rekeying and reducing costs.

In a separate initiative, Dell launched a B2B marketplace aimed at discounted office goods and services procurements including PCs, peripherals, software, stationery and travel (www.dellmarketplace.com). To illustrate the importance of taking the right business model decision see *case study 5.2*. This article is informative since it shows how the online marketplace for car sales has changed during its five-year infancy from the initial success of new intermediaries to the increasing influence of the car manufacturers as they develop their e-business strategies. It again emphasizes the need for a dynamic strategy that produces new strategies to deal with changes in the marketplace.

To sound a note of caution, flexibility in the business model should not be detrimental to the extent of losing focus on the core business. An example of business model flexibility is the diversification of Amazon from books and CDs to a range of products more typical of a department store. It remains to be seen whether this results in more profitability. A 2000 survey of CEOs of leading UK Internet companies such as Autonomy, Freeserve, NetBenefit and QXL (Durlacher, 2000) indicates that although flexibility is useful this may not apply to business models. The report states:

> *A widely held belief in the new economy in the past, has been that change and flexibility is good, but these interviews suggest that it is actually those companies who have stuck to a single business model that have been to date more successful. ... CEOs were not moving far from their starting vision, but that it was in the marketing, scope and partnerships where new economy companies had to be flexible.*

So with all strategy options, managers should also consider the 'do nothing option'. Here a company will not risk a new business model, but adopt a 'wait and see' approach to see how competitors perform. The benefits of such an approach are that it is possible to learn from other companies' mistakes and also gauge the market potential without incurring any costs. The counter-argument is that once a company has fallen behind its competitors it may prove impossible to regain lost customers or catch up in terms of how to use the new technologies and how to revise business processes. This is a powerful counter-argument, and one that e-commerce solutions providers use to persuade companies to buy their solutions.

Decision 4: Marketplace restructuring

A related issue to reviewing new business and revenue models is to consider the options created through *disintermediation and reintermediation* (*Chapter 2, p. 37*) within a marketplace. These options can be taken from both a buy-side and sell-side perspective.

Sell-side

- Disintermediation (sell-direct)
- Create new online intermediary (countermediation)
- Partner with new online or existing intermediaries
- Do nothing!

Buy-side

- Disintermediation (buy-direct, bypassing distributors)
- Buy through new intermediaries such as B2B exchanges
- Do nothing!

Prioritizing strategic partnerships as part of the move from a *value chain to a value network* (*Chapter 6, p. 227*) should also occur as part of this decision.

For all options tactics will be needed to manage the channel conflicts that may occur as a result of restructuring.

Decision 5: Market and product development strategies

Managers of e-business strategy also have to decide whether to use new technologies to expand the scope of their business into new markets and products. As for decision 1 the decision is a balance between fear of the do-nothing option and fear of poor return on investment for strategies that fail. The model of Ansoff (1957) is still useful as a means for marketing managers to discuss market and product development using electronic technologies. This decision is considered from an e-marketing perspective in *Chapter 8*. Options to be considered in an e-commerce context are:

1. *Market penetration.* Digital channels can be used to sell more existing products into existing markets. Online channels can help consolidate or increase market share by providing additional promotion and customer service facilities amongst customers in an existing market. The Internet can also be used for *customer retention management* (*Chapter 9, p. 353*). This is a relatively conservative use of the Internet.
2. *Market development.* Here online channels are used to sell into new markets, taking advantage of the low cost of advertising internationally without the necessity for a supporting sales infrastructure in the customers' country. This is a relatively conservative use of the Internet, but is a great opportunity for SMEs to increase exports at a low cost, but it does require overcoming the barriers to exporting (*Chapter 4, p. 144*).

   A less evident benefit of the Internet is that as well as selling into new geographical markets, products can also be sold to new market segments or different types of customers. This may happen simply as a by-product of having a web site. For example, RS components (www.rswww.com) a supplier of a range of

MRO items, found that 10 per cent of the web-based sales were to individual consumers rather than traditional business customers. The UK retailer Argos found the opposite was true with 10 per cent of web site sales from businesses, when their traditional market was consumer based. The Internet may offer further opportunities for selling to market sub-segments that have not been previously targeted. For example, a product sold to large businesses may also appeal to SMEs, or a product targeted at young people could also appeal to some members of an older audience. Target market strategies and positioning are described in *Chapter 8*.

3. *Product development.* New digital products or services can be developed that can be delivered by the Internet. These are typically information products, for example online trade magazine Construction Weekly has diversified to a B2B portal Construction Plus (www.constructionplus.com) which has new revenue streams. This is innovative use of the Internet.
4. *Diversification.* In this sector, new products are developed which are sold into new markets. For example Construction Plus is now international while formerly it had a UK customer base.

These options are shown in *Figure 5.16* for The B2B Company.

The benefits and risks of adopting a market and product development approach are highlighted by the creation of Smile (www.smile.co.uk) – an Internet specific bank – by the Co-operative Bank of the UK. Smile opened for business in October 1999 and in its first year added 200,000 customers at a rate of 20,000 per month. Significantly, 80 per cent of these customers were market development in the context of the

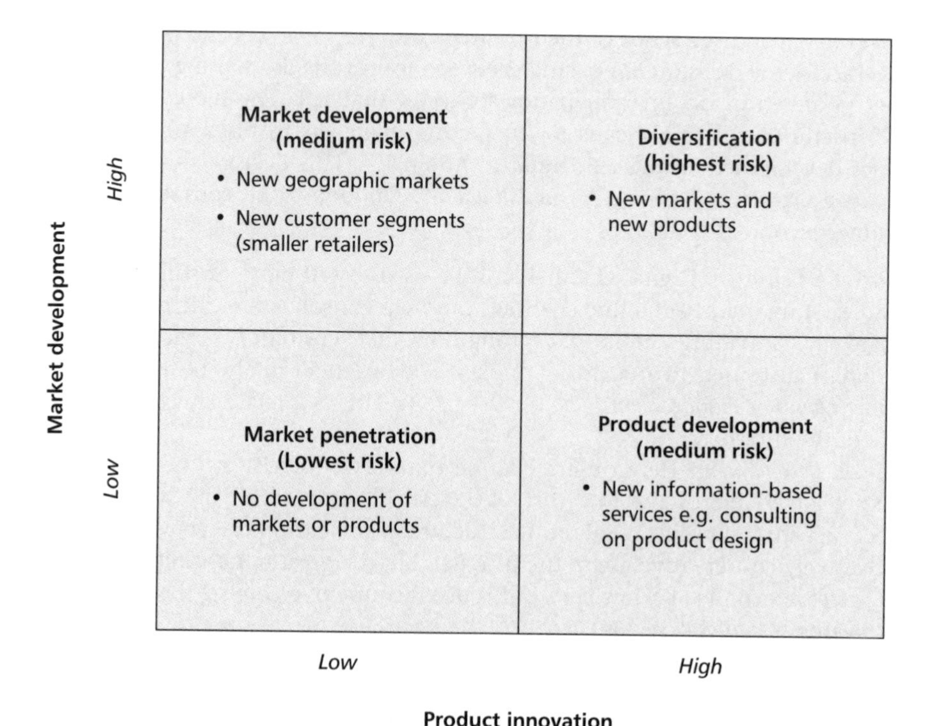

Figure 5.16 Assessment of risk for market and product development for The B2B Company

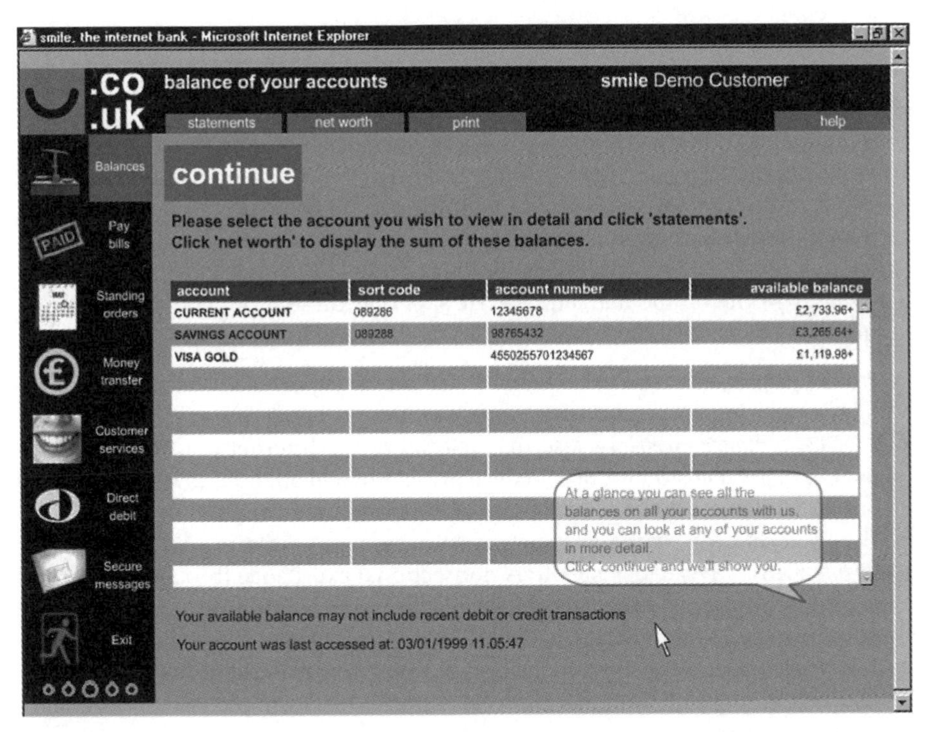

Figure 5.17 New product development – Smile online banking (www.smile.co.uk)

parent, since they were not existing Co-op customers and typically belonged to a higher income segment. As well as the new online banking products available from Smile, a secure shopping zone (*Figure 5.17*) had been developed which is a new revenue model since each purchase made from the site will provide affiliate revenue (a small percentage of sales price paid by the retailer to Smile). Retailers also pay Smile for placing advertisements and promotions within the shopping zone. The risks of the new approach are highlighted by the costs of these innovations. It is estimated that in its first year, costs of creation and promotion of Smile increased overall costs of the Co-op bank by 5 per cent. However, overheads are relatively low since Smile only employs 130 people and it is targeted for profit three years from launch.

The danger of diversification into new product areas is illustrated by the fortunes of Amazon, which is infamous for not delivering profitability despite multi-billion dollar sales. Philips (2000) reported that for books and records, Amazon sustained profitability through 2000, but it is following a strategy of product diversification into toys, tools, electronics and kitchenware. This strategy gives a problem through the cost of promotion and logistics to deliver the new product offering. Amazon is balancing this against its vision of becoming a 'one-stop shop' for online retailers.

Decision 6: Positioning and differentiation strategies

Companies can position their products relative to competitors according to four main variables: product quality, service quality, price and fulfilment time. As mentioned earlier Deise *et al.* (2000) suggest it is useful to review these as an equation of how they combine to influence customer perceptions of value or brand.

$$\text{Customer value (brand perception)} = \frac{\text{Product quality} \times \text{Service quality}}{\text{Price} \times \text{Fulfilment time}}$$

Strategies should review the extent to which increases in product and service quality can be matched by decreases in price and time. We will now look at some other opinions of positioning strategies for e-businesses. As you read through, refer back to the customer value equation to note similarities and differences.

Chaston (2000) argues that there are four options for strategic focus to position a company in the online marketplace. He says that these should build on existing strengths, but can use the online facilities to enhance the positioning as follows:

- *Product performance excellence*. Enhance by providing online product customization.
- *Price performance excellence*. Use the facilities of the Internet to offer favourable pricing to loyal customers or to reduce prices where demand is low (for example, British Midland airlines use auctions to sell underused capacity on flights).
- *Transactional excellence*. A site such as software and hardware e-tailer Dabs.com (*Figure 5.18*) (www.dabs.com) offers transactional excellence through combining pricing information with dynamic availability information on products listing number in stock, number on order and when expected.
- *Relationship excellence*. Personalization features to enable customers to review sales order history and place repeat orders; for example RS Components (www.rswww.com).

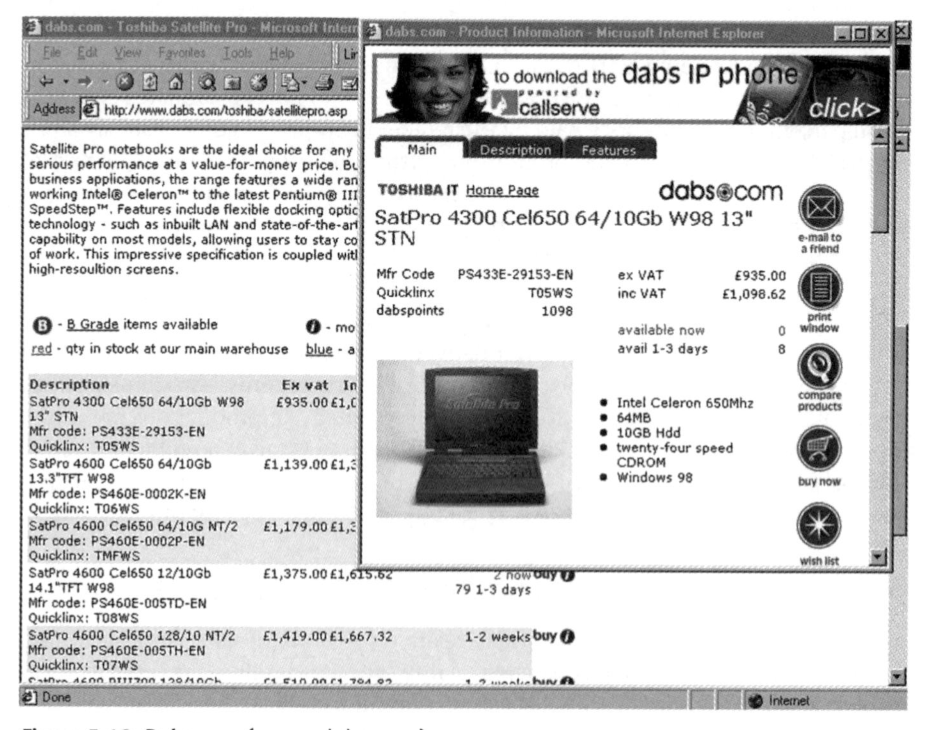

Figure 5.18 Dabs.com (www.dabs.com)

These positioning options have much in common with Porter's competitive strategies of cost leadership, product differentiation and innovation (Porter, 1980). Porter has been criticized since many commentators believe that to remain competitive it is necessary to combine excellence in all of these areas. It can be suggested that the same is true for sell-side e-commerce. These are not mutually exclusive strategic options, rather they are prerequisites for success. Customers will probably not judge on a single criteria, but on multiple criteria. The type of criteria that customers judge performance on have been analysed by retail analyst Gomez (www.gomez.com), who publish rankings of e-tailers such as banks and supermarkets using a scorecard methodology that is based on customer concerns. *Table 5.6* summarizes the criteria used by Gomez analysts. It can be seen that the criteria are consistent with the strategic postioning options of Chaston (2000). Significantly, the retailers with the best overall score at the time of writing such as Tesco (grocery retail), Smile (online banking) and Amazon (books) are also perceived as the market leaders and are strong in each of the scorecard categories. These ratings have resulted from strategies that enable the investment and restructuring to deliver customer performance.

Plant (2000) also identifies four different positional e-strategic directions which he refers to as technology leadership, service leadership, market leadership and brand leadership. The author acknowledges that these aren't exclusive. It is

Scorecard category	*Scorecard criteria*
1. Ease of use	● Demonstrations of functionality. ● Simplicity of account opening and transaction process. ● Consistency of design and navigation. ● Adherence to proper user interaction principles. ● Integration of data providing efficient access to information commonly accessed by consumers.
2. Customer confidence	● Availability, depth, and breadth of customer service options, including phone, e-mail, and branch locations. ● Ability to resolve accurately and readily a battery of telephone calls and e-mails sent to customer service, covering simple technical and industry-specific questions. ● Privacy policies, service guarantees, fees, and explanations of fees. ● Each ranked web site is monitored every five minutes, seven days a week, 24 hours a day for speed and reliability of both public and secure (if available) areas. ● Financial strength, technological capabilities and independence, years in business, years online, and membership organizations.
3. On-site resources	● Availability of specific products. ● Ability to transact in each product online. ● Ability to seek service requests online.
4. Relationship services	● Online help, tutorials, glossary and FAQs. ● Advice. ● Personalization of data. ● Ability to customize a site. ● Reuse of customer data to facilitate future transactions. ● Support of business and personal needs such as tax reporting or repeated-buying. ● Frequent buyer incentives.
5. Overall cost	● A basket of typical services and purchases. ● Added fees due to shipping and handling. ● Minimum balances. ● Interest rates.

Table 5.6 Gomez scorecard criteria for rating e-tailers.
Source: www.gomez.com

interesting that this author does not see price differentiation as important, rather online he sees brand and service as important to success.

In *Chapter 8* we look further at how segmentation, positioning and creating differential advantage through an online value proposition are part of target market strategies for sell-side e-commerce (p. 304).

To conclude this section on e-business strategies, complete *activity 5.3* for a different perspective on e-business strategies and read *case study 5.2* to look at how car manufacturers have had to substantially review the business and revenue model elements of their e-business strategies over the past five years.

Activity 5.3 E-business strategies for The B2C Company

Purpose

To evaluate the suitability of different e-business strategies.

Introduction

Many industry analysts such as the Gartner Group, Forrester, IDC Research and the 'big-five' consulting firms are suggesting e-business strategies. Many of these will not have been trialled extensively, so a key management skill becomes evaluating suggested approaches from reports and then selecting appropriate measures.

Questions

1. Review the summaries of the approaches recommended by IDC Research below (Picardi, 2000). Which elements of these strategies would you suggest are most relevant to The B2C Company?
2. Alternatively for a company with which you are familiar review the six strategy definition choices presented in the previous section.

Summary of IDC approach to e-business strategies

Picardi (2000) identifies six strategies for sell-side e-commerce. The approaches are interesting since they also describe the timeframe in which response is required in order to remain competitive.

The six strategies are:

1. *Attack e-tailing.* As suggested by the name, this is an aggressive competitive approach that involves frequent comparison with competitors' prices and then matching or bettering them. This approach is important on the Internet because of the transparency of pricing and availability information made possible through shopping comparison sites such as ShopSmart (www.shopsmart.com) and Kelkoo (www.kelkoo.com). As customers increasingly use these facilities then it is important that companies ensure their price positioning is favourable. High-street white goods retailers have long used the approach of matching competitors' prices, but the Internet enables this to be achieved dynamically. Shopping sites such as Buy.com (www.buy.com) and Evenbetter.com (www.evenbetter.com) can now find the prices of all comparable items in a category but also guarantee that they will beat the lowest price of any competing product. These sites have implemented

real-time adjustments in prices with small increments based on price policy algorithms that are simply not possible in traditional retailing.

2. *Defend e-tailing*. This is a strategic approach that traditional companies can use in response to 'attack e-tailing'. It involves differentiation based on other aspects of brand beyond price. The IDC research quoted by Picardi (2000) shows that while average prices for commodity goods on the Internet are generally lower, less than half of all consumers purchase the lowest-priced item when offered more information from trusted sources i.e. price dispersion may actually increase online. Reasons why the lowest price may not always result in the sale are:

   - Ease of use of site and placing orders (e.g. Amazon One-Click makes placing an order with Amazon much easier than using a new supplier).
   - Ancillary information (e.g. book reviews contributed by other customers enhances Amazon service).
   - After-sales service (prompt, consistent fulfilment and notification of dispatch from Amazon increases trust in the site).
   - Trust with regard to security and customer privacy.

   These factors enable Amazon to charge more than competitors and still achieve the greatest sales volume of online booksellers (although not, to date, profitability). In summary, trust becomes the means of differentiation and loyalty. As a result, price comparison sites are being superseded by sites that independently rate the overall service such as Gomez (www.gomez.com) or use customers' opinions to rate the service such as Bizrate (www.bizrate.com) and E-pinions (www.epinions.com).

3. *E2E (end-to-end) integration*. This is an efficiency strategy that uses the Internet to decrease costs and increase product quality and shorten delivery times. This strategy is achieved by moving towards an automated supply chain (*Chapter 8*) and internal value chain. A key issue in moving towards the automated supply chain is determining which process should be owned internally, which should be achieved via partnerships, and which should be outsourced.

4. *Market creation*. Picardi (2000) defines market creation as '*the business of supplying market clearing and ancillary services in cyberspace, resulting in the creation of an integrated ecosystem of suppliers*'. The term ecosystem was coined in the new millennium to emphasize the move from relatively static supply chains with defined suppliers, partners and customers for an organization to a more dynamic environment in which such links are formed more readily. In tangible terms, this strategy involves integrating and continuously revising supply chains with market maker sites such as business-to-business exchanges (*Chapter 8*).

5. *Customer as designer*. This strategy uses the technology to enable customers to personalize products, again as a means of differentiation. This approach is particularly suited to information products, but manufactured products such as cars can now be specified to a fine degree of detail by the customer.

6. *Open-source value creation*. The best-known example of this is the creation and commercial success of the operating system Linux by over 300,000 collaborators worldwide. Picardi (2000) suggests that organizations will make more use of external resources to solve their problems.

For answers see p. 209

CASE STUDY 5.2

Evolving business models in the Internet car sales market

FT

Some of Internet retail's magic-wand promises of an instant revolution appear to be drying up, and perhaps nowhere is this more apparent than in the US auto retail market. Car web retailing is in the midst of change – again. Take, for example, this headline from the industry trade magazine, *Automotive News*, published in August: 'Reports of the dealer's demise appear to have been premature.'

The first wave of web retailing of cars is already past with some very notable casualties, including the cessation of operations at carOrder.com and doom-and-gloom parting shots by the former head of Priceline.com's auto sales.

Nevertheless, selling cars via the World Wide Web is far from dead. The model has simply shifted back in favour of the traditional strengths of dealers, manufacturers and some mega auto retail sites: access to a network of cars to sell.

The Internet was supposed to help consumers to bypass, if not to kill off, the unpleasantness in buying a car: haggling with the car dealers.

Buyers would log on to the Internet, configure a car to their own specification, or just browse and negotiate anonymously in serenity.

The promises came fast and furious. Venture capital was thrown at new ideas designed to sell cars over the Internet.

Hopes were high all around except at the dealers, who became defensive at the thought of their business being undermined. Many started started to use the web for themselves.

Many harboured the suspicion that the big car manufacturers were manoeuvring to use the Internet as a way of pushing dealers out in order to increase profits.

However, as many dot-com companies and ideas fall to earth, the shakeout has also changed the initial perceptions of how cars would sell and who would sell them over the Internet.

The new thinking was crystallized by the recent resignation of Maryann Keller as the head of Priceline.com's auto business. Ms Keller, a former Wall Street auto analyst, who joined the site with hopes of 'revolutionizing' car retail, left on a more disillusioned note.

'For car buying, the Internet is an idea whose time has not yet come and may never,' she says.

Many industry analysts, however, see a bright future in online car retail on sites that can actually improve the buying process, something not achieved by the web brokering or price-naming model of Priceline.com.

That improvement could come with offering a searchable, unlimited virtual warehouse of cars. This process, called Locate-To-Order (LTO), allows consumers to search an inventory of dealers and the factory to find a match close to their desired specifications.

Transactions could occur through dealerships still, but demand could move close to supply with customers able to reserve cars still on the factory line.

'We think we are going to see an evolution of this process over the next few years,' says Baba Shetty, senior automotive analyst at Forrester Research. 'The Internet enables some fundamental process improvements, but that doesn't blow up the existing retail distribution system.'

Both General Motors and Ford have offered dealers an olive branch and started to build systems heading in this direction. GM's BuyPower.com launched in October a Minneapolis pilot programme, where it linked Oldsmobile dealerships and offered e-prices. It plans to expand its testing of this system.

Ford has launched a site, FordDirect.com, in which its dealers own an 80 per cent stake and offer combined inventories with e-prices that vary according to region. Other early leaders include AutoNation.com, and its AOL partnership, and Microsoft's auto portal, CarPoint.com.

AutoNation, the US's largest dealer holding group, says it will sell $1.5 bn in new cars online this year, and is now running a system that could be considered a prototype for the larger-scale LTO.

CarPoint.com has established 3000 dealer links with a relationship with Ford and has the highest traffic of car sites to date. Right now it only refers customers to dealers, but is likely to change early next year.

Another big referral site, Autobytel.com, is thought likely to struggle if it does not change, while direct sellers, such as Greenlight.com – which is linked with Amazon.com and finds cars for buyers – also could gravitate to this model to compete.

In five years, Forrester Research estimates that 6.5 per cent of new vehicle sales, or $33 bn, will happen over the Internet, compared with about 1 per cent, or $2.8 bn, currently.

Also, by 2005, Internet research is expected to influence 55 per cent of car sales, with 40 per cent of buyers at least visiting an online selling site. In the meantime, data about vehicles being sold on the Internet should be more detailed.

Source: Article by Christopher Bowe, *Financial Times*, 8 December 2000.

Questions

1. Evaluate the overall success of the Internet as a mechanism for car sales.
2. Which business models and revenue models appear to be effective on the Internet? Can other success factors be identified?
3. Summarize the approach taken by the car manufacturers to the Internet marketplace.

Strategy implementation

Strategy implementation includes all tactics used to achieve strategic objectives. The main tactics and actions required are summarized in *Figure 5.19*. These actions are described in more detail in the remainder of Part 2 and in Part 3 as indicated in the figure and also *Table 5.6*.

Strategy implementation
Planning, actions and controls needed to achieve strategic goals.

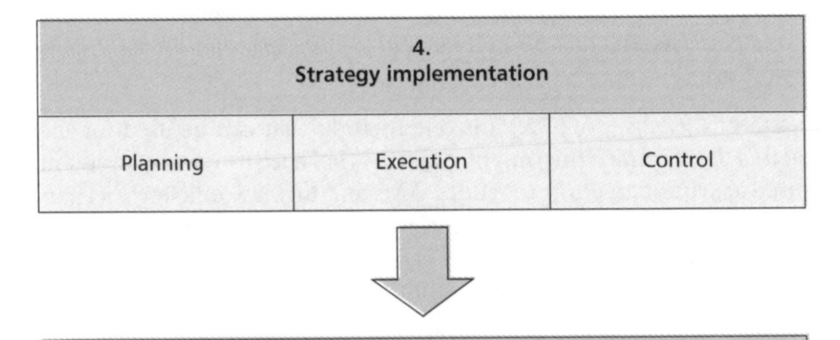

Figure 5.19 Elements of strategy implementation for the e-business

Focus on information systems strategy and e-business strategy

F

An essential part of any e-business strategy is consideration of how information systems strategy supports change. The importance to e-business success of utilizing information systems to manage information is highlighted by Willcocks and Plant (2000) who found in a study of 58 major corporations in the US, Europe and Australasia that the leading companies were astute at *distinguishing the contributions of information and technology, and considering them separately*. They make the point that competitive advantage *comes not from technology, but how information is collected stored, analysed and applied.*

An established aspect of information systems strategy development is the focus of IS strategy on business impact or alignment. In the **business alignment** approach, a top-down approach is used to review how information systems can be used to directly support a defined business strategy. Referring to e-business strategy Pant and Ravichandran (2001) say:

Business alignment IS strategy
The IS strategy is generated from the business strategy through techniques such as CSF analysis.

> *Alignment models focus on aligning the information system's plans and priorities with organizational strategy and business goals.*

Linking information systems to objectives and critical success factors (Table 5.3), is one approach for using the alignment approach. Another is the use of business systems planning methodology which focuses on deriving data and applications needs by analysis of existing business processes.

In the **business impacting** approach, a bottom-up approach is used to determine whether there are new opportunities from deploying information systems that may impact positively on a business strategy. New hardware and software technologies are monitored by the IS manager and other managers to evaluate whether they can achieve competitive advantage. Pant and Ravichandran (2001) say:

Business impacting IS strategy
IS strategy analyses opportunities for new technologies and processes to favourably impact the business strategy.

> *impact models focus on the potential impact of information technology on organizational tasks and processes and use this as a basis to identify opportunities for deploying information systems.*

Value chain analysis (*Chapter 6, p. 225*) is one method that can be used for the impact approach. For example, this might identify the need for e-procurement which can be used as part of an effort to reduce costs and increase efficiency as part of business strategy. This technique has merit in that it not only considers internal use of information systems, but also how they can be used to integrate with external organizations such as suppliers, perhaps through innovative methods such as marketplace exchanges.

The impact and alignment techniques need not be mutually exclusive. During initial development of an e-business strategy, a business alignment approach can be applied to ensure that IS strategy supports e-business strategy. A business impacting approach is also useful to see which new opportunities IS produces. For instance, managers could consider how a relatively new technology such as workflow management software (*Chapter 11, p. 421*) be used to improve efficiency and customer service.

The business impacting approach can be achieved through the use of value chain analysis or re-engineering where an organization, through an analysis of the potential for the use of IS within and between value chain elements, may seek to identify strategic IS opportunities. Perhaps the ultimate expression of using IS to impact business performance is through business process re-engineering which is considered in a later section.

The application of an impacting or aligning strategy with respect to IS and business strategy is dependent on the importance attached to IS within an organization. *Case study 5.3* indicates changes in the way that IT is perceived at board level as it increases in prominence.

CASE STUDY 5.3

The IT expertise of directors worldwide

Two years ago there were still industries and regions in which board directors could safely joke about their computer illiteracy. Now there is no longer anywhere to hide.

This stark warning comes from Rudy Puryear, chief executive of Lante, a Chicago-based e-commerce consultancy. Mr Puryear says the best directors of traditional companies across the globe have progressed over the past 18 months from basic awareness of new technologies to genuine insight into how they are transforming business. But he suspects some business leaders are treating this year's turbulence in dot-com stocks as an excuse for not taking any action.

'I would hope that this falling away of the dot-coms does not take the pressure off,' he says. 'I think the pressure is healthy.'

So how 'IT-literate' do board directors need to be these days? Experts such as Mr Lante argue that it is strategy not software that directors need to master. 'They don't need to be so deep in the details that they can talk bits and bytes at cocktail parties. But they need to comprehend how technology eliminates the traditional constraints of space, time and physical form – how eliminating distance can take a supplier and buyer who have never met and connect them in an ultra-efficient marketplace as if they were in the same room.'

He believes boards would benefit from having at least one member with a deeper understanding of IT. Because of the difficulty of finding such people with board-level qualifications, an existing director could be given the task of looking out for relevant new technologies that might determine corporate strategy.

The best directors have moved from debating whether to sell their products off the company web site to examining how they might emulate General Electric or Dell, the computer company, in deriving value from Internet-based business processes. 'Perhaps it's not as glamorous, but it's far more lucrative and revolutionary over the long run.'

That may all sound rather daunting to directors who still rely on their secretaries to handle their e-mails and have yet to surf the web. There are still some of them about, says Jim Norton, visiting professor of electrical engineering at the University of Sheffield and head of e-business policy at the UK's Institute of Directors. Professor Norton travels the length and breadth of the country, talking to directors about how to prepare for e-business.

He says small businesses in the UK are a long way behind the US. 'The US is more open to new ideas and much more economically rational. Small business in the UK assumes that getting a web site built and hosting it will cost much more than it does.'

Directors do not need to be experts in Java programming, but a basic familiarity with new technology is essential. 'It's absolutely imperative that every single member of the board should have been helped to use the Internet, should have bought something on it and visited competitors' web sites. People are embarrassed about being shown up among their peers. So do it late at night – at midnight if necessary.' Outside consultants are not necessary – board directors could be assisted by more technophile colleagues in the business.

'E-business strategy can't be shoved into an IT ghetto,' says Professor Norton. 'It affects every function around that board table. A classic mistake is to say: "Our competitors are going into e-business, we must do something – why not appoint an e-business director?" By doing that (the other directors) disown the process.'

Boards need to thrash out how e-business will change what their company does. This strategic planning may need the help of a facilitator, but not a management consultant, he argues. 'The management consultant says: "Here are the answers." That's death. The technique has to be to make the board collectively answer these questions.'

He cites what he calls the 'eight Cs' that directors should address. These are: how e-business will affect costs, the relationship with customers, the company culture, the way value is created, cooperation with partners, how it fulfils its commitments, how it charges and how it deals with new competitors.

'Only when the business has decided what to do with this do you call in the technologist,' he says. 'If you're making a major transformation, you might want to appoint to the board whoever is in charge of implementation. This will not necessarily be the manager of information systems, it could be the HR person or the specialist in business change. The role

▶

▶ CASE STUDY *continued*

of the board is to set the business principles and then trust the competent person to implement them.'

There are dangers in directors becoming involved in the nitty-gritty of technology. The chairman of one international company returned from an e-commerce conference so enthusiastic that 'they spent eight weeks talking him off the ceiling', says Jonathan Steel, chairman of The Bathwick Group, a London-based research and corporate counselling company.

At the other extreme are boards who marginalize IT. This leads to the complaint that 'the IT department doesn't understand the needs of the business' or 'the board doesn't understand IT'. E-commerce, internal company networks and e-procurement should be seen as interrelated, not as separate issues, says Mr Steel.

He believes more European companies should introduce US-style chief information officers (CIOs), who have a broad remit for how information flows across a company and how this affects the business and who do not focus only on the systems technology.

Many companies prefer to outsource their IT, but there can be dangers here too. 'A lot of companies have come to grief,' says Patrick Dunne, a director of 3i, the venture capitalists. 'You need to know that your supplier is up to the mark. You need to do incredibly careful referencing and make sure you're not their least important customer.'

Directors also need to consider IT when making acquisitions. 'Systems integration is one of the things people leave till last. You think about the people and the financial issues. But understanding the level of your systems capability and theirs and whether they are compatible is really important.'

Source: Article by Alison Maitland, *Financial Times*, 17 November 2000.

Questions

1. What involvement in IT does the article suggest for board directors?
2. Does the article suggest it is essential to have an IT or IS manager on the board of the company?

Elements of IS strategy

Developing an IS strategy for e-business involves many different perspectives, rather than a single perspective such as hardware technologies or applications to deploy. Ward and Griffiths (1996) suggest an IS strategy plan contains three elements:

1. *Business information strategy*. How information will support the business. This will include applications to manage particular types of business.
2. *IS functionality strategy*. Which services are provided?
3. *IS/IT strategy*. Earlier in this book we have referred to providing a suitable *technological, applications and process infrastructure* (*Chapter 3, p. 88*).

The advent of e-business clearly increases the strategic importance of information systems resources of an organization. However, developing an IS strategy to achieve e-business goals is complex because it can be viewed from many different perspectives (*Table 5.7*). This table is essentially a checklist of different aspects of IS strategy that have to be implemented by an IS manager in the e-business. Many of these aspects are solutions to business and technical problems that are described in Parts 2 and 3 of this book as summarized in the table.

We will now consider one of the most important issues facing IS managers in more detail.

Table 5.7 Different elements of IS strategy

IS strategy element	*What needs to be specified*	*Approaches to aid specification*	*Selected tactics (applications)*
1. Business contribution perspective (Chapter 5)	How applications achieve e-business objectives	Impact and alignment Portfolio analysis Investment types	Implementation of key systems
2. Information management strategy (Chapter 10)	Strategy for integrated information and knowledge management	Audit information management and knowledge management requirements by internal and external resources Security audit	Committee to standardize company information Enterprise resource planning, knowledge management, data warehousing, intranet and extranet projects
3. Applications perspective (Chapters 3 and 11)	Priorities for applications acquisition	Portfolio analysis Investment appraisal	As above
4. Process perspective (supply chain perspective to e-business) (Chapters 6 and 11)	How do applications and infrastructure support processes and value chain activities? Are new processes required?	Process mapping and analysis Value chain analysis	Enterprise resource planning integrated with transactional e-commerce
5. Departmental (functional) perspective (Chapters 3 and 10)	Which applications support different departments?	Portfolio analysis	Standardization of applications
6. Infrastructure perspective (Chapters 3 and 11)	Network capacity and service levels	Cost/benefit feasibility study of applications	Managing total cost of ownership Outsourcing
7. Communications perspective (Chapter 9)	Using technology to improve process efficiency and customer service quality	Audit communications volume and complexity. Prioritize.	E-mail, groupware and workflow systems Knowledge management
8. User services perspective (Chapter 9)	Help desk services for internal and external system users	Audit service levels, impact on business and then prioritize	Outsourcing Enquiry management systems
9. Customer and partner relationship management perspective (Chapters 6 and 9	Investment in systems for managing customer and partner relationships	Customer relationship management and partner relationship management systems Use of standards for integration: EDI and XML	CRM facilities on web site Integration
10. Resourcing perspective (Chapters 10)	How are relevant IS skills acquired and developed?	Skills audit and industry comparison End user computing	Technology partners Outsourcing Recruitment tactics E-learning and skills transfer
11. Change management perspective (Chapter 10)	How organizational culture and structure change to achieve e-business are managed	Apply existing change management approaches	Risk management Project management
12. Internal integration perspective (Chapters 3 and 11)	Overall applications architecture across the value chain	Analyse information access constraints, rekeying	Enterprise resource planning
13. External integration perspective (Chapters 3 and 11)	How are links between internal applications and partners managed	Analyse ease of setting up links, prioritize	Outsourcing to systems integrator Standardization through ERP. Integration of IS systems with buy- and sell-side intermediaries
14. Legal constraints approach (Chapter 4)	How do we ensure company stays within international legal and ethical constraints?	Seek specialist advice, e.g. www.itcompliance.com	Specialist lawyers and privacy statements

Investment appraisal

In the e-business context, investment appraisal can refer to:

1. Overall levels of spending on information systems to support e-business.
2. Decisions about which business applications to invest in (portfolio analysis).
3. Assessment of the cost/benefit for individual applications.

Overall levels of spending on information systems to support e-business.

Figure 5.12 suggests that companies should aim to invest in e-business in line with the objectives set. Since e-business investment is only 11.1 per cent compared to revenues of 14.9 per cent, this suggests that companies are underinvesting in e-commerce. The PricewaterhouseCoopers (2000) analysis also breaks down revenue and spending for product and service companies. Service companies achieve 20.6 per cent of total revenues online while product companies achieve 9 per cent of their revenues online. In terms of spending, service companies spend 10 per cent of operating budget on IT, split 57 per cent for IT personnel and 43 per cent for hardware and software. Product companies spend just 3.1 per cent of operating budget split 44 per cent for IT personnel and 56 per cent for hardware and software. Lower revenues in these companies seems consistent with lower investment. Hackbarth and Kettinger (2000) suggest that one element of e-business strategy development is whether to focus on the sell-side or buy-side for applications development.

Decisions about which business applications to invest in

A portfolio analysis such as that illustrated for The B2C Company in *Figure 5.3* can also be used to decide priorities for application by selecting those that fall within the strategic and turnaround categories for further investment. Relative priorities and the amount of investment in different applications can also be assisted if priorities for e-business objectives have been assigned, as is the case with *Table 5.3*.

Traditionally investments in information systems have been categorized according to their importance and contribution to the organization. For example, Robson (1997) describes four types of BIS investment:

1. *Operational value investment*. These investments are in systems that are key to the day-to-day running of the organization such as transaction processing systems for processing orders received by phone or a workflow system for managing booking staff training and leave. Such systems are often valuable in increasing efficiency or reducing costs, but they do not contribute directly to the performance of the business.
2. *Strategic value investment*. Strategic investments will enhance the performance of a business and should help in developing revenue. A customer relationship management system would be a strategic investment. This will be intended to increase customer loyalty resulting in additional sales from existing customers.
3. *Threshold investment*. These are investments in BIS that a company must make to operate within a business. Investments may have a negative return on investment but are needed for competitive survival.
4. *Infrastructure investment*. These can be substantial investments which result in gain in the medium to long term. Typically this includes investment in internal networks, electronic links with suppliers, customers and partners and investment in new hardware such as client PCs and servers.

As part of developing e-business strategies, companies can prioritize potential information systems investments in the above categories according to their impact on the business. A similar approach is to specify the applications portfolio described in the section on situation analysis. It is evident that priority should be given to applications that fall into the strategic and high potential categories in *Figure 5.4*. Now complete *activity 5.4*.

E-business investment types

Activity 5.4

Purpose

To gain an appreciation of how to prioritize IS investments.

Questions

1. Referring to the four investment categories of Robson (1997), discuss in groups which category the following investments would fit into:
   (a) E-procurement system
   (b) Transactional e-commerce web site
   (c) Contract with ISP to host web server and provide Internet connectivity for staff
   (d) Workflow system to manage complex customer orders (e.g. processing orders)
   (e) Upgrading a company network.
2. Assume you only had sufficient funds to invest in two of these options. Which two would you choose?

For answer see p. 209

The productivity paradox

All discussion of investment appraisals in information systems should acknowledge the existence of the **productivity paradox**. Studies in the late 1980s and 1990s summarized by Brynjolfsson (1993) and Strassman (1997) suggest that there is little or no correlation between a company's investment in information systems and its business performance measured in terms of profitability or stock returns. Strassman's early work, based on a study of 468 major North American and European firms, showed a random relationship between IT spending per employee and return on equity.

Productivity paradox
Research results indicating a poor correlation between organizational investment in information systems and organizational performance measured by return on equity.

To the present day, there has been much dispute about the reality of the productivity paradox with most authors such as Brynjolfsson and Hitt (1998) refuting the productivity paradox and concluding that it results from mismeasurement, the lag occurring between initial investment and payback and the mismanagement of information systems projects. More recent detailed studies such as that by Sircar *et al.* (2000) confirm the findings of Brynjolfsson and Hitt (1998). They state that

> *Both IT and corporate investments have a strong positive relationship with sales, assets, and equity, but not with net income. Spending on IS staff and staff training is positively correlated with firm performance, even more so than computer capital.*

In conclusion they state:

The value of IS staff and staff training was also quite apparent and exceeded that of computer capital. This confirms the positions of several authors, that the effective use of IT is far more important than merely spending on IT.

As they say, this will not be a surprise to many managers, but it is a reminder that it is not how much is spent on information systems, but the way in which it is spent which is important in delivering business benefits and achieving the e-business.

Summary

1. E-business strategy process models tend to share the following characteristics:
   - Continuous internal and external environment scanning or analysis are required.
   - Clear statement of vision and objectives is required.
   - Strategy development can be broken down into formulation and selection.
   - After strategy development, enactment of the strategy occurs as strategy implementation
   - Control is required to detect problems and adjust the strategy accordingly.
   - They must be responsive to changes in the marketplace.
2. In this chapter a four-stage model is used as a framework for e-business strategy development. Key e-business issues within this framework are outlined below.
3. *Strategic analysis*. Continuous scanning of the micro- and macro-environment of an organization are required with particular emphasis on the changing needs of customers, actions and business models of competitor and opportunities afforded by new technologies. Techniques include resource analysis, demand analysis and competitor analysis, applications portfolio analysis, SWOT analysis and competitive environment analysis.
4. *Strategic objectives*. Organizations must have a clear vision on whether digital media will complement or replace other media and their capacity for change. Clear objectives must be defined and in particular goals for the online revenue contribution should be set.
5. *Strategy definition*. Six key elements of e-business strategy that were reviewed are:
   - E-business priorities – significance to organization (replace or complement) and emphasis on buy-side or sell-side.
   - Form of restructuring required.
   - Business and revenue models.
   - Marketplace restructuring.
   - Market and product development strategies.
   - Positioning and differentiation strategies.
6. Strategy implementation. Detailed in the remainder of Part 2 and Part 3.
7. Information systems strategy should use a combination of impact and alignment techniques to govern e-business strategy. IS strategy can take a number of

perspectives of which those that focus on information or knowledge management and technological and applications infrastructure are most important.

ACTIVITY ANSWERS

5.1 Selecting an e-business strategy process model

1. (a) +: Strategy is based on thorough environment analysis, clear statement of vision and objectives, emphasizes the feedback loop necessary for control.
   –: Implies protracted, non-responsive strategy development which is not sufficiently dynamic. Strategy development process is not emphasized.
   (b) +: Highlights detailed elements of analysis and strategy development
   –: Doesn't highlight sequence in process. Importance of objective setting and control not element.
   (c) +: A dynamic responsive model that highlights the importance of continuous environment scanning in e-business.
   –: Doesn't emphasize the detailed strategy development elements of (a) and (b).
2. Study of the four models suggests that the following elements are significant:

   One: Continuous internal and external environment scanning or analysis are required.

   Two: Clear statement of vision and objectives required.

   Three: Strategy development can be broken down into formulation and selection.

   Four: After strategy development, enactment of the strategy occurs as strategy implementation

   Five: Control is required to detect problems and adjust the strategy accordingly.

In addition, the models suggest that these elements, although generally sequential, are also iterative and require reference back to previous stages.

5.3 E-business strategies for The B2C Company

In brief, it can be suggested that the first three strategies apply to most organizations, and in particular to B2C organizations. The attack e-tailing and defend e-tailing approaches do not have to be mutually exclusive and can be applied to most commodity products such as books, holidays and records. However, it is arguable whether a purchaser of kitchenware in the B2C case would be that price sensitive. In this case the emphasis on trust leading to loyalty as suggested by the defend e-tailing approach would be most relevant.

5.4 E-business investment types

1. You will notice that the categories are not mutually exclusive.

   (a) E-procurement system. This is an operational system, but as will be shown in *Chapter 8*, the potential cost savings are such that this could also be considered to be a strategic value investment.

   (b) Transactional e-commerce web site (*Chapter 9*). This is a customer facing system which if it increases the customer base of a company can be considered to be a strategic value investment. Within the e-business era, it can be thought of as a threshold investment to remain competitive.

   (c) Contract with ISP to provide Internet connectivity for staff. An infrastructure investment, with elements of threshold investment and operational investment.

   (d) Workflow system to manage complex customer orders (e.g. processing orders). This may appear to be an operational investment, but since it is a customer facing system that should improve customer service, it can be viewed as a strategic value investment.

(e) Upgrading a company network. An infrastructure investment.

2. If you think it is unrealistic to decide on just two investments, this is a genuine problem faced by many companies. An information system manager at a regional airline described how they had an applications backlog numbering more than one hundred of which only 20 or so could be funded immediately. The e-procurement system and transactional web site are clearly the best strategic value investments.

EXERCISES

Self-assessment questions

1. What are the key characteristics of an e-business strategy model?
2. Select a retailer or manufacturer of your choice and describe what the main elements of its situation analysis should comprise.
3. For the same retailer or manufacturer suggest different methods and metrics for defining e-business objectives.
4. For the same retailer or manufacturer assess different strategic options to adopt for e-business.

Essay and discussion questions

1. Evaluate the range of restructuring options for an existing 'bricks and mortar' organization to move to a 'bricks and clicks' or 'clicks only' contributing a higher online revenue.
2. Explain the main strategy definition options or decisions available to an organization intending to become an e-business.
3. Between 1994 and 1999 Amazon lost more than $500 m, but at the end of this period its valuation was still more than $20 bn. At the start of 2000 Amazon.com underwent its first round of job cuts, sacking 150 staff or 2 per cent of its worldwide workforce. Later in 2000 its valuation was more than halved.
   Write an essay on the strategy of Amazon.com exploring its history, different criteria for success and its future. See the Wired Magazine archive for profiles of Amazon (www.wired.com).
4. Analyze the reasons for the failure of the original boo.com. Research and assess the sustainability of the new boo.com business model.
5. What can existing businesses learn from the business approaches of the dot-com organizations?
6. What are the similarities and differences between the concepts of business process re-engineering (BPR) and e-business? Will the e-business concept face the same fate as BPR?
7. Discuss this statement by David Weymouth, Barclays Bank chief information officer (Simons, 2000b) who says:

There is no merit in becoming a dot-com business. Within five years successful businesses will have embraced and deployed at real-scale across the whole enterprise, the processes and technologies that we now know as dot-com.

8. Compare and contrast different approaches to developing e-business strategy.

Examination questions

1. Define the main elements of an e-business strategy?
2. You are incumbent e-business manager for a domestic airline. What process would you use to create objectives for the organization? Suggest three typical objectives and how you would measure them.
3. Explain the productivity paradox and its implications for managers.
4. What choices do executives have for the scope and timeframe of implementing e-business?

REFERENCES

Ansoff, H. (1957) Strategies for diversification. *Harvard Business Review* (September–October), 113–24.

Brynjolfsson, E. (1993) The productivity paradox of information technology. *Communications of the ACM*, 36(12), 67–77.

Brynjolfsson, E. and Hitt, L. (1998) Beyond the productivity paradox. *Communications of the ACM*, 41(8), 49–55.

Chaffey, D., Mayer, R., Johnston, K. and Ellis-Chadwick, F. (2000) *Internet Marketing: Strategy, Implementation and Practice*. Financial Times Prentice Hall, Harlow, UK.

Chase, L. (1998) *Essential Business Tactics for the Net*. John Wiley and Sons, New York, NY.

Chaston, I. (2000) *E-marketing strategy*. McGraw-Hill, UK.

Davenport, T.H. (1993) *Process Innovation: Re-engineering Work through Information Technology*. Harvard Business School Press, Boston.

Deise, M., Nowikow, C., King, P. and Wright, A. (2000) *Executive's Guide to E-business. From Tactics to Strategy*. John Wiley and Sons, New York, NY.

Der Zee, J. and De Jong, B. (1999) Alignment is not enough: Integrating business and information technology management with the balanced business scorecard. *Journal of Management Information Systems*, 16(2), 137–57.

Diamantopoulos, A. and Matthews, B. (1993) *Making Pricing Decisions. A Study of Managerial Practice*. Chapman and Hall, London.

Durlacher (2000) *Trends in the UK New Economy*. Durlacher Quarterly Internet Report, November, pp. 1–12.

DTI (2000) *Business In The Information Age – International Benchmarking Study 2000*. UK Department of Trade and Industry. Available online at: www.ukonlineforbusiness.gov.uk.

Economist (2000) Enter the Ecosystem. 11 November.

Goodwin, R. (2000) IT vital to high-street e-commerce boost, *Computer Weekly*, 13 July, p. 6.

Gulati, R. and Garino, J. (2000) Getting the right mix of bricks and clicks for your company. *Harvard Business Review*, May–June, 107–14.

Hackbarth, G. and Kettinger, W. (2000) Building an e-business strategy. *Information Systems Management*, Summer, 78–93.

Institute of Directors (2000) *E-business – Helping Directors to Understand and Embrace the Digital Age*. Director Publications, London, UK.

Johnson, G. and Scholes, K. (1999) *Exploring Corporate Strategy*. Prentice Hall Europe, Hemel Hempstead, UK.

Kalakota, R. and Robinson, M. (2000) *E-business. Roadmap for Success*. Addison-Wesley, Reading, MA.

Kaplan, R.S. and Norton, D.P. (1993) Putting the balanced scorecard to work. *Harvard Business Review*, September–October, 134–42.

de Kare-Silver, M. (2000) *eShock 2000. The Electronic Shopping Revolution: Strategies for Retailers and Manufacturers*. Macmillan, London.

Kotler, P. (1997) *Marketing Management – Analysis, Planning, Implementation and Control*. Prentice Hall, Englewood Cliffs, NJ.

Kumar, N. (1999) Internet distribution strategies: dilemmas for the incumbent. *Financial Times*, Special Issue on Mastering Information Management, no. 7, Electronic Commerce.

Lynch, R. (2000) *Corporate Strategy*. Financial Times Prentice Hall, Harlow, UK.

McFarlan, F. and McKenney, J. (1993) *Corporate Information Systems Management*, Prentice Hall, London.

McDonald, M. (1999) Strategic marketing planning: theory and practice. In *The CIM Marketing Book* 4th edn. Ed. M. Baker, Butterworth Heinemann, pp. 50–77.

Mintzberg and Quinn (1991) *The Strategy Process*, 2nd edn . Prentice Hall, Upper Saddle River, NJ.

Nolan, R. (1979) Managing the crisis in data processing. *Harvard Business Review*, March–April, 115–26.

Oleson (2000) The return on investment associated with ebusiness and ecommerce. Research report. IDC #W21462 (www.idcresearch.com)

Olve, N., Roy, J. and Wetter, M. (1999) *Performance Drivers. A Practical Guide to Using the Balanced Scorecard*. John Wiley and Sons, Chichester, UK.

Pant, S. and Ravichandran, T. (2001) A framework for information systems planning for e-business. *Logistics Information Management*, 14(1), 85–98.

Phillips, S. (2000) Retailer's crown jewel is a unique customer database. *Financial Times*, 4 December.

Picardi, R. (2000) *eBusiness Speed: Six Strategies for eCommerce Intelligence*. IDC Research Report. IDC Framlington, MA.

Plant, R. (2000) *eCommerce: Formulation of Strategy*. Prentice Hall, Upper Saddle River, NJ.

Porter M., 1980, *Competitive Strategy*. Free Press, USA

PricewaterhouseCoopers (2000) Trendsetter Barometer Report, Q2, 00. Available online only at www.barometersurveys.com.

Quelch, J. And Klein, L. (1996) The Internet and international marketing. *Sloan Management Review*, Spring, 60–75.

Robson, W. (1997) *Strategic Management and Information Systems: An Integrated Approach*. Pitman, London.

Simons, M. (2000a) Barclays gambles on web big bang. *Computer Weekly*, 13 July, p. 1.

Simons, M. (2000b) Setting the banks alight, *Computer Weekly*, 20 July, p. 6.

Sircar, S., Turnbow, J. and Bordoloi, B. (2000) A framework for assessing the relationship between information technology investments and firm performance. *Journal of Management Information Systems*, Spring, 16(4), 69–98.

Strassman, P. (1997) *The Squandered Computer*. Information Economics Press, New Canaan, CN.

Venkatraman, N. (2000) Five steps to a dot-com strategy: how to find your footing on the web. *Sloan Management Review*, Spring, 15–28.

Ward, J. and Griffiths, P. (1996) *Strategic Planning for Information Systems*, John Wiley and Sons, Chichester, UK.

Willcocks, L. and Plant, R. (2000) Business Internet Strategy – moving to the Net. In L. Willcocks and C. Sauer (eds) *Moving to E-business*. Random House, London, pp. 19–46.

Willcocks, L. and Sauer, C. (2000) Introduction to *Moving to E-business*. Random House, London, pp. 1–18.

FURTHER READING

Deise, M., Nowikow, C., King, P. and Wright, A. (2000) *Executive's Guide to E-business. From Tactics to Strategy*. John Wiley and Sons, New York, NY. An excellent practitioner's guide.

Gulati, R. and Garino, J. (2000) Getting the right mix of bricks and clicks for your company. *Harvard Business Review*, May–June, 107–14. A different perspective on the six strategy decisions given in the strategic definition section with a road map through the decision process.

Hackbarth, G. and Kettinger, W. (2000) Building an e-business strategy. *Information Systems Management*, Summer, 78–93. An information systems perspective to e-business strategy.

Porter, M. (2001) Strategy and the Internet. *Harvard Business Review*, March, 63–78. Michael Porter defends his existing models in the new economy context.

Willcocks, L. and Sauer, C. (2000) Introduction to *Moving to E-business*. Random House, London, pp. 1–18. Combines traditional IS strategy-based approaches with up-to-date case studies.

WEB LINKS

BRINT.com (www.brint.com): a business researcher's interests. Extensive portal with articles on e-business, e-commerce, knowledge management, change management and IS strategy.

CIO Magazine e-commerce resource centre (www.cio.com/forums/ec/): one of best online magazines from business/technical perspective – see other research centres also, e.g. intranets, knowledge management.

E-commerce innovation centre (www.ecommerce.ac.uk) at Cardiff University. Interesting case studies for SMEs and basic explanations of concepts and terms.

E-commerce Times (www.ecommercetimes.com): an online newspaper specific to e-commerce developments.

Financial Times IT surveys (www.ft.com/ftit): excellent monthly articles based on case studies. Also see Connectis for more European examples.

E-commerce About.com (www.ecommerce.about.com): portal about all aspects of e-commerce.

US Centre for e-business (www.ebusiness.mit.edu): useful collection of articles.

Net Academy (www.netacademy.org): business resources including e-business articles.

E-consultancy (www.e-consultancy.com): e-business portal with links to news and white papers on other sites.

IT Toolbox (www.ittoolbox.com): guidelines and articles on e-business including ERP, CRM and data warehousing.

PwC Barometer Surveys (www.barometersurveys.com): research on e-business strategy and implementation in the New Economy.

Chapter 6

Supply chain management

CHAPTER AT A GLANCE

LEARNING OBJECTIVES

After completing this chapter the reader should be able to:

- Identify the main elements of supply chain management and their relationship to the value chain and value networks.
- Assess the potential of information systems to support supply chain management and the value chain.

MANAGEMENT ISSUES

The issues for the manager:

- Which technologies should we deploy for supply chain management and how should they be prioritized?
- Which elements of the supply chain should be managed within and beyond the organization and how can technology be used to facilitate this?

Links to other chapters

The main related chapters are:

- *Chapter 1* introduces the supply chain as a key element of e-business.
- *Chapter 7* considers the e-procurement part of the supply chain in more detail.

Introduction

In the end business all comes down to supply chain vs supply chain. (Robert Rodin, CEO of Marshall Industries, one of the largest global distributors of electronic components)

Supply chain management is presented as the premier application of e-business in Part 2 of this book since it is a unifying concept that incorporates both e-procurement (*Chapter 7*) and sell-side e-commerce (*Chapters 8 and 9*). By applying information systems, companies can enhance or radically improve many aspects of the supply chain. In the context of *Figure 1.1*, which was used to introduce the concept of e-business, supply chain management can be enhanced through buy-side e-commerce, internal communications, relationships with partners and sell-side e-commerce.

Much of the excitement generated by the e-business concept concerns the benefits that companies can achieve through increasing the efficiency of the whole supply chain. Companies that have enthusiastically embraced technology to manage the supply chain such as Tesco (*case study 6.1*) are already starting to reap these benefits.

What is supply chain management?

Supply chain management (SCM)
The coordination of all supply activities of an organization from its suppliers and partners to its customers.

Upstream supply chain
Transactions between an organization and its suppliers and intermediaries, equivalent to buy-side e-commerce.

Downstream supply chain
Transactions between an organization and its customers and intermediaries, equivalent to sell-side e-commerce.

Supply chain network
The links between an organization and all partners involved with multiple supply chains.

Supply chain management (SCM) involves the coordination of all supply activities of an organization from its suppliers and delivery of products to its customers (*Figure 6.1*). *Figure 6.1* introduces the main players in the supply chain. In *Figure 6.1(a)* the main members of the supply chain are the organizations that manufacture a product and/or deliver a service.

For most commercial and not-for-profit organizations we can distinguish between **upstream supply chain** activities which are equivalent to buy-side e-commerce and **downstream supply chain** activities which equate to sell-side e-commerce. In this chapter and the next we focus mainly on improving the efficiency of upstream supply chain activities while in *Chapters 8 and 9* the emphasis is on the marketing aspects of improving downstream supply chain activities.

Remember also from *Figure 1.1* that supply chain management includes not only supplier and buyer, but also the intermediaries such as the supplier's suppliers and the customer's customers (*Figure 6.1(b)*). Indeed *Figure 6.1(b)* is a simplification of some companies which may have first-tier suppliers, second-tier or even third-tier suppliers and first-tier, second or more-tier customers. Because each company effectively has many individual supply chains for different products, the use of the term 'chain' is limiting and **supply chain network** is a more accurate reflection of the links between an organization and its partners. The existence of this network increases the need for electronic communications technology to manage and optimize this network.

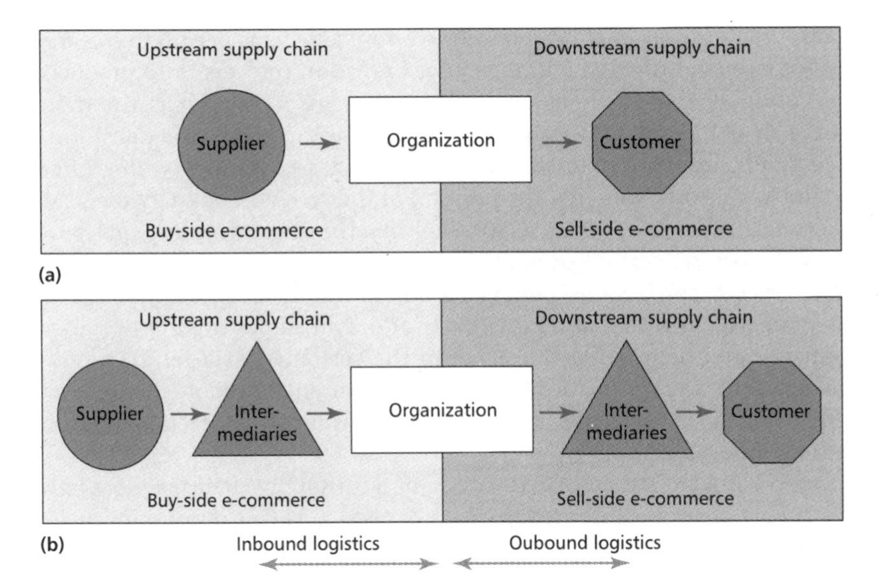

Figure 6.1 Members of the supply chain (a) simplified view (b) including intermediaries

Technology is vital to supply chain management since managing relationships with customers, suppliers and intermediaries is based on the flow of information and the transactions between these parties. The main strategic thrust of enhancing the supply chain is to provide a superior value proposition to the customer; see the box *Efficient consumer response*. As explained in *Chapter 5* improving customer value involves improving product quality, customer service quality and/or reducing price and fulfilment times. An alternative emphasis is on increasing efficiency in obtaining resources from a supplier organization or distributing products to customers. This emphasis is about reducing operational costs and so increasing profitability.

Efficient consumer response (ECR)

The ECR concept was developed for the food retailing business in the US but since then it has been applied to other products and other countries. It was originally developed by David Jenkins, then chairman of Shaw's supermarkets to compete with other players such as Walmart. *Table 6.1* shows that some of the aims and strategic approaches generated by ECR can also apply to business customers.

Table 6.1 Objectives and strategies for effective consumer response (ECR)

Objective	*Strategy*
Timely, accurate, paperless information flow	Revision of organization processes supported by information systems
Smooth, continual product flow matched to consumption	See strategies below
Optimize productivity of retail space and inventory	Efficient store assortments
Optimize for time and cost in the ordering process	Efficient replacement
Maximize efficiency of promotions	Promotions are integrated into entire supply chain planning
Maximize effectiveness of new product development (NPD)	NPD process improved and better forward planning with other partners

An organization's supply chain can be viewed from a systems perspective as the acquisition of resources (inputs) and their transformation (process) into products and services (outputs) that are then delivered to customers. Such a perspective indicates that as part of moving to e-business, organizations can review the transformation process and optimize it in order to deliver products to customers with greater efficiency and lower cost. Note that the position of the systems boundary for SCM extends beyond the organization – it not only involves improving internal processes, but also processes performed in conjunction with suppliers, distributors and customers. However, this process perspective misses the strategic importance of supply chain management – it also provides great opportunities to improve product performance and deliver superior value to the customer. As a result, supply chain management can dramatically impact the profitability of a company through reducing operating costs and increasing customer satisfaction and so loyalty and revenue.

Since *Figure 6.1* is a grossly simplified version of most supply chains, a more representative supply chain is illustrated in *Figure 6.2* which shows the supply chain for The B2B Company. Complete the introductory activity (*activity 6.1*) to consider the issues involved in modifying the supply chain in response to e-business. Note

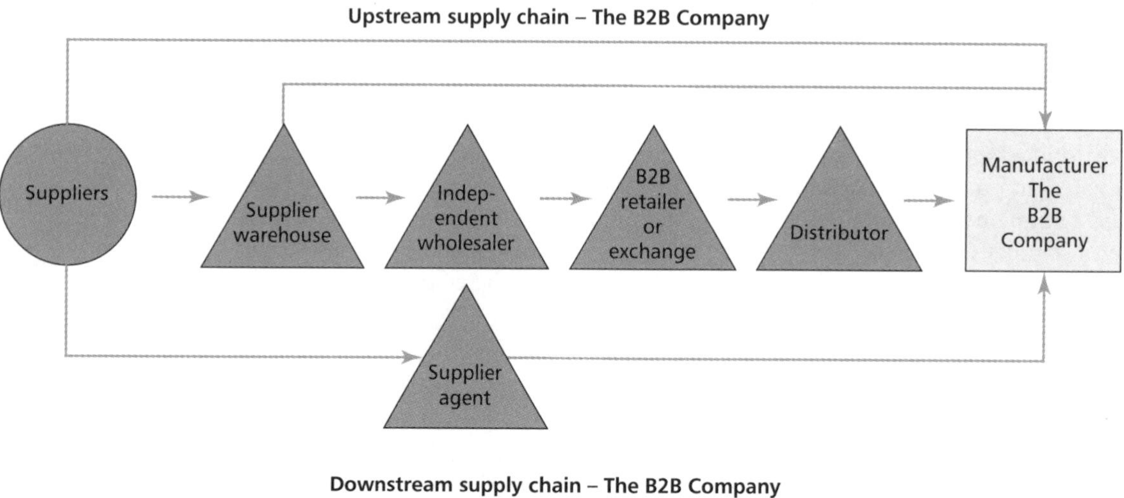

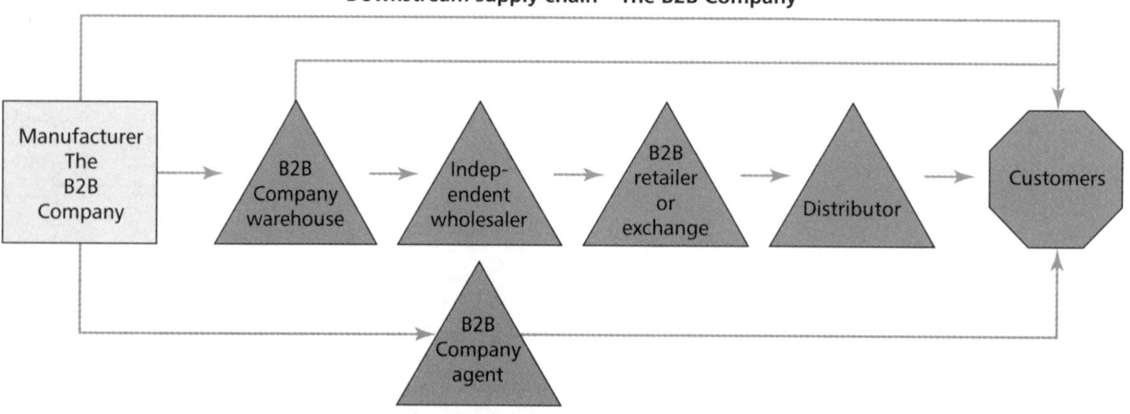

Figure 6.2 A typical supply chain (an example from The B2B Company)

that although this example is based on a business-to-business scenario, supply chain management is also vital to the management of business-to-consumer and service companies. With service companies such as financial services, the resources managed tend not to be physical but human, financial and information resources. However, the same principles of using e-commerce technology to enhance supply chain activities can still be applied.

The supply chain for The B2B Company

Activity 6.1

Purpose

To examine the nature of a B2B supply chain and its potential for modification through restructuring and information systems as part of e-business development.

Questions

1. Referring to *Chapter 2* and the section on *disintermediation and reintermediation* discuss the opportunities for The B2B Company to restructure its supply chain as part of the move to e-business, and the benefits this may bring.
2. How can information systems be used to accomplish the changes you have identified in question 1?

For answer see p. 251

What is logistics?

Logistics is a concept closely related to supply chain management. According to the Institute of Logistics and Transportation (www.iolt.org):

> *Logistics is the time-related positioning of resource, or the strategic management of the total supply chain. The supply chain is a sequence of events intended to satisfy a customer. It can include procurement, manufacture, distribution, and waste disposal, together with associated transport, storage and information technology.*

This definition of logistics is broad, reflecting its provenance. More typically, logistics is used to refer not to all supply chain activities, but specifically to the management of **outbound logistics** or **inbound and outbound logistics** (*Figure 6.1*). Logistics is essential to the efficient management of the supply chain, for example resource management and transport are integral parts of the supply chain, not only between supply chain processes, but within these processes.

Inbound logistics
The management of material resources entering an organization from its suppliers and other partners.

Outbound logistics
The management of resources supplied from an organization to its customers and intermediaries such as retailers and distributors.

To understand why supply chain management plays an important role in modern management thinking, read the box *Developments in supply chain management*.

Developments in supply chain management

In order to understand how e-commerce can be used to enhance supply chain and logistics management it is useful to consider the historical context of management approaches to supply chain management and how information systems have been used to support them. The following stages can be identified:

▶

1960s/70s: Physical distribution management (PDM)

Physical distribution management (PDM) focused upon the physical movement of goods by treating stock management, warehousing, order processing and delivery as related rather than separate activities. Although information systems were developed to manage these processes they were often paper-based and not integrated across different functions. However, some leading companies started using EDI at this time. PDM was essentially about the management of finished goods but not about the management of materials and processes that impacted upon the distribution process. PDM was superseded by logistics management which viewed manufacturing storage and transport from raw material to final consumer as integral parts of a total distribution process.

1970s/80s: Logistics management (Materials Requirement Planning (MRP) and Just in Time – JIT)

The Just in Time philosophy (JIT) is still a relatively recent development of logistics management, its aim to make the process of raw materials acquisition, production and distribution as efficient and flexible as possible in terms of material supply and customer service. Minimum order quantities and stock levels were sought by the customer and therefore manufacturers had to introduce flexible manufacturing processes and systems that interfaced directly with the customer who could call an order directly against a pre-arranged schedule with a guarantee that it would be delivered on time. Materials Requirement Planning systems were important in maintaining resources at an optimal level. The Design for Manufacture technique was used to simplify the number of components required for manufacture. However, none of the above methods looked at the management of the total supply chain. An associated phenomenon is *lean production and lean supply* where supply chain efficiency is aimed at eliminating waste and minimizing inventory and work in progress.

1980s/90s: Supply chain management and efficient consumer response (ECR)

Effective management of the supply chain involved much closer integration between the supplier, customer and intermediaries and in some instances involved one organization in the channel taking over functions that were traditionally the domain of the intermediary. Bottlenecks or undersupply/oversupply can have significant impacts on an organization's profitability. The two primary goals of supply chain management are to maximize the efficiency and effectiveness of the total supply chain for the benefit of all the players, not just one section of the channel, and to maximize the opportunity for customer purchase by ensuring adequate stock levels at all stages of the process. These two goals impact upon the sourcing of raw materials and stockholding. A recent phenomenon has been the rapid growth in global sourcing of supplies from preferred suppliers, particularly amongst multinational and/global organizations. The Internet will provide increased capability for smaller players to globally source raw materials and therefore improve their competitivness. Quelch and Klein (1996) argue that the Internet will revolutionize the dynamics of international commerce and in particular lead to the more rapid internationalization of small and medium-sized enterprises. The web will reduce the competitive advantage of economies of scale in many industries making it easier for smaller companies to compete on a worldwide basis. New integrated information systems such as the SAP enterprise resource planning (ERP) system have helped manage the entire supply chain. ERP systems include modules which are deployed throughout the business and interface with suppliers. Technology has enabled the introduction of faster, more responsive and flexible ordering, manufacturing and distribution systems, which has diminished even further the need for warehouses to be located near to markets that they serve.

1990s/00s: Technological interface management (TIM)

According to Hamill and Gregory (1997) the challenge facing suppliers, intermediaries and customers in the supply chain will shift from a focus on physically distributing goods to a process of collection, collation, interpretation and dissemination of vast amounts of information. Enterprise resource planning systems are continuously being updated to support first direct data interfaces with suppliers and customers, for example to support EDI. A more recent development is interfacing of ERP systems with B2B intermediary sites or exchanges such as Commerce One (www.commerceone.com). See the focus on B2B exchanges in *Chapter 7* for further discussion of these. SAP has also created mySAP facility to help customers manage and personalize their interactions with these exchanges. XML (*Chapter 3*) is increasingly used as the technical means by which technological interface management is achieved. (The critical resource possessed by these new intermediaries will be information rather than inventory. Hagel and Rayport (1997) take this a stage further by suggesting that customer information capture will serve customers rather than vendors in future. Currently customers leave a trail of information behind them as they visit sites and make transactions. This data can be captured and then used by suppliers and agents to improve targeting of offers. However, as customers become more aware of the value of information and as technology on the Internet enables them to protect private information relating to site visits and transactions, then the opportunity for intermediaries to act as customer agents and not supplier agents grows.)

Push and pull supply chain models

A change in supply chain thinking, and also in marketing communications thinking, is the move from push models of selling to pull models or combined push-pull approaches. The push model is illustrated by a manufacturer who perhaps develops an innovative product and then identifies a suitable target market. A distribution channel is then created to push the product to the market. This situation is shown in *Figure 6.3(a)* where it can be characterized by the statement '*This is a great product, now who shall we sell it to*' or the quip about the original model T Ford – 'you can have any colour, so long as it is black'. The typical motivation for a push approach is to optimize the production process for cost and efficiency.

The alternative approach consistent with ECR is focused on the customer's needs and it starts with analysis of their requirements through market research and close cooperation with customers and suppliers in new product development (*Figure 6.3(b)*). Here the supply chain is constructed to deliver value to the customer by reducing costs and increasing service quality. *Figure 6.3(b)* shows how there are much closer links between the elements of the supply chain through use of technology such as EDI to minimize document transfer and rekeying. This approach can be characterized by the question '*What do our customers demand in the ideal product and service?*' Modern car manufacturers now not only provide a choice of colour, but thousands of permutations of trim and accessories backed up by service promises such as three-year warranties. The typical motivation for a pull approach is to optimize the production process for customer response, cost and efficiency. It will be apparent that such an approach is also consistent with management thinking about the similar concept of the value chain as illustrated in the *Focus on the value chain* section.

Push supply chain
A supply chain that emphasizes distribution of a product to passive customers.

Pull supply chain
An emphasis on using the supply chain to deliver value to customers who are actively involved in product and service specification.

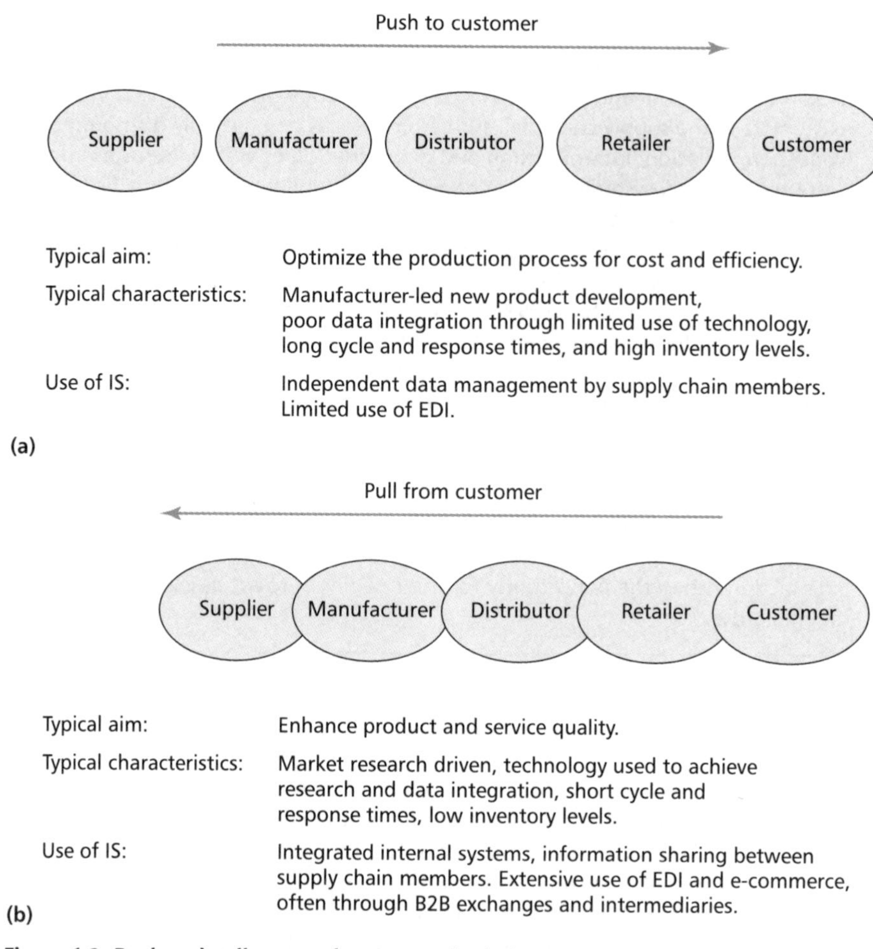

Figure 6.3 Push and pull approaches to supply chain management

F *Focus on* the value chain

Value chain
A model that considers how supply chain activities can add value to products and services delivered to the customer.

Michael Porter's **value chain** is a well-established concept for considering key activities that an organization can perform or manage with the intention of adding value for the customer as products and services move from conception to delivery to the customer (Porter, 1980). The value chain is a model that describes different value-adding activities that connect a company's supply side with its demand side. We can identify an *internal* value chain within the boundaries of an organization and an *external* value chain where activities are performed by partners. By analysing the different parts of the value chain managers can redesign internal and external process to improve their efficiency and effectiveness. Value can be added to the customer by reducing cost *and* adding value to customers:

- *within each* element of the value chain such as procurement, manufacture, sales and distribution;
- *at the interface between* elements of the value chain such as between sales and distribution.

In equation form:

Value = (Benefit of each VC activity − its cost) +
(Benefit of each interface between VC activities – its cost)

Electronic communications can be used to enhance the value chain by making value chain activities such as procurement more efficient (see *Chapter 7*) and also enabling data integration between activities. For, example if a retailer shares information electronically with a supplier about demand for its products, this can enhance the value chain of both parties since the cycle time for ordering can be reduced, resulting in lower inventory holding and hence costs for both. *Case study 6.1* illustrates this point.

Traditional value chain analysis (*Figure 6.4(a)*) distinguishes between *primary activities* that contribute directly to getting goods and services to the customer (such as inbound logistics, including procurement, manufacturing, marketing and delivery to buyers, support and servicing after sale) and *support activities* which provide the inputs and infrastructure that allow the primary activities to take place. Support activities include finance, human resources and information systems. It can be argued that, with the advent of e-business, the support activities offer much more than support; indeed having effective information systems and management of human resources is critical to contribute to the primary activities. Michael Porter now acknowledges that this is the case.

Internet technologies can reduce production times and costs by increasing the flow of information as a way to *integrate* different value-chain activities. Through doing this the value chain can be made more efficient and services delivered to customers more readily. Rayport and Sviokla (1996) contend that the Internet enables value to be created by gathering, organizing, selecting, synthesizing and distributing

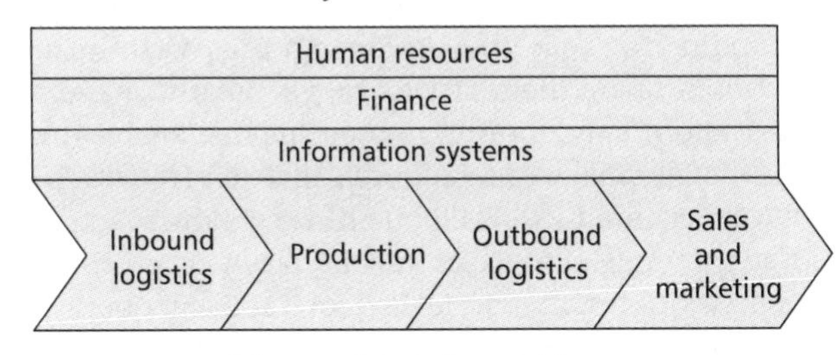

(a)

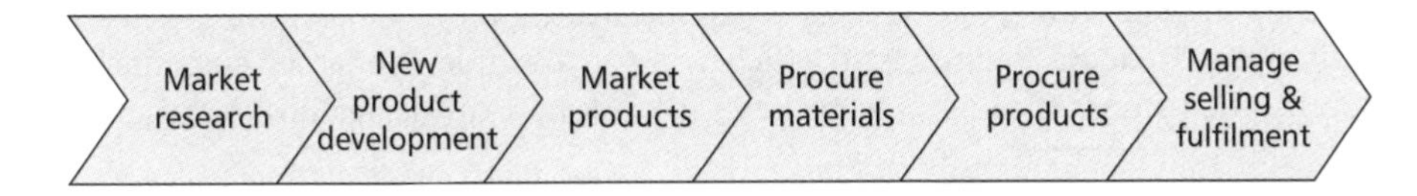

(b)

Figure 6.4 Two alternative models of the value chain: (a) traditional value chain model (b) revised value chain model

information. They refer to a separate parallel *virtual value chain* mirroring the physical value chain. The virtual value chain involves electronic commerce used to mediate traditional value chain activities such as market research, procurement, logistics, manufacture, marketing and distributing. The processing is machine-based or virtual rather than paper-based. The situation is not truly virtual in that human intervention is still required in many value chain activities such as procurement. The 'virtuality' of the virtual value chain will increase as software agents increasingly perform these activities.

Restructuring the internal value chain

Traditional models of the value chain (such as *Figure 2.11* and *Figure 6.4(a)*) have been re-evaluated with the advent of global electronic communications. It can be suggested that there are some key weaknesses in the traditional value chain model:

- It is most applicable to manufacturing of physical products as opposed to services.
- It is a one-way chain involved with pushing products to the customer (see section on *push and pull supply chain models*); it does not highlight the importance of understanding customer needs through market research and responsiveness through innovation and new product development.
- The internal value chain referred to in *Figure 2.11* does not emphasize the importance of value networks (although Porter (1980) did produce a diagram that indicated network relationships).

A revised form of the value chain has been suggested by Deise *et al.* (2000); an adaptation of this model is presented in *Figure 6.4(b)*. This value chain starts with the market research process, emphasizing the importance of real-time environment scanning made possible through electronic communications links with distributors and customers. For example, leading e-tailers now monitor, on an hourly basis, how customers are responding to promotional offers on their web site and review competitors' offers and then revise them accordingly. Similarly, manufacturers such as Cisco have feedback forms and forums on their site that enable them to collect information from customers and channel partners that can feed through to new product development. As new product development occurs the marketing strategy will be refined and at the same time steps can be taken to obtain the resources and production processes necessary to create, store and distribute the new product. Through analysis of the value chain and looking at how electronic communications can be used to speed up the process, manufacturers have been able to significantly reduce time to market from conception of a new product idea through to launch on the market. For example, car manufacturers have reduced time to market from over 5 years to 18 months. At the same time the use of technology increases value chain efficiency, for example it enables customers to specify their needs through a web site or a kiosk in a car dealership and then the car will be manufactured to order.

In addition to changes in the efficiency of value chain activities, electronic commerce also has implications for whether these activities are achieved internally or externally. These changes have been referred to as value chain *disaggregation* (Kalakota and Robinson, 2000) or *deconstruction* (Timmers, 1999) and value chain *reaggregation* (Kalakota and Robinson, 2000) or *reconstruction* (Timmers, 1999).

Value chain disaggregation can occur through deconstructing the primary activities of the value chain. Each of the elements can be approached in a new way, for instance by working differently with suppliers. In value chain reaggregation the value chain is streamlined to increase efficiency between each of the value chain stages. Indeed Timmers (1999) notes that the conventional wisdom of the value chain as a separate series of discrete steps may no longer be tenable as steps such as inbound logistics and operations become more tightly integrated through technology. We have only touched upon changes to the structure of the value chain here, since there is great similarity with the changes possible in the structure of the supply chain. This is evaluated in more depth in the sections on vertical integration and models for redefining the supply chain.

The value stream

The **value stream** is a closely related concept to the value chain. The difference is that it considers different types of tasks that are involved with adding value and looks at how the efficiency of these tasks can be improved. Womack and Jones (1998) define the value stream as:

Value stream
The combination of actions required to deliver value to the customer as products and services.

the set of all the specific actions required to bring a specific product through the three critical management tasks of any business:

1. *the problem-solving task* [the processes of new product development and production launch]
2. *the information management task* [the processes of order taking, scheduling to delivery]
3. *the physical transformation task* [the processes of transforming raw materials to finished product delivered to customers]

Tasks 2 and 3 are traditional value chain activities (*Figure 6.4(a)*) but task 1 is not.

Returning to the definition of customer value from Deise *et al.* (2000) shown in the equation below, we can see that the lean thinking approach proposed by Womack and Jones is aimed at adding value by cutting out waste in each of these three management tasks. By reducing new product development and production times and costs, organizations can then either increase customer value by decreasing fulfilment time or if they wish decreasing price, and/or increasing product and service quality. Clearly e-commerce plays a key role in decreasing time to market and production times and costs.

$$\text{Customer value (brand perception)} = \frac{\text{Product quality} \times \text{Service quality}}{\text{Price} \times \text{Fulfilment time}}$$

Value chain analysis

This is an analytical framework for decomposing an organization into its individual activities and determining value added at each stage. In this way the organization can then assess how effectively resources are being used at the various points within the value chain. The relevance for information systems is that for each element in the value chain it may be possible to use IS to increase the efficiency of resource usage in that area. In addition, IS may be used *between* value chain activities to increase organizational efficiency.

How can an organization positively impact on its value chain by investing in new or upgraded information systems? Porter and Millar (1985) propose the following five-step process.

- *Step 1.* Assess the information intensity of the value chain (i.e. the level and usage of information *within* each value chain activity and *between* each level of activity). The higher the level of intensity and/or the higher the degree of reliance on good quality information, the greater the potential impact of new information systems.
- *Step 2.* Determine the role of IS in the industry structure (for example banking will be very different from mining). It is also important here to understand the information linkages between buyers, suppliers within the industry and how they and competitors might be affected by and react to new information technology.
- *Step 3.* Identify and rank the ways in which IS might create competitive advantage (by impacting one of the value chain activities or improving linkages between them). High cost or critical activity areas present good targets for cost reduction and performance improvement.
- *Step 4.* Investigate how IS might spawn new businesses (for example the Sabre computerized reservation system spawned a multi-billion dollar software company which now has higher earnings than the original core airline business).
- *Step 5.* Develop a plan for taking advantage of IS. A plan must be developed which is business-driven rather than technology-driven. The plan should assign priorities to the IS investments (which of course should be subjected to an appropriate cost-benefit-analysis).

In the five-step analysis above we have mainly been looking at how value chain analysis can be applied to the internal value chain. Such a process can also be applied to an organization's external value chain. Womack and Jones (1998) refer to the related concept of *value stream analysis*. This considers how the whole production and delivery process can be made more efficient. To conduct this analysis, they suggest that companies should map every activity that occurs in creating new products and delivering products or services to customers and then categorize them as:

1. Those that create value as perceived by the customer.
2. Those which create no value, but are required by product development or production systems so cannot immediately be eliminated.
3. Those that don't add value, so can be immediately eliminated.

Having performed this analysis, plans for removing the category 3 activities can be made and managers can then concentrate on eliminating category 2 activities and enhancing category 1 activities. Womack and Jones give the example of the value stream for a cola can. Even a superficially simple product such as canned cola can have many activities involved in its production. Indeed there are several value streams: that in producing the can itself, those to produce the contents from beet field to sugar and corn field to caramel and to produce the packaging. Taking the example of the can itself, value stream analysis can be performed to identify the stages in production as follows:

1. Mine bauxite.
2. Reduction mill.
3. Smelter.
4. Hot rolling mill.
5. Cold rolling mill.
6. Can maker.
7. Bottler
8. Regional distribution centre (RDC)
9. Retail unit storage.
10. Home storage.

In value stream analysis, efficiency for each of the stages above will be calculated. For example, at stage 7, the bottler (adding the drink to the can), Womack and Jones (1998) give the example of incoming storage four days, processing time one minute, finished storage five weeks. The need for such analysis is shown by the delays in the whole process which give incoming storage of five months, finished storage of six months, but processing time of only three hours. This gives a total cycle time of nearly a year from mine to home. Clearly if information management can be used to reduce these storage times, it can create large savings in terms of reduced storage capacities. The benefits are evident for a retailer such as Tesco (*case study 6.1*) that has already undertaken value-stream analysis and deployed e-commerce in the Tesco Information Exchange to reduce its storage in the RDC and instore to only two and three days respectively. It has also been able to move to a system of continuous replenishment in 24 hours. Orders made by a Tesco store on a Monday night are delivered from suppliers via the RDCs to arrive before a store on Wednesday morning!

Value networks

Reduced time to market and increased customer responsiveness are not simply the result of reviewing the efficiency of internal processes and how information systems are deployed, but also through consideration of how partners can be involved to outsource some processes that have traditionally been considered to be part of the internal value chain of a company. Porter's original work considered both the internal value chain, but also the **external value chain or network**. Since the 1980s there has been a tremendous increase in outsourcing of both core value chain activities and support activities. As companies outsource more and more activities, management of the links between the company and its partners become more important. Deise *et al.* (2000) describe value network management as:

Value network
The links between an organization and its strategic and non-strategic partners that form its external value chain.

> *the process of effectively deciding what to outsource in a constraint-based, real-time environment based on fluctuation.*

Electronic communications have enabled this shift to outsourcing, enabling the transfer of information necessary to create, manage and monitor partnerships. These links are not necessarily mediated directly through the company, but also through intermediaries known as value chain integrators or directly between partners. As a result the concept of managing a value network of partners has become commonplace.

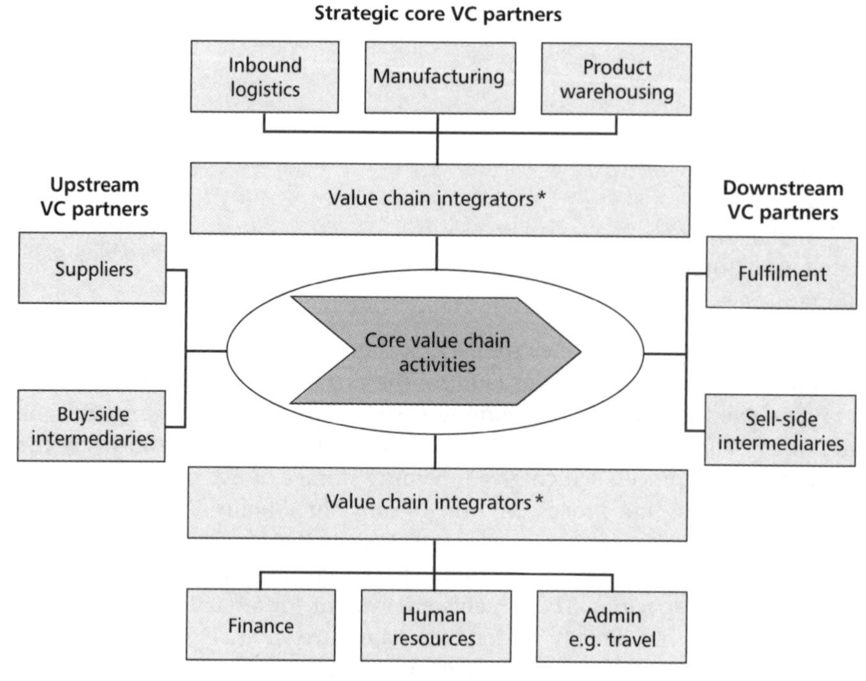

***includes IS partners, for example:**

- **Strategic outsourcer**
- **System integrator**
- **ISP/WAN provider**
- **ASP provider**

Figure 6.5 Members of the value network of an organization

Figure 6.5, which is adapted from the model of Deise *et al.* (2000), shows some of the partners of a value network that characterizes partners as:

1. Supply-side partners (upstream supply chain) such as suppliers, business to business exchanges, wholesalers and distributors.
2. Partners who fulfil primary or core value chain activities. The number of core value chain activities that will have been outsourced to third parties will vary with different companies and the degree of virtualization of an organization. In some companies the management of inbound logistics may be outsourced, in others different aspects of the manufacturing process. In the virtual organization all core activities may be outsourced.
3. Sell-side partners (downstream supply chain) such as business-to-business exchanges, wholesalers, distributors and customers (not shown, since conceived as distinct from other partners).
4. Value chain integrators or partners who supply services that mediate the internal and external value chain. These companies typically provide the electronic infrastructure for a company and include strategic outsourcing partners, system integrators, ISP/WAN providers and ASP providers.

The similarity between elements of the value network of *Figure 6.5* and the supply chain of The B2B Company of *Figure 6.2* will be apparent. But the value network offers a different perspective that is intended to emphasize:

- The electronic interconnections between partners and the organization and directly between partners that potentially enables real-time information exchange between partners.
- The dynamic nature of the network. The network can be readily modified according to market conditions or in response to customer demands. New partners can readily be introduced into the network and others removed if they are not performing.
- Different types of links can be formed between different types of partners. For example, EDI links may be established with key suppliers, while e-mail links may suffice for less significant suppliers.

The Waterstone's book chain (www.waterstones.co.uk) provides an example of the importance of developing a value network of infrastucture partners. Field (2000) describes how initially the web site was designed and hosted a single company, Hyperlink, and offered book searching among 1.2 m books, secure ordering, diary, Waterstone's club and online chat. But Field states that, according to Andrew Hatton, project manager, the technology was holding the company back, particularly as Amazon continued to use its huge market capitalization to invest in web interface and back-end fulfilment systems. Using an in-house developed application and web server, the site was unable to deliver new functionality quickly or cost-effectively since the supplier had to perform a time-consuming software upgrade to meet our request for the site's pages to change more rapidly. Waterstones decided to expand the network of suppliers to get best of breed suppliers. Partners included numerous hardware and software vendors, as well as integration and design consultants; these included Siemens, web site designers Brainstormers and e-commerce integrator Nvision. Nvision achieved the key back-end integration to link the new solution to Waterstones' existing business systems in 12 weeks. The integrator performed a 'Swot' (strength, weakness, opportunities, threats) analysis to identify the market opportunities for an online bookstore, and these were then matched against Waterstone's existing capabilities, both on the web site and in the supply chain.

In this section, we refer to wholesale outsourcing the elements of a value network to third parties. In fact, the options are more complex than this. The different types of partnership that can be formed are described in more detail in the later section on managing partnerships. Remember also that outsourcing does simply imply cost reduction. Michael Dell relates that Dell do not see outsourcing as getting rid of a process that does not add value, rather they see it as a way of *'coordinating their activity to create the most value for customers'* (Magretta, 1998). Dell has improved customer service by changing the way it works with both its suppliers and distributors to build a computer to the customer's specific order within just six days.

Virtual organization
An organization which uses information and communications technology to allow it to operate without clearly defined physical boundaries between different functions. It provides customized services by outsourcing production and other functions to third parties.

Towards the virtual organization

The implication of increasing outsourcing of core activities is that companies will move towards the **virtual organization**. Benjamin and Wigand (1995) state that *'it is becoming increasingly difficult to delineate accurately the borders of today's* *organizations*'. A further implication of the introduction of electronic networks such as the Internet is that it becomes easier to outsource aspects of the production and distribution of goods to third parties (Kraut *et al.*, 1998). This can lead to the boundaries between supplier and organization becoming blurred. Employees may work in any time zone and customers are able to purchase tailored products from any location. The absence of any rigid boundary or hierarchy within the organization should lead to a more responsive and flexible company with greater market orientation.

Davidow and Malone (1992) describe the virtual corporation as follows:

> *To the outside observer, it will appear almost edgeless, with permeable and continuously changing interfaces between company, supplier and customer. From inside the firm, the view will be no less amorphous, with traditional offices, departments, and operating divisions constantly reforming according to need. Job responsibilities will regularly shift.*

Kraut *et al.* (1998) suggest that the features of a virtual organization are:

1. Processes transcend the boundaries of a single form and are not controlled by a single organizational hierarchy.
2. Production processes are flexible with different parties involved at different times.
3. Parties involved in the production of a single product are often geographically dispersed.
4. Given this dispersion, coordination is heavily dependent on telecommunications and data networks.

All companies tend to have some elements of the virtual organization. As these characteristics increase this is known as **virtualization**. Malone *et al.* (1987) argued that the presence of electronic networks tends to lead to virtualization since the governance and coordination of business transactions can be conducted effectively at lower costs.

Virtualization
The process of a company developing more of the characteristics of the virtual organization.

Options for restructuring the supply chain

As part of strategy definition for e-business, managers will consider how the structure of the supply chain can be modified. These choices are not primarily based on Internet technology choices, rather they are mainly choices that have existed for many years. What Internet technology provides a more efficient enabler and lower cost communications within the new structures.

Supply chain management options can be viewed as a continuum between internal control of the supply chain elements and external control of supply chain elements through outsourcing. The two end elements of the continuum are usually referred to as **vertical integration** and **virtual integration**. The intermediate situation is sometimes referred to as vertical disintegration or supply chain disaggregation. This continuum is illustrated in *Figure 6.6*.

Vertical integration
The extent to which supply chain activities are undertaken and controlled *within* the organization.

Virtual integration
The majority of supply chain activities are undertaken and controlled *outside* the organization by third parties.

There has been a general trend during the second half of the twentieth century from vertical integration through vertical disintegration to virtual integration. A good example is provided by the car manufacturing industry where traditionally car plants would be located near to steel works so that the input to the car plant would be raw materials with finished cars produced as the output. Other components of the car such as the engine and passenger equipment would also be

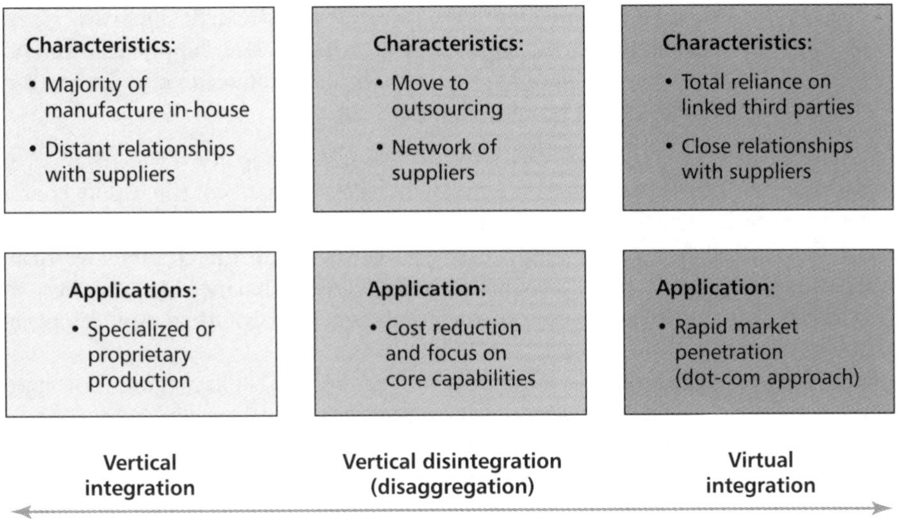

Characteristics:	Characteristics:	Characteristics:
• Majority of manufacture in-house • Distant relationships with suppliers	• Move to outsourcing • Network of suppliers	• Total reliance on linked third parties • Close relationships with suppliers
Applications: • Specialized or proprietary production	**Application:** • Cost reduction and focus on core capabilities	**Application:** • Rapid market penetration (dot-com approach)
Vertical integration	**Vertical disintegration (disaggregation)**	**Virtual integration**

Figure 6.6 The characteristics of vertical integration, vertical disintegration and virtual integration

manufactured by the company. In addition, other value chain activities such as marketing would also largely be performed in-house. There has been a gradual move to sourcing more and more components such as lights, upholstery and trim and even engines to third parties. Marketing activities such as web site development, brochure fulfilment and advertising campaigns are now largely outsourced to marketing agencies. Another example is the purchase by pharmaceutical companies of pharmacy benefit managers (companies that manage drug distribution with private and company health schemes). By acquiring these companies which are part of a pharmaceutical company's downstream supply chain the aim is to 'get closer to the customer' while at the same time favourably control the distribution of its own drugs.

Hayes and Wheelwright (1994) provide a useful framework that summarizes choices for an organization's vertical integration strategy. The three main decisions are:

1. *The direction of any expansion.* Should the company aim to direct ownership at the upstream or downstream supply chain? The pharmaceuticals companies referred to above have decided to buy into the downstream part of the supply network (downstream vertical integration). This is sometimes referred to as an *offensive* strategic move since it enables the company to increase its power with respect to customers. Alternatively, if the pharmaceuticals company purchased other research labs this would be upstream-directed vertical integration which is strategically *defensive*.
2. *The extent of vertical integration.* How far should the company take downstream or upstream vertical integration? Originally car manufacturers had a high degree of vertical integration, but more recently they have moved from a *wide process span* to a *narrow process span*. This change is the main way in which e-business can impact upon vertical integration by assisting the change from wide to narrow process span.

3. *The balance among the vertically integrated stages*. To what extent does each stage of the supply chain focus on supporting the immediate supply chain? For example if a supplier to a motor manufacturer also produced components for other industries this would be an unbalanced situation.

Combining these concepts, we can refer to The B2B Company (*Figure 6.2*). If it owned the majority of the upstream and downstream elements of the supply chain and each element was focused on supporting the activities of The B2B Company, its strategy would be to follow upstream and downstream directions of vertical integration with a wide process span and high degree of balance. Alternatively if the strategy was changed to focus on core competencies it could be said to have a narrow process span.

How then, can electronic communications support these strategies? Through increasing the flow of information between members of the supply chain, a strategy of narrower process span can be supported by e-commerce. However, this relies on all members of the supply chain being e-enabled. If only immediately upstream suppliers have adopted e-commerce then the efficiency of the supply chain as a whole will not be greatly increased. It may be difficult for a manufacturer to encourage companies further up the supply chain to adopt e-commerce. So companies undertaking offensive or defensive strategies will be in a better position to stipulate adoption of e-commerce, and so increase the overall efficiency of the supply chain. As we saw in *case study 1.1*, a company such as Shell helps e-enable the supply chain by sharing information in its own databases with customers to increase the efficiency of the supply chain.

Our final example is the manufacture of personal computers also illustrates the concept of the two different supply chain products well. Complete *activity 6.2* to review the benefits of each approach.

Activity 6.2 Supply chain models in personal computer manufacture

Activity

1. Review the approaches of the two companies illustrated below. Which tends to vertical integration and which tends to virtual integration?
2. Produce a table summarizing the benefits and disadvantages of each approach. Which do you think is the best approach?
3. How can information systems to facilitate each approach?

Approach 1 IBM during 1980s and early 1990s

Manufacture of many components by IBM plants in different locations including IBM processors, IBM hard disks, IBM cases and IBM monitors and even IBM mice. Distribution to companies by IBM logistics.

Approach 2 Dell during 1990s and 2000

Manufacture of all components by third parties in different locations including Intel processors, Seagate hard disks, Sony monitors and Microsoft mice. Assembly of some components in final product by third parties e.g. adding appropriate monitor to system unit for each order. For more information on Dell see Magretta (1998).

For answer see p. 251

Using information systems to restructure the supply chain

In this section we start by reviewing the extent of adoption of different types of information systems to support supply chain management as part of e-business strategy. The benefits of implementing these technologies are also described. We then consider, through referring to case studies, how companies can use technologies to support the management of the upstream and downstream supply chain.

A report from the UK trade and industry department (DTI, 2000) provides useful evidence of the extent to which technologies are being adopted by firms to enable supply chain management. This report benchmarks businesses in the UK against those in France, Germany, Italy, Sweden, the US, Canada and Japan. The survey is based on the results of nearly 6000 telephone interviews in businesses of all sizes. Note that the results are not reported by number of businesses, but have been weighted according to size of business based on number of employees. *Figure 6.7* shows the range of technologies that companies use to allow customers to order. It is evident that the humble e-mail is the most common form of ordering method. Web-based ordering, where a user enters their order details into a form is the second most common method of ordering which is used by over 50 per cent of companies in the sample countries. Note that this ordering can vary in sophistication from a simple form that is converted into an e-mail without secure payment through to a secure integrated catalogue and merchant server ordering system. The

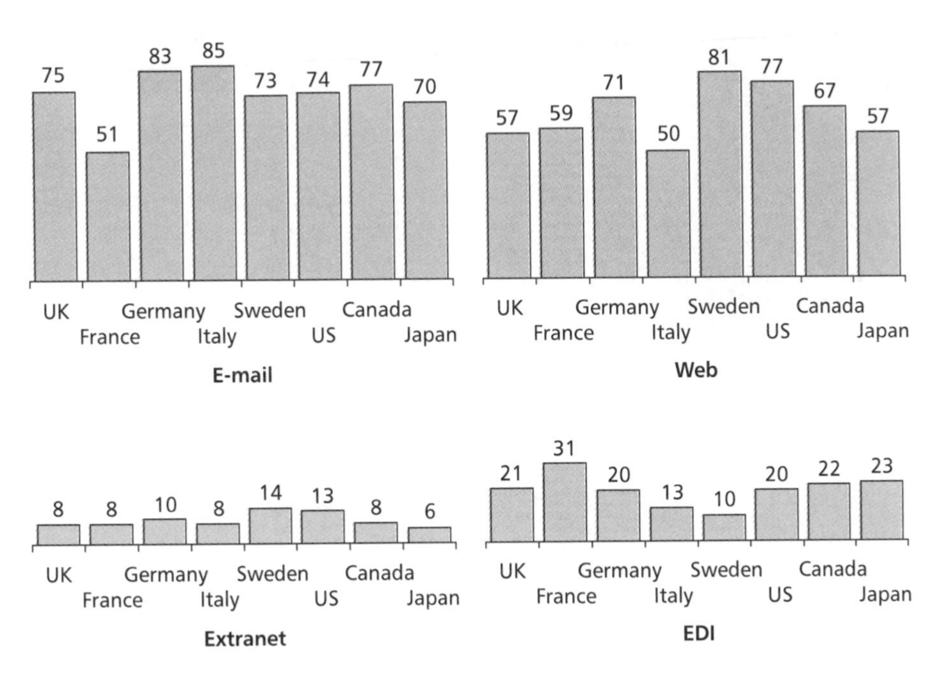

Figure 6.7 Technologies used by customers to order online
Source: DTI (2000)

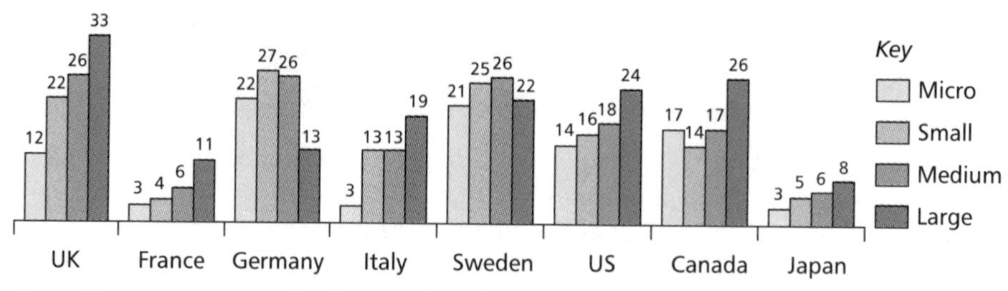

Figure 6.8 Businesses that make payments online to customers by business size
Source: DTI (2000)

lower proportion of companies that have adopted EDI and extranet methods of ordering indicates that these approaches are mainly limited to the largest companies involved with B2B trading. This is supported by *Figure 6.8* which shows that in most countries online payment is of greater popularity in the largest companies compared with the smallest companies.

While *Figure 6.7* suggests that online ordering is fairly widespread, the sophistication of technologies used for online ordering varies considerably. *Figure 6.9*

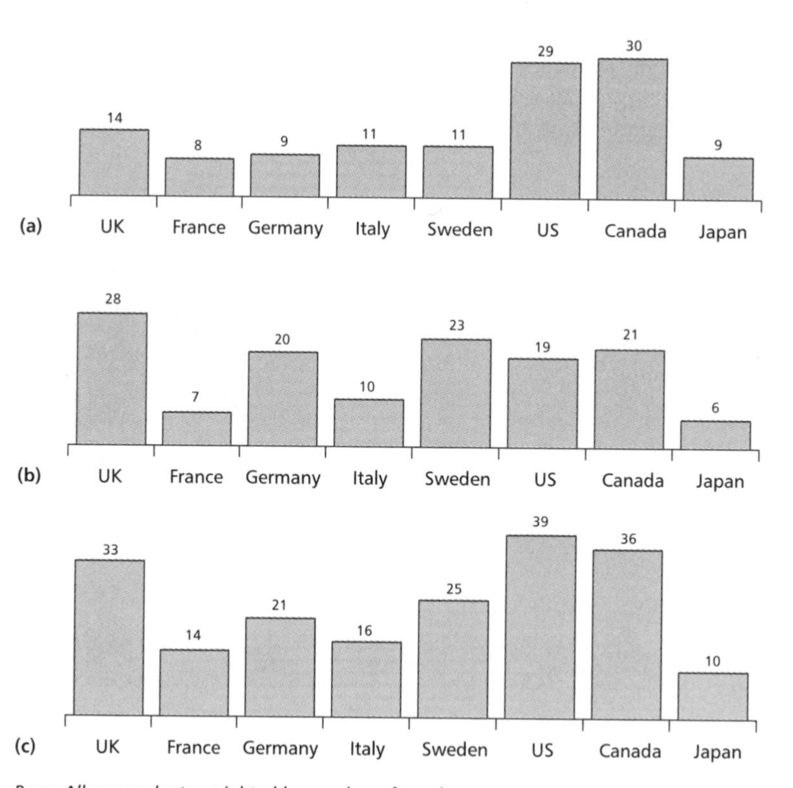

Figure 6.9 Use of e-commerce at different stages of the buying process: (a) business that accept invoices online from suppliers (%), (b) businesses that make online payments to suppliers (%), (c) businesses that track progress of supplies (5%)
Source: DTI (2000)

shows that *structured* transfer of information related to invoices and payments is typically less than half that of web ordering (*Figure 6.7*). This suggests that although orders can be placed electronically, it may be necessary to reconcile invoices and payments using separate, possibly paper-based systems. Organizations where payment involves paper copies of orders and invoices or rekeying between systems have yet to achieve the full degree of automation of order processing.

Based on these results, the authors of the benchmarking study (DTI, 2000) have suggested there is staged adoption of the technologies as summarized in *Figure 5.6*. They liken the process of adoption as similar to moving up the steps of a ladder. Companies start off using e-mail to communicate internally and with suppliers (step 1) before moving to offering product information and availability checking (step 2); online ordering (step 3); online payment (step 4); online progress tracking (step 5) and finally when the e-business is achieved all stages are integrated (step 6).

Considering the use of software for supply chain management in particular, a survey of UK manufacturing companies (Conspectus, 2000) showed that the use of information systems, and the web in particular, for supply chain management is increasing rapidly. In 2000, around a quarter of respondents were utilizing the web for their supply chain, but within a year it was anticipated this would increase to 75 per cent. Furthermore, coupled with this increased use of information systems was the intention of the majority to perform associated process redesign and re-engineering.

Information systems, and in particular electronic communications can be used to impact supply chain management in a number of ways. We will consider these changes with respect to The B2B Company; they include:

1. *Increased efficiency of individual processes*. Here the cycle time to complete of a process and the resources needed to execute it are reduced. If The B2B Company adopts e-procurement this will result in a lower faster cycle time and cost per order as described in *Chapter 7*.
   Benefit: reduced cycle time and cost per order as described in *Chapter 7*.
2. *Reduced complexity of the supply chain*. This is the process of disintermediation referred to in *Chapter 2*. Here The B2B Company will offer the facility to sell direct from its e-commerce site rather than through distributors or retailers.
   Benefit: reduced cost of channel distribution and sale.
3. *Improved data integration between elements of the supply chain*. The B2B Company can share information with its suppliers on the demand for its products to optimize the supply process in a similar way to that described for Tesco in *case study 6.1*.
   Benefit: reduced cost of paper processing.
4. *Reduced cost through outsourcing*. The company can outsource or use virtual integration to transfer assets and costs such as inventory holding costs to third party companies. Technology is also an enabler in forming value networks, and in making it faster to change suppliers on the basis of cost and quality.
   Benefits: lower costs through price competition and reduced spend on manufacturing capacity and holding capacity. Better service quality through contractual arrangements?
5. *Innovation*. It may be possible to offer new products or new ways of ordering and servicing products to customers. For example The B2B Company may use e-commerce to enable its customers to specify the mixture of chemical

compounds and additives used to formulate their plastics and refer to a history of previous formulations.
Benefit: Better customer responsiveness.

An alternative perspective is to look at the benefits that technology can deliver to customers at the end of the supply chain. For The B2B Company these could include:

- Increased convenience through 24 hours a day, 7 days a week, 365 days ordering.
- Increased choice of supplier leading to lower costs.
- Faster lead times and lower costs through reduced inventory holding.
- The facility to tailor products more readily.
- Increased information about products and transactions such as technical data sheets and order histories.

There are two alternative, but contradictory implications of supply chains becoming electronically mediated networks. Malone *et al.* (1987) and Steinfield *et al.* (1996) suggests that networks may foster electronic marketplaces that are characterized by more *ephemeral* relationships. In other words, since it is easier to form an electronically mediated relationship, it is also easier for the customer to break it and choose another supplier. Counter to this is the suggestion that electronic networks may *lock-in* customers to a particular supplier because of the overhead or risk in changing to another supplier. Here networks are used to strengthen partnerships. An example of this is when the use of an EDI solution is stipulated by a dominant customer.

The popular conception of the introduction of the Internet into a channel is that it will tend to lead to more ephemeral relationships. This may yet prove to be the case as more intermediaries evolve and this becomes an accepted way of buying. However, a review by Steinfield *et al.* (1996) seems to suggest that EDI and the Internet tend to cement existing relationships. Furthermore, research indicates that the use of networks for buying may actually reduce outcomes such as quality, efficiency and satisfaction with suppliers. If the findings of Steinfield *et al.* (1996) are confirmed in practice, then this calls into doubt the future of many B2B marketplaces (*Chapter 7, p. 272*). Personal relationships between the members of the buying unit and the supplier still seem to be important. It will be interesting to see which type of arrangement predominates in the future, or it may well be that there is a role for both according to the nature of the product purchased.

IS supported upstream supply chain management

The key activities of upstream supply chain management are procurement and upstream logistics. The way in which information systems can be used to support procurement in the e-business is of such importance that a whole chapter is devoted to this (*Chapter 7*). However, in the current chapter we look at some examples of how technologies are used to improve upstream supply chain management.

Many grocery retailers have been at the forefront of using technology to manage their upstream supply chain. The major example we will review here is the system created by Tesco, but other UK retailers have developed systems such as 'Sainsbury

Information Direct' and 'Safeway Supplier Information Service'. *Case study 6.1* illustrates the use of technology to manage the upstream supply chain from the retailer's perspective, but also highlights the benefits for their suppliers. The Tesco Information Exchange (TIE) was developed in conjunction with GE Information Services (GE), and is an extranet solution that allows Tesco and its suppliers to collaboratively exchange trading information. *Figure 6.10* shows how TIE is linked to Tesco's key systems to give suppliers access to relevant and up-to-date information such as Electronic Point of Sale (EPOS) data, to track sales and the Internal telephone/mail directory, so that suppliers can quickly find the right person to talk to.

CASE STUDY 6.1

Tesco develop buy-side e-commerce system for supply chain management

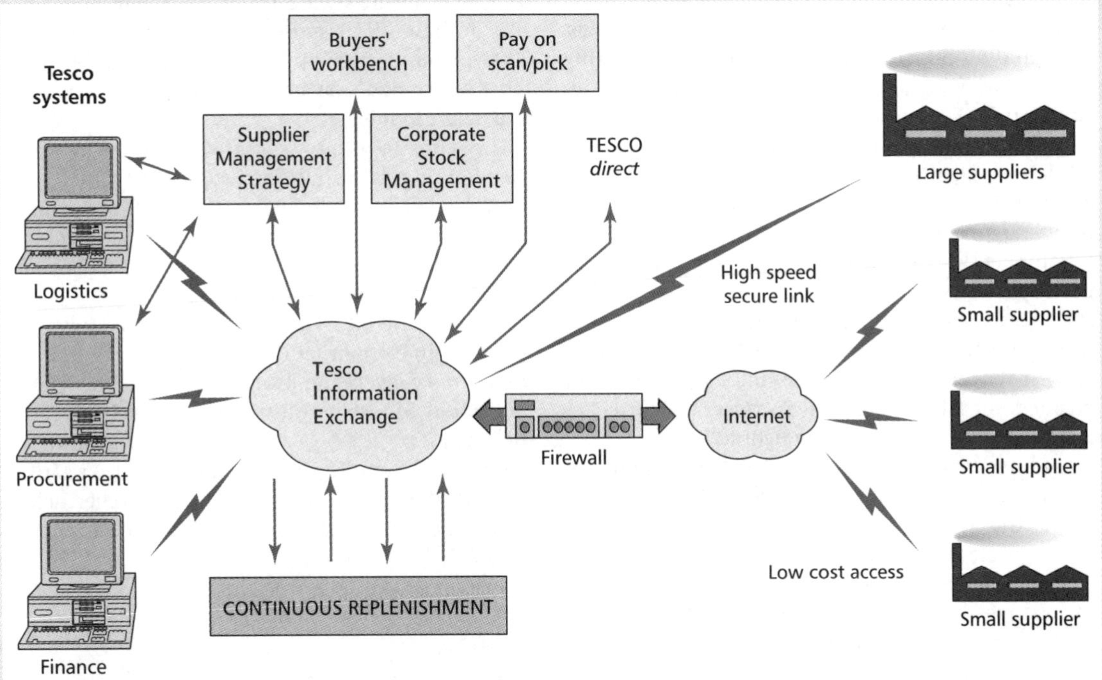

FT

Figure 6.10 Infrastructure for Tesco Information Exchange (TIE)
Source: Tesco web site

Retailers have long sought greater collaboration in their supply chains, but few have managed to achieve it. One that has is Tesco, the UK's largest grocery retailer, which has built a reputation as one of Europe's most innovative retailers in its use of information technology.

As with many retailers, Tesco has long used electronic data interchange (EDI) to order goods from suppliers and the network links 1300 of Tesco's 2000 suppliers, representing around 96 per cent by volume of goods sold in Tesco stores.

The EDI system started operating in the 1980s and its use was initially limited to streamlining store replenishment. In 1989, Tesco took its first steps on

▶ CASE STUDY *continued*

the road to collaboration and began using its EDI network to help its suppliers better forecast demand.

About 350 suppliers receive EDI messages with details of actual store demand, depot stockholdings and Tesco's weekly sales forecasts.

According to Barry Knichel, Tesco's supply chain director, this forecasting project has been successful as average lead times have fallen from seven to three days. 'Nevertheless, the information flow is strictly one way,' he says. 'We still do not know the true value of this sales data because we never get any feedback.'

In 1997, Tesco thus started its Tesco Information Exchange (Tie) project in an attempt to achieve much more sophisticated two-way collaboration in its supply chain.

'This really was a big development for us,' he says. 'The guiding principle was to combine our retailing knowledge with the product knowledge of our suppliers.'

A large Tesco store may carry 50,000 products while a supplier will have at most 200. An important aim of the Tie project was thus to shift responsibility for managing products down to the relevant supplier.

'Suppliers clearly have a better understanding of their specific product lines, so if you can engage the supplier to manage the supply chain you are going to get much better product availability and reduce your inventory,' says Jorge Castillo, head of retail business for GE Information Services, which developed the extranet technology behind Tie.

Suppliers pay from £100 to £100,000 to join Tie, depending on their size. This then allows them to access the Tie web site and view daily electronic point-of-sale (Pos) data from Tesco stores.

According to Mr Castillo, Tie lets suppliers monitor changes in demand almost in real time and so gives them more time to react. 'Before, Tesco's suppliers would not have seen a problem until Tesco got on the phone to them,' he says. 'Now, it is the suppliers who get on the phone to Tesco and they can see much earlier on if a product is not selling well.'

The data can be analysed in a number of ways to allow suppliers to see how sales perform by distribution centre, by individual store or even by TV region – important for promotions.

The management of promotions is a complex process requiring close cooperation between supplier and retailer. However, it has traditionally been difficult to do well because of the lack of shared data to support collaborative decisions.

'Promotions can be a nightmare,' says Mr Knichel. Tesco and GEIS added a promotions management module to the service in 1999. It allows retailers and suppliers to collaborate in all stages of the promotion: initial commercial planning, supply chain planning, execution and final evaluation.

According to St Ivel, one of Tesco's bigger food suppliers, Tie has saved 30 per cent of its annual promotional costs.

More than 600 suppliers, representing 70 per cent of Tesco's business, are using Tie today and Tesco aims to have all its suppliers onboard by the end of 2000. Around 40 suppliers are participating in the most recent addition to the Tie system, a collaborative data module.

This aims to allow 'seamless' planning in which the planning data on the screen is jointly filled in by both retailer and supplier. Mr Knichel sees this as radical change for the retail industry as suppliers and retailers have traditionally worked to separate agendas.

He feels Tie has much potential to streamline Tesco's supply chain and to help suppliers improve their service levels and promotions. But retailing is a traditional industry and many suppliers are set in their ways.

'Only two suppliers have fundamentally changed the way they work as a result of Tie. Nevertheless, they can bring products to market much faster than any of their competitors,' he says.

Source: Article by Geoffrey Nairn, *Financial Times*, 3 May 2000.

Questions

1. What benefits does Tesco's information exchange offer to the retailer and its suppliers?
2. What differences have the use of TIE added over the original EDI system?
3. Discuss reasons why only two of Tesco's suppliers have fundamentally altered the way they work as a result of TIE.

The Tesco case study illustrates the benefits and difficulties of implementing EDI for supply chain optimization from a retailer perspective. We will now consider it from the perspective of the manufacturer. Fisher (1997) makes the distinction between two strategies that manufacturers can follow according to the type of product and the nature of its demand.

For functional products, particularly those with easily predictable demand, such as consumer goods like toothpaste or shampoo, the product does not need to be modified frequently in response to consumer demand. Here the implication is that the supply chain should be directed at cost reduction and efficiency. For more complex products, including those with less predictable demand, Fisher (1997) gives the example of two contrasting products, Skiwear from Sport Obermayer and Soup from Campbells. Each year, 95 per cent of Sport Obermayers products are new designs and demand forecasts may err by over 200 per cent. In contrast, 95 per cent of Campbell's products are similar each year with predictable demand levels. The strategic response for these products is to develop a physically efficient supply chain in the former case and a market responsive supply chain in the latter case.

Cost cutting within a company such as Campbells may soon give diminishing returns. In these cases the biggest cost savings are possible by reviewing the structure of the supply chain as a whole. In 1991 the company operationalized what it referred to as a continuous replenishment programme. It set up EDI links with major retailers and each morning retailers electronically inform Campbells of their demand for all products. Campbells then uses this information to determine which products require replenishment based on upper and lower limits of inventory agreed with each retailer. Trucks leave Campbells shipping plants and then arrive at the retailers' distribution centres each day. This approach reduced the inventory of participating retailers from about four weeks to two weeks with the associated cost reductions. This two-week inventory reduction is this equivalent of a 1 per cent increase in sales. This does not sound like a large improvement, but retailers' margins are thin so this translates to a large increase in profitability on these product lines. This example is instructive since it illustrates not only the savings possible with this approach, but the pitfalls of minimizing inventory through the use of EDI. The problem that Campbells encountered was that when it ran price promotions this could lead to up to five times the demand. This cannot be fulfilled on a short timescale so manufacture and retailer have to cooperate on advanced buying to meet these peaks in demand.

IS supported downstream supply chain management

The key activities of downstream supply chain management are outbound logistics and fulfilment. It is evident that in a B2B context the benefits for downstream customers are, of course, similar to the benefits that the organization receives through automating its upstream supply chain. These issues are considered from a marketing perspective in *Chapters 8 and 9*, but in this chapter we review the importance of fulfilment in achieving e-commerce success.

We also use the grocery retail market to illustrate the implications of e-commerce for management of the downstream supply chain. In addition to being one of the leaders in using technology to improve upstream supply change management, Tesco is also one of the leaders in using e-commerce for downstream supply chain management. Tesco's downstream supply chain involves selling direct to customers, in other words it is operating a strategy of disintermediation (*Chapter 2, p. 37*) by reducing the role of its branches. Through being an early adopter,

Tesco.com has developed as the world's largest online grocery site. By the end of 2000 annualized sales were running at nearly £300 million, with 48,000 orders per week – the most transactions for any online supermarket. Over 500,000 people have signed up for the grocery service.

Outbound logistics management

The importance of outbound logistics relates to the expectations of offering direct sales through a web site. In a nutshell, logistics are crucial to delivering the service promise established on the web site. If a customer is informed on the web site that a book will take two days to arrive, they will not be a repeat customer if the book arrives two weeks later.

A different angle on the importance of logistics and how it relates to the bottom line is illustrated by the fortunes of Amazon, which is infamous for not delivering profitability despite multi-billion dollar sales. Phillips (2000) reported that the fulfilment mechanism was adding to Amazon's costs because of split shipments, where multiple deliveries of items are necessary from a single order. Evidence suggests that Amazon may require over three shipments to fulfil some orders. This is a particular problem in the US, which is the source of 86 per cent of Amazon's revenue. Here the distance between population centres requires a network of seven distribution centres for shipments. Phillips (2000) explains that the need to fulfil a single order by shipping items from multiple locations increases costs for postage and the labour to assemble and dispatch goods. The alternative situation of stocking all distribution centres with every product is financially prohibitive. Some analysts suggest that Amazon should change its logistics strategy by separating out its distribution operation as a separate revenue source and outsource fulfilment to reduce costs.

A final indication of the importance of logistics is its scale – Phillips (2000) reports that e-fulfilment including warehousing, logistics and dispatch of online orders could be worth £5 bn per year in the UK by 2008.

The challenge for distribution companies is to deliver on time and provide services to enable customers to track shipment of products ordered online. While an order-tracking facility has been the reality for international parcel carriers such as Federal Express since the mid 1990s, this is a challenge that needs now to be met by all distribution companies of consumer and business goods. The scale of challenge can be gauged by looking at Van Gend & Loos (VG&L, www.vgl.nl), a Dutch distribution company based within the Benelux countries. With over 4000 employees, a fleet of 1500 trucks, and annual revenues of approximately $500 million, VG&L wanted to offer its 40,000 customers the ability to track and trace their shipments over the Internet. While some distribution companies offer the facility for the sender to trace a package based on a consignment number, VG&L lets both the sender and the recipient track and trace packages based on date and destination searches. This key feature means that the sending parties can look at their information without the need for a special number, and they can look at all past shipments for the previous two months. At the same time, VG&L customers can also request pickups and shipments over the Internet.

To conclude this section *case study 6.2* highlights many of the issues that make fulfilment difficult to manage for e-tailers.

CASE STUDY 6.2

A short history of Sainsbury's approach to e-fulfilment models

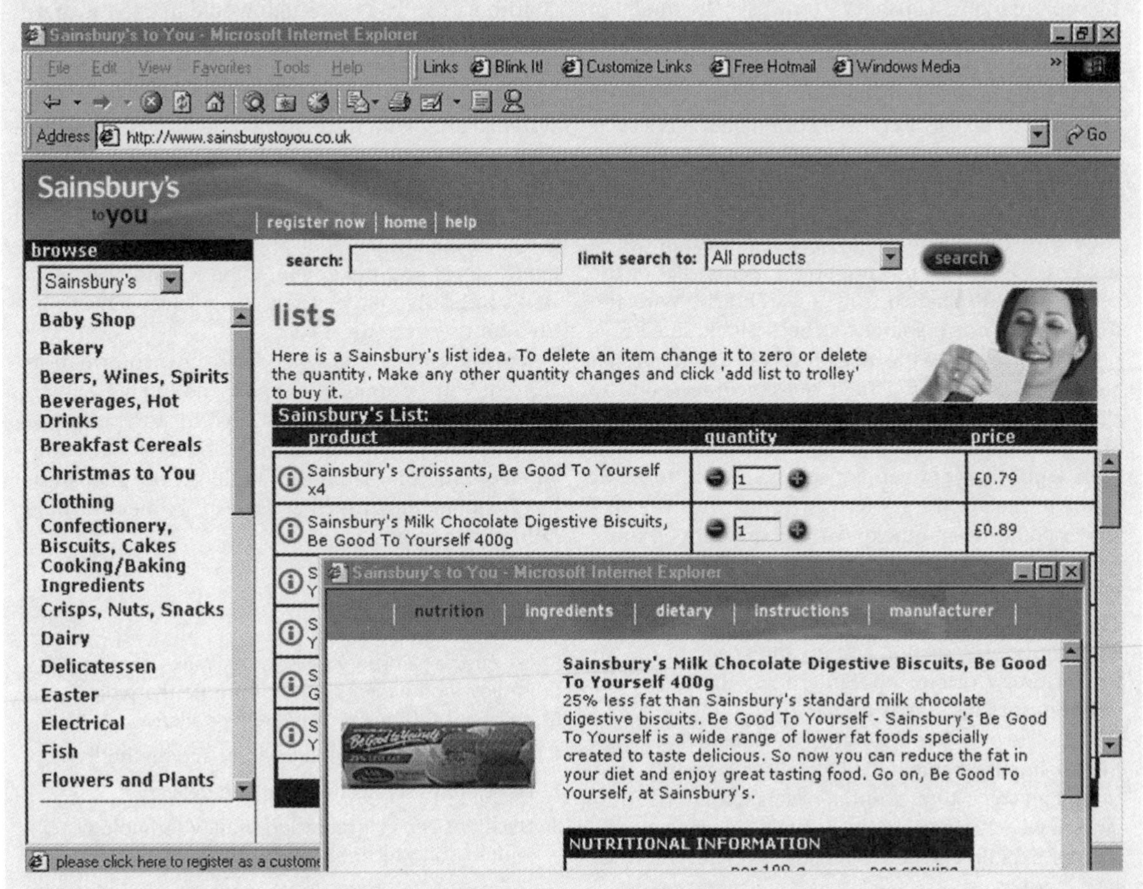

Figure 6.11 Sainsbury's web site (www.sainsburystoyou.co.uk)

Background

UK grocery retailer Sainsbury's commenced its online service in 1995 when there was a first pilot at Solihull in the West Midlands. In spring 1998 its Orderline service was launched. This was eventually rolled out to 27 stores, but in 1999 it was rationalized to eight stores near London. A rebranded 'Sainsbury's to you' e-commerce service was launched in 1999 and this is targeted to reach 60 per cent of the UK population by 2001. Ody (2000) reports that Patrick McHugh, the group e-commerce director, is hoping that within four years there will be an online revenue contribution of 20 per cent.

The actions Sainsbury's and other grocers are taking are instructive since they highlight some of the practical problems of fulfilment faced by retailers when e-commerce services are developed. The difficulties are magnified in this instance by the range of products and the limited shelf life of some items. We will now highlight some of the issues raised by the Sainsburys case.

Initially, as with the Tesco operation, the Orderline fulfilment was via individual stores. This proved to be too expensive, the chief executive at the time was quoted as saying: 'a store-based home shopping service is not a viable proposition'. Estimates for the cost of selecting or picking each Tesco Direct order range from £12 to £15. This is a significant amount when the customer only pays a £5 service charge for each purchase. This shows that

▶ CASE STUDY *continued*

moving from customer self-service to a more personal service reverses the economies of scale built up by supermarkets. Sainsbury's now uses the model of regional picking centres. It is planning to build a network of regional picking centres. Currently there is one in London, but others are planned. Managing the rate of expansion of e-commerce services is important since previous initiatives appear to have involved expansion that was too rapid, resulting in over-capacity. A mixed fulfilment model is currently used with the customer having the option of ordering direct and then picking up a supermarket or the order being dispatched from a warehouse. With the former it is not possible to check stock since it is dependent on how the stock levels in an individual store vary. Both approaches place constraints on the time the order must be picked by. Home delivery also gives issues of scheduling delivery vans in line with when it is convenient for customers to be at home to receive the goods. Convenient for the customer could mean quickly, or at a pre-defined time, or at a pre-defined location at work, home or elsewhere, but such flexibility is difficult to schedule. The difficulty for the e-tailer is that the speed of e-commerce transaction sets up an expectation with the customer of rapid fulfilment or what has been referred to as fulfilment velocity.

The scale of orders also varies considerably according to buying behaviour. Ody (2000) reports that from a given customer, initial orders tend to be similar to a weekly shop; the value then increases as customers experiment, and then declines to a core of staple orders.

In terms of technology 'Orderline' ran as a standalone operation. This is also the case with 'Sainsbury's to You'. McHugh would like to integrate the system with IT from the main system, but says this may take five years. This suggests the difficulty of getting a sufficiently fast integration with existing systems and which perform adequately. It often proves easier to purchase an off-the-shelf system. The 14 million customer loyalty card customers are not yet integrated with the site. A further data issue is that there are regional price differences with different stores and prices can change frequently. As a result indicative rather than exact prices have to be used on the web site.

Sainsbury's has also considered how information content can be used to support the buying experience. Mirroring the approach used in store, in a separate initiative 'Taste for Life' is aimed at providing an electronic magazine that build on the success of the instore magazine that is read by nearly three million shoppers.

Source: Based on Ody (2000).

Questions

Based on the Sainsbury's case study make notes under the following headings which illustrate the typical problems of fulfilment facing any e-tailer:

1. Decisions about picking location and method.
2. Decisions about distribution and delivery.
3. Decisions about integration of new technology with existing technology

IS infrastructure for supply chain mangement

Supply chain visibility
Access to up-to-date, accurate, relevant information about supply chain process to different stakeholders.

Information systems need to deliver **supply chain visibility** to different parties who need to access the supply chain information of an organization, whether it is employees within an organization, suppliers, logistics service providers or customers. Information systems have a key role in providing this visibility. Since a huge volume of information defines supply chain processes for each organization, users of this information need to be able to personalize their view of the information according to their needs – customers want to see the status of their order, suppliers want to access the organization's database to know when their customer is next likely to place a major order. Security is also important – if a company has differential pricing, it will not want customers to see price differences.

These requirements for delivering supply chain information imply the need for an integrated supply chain database with different personalized views for different

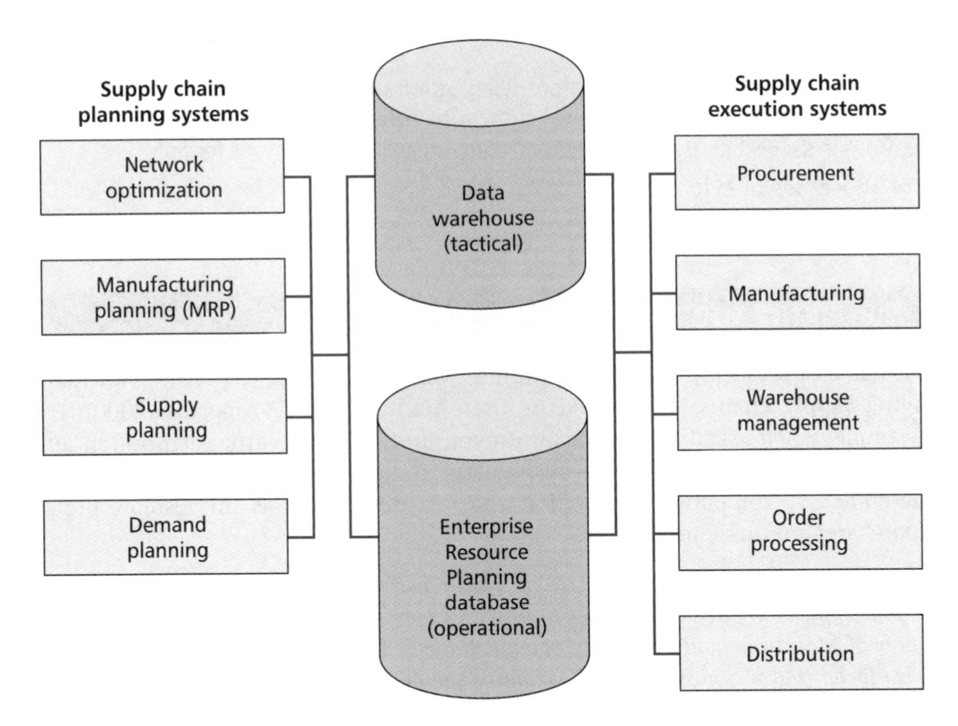

Figure 6.12 A typical IS infrastructure for supply chain management

parties. A typical integrated information systems infrastructure for delivering supply chain management is illustrated in *Figure 6.12*. It can be seen that applications can be divided into those for planning the supply chain and those to execute the supply chain processes. A key feature of a modern supply chain infrastructure is the use of a central operational database that enables information to be shared between supply chain processes and applications. This operational database is usually part of an enterprise resource planning system such as SAP, Baan or Prism and is usually purchased with the applications for supply chain planning and execution. Some of the planning applications such as network simulation and optimization are more likely to be supplied by separate software suppliers. The use of Internet technologies to deliver information over a TCP/IP protocol is becoming standard to reduce the costs of proprietary leased line networks (*Chapter 3*). Information needed by managers to intervene in the supply chain process when problems occur is delivered as alerts or through continuous monitoring across secure private intranets of extranets used to link to partners.

To conclude this section on the IS infrastructure to facilitate e-commerce, complete *activity 6.3* on IS applications for e-commerce.

Software applications to facilitate supply chain management

Activity 6.3

Purpose

To summarize the range of applications that can support supply chain management.

Activity

From your knowledge of the different types of information system and software application, the case studies in this section or by referring to a text on information systems (e.g. Bocij *et al.*, 1999), name specific software applications for SCM.

For answer see p. 251

Managing the supply chain

The difficulties facing managers within a company who are responsible for managing supply chains is indicated by these quotes from Conspectus (2000). For example, when asked 'How difficult do you find it coordinating distribution and logistic plans at your sites?', a respondent from a UK mobile phone operator described his company's distribution and logistics process as 'an absolute nightmare' and another commented:

> *Everything is moving so quickly within our industry at the moment that sourcing suppliers and changing our processes to fit with them is a constant battle. We are hoping our SCM software and the roll-out of our extranet will grow end-to-end ROI but it is easy to forget that we must constantly examine the business model to ensure we are doing things right.*

If you are unfamiliar with the responsibilities managers tasked with supply chain management face complete *activity 6.4*.

Activity 6.4 Who manages the supply chain?

Purpose

To highlight the roles required of staff involved in supply chain management.

Questions

1. Review the job adverts below and for each list the processes that the manager is responsible for and the skills that are required.
2. Discuss the practicality of recruiting a person to this position with the necessary skills and experience.

Advert 1

Supply Chain Manager – The Healthcare Company

The opportunity
With annual turnover of $27 billion The Healthcare Company is a world leader in healthcare products, servicing over 150 countries in pharmaceutical, consumer diagnostic and professional markets. Manufacturing excellence coupled with exceptional customer service delivery is being met with repeat purchase and new account development. To reinforce business growth and profitability, The Healthcare Company seek to appoint an experienced supply chain professional to lead a team of supply chain experts.

The challenge
Reporting to the General Manager, UK, you will provide strategic and tactical leadership to the UK operation, reinforcing customer service excellence while simultaneously delivering supply chain profitability. You will be instrumental in developing and implementing supply

chain initiatives that impact positively across procurement, product development, manufacturing and distribution supply chains. Your team will be measured against the optimal use of business resources, lead time reductions, access to real-time data, stock turns, working capital costs and on time in full delivery to customers. Through the effective coordination of all business operating departments and the leadership of functional reports, purchasing, master scheduling / manufacturing control and data management, you will be the ambassador of customer service and supply chain excellence.

The solution

An ambitious and commercially mature business professional, your breadth of management exposure will ideally encompass supplier liaison, systems development, implementation and maintenance, material management, sales forecasting and capacity planning. Career progression to date has been enhanced by your ability to lead business professionals in the effective implementation of supply chain systems and their ongoing development (preferably MRPII). Personal qualities should include outstanding communication and influencing skills, combined with excellent analytical skills and a thorough working knowledge of IT business management tools (SAP/Oracle/BPEX) which have allowed your teams to deliver business supply excellence.

£50,000 + Bonus + Car

Advert 2

Supply Chain Manager – The Manufacturing Company

The Manufacturing Company is an international manufacturer operating throughout Northern and Continental Europe. The job will involve the management of information channels between customer, company suppliers and partners. The role requires constant monitoring of production against cost to achieve optimum performance levels.

The responsibilities of this role will include:

- The design and implementation of information flows that are consistent and appropriate to achieve minimum cost to the business.
- Manage trade-off between production efficiency, inventory and customer service.
- Analysis of data to ensure that valid business decisions can be made.
- Management of service level agreements to maximize service whilst minimizing inventory.
- Championing the use of IT planning systems.
- The development of team members to ensure standards are set and achieved.

Candidates should have:

- Been educated to a high standard, ideally a relevant degree.
- Excellent analytical and problem solving skills, strong systems knowledge (ERP/MRP, finite scheduling) and experience in planning and inventory control preferably in a short lead time environment. You should be highly motivated with strong influencing and communication skills.

£ 40,000 + car allowance

Advert 3

Logistics Manager – The Engineering Company

A market leader with turnover in excess of £100m and approaching 1000 employees. The business is engaged in sourcing, manufacturing and direct sales benefiting from strong brands and a good customer base.

Supply chain and logistics are recognized as critical with 40,000 product lines and 20,000 suppliers. Over 10,000 orders are processed daily with a substantial third party transport budget and a large in-house NDC.

You will be the logistics champion for the business, coordinating activities between operations and function. Successes will be measured by the achievement of positive change in continuous improvement environment. In addition it will involve direct control of distribution and third parties.

Candidates should be of graduate calibre from a background involving commercial and budget responsibility, customer focused with character, drive and energy.
To $45,000 plus car

Advert 4

Transport Manager – The Food Manufacturer

A long established, family-owned food manufacturer with an annual turnover of £100 m.
Responsible for efficient distribution operation from three sites utilizing a range of owned specialist vehicles supported by approved subcontractors. You will possess extensive transport and management experience operating a fleet size in excess of 30 vehicles. Analytical and planning skills are essential in order to monitor and optimize fleet efficiency in response to customer requirement.

To £36,000 + Benefits

A new concept are integration managers who enable supply chain partnerships to be redesigned. Approaches include launching 100-day projects to achieve short-term bottom line results, transfer of best practice between companies and mobilization of joint teams.

The supply chain management strategy process

A strategic approach for supply chain management can also be defined using the SOSTAC™ approach referred to in *Chapters 5* and *8*. *Table 6.2* summarizes a SOSTAC™ approach to supply chain management strategy development based on the guidance of Hughes *et al.* (1998). *Table 6.2* implies a linear approach to strategic thinking, but as was pointed out in *Chapters 4 and 5*, an iterative approach in which there is a joint development between the organization, suppliers and other third parties.

Table 6.2 A SOSTAC™ approach to supply chain management

Strategy element	*SCM approach of Hughes* et al. *(2000)*
Situation analysis	Gather the data: ● Internal assessment of current approaches to the supply chain ● External analysis of marketplace trends and customer opportunities
Objective setting	Set the objectives ● Definition of required target returns and release of shareholder value
Strategy	Frame the strategies: ● Development of supply chain strategies to achieve these goals (actions)
Tactics	Prioritization of operational improvement strategies and quick wins
Actions	Implement the change and challenge the thinking: ● Formation of a supply chain strategy forum to assess the needs ● Analysis of value-added, cost and cycle time of supply chain activities ● Cascade of executive-led project groups to scrutinize key processes ● Allocation of business development strategies to sponsor executives
Control	Measure the outcome: ● Integration of supply chain measurement in corporate-wide reviews ● Baselining to maintain pressure for performance delivery

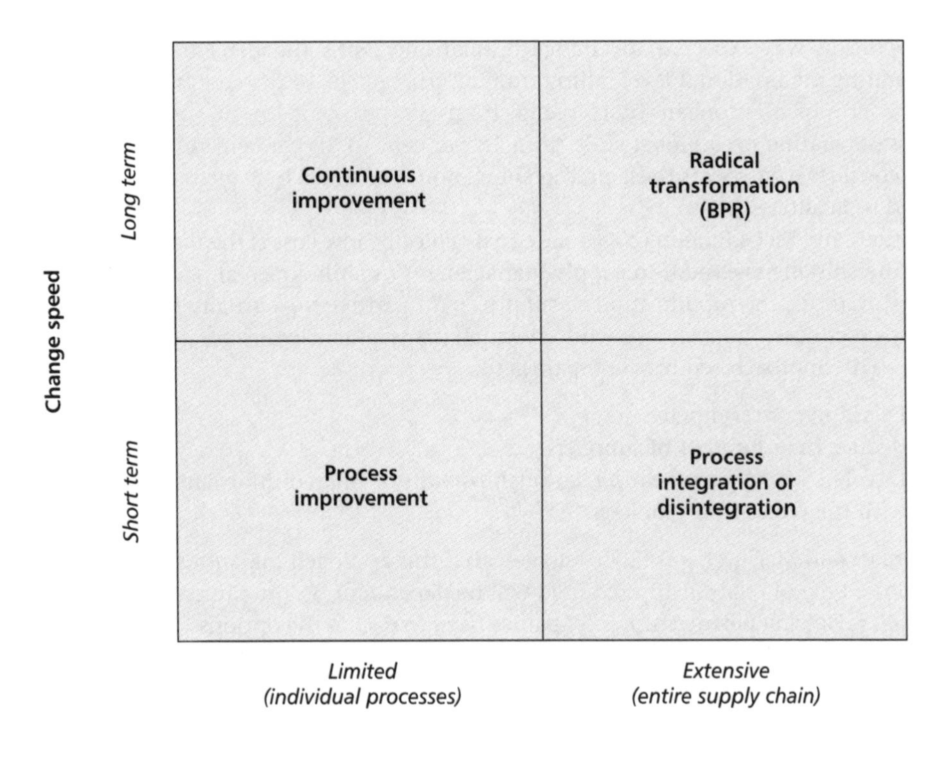

Figure 6.13 Alternative strategies for modification of the e-business supply chain

Strategies for supply chain improvement have been categorized by Hughes *et al.* (1998) according to the scope of change and the speed of change. These dimensions of change are similar to those that are associated with business process re-engineering and business process improvement (Bocij *et al.*, 1999). *Figure 6.13* illustrates four strategic options for the supply chain. The two strategies that are relatively limited in scope apply to individual processes such as procurement or outbound logistics and can be thought of as delivering improvement at an operational level. These may give short-term benefits while minimizing the risk of more radical change. Conversely where the scope of change is more extensive there is a greater risk, but also greater potential reward. These changes include complete re-engineering of processes or major changes to the supply chain.

Managing partnerships

A key element of restructuring of the supply chain is examining the form of relationships with partners such as suppliers and distributors. This need to review the form of partnership has been accentuated with the globalization enabled by e-commerce. The importance of forming new international partnerships is indicated by the survey of UK manufacturing companies with a turnover greater than £100 m reported by Conspectus (2000). This showed that, at the time of the survey, 52 per cent of the sample operated their supply chain at a national level, with 30 per cent at a pan-European level and 18 per cent on a global scale. By 2002 the proportion was expected to change dramatically with the percentage of those operating on a national level falling from 52 per cent to 14 per cent, those operating on a pan-European basis rising from 30 per cent to 58 per cent and those operating on a global scale from 18 per cent to 28 per cent. In this section we consider what forms these partnerships should take and how technology can be used to facilitate them.

Stuart and McCutcheon (2000) state that typically, low cost is the main driver for partnership management in supply management (mainly upstream). According to these authors, the modification of supply chain partnerships usually follows what they describe as the 'received wisdom which many practitioners are rigidly following'. This approach requires companies to:

1. Focus on core competencies.
2. Reduce their number of suppliers.
3. Develop strong partnership relationships built on shared information and trust with the remaining suppliers.

Stuart and McCutcheon (2000) suggest that this approach may not suit all needs and the type of relationship required will be dependent on the ultimate objective. When reviewing partnerships, companies need to decide the options for the extent of their control of the supply chain process. *Table 6.3* presents some strategic

Table 6.3 Strategic options for partnerships

Partnering arrangement	*Technical infrastructure integration*	*Examples*
1. Total ownership (more than 51% equity in company)	Technical issues in merging company systems	Purchase of Booker (distribution company) by (Iceland) retailer. Since 1993 Cisco has made over 30 acquisitions (not all SCM related)
2. Investment stake (less than 49% equity)	Technical issues in merging company systems	Cisco has also made over 40 investments in hardware and software suppliers
3. Strategic alliance	Collaboration tools and groupware for new product development	Cable and Wireless, Compaq and Microsoft new e-business solution called a-Services
4. Profit sharing partnership	As above	Arrangement sometimes used for IS outsourcing
5. Long-term contract	See above. Tools for managing service level agreements important	ISPs have performance and availability SLAs with penalty clauses
6. Preferred suppliers	Permanent EDI or Internet EDI links set up with preferred partners	*Tesco information exchange* case study 6.1
7. Competitive tendering	Tenders issued at intermediary or buyer's web site	Buyer-arranged auctions e.g. SmithKline Beecham (*Chapter 2*)
8. Short-term contracts	As above	As above
9. Spot markets and auctions	Auctions at intermediary or buyer's web site	Business-to-business marketplaces e.g. www.itoi.com

options for partnerships in order of increasing control and ownership over the process by the organization. In Table 6.3 option 1 is total insourcing of a particular process while 2 to 9 give varying degrees of outsourcing. There is also a continuum between collaborative partnerships where risks are shared (options 1 to 5) and competitive sourcing where market competition is used to achieve the best combination of price and value. Note that although an organization may lose control of the *process* through outsourcing, a contractual arrangement will still enable them to exert a strong control over the *outputs* of the process. Although there is a general trend to outsourcing, this does not mean that ownership arrangements are not uncommon, as the Iceland acquisition of Booker shows.

From *Table 6.3* it can be seen that as the depth of relationship between partners increases, the volume and complexity of information exchange requirements will increase. For a long-term arrangement information exchange can include:

- Short-term orders
- Medium to long-term capacity commitments
- Long-term financial or contractual agreement
- Product design, including specifications
- Performance monitoring, standard of product and service quality.
- Logistics

For a short-term relationship simple information on transactions only such as the EDI purchase order example in *Chapter 3* are all that are required.

Stuart and McCutcheon (2000) present a more simplified set of partnership choices than those in *Table 6.3*. They suggest that the partnering option chosen should be dependent on the core objective. If this is cost reduction, then a relationship with competitive tension is required (equivalent to options 6 to 9 in *Table 6.3*). Alternatively, if the core objective is value-added benefits such as improved delivery speed, additional design features or the need for customization, then the 'arms-length' approach of options 6 to 9 may not be appropriate. In this case they suggest a strategic alliance or cooperative partnership is the best option. Stuart and McCutcheon point out that the competitive advantages achieved through cost reduction are likely to be short-lived so companies will increasingly need to turn to value-added benefits. Each supplier has to be considered for whichever type of partnership is most appropriate. For example, ICL, the UK computer supplier, has strategic alliances with only 2 to 3 per cent of suppliers, with the majority in the cost reduction category.

Managing global distribution

Arnold (2000) suggests action that manufacturers should follow as they enter new overseas markets enable by the Internet. The seven actions are:

1. Select distributors. Don't let them select you.
2. Look for distributors capable of developing markets rather than those with new customer contacts.
3. Treat the local distributors as long-term partners, not temporary market entry vehicles.
4. Support market entry by committing money, managers and proven marketing ideas.

5. From the start, maintain control over marketing strategy.
6. Make sure distributors provide you with detailed market and financial performance data.
7. Build links among national distributors at the earliest opportunity.

Summary

1. Supply chain management involves the coordination of all supply activities of an organization from its suppliers and partners to its customers. Upstream supply chain activities (procurement and inbound logistics) are equivalent to buy-side e-commerce and downstream supply chain activities (sales, outbound logistics and fulfilment) equate to sell-side e-commerce.
2. There has been a change in supply chain management thinking from a push-oriented supply chain that emphasizes distribution of a product to passive customers to a pull-oriented supply chain that utilizes the supply chain to deliver value to customers who are actively involved in product and service specification.
3. The value chain concept is closely allied to supply chain management. It considers how value can be added both between and within elements of the supply chain and at the interface between them.
4. Electronic communications enable value networks to be created that enable the external value chain to be dynamically updated in response to marketplace variables.
5. Supply chains and value chains can be revised by disaggregation or re-aggregation. Disaggregation may involve outsourcing core supply chain activities to external parties. As more activities are outsourced a company moves towards a virtual organization.
6. Electronic communications have played a major role in facilitating new models of supply chain management. Technology applications that have facilitated supply chain management are:
   - E-mail
   - Web-based ordering
   - EDI of invoices and payment
   - Web-based order tracking
7. Benefits of deploying these technologies include:
   - More efficient, lower cost execution of processes
   - Reduced complexity of the supply chain (disintermediation)
   - Improved data integration between elements of the supply chain
   - Reduced costs through ease of dynamic outsourcing
   - Enabling innovation and customer responsiveness
8. Intranets connecting internal business applications such as operational enterprise resource planning systems and decision support oriented data warehouses enable supply chain management. Such systems increasingly support external links to third parties such as suppliers.
9. Key strategic issues in supply chain management include:
   - Redesigning supply chain activities.
   - Restructuring partnerships which support the supply chain through outsourcing or ownership.

ACTIVITY ANSWERS

6.1 The supply chain for The B2B Company

1. Upstream supply chain:
   - Disintermediation offers the opportunity to *buy* direct from the supplier with reduced costs and shorter cycle times.
   - Reintermediation offers the chance to use business-to-business exchanges to source products at lower costs.

   Downstream supply chain:
   - Disintermediation offers the opportunity to *sell* direct to the customer with lower cost of sales and improved lead time for customers.
   - Reintermediation offers the opportunity to compete in new marketplaces through B2B exchanges.

A more detailed discussion can review the different options for disintermediation and reintermediation.

2. Without any restructuring of the supply chain technologies such as e-mail, web-based ordering, EDI and order tracking can be used to reduce costs and cycle times. Distintermediation and reintermediation options are also facilitated through e-mail, web sites, EDI and e-commerce.

6.2 Supply chain models in personal computer manufacture

1. Approach 1: IBM – Vertical integration. Approach 2: Dell – Virtual integration.
2. Some of the main advantages and disadvantages are shown in *Table 6.4*.

Table 6.4 Advantages and disadvantages of vertical integration and virtual integration

Approach 1: IBM – Vertical integration		*Approach 2: Dell – Virtual integration*	
Advantages	*Disadvantages*	*Advantages*	*Disadvantages*
Control of manufacturing quality	Less pressure on manufacturing costs	Excellent control of costs through supplier competition	Less direct control on quality (although can swap to other suppliers)
Lower overhead in dealing with third parties (easier to integrate systems internally)	Costs of systems all borne by manufacture	Fewer assets. Costs of inventory borne by suppliers. Costs of data integration shared with partners	Emphasis on management of suppliers
–	More responsive to short- and medium-term market demand variations	More responsive to short- and medium-term market demand variations	–

The market success of Dell suggests their approach is superior.

3. Information systems can help both situations through using enterprise resource planning systems, EDI and groupware systems to integrate market research, product design, sourcing, material requirements planning, production, warehousing and distribution. As is pointed out in the table it may be easier to integrate systems with vertical integration, but more of the cost is borne by the manufacturer.

6.3 Software applications to facilitate supply chain management

- E-mail messaging and WAP
- Groupware for new product development (across intranets and partner extranets)

- Auctions on business to business exchanges
- On-line catalogues tailored for buyers
- Price comparison engines (agents)
- Extranet facilities (Dell Premier Pages)
- Order tracking
- CAD/CAM systems
- Barcodes for traceabilty
- Document management systems for sharing standards, technical specifications, engineering drawings and user guides.

EXERCISES

Self-assessment questions

1. Define supply chain management; how does it relate to:
   - logistics;
   - the value chain concept;
   - value networks?
2. What is the difference between a push orientation to the value chain and pull orientation?
3. How can information systems support the supply chain?
4. What are the key strategic options in supply chain management?

Essay and discussion questions

1. How does electronic communications enable restructuring of the value chain network?
2. The concept of a linear value chain is no longer tenable with the advent of electronic commerce. Discuss.
3. Select an industry of your choice and analyse how business-to-business exchanges will change the supply chain.
4. *'In the end business all comes down to supply chain vs supply chain'*. Discuss.
5. Select a retailer of your choice and analyse their strategy for management of the upstream and downstream supply chain.

Examination questions

1. Explain how the concepts of disintermediation, reintermediation and countermediation apply to the supply chain.
2. You have recently been appointed as supply chain manager for a pharmaceutical company. Summarize the main Internet-based applications you would consider for communicating with your suppliers.
3. How has the increase in electronic communications contributed to the development of value networks?

4. What are the characteristics of a virtual organization? Using examples, explain how e-commerce can support the virtual organization.
5. Explain how information technologies can be employed for different elements of a purchaser–supplier relationship.
6. Using industry examples, summarize three benefits of using e-commerce to streamline the supply chain.
7. How can electronic commerce be used to support restructuring of the supply chain?
8. What are the differences and similarities of using information technology to support:
   (a) the upstream supply chain;
   (b) the downstream supply chain?

REFERENCES

Arnold, D. (2000), Seven rules of international distribution. *Harvard Business Review,* November–December, 131–7.

Benjamin, R. and Wigand, R. (1995) Electronic markets and virtual value-chains on the information superhighway. *Sloan Management Review*, Winter, 62–72.

Bocij, P., Chaffey, D., Greasley, A. and Hickie, S. (1999) *Business Information Systems. Technology, Development and Management.* FT Management, London.

Chandra, C. and Kumar, S. (2000) An application of a system analysis methodology to manage logistics in a textile supply chain. *Supply Chain Management: An International Journal*, 5(5), 234–45.

Conspectus (2000) Supply chain management software issue. Prime Marketing Publications, June 2000. PMP Research www.pmp.co.uk

Davidow, W.H. and Malone, M.S. (1992) *The Virtual Corporation. Structuring and Revitalizing the Corporation for the 21st Century*. HarperCollins.

Deise, M., Nowikow, C., King, P. and Wright, A. (2000) *Executive's Guide to E-business. From Tactics to Strategy*. John Wiley and Sons, New York, NY.

DTI (2000) *Business In The Information Age – International Benchmarking Study 2000.* UK Department of Trade and Industry. Available online at: www.ukonlineforbusiness.gov.uk.

Field, C. (2000). Waterstone's: Fully integrated into existing fulfilment systems. *Financial Times*, 3 May.

Fisher, M. (1997) What is the right supply chain for your product? *Harvard Business Review*, March–April, 105–16.

Hagel III, J. and Rayport, J. (1997) The new infomediaries. *The McKinsey Quarterly* no. 4, 54–70.

Hamill, J. and Gregory, K. (1997) Internet marketing in the internationalisation of UK SMEs. *Journal of Marketing Management*, 13, 1–3.

Hayes, R. and Wheelwright, S. (1994) *Restoring our Competitive Edge*. John Wiley and Sons, New York.

Hughes, J., Ralf, M. and Michels, B. (1998) *Transform Your Supply Chain*. International Thomson Business Press.

Kalakota, R. and Robinson, M. (2000) *E-business. Roadmap for Success*. Addison-Wesley, Reading, MA.

Kraut, R., Chan, A., Butler, B. and Hong, A. (1998) Coordination and virtualisation: the role of electronic networks and personal relationships. *Journal of Computer Mediated Communications*, 3(4).

Magretta, J. (1998) The power of virtual integration. An interview with Michael Dell. *Harvard Business Review*, March–April, 72–84.

Malone, T., Yates, J. and Benjamin, R. (1987) Electronic markets and electronic hierarchies: effects of information technology on market structure and corporate strategies. *Communications of the ACM,* 30 (6), 484–97.

Ody, P. (2000) Taste for the Web. *e.business Review,* 1(9), 56–9.

Phillips, S. (2000) Retailer's crown jewel is a unique customer database. *Financial Times,* 4 December.

Porter, M. (1980) *Competitive Strategy*. Free Press, USA.

Porter, M. and Millar, V. (1985) How information gives you competitive advantage. *Harvard Business Review*, July/August, 149–60.

Quelch, J. and Klein, L. (1996) The Internet and international marketing. *Sloan Management Review*, Spring, 60–75.

Rayport, J. and Sviokla, J. (1996) Exploiting the virtual value-chain. *The McKinsey Quarterly*, no. 1, 20–37.

Ritchie, L., Burnes, B., Whittle, P. and Hey, R. (2000) The benefits of reverse logistics: the case of the Manchester Royal Infirmary Pharmacy. *Supply Chain Management: An International Journal*, 5(5), 226–34.

Steinfield, C., Kraut, R. and Plummer, A. (1996) The impact of interorganizational networks on buyer–seller relationships. *Journal of Computer Mediated Communication*, 1(3).

Stuart, F. and McCutcheon, D. (2000) The manager's guide to supply chain management. *Business Horizons*, March–April, 35–44.

Timmers, P. (1999) *Electronic Commerce Strategies and Models for Business-to-Business Trading*. John Wiley series in information systems. John Wiley and Sons, Chichester, UK.

Womack, J. and Jones, D. (1998) *Lean Thinking*. Touchstone, Simon and Schuster, London, UK.

FURTHER READING

Deise, M., Nowikow, C., King, P., Wright, A. (2000) *Executive's Guide to E-business. From Tactics to Strategy*. John Wiley and Sons, New York, NY. See Chapter 5, Industry transformation for description of value networks and partnering arrangements.

Fingar, P., Kumar, H. and Sharma, T. (2000) *Enterprise E-commerce*. Meghan-Kiffler Press, Tampa, FL. See Chapter 6, Extended supply chain management.

Hughes, J., Ralf, M. and Michels, B. (1998) *Transform your Supply Chain*. International Thomson Business Press. An accessible introduction to supply chain management, with many examples. See Chapter 9, The electronic supply chain.

Westland, J.C. and Clark, T.H. (2000) *Global Electronic Commerce: Theory and Case Studies*. Massachusetts Institute of Technology. Chapter 4, Supply chain management use – a value chain perspective on the application of e-commerce to SCM.

WEB LINKS

ASCET Project (www.ascet.com): excellent collection of articles coordinated by Accenture and Montgomery research.

Conspectus (www.conspectus.com): articles on different aspects of e-business including supply chain management.

Institute of Logistics and Transport (www.iolt.org.uk): overview of logistics, plus links to related sites.

CIO Magazine E-commerce resource centre (www.cio.com/forums/ec/): one of the best online magazines from business/technical perspective – see other research centres also, e.g. intranets, knowledge management.

Chapter 7

E-procurement

CHAPTER AT A GLANCE

Main topics

Focus on . . .

Case studies

LEARNING OBJECTIVES

After reading this chapter the reader should be able to:

- Identify the benefits and risks of e-procurement
- Analyze procurement methods to evaluate cost savings
- Assess different options for integration of organizations' information systems with e-procurement suppliers

MANAGEMENT ISSUES

Managers will be concerned with the following e-procurement issues:

- What benefits and risks are associated with e-procurement?
- Which method(s) of e-procurement should we adopt?
- What organizational and technical issues are involved in introducing e-procurement?

Links to other chapters

The main related chapters are:

- *Chapter 2* – introduces business-to-business marketplaces, models of electronic trading and B2B auctions
- *Chapter 6* – covers the role of purchasing within supply chain management
- *Chapters 8 and 9* – describe the implications of e-procurement from a sell-side perspective.

Introduction

Procurement has not traditionally been a significant topic for management study in comparison other areas such as marketing, operations or strategy. The concept of e-business, has however, highlighted its importance as a strategic issue since introducing electronic procurement or e-procurement can achieve significant savings and other benefits which directly impact upon the customer. Issues involved with electronic trading between a supplier and their customers are often considered as in *Chapters 8 and 9* from the marketing perspective of the supplier of goods. In this chapter, we consider the same transaction, but from the alternative perspective of the purchaser of goods. It will be seen that there is a wide range of methods of implementing electronic trading with suppliers which will be assessed by purchasing, information systems and marketing managers. Meanwhile company directors will need to assess the strategic benefits and risks of e-procurement. In the context of *Chapter 1* definitions, supply chain procurement is an aspect of buy-side e-commerce within the B2B arena.

The growing importance of e-procurement was highlighted by a Tranmit plc (1999) report that showed that around 90 per cent of companies said that they planned to implement an electronic procurement management system within the next five years, with the majority identifying cost savings as their primary goal. The biggest barrier to automation is integration of these systems with existing financial systems, according to 60 per cent of the respondents. Furthermore, the survey suggested that only 13 per cent of these businesses have computerized the procurement process and integrated it with other financial processes; 25 per cent of organizations continue to rely on entirely paper-based procurement. The majority (62 per cent) continue to rely on a mixture of electronically supported and manual processes. The respondents in the survey were procurement directors and senior managers in 112 UK organizations with an annual turnover of more than £30 million; they were approached to establish the adoption levels, drivers and barriers for e-procurement.

In this chapter we consider the benefits and risks of e-procurement together with techniques that can be used to assess these benefits and risks. We also consider the selection of the different types of e-procurement including the hyped business-to-business marketplaces.

What is e-procurement?

The terms purchasing and procurement are sometimes used interchangeably, but as Kalakota and Robinson (2000) point out, procurement generally has a broader meaning. Procurement refers to all activities involved with obtaining items from a supplier; this includes purchasing, but also inbound logistics such as transportation, goods-in and warehousing before the item is used. The key procurement activities and associated information flows within an organization are shown in *Figure 7.1*. In this chapter we focus on these activities which include searching and specification of product by the end-user, purchasing by the buyer, payment by an account and receipt and distribution of goods within a warehouse.

E-procurement should be directed at improving performance for each of the 'five rights' of purchasing' (Baily *et al.*, 1994) which are sourcing items:

Electronic procurement (e-procurement)
The electronic integration and management of all procurement activities including purchase request, authorization, ordering, delivery and payment between a purchaser and a supplier.

1. At the right price.
2. Delivered at the right time.
3. Are of the right quality.
4. Of the right quantity.
5. From the right source.

E-procurement is not new; there have been many attempts to automate the process of procurement for the buyer using **electronic procurement systems (EPS)**, workflow systems and links with suppliers through EDI (*Chapter 3*). These involved online entry, authorization and placing of orders using a combination of data entry forms, scanned documents and e-mail-based workflow. It is convenient to refer to these as first generation e-procurement. *Figure 7.2* is an example of an electronic procurement system that is available through a company intranet.

Electronic procurement systems (EPS)
An electronic system used to automate all or part of the procurement function by enabling the scanning, storage and retrieval of invoices and other documents; management of approvals; routing of authorization requests; interfaces to other finance systems; and matching of documents to validate transactions.

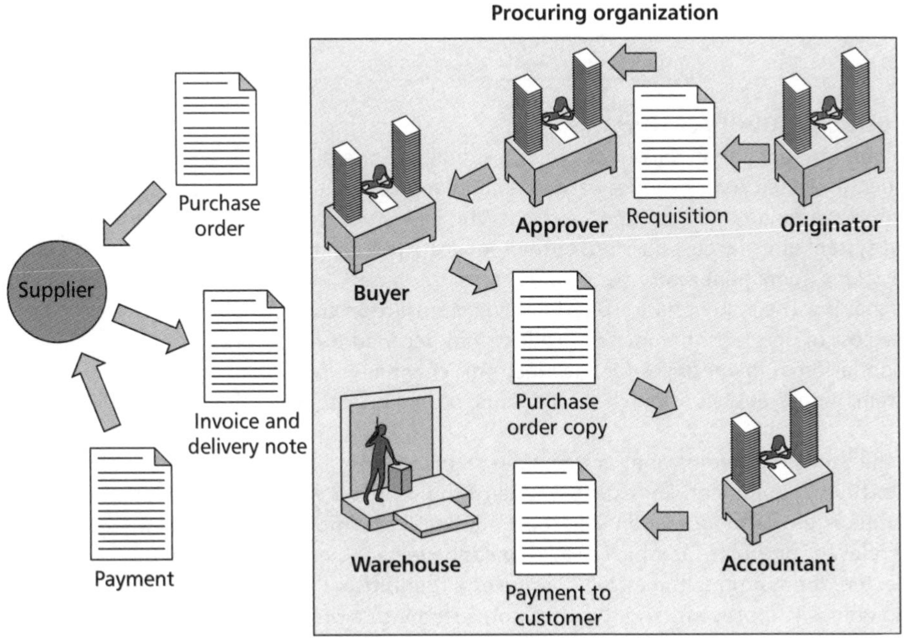

Figure 7.1 Key procurement activities within an organization

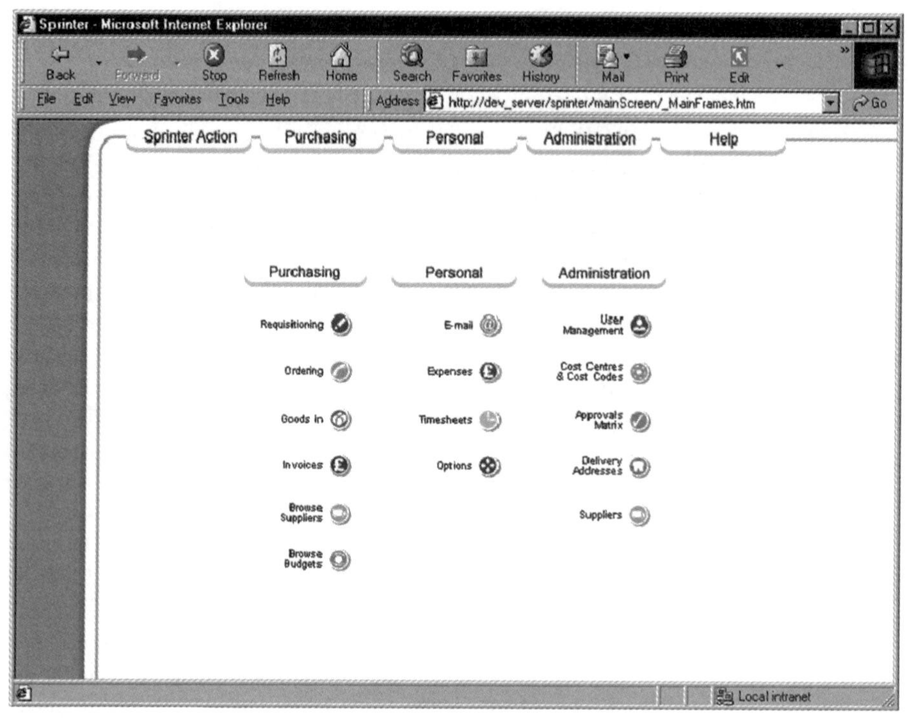

Figure 7.2 Electronic procurement system
Source: Tranmit plc

Read the box *E-procurement at Schlumberger in Paris* to understand how e-procurement occurs within an organization.

E-procurement at Schlumberger in Paris

Schlumberger is a global company that started its life as a supplier in the oil and gas exploration industry with revenues. In 2000 it had revenues of $8.5 million and 60,000 employees across 100 countries. It now provides a range of information services. This case study describes the installation of an e-procurement system at its largest division, oilfield services. The aim of the new system was to replace existing systems, some paper-based and some computer-based, with a single system that would speed up purchasing. The system has resulted in lower transaction costs for placing orders and also reduced the cost of goods as the price of products has declined through greater competition and negotiation of lower prices for the electronic channel.

With the new system, employees act as purchasing agents, ordering directly via their desktop PCs.

The system runs on the Schlumberger intranet and enables staff to access a simplified catalogue of office supplies and technical equipment. For example, one of the suppliers is OfficeDepot. Although OfficeDepot can post its entire catalogue at an electronic marketplace, employees at Schlumberger only see a subset of relevant products for which special prices have been negotiated. Once the items have been selected, the system automatically produces a requisition that is electronically routed to the person who will approve it, and it is then converted into a purchase order without the intervention from purchasing staff.

The technical solution is based on Commerce One Buysite procurement software for selection and approval and Marketsite from the same supplier for the transaction between Schlumberger and their suppliers. Schlumberger report that Marketsite tends to give access to a wider range of suppliers than when it used one-to-one EDI transactions with suppliers. The solution was implemented gradually through introducing new items in stages.

Source: Based on a summary of a dialogue between Alain-Michel Diamant-Berger and Andrea Ovans (Ovans, 2000).

Understanding the procurement process

Before the advent of e-procurement, organizational purchasing processes had remained similar for decades. *Table 7.1* highlights the paper-based process. It can be seen that it involves the end-user of the item selecting an item by conducting a search and then filling in a paper requisition form that is sent to a buyer in the purchasing department (often after authorization by a manager, which introduces further delay). The buyer then fills out an order form that is dispatched to the supplier. After the item is delivered, the item and a delivery note are usually reconciled with the order form and an invoice and then payment occurs. Procurement also includes the transport, storage and distribution of goods received within the business referred to as inbound logistics. *Activity 7.1* explains how the procurement process can be simplified through e-procurement.

Evaluating the benefits of the e-procurement process for The B2B Company

Activity 7.1

Purpose

To highlight the tasks involved in organizational purchasing and to indicate the potential time savings from e-procurement.

Introduction

Table 7.1 illustrates a typical traditional procurement process using the flow process chart symbols that are explained in more detail in *Chapter 11*. It is based on the actual

Table 7.1 Process flow analysis for traditional procurement (typical cycle time, 5½ days)

	Task description	*Chart symbols*	*Time*
1.	Search for goods	●⇨□D▽	1 hour+
2.	Fill in paper requisition	●⇨□D▽	10 min
3.	Send to buyer	○➡□D▽	1 day
4.	In buyer's intray	○⇨□◗▽	½ day
5.	Buyer enters order number	●⇨□D▽	10 min
6.	Buyer authorizes order	●⇨□D▽	10 min
7.	Buyer prints order	●⇨□D▽	10 min
8.	Order copies to supplier and goods in	○➡□D▽	1 day
9.	Delivery from supplier	○⇨□D▼	1 day
10.	Order copy to accounts	○➡□D▽	1 day
11.	3 way invoice match	●⇨□D▽	1 day
12.	Cheque payment	●⇨□D▽	10 min

Activity 7.1 *continued*

procurement process for Cambridge Consultants described in *case study 7.1*. Note that this process is for relatively low-value items that do not need authorization by senior managers. The timings are for a new item rather than a repeat buy for which searching would not be required. *Table 7.2* summarizes the new procurement process.

Table 7.2 Process flow analysis for new procurement (typical cycle time, 1½ days)

	Task description	*Chart symbols*	*Time*
1.	Search for goods	●⇨□D▽	20 min
2.	Order on web	●⇨□D▽	10 min
3.	Delivery from supplier	○⇨□D▼	1 day
4.	Generate invoice	●⇨□D▽	10 min
5.	Cheque payment	●⇨□D▽	10 min

Key to flow process chart symbols

○ Process
⇨ Transport
□ Inspection
D Delay
▽ Inbound goods

Questions

1. Identify inefficiencies in the traditional procurement process (Table 7.1).
2. Identify process benefits to Table 7.1 that would be possible through the automation of a system through an e-mail-based workflow system.
3. Summarize why the e-procurement process in Table 7.2 is more efficient.

For answers see p. 279

Types of procurement

To understand the benefits of e-procurement, and also to highlight some of the practical considerations with introducing e-procurement, we need to briefly consider the different types of items that are obtained by procurement (what is bought?) and types of ordering (how is it bought?).

Let us start us by reviewing what is bought by businesses. The B2B Company, for example, will buy everything from steel for manufacturing products, through equipment to help machine products to paper-clips and pens for office use. There are two broad categories of procurement; those that relate to *manufacturing* of products (*production-related procurement*) and *operating* or *non-production related procurement* that supports the operations of the whole business and includes office supplies, furniture, information systems, **MRO goods** and a range of services from catering, buying travel to professional services such as consulting and training. Raw materials for the production of goods and MRO goods are particularly important since they are critical to the operation of a business. For the B2B Company, they would include manufacturing equipment, network cables and computers to control the process.

MRO goods
Maintenance, repairs and operations of manufacturing facilities.

Moving to how items are bought, businesses tend to buy either by:

- *Systematic sourcing* – negotiated contracts with regular suppliers typically in long-term relationships.

- *Spot sourcing* – fulfilment of an immediate need, typically of a commoditized item for which it is less important to know the credibility of the supplier.

A further characteristic of corporate procurement is that often items such as stationery are purchased repeatedly, either for identical items (straight rebuy) or with some changes (modified rebuy). E-procurement systems can assist in purchase if they make rebuys more straightforward.

Drivers of e-procurement

Case study 7.1 illustrates many of the reasons why many companies are now introducing e-procurement. The primary driver is cost reduction, in this case from an average of £60 per order to £10 per order. In many cases the cost of ordering exceeds the value of the product purchased. Internet Business indicates that the figures in the case are representative, suggesting that the average cost of ordering is £80. If these types of savings are scaled across the whole of the UK it is estimated that UK businesses could save £100 billion per year and as a result it is estimated that global B2B trading will reach over $1 trillion by 2003 from $60 billion in 1999 (eMarketer, 2000). Savings may also be made through the need for less material in stock due to faster purchase cycle times.

Kluge (1997) and Kalakota and Robinson (2000) consider procurement to be a strategic issue since, as the figures above show, significant savings can be made and these cost reductions should increase in greater profitability. Kluge (1997) reports on a survey of electronics companies in which there was a 19 per cent difference in profitability between the most successful and least successful companies. Of this difference, 13 per cent was due to differences in the cost of goods sold of which between 40 and 70 per cent was accounted for by differences in the cost of purchased goods and services.

Direct cost reductions are achieved through efficiencies in the process as indicated by *case study 7.1* and *Tables 7.1 and 7.2*. Process efficiencies result in less staff time spent in searching and ordering products and reconciling deliveries with invoices. Savings also occur due to automated validation of pre-approved spending budgets for individuals or departments, leading to fewer people processing each order, and in less time. It is also possible to reduce the cost of physical materials such as specially printed order forms and invoices that are important to the process as is evident from *Figure 7.1*.

There are also indirect benefits from e-procurement; Tables 7.1 and 7.2 show how the cycle time between order and use of supplies can be reduced. In addition e-procurement may enable greater flexibility in ordering goods from different suppliers according to best value. This is particularly true for *electronic B2B marketplaces* (p. 272). E-procurement also tends to change the role of buyers in the purchasing department. By removing administrative tasks such as placing orders and reconciling deliveries and invoices with purchase orders, buyers can spend more time on value-adding activities. Such activities may include more time spent with key suppliers to improve product delivery and costs or analysis and control of purchasing behaviour.

CASE STUDY 7.1

Cambridge Consultants reduce costs through e-procurement

Introduction

Cambridge Consultants offers technical product design and development services to commerce and industry. It has over 300 employees, all based in Cambridge, 200 of whom are engineers, consultants, and technicians. They work on products in health care, industrial consumer development (ICD), and telecommunications, information, media and electronics (TIME). Although it is not a volume manufacturer, Cambridge Consultants must design to production standards. This means building several production prototypes for each project. With 120 projects in hand at any one time, Cambridge needs a diverse range of components every day.

Purchasing is centralized across the company and controlled by its Purchasing Manager, Francis Pullen. Because of its varied and often unique requirements, Cambridge has a supplier base of nearly 4000 companies, with 20 new ones added each month. Some of these companies are providing items so specialized that Cambridge purchases from them no more than twice a year. Of the total, only 400 are preferred suppliers. Of those, just 10 per cent – 1 per cent of the overall supplier base – have been graded key supplier by Cambridge. That number includes RS Components. Francis Pullen says, 'We charge our clients by the hour, so if a product is faulty or late we have engineers waiting for new parts to arrive. This doesn't align with our fast time to market business proposition. RS Components' guarantee of service and range of products fits in with our business ethos.'

The existing purchasing process

Pullen has seen many changes and improvements in the company's purchasing process as its suppliers have used new technology to introduce new services. The first was moving to CD-ROM from the paper-based catalogue. Next was an online purchasing card – an account card with detailed line item billing, passwords and controls. Using industry standard guidelines from the Chartered Institute of Purchasing and Supply (CIPS), Francis Pullen analysed the internal cost of raising an order. This took into account every step, from the engineer raising a paper requisition, through processing by purchasing, the cost of handling the delivery once it arrived, invoice matching and clearance and even the physical cost of a four-part purchase order form. The whole process involved between eight and ten people and cost the company anywhere from £60 to £120, depending on the complexity of the order.

The main cost is in requisitioning, when engineers and consultants spend their revenue-producing time in identifying their needs and raising paperwork. (Centralized purchasing, by contrast, is very efficient, costing around £50 an order.)

Using the RS purchase card removes the need for engineers and consultants to raise a paper requisition. This makes low-value ordering much more cost efficient. Invoice matching costs are also reduced, since the purchase card statement lists all purchases made each month.

Although the purchase card is undoubtedly an advance, on its own it does not allow costs to be assigned to jobs in the system each day. The purchase card statement takes a month to arrive, giving rise to an equivalent lag in showing the real costs on internal project accounts.

The e-procurement process

To enable the company to order online immediately, RS put Cambridge's pre-Internet trading records on the Web server. Purchasing agreements and controls were thus automatically set up on the Internet order form, including correct pricing and special payment terms.

The benefit was instantly apparent. The use of the RS purchase card when ordering from the web site meant that the complete order was automatically collated, with all controls in place. Accuracy was assured and the purchase process was speeded up with the cost per transaction reduced significantly.

Pullen describes the change this has had on Cambridge's purchasing process. 'For the first time in our purchasing history, our financial controllers saw the benefit of distributed purchasing because of the cost savings, reassured by the central purchasing controls as back up.

'This has benefited us enormously. We have allowed three department heads to have their own purchasing cards, so that they can order independently from the web site.

'We have implemented a very efficient electronic

workflow requisition system which is initiated by the purchase card holders and mailed to central purchasing. The orders are held in a mailbox and checked against physical delivery. This has cut out two layers of order activity.

'In purchasing, we no longer spend our time passing on orders that they have raised, and there is no generation of paper during the order process. It doesn't just save time and money – it's also far more environmentally friendly. Passing on low value orders each day adds very little value, so devolving this function back to our internal customers frees up our time in purchasing to work on higher value tasks.'

Benefits for staff

Francis Pullen continues: 'Our internal customers are also much happier. We leave at 6pm but the engineers will often work late if they are on a deadline. Because they can order off the web site from their desks (everyone at Cambridge has Internet access), they can add items to the order right up until RS's 8pm deadline without our involvement. We maintain control because of the reporting functions on the site.'

Phase 2 of the rswww.com design has also made it possible for multiple orders to be opened during the day and then put against different cost centres internally.

Results

In the year to June 1999, Cambridge Consultants placed 1200 orders with RS Components, totalling more than £62,000 in value. Of those transactions, 95 per cent went via the Internet. Average order value over the Internet was £34 and accounted for £43,000 of the total business done. The remaining 60 orders were placed though traditional channels but had an average value of £317.

The cost to Cambridge of raising a paper-based order was identified as being £60. Using the combination of the RS purchasing card and rswww.com, this has been reduced to £10 an order. Over a year, this represents a saving of £57,000 to Cambridge. The net effect, therefore, is that its purchases from RS Components now cost it a mere £5000 a year!

Francis Pullen again: 'RS has demonstrated its commitment to its customers in spending time and investing money in developing a world-class purchasing system that delivers tangible customer cost savings and benefits. We have welcomed their innovative approach to purchasing and believe they are way ahead of their competition in this sector.'

Source: RS Components White Paper (www.rswww.com) © RS Components Ltd 2001.

Questions

1. Given the scale of the purchasing operation at Cambridge Consultants, what benefits do you think e-procurement has brought?
2. Why are procurement costs currently as high as £60 to £100 per order?
3. How are procurement costs reduced through e-procurement?
4. What staff benefits accrue to Cambridge Consultants as a result of e-procurement?

Turban *et al.* (2000) summarize the benefits of e-procurement as follows:

- Reduced purchasing cycle time and cost
- Enhanced budgetary control (achieved through rules to limit spending and improved reporting facilities)
- Elimination of administrative errors (correcting errors is traditionally a major part of a buyer's workload)
- Increasing buyers' productivity (enabling them to concentrate on strategic purchasing issues)
- Lowering prices through product standardization and consolidation of buys
- Improving information management (better access to prices from alternative suppliers and summaries of spending)
- Improving the payment process (this does not often occur currently since payment is not always integrated into e-procurement systems).

Focus on estimating e-procurement cost savings

While cost savings are commonly cited as the key benefit of e-procurement, more than half the companies in the Tranmit (1999) survey (54 per cent) did not know the procurement costs of their organization! This suggests that calculating costs is not straightforward, but is clearly an important part of the cost-justification of introducing an e-procurement system.

The general approach to estimating procurement costs is straightforward. First we calculate the average procurement cost per item, then we multiply by the average number of requisitions. The Tranmit (1999) report provides some illustrations – typical medium to large companies issue between 1000 and 5000 requisitions a month and are spending between £600,000 and £3 million annually on the procurement process based on the £50 median cost per item. In exceptional cases, the number of requisitions was between 30,000 and 40,000 per month. In these cases, the annual cost of procurement could be between £18 million and £43 million!

To calculate cost savings from e-procurement we perform the following calculation:

$$\text{Savings} = \text{No. requisitions} \times (\text{original cost} - \text{new cost})$$

For Cambridge Consultants (*case study 7.1*) cost savings from orders placed with RS Components alone are as follows:

$$\text{Savings} = 1300 \times (£90 - £10)$$

$$\text{Savings} = £104{,}000$$

These are relative to a typical order value of £70, i.e. savings of £104,000 on purchase item costs of £91,000.

The impact of cost savings on profitability

The study by Kluge (1997) referred to above suggested that cost savings achieved through e-procurement may have a significant effect on profitability. *Activity 7.2* illustrates how the savings will vary between companies according to their buying characteristics. The largest savings and impact on profitability will typically be for manufacturing companies in which procurement is a major cost element and there are many requisitions for relatively low value items. Service industries have lower potential for savings. The consequence for this is that there will be a wide variation in potential savings according to industry as illustrated in *Table 7.3*.

Table 7.3 Procurement as a percentage of costs of goods sold for different industry sectors (estimates from Kluge (1997))

Industry	*Procurement costs as a percentage of cost of goods sold*
Consumer electronics	60–70%
Mini and personal computers	50–70%
Consumer goods	50–70%
Automotive	50–60%
Pharmaceuticals	25–50%
Service industry	10–40%

Modelling cost savings and profitability arising from e-procurement

Activity 7.2

Purpose

To explore the different characteristics of purchasing in organizations that will govern the scale of savings made through e-procurement.

Activity

Imagine you are a procurement manager, IS manager or consultant who needs to demonstrate the cost savings of e-procurement to a senior management team in order to obtain approval for investment in an e-procurement system. Develop two spreadsheet models for two hypothetical companies to demonstrate the case as follows:

1. *Cost saving calculations.* Using the input parameters for the two companies in *Table 7.4*, develop a spreadsheet model to calculate traditional overall purchasing cost, new overall purchasing cost, % change in cost per order and % change in overall purchasing cost.

Table 7.4 Input parameters for cost saving calculations for two companies

Input parameters (Company A)		*Input parameters (Company B)*	
Number of orders	25,000	Number of orders	2500
Traditional cost per order (average)	£50	Traditional cost per order (average)	£50
New cost per order (average)	£10	New cost per order (average)	£10
Average value of order	£150	Average value of order	£1500

2. *Profitability calculations.* Using input parameters of turnover, traditional purchasing costs, other costs and a 5 per cent reduction in purchasing costs as shown in *Table 7.5* develop a model that calculates the profitability before and after introduction of e-procurement and also shows the change in profitability as an absolute (£) and as a percentage.

Table 7.5 Input parameters for profitability calculations for two companies

Parameter	*Company X*	*Company Y*
Turnover	£10,000,000	£10,000,000
Traditional purchasing costs	£5,000,000	£1,000,000
Other costs	£4,000,000	£8,000,000
Reduction in purchasing costs	20%	20%

3. Analyze the sensitivity of the models to differences in volume of orders and values of purchases (*Table 7.4*) and the balance between traditional purchasing costs and other costs such as salaries and capital by using the parameters (*Table 7.5*). Explain to the managers the typical characteristics of a company that will make significant changes to profitability from introducing e-procurement.

For answers see p. 280

To conclude this *Focus on* topic, a note of caution should be struck. Many of the models used to calculate savings and return on investment are, of course, only as good as the assumptions they use. Refer to the *activity 7.4, Purchasing ROI myths* to review why savings may be lower than those predicted by models.

Risks and impacts of e-procurement

The Tranmit (1999) report at the start of the chapter indicated that in the UK and throughout Europe, adoption of e-procurement is low, with less than a fifth of large companies adopting this technology. It may be possible to explain low adoption through a consideration of the risks and impacts involved with e-procurement. A PricewaterhouseCoopers survey of 400 senior European business leaders indicates that security concerns and lack of faith in trading partners are the most significant factors holding back e-procurement (Potter, 2000). Although 62 per cent said they expected 30 per cent of procurement to be online by the end of 2001, the typical online spend in early 2000 was 5 per cent. Potter states that authentication of identity is the main issue. He says 'People need to be satisfied about who they are dealing with. They need to know that their messages have not been intercepted or corrupted on the way, and most importantly they are legally non-repudiable – meaning that the other party can't walk away from it in a court of law'. He goes on to say that the security fears are well-founded with nearly two thirds of companies relying solely on password protection when dealing with suppliers. Trusted third party certification is required for the level of trust to increase. While the Internet may give the impression of making it readily possible to swap between suppliers and use new suppliers, two-thirds of those interviewed said building a trusted relationship with suppliers is necessary before they would trade using the Internet.

Organizational risks

If the cost savings referred to earlier in the chapter are to be achieved it may be necessary to redeploy staff, or in the worst case make them redundant. For a medium-sized company such as Cambridge Consultants the purchasing team of five people was reduced to four. The threat of redundancy or redeployment is likely to lead to resistance to the introduction of the system and this needs to be managed. The purchasing manager will have to carefully explain the reasons for introducing the new system, emphasizing the benefits to the company as a whole and how it should enable more variety to be introduced to the buying role.

Since the cost savings of e-procurement are achieved through empowerment of originators throughout the business to directly purchase their own items rather than through purchasing there is a risk that some originators may take advantage of this. This is known as maverick or off-contract purchasing, and it has always happened to an extent. Maverick purchasing occurs when items are ordered that are unnecessary or too expensive. Complete *activity 7.3* to review the mechanisms that can be used to reduce this risk.

Activity 7.3 **Avoiding maverick purchasing**

Purpose

To identify responses to problems of maverick purchasing.

Activity

To avoid maverick purchasing, businesses introducing e-procurement need to introduce safeguards into the e-procurement system. Think about the type of rules that could be written into an e-procurement system.

For answer, see p. 281

Failure to achieve real cost reductions

There is a risk that the return on investment from introducing e-procurement may be lower than that forecast and the introduction of the e-procurement system may not pay for itself. This may occur if the assumptions used to calculate savings from e-procurement such as those in *activity 7.2* are too simplistic. Complete *activity 7.4* to review why savings may be lower than anticipated.

Purchasing ROI myths

Activity 7.4

Purpose

To highlight reasons why not all the benefits of e-procurement may be delivered.

Activity

There are many proponents of the benefits of e-procurement, but a cautionary note is struck by Brian Caffrey of the Purchasing web guide on About.com (http://purchasing.about.com). Visit this site and review his editorial comments on why caution should be exercised when assessing the financial savings that accrue through e-procurement. The most relevant article is Caffrey (1998) Dispelling e-commerce ROI myths (http://purchasing.about.com/industry/purchasing/library/weekly/aa032798.htm). This article also gives a more detailed model from a supplier of how cost savings may be achieved.

For answer, see p. 281

Technology risks

Tranmit (1999) reported the biggest barrier to automation of e-procurement is integration with existing financial systems, according to 60 per cent of respondents.

The section on implementing e-procurement shows that there is a range of different models for procurement. The models are evolving fast, so it is difficult to know which to select. Likewise there is a range of different marketplaces, many of which have not yet reached critical mass. It will be wasteful to become involved in a marketplace which fails in a year's time. Problems introduced by large-scale ERP systems may also not dispose organizations to e-procurement.

Implementing e-procurement

To introduce e-procurement the IS manager and procurement team must work together to find a solution that links together the different people and tasks of procurement shown in *Figure 7.1*. Historically, it has been easier to introduce systems that only cover some parts of the procurement cycle. *Figure 7.3* shows how different types of information system cover different parts of the procurement cycle. The different type of systems are shown below.

- *Stock control system* – this relates mainly to production-related procurement; the system highlights when re-ordering is required when the number in stock fall below re-order thresholds.

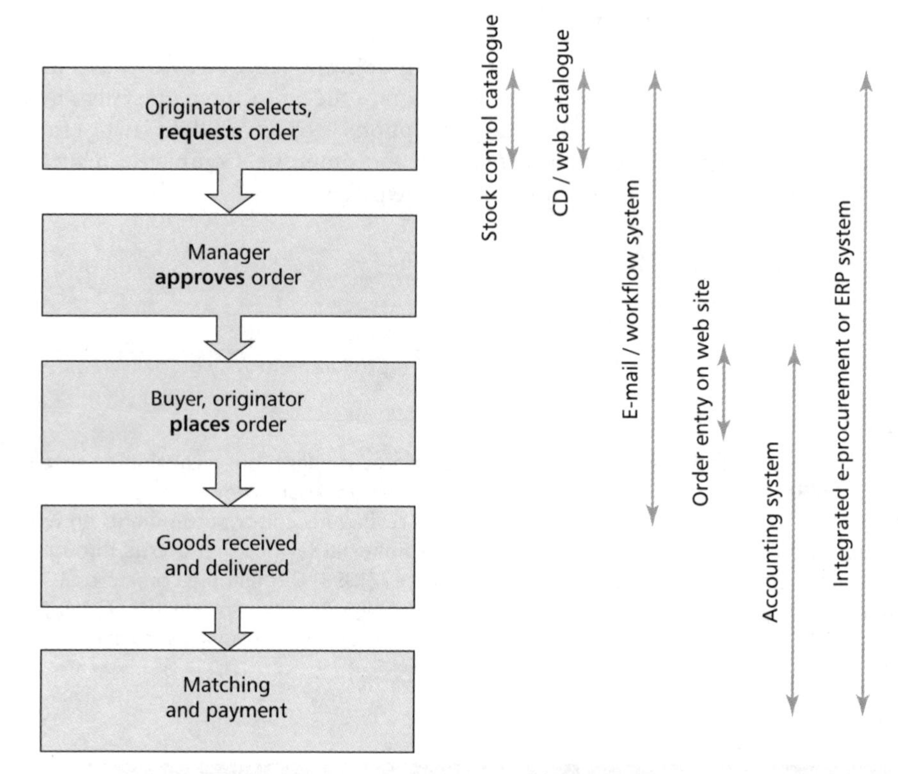

Figure 7.3 Use of different information systems for different aspects of the fulfilment cycle

- *CD / web-based catalogue* – paper catalogues have been replaced by electronic forms that make it quicker to find suppliers.
- *E-mail or database-based workflow systems* integrate the entry of the order by the originator, approval by manager and placement by buyer. The order is routed from one person to the next and will wait in their in-box for actioning. Such systems may be extended to accounting systems. *Figure 7.4* shows an e-mail generated by an electronic procurement system as part of a workflow, it shows that a manager has approved the purchase requisition.
- *Order-entry on web site* – the buyer often has the opportunity to order directly on the supplier's web site, but this will involve rekeying and there is no integration with systems for requisitioning or accounting.
- *Accounting systems* – networked accounting systems enable staff in the buying department to enter an order which can then be used by accounting staff to make payment when the invoice arrives.
- *Integrated e-procurement or ERP systems* – these aim to integrate all the facilities above and will also include integration with suppliers' systems. *Figure 7.5* shows document management software as an integrated part of an e-procurement system. Here a paper invoice from a supplier (on the left) has been scanned into the system and is compared to the original electronic order information (on the right).

Companies face a difficult choice in achieving full-cycle e-procurement since they have the option of trying to link different systems or purchasing a single new system that integrates the facilities of the previous systems. Purchasing a

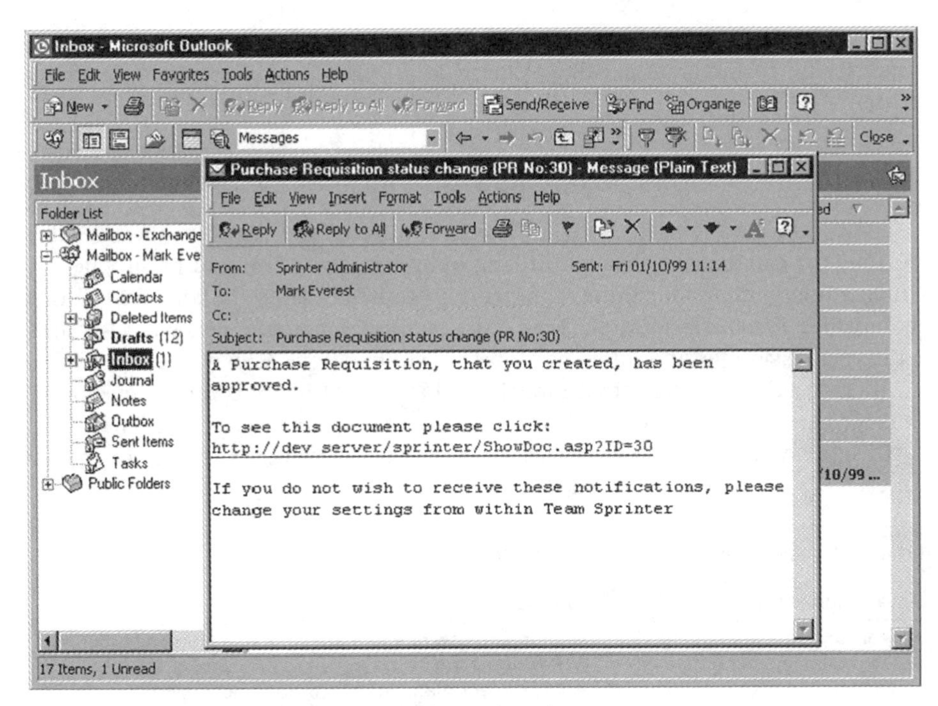

Figure 7.4 E-mail notification of requisition approval
Source: Tranmit plc

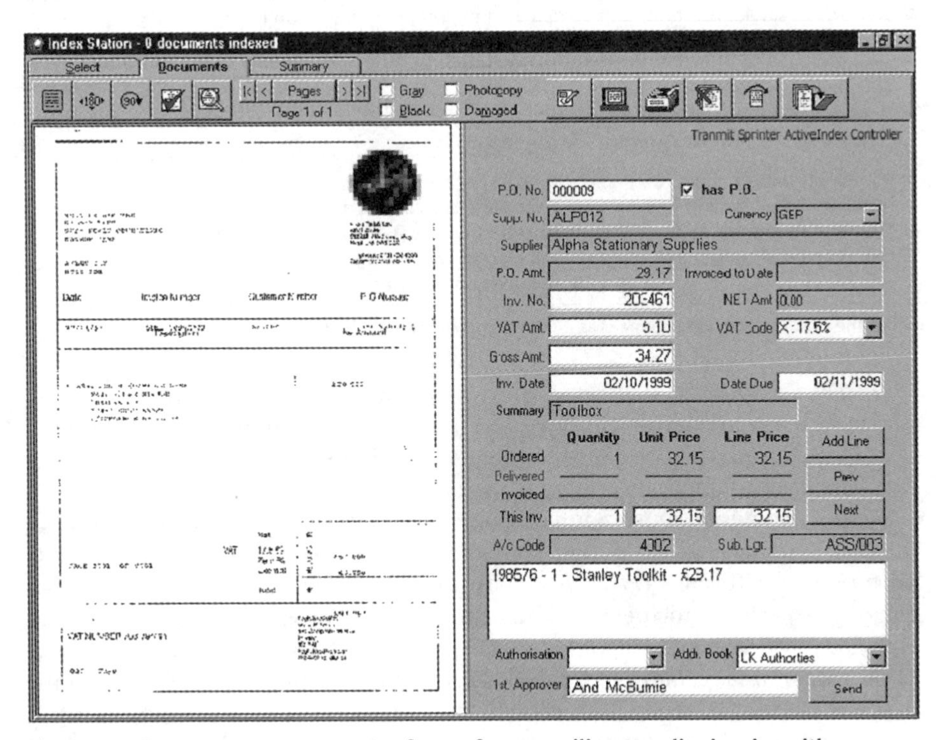

Figure 7.5 Document management software for reconciling supplier invoice with purchase order data
Source: Tranmit plc

new system may be the simplest technical option, but it may be more expensive than trying to integrate existing systems and it also requires re-training in the system.

Integrating company systems with supplier systems

We saw from the Shell case study in *Chapter 1*, the cost and cycle-time benefits that a company can achieve through linking its systems with those of its suppliers. If integrating systems within a company is difficult, then linking with other companies' systems is more so. This situation arises since suppliers will use different types of systems and different models for integration. As explained in *Chapter 2*, there are three fundamental models for location of B2B e-commerce: sell-side, buy-side and marketplace based. These alternative options for procurement links with suppliers are summarized in *Figure 7.6* and the advantages and disadvantages of each are summarized in *Table 7.6*.

Table 7.6 Assessment of the procurement model alternatives for buyers

Procurement model	*Advantages to buyer*	*Disadvantages to buyer*
Sell-side e.g. Many catalogue-based B2B suppliers e.g. www.rswww.com	● Searching ● Onus of maintaining data on supplier	● Different interface on each site (catalogue and ordering) ● Restricted choice ● Poor integration with ERP/procurement systems ● Limited purchase control
Buy-side e.g. Solutions developed by www.sap.com www.ariba.com	● Simplicity – single interface ● Wider choice than sell-side ● Integration with ERP/procurement systems ● Good purchase control	● Onus of maintaining data is on buyer ● Software licence costs ● Retraining
Marketplace e.g. www.itoi.com www.vertical.net www.chemdex.com www.itoi.com	● Simplicity – single interface ● Potentially widest choice of suppliers, products and prices ● Often unified terms and conditions and order forms	● Difficult to know which marketplace to choose (horizontal and vertical) ● Poor purchase controls* ● Uncertainty on service levels from unfamiliar suppliers ● Interfacing with marketplace data format* ● Relatively poor integration with ERP*

* Note that these disadvantages of the marketplace will disappear as marketplaces develop ERP integration

Chapter 2 explained that companies supplying products and services had to decide which combination of these models would be used to distribute their products. From the buyers' point of view, they will be limited by the selling model their suppliers have adopted.

Figure 7.7 shows options for integration for a buyer who is aiming to integrate an internal system such as an ERP system with external systems. Specialized e-procurement software may be necessary to interface with the ERP system. This could be a special e-procurement application or it could be middleware to interface with an e-procurement component of an ERP system. How does the e-procurement system access price catalogues from suppliers? There are two choices shown on the diagram. Choice (a) is to house electronic catalogues from different suppliers inside the company firewall. This traditional approach has the benefit that the data is housed inside the company so can be readily accessed. However, electronic links beyond the firewall will be needed to update the catalogues, or this is sometimes

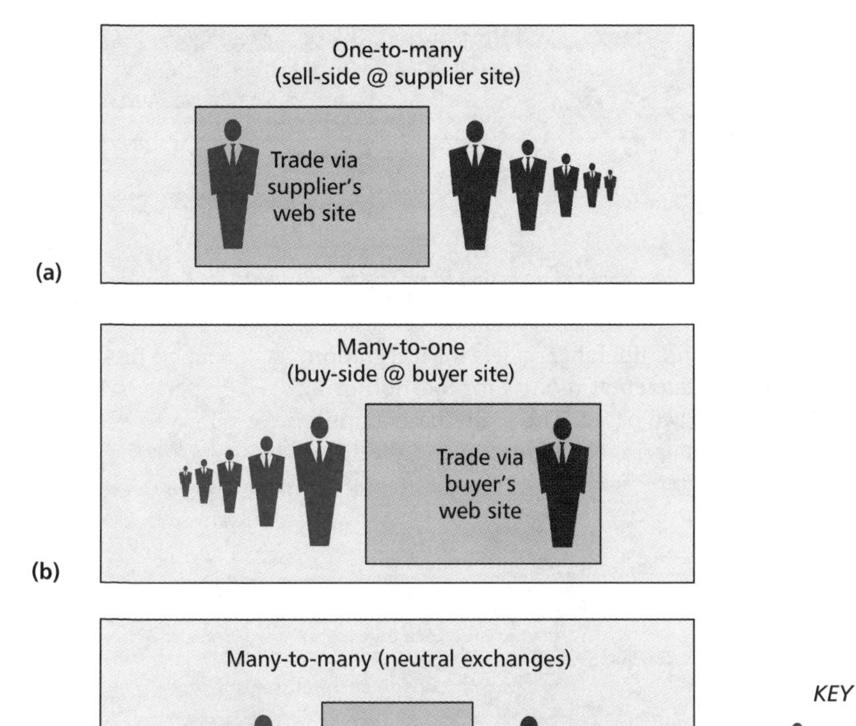

Figure 7.6 The three main e-procurement model alternatives for buyers

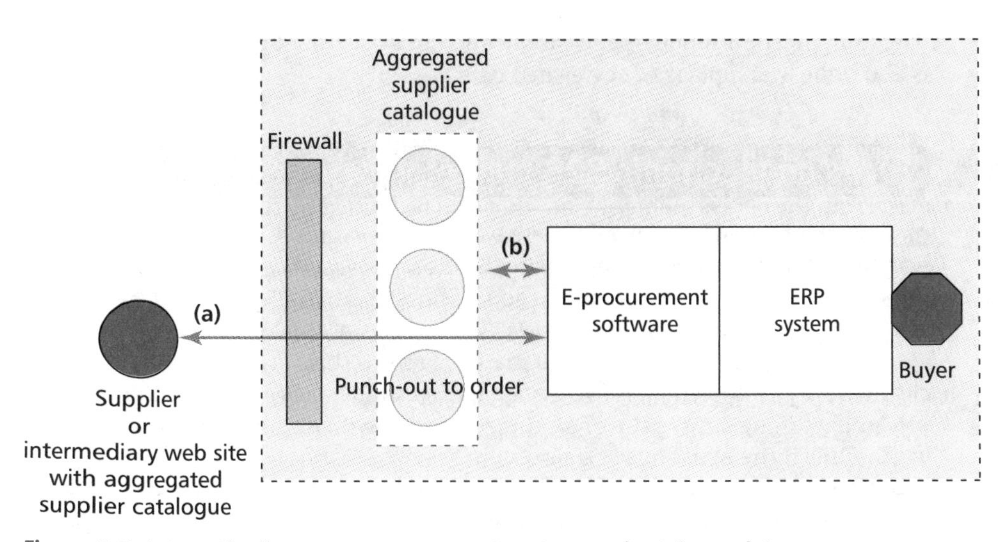

Figure 7.7 Integration between e-procurement systems and catalogue data

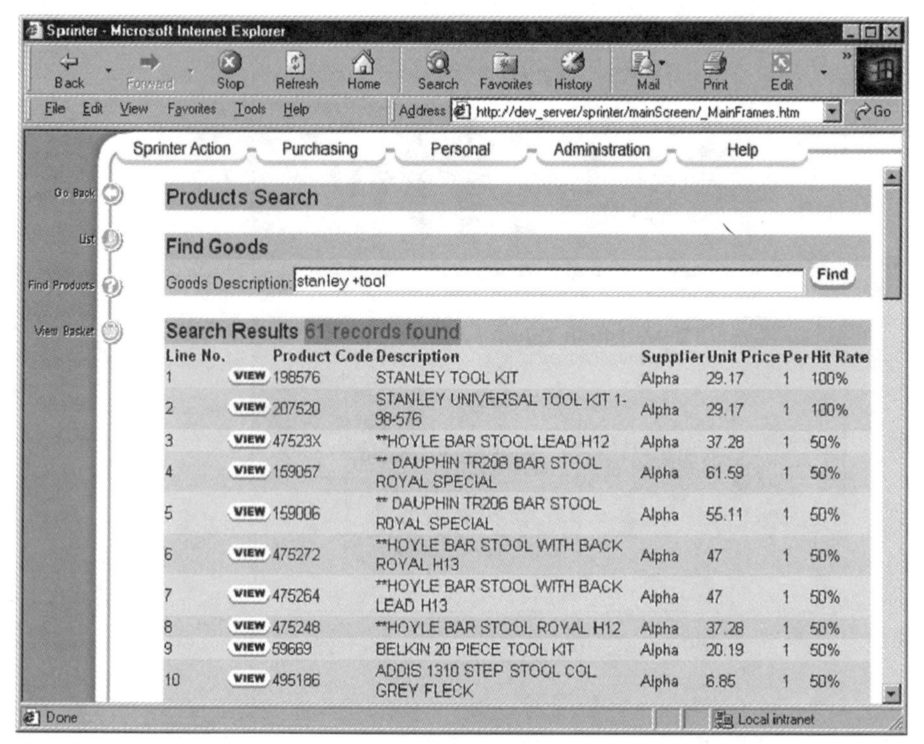

Figure 7.8 An online catalogue of items for purchase

Source: Tranmit plc

achieved via delivery of a CD with the updated catalogue. Purchasers will have a single integrated view of products from different suppliers as shown in *Figure 7.8*. Choice (b) is to punch-out through the firewall to access catalogues either on a supplier site or at an intermediary site. One of the benefits of linking to an intermediary site such as a B2B exchange is that this has done the work of collecting data from different suppliers and producing it in a consistent format. However, this is also done by suppliers of aggregated data.

F *Focus on* electronic B2B marketplaces

As the new millennium dawned there was a proliferation of B2B marketplaces. A search on 'marketplaces' at the Open Directory (www.dmoz.org) will reveal that there are over 100. However, as start-up businesses, many have had difficulty in achieving sustainable business models. This creates a difficult decision for managers exploring the relevance of B2B marketplaces to their organization since they clearly have great potential for achieving greater supplier choice and reduced costs, yet going through the pain of setting up links with B2B marketplaces is only worthwhile if the marketplace is persistent.

B2B marketplaces, exchanges and hubs
Virtual locations with facilities to enable trading between buyers and sellers.

Electronic B2B marketplaces are variously known as marketplaces, exchanges and hubs. Typically they are intermediaries who are part of the *reintermediation* (*Chapter 2, p. 39*) phenomenon and are independent of buyers and suppliers.

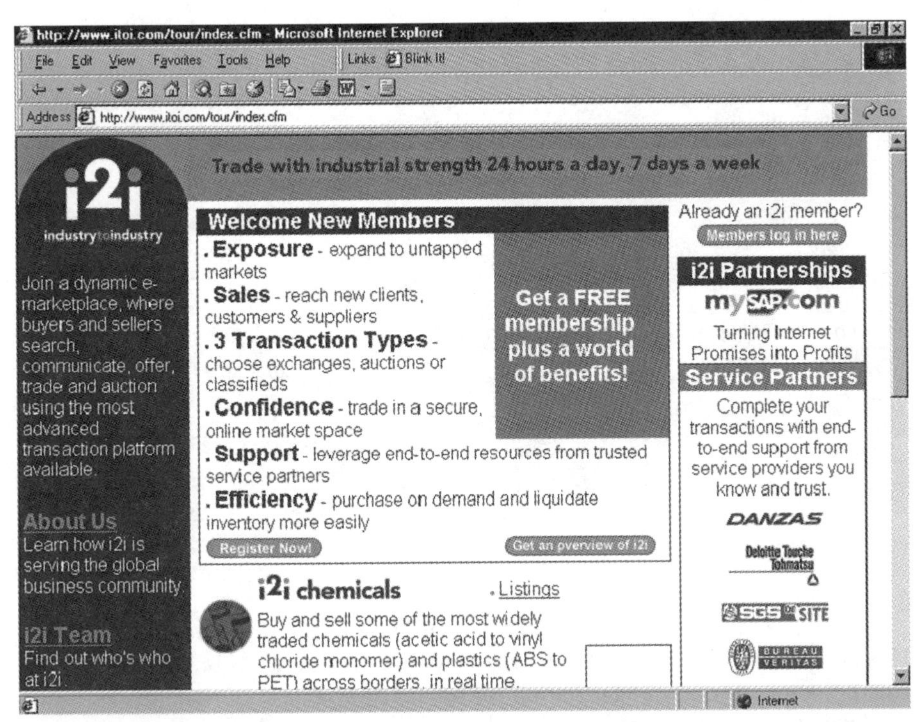

Figure 7.9 industry2industry (www.ind2ind.com), an example of a B2B marketplace

An example of a market exchange of European origin is industry2industry (www.ind2ind.com) that was originally a vision of Professor Klaus Schwab, President and Founder of the World Economic Forum that was launched at the WEF's 1999 Annual Meeting in Davos, Switzerland. *Figure 7.9* shows how industry2industry has separate spot markets for commodities such as Chemicals, Plastics and Energy. Industry2industry has partnered with companies who specialize in other aspects of the supply chain, for example SGS and Bureau Veritas handle the inspection of goods, Danzas covers logistics and transportation, and Deloitte Touche Tohmatsu takes care of import/export and taxation issues. It is interesting to note that although it has started as a global exchange it has introduced country specific exchanges such as i2iexchangeitaly (www.i2iexchangeitaly.com) and marketplaceitaly.com for small and medium-sized enterprises (SMEs). This suggests that even in the global economy localization of services is necessary for success.

Improved methods for facilitating purchasing using these types of sites will undoubtedly increase the adoption of the Internet for e-commerce since consumers will become aware of the lower prices available by these buying methods. For the business-to-business case this needs to be linked in with methods of making payment easier such as the Open Buying Initiative (www.obi.org).

Types of marketplace

Kaplan and Sawhney (2000) have developed a taxonomy of B2B marketplaces by applying existing classifications of corporate purchasing, namely *how* business businesses buy (systematic purchasing or spot purchasing) and *why* businesses buy (manufacturing inputs or operating resource inputs). They identify the types of marketplace shown in *Table 7.7*. Note that manufacturing input marketplaces tend to be vertical marketplaces set up for particular industry such as Steel, Construction or Chemical while Operating resources tend to be horizontal marketplaces offering a range of products to differing industries

Table 7.7 Types of B2B marketplaces identified by Kaplan and Sawhney (2000) with examples

	What businesses buy?	
How businesses buy?	*Operating resources*	*Manufacturing resources*
Systematic sourcing	MRO Hubs Commerce One www.commerceone.net	Catalogue Hubs www.chemdex.com
Spot sourcing	Yield Managers www.elance.com	Exchanges www.itoi.com www.vertical.net Chemicals www.plastics.net

Kaplan and Sawhney introduce another variation in the way marketplaces differ. This is according to whether the marketplace is direct between buyer and seller or whether some degree of aggregation occurs. In the same way that for consumer products, volume discounts can be achieved through combining the purchasing power of individuals, this can also occur for small and medium businesses. Kaplan and Sawhney refer to this type of aggregation as reverse aggregation since aggregation is back through the supply chain *from* customers to suppliers. They also identify forward aggregation in which the supply chain operates through distributors in a traditional way. A distributor of PCs from different manufacturers aggregates supply from the different manufacturers. Marketplaces can also act as value-chain integrators when they combine supply chain functions referred to in *Chapter 6*.

According to Sawhney (1999a) companies looking to create exchanges typically specialize in one of the four sectors of Table 7.7, although some B2B marketplaces do offer both catalogue hubs and exchanges.

Some marketplaces also differ in the range of services they may offer – some may go beyond procurement to offer a range of services that integrate the supply chain. Sawhney (1999a) refers to these marketplaces as **metamediaries**. An example of a metamediary is Plastic Net (www.plasticsnet.com).

Metamediaries
Third parties that provide a single point of contact and deliver a range of services between customers and suppliers.

This provides services of supplier evaluation, procurement, tracking, marketplace information, certification monitoring, auctions and catalogues.

How successful will exchanges be? Kaplan and Sawhney (2000) note that neutral exchanges face a chicken and egg situation when recruiting buyers and suppliers to their service – buyers may not want to participate if there are insufficient suppliers, and suppliers may not join if the site is not used by many purchasers. Procurement managers will naturally select a marketplace that is most active.

Case study 7.2 illustrates the benefits and risks of using an exchange from the purchaser perspective.

CASE STUDY 7.2

Worldwide oil exchange – the Shell perspective

On 5 July 2000, the world's biggest online exchange started trading. In all, 14 oil and gas companies with names like BP, Statoil, Conoco, Tosco, Unocal and Shell with a combined annual spend of $125 bn started to buy what they need to stay in business over the Web. The oil, gas and petrochemical exchange is the latest in the global rush to electronic procurement that is already being pursued by the aerospace, automobile and telecoms industries. Setting up of the exchange was agreed after a 40-minute discussion in January, and announced on 11 April.

So why are all the partners so keen? 'The real key to e-procurement is the completeness of the data,' says Chris Miller, group adviser of strategic sourcing at Shell International. 'All the procurement flows through a common database where you can analyse what's going on in order to make better commercial decisions.' 'The competitive advantage goes to those which become masters of the data created and make the best procurement deals,' he added.

To date there have been buyers facing off to suppliers individually, says Miller. Now they'll be facing off in a marketplace. In the exchange, the catalogues will be maintained by suppliers which have control of changes in prices, even minute by minute if they want.

'Up till now we've maintained the catalogues,' says Miller. This has been both costly and inaccurate, owing to the ease of duplication. 'At a stroke [the exchange] takes a massive amount of cost out, making oil and gas more competitive in the 21st century,' he points out.

Reducing costs for everyone is the key. The exchange reduces procurement effort via one hub for transaction flow. 'E-procurement is not about screwing suppliers,' Miller emphasizes. 'It's about taking cost out for both suppliers and buyers and reducing institutionalized inefficiencies. Plus it supports smaller buyers and suppliers just as much as larger ones. It's not a big boys' club.'

The greater transparency of pricing over the exchange, will, he argues, be commercially healthier all round than the current practice of sealed bids. Having a single, transparent marketplace will also, the participants hope, attack the costly, but all too frequent, practice of off-contract, maverick buying by departments evading their own corporate purchasing policies and standards.

Shell expects 23 per cent of the savings it anticipates from e-procurement to come from the greater efficiency it will get from doing volume deals it had previously been unable to guarantee because it did not know its spend accurately enough. But the biggest tranche of savings, 40 per cent, will come, says Miller, from cutting out maverick procurement and complying with corporate standards. He also expects about 20 per cent to come from auctions. 'They're a terrific opportunity,' he enthuses.

Altogether, Miller anticipates the transaction cost of purchasing should plunge. 'Most companies have no idea [what each purchase costs them] – it's something like $200–$250 per transaction. Now it will be under $1,' he says. E-procurement will also change the way orders are put together and issued. Most purchases, he points out, are done on the basis of the specification of the equipment needed, which is affected by the conditions in which it has to be used. On an exchange, a supplier could simply ask the buyer to tell them what conditions the kit has to be suitable for, and they can select what meets that requirement and offer it, instead of the buyer having to specifically request it.

'The condition of use could become the purchase order,' suggests Miller. As the exchange gets under way more innovations in how suppliers could do business with purchasers, more cheaply and efficiently, are bound to emerge. And already, e-procurement also promises other value-added services, such as cheap capital, logistics and auctions.

'We can even book our travel over it,' says Miller. Eventually, he believes, the transaction charges that the exchange levies 'will disappear, and it will exist on the value-added services themselves.'

Vertical exchanges in specific industry sectors, believes Miller, grow very quickly once trading starts. Market liquidity will increase as more suppliers come on to the exchange. They get a shop window seen by all their customers. Their customers get yet more choice in what to buy, from whom, at what price.

'It means we can be far more imaginative about sourcing – we were a very conservative industry,' says Miller.

▶

▶ CASE STUDY *continued*

As the market liquidity increases and the conservative tradition erodes, there is an opportunity for oil and gas companies to tighten inventory. 'Our industry has massive inventory – we have lots of duplicates sitting in warehouses 100 metres apart,' he points out. Miller believes the exchange has allayed any initial fears that the industry's suppliers felt would distance them from their customers. 'We feared they thought we wouldn't be able to differentiate between them,' he says.

In fact, he argues, the reverse is true – exchanges offer suppliers the chance of getting even closer to their customers. 'Suppliers can use the software to get to the desk of the manager calling off the service,' he says. Even out on an oil platform, for example, offshore workers can go to the exchange and look at all the data they need about a drilling tool. 'The exchange makes for a far closer relationship than they were able to have before,' says Miller.

With all the upside, is there any downside to e-procurement? Certainly there are some caveats, warns Miller. Firstly, the very ease of purchasing can mean that not every purchase is the best possible automatically, without effort. 'The system can support bad deals as well as good,' he points out.

Dangerously, at any rate to begin with, having an exchange can 'create a legitimacy for bad deals'. Keyboard-happy purchasers let loose on the exchange can get literally carried away, buying is so easy. 'Three clicks and you've spent a quarter of a million dollars,' warns Miller. 'And you've done it in three seconds, not three weeks.' Second, is the tricky issue of data confidentiality. There is so much data generated by, or passing through, the exchange that ownership and levels of access have to be scrupulously worked out and adhered to. It may be in the interests of rival oil and gas industries to reduce the cost of procurement across the board, and ditto for their rival suppliers, but respect for each other's commercially sensitive data is crucial for the overall success of the exchange. Thirdly, a global, industry-wide exchange will, inevitably, operate globally. Will that mean that local suppliers are squeezed out, or their support costs are exposed as higher than lower cost suppliers in cheaper parts of the world, which will now become more accessible through a cyberspace marketplace? 'It's true to an extent,' concedes Miller, 'but we must get suppliers on the exchange.'

The final caveat has to be issued in the direction of the IT department. Inevitably, every business opportunity is an IT challenge to make happen and e-procurement is no exception. 'How on earth is the exchange going to integrate with our enterprise resource planning systems? It's an enormous headache,' allows Miller.

However it's done, integration must be fully automatic, he stipulates. The sheer scale of the user community within a major company like Shell is a challenge for IT. 'We'll have 100,000 users in 120 countries,' says Miller. Just training them how to use the e-procurement system is a significant task. Shell is rolling out training across countries that are as different in scale and culture as the US and Gabon – not forgetting its tanker fleet and offshore platforms. Operational management will also be a challenge. 'It's important to maintain a data hierarchy,' says Miller. 'We must gather data in regional and global hubs. We have to put lots of management in place to make it work.' One thing though is clear. E-procurement is not IT-led. 'It has been a business-led initiative – it did not come from the IT department,' says Miller. Being business-led 'the business demanded IT service – IT has had to make it integrate with our ERP, and make the speed up to scratch'. That business commitment to e-procurement marks, says Miller, a sea-change in Shell. 'For 15 years IT has said, "we've got a new idea, we've got to have it!" For example, ERP, that the business has then been puzzled about how to use. Now [with e-business] there's a new self-confidence in business about making IT systems increase profits and get costs down.'

Profit, should, hopefully, be arriving even more directly. This latest exchange on the web has a chief executive from outside the oil and gas industry, and with outside equity partners is looking to float shortly.

Challenge for IT and business

- ERP interfaces
- Supporting the infrastructure
- Speed and integrity of transactions (security; intranet vs extranet)
- Maintaining the data hierarchy (management information)
- Controlling the external interfaces
- Business-led initiatives in the IT domain

Commercial challenges

- Extending the use of contractual agreements for purchasing – but what will the contractual relationships be in the e-world?
- How will suppliers differentiate their products?
- At the end of the day, who will actually be the masters of the data being created?

Benefits

What value will buyers get from the exchange?

- Cut down maverick purchasing by enforcing corporate contracts and standards
- Cut transaction costs and boost internal productivity by saving time and effort in purchasing
- Better demand management and inventory control
- Better information leading to better decision making

Suppliers will benefit from:

- Closer integration with buyers
- Lower catalogue content management costs
- Lower cost electronic sales channels
- Lower inventory, better planning and less volatility
- Global reach and visibility for all, irrespective of size
- Better management information

Source: Article in *Computer Weekly*, 6 July 2000, pp. 26–7.

Questions

1. Using your judgement and by referring to the article summarize the benefits to Shell of using an exchange rather than buy-side or sell-side e-procurement.
2. Which of the commercial and technical challenges do you think are unique to an exchange, and which may occur for other forms of e-procurement?

It remains to be seen whether B2B marketplaces deliver on their potential. For an update, complete *activity 7.5*.

Reviewing the success of B2B exchanges

Activity 7.5

A number of B2B exchanges created by buyers have been announced or launched in 2000 sponsored by major global companies. Examples include:

- Covisint in motor industry (Ford, DaimlerChrysler and GM). Here former exchanges created by Ford (AutoXchange) and GM (Tradexchange) have merged. Tait (2000) reports on research that suggests between $1000 and $3600 savings on a $26,000 car could be achieved for a car where all purchasing from manufacturer and end-customer is completed electronically. By end 2000 Covisint already had completed $200 million worth of transactions.
- WorldWide Retail Exchange (Kingfisher, Kmart, Marks and Spencer).
- T2 US airline trading exchange.
- GlobalNetExchange (Retailers Sears and Carrefour). Note that Transora has been created by fifty of the world's major FMCG suppliers including Coca Cola and Kelloggs in response to retailers.
- PaperX Paper industry designed for one-to-one deals.

1. Visit the sites of these companies and search news sources (for example, Moreover (www.moreover.com)) to summarize the success of these initiatives.
2. Identify other hubs operating in your own country, classify them under this scheme of *Table 7.7*, evaluate their success.

The future of e-procurement?

Software (intelligent) agents
Software programs that can assist humans to perform tasks.

In the future, some suggest that the task of searching for suppliers and products may be taken over by **software agents** which have defined rules or some degree of intelligence that replicate that in humans. An agent is a software program that can perform tasks to assist humans. On the Internet, agents can already be used for marketing research by performing searches using many search engines and in the future they may also be used to search for products or even purchase products. Agents work using predetermined rules or may learn rules using neural network techniques. Such rules will govern whether purchases should be made ot not.

Some of the implications of agent technology on marketing are explored by Gatarski and Lundkvist (1998). They suggest that agent technology may create artificial consumers who will undertake supplier search, product evaluation and product selection functions. The authors suggest that such actors in a supplier-to-consumer dialogue will behave in a more rational way than their human equivalent and existing marketing theories may not apply.

Tucker and Jones (2000) also review the use of intelligent agents for sourcing. They foresee agents undertaking evaluation of a wide range of possible alternative suppliers based on predefined quantitative selection criteria including price, availability and delivery. They believe the technology is already available, indeed similar intelligent software is used for making investments in financial markets. What is not clear is how the software will assess trustworthiness of a supplier or their competence as business partners/associates.

An example of an exchange using such an agent is TheBuilding-Site.com (www.thebuilding-site.com) who use Exterprise Activemarket to match online buyers and sellers. The software is intended to look through online alternatives to see which one best meets a business requirement.

As a summary to this chapter, *activity 7.6* illustrates some of the decisions faced by purchasing managers when deciding how they will link to suppliers through e-procurement.

Activity 7.6 The B2B Company decides how to integrate its procurement with suppliers

Purpose

To highlight issues involved in selecting online suppliers

Activity

Assume The B2B Company has three favoured suppliers of office items (A, B and C). Supplier A may have set up a web site through which it is possible to place orders, Supplier B may have used a marketplace solution such as Commerce One to sell products and Supplier C may not have developed e-commerce.

Questions

1. Identify the different alternatives for The B2B Company if it wishes to adopt e-procurement.
2. Evaluate the alternatives and recommend your favoured alternative.

For answers see p. 281

Summary

1. Procurement activities involved with purchasing items from a supplier include purchasing, but also transportation, goods-in and warehousing before the item is used.
2. E-procurement involves the electronic integration of all procurement activities.
3. The number of staff and stages involved in procurement is reduced through e-procurement by empowering the originator of orders and changing the role of buying staff.
4. E-procurement is intended to achieve reduced purchasing cycle time and cost savings, principally through reduced staff time spent in procurement and lower inventory.
5. Options for introducing e-procurement include:
   - Sell-side e-procurement – purchase direct from a seller's web site that is typically not integrated with the buyer's procurement system.
   - Buy-side e-procurement – integration of seller's catalogues with the buyer's procurement system.
   - Marketplace procurement – trading through an intermediary with many suppliers (may or may not be integrated with buyer's procurement system).
6. The main types of electronic marketplace in the terminology of Kaplan and Sawhney (2000) are combinations of:
   - Systematic sourcing of operating resources (MRO hubs)
   - Systematic sourcing of manufacturing resources (Catalogue hubs)
   - Spot sourcing of operating resources (Yield managers)
   - Spot sourcing of manufacturing resources (Exchanges)
7. Organizational hurdles involved with the introduction of e-procurement include redeployment or redundancy of staff and overcoming fears of trust in suppliers.
8. The main technical challenges are the integration or replacement of a range of existing purchasing systems with a variety of supplier or marketplace systems.

ACTIVITY ANSWERS

7.1 Evaluating the benefits of the e-procurement process for The B2B Company

1. It is evident that the major delays are introduced through the transport of material (this may have been through an internal post system with only one or two collections per day) and while the item was waiting for processing in the buyer's in-tray. Further inefficiencies occurred through duplicating ordering of information – the order had to be specified separately on the requisition and again on the order for the supplier. If a more senior manager is required to authorize an expensive purchase then this would introduce further delay through a cycle of transport, delay (in-tray), process (authorize), transport, delay (in-tray).
2. Before the advent of e-business it was possible to improve the paper-based process indicated in

Table 7.1 through using a workflow system to automate the entry of purchasing information and passing information on via e-mail rather than internal post. This would certainly reduce the delays due to transport, but delays still occur while the order is in the e-mail inbox of the authorizer and purchaser.

3. The real benefits of applying technology accrue through changing the process. In *Table 7.2* the process has been changed such that involvement by the purchaser is not required at all. It is also easier to find products using the web than traditional catalogues. Large savings in time and expense are possible by removing this person from the process.

Note to lecturers:
A description of the old and new processes and a blank version of this chart is available on the CWS to enable students to conduct the analysis themselves.

7.2 Modelling cost savings and profitability arising from e-procurement

1. *Table 7.8* shows that much greater savings are possible where there is combination of a large number of orders and low order value.

Table 7.8 Answers for cost-saving calculations for two companies A and B

Input parameters (Company A)		*Input parameters (Company B)*	
Number of orders	25,000	Number of orders	2,500
Traditional cost per order (average)	£50	Traditional cost per order (average)	£50
New cost per order (average)	£10	New cost per order (average)	£10
Average value of order	£150	Average value of order	£1,500
Traditional overall purchasing cost	£5,000,000	Traditional overall purchasing cost	£3,875,000
New overall purchasing cost	£4,000,000	New overall purchasing cost	£3,775,000
% change in cost per order	–80%	% change in cost per order	–80%
% change in overall purchasing cost	–20%	% change in overall purchasing cost	–3%

2. *Table 7.9* shows that change in profitability is much greater for a company such as Company X where purchasing costs are a higher proportion of overall costs. Company X is more typical of a manufacturing company, and company B a services company. In both cases, however, significant changes in profitability are achieved. A further exercise would be to calculate the increase in turnover necessary to achieve this through increased sales (it would be potentially more difficult to achieve).

Table 7.9 Input parameters for profitability calculations for two companies X and Y

Input parameters (Company X)			*Input parameters (Company Y)*		
Turnover		£10,000,000	Turnover		£10,000,000
Traditional purchasing costs		£5,000,000	Traditional purchasing costs		£1,000,000
Other costs		£4,000,000	Other costs		£8,000,000
% Reduction in purchasing costs		20%	% Reduction in purchasing costs		20%
	Before	After		Before	After
Turnover	£10,000,000	£10,000,000	Turnover	£10,000,000	£10,000,000
Purchasing costs	£5,000,000	£4,000,000	Purchasing costs	£1,000,000	£800,000
Other costs	£4,000,000	£4,000,000	Other costs	£8,000,000	£8,000,000
Profitability	£1,000,000	£2,000,000	Profitability	£1,000,000	£1,200,000
Profit change (£)	–	£1,000,000	Profit change (£)	–	£200,000
Profit change (%)	–	100%	Profit change (%)	–	20%

3. Combining the answers from Q1 and Q2, the greatest benefits will be achieved by a company with:
   - Large volume of orders
   - Typically low value purchases
   - High current purchasing cost per order
   - A high proportion of costs involved in purchasing

These spreadsheet models can be downloaded from the web.

7.3 Avoiding maverick purchasing

You may have identified the following:

- Overall limits on purchasing for each individual over a time period (e.g. spend limit/month);
- Limits on cost of individual items (spend limit/item);
- Limits on each order value (spend limit.order);
- Limit types of product that can be purchased by a certain individual; books, for example, could be excluded.

If these limits are exceeded there is still an important role for the procurement department in checking and controlling excesses.

7.4 Purchasing ROI myths

Caffrey's argument is that although calculations such as those illustrated in *Table 7.9* appear to demonstrate significant savings, these savings will only be translated to the bottom-line profitability if staff expenses are reduced. This may occur through fewer overtime payments to staff, less use of temporary staff or redundancies (staff salaries reduced). If the staff are simply redeployed to perform other work then there will not be a real saving although intangible benefits may result. When time savings are spread across the organization which is the case for savings that accrue from less time being taken in placing orders by the originator, it is unlikely there will be any potential to save money.

7.6 The B2B Company decides how to integrate its procurement with suppliers

1. The main alternatives are as follows:
   - To move to one preferred supplier for these products (sell-side), say supplier A and integrate with their sell-side infrastructure (this is what Cambridge Consultants have done with supplier RS Components)
   - To develop different types of sell-side links to work with suppliers (A and B)
   - To set up buy-side links and encourage suppliers to link to your standard
   - To use marketplaces and start using new suppliers
   - To give up the e-procurement initiative because of the complexity of it!
2. Evaluation of alternatives:
   - To move to one preferred supplier for these products (sell-side) – this alternative could lead to lock-in with this supplier and price competition is not encouraged, but it is the most straightforward to implement.
   - To develop different types of links to work with suppliers (A and B) – this option is best for encouraging price competition.
   - To set up buy-side links and work with several suppliers – this option may result in the best competition and has the lowest cost since suppliers are forced to integrate with your system, but is only really an option for large companies (General Electric is the best known example) or for purchase of high-value option such as raw materials.

- To use marketplaces and start using new suppliers – this is the most innovative option, but is a step in the dark; it is probably best to combine with setting up a link with a favoured supplier.
- To give-up the e-procurement initiative because of the complexity of it! Giving up long-term will not realize the benefits, but perhaps putting on hold will enable the situation on marketplaces to become clearer.

EXERCISES

Self-assessment questions

1. Outline the two main methods by which companies purchase supplies and the two broad divisions of supplies needed.
2. Taking your answer from one, give examples of B2B exchanges that have been created to meet these purchasing needs.
3. Draw a sketch that shows the main stages and people involved in traditional and e-procurement.
4. Outline the main reasons for e-procurement.
5. What is maverick purchasing? What safeguards need to be introduced into e-procurement to avoid this?
6. Explain the differences between the buy-side, sell-side and marketplace options for e-procurement.
7. Outline the benefits and disadvantages of each of the options in 6.
8. What are the organizational implications of introducing e-procurement?

Essay and discussion questions

1. In the Shell case study, Chris Miller states *'E-procurement is not about screwing suppliers. It's about taking cost out for both suppliers and buyers and reducing institutionalized inefficiencies. Plus it supports smaller buyers and suppliers just as much as larger ones. It's not a big boys' club.'*

   Discuss this statement through reviewing the benefits and disadvantages of e-procurement to both buyers and suppliers.
2. For an industry sector of your choice review the current alternative options for, and business adoption of B2B marketplaces available to purchasing and IS professionals and attempt to forecast the situation in five years.
3. Critically assess the claims made for cost savings and increased profitability available from e-procurement.
4. Analyze the procurement process for an organization with which you are familiar. Explain the changes and possible problems involved with introducing e-procurement.
5. Fully automated end-to-end procurement is not practical. Discuss.

Examination questions

1. Draw a diagram explaining four types of B2B exchanges that are dependent on the type of purchasing and what is purchased. Give one example of a product that could be purchased at each, and the name of an exchange offering this service.
2. Describe the different elements of an e-procurement system.
3. Draw a diagram that summarizes the main differences in processes within an organization for traditional procurement and e-procurement.
4. Outline the main benefits of e-procurement.
5. Explain the differences between buy-side and sell-side e-procurement. Give an advantage for each type for the purchasing company.
6. Current adoption levels of e-procurement are low. Identify the main reasons for this.
7. Explain how cost savings may arise from e-procurement.
8. Why do some commentators suggest real cost savings from e-procurement may be nearer to 10 per cent than higher figures suggested by e-procurement solutions providers?

REFERENCES

Baily, P, Farmer, D., Jessop, D. and Jones, D. (1994) *Purchasing Principles and Management*. Pitman.

Caffrey, B. (1998) Dispelling e-commerce ROI myths. Published online only at http://purchasing.about.com/industry/purchasing/library/weekly/aa032798.htm, 18 July 1997.

Internet Business (1999) A world without e-procurement is costing billions of pounds a year.

eMarketer (2000) B2B revenues to top US$1 trillion by 2003. Analyst report 25 July.

Fingar, P., Kumar, H. and Sharma, T. (2000) *Enterprise E-commerce*. Meghan-Kiffler Press, Tampa, FL.

Gatarski, R. and Lundkvist, A. (1998) Interactive media face artificial customers and marketing theory must rethink. *Journal of Marketing Communications*, 4, 45–59.

Kalakota, R. and Robinson, M. (2000) *e-business. Roadmap for Success*. Addison Wesley, Reading, MA.

Kaplan, S. and Sawhney, M. (2000) E-hubs: the new B2B marketplaces. *Harvard Business Review*, May–June, 97–103.

Kluge, J. (1997) Reducing the cost of goods sold: role of complexity, design relationships. *McKinsey Quarterly*, 2, 212–15.

Ovans, A. (2000) E-procurement at Schlumberger. *Harvard Business Review*, May–June, 21–3.

Potter, C. (2000) Trust . . . Not built at e-speed: trust issues in B2B e-procurement. Pricewaterhouse Report, July, London.

Robinson, E. (2000) Battle to the bitter end. *Business 2.0*, July, 134–44.

Sawhney, M. (1999a) Making new markets. *Business 2.0*, May, 116–21.

Sawhney, M. (1999b) Let's get vertical. *Business 2.0*, September, 113–16.

Tait, N. (2000) Top dogs push web sales pitch. *Financial Times*, 8 December.

Tranmit plc (1999) *Procurement Management Systems: a corporate black hole. A survey of technology trends and attitudes in British industry*. Published by Tranmit plc, UK. Survey conducted by Byline Research. Report available at www.rswww.com/purchasing.

Tucker, D. and Jones, L. (2000) Leveraging the power of the Internet for optimal supplier sourcing. *International Journal of Physical Distribution & Logistics Management*, 23 May, 30(3/4), 255–67.

Turban, E., Lee, J., King, D. and Chung, H. (2000) *Electronic Commerce: A Managerial Perspective*. Prentice Hall, Upper Saddle River, NJ.

FURTHER READING

Fingar, P., Kumar, H. and Sharma, T. (2000) *Enterprise E-commerce*. Meghan-Kiffler Press, Tampa, FL. Chapter 5 covers e-procurement from an applications perspective. E-procurement is described under the heading of 'Vendor management systems'. Chapter 3 describes electronic marketplaces under the heading of 'I-markets'.

Kalakota, R. and Robinson, M. (2000) *E-business. Roadmap for Success*. Addison-Wesley, Reading, MA. E-procurement is considered in Chapter 9, states procurement to be a senior manager issue and describes implementation of e-procurement from both buy-side and sell-side perspectives.

Turban, E., Lee, J., King, D. and Chung, H. (2000) *Electronic Commerce: A Managerial Perspective*. Prentice Hall, Upper Saddle River, NJ. Briefly refers to some of the benefits of what they describe as procurement re-engineering in Chapter 6, p. 210.

WEB LINKS

The Purchasing Web Guide on **About.com** (http://purchasing.about.com) gives an excellent collection of links on the benefits *and* disadvantages of e-procurement.

Ariba.com (www.ariba.com): guidelines on B2B e-commerce procurement.

Buy IT (www.buyitnet.org): UK-based.

The Chartered Institute of Purchasing and Supply (CIPS) (www.cips.org.uk): industry body in UK.

Chapter 8

E-marketing

CHAPTER AT A GLANCE

Main topics

Focus on ...

Case studies

LEARNING OBJECTIVES

After completing this chapter the reader should be able to:

- Assess the need for separate e-business and e-marketing strategies
- Create an outline e-marketing plan intended to implement the e-marketing strategy
- Distinguish between marketing communication characteristics of traditional and new media

MANAGEMENT ISSUES

The issues for managers raised in this chapter include:

- How do we integrate traditional marketing approaches with e-marketing?
- How can we use electronic communications to differentiate our products and services?
- How do we redefine our marketing and communications mixes to incorporate new media?

Links to other chapters

The main related chapters are:

- *Chapter 4* – e-environment provides underpinning on the macro-economic factors that support e-marketing planning;
- *Chapter 5* – on e-business strategy; this chapter acts as an introduction to Part 2 and the chapters that follow;
- *Chapter 9* – CRM details practical implementation of e-marketing plans through promotional techniques and customer relationship management.

Introduction

In *Chapter 5* we explored approaches to developing e-business strategies. In this chapter we examine e-marketing planning separately since, typically, an e-marketing plan will be developed separately by the marketing or e-commerce team within a company. It will be based on the aims of the e-business strategy. A sell-side e-commerce perspective often leads to a separate e-commerce division for which a strategy must be developed to deliver services to customers. This e-marketing plan, will, of course, be driven by the wider business objectives and e-business strategy. This chapter assumes limited previous knowledge of marketing hence it introduces the marketing concept in order to relate it to e-business. It also reviews how marketing differs when using digital media such as the Internet, interactive TV and wireless mobile communications.

What is e-marketing?

Internet marketing has been described simply as '*the application of the Internet and related digital technologies to achieve marketing objectives*' (Chaffey *et al.*, 2000). In practice Internet-based marketing will include the use of a company web site in conjunction with promotional techniques such as banner advertising, direct e-mail and links or services from other web sites to acquire new customers and provide services to existing customers that help develop the customer relationship. The term 'Internet marketing' tends to refer to an external perspective of how the Internet can be used in conjunction with traditional media to acquire and deliver services to customers. An alternative term is **e-marketing** (for example McDonald and Wilson, 1999) which can be considered to have a broader scope since this refers to any use of technology to achieve marketing objectives and has an external and internal perspective.

E-marketing
Achieving marketing objectives through use of electronic communications technology.

As with many terms with the 'e' prefix, we need to return to an original definition of the topic to more fully understand what e-marketing involves. The definition of marketing by the UK's Chartered Institute of Marketing is:

> *Marketing is the management process responsible for identifying, anticipating and satisfying customer requirements profitability.*

This definition emphasizes the focus of marketing on the customer, while at the same time implying a need to link to other business operations to achieve this profitability. In this chapter, and in *Chapter 9*, we will focus on how the Internet can be used to achieve the processes implied by this statement:

- Identifying – how can the Internet be used for marketing research to find out customers' needs and wants?
- Anticipating – we have seen in *Chapter 5* that anticipating the demand for digital services (the online revenue contribution) is key in governing the resource allocation to e-business.
- Satisfying – a key issue for e-marketing is how to achieve customer satisfaction through the electronic channel; this raises issues such as is the site easy to use, does it perform adequately, what is the standard of associated customer service and how are physical products dispatched?

A broader definition of marketing has been developed by Dibb *et al.* (2000):

> *Marketing consists of individual and organizational activities that facilitate and expedite satisfying exchange relationships in a dynamic environment through the creation, distribution, promotion and pricing of goods, services and ideas.*

This definition is useful since it highlights different marketing activities necessary to achieve the 'exchange relationship', namely product development, pricing, promotion and distribution.

According to Chaffey *et al.* (2000) the term 'marketing' tends to be used in two distinct respects in modern management practice. It can describe:

1. The range of specialist marketing functions carried out within many organizations. Such functions include market research, brand/product management, public relations, and customer service.
2. An approach or concept (the marketing concept) that can be used as the guiding philosophy for all functions and activities of an organization. Such a philosophy encompasses all aspects of a business. Business strategy is guided by an organization's market and competitor focus and everyone in an organization should be required to have a customer focus in their job.

The modern **marketing concept** (Houston, 1986) unites these two meanings and stresses that marketing encompasses the range of organizational functions and processes that seek to determine the needs of target markets and deliver products and services to customers and other key stakeholders such as employees and financial institutions. From the marketer's perspective marketing has to be seen as the essential focus of all activities within a organization (Valentin, 1996). They argue that the marketing concept should lie at the heart of the organization, and the actions of directors, managers and employees guided by its philosophy.

The marketing concept
The management of the range of organizational activities that impact on the customer as part of marketing.

Modern marketing philosophy also requires that organizations be committed to a **marketing or customer orientation** (Jaworski and Kohli, 1993). This concept involves all parts of the organization coordinating activities to ensure that customer needs are met efficiently, effectively and profitably. In this case, marketing may encompass activities traditionally seen as the sole domain of accountants, production, HRM and information technology.

Marketing orientation
Coordinating all organizational activities that impact on the customer to deliver customer requirements.

It is apparent that the modern concept of marketing is much broader than the lay person's view of marketing simply as advertising and sales. Given that the marketing concept implies a broad meaning for marketing, how can we distinguish

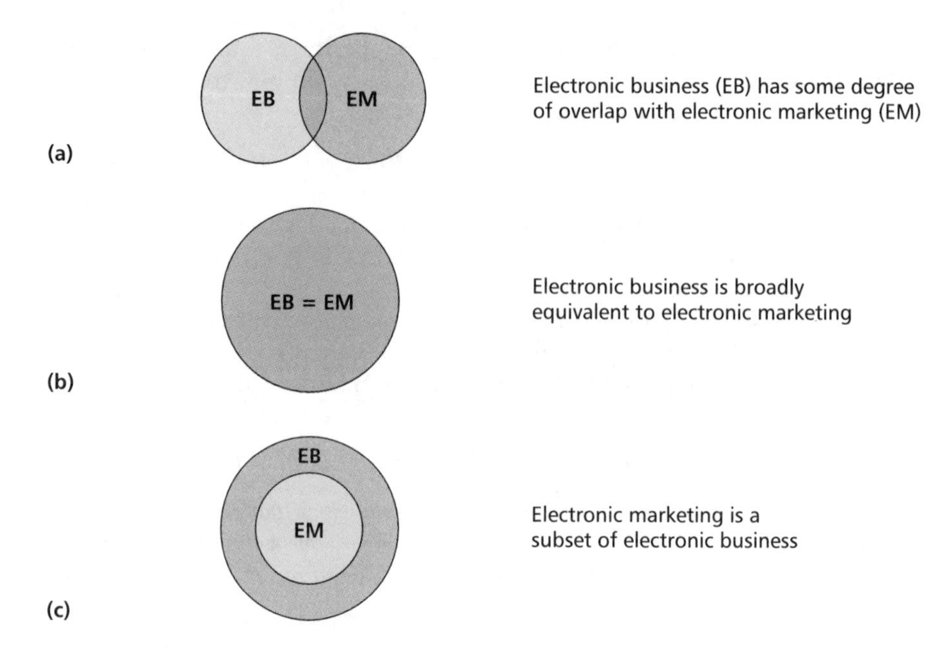
EB
EM
Electronic business (EB) has some degree of overlap with electronic marketing (EM)
(a)
EB = EM
Electronic business is broadly equivalent to electronic marketing
(b)
EB
EM
Electronic marketing is a subset of electronic business
(c)

Figure 8.1 Alternative relationships between e-business and e-marketing

between e-business and e-marketing? In fact, we can use a similar to device to that of *Figure 1.2* to help distinguish between them. *Figure 8.1* is similar to *Figure 1.2*; it shows that there are essentially three alternatives by which we can relate e-business and e-marketing. In Figure 8.1(a) there is a relatively small overlap between e-business and e-marketing. From the discussion of the marketing concept above we can reject Figure 8.1(a) as a suitable representation. Figure 8.1(b) is perhaps more realistic, and indeed some marketers would consider e-business and e-marketing to be synonymous. It can be argued, however, that Fig 8.1(c) is most realistic since e-marketing is essentially customer-oriented and it has less emphasis on supply chain and procurement activities in comparison with e-business. In summary, e-marketing can best be conceived as a subset of e-business. Referring back to *Figure 1.2* for a final time, you may ask, if e-commerce is best considered as a subset of e-business and e-marketing is also subset of e-business, then what is the relationship between e-commerce and e-marketing? The implication is that they are similar, but e-commerce is perhaps broader than e-marketing since it involves both buy-side and sell-side transactions, whereas e-marketing concentrates on sell-side transactions and communications.

E-marketing planning

E-marketing plan
A plan to achieve the marketing objectives of the e-business strategy.

An **e-marketing plan** is needed in addition to a broader e-business strategy to detail how the objectives of the e-business strategy will be achieved through marketing activities such as marketing research and marketing communications. Since the e-marketing plan is based on the objectives of the e-business or business strategy there is overlap between the elements of each approach, particularly for environment analysis, objective setting and strategic analysis. *Figure 5.1* shows how e-marketing activities will inform the e-business strategy which, in turn, will inform the e-marketing plan. For each of these elements of e-business strategy development shown in *Figure 5.3* there will be overlap with the e-marketing plan.

A necessary starting point for achieving successful e-marketing, as for any business or marketing strategy, is creation of a clearly defined strategic process that links the objectives of e-marketing through to the marketing communications and design tactics intended to achieve these objectives. Chaston (2000) and Chaffey *et al.* (2000) have suggested that e-marketing strategy development should include similar elements to a traditional marketing strategy, such as those defined by McDonald (1999) and Kotler (1997). A similar framework (SOSTAC™) has been developed by Paul Smith (1999) that summarizes the different stages that should be involved in a marketing strategy (*Figure 8.2*). The stages involved can be summarized as:

- Situation – where are we now?
- Objectives – where do we want to be?
- Strategy – how do we get there?
- Tactics – how exactly do we get there?
- Action – what is our plan?
- Control – did we get there?

Measurement of the effectiveness of e-marketing is an integral part of the strategy process in order to assess whether objectives have been achieved. The loop is closed by using the analysis of metrics collected as part of the control stage to continuously improve e-marketing through making enhancements to the web site and associated marketing communications.

We will use the SOSTAC™ framework of *Figure 8.2* in this chapter to structure our discussion of developing an e-marketing plan. Is such a traditional framework relevant when some commentators such as Hoffmann and Novak (1997) have stated that the web represents a new paradigm? Our belief is that for profitability, traditional companies or dot-coms still need to follow the well-established approaches such as assessing the marketplace and environment, setting clear

Figure 8.2 SOSTAC™ – a generic framework for e-marketing planning

objectives and defining approaches to achieve these objectives. It can be argued that many of the dot-com failures such as that of Boo.com were because elements of the strategy were flawed. It is clear though that the details of planning will need to differ for the new e-marketplace. Differences in the e-environment do need to be considered, specific objectives may need to be set and tactics often need to different to traditional approaches. As we run through the elements of e-planning we will highlight what the key differences are. A further difference is the time frame of the strategic marketing planning process. In the past, the planning process has been conceived as an annual event, but as McDonald (1999) points out, this is no longer relevant in a dynamic business environment. The era of e-business accentuates this trend and strategies will need to be reviewed frequently, as suggested in *Chapter 5*, due to events in the marketplace.

We will now review the six elements of the SOSTAC™ approach to e-marketing planning. Overlap between this coverage and that in *Chapter 5* is minimized by cross-referencing between these chapters.

Situation analysis

Situation analysis
Environment analysis and review of internal processes and resources to inform strategy.

The aim of **situation analysis** is to understand the current and future environment in which the company operates in order that the strategic objectives are realistic in light of what is happening in the marketplace. *Figure 8.3* shows the inputs from situation analysis that inform the e-marketing plan. These mainly refer to a company's external environment. The study of an organization's environment was introduced in *Figure 2.1* where it was noted that there was the immediate (micro) environment of customers, competitors, suppliers and intermediaries and a broader (macro) environment of social, legal, political, economic and technological characteristics. Situation analysis will involve consideration of all of these factors and will form the basis for defining objectives, strategies and tactics. Consideration of the SLEPT or macro-environment factors is a major topic that is covered in *Chapter 4*. In this chapter we will concentrate on what needs to be analysed about the more immediate marketplace in terms of customers, competitors, intermediaries and market structure. An internal audit of the capability of the resources of the company such as its people, processes and technology also needs to take place.

Demand analysis

Demand analysis for e-business
Assessment of the demand for e-commerce services amongst existing and potential customer segments.

A key factor driving e-marketing and e-business strategy objectives is the current level and future projections of customer demand for e-commerce services in different market segments. (See *strategic analysis, Chapter 5, p. 169.*) This will influence the demand for products online and this, in turn, should govern the resources devoted to different online channels. **Demand analysis** examines current and projected customer use of each digital channel within different target markets. It can be determined by asking for each market:

- What percentage of customer businesses have access to the Internet?
- What percentage of members of the buying decision in these businesses have access to the Internet?

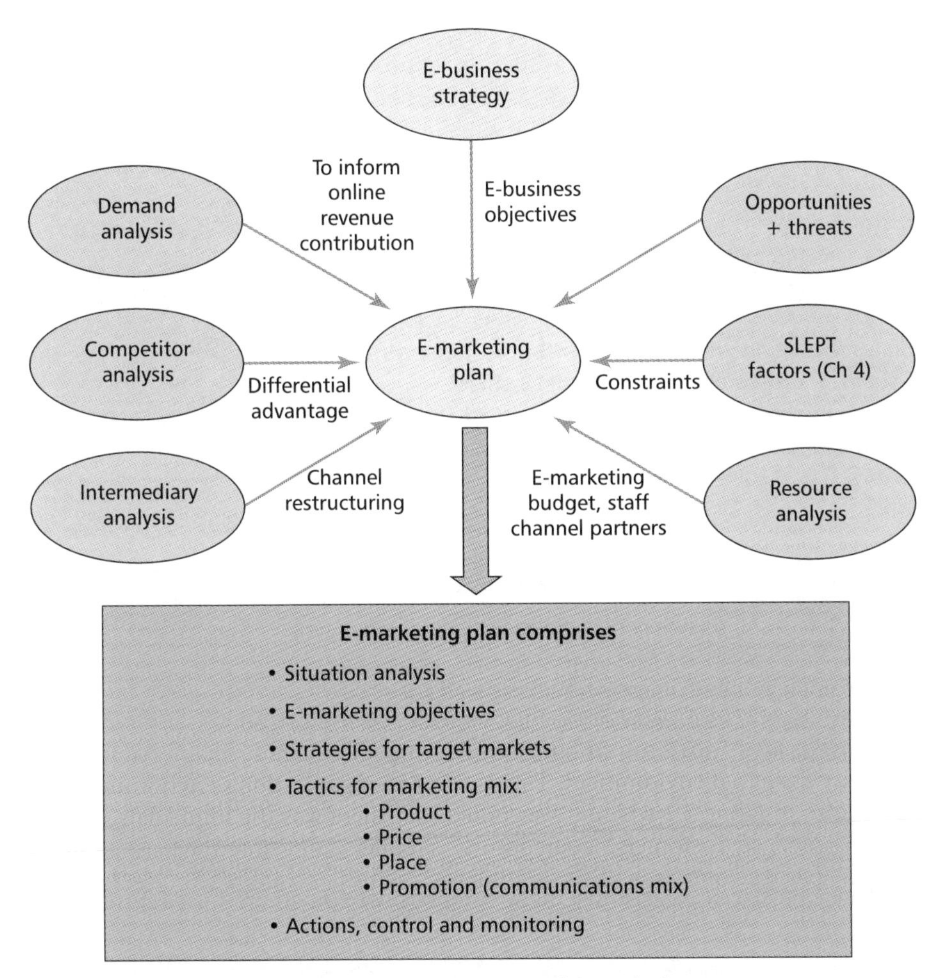

Figure 8.3 Inputs to the e-marketing plan from situation analysis

- What percentage of customers are prepared to purchase your particular product online?
- What percentage of customers with access to the Internet are not prepared to purchase online, but are influenced by web-based information to buy products offline?
- What are the barriers to adoption amongst customers and how can we encourage adoption?

Thus the situation analysis as part of e-marketing planning must determine levels of access to the Internet in the marketplace and propensity to be influenced by the Internet to buy either offline or online. In a marketing context, the propensity to buy is an aspect of buyer behaviour (*Focus on buyer behaviour* section, (*Chapter 9, p. 342*).

Figure 8.4 summarizes the type of picture the e-marketing planner needs to build up. For each geographic market the company intends to serve research needs to establish:

1. Percentage of customers with Internet access.

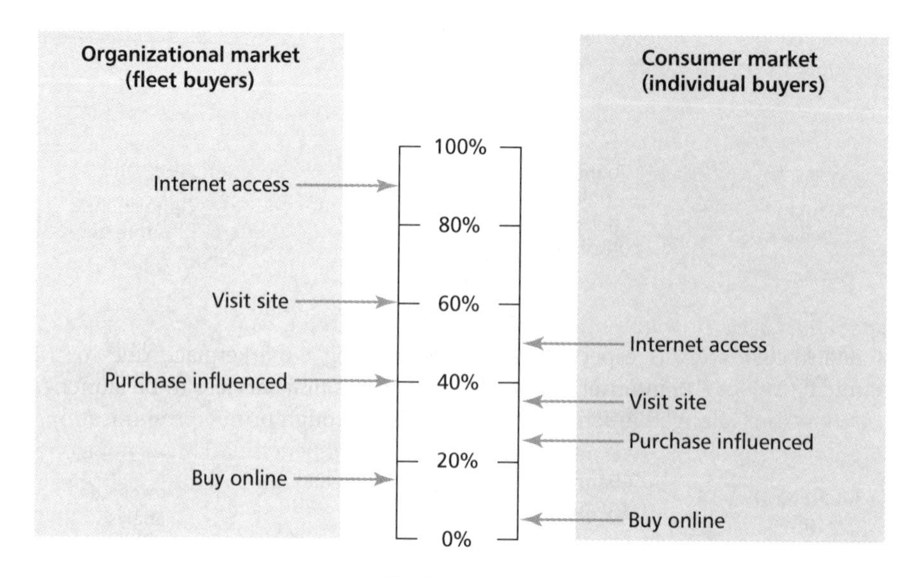

Figure 8.4 Customer demand analysis for the car market

2. Percentage of customers who access web site.
3. Percentage of customers who will be favourably influenced.
4. Percentage of customers who buy online.

Now refer to *activity 8.1* where this analysis is performed for the car market. This picture will vary according to different target markets, so the analysis will need to be performed for each of these. For example, customers wishing to buy 'luxury cars' may have web access and a higher propensity to buy than those for small cars.

Activity 8.1 Customer activity in the car market in your country

Purpose

To illustrate the type of marketing research needed to inform demand analysis for e-marketing planning and approaches to finding this information.

Activity

For your country update *Figure 8.4* to reflect current and future projections:

A. For corporate buyers (fleet market)
1. Percentage of customers with Internet access.
2. Percentage of customers who access web site.
3. Percentage of customers who will be favourably influenced (may be difficult to determine).
4. Percentage of customers who buy online.

If possible, try to gauge how these figures vary according to age, sex and social class.

B. For individual buyers
1. Percentage of customers with Internet access.
2. Percentage of customers who access web site.
3. Percentage of customers who will be favourably influenced.
4. Percentage of customers who buy online.

If possible, try to gauge how these figures vary according to companies of different sizes and different members of the buying unit.

Examples of data sources are given in the *assessing demand for e-commerce services* section (*Chapter 4, p. 126*).

Competitor analysis

Competitor analysis for e-business
Review of e-business services offered by existing and new competitors and adoption by their customers.

Competitor analysis or the monitoring of competitor use of e-commerce to acquire and retain customers is especially important in the e-marketplace due to the dynamic nature of the Internet medium. This enables new services to be launched and promotions changed much more rapidly than through print communications. The implications of this dynamism are that competitor benchmarking is not a one-off activity while developing a strategy, but needs to be continuous. Trainmaker ADTRanz now employs a member of marketing staff to continuously scan their competitors' sites and to track major customer orders and other industry news. This approach is particularly necessary for a business-to-business environment with a small number of clearly identified competitors. In this environment, it is also prudent to monitor customers' web sites frequently.

Benchmarking is used to compare e-commerce services within a market. For a retailer, conducting a benchmarking audit of Internet-based competitors may be more difficult than a traditional audit of competitors. Traditionally competitors will be well known. With the Internet and the global marketplace there may be new entrants that have the potential to achieve significant market share. This is particularly the case with retail sales. For example, successful new companies have developed on the Internet that sell books, music, CDs and electronic components. As a consequence, companies need to review the Internet-based performance of both existing and new players. Companies should review:

- well-known local competitors (for example, UK/European competitors for British companies);
- well-known international competitors;
- new Internet companies local and worldwide (within sector and out of sector).

Chase (1998) advocates that when benchmarking, companies should review competitors' sites identifying best practices, worst practices and next practices. Next practices are where a company looks beyond their industry sector at what leading Internet companies such as Amazon (www.amazon.com) and Cisco (www.cisco.com) are doing. For instance a company in the financial services industry could look at what portal sites are providing and see if there are any lessons to be learnt on ways to make information provision easier. When undertaking scanning of competitor sites, the key differences that should be watched out for are:

- new approaches from existing companies;
- new companies starting on the Internet;
- new technologies, design techniques and customer support on the site which may give a competitive advantage.

Deise *et al.* (2000) suggest an 'equation' that can be used in combination to assess competition when benchmarking:

$$\text{Competitive capability} = \frac{\text{Agility} \times \text{Reach}}{\text{Time-to-market}}$$

Agility refers to the speed at which a company is able to change strategic direction and respond to new customer demands. Reach is the ability to connect to, or to promote products and generate new business in new markets. Time-to-market is the product lifecycle from concept through to revenue generation. Companies can also turn to benchmarking organizations such as Gomez (www.gomez.com) to review e-commerce scorecards such as that of *Table 5.5*.

Deise *et al.* (2000) also suggest a further 'equation' that can be used to appraise competitors from their customer's viewpoint. This is

$$\text{Customer value (brand perception)} = \frac{\text{Product quality} \times \text{Service quality}}{\text{Price} \times \text{Fulfilment time}}$$

Some companies such as NSK bearings (www.nsk-rhp.co.uk) ask customers to complete a questionnaire on their site to rank their offering relative to competitors in these areas of customer value.

Now complete *activity 8.2* to gain an appreciation of how this can be approached.

Activity 8.2 **Competitor benchmarking**

Purpose

To understand the characteristics of competitor web site it is useful to benchmark and to assess the value of benchmarking.

Activity

Choose a B2C industry sector for such as an airline, book retailers, book publishers, CDs or clothing or for B2B such as oil companies, chemical companies, construction industry companies or B2B exchanges. Work individually or in groups to identify the type of information that should be available from the web site (and which parts of the site you will access it from) which will be useful in terms of competitor benchmarking. Once your criteria have been developed, you should then benchmark companies and summarize which you feel is making best use of the Internet medium. Web links that may help with this activity are, for the UK, Zenith Media (www.zenithmedia.co.uk), which presents the main operators in sectors such as finance, construction and industry; in the US Advertising Magazine (www.netb2b.com) reviews sites and classifies them according to an assessment of how successful a site is. By viewing the relevant industry sections in a directory such as (www.yahoo.com) it is also possible to review competitors who are proactively promoting their web sites through an entry in a directory.

For answer see p. 324

Intermediary analysis

Chapter 2 highlighted the importance of web-based intermediaries such as portals in driving traffic to an organization's web site. Situation analysis will also involve identifying relevant intermediaries for a particular marketplace and looking at how the organization and its competitors are using the intermediaries to build traffic and provide services. For example, a book e-tailer needs to assess which comparison services such as Kelkoo (www.kelkoo.com) and Shopsmart (www.shopsmart.com) it and its competitors are represented on. Do competitors have any special sponsorship arrangements or microsites created with intermediaries? The other aspect of situation analysis for intermediaries is to consider the way in which the marketplace is operating. To what extent are competitors using disintermediation or reintermediation? How are existing channel arrangements being changed?

Internal marketing audit

An internal audit will assess the capability of the resources of the company such as its people, processes and technology to deliver e-marketing compared with its competitors. So benchmarking is also included here. The internal audit will review the way in which a current web site or e-commerce services perform. The audit is likely to review the following elements of an e-commerce site that are described in more detail in *the Focus on e-marketing measurement* section (p. 507).

1. *Business effectiveness*. This will include the contribution of site to revenue (see Internet contribution section above), profitability and any indications of the corporate mission for the site. The costs of producing and updating the site will also be reviewed, i.e. cost-benefit analysis.
2. *Marketing effectiveness*. These measures may include:
   - leads;
   - sales;
   - retention;
   - market share;
   - brand enhancement and loyalty;
   - customer service.

   These measures will be assessed for each of the different product lines delivered through the web site. The way in which the elements of the marketing mix are utilized will also be reviewed.
3. *Internet effectiveness*. These are specific measures that are used to assess the way in which the web site is used, and the characteristics of the audience. Such measures include specialist terms such as hits and page impressions that are collected from the log file, and also more typical techniques such as focus groups and questionnaires to existing customers. From a marketing point of view, how clear the value proposition of the site for the customer is should be noted.

Objective setting

Effective e-marketing plans are based on clearly defined objectives since these will inform the strategies and tactics used to achieve the objectives and help in communicating the strategic aims to the workforce and investors. Evidently, many companies have found it difficult to establish objectives for e-marketing when responding to the Internet. This may be because the Internet was not integrated into company culture or management – it may have been seen as a separate responsibility from marketing.

Objectives can be based on achieving the sought-after benefits of e-commerce described in *Chapter 1* such as cost reduction and sales together with less tangible benefits such as improving the image of the company. The value of objectives can be tested using the widely used SMART mnemonic, i.e. are they Specific, Measurable, Achievable, Realistic and Time-constrained? Examples of SMART e-marketing objectives are:

- Start-ups – acquiring a specific number of new customers or to sell advertising space to generate a specified revenue that will hopefully exceed investment in site creation and promotion!
- Established mobile phone operator – increase customer retention by reducing churn from 25 per cent to 20 per cent.
- Established media company – increase online revenue, target of 20 per cent online contribution to revenue by offering new online services and media sales.
- Established business-to-business engineering company – increase overall revenue by 5 per cent, through targeting sales in new international markets.
- Reduce costs of routine customer service by 10 per cent to enable focus on delivery of specialized customer service.

It can be suggested that there is a single key objective that should be part of every e-marketing plan. This is the online revenue contribution.

The online revenue contribution

Online revenue contribution
An assessment of the direct contribution of the Internet or other digital media to sales, usually expressed as a percentage of overall sales revenue.

The **online revenue contribution** is a measure of the extent to which a company's online presence directly impacts on the sales revenue of an organization. Online revenue contribution objectives can be specified for different types of products, customer segments and geographic markets. They can also be set for different digital channels such as web, mobile or interactive digital TV.

Companies that can set a high online revenue contribution objective of, say, 25 per cent for two years' time will need to provide more resource allocation to the Internet than those companies who anticipate a contribution of 2.5 per cent. Cisco Systems Inc (www.cisco.com), maker of computer networking gear, is now selling over three quarters of its 20 billion dollars sales online. This was achieved since senior executives at Cisco identified the significance of the medium, setting aggressive targets for the online revenue contribution and resourcing the e-commerce initiative accordingly. Note that through using the Internet, Cisco has achieved strategic benefits beyond increased revenue. It has also dramatically increased profitability. This has partly been achieved through the web site which is thought to have been responsible for a 20 per cent reduction in overall operating costs.

For some companies such as an FMCG manufacturer like a beverage company, it is unrealistic to expect a high direct online revenue contribution. In this case, an indirect online contribution could be stated. This considers the Internet as part of the promotional mix and its role in influencing a proportion of customers to purchase the product or in building the brand. In this case a company could set an **online promotion contribution (reach)** of 5 per cent of its target market visiting the web site or seeing banner adverts.

Online promotion contribution (reach)
An assessment of the proportion of customers (new or retained) who use the online information sources and are influenced as a result.

Figure 8.5 combines the online revenue contribution and the online promotion contribution as a forecast based on marketing research of demand analysis and competitor analysis for The B2B Company. It can be seen that currently 10 per cent

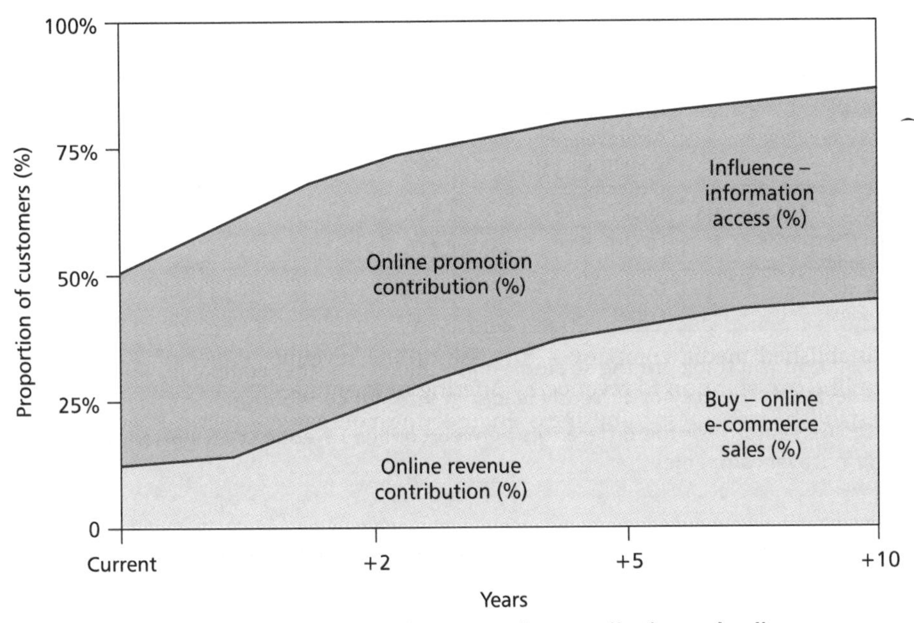

Figure 8.5 Assessment of the future online promotion contribution and online revenue for The B2B Company, for Product A, Europe

of sales are achieved online. This could be because The B2B Company has taken the decision to persuade its three largest customers to migrate online. It anticipates that over the next two to five years as more medium and large customers move to online purchasing this figure could increase to around 30 per cent. However it does not anticipate significant growth in online revenue contribution beyond this point since research indicates that smaller customers of 5 to 15 employees do not see the need for using e-procurement – they are satisfied with using faxes and invoicing and cannot see this changing. *Figure 8.5* also shows that the online promotion contribution is of greater magnitude. This suggests that even if smaller customers do not buy online, their purchase decision may well be influenced by online communications. Investment in informational and customer service elements of an e-commerce site therefore continues to be important.

Now complete *activity 8.3* to look at how the online contribution varies for different types of company.

Variations in online revenue contribution

Activity 8.3

Table 8.1 shows the online revenue contribution for some companies. Note that there is a wide variety in online contribution according to the market sector the company operates in.

Questions

1. Explain the varying percentage contribution to revenue according to the industry sector the companies operate in.
2. Comment on the variation in total Internet based revenue for the companies shown.

Activity 8.3 *continued*

Table 8.1 Variations in online revenue contribution (source: company web sites, end 2000)

Organization	*Sector*	*Online contribution*	*Overall turnover*
Cisco	Networking hardware	90%	$19bn
easyJet	Air travel	85%	£264m
Dell	Computers	48%	$25bn
Lands End Clothing	Clothing	11%	$1.3bn
Book Club Associates	Books	10%	£100m
Electrocomponents	Electronics	7%	£761m Group
Domino's Pizza	Food	3.4%	£76m
Tesco	Grocery	1.4%	£18.4bn
Thomas Cook	Travel	<1%	£1.8bn

3. What do you think are the strategic implications for other companies operating in a sector if they are not currently leader in Internet contibution?
4. Discuss reasons for the differences between online revenue contribution for the two travel companies.

Complete *case study 8.1* to review how easyJet achieved an online revenue contribution of over 50 per cent.

CASE STUDY 8.1

The e-volution of easyJet's online revenue contribution

This case study examines the development of the easyJet web site (*Figure 8.6*) from its launch in 1998.

easyJet was founded by Stelios Haji-Ioannou, the son of a Greek shipping tycoon who reputedly used to 'hate the Internet'. In the mid 1990s Haji-Ioannou reportedly denounced the Internet as something 'for nerds', and swore that it wouldn't do anything for his business. This is no longer the case since by August 1999, the site accounted for 38 per cent of ticket sales or over 135,000 seats. This was past the company's original Internet contribution target at launch of 30 per cent of sales by 2000. In the period from launch, the site had taken more than 800,000 bookings since it was set up in April 1998 after a shaky start of two sales in the first week and one thousand within the first month.

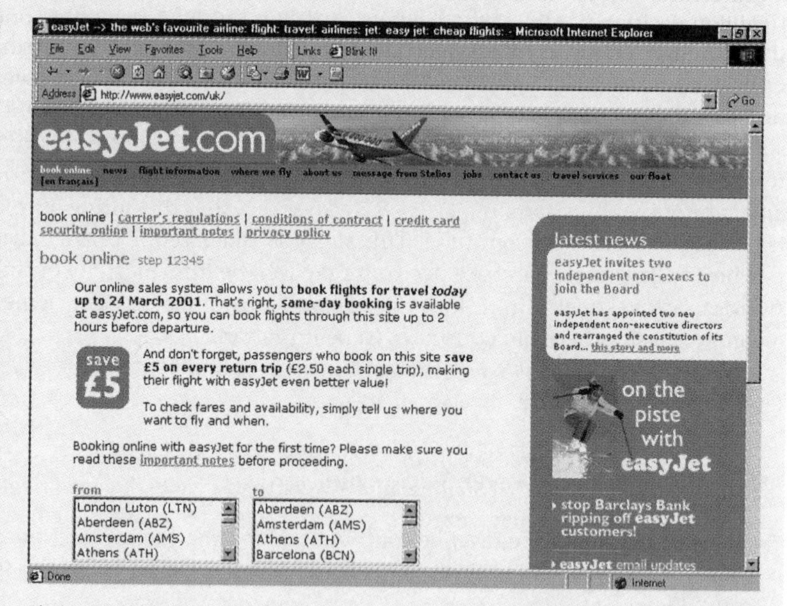

Figure 8.6 easyJet web site (www.easyjet.com)

The articles relate the tale of the owner's office being graced by a photo of the owner with horns on his head and a Mexican moustache on his upper lip. The image was contributed as a complaint by an aggrieved customer. The nature of the entrepreneur was indicated since he sent the customer two free tickets.

The company was originally set up in 1994. As a low-cost airline, looking to undercut traditional carriers such as British Airways, it needed to create a lean operation. To achieve this, Haji-Ioannou decided on a single sales channel in order to survive. He chose the phone. At the time this was groundbreaking, but the owner was encouraged by companies such as Direct Line insurance, and the savings which direct selling would bring.

Although Haji-Ioannou thought at the time that there was no time to worry about the Internet and that one risk was enough, he was adaptable enough to change. When a basic trial site was launched, he kept a close eye on how popular the dedicated information and booking phone line was (having a web-specific phone number advertised on the site can be used to trace the volume of users on the site). A steady rise in the number of calls occurred every week. This early success coincided with the company running out of space at its call centre due to easyJet's growth. Haji-Ioannou related, 'We either had to start selling over the Internet or build a new call centre. So our transactional site became a £10 million decision.'

Although the success of easyJet could be put down solely to the founder's adaptability and vision, the company was helped by the market it operated in and its chosen business model – it was already a 100 per cent direct phone sales operation. This meant it was relatively easy to integrate the web into the central booking system. There were also no potential channel conflicts with intermediaries such as travel agents. The web also fitted in with the low-cost easyJet proposition of no tickets, no travel agents, no network tie-ups and no in-flight meals. Customers are given a PIN number for each order on the web site which they give when they get to the airport.

Sales over the Internet began in April 1998, and although easyJet's new-media operations were then handled by Tableau, a few months ago easyJet took them in-house.

The Internet is important to easyJet since it helps it to reduce running costs, important for a company where each passenger generates a profit of only £1.50. Savings to easyJet made through customers booking online enable it to offer at least £1 off to passengers who book online – this is part of the online proposition. Online buyers also benefit from paying the price of a local call, instead of the standard national rate of easyJet's booking line.

The owner says that 'the savings on the Internet might seem small compared to not serving a meal on a plane, which saves between £5 and £10, but when you think how much it would cost to build a new call centre, pay every easyJet reservation agent 80 pence for each seat sold – not to mention all the middlemen – you're talking much more than the £1 off we give online buyers.'

What about the risks of alienating customers who don't want to book online? This doesn't worry the owner. He says 'I'm sure there are people who live in the middle of nowhere who say they can't use the Internet and will fly Ryanair instead. But I'm more worried about keeping my cost base down, and finding enough people to fill my aeroplanes. I only need six million people a year, not all 56 million.'

Promotion

The Internet marketing gurus say 'put the company URL everywhere'. easyjet has taken this literally with its web address alongside its Boeing 737s.

easyjet frequently varies the mix by running Internet-only promotions in newspapers. easyJet ran its first Internet-only promotion in a newspaper in *The Times* in February 1999, with impressive results. Some 50,000 seats were offered to readers and 20,000 of them were sold on the first day, rising to 40,000 within three days. And, according to the marketing director, Tony Anderson, most of these were seats that otherwise would have been flying along at 600 mph – empty. The scalability of the Internet helped deal with demand since everyone was directed to the web site rather than the company needing to employ an extra 250 telephone operators. However, risk management did occur with a microsite built for *Times* readers (www.times.easyjet.com) to avoid putting a strain on easyJet's main site.

Anderson says, 'The airline promotions are basically designed to get rid of empty seats'. He adds, 'If we have a flight going to Nice that's leaving in 20 minutes' time, it costs us very little to put some extra people on board, and we can get, say, £15 a head for it'. Flight promotions are intended to avoid attracting people who'd fly with easyJet, so advanced booking schemes are intended to achieve that.

A later five-week promotion within *The Times* and *The Sunday Times* newspaper offered cheap flights to

▶ CASE STUDY *continued*

a choice of all easyJet destinations when 18 tokens were collected. In total, 100,000 seats were sold during the promotion, which was worth more than £2m to the airline. Thirty per cent of the seats were sold online, with the rest of the transactions being completed by phone; 13,000 orders were taken over the Internet in the first day alone with over 15,000 people on the site at one point.

The web site also acts as a PR tool. Haji-Ioannou uses its immediacy to keep newspapers informed about new promotions and offers by phoning and e-mailing journalists and referring them to the web site rather than faxing.

The web site is also used as an aggressive tool in what is a very competitive marketplace. Haji-Ioannou says 'Once we had all these people coming to our site, I asked myself: "Why pay a PR company to publicise what we think when we have a captive audience on the site?"' For example, easyJet ran a competition in which people had to guess what BA's losses would be on 'Go', its budget rival to easyJet (the figure turned out to be £20m). Within minutes of the BA results being announced on 7 September, the easyJet site had the 50 flight-ticket winners from an incredible 65,000 people who had entered. In a similar vein a section of the site was entitled 'Battle with Swissair', giving easyJet's view that Swissair's head had persuaded the Swiss government to stop easyJet being granted a commercial scheduled licence on the Geneva–Barcelona route. easyJet also called itself 'The web's favourite airline', in 1999, a direct counterpoint to British Airways slogan of 'The world's favourite airline' for which it enjoyed a court battle.

easyEverything

Following the brand extension success of Virgin, easyJet has used the 'easy' prefix to offer additional services as part of the easyGroup:

- easyEverything, a chain of 400-seat capacity Internet cafes originally offering access at £1/hour. This is run as an independent company and will charge easyJet for banner ads, but clearly the synergy will help with clickthrough between two to three per cent. The only concession easyEverything makes towards easyJet is that cafe customers can spend time on the easyJet site for free.
- easyRentacar, a low-cost car rental business offering car rental at £9 a day. These costs are possible through offering a single car type and being an Internet-only business.

Implementation

The articles report that Russell Sheffield, head of new-media agency Tableau, who initially worked with easyJet had an initial problem of colour! 'He says there was a battle to stop him putting his favourite colour all over the site'. The site was intended to be highly functional, simply designed and without any excess baggage. He says 'the home page (orange) only had four options – buy online, news, info, and a topic of the moment such as BA "go" losses – and the site's booking system is simpler to use than some of its competitors'. He adds: 'great effort was put into making the navigation intuitive – for example, users can move directly from the timetables to the booking area, without having to go via the home page'.

The site was designed to be well integrated into easyJet's existing business processes and systems. For example, press releases are fed through an electronic feed into the site, and new destinations appear automatically once they are fed into the company's information system.

Measurement of the effectiveness of the site occurred through the dedicated phone number on the site which showed exactly how many calls the site generated, and the six-month target within six weeks. Web site log file analysis showed that people were spending an average of eight minutes a time on the site, and better still, almost everyone who called bought a ticket, whereas with the normal phone line, only about one in six callers buys. Instead of having to answer questions, phone operators were doing nothing but sell tickets.

Once the web site generated two-fifths of easyJet business, it was taken in-house and Tableau now acts solely as a strategic advisor.

Source: Based on *Revolution* articles: EasyJet site a success in first month, 1 August 1998; EasyJet promotion sells 30,000 seats, 1 November 1998; Say hello to Mr e-Everything, 13 October 1999. Available in archive at: www.revolution.haynet.com.

Questions

1. To what extent was the Internet contribution of nearly 50 per cent achieved more 'by luck than judgement'?

2. Describe the proposition of using the Internet for the customer and the benefits for the company.
3. Explain how easyJet uses the web site to vary the different elements of the marketing mix or as a marketing communications tool.
4. Use a news source such as www.moreover.com or www.ft.com to update the latest fortunes of easyjet.

Strategy

The strategy element of an e-marketing plan defines how e-marketing objectives will be achieved. Strategy definition has to be tightly integrated into the e-marketing planning process since e-marketing planning is an iterative process from situation analysis, to objective setting to strategy definition (*Figure 8.2*). McDonald (1999) points out that models of the stages of strategic marketing planning do not pass sequentially from one stage to the next, rather there is iteration between stages.

Six key decisions in strategy definition for e-business were described in *Chapter 5* (p. 189). To avoid significant overlap here, the reader is referred to that section.

The amount invested on the Internet should be based on the anticipated contribution the Internet will make to a business as explained in the sections on objectives. In *Chapter 5, p. 183* we saw how Kumar identified four different criteria for deciding whether the Internet would replace or complement other channels to market. In this chapter, we consider an alternative model, the Electronic Shopping Test, for reviewing the likely strategic importance of the Internet to a company as developed by de Kare-Silver (2000).

The Electronic Shopping or ES test

This test was developed by de Kare-Silver to assess the extent to which consumers are likely to purchase a retail product using the Internet. De Kare-Silver suggests factors that should be considered in the ES test:

1. *Product characteristics*. Does the product need to be physically tried, or touched before it is bought?
2. *Familiarity and confidence*. Considers the degree the consumer recognizes and trusts the product and brand.
3. *Consumer attributes*. These shape the buyer's behaviour – are they amenable to online purchases in terms of access to the technology skills available and do they no longer wish to shop for a product in a traditional retail environment? For example, a student familiar with technology may buy a CD online because they are comfortable with the technology. An elderly person looking for a classical CD would probably not have access to the technology and might prefer to purchase an item in person.

In his book, de Kare-Silver describes a method for ranking products. Product characteristics, familiarity and confidence are each marked out of 10, and consumer attributes are marked out of 30. Using this method, he scores products as shown in *Table 8.2*.

Table 8.2 Product scores in de Kare-Silver (2000), electronic shopping potential test

Product	*1. Product characteristics (10)*	*2. Familiarity and confidence (10)*	*3. Consumer attributes (30)*	*Total*
1. Groceries	4	8	15	27
2. Mortgages	10	1	4	15
3. Travel	10	6	15	31
4. Books	8	7	23	38

De Kare-Silver states that any product scoring over 20 has good potential, since the score for consumer attributes is likely to increase through time. Given this, he suggests companies will regularly need to review the score for their products.

Market and product positioning

The Internet offers new opportunities for selling new products into new markets. These present strategic alternatives that need to be evaluated. These alternatives can be evaluated using the options first stated by Ansoff (1957). The risks involved with the four options of market penetration, market development, product development or both market and product development (diversification) vary as shown in *Figure 5.15* and explained in the commentary.

There may also be options for new digital products that could include information products that can be delivered over the web. Such products may not be charged for, but will add value to existing products. Ghosh (1998) talks about developing new products or adding 'digital value' to customers. He says companies should ask the following questions:

1. Can I offer additional information or transaction services to my existing customer base?
2. Can I address the needs of new customer segments by repackaging my current information assets or by creating new business propositions using the Internet?
3. Can I use my ability to attract customers to generate new sources of revenue such as advertising or sales of complementary products?
4. Will my current business be significantly harmed by other companies providing some of the value I currently offer?

In addition Ghosh (1998) suggests that companies should provide free digital value to help build an audience. He refers to this process as building a 'customer magnet'; today this would be known as a portal or community. There is good potential for customer magnets in specialized vertical markets served by business-to-business companies. For example, a customer magnet could be developed for the construction industry, agrochemicals, biotechnology or independent financial advisers.

These issues of market and product development options are explored from the context of a particular company in the case study – personalized 'cybercycles' from DBS Oegland, Norway.

CASE STUDY 8.2

Personalized ‘cybercycles’ from DBS Oegland, Norway

The company and its proposition

DBS Oegland is a well-established Norwegian bicycle manufacturer catering to the high-end market with its core customer professionals and those with a passion for cycling as a sport. Via its web site customers can interactively design a personalized bike. Customers can select a type (men’s, women’s, children’s) and then pick from a choice of generic models such as the Cyber Track, Tricky Track and Bambo. Customers then decide on specific frames, wheels, pedals, saddles, gear systems and colours. Once customers have electronically configured their personalized bike, the on-screen search facility identifies the nearest DBS dealer and the bike is then delivered to the nearest store within 14 days where the customer can pick it up. John T. Roenneberg, the Managing Director for DBS, explains how possible channel conflicts are avoided: ‘We alert the store that a Cyber cycle order is on the way, and dealers get their commission as usual, so no one loses out’.

The DBS marketplace

In 2000, 1.5 million Norwegians and 390,000 households had access to the Web, an increase of 40 per cent since May 1997. According to recent figures from Norsk Gallup, the market research company,15 per cent of these shop via the Net, while 50 per cent express a positive attitude toward Internet shopping.

DBS produces over 150,000 bicycles a year, over 95 per cent of which are currently sold nationally. ‘Our business was initially aimed at Norwegian customers, but this new way of using the Internet suddenly gives us the potential to market worldwide,’ says Roenneberg. ‘Launching the site has given the company the opportunity to create an international presence at a fraction of the cost required to advertise outside the domestic market.’

Implementation

A secure site is necessary since customers are asked to pay 15 per cent of their total order over the web. The customer’s payment data is encrypted using Secure Socket Layer (SSL) technology. In addition, supplier IBM also installed an eNetwork Firewall solution. This allows the secure exchange of information across an extranet between business partners, customers and suppliers while restricting access to non-public parts of the site.

DBS and its supplier implemented the system using as much as the existing IT infrastructure as possible to create the site. Customer and product information was traditionally held on IBM AS/400 servers and this has been used as the basis for the new web site. The data on the different bicycle configurations is stored in a Lotus Notes database, which is made available on the web through Lotus Domino. The managing director believes that this solution gives customers and internal users the benefits of integration, ease-of-use, reliability and scalability.

Questions

1. Comment on the strategy DBS has used to exploit the Internet with reference to *Figure 8.7*.
2. Explain how DBS has used technology to vary the marketing mix from the extract and explain other opportunities for varying the mix.
3. What marketing issues were involved with the implementation of the DBS e-business solution?

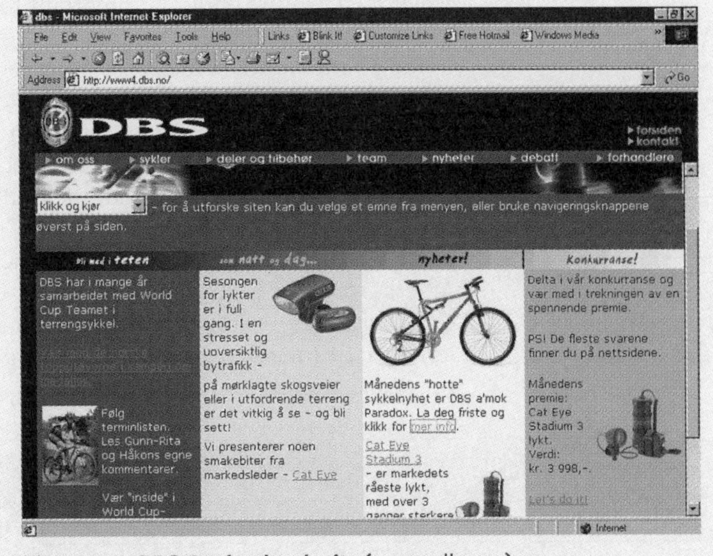

Figure 8.7 DBS Oegland web site (www.dbs.no)

Target market strategies

We have seen that we need to review the options for using the digital media to reach new markets or develop existing markets. Within both of these markets we need to analyse the target market in more detail to understand their needs and potential and then develop a strategy to satisfy these markets to maximize revenue. This process is referred to as **segmentation**. Dibb *et al.* (2000) say that:

Segmentation
Identification of different groups within a target market in order to develop different offerings for the groups.

> *Market segmentation is the key of robust marketing strategy development . . . it involves more than simply grouping customers into segments . . . identifying segments, targeting, positioning and developing a differential advantage over rivals is the foundation of marketing strategy.*

In an e-marketing planning context market segments will be analysed to assess:

1. Their current market size or value, future projections of size and the organization's current and future market share within the segment.
2. Competitor market shares within segment.
3. Needs of each segment, in particular unmet needs.
4. Organization and competitor offers and proposition for each segment across all aspects of the buying process.

Since we do not have time here to detail the process of segmentation, we will spend a little time looking at its significance from an e-marketing planning perspective. *Figure 8.8* shows questions that Seybold (1999) has identified as important when developing a customer-centric strategy for e-marketing. The questions are:

1. *Who are our customers?* This involves identifying target segments that share certain characteristics and needs. It was seen in *Chapter 4* that different criteria for identifying segments include demographics and geographic location for the B2C market and organizational characteristics and members of the buying unit for the B2B market.
2. *How are their needs changing?* Understanding the needs of different segments when they venture online is important to the next stages of delivering value to the customer. Some segments may have originally been motivated by price, but in the online world, perhaps customer service becomes more important. This is closely related to buyer behaviour (*Chapter 9, p. 342*).
3. *Which do we target?* This is an important strategic decision in e-marketing. We saw from *activity 8.1* that the Internet access levels for the organizational car-buying segment was higher than the individual buyer segment. On this basis a company may decide to allocate more of their e-marketing budget towards using electronic channels to communicate with members of this segment. Alternatively, for a B2C marketplace an insurer may decide to target a young (21–35 year old) segment rather than an older segment which has lower access levels to the Internet and is less likely to purchase online. Dibb *et al.* (2000) suggest these options for targeting strategy:

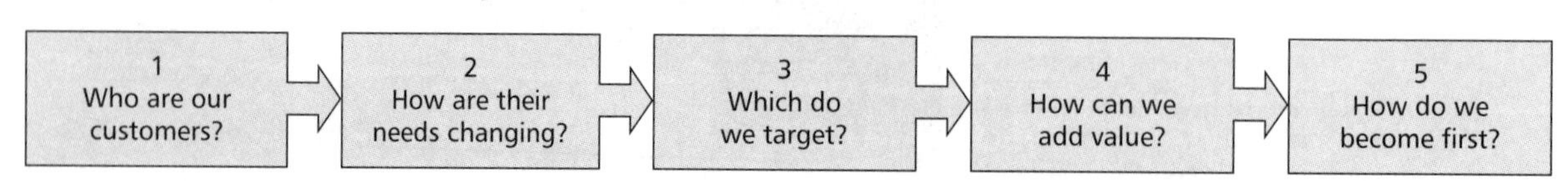

Figure 8.8 Stages in online customer segmentation according to Seybold (1999)

- Concentrate on a single segment with one product and marketing programme (this is a common approach when launching an online service).
- Offer one product and use one marketing program across segments (again an appropriate online option).
- Target different segments with different products and marketing programmes.

4. *How can we add value?* We have seen in *Chapters 5 and 6* that customer value is mainly dependent on the combination of product quality, customer service quality, fulfilment time and price. Companies need to decide for each segment which of these is most important and then seek to adjust these elements accordingly as part of the marketing mix described in the next section.
5. *How do we become first choice?* To decide on this it is necessary to know how to position within the marketplace relative to competitor offerings. **Positioning** is related to how a consumer perceives a product in terms of the elements of value described above. A positioning statement is often developed to encapsulate this. Companies then need to decide how to highlight the benefits as a **differential advantage** over rivals' products.

Positioning
Influencing the customer's perception of a product within a marketplace.

Differential advantage
A desirable attribute of a product offering that is not currently matched by competitor offerings.

Online value proposition (OVP)
A statement of the benefits of e-commerce services that ideally should not be available in competitor offerings or offline offerings.

In an e-marketing context the differential advantage and positioning can be clarified and communicated by developing an **online value proposition (OVP)**. This is similar to a unique selling proposition, but is developed for e-commerce services. In developing a proposition managers should identify:

- A clear differentiation of the proposition from competitors based on product features or service quality.
- Target market segment(s) that the proposition will appeal to.
- How the proposition will be communicated to site visitors and in all marketing communications. Developing a tag line can help this.
- How the proposition is delivered across different parts of the buying process (*Chapter 9, p. 335*).
- How the proposition will be delivered and supported by resources – is the proposition genuine? Will resources be internal or external?

Ideally, the e-commerce site should have an additional value proposition to further differentiate the company's products or services.

Having a clear online value proposition has several benefits:

- it helps distinguish an e-commerce site from its competitors (this should be a web site design objective);
- it helps provide a focus to marketing efforts and enables company staff to be clear about the purpose of the site;
- if the proposition is clear it can be used for PR and word-of-mouth recommendations may be made about the company. For example, the clear proposition of Amazon on its site is that prices are reduced by up to 40 per cent and that a wide range of three million titles is available;
- it can be linked to the normal product propositions of a company or its product.

Examples of OVPs are given in the *Focus on marketing communications for customer acquisition* section (*Chapter 9, p. 335*). Once e-marketing strategies have been developed as part of the e-marketing plan, tactics need to be implemented to achieve these strategies. These tactics, and in particular the promotion or communications tactics, will be informed by the special marketing characteristics of electronic media. The *Focus on* section below summarizes some of the key differences before we review tactics.

Focus on characteristics of new media marketing communications

In this section, we explore the main differences between marketing communications in the traditional media such as TV, print and radio and new digital media such as web sites, interactive TV and mobile commerce. This section is based on the summary presented in Chaffey (2000). Recognizing the differences between the Internet and other media is important to achieving success in channel promotion and channel satisfaction, and will lead in turn to positive channel outcomes and profitability.

A useful summary of the differences between the new media and traditional media has been developed by McDonald and Wilson (1999) as the '6Is' of e-marketing. The '6Is' are useful since they highlight factors that apply to practical aspects of Internet marketing such as personalization, direct response and marketing research, but also strategic issues of industry restructuring and integrated channel communications. By considering each of these facets of the new media, marketing managers can develop marketing plans that accommodate the characteristics of the new media. This presentation of the '6Is' is a new interpretation of these factors using new examples and diagrams to illustrate these concepts.

1. Interactivity

Deighton (1996) was one of the first authors to explain that one of the key charac-

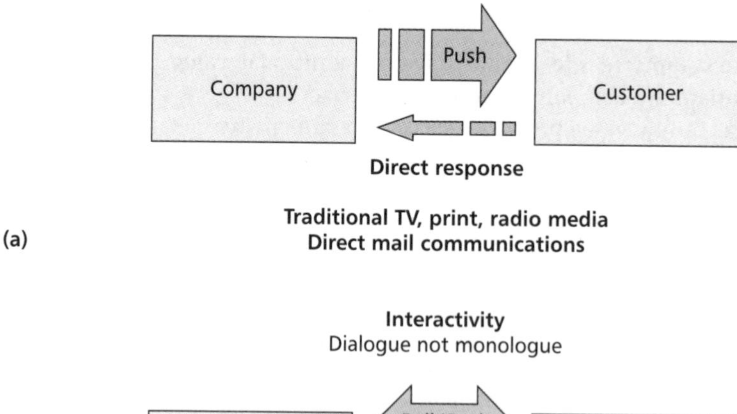

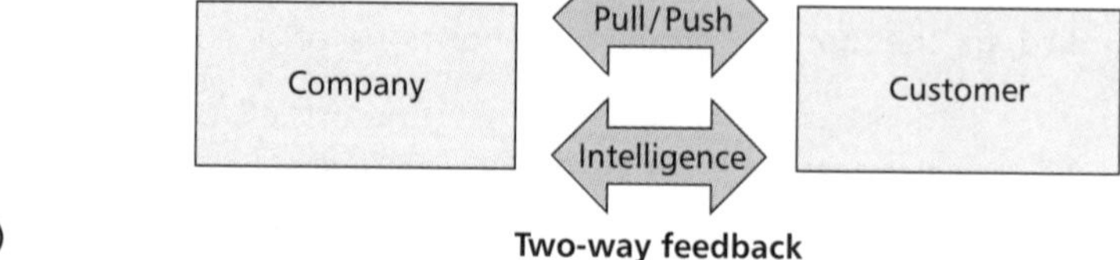

Figure 8.9 Summary of communication models for (a) traditional media (b) new media

teristics of the Internet was the opportunities that the Internet provided for interactivity. *Figure 8.9(a)* shows how traditional media are predominantly *push media* where the marketing message is broadcast from company *to* customer and other stakeholders. During this process, there is limited interaction with the customer, although interaction is encouraged in some cases such as the direct response advert or mail-order campaign. On the Internet, it is usually a customer who initiates contact and is *seeking* information on a web site. In other words it is a *'pull'* mechanism unless e-mail is used (this can be considered as a push technique). Figure *8.9(b)* shows how the Internet should be used to encourage two-way communication; these may be extensions of the direct-response approach. For example, FMCG suppliers such as Nestlé (www.nescafe.co.uk) use their web site as a method of generating interaction by providing incentives such as competitions and sales promotions to encourage the customer to respond with their names, addresses and profile information such as age and sex.

Hoffman and Novak (1997) believe that this change is significant enough to represent a new model for marketing or a new marketing paradigm. They suggest that the facilities of the Internet including the web represent a computer-mediated environment in which the interactions are not between the sender and receiver of information, but with the medium itself. They say: *'consumers can interact with the medium, firms can provide content to the medium, and in the most radical departure from traditional marketing environments, consumers can provide commercially-oriented content to the media'*. The content customers can provide may be directly commercial such as auctioning of their possessions such as via QXL (www.qxl.com) or could include comments on companies and products submitted via a newsgroup.

2. Intelligence

The Internet can be used as a relatively low cost method of collecting marketing research, particularly about customer perceptions of products and services. In the competitions referred to above Nescafé are able to profile their customers on the basis of the information received in questionnaires. The Internet can be used to create two-way feedback which does not usually occur in other media. Financial services provider Egg (www.egg.com) collects information about their online service levels through a questionnaire that is continuously available in the customer service part of their site. What is significant is that the company responds via the web site to the main concerns from customer; if the length of time it takes to reply to customer service e-mails is seen as a problem it will explain what the organization is trying to do to resolve this problem.

A wealth of marketing research information is also available from the web site itself, since every time a user clicks on a link this is recorded in a transaction log file summarizing what information on the site the customer is interested in. Since these log files quickly grow to be many thousands of lines long, analysis software tools are needed to summarize the information contained within them. Log file analysers, of which Webtrends (www.webtrends.com) is the most widely used, will highlight which type of products or promotions customers are responding to and how patterns vary through time. This enables companies to respond in real-time to buyer behaviour. UK e-tailer Jungle.com uses this technique to change the offers on its home page if customers are not responding to a special offer.

3. Individualization

Another important feature of the interactive marketing communications referred to above is that they can be tailored to the individual (*Figure 8.10(b)*) unlike traditional media where the same message tends to be broadcast to everyone (*Figure 8.10(a)*). The process of tailoring is also referred to as *personalization* and is an important aspect of achieving customer relationship management online. Personalization is often achieved through extranets which are set up with key accounts to manage the buying and after-sales processes. Dell (www.dell.com/premierpages) has set up 'Premier Pages' for key accounts such as the Abbey National where special offers and bespoke customer support are delivered. Another example of personalization is that achieved by business-to-business e-tailer RS Components (www.rswww.com). Every customer who accesses their system is profiled according to their area of product interest and information describing their role in the buying unit. When they next visit the site information will be displayed relevant to their product interest, for example office products and promotions if this is what was selected. This is an example of what is known as *mass customiza-*

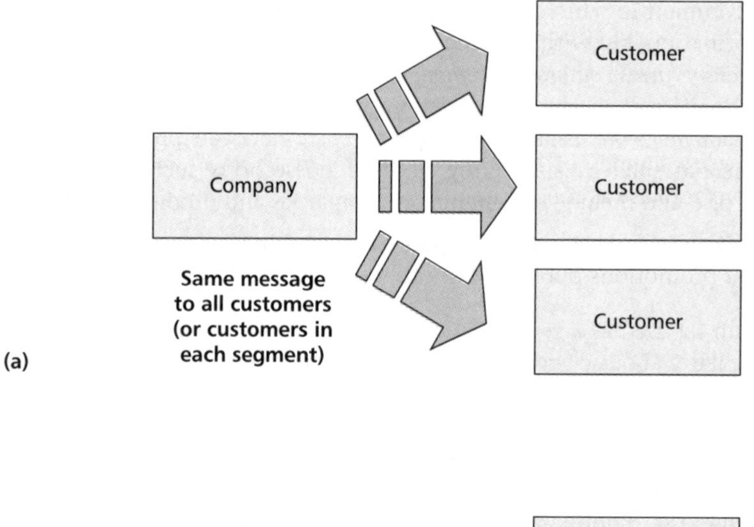

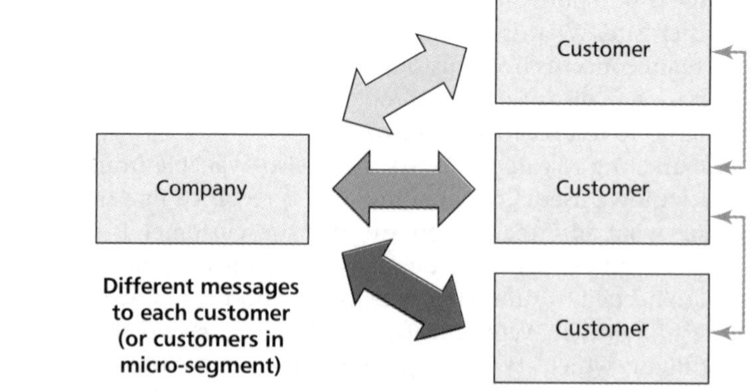

Figure 8.10 Summary of degree of individualization for (a) traditional media (same message) (b) new media (unique messages and more information exchange between customers)

tion where generic customer information is supplied for particular segments i.e. the information is not unique to individuals, but to those with a common interest. The online booksellers such as Amazon (www.amazon.co.uk) use this approach to communicate new books to groups of customers. Gardeners for instance, who have previously purchased a gardening book, will receive a standard e-mail advertising the latest gardening tome. This is again mass customization.

4. Integration

The Internet provides further scope for integrated marketing communications. *Figure 8.11* shows how it is just one of many different media channels (these channels are also offered by intermediaries). When assessing the success of a web site, the role of the Internet in communicating with customers and other partners can best be considered from two perspectives. First, organization to customer direction: how does the Internet complement other channels in communication of proposition for the company's products and services to new and existing customers with a view to generating new leads and retaining existing customers? Second, customer to organization: how can the Internet complement other channels to deliver customer service to these customers? Many companies are now considering how they integrate e-mail response and web-site call-back into their existing call centre or customer service operation. This may require a substantial investment in training and new software.

Some practical examples of how the Internet can be used as an integrated communications tool are as follows:

- The Internet can be used as a direct response tool enabling customers to respond to offers and promotions publicized in other media.

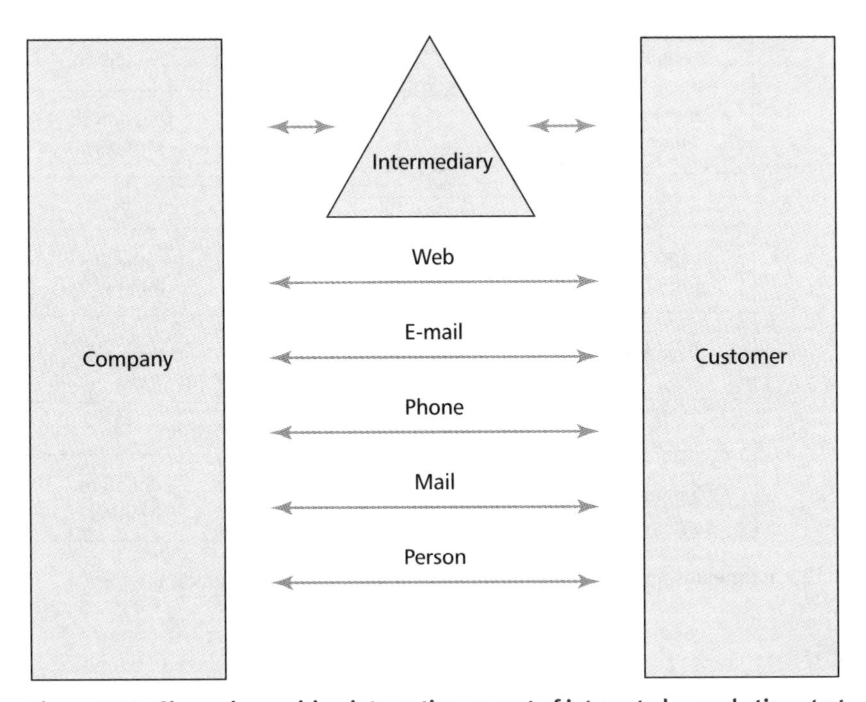

Figure 8.11 Channels requiring integration as part of integrated e-marketing strategy

- The web site can have a direct response or call-back facility built into it. The Automobile Association have a feature where a customer service representative will contact a customer by phone when the customer fills in their name, phone number and a suitable time to ring.
- The Internet can be used to support the buying decision even if the purchase does not occur via the web site. For example, Dell has a prominent web-specific phone number on their web site that encourages customers to ring a representative in the call centre to place their order. This has the benefits that Dell are less likely to lose the business of customers who are anxious about the security of online ordering and Dell can track sales that result partly from the web site according to the number of callers on this line. This is alternative 3 on *Figure 8.12*. Considering how a customer changes from one channel to another during the buying process is referred to as **mixed-mode buying**. It is a key aspect of devising online marketing communications since the customer should be supported in changing from one channel to another.

Mixed-mode buying
The process by which customer changes between online and offline channels during the buying process.

- Customer information delivered on the web site must be integrated with other databases of customer and order information such as those accessed via staff in the call centre to provide what Seybold (1999) calls a '360 degree view of the customer'.
- The Internet can be used to support customer service. For example EasyJet (www.easyjet.com), who receive over half their orders electronically, encourage users to check a list of frequently asked questions (FAQ) compiled from previous customer enquiries before contacting customer support via phone.

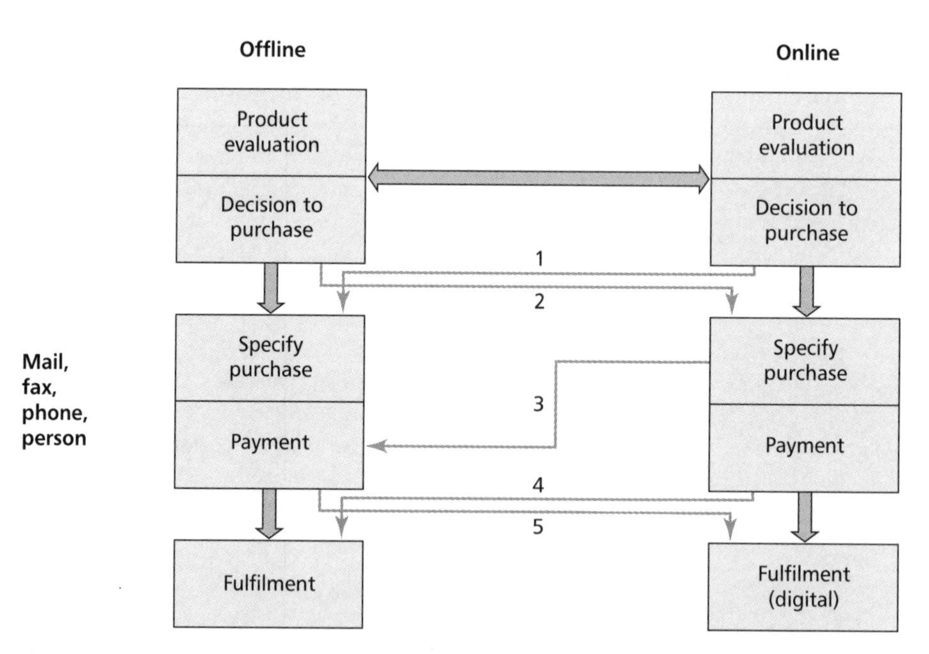

Figure 8.12 Channel integration required for e-marketing and mixed-mode buying

Integrating online and offline communications

Activity 8.4

Purpose

To highlight differences in marketing communications introduced through the use of the Internet as a channel and the need to integrate these communications with existing channels.

Activity

List communications between PC vendor and a home customer over the lifetime of a product such as a PC. Include both communications using the Internet and traditional media. Refer to channel swapping alternatives in the buying decision shown in *Figure 8.11* to develop your answer.

For answer see p. 325

5. Industry restructuring

Disintermediation and reintermediation, key concepts of industry restructuring that should be considered by any company developing an e-marketing strategy, were introduced in *Chapter 2*. For the marketer defining their company's communications strategy it becomes very important to consider a company's representation on these intermediary sites by answering questions such as 'which intermediaries should we be represented on?' and 'how do our offerings compare to those of competitors in terms of features, benefits and price?'

6. Independence of location

Electronic media also introduce the possibility of increasing the reach of company communications to the global market. This gives opportunities to sell into international markets that may not have been previously possible. Scott Bader (www.scottbader.com), a business-to-business supplier of polymers and chemicals for the paints and coatings industry, can now target countries beyond the forty or so it has traditionally sold to via a network of local agents and franchises. The Internet makes it possible to sell to a country without a local sales or customer service force (although this may still be necessary for some products). In such situations and with the restructuring in conjunction with disintermediation and reintermediation, strategists also need to carefully consider channel conflicts that may arise. If a customer is buying direct from a company in another country rather than via the agent, this will marginalize the business of the local agent who may want some recompense for sales efforts or may look to partner with competitors.

Tactics

Marketing tactics to implement strategies and objectives are traditionally based around the elements of the marketing mix. There are other methods for approaching tactics that are detailed in further sections. One approach is to use customer-driven tactics that impact both the design and services provided by an e-commerce site. The principles of customer orientation as stated by Seybold (1999) are described in *Chapter 11*. A further approach to tactics is that of customer relationship management described in the next chapter.

The marketing mix – the 4Ps originally proposed by Jerome McCarthy (1960) – is used as an essential part of implementing marketing strategy by many practitioners. The 4Ps has been extended to include three (or more) further elements that better reflect service delivery: people, processes and physical evidence (Booms and Bitner, 1981), although others argue that these are subsumed within the 4Ps. The marketing mix is applied frequently since it provides a simple framework for varying different elements of the product offering to influence the demand for products within target markets. For example, to increase sales of a product the price can be decreased or the amount or type of promotion changed, or some combination of these elements. E-commerce provides new opportunities for the marketer to vary the marketing mix, so it is worthwhile outlining these. However, it should be noted that many marketers now consider it as only one tool for developing tactics and other approaches such as branding (see *Focus on online branding*, p. 317) or a *customer relationship management perspective* (*Chapter 9, p. 330*) can be used to develop tactics, particularly for marketing communications. One difficulty is that the marketing mix is symptomatic of a push approach to marketing and does not recognize the needs of customers. For this reason it is important that mix is based up by detailed knowledge of buyer behaviour collected through market research. Furthermore, the mix should be adjusted according to different target markets or segments to better meet the needs of customers.

We will now consider how each element of the marketing mix can be varied or how we 'mix the mix' in more detail.

Product

There are many alternatives for varying the product when a company is developing its online strategy. Options should be reviewed for how a company can add value to its core and extended services. In the section above we looked at the recommendations of Ghosh (1998) for creating digital value, and in *Chapter 2* we reviewed some of the new revenue models that are available. Features of existing products can be varied using the Internet, in particular, features of the extended product such as the quality of customer support information can be enhanced. The advertising directing BRAD (www.brad.net) has been enhanced online to provide searching facilities that were not available in the paper-based version. As we saw in the section on target market strategies we will also want to enhance the product to provide differential advantage. Questions that can be asked to achieve this include:

- How do we differentiate? How can we make our online presence different to our competitors?
- How do we migrate the current brand online? Do we use a brand variant?
- Do we become a portal or ISP?
- Do we offer an extranet for key customers? What are the facilities?
- Do we offer personalized services that help build relationships with customers?
- Are there any other features of extended product we can charge a premium for? For example, some online booksellers charge for a gift-wrapping service.

Price

The price element of the marketing mix is key in achieving objectives such as customer acquisition and retention for particular target markets, but of course this will be tempered by profitability aims. *Case study 8.1* showed how easyJet discounted online prices in an effort to meet its objectives of online revenue contribution. The case also showed how this price reduction was possible because of the lower overhead of processing a customer transaction online in comparison to phone. Similarly, to acquire customers online booksellers may decide to offer a discount of 50 per cent on the top 25 best-selling books in each category, for which no profit is made, but offer a relatively small discount on less popular books to give a profit margin.

Bickerton *et al.* (2000) identify a range of options that are available for setting pricing:

1. Cost plus pricing

This involves adding on a profit margin based on production costs.

2. Target profit pricing

This is a more sophisticated pricing method, which involves looking at the fixed and variable cost in relation to income for different sales volumes and unit prices. Using this method the breakeven amount for different combinations can be calculated. For e-commerce sales the variable selling costs, i.e. the cost for each transaction, is small. This means that once breakeven is achieved each sale has a large margin. With this model differential pricing is often used in a B2B context according to the volume of goods solved. Care needs to be taken that differential prices are not evident to different customers. One company, through poor implementation, made prices for different customers available for all to see with disastrous results.

3. Competition-based pricing

This approach is common online. The advent of price-comparison engines such as Kelkoo (www.kelkoo.com) for B2C consumables has increased price competition and companies need to develop online pricing strategies that are flexible enough to compete in the market place, but are still sufficient to achieve profitability in the channel. Diamantopoulos and Matthews (1993) suggest there are two aspects of competition that affect an organization's pricing. The first is the structure of the market – the greater number of competitors and the visibility of their prices the nearer a *perfect market* is approached. The implication of a perfect market is that an organization will be less able to control prices, but must respond to competitors' pricing strategies. The second is the perceived value of the product. If a brand is differentiated in some way, it may be less subject to downward pressure on price. As well as making pricing more transparent, the Internet does lead to opportunities to differentiate in information describing products or through added-value services. Whatever the combination of these factors, it seems clear that the Internet will lead to more competition-based pricing.

Kotler (1997) suggests that in the face of price-cuts from competitors in a market, a company has the following choices that can be applied to e-commerce.

(a) Maintain the price (assuming that e-commerce-derived sales are unlikely to decrease greatly with price since other factors such as customer service are equally or more important).
(b) Reduce the price (to avoid losing market share).
(c) Raise perceived quality or differentiate product further by adding value services.
(d) Introduce new lower-priced product-lines.

4. Market-oriented pricing

Here the response to price changes by customers comprising the market is considered. This is known as the elasticity of demand. There are two approaches: *premium pricing (or skimming the market)* involves setting a higher price than the competition to reflect the positioning of the product as a high quality item. *Penetration pricing* is when a price is set below the competitors' prices either to stimulate demand and/or increase penetration. This approach was commonly used by dot-com companies to acquire customers. The difficulty with this approach is that if customers are price sensitive then the low price has to be sustained otherwise customer may change to a rival supplier. This has happened with online banks – some customers will move to reduce costs of overdrafts, for example. Alternatively if a customer is concerned by other aspects such as service quality it may be necessary to create a large price differential in order to encourage a customer to change supplier.

Tactical discounts may also be used to achieve online revenue contributions. Offering an online discount as described for easyjet is one approach. This may lead to channel conflicts with other distributors if they are being undercut. easyjet is fortunate in that it has only ever sold direct, so the only conflict is with its own telesales channel. Another discount approach is the use of coupons. For example, a £5 discount is offered if the customer types in a redemption code from a coupon they have received via a mail-order promotion or in a magazine. Online loyalty schemes such as Beenz effectively offer a discount since this can be redeemed on other sites. Volume discounts according to number of items purchased may be used on B2B e-commerce sites. Another approach that is based on loyalty offers discounts according to the amount previously spent on the site.

As well as these traditional pricing methods, the Internet has led to an increase in certain pricing techniques such as auctions (*Chapter 2, p. 46*). Some new price models such as the Priceline 'name your price' approach (*Chapter 2, p. 46*) have also been developed. For some downloadable services such as information or software there has been a move from fixed price to pay per view or rental techniques.

Place

Place refers to place of purchase, distribution or the place of consumption. The changes in market structure such as disintermediation and reintermediation referred to in *Chapter 2* (*p. 36*) and *Chapter 5* (*p. 193*) are one of the decisions associated with place. Reducing channel conflicts where disintermediation and reintermediation occur has also to be countered as part of the tactic. A further issue is the location of e-commerce (*Chapter 2, p. 43*), that is, in a B2B context e-commerce is conducted on the manufacturer's own site, at an intermediary or procured on a customer's site. Place tactics will have to review all these opportunities and decide which are appropriate. In a B2B context they may vary on a case-by-case basis, for example special links may be set up to sell on a large customer's own procurement site. Issues in distribution and fulfilment are described in *Chapter 5, p. 240*.

Promotion

Specification of the promotion is usually part of a communications strategy. This will include selection of target markets, positioning and integration of different communications tools. The Internet offers a new, additional marketing communications channel to inform customers of the benefits of a product and assist in the buying decision. One approach for developing promotion tactics is to specify the communications techniques required for different stages of the buying process (see *Focus on buyer behaviour, Chapter 9, p. 342*). Another approach is to look at how the Internet can supplement the range of promotional activities such as advertising, sales promotions, PR and direct marketing. How these techniques can be used to drive customer traffic to a web site is described in more detail in the *Focus on marketing communications for customer acquisition* section (*Chapter 9, p. 335*). In *Chapter 9* we also look at how customers can be persuaded to return to a site for future purchases. This is a perplexing problem since the Internet is a pull medium (see below). It is the customer who decides to visit a site. The promotional strategy should acknowledge this and identify tactics to make the customer return to the site. Methods for achieving this include:

- reminders in traditional media campaigns why a site is worth visiting such as online offers and competitions;
- direct e-mail reminders of site proposition – new offers;
- frequently updated content including promotional offers, or information that helps your customer do their job, which reminds them to visit.

The promotion element of the marketing plan also requires three important decisions about investment for the online promotion or the online communications mix:

1. *Investment in promotion compared to site creation and maintenance* (*Figure 12.15*). Since there is often a fixed budget for site creation, maintenance and promotion, the e-marketing plan should specify the budget for each to ensure there is a sensible balance and the promotion of the site is not underfunded.
2. *Investment in online promotion techniques in comparison to offline promotion*. A balance must be struck between these techniques. *Figure 8.13* summarizes the tactical options that companies have. Which do you think would be the best option for an established company as compared to a dot-com company? It seems that in both cases, offline promotion investment often exceeds that for online promotion investment. For existing companies traditional media such as print are used to advertise the sites, while print and TV will also be widely used by dot-com companies to drive traffic to their sites.
3. *Investment in different online promotion techniques*. For example, how much to pay for banner advertising as against online PR about online presence; how much to pay for search engine registration. These and other traffic building techniques are described in *Chapter 9, p. 335*.

The Revolution 'Campaign of the week' articles (www.revolution.haynet.com) give good examples of how these investment decisions are made, and the

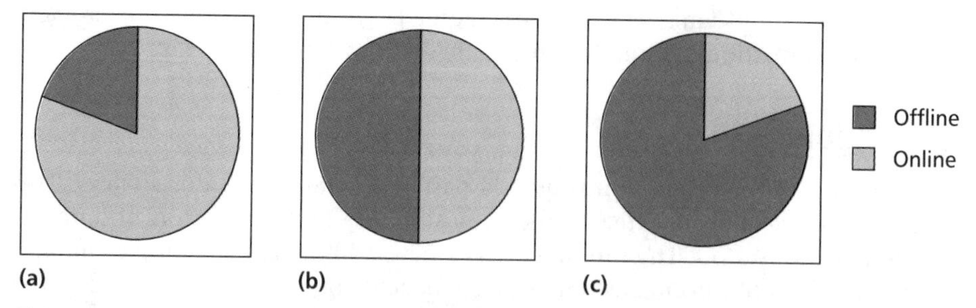

Figure 8.13 Options for the online vs offline communications mix (a) online > offline (b) similar online and offline (c) offline > online

creative techniques used. For example it reported that a campaign run by *Sporting Life* had a starting base of 25 million page impressions. The campaign consisted of:

- £250,000 online of which 60 per cent was spent on banners with live sports feeds appearing on sites such as The Times, Excite, This is Local Sport, E*Trade and Arsenal Football Club.
- £400,000 offline campaign in the national press tied in with Wimbledon tennis stars.

The results were that page impressions have increased by 20 per cent after the offline campaign and click-throughs of 2 to 5 per cent were achieved for the banner ads.

People, process and physical evidence

People, process and physical evidence are particularly important for service delivery. Since service delivery is an important aspect of e-commerce site this is referred to in *the Focus on providing quality customer service* in *Chapter 9*; managing organizational change is the focus of *Chapter 10* and user-centred design in *Chapter 11*. Enhancing service is also an important element of online branding which is described in the next *Focus on* section. Physical evidence could be applied to site design or the accompanying packaging when products are delivered. Alternatively these could be interpreted as part of the extended product.

F *Focus on* online branding

The importance of building an effective online brand is often referred to when start-ups launch e-commerce sites, but what does this mean and how important an aspect of e-marketing planning is branding for existing companies?

What is a successful online brand? Is an e-commerce site with high-levels of traffic and online sales or good name recognition a successful brand? Or is it a site with more modest sales levels, but one that customers perceive as having good service? Although such sites are often described as successful brands, as we will see a successful brand is dependent on a wide range of factors.

Branding seems to be a concept that is difficult to grasp since it is often used in a narrow sense. Many think of branding only in terms of aspects of the brand identity such as the name or logo associated with a company or products, but branding gurus seem agreed it is much more than that. A **brand** is described by Leslie de Chernatony and Malcolm McDonald in their classic 1992 book, *Creating Powerful Brands*, as

Branding
The process of creating and developing successful brands.

Brand
The sum of the characteristics of a product or service perceived by a user.

> *an identifiable product or service augmented in such a way that the buyer or user perceives relevant unique added values which match their needs most closely. Furthermore, its success results from being able to sustain these added values in the face of competition.*

This definition highlights three essential characteristics of a successful brand:

- brand is dependent on customer perception;
- perception is influenced by the added-value characteristics of the product;
- the added-value characteristics need to be sustainable.

To summarize, a brand is dependent on a customer's psychological affinity for a product, and is much more than physical name or symbol elements of brand identity.

An alternative perspective on branding is provided by Aaker and Joachimstahler (2000) who refer to **brand equity**. Aaker has said that brand equity is made up of four dimensions:

Brand equity
The brand's assets (or liabilities) linked to a brand's name and symbol that add to (or subtract from) a service.

1. *Brand awareness*. This is achieved through marketing communications to promote the brand identity and the other qualities of the brand. Aaker and Joachimstahler note that brand awareness is not only important in terms informing customers about a product, but also because people like the familiar and it links through to other aspects of brand equity. For example, the Intel Inside awareness campaign not only increased awareness, but also provides a perception of technological innovation and quality.
2. *Perceived quality*. Awareness counts for little if the customer has a bad experience of a product or associated customer service. If quality of a brand is negatively perceived this affects its equity since word-of-mouth will quickly be relayed to many people.
3. *Brand associations*. There are many brand associations that connect a customer to a brand including imagery, the situation in which a product is used, its personality and symbols. Intel Inside aims to create a fun and funky, but technical brand association through the use of dancing clean-lab technicians.
4. *Brand loyalty*. This refers to the commitment of customer segments to a brand. For example Intel may have good brand awareness, quality and clear associations, but its brand equity is undermined if customers are happy to buy a computer with an AMD or Cyrix chip when they next upgrade their computer.

Brand identity

Aaker and Joachimstaler also emphasize the importance of developing a plan to communicate the key features of the **brand identity** and increase brand awareness. Brand identity is again more than the name. These authors refer to it as a set of brand associations that imply a promise to customers from an organization. Refer to the box *Jungle.com's brand identity* to see the different elements of brand identity which is effectively a checklist of what many e-tailers are looking to achieve.

Brand identity
The totality of brand associations including name and symbols that must be communicated.

Jungle.com's brand identity

Aaker and Joachimstaler (2000) suggest the following characteristics of identity need to be defined at the start of a brand building campaign. Marketing communications can then be developed that create and reinforce this identity.

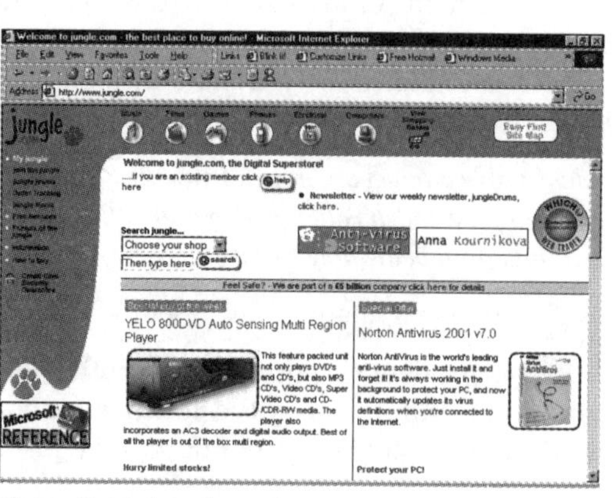

Figure 8.14 Jungle.com

Brand essence (a summary of what the brand represents)

This is not necessarily a tag line, but for Jungle it could be 'Making technology fun and affordable'.

Core identity (its key features)

- Service quality – next day delivery
- Value for money – price pledge policy
- Reliable, secure, backed by larger company (GUS/Argos) so support should be available
- An entertaining, down-to-earth buying experience

Extended identity

- Personality – flaunts what is standard for technology suppliers
- Symbols – Jungle.com logo and typeface and the Stanley monkey and footprint brand icons

Value proposition

- Functional benefits – four reasons listed in catalogue are: 1. Huge stocks; 2. Next day delivery; 3. Lines open seven days a week; 4. Internet security – a member of the Argos group.
- Emotional benefits – good to make technology accessible and friendly, backed up by a larger company.
- Self-expressive benefit – willingness to go against the usual way of selling products.

Relationship

- Customers value and will be loyal to a company that isn't stuffy.

This is an interpretation of Jungle.com's brand identity based on evaluation of their marketing communications. The intention is to indicate the depth with which identity is defined; interpretations may not be accurate for Jungle.com.

A further decision for marketing managers is whether to redefine the name element of brand identity to support the move online. Brands that are newly created for the Internet such as Expedia and Quokka.com do not risk damaging existing brands, although it is suggested by de Chernatony and McDonald (1992) that new brand launches are risky activities and that even in the offline world less than 10 per cent of new brands prove successful. Chaffey *et al.* (2000) describe four options for a company migrating their brands online. When a company launches or relaunches an e-commerce site it has the following choices with regards to brand identity:

1. Migrate traditional brand online

This is probably the most common approach. Companies with brands that are well established in the real world can build on the brand by duplicating it online. Sites from companies such as Ford, Orange and Disney all have identical brand identities and values that would be expected from experience of their offline brands. The only risks of migrating existing brands online are that the brand equity may be reduced if the site is of poor quality in terms of performance, structure or information content. There may also be a missed opportunity as explained below.

2. Extend traditional brand: variant

Some companies decide to create a slightly different version of their brand when they create their web site. The DHL site (www.dhl.co.uk) is based on an online brand 'Red Planet' which is based on a spaceship concept. Users order couriers and track using controls on a spaceship console. Through using this approach, the advantages of a brand variant are illustrated well. The company is able to differentiate itself from similar competing services and this can be used in online and offline promotion to distinguish the site from its rivals. Cisco uses a similar approach with its Cisco Online Connection brand. The use of an online brand variant helps raise the profile of the web site and helps the customer think of the site in association with the company. Aaker suggests that when a brand variant is created there may still be problems with recognition and also brand trust and quality associations may be damaged.

3. Partner with existing digital brand

It may be that a company can best promote its products in association with a strong existing digital or Internet brand such as Yahoo, Freeserve or LineOne. For example, the shopping options for record and book sales on Freeserve are branded as Freeserve although they are actually based on sites from other companies such as record seller Audiostreet.com. Freeserve is given brand prominence since this is to the advantage of both companies.

4. Create a new digital brand

It may be necessary to create an entirely new digital brand if the existing offline brand has negative connotations or is too traditional for the new medium. An example of a new digital brand is the Egg banking service which is part of Prudential, a well-established company. Egg can take new approaches without damaging Prudential's brand, and at the same time, not being inhibited by the Prudential brand. Egg is not an entirely online brand since it is primarily accessed by phone. Egg now encourage some of their million plus customers to perform all their transactions online. Another example of a new digital brand was the Go portal which was created by Disney, who desired to be able to 'own' some of the many online customers who are loyal to one portal. It was felt they could achieve this best through using a completely new brand. The Disney brand might be thought to appeal to a limited younger audience. However the new brand was not sufficiently powerful to compete with the existing Yahoo! brand and has now failed.

Some of the characteristics of a successful brand name are suggested by de Chernatony and McDonald (1992) are that ideally it should be simple, distinctive, meaningful, and compatible with the product. These principles can be readily applied to web-based brands. Examples of brands that fulfil most of these characteristics are CDNow, CarPoint, BUY.COM and e-STEEL. Others suggest that distinctiveness is most important are Amazon, Yahoo!, Expedia, Quokka.com (extreme sports), E*Trade, and FireandWater (HarperCollins) books.

Ries and Ries (2000) suggest two rules for naming brands. (1) The Law of the Common Name – they say 'The kiss of death for an Internet brand is a common name'. This argues that common names such as Art.com or Advertising.com are poor since they are not sufficiently distinctive. (2) The Law of the Proper Name – they say 'Your name stands alone on the Internet, so you'd better have a good one'. This suggests that proper names are to be preferred to generic names e.g. Handbag.com against Woman.com or Moreover.com against Business.com. The authors suggest that the best names will follow most of these eight principles: (1) short, (2) simple, (3) suggestive of the category, (4) unique, (5) alliterative, (6) speakable, (7) shocking, and (8) personalized. Although these are cast as 'immutable laws', of course there will be exceptions to these laws!

To summarize this *Focus on* section, complete *activity 8.5* to see how different elements of branding relate to e-commerce services.

Activity 8.5 Applying branding concepts to The B2C Company e-commerce site

Purpose

To illustrate the importance of branding for e-commerce services.

Activity

You are putting together a business plan for a start-up company. Show how each of Aaker's dimensions of brand equity relate to a start-up dot-com. To what extent do these factors also apply to the e-commerce service of an existing company?

For answer see p. 325

The activity illustrates the importance of building brand awareness for an e-commerce service in a cost effective manner at the same time as achieving good levels of service quality. This is described further in the 'excelling in service quality' section in *Chapter 9* and summarized in *Table 9.5*. Success factors can be summarized as creating a positive customer experience through:

- Content quality (Can the customer easily find relevant, up-to-date content? Are there errors?)
- Adequate performance of web site infrastructure in terms of availability and download speed
- Ease of contacting a company for support by e-mail or the customer's preferred channel.
- Quality of response to e-mail enquiries and fulfilment quality
- Acknowledgement of customer privacy
- Reflecting and supporting the characteristics of the offline brand

Managing the technology and customer database necessary to deliver service is a key aspect of e-marketing and requires close interaction between marketers and IS department or external consultants.

Actions

The actions component of e-marketing planning refers to activities conducted by managers to execute the plan. Questions that need to be resolved when specifying actions include:

- What level of investment in the Internet channel is sufficient to deliver these services? What will be the payback?
- What training of staff is required?
- What new responsibilities are required for effective Internet marketing?
- Are changes in organizational structure required to deliver Internet-based services?
- What activities are involved in creating and maintaining the web site?

At this stage an e-marketing plan will be finalized to summarize actions that need to occur. An example of what appears in a typical e-marketing plan is presented in the box *The B2B Company e-marketing plan*. This also acts as a summary for the chapter.

The B2B Company e-marketing plan

1. Situation analysis

Internal audits

- Current Internet marketing audit
  (business, marketing and Internet marketing effectiveness)
- Audience composition and characteristics
- Reach of web site, contribution to sales and profitability
- Suitability of resources to deliver online services in face of competition

External audits

- Macro-economic environment (*Chapter 4*)
- Micro environment – new marketplace structures, predicted customer activity
- Competition – threats from existing rivals, new services, new companies and intermediaries

Assess opportunities and threats (SWOT analysis)

- Market and product positioning
- Methods of creation of digital value and detailed statement of customer value proposition
- Marketplace positioning (buyer, seller and neutral marketplaces)
- Scope of marketing functions

2. Objectives statement

- Corporate objectives of online marketing (mission statement)
- Detailed objectives: tangible and intangible benefits, specific critical success factors
- Contribution of online marketing to promotional and sales activities
- Online value proposition

3. Strategy definition

- Investment and commitment to online channels (mixture of bricks and clicks)

▶

- Market and product positioning – aims for increasing reach, new digital products and new business and revenue models
- Target market strategies – statement of prioritized segments, new segments, online value proposition and differential advantage. Significance of non-customer audiences?
- Change management strategy (which new processes, structures and responsibilities will be required, *Chapter 10*)

4. Tactics

- **Product**. Creating new core and extended value for customers, options for migrating brand online
- **Promotion**. Specify balance of online and offline promotion methods. Role of CRM (incentivization to acquire new customer registrations and opt-in e-mail to retain customers, *Chapter 9*)
- **Price**. Discounting online sales, options for setting pricing, new pricing options, e.g. auctions
- **Place**. Disintermediation and reintermediation, seller, buyer or neutral sales
- **People, process and physical evidence**. Online service delivery through support and characteristics of web site

5. Actions

Specify:

- Tasks
- Resources
- Partnering and outsourcing
- Budget including costs for development, promotion and maintenance
- Timescale
- Staff

Implementation

- Key development tasks (*Chapters 11 and 12*): analysis of business and audience needs, scenario-based design, development of content, integration of databases, migration of data, testing and changeover
- Project and change management (*Chapter 10*)
- Team organization and responsibilities
- Risk assessment (identify risks, measures to counter risks)
- Legal issues
- Development and maintenance process

6. Control

Identify a measurement process and metrics (*Chapter 12*) covering:

- Business contribution (channel profitability – revenue, costs, return on investment)
- Marketing effectiveness (channel outcomes – leads, sales, conversion rate; channel satisfaction)
- Online marketing effectiveness (channel behaviour – page impressions, visitors, repeat visits, conversion rates)

Control

The control element of the e-marketing plan can be achieved through a combination of traditional techniques such as marketing research to obtain customer views and opinions and novel techniques such as analysis of web server log files that use technology to monitor whether objectives are achieved. These techniques are reviewed in detail in *Chapter 12* (*p. 507*). Intranets can be used to share information among marketers and consultants within an organization. An example of such an approach is Truffles intranet (*Figure 8.15*) within OgilvyOne Worldwide which is described by Cody (2001).

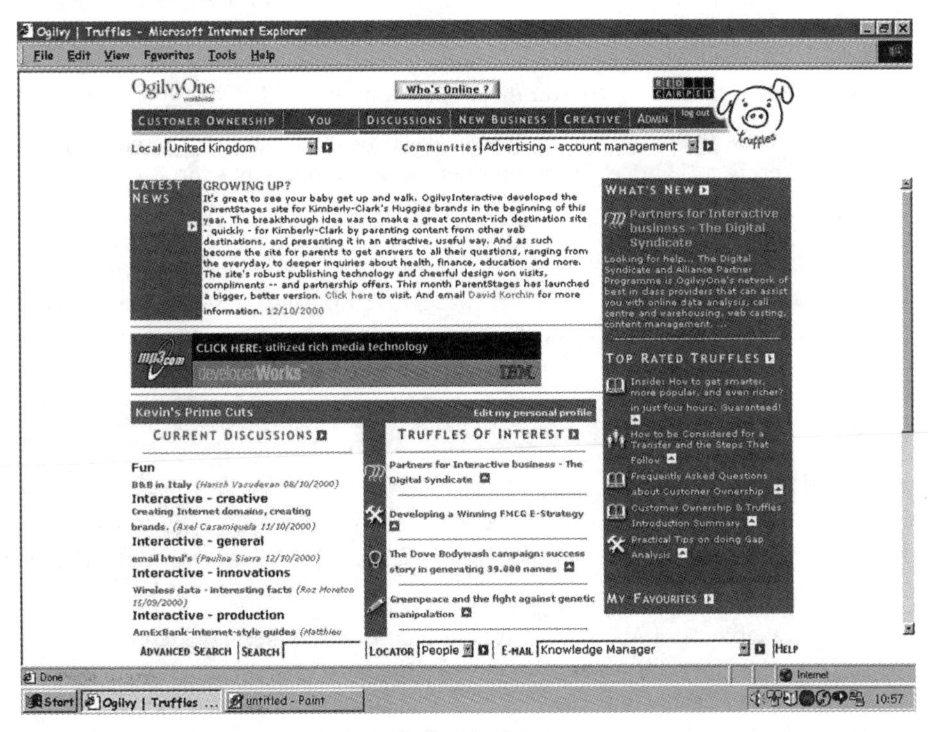

Figure 8.15 Truffles intranet for knowledge sharing

Summary

1. E-marketing is the application of technology to achieve marketing objectives, defined by the Chartered Institute of Marketing as: *'the management process responsible for identifying, anticipating and satisfying customer requirements profitability'*.

2. E-marketing can be considered a subset of e-business and is equivalent to sell-side e-commerce.

3. An e-marketing plan is often developed separately to an e-business strategy. The SOSTAC framework is used to introduce the elements of an e-marketing plan.

4. Situation analysis – involves a consideration of the external environment with the emphasis on levels of customer access to the Internet, benchmarking of competitors and new entrants.
5. Objectives setting – a key objective is setting the online revenue contribution or the percentage of sales that will be achieved online. For companies where direct sales are not practical because of the nature of the product companies may set objectives for how the web will affect marketing communications, customer service and cost reductions.
6. Strategies – through evaluating the suitability of product for direct sale a company may define a replacement (product suitable for direct sale e.g. airline tickets) or complementary strategy (product unsuitable for direct sale e.g. FMCG or consultancy services). Replacement strategies may involve changing distribution networks. Complementary strategies will involve using the Internet as an additional marketing communications channel.
7. Tactics – e-marketing tactics can be reviewed through varying the elements of the marketing mix: price, place, product, promotion, people and processes.
8. Actions – the planning of e-marketing strategy by identifying resources and timescales.
9. Control – control can be achieved through monitoring customer satisfaction and channel performance via the web site and traditional channels.

ACTIVITY ANSWERS

8.2 Competitor benchmarking

You should have identified the need to distinguish between benchmarking criteria that define the company's marketing performance in the industry and those that are specific to web marketing as follows:

- *Financial performance* (available from About Us, Investor relations and electronic copies of company reports). This information is also available from intermediary sites such as finance information or share dealing sites such as Interactive Trader International (www.iii.com) or Bloomberg (www.bloomberg.com) for major quoted companies.
- *Marketplace performance* – marketshare and sales trends and significantly the proportion of sales achieved through the Internet. This may not be available directly on the web site, but may need to use other online sources. For example, new entrant to European aviation easyJet (www.easyjet.com) has achieved over two thirds of its sales via the web site and competitors need to respond to this
- *Business and revenue models (see Chapter 2)* – do these differ from other marketplace players?
- *Marketing communications techniques* – is the customer value proposition of the site clear? Does the site support all stages of the buying decision from customers who are unfamiliar with the company through to existing customers, are special promotions used on a monthly or periodic basic? Beyond the competitor's site, how do they make use of intermediary sites to promote and deliver their services?
- *Services offered* – what is offered beyond brochureware? Is online purchase possible, what is the level of online customer support and how much technical information is available?

- *Implementation of services* – these are the practical features of site design that are described in *Chapter 12* such as aesthetics, ease of use, personalization, navigation and speed.

8.4 Integrating online and offline communications

Table 8.3 shows the integration between the channels.

Table 8.3 Examples of communications initiated by customer and company

Communication initiated by customer	*Communication initiated by company*
Phone call to company	Advert to generate awareness placed in newspaper or PC magazine
Visit to web site to review prices and specification	Phone call or e-mail by courier company to arrange delivery of PC
Phone-call or e-commerce purchase of PC	Traditional mail-out or e-mail after one year to describe upgrade service
Support call to solve problem	Traditional mail-out or e-mail after three years to describe new product offers
Complaint about repair	Call to arrange visit (from sub-contracted company)

8.5 Applying branding concepts to The B2C Company e-commerce site

1. *Brand awareness.* This is vital to the dot-com and explains the importance of their mounting large offline marketing campaigns. However, since the cost of customer acquisition using this approach is so high, some of the more successful start-ups have used more cost-effective methods such as PR or viral marketing techniques.
2. *Perceived quality.* This is a key difficulty for dot-coms. While it is straightforward, if costly, to create awareness, to build up a perception of quality may take several transactions. If a customer has one bad experience in terms of site performance or fulfilment then the rest of the branding counts for nothing and the company has lost this customer forever.
3. *Brand associations.* These are relatively unimportant compared to awareness and quality, yet sometimes branding progresses no further than describing the associations.
4. *Brand loyalty.* As mentioned in 2, loyalty is the key to success. This may be a problem for the dot-com if it is thinking in terms of customer acquisition rather than retention.

For the existing company developing an e-commerce service, the task is easier than for the dot-com. It has probably spent some years building its brand equity. Brand awareness exists already, so this needs to be reinforced to communicate to customers the online value proposition and how this enhances the brand identity. Developing an online service quality that is well received by customers is still equally important.

Many of the concepts in this activity also relate to *Chapter 9* which reviews how companies can achieve acquisition, retention and extension.

EXERCISES

Self-assessment questions

1. Explain the link between e-marketing and e-business and why they may be considered separately.
2. Outline the stages in a strategic e-marketing planning process, for each stage noting two aspects that are of particular importance for e-marketing.
3. What is the Internet contribution and what is its relevance to e-marketing strategy?
4. What factors will govern the Internet contribution that is set for a given organization?
5. Why and how should a company approach benchmarking of online competitors?
6. Describe what is meant by a complementary and replacement Internet channel strategy and give examples of products for which companies follow a particular approach.
7. Summarize new opportunities to vary the marketing mix that arise through deploying the Internet.
8. How can online and offline techniques be used in the control stage of strategy?

Essay and discussion questions

1. Select a particular market sector and assess the past, current and future customer use of the Internet as a medium to select and buy products.
2. Develop an outline strategic e-marketing plan for an organization with which you are familiar.
3. Traditional strategic planning has no relevance for the start-up company given the dynamism of the marketplace. Discuss.
4. Assess the value and importance of the Internet contribution in setting e-marketing objectives in relation to other possible objectives.
5. Explain how the e-business can make use of technology to monitor and control its operations.

Examination questions

1. Outline the stages involved in developing a strategic e-marketing plan.
2. Explain what is meant by the Internet contribution and outline how companies will decide on a realistic objective.
3. What opportunities may there be to vary the price and place components of the marketing mix when delivering services through the Internet?
4. What is a complementary Internet channel strategy and for which companies will this be most appropriate?

5. What different aspects of e-marketing should be monitored as part of controlling e-marketing? Name three examples of how technology can be used to assist monitoring.
6. Explain the strategic options available for a company currently selling the majority of its products to in a single country for product and marketplace positioning.
7. What do the concepts of reintermediation and disintermediation imply for the tactics a company employs for the promotion and place elements of the marketing mix?
8. Outline how the electronic medium requires different tactics for effective marketing communications.

REFERENCES

Aaker, D. and Joachimstahler, E. (2000) *Brand Leadership*. Free Press, New York, NY.

Ansoff, H. (1957) Strategies for diversification. *Harvard Business Review* (September–October), 113–24.

Bickerton, P., Bickerton, M. and Pardesi, U. (2000) *CyberMarketing*, 2nd edn. Butterworth-Heinemann, Oxford. Chartered Institute of Marketing series.

Breitenbach, C. and van Doren, D. (1998) Value-added marketing in the digital domain: enhancing the utility of the Internet. *Journal of Consumer Marketing*, 15(6), 559–75.

Booms, B. and Bitner, M. (1981) Marketing strategies and organization structure for service firms, in *Marketing of Services*, eds. J. Donelly, and W. George, American Marketing Association.

Chaffey, D. (2000) Achieving success in Internet marketing. *The Marketing Review*, 1, 1–23.

Chaffey, D. and Edgar, M. (2000) Measuring online service quality. *Journal of Targeting, Analysis and Measurement for Marketing*, May.

Chaffey, D., Mayer, R., Johnston, K. and Ellis-Chadwick, F. (2000) *Internet Marketing: Strategy, Implementation and Practice*. Financial Times Prentice Hall, Harlow, UK.

Chase, L. (1998) *Essential Business Tactics for the Net*. John Wiley and Sons, New York.

Chaston, I. (2000) *E-commerce Marketing*. McGraw-Hill, UK.

de Chernatony, L. and McDonald, M. (1992) *Creating Powerful Brands*. Butterworth-Heinemann, Oxford, UK.

Cody, K. (2001) Exploiting knowledge within a global company: The Truffles intranet. *Interactive Marketing*, 2(3), 264–71.

Deighton, J. (1996) The future of interactive marketing. *Harvard Business Review*, November–December, 151–62.

Deise, M., Nowikow, C., King, P. and Wright, A. (2000) *Executive's Guide to E-business. From Tactics to Strategy*. John Wiley and Sons, New York, NY.

Diamantopoulos, A. and Matthews, B. (1993) *Making Pricing Decisions. A Study of Managerial Practice*. Chapman and Hall, London.

Dibb, S., Simkin, L., Pride, W. and Ferrell, O. (2000) *Marketing. Concepts and Strategies*, 4th edn. Houghton Mifflin, Boston, MA.

Friedman, L. and Furey, T. (1999) *The Channel Advantage*. Butterworth-Heinemann, Oxford, UK.

Ghosh, S. (1998) Making business sense of the Internet. *Harvard Business Review*, March–April, 126–35.

Godin, S. (1999) *Permission Marketing*, Simon and Schuster.

Hanson, W. (2000) *Principles of Internet Marketing*. South Western College Publishing, Cincinnati.

Hoffman, D.L. and Novak, T.P. (1996) Marketing in hypermedia computer-mediated environments: conceptual foundations. *Journal of Marketing*, 60 (July), 50–68.

Hoffman, D.L. and Novak, T.P. (1997) A new marketing paradigm for electronic commerce. *The Information Society*, Special issue on electronic commerce, 13 (January–March), 43–54.

Hoffman, D.L., and Novak, T.P. (2000) How to acquire customers on the web. *Harvard Business Review*, May–June, 179–88.

Houston, F. (1986) The marketing concept: what it is and what it is not. *Journal of Marketing*, 50 (April), 81–7.

Jaworski, B. and Kohli, A. (1993) Market orientation: antecedents and consequences. *Journal of Marketing*, July, 53–70.

de Kare-Silver, M. (2000) *eShock 2000. The Electronic Shopping Revolution: Strategies for Retailers and Manufacturers*. Macmillan, London.

Kiani, G. (1998) Marketing opportunities in the digital world. *Internet Research: Electronic networking applications and policy*, 8(2), 185–94.

Kierzkowski, A., McQuade, S., Waitman, R. and Zeisser, M. (1996) Marketing to the digital consumer, *The McKinsey Quarterly*, 3, 4–21.

Kotler, P. (1997) *Marketing Management – Analysis, Planning, Implementation and Control*. Prentice Hall, Englewood Cliffs, NJ.

Levine, R., Locke, C., Searls, D. and Weinberger, D. (2000) *The Cluetrain Manifesto*. Perseus Books, Cambridge, MA.

Lewis, H and Lewis, R. (1997) Give your customers what they want. *Selling on the Net. Executive Book Summaries*, 19(3), March.

Lynch, P. and Horton, S. (1999) *Web Style Guide. Basic Design Principles for Creating Web Sites*. Yale University Press. Available online at http://info.med.yale.edu/caim/manual/contents.html.

McCarthy, J. (1960) *Basic marketing: a Managerial Approach*. Irwin, Homewood, IL.

McDonald, M. (1999) Strategic Marketing Planning: theory and practice. In *The CIM Marketing Book*, 4th edn, ed. M. Baker, Butterworth-Heinemann, Oxford, UK, pp. 50–77.

McDonald, M. and Wilson, H. (1999) *e-Marketing: Improving Marketing Effectiveness in a Digital World*. Financial Times Management, Pearson Education, Harlow, UK.

Pak, J. (1999) Content dimensions of web advertising: a cross-national comparison. *International Journal of Advertising*, 18(2), 207–31.

Parasuraman, A., Zeithaml, V. and Berry, L. (1985) A conceptual model of service quality and its implications for future research. *Journal of Marketing*, 49, Fall, 41–50.

Resnik, A. and Stern, A. (1977) An analysis of information content in television advertising. *Journal of Marketing*, January, 50–53.

Ries, A. and Ries, L. (2000) *The 11 Immutable Laws of Internet Branding*. HarperCollins Business, London, UK.

Smith, P. (1999) *Marketing Communications: An Integrated Approach*, 2nd edn. Kogan Page, London, UK.

Seybold, P. (1999) *Customers.com*. Century Business Books, Random House, London.

Valentin, E. (1996) The marketing concept and the conceptualisation of marketing strategy. *Journal of Marketing Theory and Practice*, Fall, 16–27.

FURTHER READING

Bickerton, P., Bickerton, M. and Pardesi, U. (2000) *CyberMarketing*, 2nd edn. Butterworth-Heinemann, Oxford, Chartered Institute of Marketing series. Considers each element of the marketing mix in a separate chapter.

Chaffey, D., Mayer, R., Johnston, K. and Ellis-Chadwick, F. (2000) *Internet Marketing: Strategy, Implementation and Practice*. Financial Times Prentice Hall, Harlow, UK. Chapters 5, 6 and 7 cover e-marketing strategy.

WEB LINKS

Iconcast (www.iconocast.com): weekly newsletter and supporting site, giving industry news across a range of sectors.

eMarketer (www.emarketer.com): regular reports about online marketing approaches.

Marketing Sherpa (www.marketingsherpa.com): case studies and new about e-marketing.

Marketing Online (www.marketing-online.co.uk): links and articles about different stages in achieving e-marketing.

Brand Channel (www.brandchannel.com): forum and articles about branding, produced by Interbrand.

Chapter 9

Customer relationship management

CHAPTER AT A GLANCE

LEARNING OBJECTIVES

After completing this chapter the reader should be able to:

- Outline different methods of acquiring customers via electronic media;
- Evaluate different buyer behaviour amongst online customers;
- Describe techniques for retaining customers and cross and up-selling using new media.

MANAGEMENT ISSUES

Customer relationship management involves these management issues:

- What is the balance between online and offline investment for customer acquisition?
- What technologies can be used to build and maintain the online relationship?
- How do we deliver superior service quality to build and maintain relationships?

Links to other chapters

The main related chapters are:

- *Chapter 4* – CRM techniques are constrained by social, legal and ethical factors;
- *Chapter 5* – CRM supports e-business strategy;
- *Chapter 8* – CRM is one of the tactics aimed at fulfilling the objectives defined in the e-marketing plan.

Introduction

Customer relationship management (CRM)
An approach to building and sustaining long-term business with customers.

The application of technology to achieve **customer relationship management (CRM)** is a key element of e-business. Building long-term relationships with customers is essential for any sustainable business. Failure to build relationships largely caused the failures of many dot-coms following huge expenditure on customer acquisition as explained in *Chapter 4*. The importance of customer retention to long-term profitability is well known from modelling of the type referred to in *Chapter 4*. But research summarized by Reicheld and Schefter (2000) shows that acquiring online customers is so expensive (20–30 per cent higher than for traditional businesses) that start-up companies may remain unprofitable for at least two to three years. The research also shows that by retaining just 5 per cent more customers, online companies can boost their profits by 25 per cent to 95 per cent. They say:

> *but if you can keep customers loyal, their profitability accelerates much faster than in traditional businesses. It costs you less and less to service them.*

This chapter evaluates different techniques to initiate and build relationships with customers by using a combination of online and offline techniques. The chapter is structured around three key stages of a relationship from initial customer acquisition, to retention and extension as shown by *Figure 9.1*. An alternative view of how this can be achieved in a web site is the approach Yahoo! has used to build a profitable site. The managers of the site have reported at industry conferences that an effective web site should have three characteristics:

- *Magnetic*. Acquisition of visitors by promotion and making it attractive.
- *Sticky*. Retention – keeping customers on the site once they arrive and encouraging them to engage in revenue-generating activities.
- *Elastic*. Extension – persuading customers to return, particularly for revenue-generating activities.

Customer acquisition
Techniques used to gain new customers.

Customer acquisition involves techniques used to form relationships with new customers to achieve an online sale. We will evaluate the range of marketing communications options for acquiring new customers to use e-commerce services. In order for online and offline marketing communications techniques to be effective we also need to understand the differences in communications between the old media and new media and the way the customer behaves online; distinguishing features of online customer behaviour are described in the section later in this chapter, *Focus on online customer behaviour*.

Customer retention refers to the actions an organization takes to retain existing customers.

Customer retention
Techniques to maintain relationships with existing customers.

The phase of **customer extension** refers to increasing the depth or range of products that a company purchases for a company. For example, an online bank may initially acquire a customer through use of a credit card. The relationship will be intensified if the customer can be persuaded to purchase other financial services such as loans or insurance.

Customer extension
Techniques to encourage customers to increase their involvement with an organization.

Figure 9.1 also highlights the need for **customer selection** at each stage of customer relationship management. This links CRM with target marketing and segmentation (*Chapter 8, p. 304*). In an e-commerce context we may want to select customers for acquisition who belong to a particular segment, perhaps those with high disposable income. Our tactics for acquisition would then reflect that. The reality is that given a particular campaign a range of prospects may contact the company. Selection would use tactics to dissuade those who seem to be unlikely to be profitable, since they have a high risk of moving on to another company, from becoming customers. Alternatively if a customer is unprofitable there may not be proactive approach to retention, that is, special offers will not target unprofitable customers.

Customer selection
Picking the ideal customers for acquisition, retention and extension.

You will also notice that *Figure 9.1* emphasizes the importance of adding value at each stage. This refers to ways of distinguishing the service from that of competitors.

Although the concept of CRM is prevalent in current marketing thinking and provides a valuable framework for tactics to increase loyalty and profitability, it should be noted that it may not accurately reflect the way the customer reflects their dealings with a company. Consumers may see simply their dealings with an organization as an exchange relationship and will not believe that they are tied to any company. O'Malley and Tynan (2001) note that the concept of a long-term relationship or partnership may be more readily applied to B2B marketing rather than consumer marketing. They say consumers

> *do not consider this false intimacy an interpersonal relationship. It is not driven primarily by trust, commitment, communication and shared values, but by convenience and self-interest.*

It is useful to remember this consumer perspective on relationships when considering tactics to employ to help build and maintain relationships. The variation in the nature of the relationship according to product or service type and customer buyer

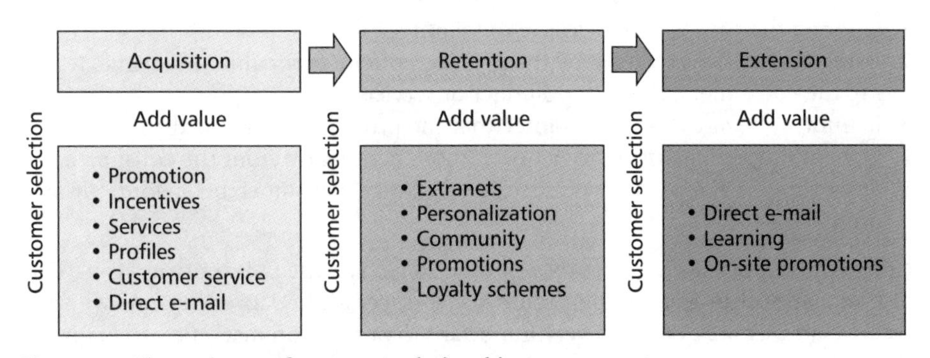

Figure 9.1 Three phases of customer relationship management

behaviour should also be considered. The article by Clemons and Row in *case study 9.1* highlights differences in the depth of relationship according to product type.

This chapter is broad in scope; in addition to looking at methods for achieving CRM, we also focus on the role of marketing communications in achieving customer acquisition and also how analysis of online buyer behaviour can be used to inform our CRM tactics.

Permission marketing

Permission marketing
Customers agree (opt-in) to be involved in an organization's marketing activities, usually as a result of an incentive.

Interruption marketing
Marketing communications that disrupt customers' activities.

To understand the thinking behind CRM, it is useful to relate it to the concept of **permission marketing** since this has been a driving force for investment in CRM. Permission marketing is a term coined by Seth Godin. Godin (1999) notes that while research used to show we were bombarded by 500 marketing messages a day, with the advent of the web and digital TV this has now increased to over 3000 a day! From an organization's viewpoint, this leads to a dilution in the effectiveness of the messages – how can the communications of any one company stand out? From the customer's viewpoint, time is seemingly in ever shorter supply, customers are losing patience and expect reward for their attention, time and information. Godin refers to the traditional approach as **interruption marketing**. Permission marketing is about seeking the customer's permission before engaging them in a relationship and providing something in exchange. The classic exchange is based on information or entertainment – a B2B site can offer a free report in exchange for a customer sharing their e-mail address which will be used to maintain a dialogue, while a B2C site can offer a screensaver in exchange. Think what the logical conclusion of this is. Companies will pay customers to view ads. This has already happened with www.alladvantage.com offering targeted customers payment in exchange for viewing ads from high-end auto brands.

From an e-commerce perspective, we can think of a customer agreeing to engage in a relationship when they agree by checking a box on a web form to indicate that they agree to receiving further communications from a company. This is referred to as **opt-in**. This is preferable to **opt-out**, the situation where a customer has to consciously agree not to receive further information.

Opt-in
A customer proactively agrees to receive further information.

Opt-out
A customer declines the offer to receive further information.

The importance of incentivization in permission marketing has been emphasized by Seth Godin who likens the process of acquisition and retention to dating someone. Likening customer relationship building to social behaviour is not new, as O'Malley and Tynan (2001) note; the analogy of marriage has been used since the 1980s at least. Godin (1999) suggests that dating the customer involves:

1. Offering the prospect an *incentive* to volunteer.
2. Using the attention offered by the prospect, offer a curriculum over time, teaching the consumer about your product or service.
3. Reinforce the *incentive* to guarantee that the prospect maintains the permission.
4. Offer additional *incentives* to get even more permission from the consumer.
5. Over time, leverage the permission to change consumer behaviour towards profits.

Notice the importance of incentives at each stage. The use of incentives at the start of the relationship and through it are key to successful relationships. As we shall see in a later section, e-mail is very important in permission marketing to maintain the dialogue between company and customer.

An allied concept to permission marketing is a movement originating in the US that is known as the Cluetrain manifesto (www.cluetrain.com). The Cluetrain relates to managers at a large organization who are unable or unprepared to listen or respond to the clues from empowered customers demanding better service and response. Clues might include high churn, rising complaints and the success of more responsive competitors. An idea of the thinking of this movement is that push marketing is inappropriate. The authors, Levine *et al.* (2000), say

> *Conversations among human beings sound human. They are conducted in a human voice. Most corporations, on the other hand, only know how to talk in the soothing, humourless monotone of the mission statement, marketing brochure, and your-call-is-important-to-us busy signal. Same old tone, same old lies. No wonder networked markets have no respect for companies unable or unwilling to speak as they do.*
>
> *Corporate firewalls have kept smart employees in and smart markets out. It's going to cause real pain to tear those walls down. But the result will be a new kind of conversation. And it will be the most exciting conversation business has ever engaged in.*

It is apparent that the Cluetrain manifesto is about using new technology to enable employees of an organization interact with and listen to their needs in a responsible way. Of course, traditional direct marketers may see this trend as dangerous and point out that to offer the incentives to form relationships in the first place and to retain customer by tempting them with new offers has long been at the heart of direct marketing and that additional push communications such as TV advertising campaigns are still important to achieve acquisition an retention.

Customer acquisition management

In an online context, **customer acquisition** can have two meanings. First, it may mean the use of the web site to acquire new customers for a company as qualified leads that can hopefully be converted into sales. Second, it may mean encouraging existing customers to engage in an *online* dialogue. Many organizations concentrate on the former, but where acquisition is well managed, campaigns will be used to achieve online conversion. For example, American Express developed a '*Go Paperless*' campaign to persuade customers to receive and review their statements online rather than by post. Phone bank *First Direct* used call centre representatives to persuade customers the benefits of bypassing them by reviewing their statements online.

Customer acquisition
Techniques used to gain qualified leads that lead to sales from new customers.

Before an organization can acquire customers through the content on its site, it must, of course, develop marketing communications strategies to attract visitors to the web site. This is vital to achieving CRM objectives, so see the *Focus on marketing communications for customer acquisition* section for a description of online and offline methods of attracting customers to an e-commerce site.

Customer profiling

To engage a customer in an online relationship, the minimum information that is needed is an e-mail address. This is the approach taken by the Pepper and Rogers site (www.1to1.com). What we really need, particularly for B2B sites, is a **qualified lead** that provides us with more information about the customer to help us decide

Qualified lead
Contact information for a customer and an indication of his or her propensity to purchase different products.

whether a customer is a good prospect who should be targeted with further communications. For B2B this could mean a visit by field sales staff or a follow-up e-mail to arrange this.

Customer profile
Information that can be used to segment a customer.

To continue the relationship it is essential to build a **customer profile** that details each customer's product interest, demographics or role in the buying decision. This will affect the type of information and services delivered at the retention stage. For the customer to give this information a company will have to offer an incentive, establish trust and demonstrate credibility. Profiling is also important for selection – to identify potential customers who are likely to be profitable and offer appropriate incentives.

Peppers and Rogers (1999) have applied their work on building *one-to-one* relationships with the customer to the web. They suggest the IDIC approach as a framework for using the web effectively to form and build relationships. IDIC stands for

1. *Customer identification.* This stresses the need to identify each customer on their first visit and subsequent visits. Common methods for identification are use of cookies or asking a customer to log on to a site.
2. *Customer differentiation.* This refers to building a profile to help segment customers. Characteristics for differentiating customers are described in *Chapter 4, p. 128.*
3. *Customer interaction.* These are interactions provided on site such as customer service questions or creating a tailored product.
4. *Customer communications.* This refers to personalization or mass-customization of content or e-mails according to the segmentation achieved at the acquisition stage. Approaches for personalization are explained in the section on *retention.*

To consider the practicalities of what is required for customer acquisition in terms of web site design complete *activity 9.1.* Remember from the section on permission marketing that incentives are key in acquisition and that they should be targeted for selection of the right customers.

Activity 9.1 Customer acquisition for the B2B and B2C companies

Purpose

To identify effective tactics for customer acquisition.

Activity

Visit the site of a B2B company such as RS Components (www.rsww.com) or a B2C company such as (www.virginmega.com) and infer the approach they use to identify customers.

For answers see p. 371

Note that although we are suggesting it is vital to capture the registration information, this should not be too 'up-front' since studies reported by Nielsen (2000) show that having to register acts as a barrier to entering sites. So the advice is delay customer registration as late as possible.

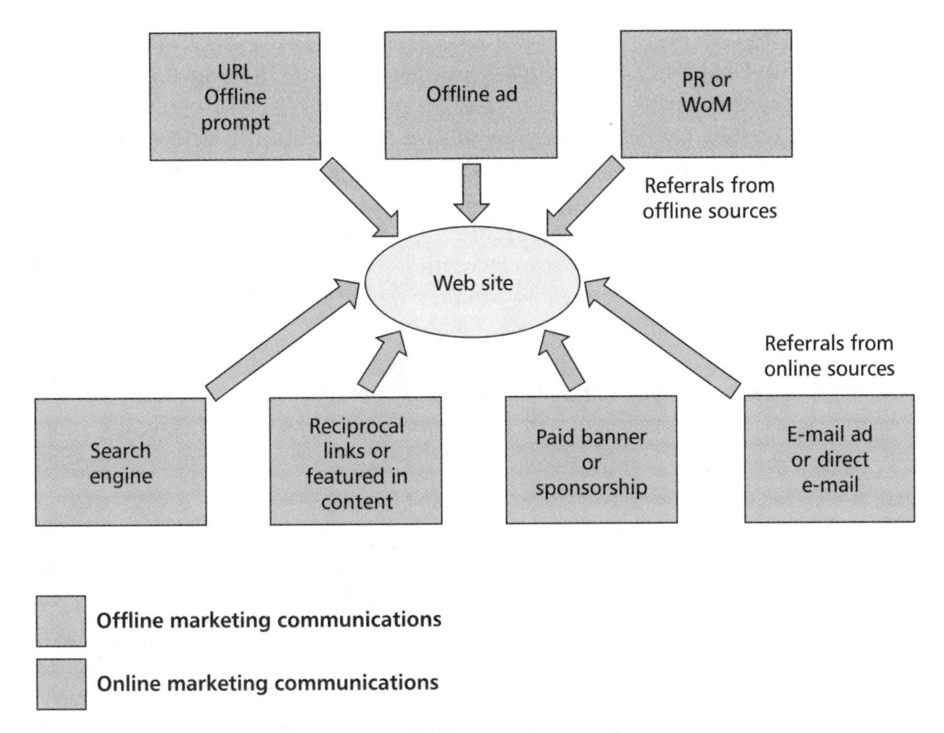

Figure 9.2 Offline and online communications techniques for e-commerce

Focus on marketing communications for customer acquisition

Managers need to consider the most effective mix of communications to drive traffic to an e-commerce site. The different techniques can be characterized as traditional **offline marketing communications** or new **online communications**. The objective of employing these techniques is to acquire new traffic on an e-commerce site using the techniques summarized in *Figure 9.2*. Many of these techniques can also be used to drive customers to a site for retention. Some other techniques to promote repeat visits are considered separately in the section on retention. Traffic volume is not the only reason for using these techniques; the method selected should also produce high quality, that is, it is consistent with the target market for an organization's services. Remember that some techniques may also have other effects such as brand building, but this is not the primary intention.

Online marketing communications
Internet-based techniques used to generate web site traffic.

Offline marketing communications
Traditional techniques such as print and TV advertising used to generate web site traffic.

As we consider the different methods of building site traffic, think about the strengths and weaknesses of each approach. These will be summarized at the end of this *Focus on* section.

Online marketing communications

In this section we shall outline the four of the main methods of online marketing communications.

1. Search engine registration

Search engines
Provide an index of content on registered sites that can be searched by keyword.

Directories or catalogues
Provide a structured listing of registered web sites and their function in different categories.

As explained in Chapter 2, **search engines** and **directories** are the primary method of finding information about a company and its products. Over 80 per cent of web users state that they use search engines to find information. It follows that if an organization is not registered with a search engine, then traffic volume will be less than optimal.

Employees who are involved with promoting a web site will want to optimize its position in listings from different search engines, so some of the factors that impact on this are outlined here. There are five main parameters on which search engines base the order of their ranking. These are mainly based on how well the keywords typed in by the searcher match against the same words on the page of your web site. They are summarized in *Table 9.1* in approximate order of importance, but note that some such as frequency of occurrence and links-in are becoming more important. For a review of current techniques refer to www.searchenginewatch.com.

Meta tags
Keywords that are part of an HTML page that result in a higher search listing if they match the typed keyword.

Table 9.1 Techniques to boost position of a web site in search engines

Factor	*Description*	*Interpretation*
1. Title	The keywords in the title of a web page that appear at the top of a browser window are indicated in the HTML code by the <TITLE></TITLE>keyword.	This is significant in search engine listings since if a keyword matches a title it is more likely to be listed highly than if it is only in the body text of a page.
2. Meta-tags	These are part of a web page, hidden from users, but used by search engines when robots or spiders compile their index. There are two types of meta tag. Example <meta name="keywords" content="book, books, shop, store"> <meta name="description" content="The largest online book store in the world.">	In most search engines, if a keyword is typed in by the user that matches the meta-tag on a site, then this site will be listed higher up the search engine listing than a site that doesn't use meta-tags.
3. Frequency of occurrence	The number of occurrences of the keyword in the text of the web page will also determine the listing. Higher listings will also occur if the keyword is near the top of the document.	Copy can be written to increase the number of times a word is used and boost position in the search engine.
4. Hidden graphic text	For example text about a company name and products can be assigned to a company logo using the 'ALT' tag as follows: <IMG NAME= 'Logo' SRC="logo.gif" ALT="The B2B Company for chemical products">	A site that uses a lot of graphical material or is less likely to be listed highly, but it is essential that the hidden graphic text keyword is used.
5. Links	Some search engines rank more highly when keywords entered are included as links. Others such as Google rank you more highly when then there are links in from other sites.	A link building campaign can help increase position in search engines also.

2. Link building

The traffic of a site will clearly increase with a greater number of links into it. Efforts to increase the number of links are sometimes referred to as link building campaigns. Techniques that can be used to increase the number of links include:

- **Reciprocal links**. These are two-way links agreed between two organizations and another organization. They have the benefit that they are free. A web ring is a similar arrangement involving more than two sites.
- *PR – content mentions*. If links to your site are featured in media sites like online newspapers or trade magazines, then this will also increase traffic.
- *Affilates*. **Affiliate networks** are widely used by e-tailers to drive traffic to a site. Amazon has in excess of 500,000 affiliates, which have links to the Amazon site. For example, a site for a particular band may have an Amazon graphic on a page which takes the user straight to CDs for that band. Of course, the benefit for the site that links to Amazon is that they will receive commission for each sale made. Building an affiliate network is now often outsourced to a specialist such as www.ukaffiliates.com.
- *Sponsorship*. Paid for sponsorship of another site, or part of it, especially a portal for an extended period is another way to develop permanent links. Co-branding is a similar method of sponsorship and can exploit synergies between different companies, but is a reciprocal arrangement.
- *Banner advertising*. This technique is widely used by large B2C companies to drive traffic to their sites so is explained in more detail.

Reciprocal links
An exchange of links between two site owners.

Affiliate networks
An e-tailer pays commission on sales referred from other sites.

3. Viral marketing

Viral marketing harnesses the network effect of the Internet and can be effective in reaching a large number of people rapidly in the same way as a computer virus can affect many machines around the world. The speed of transmission and impact of the message must be balanced by naturally negative perceptions of viruses. A simple, yet elegant method of customer acquisition is the 'e-mail a friend' facility where a form is placed on an article that enables a customer to forward the page to a colleague. Other techniques include forwarding particular info such as a screen-saver or an online postcard.

Viral marketing
E-mail is used to transmit a promotional message to another potential customer.

4. Banner advertising

The process and terminology of banner advertising is described in *Figure 9.3*.

A visitor who clicks on a banner ad on an ad site such as a portal is then trans-

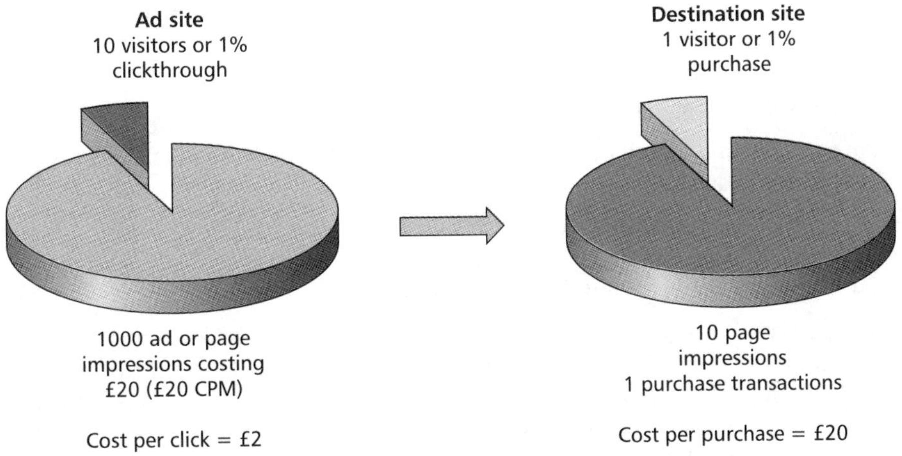

Figure 9.3 The relationship between banner ads and destination sites

ported through to the destination site of the company who paid for the banner ad. Banner ads are one of the main revenue models for the Internet so there is a lot of research into how to make them effective.

Although banner advertising can be thought of simply as a traffic-building technique, there are several alternative objectives that have been identified by Cartellieri *et al.* (1997):

- *Deliver content.* Information on-site to help communicate a company's offering.
- *Enable transaction.* An e-tailer intending to use banner ads to increase sales
- *Shape attitudes.* An advert that is consistent with a company brand can help build brand awareness.
- *Solicit response.* An advert may be intended to identify new leads or as a start for two-way communication.
- *Encourage retention.* The advert may be placed to remind about the company and its service.

Banner ads are mainly used for B2C brands, with B2B advert spend being just 5 per cent of total.

Creative content for banner ads is limited in size to the CASIE standards (www.adrelevance.com). The full banner ad is most important. Banner ads are based on .GIF graphic files that are usually hosted on a separate server. To the user, these appear as part of the web page. Interstitial adverts are incorporated within text on the page. Superstitials are pop-up adverts that require interaction by the user to close them down.

Banners can be:

- *Static* – they don't change through time.
- *Animated* – the norm with a typical rotation of three to five different images.
- *Interactive* – the user can type in an e-mail address to register for information.
- *Rich media* – using a combination of animation, video or even sound.

The top 10 banner adverts in the US can be viewed at www.nielsennetratings.com, which shows the forms of banner and creative techniques that seem to be popular.

As for traditional advertising, testing creative content is important, but banner ads have the benefit that they can be updated during the campaign in line with clickthrough response.

The creative content of many of the adverts encourages the user to click through devices such as 'Click here'.

Buying advertising

Banner advertising is purchased for a specific period. It may be purchased for the ad to be served on:

- The run-of-site (the entire site)
- A section of site
- According to keywords entered on a search engine

Payment is typically according to the number of customers who view the page as a cost per thousand (CPM) ad or page impressions. Typical CPM is in the range of £10–50. Other options that benefit the advertiser if they can be agreed are per clickthrough or per action such as a purchase on the destination site.

To target a particular segment with a banner ad, the following options are possible:

- Purchasing on a site (or part of site) with a particular visitor profile
- Purchasing at a particular time of day or week
- Buying a keyword-based advert on a portal

Banner ad campaigns can be rated by:

- Reach (the percentage of web users who see the advert)
- Recognition (spontaneous and prompted recall of advert from web users)
- Clickthrough
- Traffic quantity (thousands of visitors)
- Traffic quality (those who proactively use the site)
- Cost

Before we leave banner adverts we should note that the death of banner advertisements has been forecast since their first use, but the global value of banner advertising has increased year on year. By 1999 it had only reached $3.3 billion or 1 per cent of total global advertising value, but Forrester Research estimated that it could reach 10 per cent within five years.

The main argument for why banner ads will decline in importance is that there is currently a 'novelty value' in banner ads. New Internet users, of which there are millions each month, may click on banners out of curiosity or ignorance. More experienced users tend to filter out banner adverts concentrating mainly on the text content of the site where the ad placement is. Data at eMarketer (www.emarketer.com) shows a dramatic decline in average clickthrough rate from over 2 per cent to less than 2 per cent through time. Much ad inventory also remains unsold suggesting that supply outstrips demand.

Offline marketing communications

In this *Focus on* section we have concentrated on new techniques of online marketing communications. For detail on offline communications, the reader is referred to texts such as Fill (1999) or Smith (1999). The offline techniques that are most relevant are highlighted in *Figure 9.2*. They include advertising in established media such as print, TV and radio and using PR and word-of-mouth. A weird example of how can PR can help traffic is the case of half.com. Here, a town originally named Half, was renamed half.com for a year. In return, it received a package from company half.com totalling about $100,000, including 20 computers for its elementary school, funds for civic improvement and web site design, and support for local businesses. In the year that followed, due to national media coverage, the site half.com received over 150 million media impressions.

There are some specific management issues involved with offline marketing communications for e-commerce. A key issue is to set an appropriate objective for offline marketing communications. The main objective for much offline advertising of traditional brands seems to be simply to promote the web address (URL). Here the web site is incidental to advertising the product. If a company is serious about gaining traffic on the web site, the URL is only the starting point – the company also needs to highlight the online value proposition (*Chapter 8, p. 305*) and special sales promotions and offers to attract visitors to the site.

The use of physical reminders about an e-commerce site that are part of direct marketing is also still important to generate repeat visits since most potential customers will spend more time in the real world than the virtual world. Physical prompts to visit a site may prove effective in this case. Examples include referring to the benefits of the web sites or having special offers in brochures, catalogues, business cards, point-of-sale material, trade shows, direct mail sales promotions, postcards and inserts in magazines and password reminders. The examples in the box *Communications to encourage the customer online* show the type of copy organizations have used to encourage customers online.

Communications to encourage the customer online

B2C hardware and software e-tailer Jungle uses these messages to encourage users to adopt the Internet:

- Jungle prices ... widest choice!
  10,000s of top-brand products and big discounts
- Shop from the comfort of your home!
  No queues, no crushes, no traffic and no parking
- Online security ... Guaranteed!
- Seven-day money-back guarantee
- Part of the Argos Retail Group

B2B e-tailer RS Components promotes online ordering in its paper brochures as follows:

Why order online?

Here are some of the benefits:

- Shows stock availability as you build your order
- Checks pricing and pack quantities
- Account or credit card payment options
- Multiple delivery options

The benefits of other web site services are also highlighted:

Check the full product details online:

- Colour picture for each product
- Full technical specifications and line drawings
- Latest price information including volume discounts

Technical infozone:

- There are over 21,000 data sheets on line to view and print out
- Links to relevant datacoms sites
- Frequently asked questions

Management issues for traffic building techniques

We have reviewed a wide range of techniques that can be used to build traffic to web sites. Marketing managers have to work with agencies to agree the balance and timing of all these methods. Perhaps the easiest way to start budget allocation is to look at those activities that need to take place all year. These include search engine registration, link building, affiliate campaigns and long-term sponsorships. These

Table 9.2 Relative effectiveness of different forms of marketing communications for the B2C Company

Media	*Budget* %	*Contribution* %	*Effectiveness*
Print (Off)	20%	10%	0.5
TV (Off)	25%	10%	0.25
Radio (Off)	10%	5%	0.5
PR (Off)	5%	15%	3
WoM (Off)	0%	25%	Infinite
Banners (On)	20%	20%	1
Affiliate (On)	20%	10%	0.5
Links (On)	0%	3%	Infinite
Search engine registration (On)	0%	2%	Infinite

are often now outsourced to third-party companies because of the overhead of retaining specialist skills in-house.

Other promotional activities will follow the pattern of traditional media buying with spending supporting specific campaigns which may be associated with new product launches or sales promotions.

Managers also have to decide the overall balance of different communications techniques. A useful analytical approach to help determine overall patterns of media buying is presented in *Table 9.2*. E-commerce companies can analyse the proportion of the promotional budget that is spent on different channels and then compare this with the contribution from customers who purchased using the original channel. This type of analysis reported by Hoffman and Novak (2000) requires two different types of marketing research. First **tagging** of customers can be used. We can monitor, using cookies, the numbers of customers who are referred to a web site through a particular online technique such as search engines, affiliate or banner ads, and then track the money they spend on purchases. Secondly, for other promotional techniques, tagging will not be practical. For word-of-mouth referrals, we would have to extrapolate the amount of spend for these customers through traditional market research techniques such as questionnaires. The use of tagging enables much better feedback on the effectiveness of promotional techniques than is possible in traditional media, but it requires a large investment in tracking software to achieve it.

Tagging
Tracking of origin of customers and their spending patterns.

To summarize and conclude this section complete *activity 9.2*.

Online and offline marketing communications at Egg

Activity 9.2

Purpose

To review the balance of online and offline communications at one company and evaluate how these are achieved through site design.

Background

Financial services provider Egg (www.egg.com) was launched in October 1998. For a start-up such as Egg it is vital that the identity and proposition for the brand is clear and communicated. This is needed for the practical reason that a customer will only visit a site where a distinct, memorable web address or URL exists and the proposition of the product and site is clear. Egg has been very successful in this and has achieved name recognition with three-quarters of the UK marketplace. To communicate identity and proposition, initial expenditure on promotion in the offline media is required. Early TV campaigns featured well-known young, affluent celebrities extolling the bank's virtues. Extensive campaigns in TV and print media contributed to brand, and marketing costs for the half-year to June 2000 were £23.4 million compared to development costs of £17.7 million. Once identity is established, word of mouth is an effective method of promotion that can be facilitated by features on a web site such as 'e-mail a friend'. Online promotion methods such as banner advertising and search engine registration are also important to dot-coms and these were used by Egg on financial services-specific sites.

Once a company has been successful in attracting prospects to a site it must effectively communicate the features and benefits of its service to the potential customer. This is a challenge since this information must be communicated to create interest and desire in a few seconds before the customer loses interest! At launch, the Egg web site communicated the proposition of cash back and low interest rates very prominently with minimum words. Egg seems to have been successful in communicating this since it has recruited over one million customers in a period of three years.

The image conveyed by the web site should ideally be consistent with how the customers perceive themselves i.e. it should have a design affinity with the customer. A visit to the Egg site will show the use of images of young, dynamic people which the customer may associate with. Note, however, that a sizeable proportion of Egg's customers do not fit the ideal target customer segment, with older customers an important part of the customer base. Another aspect of affinity particularly relevant to Internet marketing is how well a company recognizes a customer's privacy as described further below.

Activity

Visit Egg.com and evaluate its success in communicating its proposition to its target audience. This site can be used to assess tools relating to a number of topics in this chapter:

1. Online buyer behaviour: how does Egg provide on-site communications for consumers at different stages of the buying process?
2. Customer service quality and community. Visit the Egg Free Zone (www.eggfreezone.com) to review customer comments about how well Egg and other e-tailers deliver their service promise.
3. Customer retention and extension. What techniques does the site use to achieve retention and achieve cross-selling?

Focus on online buyer behaviour

An understanding of novel buyer behaviour in the online environment is essential for e-marketing managers since if we understand why customers venture online we can devise effective communications that encourage them online. Chaston (2000) says:

> *Understanding consumer motivation is not an option – it's an absolute necessity for competitive survival and is now critical because of the proactive role of the customer.*

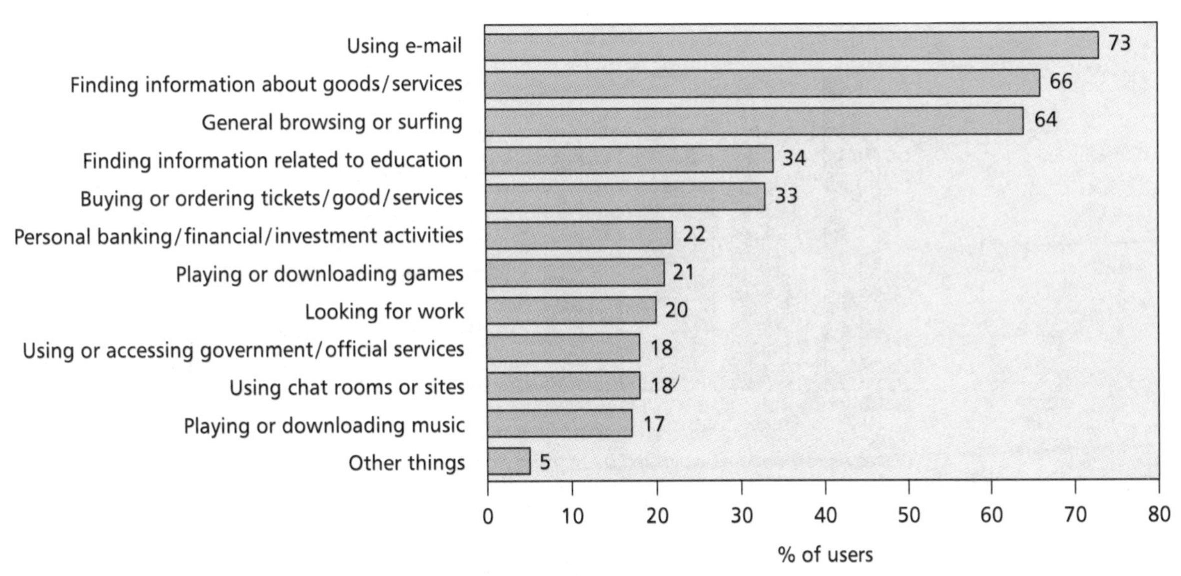

Figure 9.4 Main online activities (%) ONS data. UK source – National Statistics Omnibus Survey, October 2000. (www.statistics.gov.uk/press_release/Archive.asp)

Key online buyer activities

The drivers for online adoption are indicated by popular online activities – recent research summarized in *Figure 9.4* shows that socializing through e-mail and chat are the 'killer applications' of the Internet. It is estimated that globally four billion e-mail messages are sent daily with 300 million SMS messages. In 2000 Dell received 50,000 e-mail messages a month and 100,000 order-status-requests. Leveraging the strong desire to socialize should not be underestimated.

The second most popular activity is finding out about products, regardless of whether the purchase is to be online or offline, so we need to facilitate the process of **mixed-mode buying**. The other popular online activity is entertainment such as downloading games or music, or checking up on the latest news about a favourite band, sports team or celebrity.

Mixed-mode buying
The process by which customers change between online and offline channels during the buying process.

It is no surprise that Yahoo! is the most popular site worldwide since it offers in one place these key activities of socializing, product information, purchasing and entertainment through e-mail and chat, search engines and product guides, shopping, community and games!

For the B2B market international benchmarking studies suggest that the main drivers for adopting e-commerce for purchasing are cost/efficiency drivers. For selling, it is to tap into the global market. The DTI (2000) International Benchmarking Study showed that these were the main reasons businesses move online:

- Increasing speed with which supplies can be obtained
- Increasing speed with which goods can be despatched
- Reduced sales and purchasing costs
- Reduced operating costs

Figure 9.5 shows that looking for suppliers is an important online activity, but

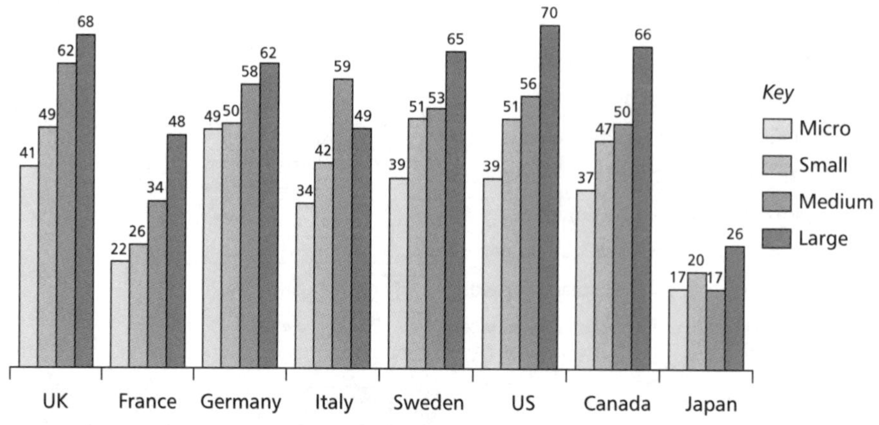

Base: All respondents weighted by number of employees

Figure 9.5 Importance of seeking suppliers online by company size.
Source: DTI (2000)

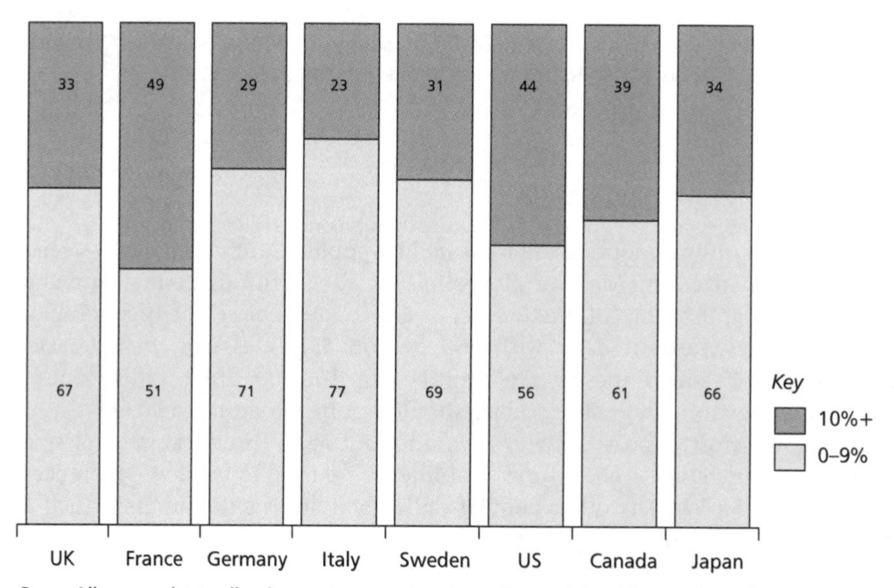

Base: All respondents allowing customers to order online weighted by number of employees

Figure 9.6 Importance of online purchasing (distinguishes between less or more than 10 per cent of puchases online)
Source: DTI (2000)

Figure 9.6 shows that although looking for suppliers is important, the proportion actually placing orders online is much lower.

In summary, for both home and business users, the Internet offers communication, information on suppliers, value-for-money and convenience in purchasing. For home users, and for business users also, it is an important social tool enabling conversations with participants known and unknown, from near and far. To encourage users online, temptation, information and reassurance should be blended into a single message as the campaign examples in the box *Communications to encourage the customer online* show.

The online buying process

Companies that understand how customers use the new media in their purchase decision making can develop integrated communications strategies that support their customers at each stage of the buying process. Considering mixed-mode buying or how a customer changes between an online channel and an offline channel during the buying process is a key aspect of devising online marketing communications since the customer should be supported in changing from one channel to another. An example of this behaviour is shown in *Figure 8.11, activity 8.4*.

The simple model of the buying process shown in *Figure 9.7* is still valuable in developing tactics to support each stage of the process, as summarized in *Table 9.3*.

Lewis and Lewis (1997) identified five different types of web users who exhibit different searching behaviour according to the purpose of using the web.

- *Directed information seekers*. Will be looking for product, market or leisure information such as details of their football club's fixtures. This type of user tends to be experienced in using the web and they are proficient in using search engines and directories.
- *Undirected information seekers*. These are the users usually referred to as surfers, who like to browse and change sites by following hyperlinks. This group tends to be novice users (but not exclusively so) and they may be more likely to click on banner advertisements.

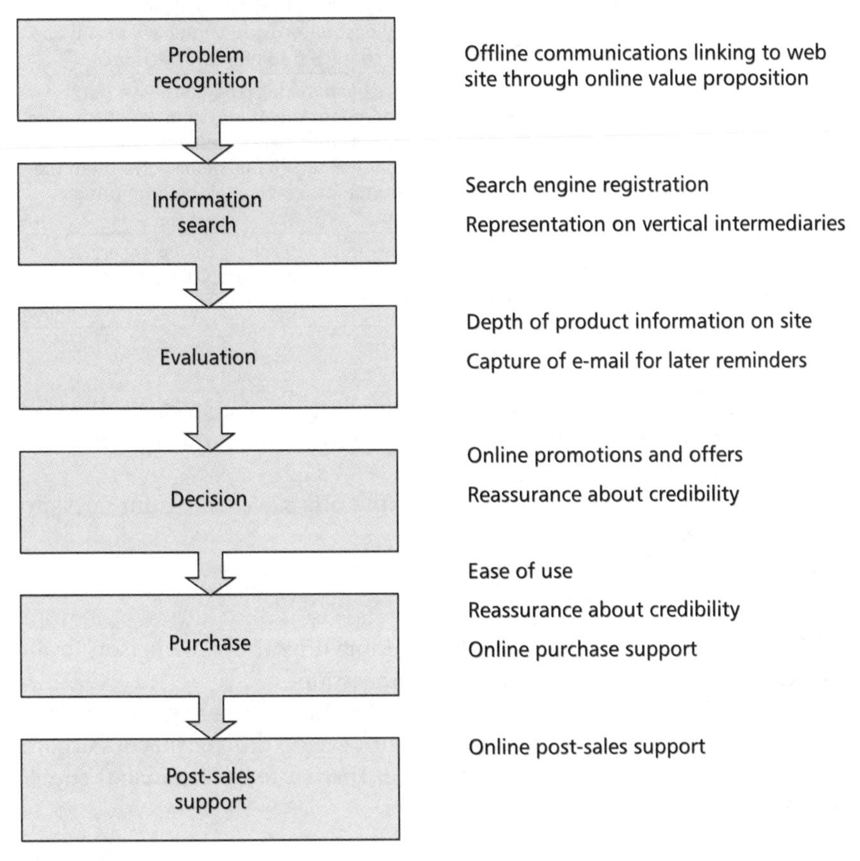

Figure 9.7 The simple buying process

Table 9.3 Tactics to support customers through different stages of the buying process

Stage	*Tactics*
1. Problem recognition	As the *Focus on marketing communications* section showed, offline advertising and media mentions are important in generating awareness of digital channels as a means by which customers can find, evaluate and purchase products.
2. Information (or supplier) search	We also need to think about different **searching behaviours**, remembering that surfing, not searching, is more important to groups with a high proportion of non-directed information seekers such as young adults. By contrast, for the B2B product, directed information seeking will be the predominant search behaviour.
3. Evaluation	Site content should communicate the features and benefits of the brand in what may be a fleeting visit to the site or an in-depth analysis. We also need to think about how to cater for different customer buying behaviour according to Internet experience. Remember that search behaviour will differ according to the four familiarities described in *Chapter 11, p. 444*.
4. Decision making	To influence decision making other channels can be used to provide mixed mode messages that reinforce the features and benefits of the product to the customer conveyed on the site. To do this we may need to provide incentives to capture an e-mail or postal address and deliver a more detailed brochure by post, or provide a call-back facility so the customer can be contacted to help the decision.
5. Purchase	Once the decision has been made to purchase, we don't want to lose the customer at this stage, so make purchasing slick through the user-centred design described in *Chapter 11* and if the customer has security anxieties, give them the choice of buying through other channels by prompting with a phone number.
6. Post purchase	Use e-mail and the web site to provide customer service and support. E-mail notifications of an order and its dispatch can help reduce post-purchase dissonance.

Searching behaviours
Approaches to finding information vary from directed to undirected.

- *Directed buyers*. These buyers are online to purchase specific products. For such users, brokers or cybermediaries who compare product features and prices will be important locations to visit.
- *Bargain hunters*. These users want to use the find offers available from sales promotions such as free samples or prizes.
- *Entertainment seekers*. Users looking to interact with the web for enjoyment through entering contests such as quizzes.

These different types of behaviour could be exhibited by the same person in different sessions online, or, less likely, in the same session.

Variation in online buyer behaviour must also be related to the type of product; read *case study 9.1* to review how companies can develop different tactics according to the type of product. The authors consider that customer behaviour should govern approaches to web retailing strategy.

CASE STUDY 9.1

Variations in online buyer behaviour and loyalty

FT

Consumer behaviour should be the principal determinant of corporate e-commerce strategy. While technology will improve, consumer loyalty, for example, is likely to differ significantly between, say, online booksellers and providers of financial services. Two factors seem critical in predicting behaviour and determining an appropriate e-commerce strategy.

First, what is the duration of the relationship between buyer and seller? That is, does the buyer have a relationship with a favourite seller, in which they come to learn about each other, or does the buyer search for a different electronic vendor for each interaction? The former suggests an opportunity for tuning offerings; the latter precludes stable relationships.

Second, what is the scope of goods and services linking buyer and seller? Does the consumer purchase a single good or service, or a bundle of related goods and services? The former suggests the consumer searches for the provider of the best individual goods and services, while the latter suggests a search for the best provider of a collection of goods and services.

Combining these indicates that different companies, in different industries, will find themselves in one or more of four competitive landscapes.

Consumers buying products that can be described as opportunistic spot purchases exhibit no loyalty; each purchase may be from a different vendor and there is no one-stop shopping. They may buy a ticket from British Airways one day and United the next, and book their hotels separately.

Opportunistic store markets occur when consumers exhibit no loyalty or relationship continuity, to brands or stores. Unlike the spot market, however, they do use intermediaries to construct bundles of goods. They may shop at Sainsbury one day and Tesco another; they may use Amazon.com one day and Buy.com another.

Consumers buying in categories that may be described as loyal links exhibit continuity when choosing vendors and service providers, but have no desire to have bundles prepared for them. They may never leave home without their American Express cards, but see no reason for their card issuer to be their insurance provider or financial planner.

Finally, consumers buying in categories that may be described as loyal chains will have preferred providers. Additionally, they will count on these providers for a range of tightly coupled offerings. They may work with a financial consultant at Merrill Lynch who helps pick stocks, reminds them to draft a will and arranges guardians for their children, helps find a lawyer and reviews their insurance. The integrated service is so effective they seldom consider switching providers or taking the time to provide these things for themselves.

Each of these environments has a different competitive feel, requires a different strategy and use of different assets. This is as true in the physical world, where companies understand it pretty well, as it is in the dot-com world, where companies are struggling to develop profitable strategies.

Note that no e-commerce company occupies just one quadrant. There are, for instance, loyal link customers and companies may pursue them with loyal link strategies, but in reality some customers may use a web site for spot purchases and others may show great loyalty. The challenge for companies is to guide the consumer to the behaviour matching the company's strategy; where this is not possible, companies should match the strategy to the customer's behaviour. The approach given here may help managers discover the forces that determine their best strategy.

Competition in opportunistic spot markets is based on price, since there is little loyalty to influence consumers' decisions. This brutal competition is exacerbated by nearly perfect web-based information. Thus, for standardized products such as the latest Harry Potter, we observe both Amazon.com and BN.com selling at cost price. Where possible, companies try to soften competition by creating quality differences and ensuring consumers are aware of them. However, this branding must be based on real differences, since with nearly perfect information it is difficult to deceive consumers. There is a limited role for intermediaries. They may reduce risk in conducting transactions, but in most instances, consumers will buy from a set of

▶ CASE STUDY *continued*

trusted, well-known manufacturers and service providers.

The Internet will be used for supply chain management and logistics to ensure the lowest cost structure and the lowest prices. It will also support access to information on consumers, both current and potential new accounts, to allow the most accurate setting of prices where differential pricing is required. That means no applicant for insurance can be undercharged based on inaccurate risk assessment and no applicant for a credit card can be given too good a deal. In a market where no one can be overcharged without losing the account, there is little margin for error and little opportunity to recover from undercharging anyone. The ability to predict the profitability of a new customer, and so to determine a price to offer, is called predictive pricing.

It is essential to recognize consumers exhibiting opportunistic spot market behaviour and to develop an appropriate marketing and pricing strategy. For example, in markets that exhibit this behaviour, buying market share is unwise since it can be acquired only temporarily; when prices are raised to cover losses, customers will flee. Similarly, a policy of offering selected items below cost as loss leaders to attract traffic will be unwise, because consumers may easily purchase loss leaders from one site and the rest of their items elsewhere. Only time will tell whether the market for books, CDs or DVDs exhibits this behaviour, so it is too early to assess the validity of Amazon.com's customer acquisition strategy or the promotional items of other web retailers.

In the absence of consumer loyalty, competition in opportunistic store markets again is based on price; however, it is the pricing of bundles rather than individual items that attracts consumers. Unlike spot markets, there are opportunities for intermediaries to add value, through logistical savings (shipping a box of books), or through assembly or integration (selling a package tour or designing a digital imaging platform where camera, printer and computer work together).

In this scenario, intermediaries enjoy power over manufacturers because consumers select bundles with little attention to components. Thus, when filling an order for paper towels, a grocer will use the product with the highest margins. This pursuit of margins, in the absence of brand loyalty from customers, shifts economic power to intermediaries.

Manufacturers will attempt to use the web for branding, to create consumer awareness of product differences and to weaken intermediaries' power. While it is dangerous to antagonize the existing channel in the opportunistic store scenario by trying to sell directly, branding offers manufacturers the ability to counter some of the power of intermediaries. As in the spot markets, manufacturers will also use the Internet to improve efficiency. Intermediaries will use the Internet to create branding for their web stores, so weakening price competition. They will use customer information, as manufacturers did in spot markets, for predictive pricing.

As in spot markets, no consumer can consistently be overcharged, so it is difficult to recover from undercharging anyone. While loss leaders can work in these markets, since a customer may fill a basket or obtain a bundle of services, there is little loyalty to assure repeat business; thus, as in spot markets, buying market share is risky since there is no assurance that initial losses can be recouped by overcharging for later purchases.

Of course there may be reasons to buy share in a 'scale-intensive' industry where volume is needed to bring down unit costs. Indeed, some aspects of online retailing, such as grocery shopping, may be extremely scale-intensive, which could initially appear to justify buying share. However, without customer loyalty, the danger is that capital will be spent more on training users to accept online shopping and less on training users to accept your online shop.

Competition in loyal link markets is based on retaining the best customers through a careful blend of service and pricing. For the customer, relationship value and pricing improve over time. For example, anecdotal evidence suggests online PC seller Dell has succeeded in creating loyal link behaviour in customers, many of whom have bought several generations of computer from Dell.

In fact, no incumbent should ever lose desirable business to an attacker. If a less well-informed competitor were to attempt to persuade a loyal customer to transfer his or her business, the current supplier could decide whether or not to match the new offer. If the current supplier, with its detailed knowledge, were to choose not to match the new offer, odds are that the new supplier is making an offer that is too low. Successful attempts to get customers to switch in loyal link markets probably represent pricing mistakes by the attacker. Relationship pricing and value work to soften pure price competition in loyal link markets.

Buying market share will work under certain conditions, since it is possible to learn enough to price effectively. However, buying market share is ineffective without loyalty, as online brokerage firms are discovering; so it is critical to assess whether the company is operating in an opportunistic spot or loyal link market.

Using loss leaders in a link market will be unrewarding; offering online banking below cost to gain credit card business is unlikely to succeed in a link market, where customers will pick the best hotel and the best air service, or the best online banking and the best credit offers, independently.

Systems will be used for branding and attracting customers and to support relationship pricing and relationship service to keep the best accounts. These markets may appear to have only a limited role for intermediaries; however, intermediaries enjoy an advantage in controlling customer information and may end up owning customer relationships.

Competition in loyal chain markets, as in loyal link markets, is based on attracting and retaining the best customers and, as in loyal link, relationship value and relationship pricing improve over time. However, in chain markets, which are composed of a tightly coupled set of links, pricing to individual customers and the value they receive are determined by a bundle of goods and services.

Taking the earlier example of the digital-imaging platform, it may not be necessary to replace all components when upgrading. However, if buying a higher-resolution camera and a faster laptop, it is helpful to determine if the new computer and the old printer are compatible, otherwise the customer may experience an unpleasant surprise if picking and choosing components in a spot or link fashion. If the previous chain supplier is used to update the components, unpleasant surprises are likely to be avoided, since his vendor can be relied upon to provide components that are compatible with those bought before. Evidence suggests Amazon has succeeded in encouraging a degree of loyal chain behaviour from its best customers, who value the book recommendations made to repeat buyers.

Loyal chain markets represent a power shift from producers to intermediaries. Online intermediaries can reconfigure the virtual store to show loyal purchasers the brands they wish to see; customers without a preference can be shown brands that earn the highest margins. Indeed, it is a small step from this relationship-based presentation to demanding rebates from manufacturers to ensure that their offerings will be shown to customers with no brand preference. While physical stores charge a fee for preferred locations such as displays near checkouts, they cannot reconfigure the store for each customer.

This shift in online power greatly increases the importance of branding for manufacturers, because a powerful brand is the best counter to pressure from retailers. It also suggests that, to the extent permitted by legislators, manufacturers should form consortia for web retailing. This would avoid loss of control to retailers with significant information advantage. However, a broad consortium is needed since online markets reward scope and breadth.

Intermediaries may effectively buy market share through pricing low, enabling them to pursue informed relationship pricing over time. Likewise, they may use loss leaders to increase traffic through their web site, selling other items to consumers interested in a complete bundle.

Systems play many roles in chain markets. Intermediaries will use them for branding, to attract customers, and for informed relationship pricing and service. Likewise, manufacturers will use the Internet for branding, so limiting price pressure from online retailers. However, efficient markets still place significant price pressure on retailers, assuring the role of systems for logistics and other forms of cost control. Likewise, manufacturers and service providers will use the web for their own cost control.

Conclusions

Three observations are true across all four competitive landscapes:

- Only differences between brands, and consumer awareness of them, can blunt pure price competition in an efficient market.
- Cost control is important: efficient access to information makes it almost impossible to overcharge.
- As online information makes markets more efficient, predictive pricing will be used in spot and store markets, and relationship pricing in link and chain markets. Pricing strategies will be limited by adverse publicity that companies receive from charging different prices for the same goods.

▶ CASE STUDY *continued*

Other conclusions follow from these:

- The role of buying market share will vary. In opportunistic markets, buyers will leave when you raise prices.
- Similarly, the role of loss leaders will vary. In spot and link markets, consumers will pick off loss leaders and do the rest of their shopping elsewhere. Once customer traffic has been acquired, there is a chance to sell extra items.

Questions

1. Summarize the characteristics of the four different types of customer behaviour by taking an example from a single market such as the financial services industry.
2. Evaluate the suitability of this framework as a method for generating e-marketing strategies.

Source: Clemons and Row (2000).

Differences in buyer behaviour in target markets

As explained in *Chapter 4*, in the section on *assessing demand for e-commerce services* (p. 124), there is great variation in the proportion of user access in different countries. This gives rises to differences in buyer behaviour within different countries or within different segments according to how sophisticated customers are in their use of the Internet. Complete *activity 9.3* to gain an appreciation of these differences.

Activity 9.3 **Differences in Internet usage in different countries**

Purpose

To highlight differences in the use of the Internet at home in different countries.

Table 9.4 Nielsen//NetRatings average Internet usage in different countries, April 2000

Measure	*United States*	*Australia*	*Ireland*	*New Zealand*	*Singapore*	*United Kingdom*
Number of sessions per month	19	12	9	15	13	11
Page views per month	671	468	358	421	506	400
Time spent per month	9:26:23	7:10:47	4:29:49	7:25:13	6:52:51	5:10:32
Duration of a page viewed	0:00:51	0:00:56	0:00:45	0:01:04	0:00:48	0:00:47
% access at home		43		44	50	42
% access at work		28		28	22	24
Current Internet universe estimate (those who had access, but did not necessarily go online)	130.2 million	6.3 million	713,000	1.3 million	1.7 million	18.0 million

Source: Nielsen//NetRatings, April 2000.

Activity

Review *Table 9.4* and summarize the differences in usage of the Internet in different countries and regions. What overall similarities are there?

For answers, see p. 371

Differences between B2C and B2B buyer behaviour

Major differences in buyer behaviour exist between B2B and B2C markets, and these must be accommodated in e-marketing communications. The main differences are:

1. Market structure
2. Nature of the buying unit
3. Type of purchase
4. Type of buying decision
5. Communication differences

Market structure

One of the main differences between business-to-business and business-to-consumer, which is important when considering the promotion of a web site, is the number of buyers. As Kotler (1997) points out, there tend to be *far fewer but larger buyers*. What are the implications of this? Firstly, with fewer buyers, the existence of suppliers tend to be well known. This means that efforts to promote the web site using methods such as banner advertising or listing in search engines are less important than for consumer brands. Existing customers can be contacted directly, by post or e-mail where this has been collected, or sales representatives can be used to make customers aware of the web site and how it can help them in their work. Of course, for business-to-business suppliers with many potential customers, then the promotion methods used will correspond more closely to those of the retail market. Secondly, the existence of larger buyers is likely to mean that each is of great value to the supplier. The supplier therefore needs to understand the buyers' needs from the web site and put effort in to develop the web-based content and services necessary to deliver these services. The type of services to support the customer relationship have been summarized well by Patricia Seybold in her book *Customers.com* and eight key factors are summarized in *Chapter 11 (p. 445)* in designing for customer orientation. An assessment of how the principles she suggests for an effective business strategy for the Internet apply particularly to the business-to-business market is presented in the mini-case study. To implement such principles for a business often implies the development of personalized web content such as Dell's Premier Pages which are accessed using an extranet.

There may also be a correspondingly small number of competitors in a market. For example, there are five main train-makers in the world such as ABB AdTranz. This is significant from a market research point of view. To provide potential and existing clients with information each will publish information about new contracts, new products and testimonials from existing customers. This information will also of be of great interest to competitors. The web provides a means of finding such information more rapidly and tends to give greater depth of information than other sources. This has led to companies employing staff specifically to find and summarize information from competitors.

With the need to put information on the web to support customers and encourage loyalty, there is a danger of giving away too much information – 'giving away the crown jewels'. Thus, a careful balance needs to be struck between disclosing too much information and supplying less information than competitors. The use of extranets where businesses have to log-in to find information is one solution to this, but passwords are notoriously insecure. An employee of a customer could be recruited on the basis of their access to a password or knowledge of competitors.

Nature of the buying unit

Business purchases typically involve a more complex decision-making process since more people are involved. Webster and Wind (1972) identified:

- Users
- Influencers
- Buyers
- Deciders
- Gatekeepers

This complexity is needed for financial control and authorization of what may be expensive products. The implications of this are that the content of the web site should be devised according to the different members of the buying unit who are going to visit the web site. While the site should make the buying process straightforward, the content should be tailored for the users, influencers and deciders. However, for situations where the buyer is the same person as the decider, as may be the case for stationery, it is important to make the whole selection and buying process as easy as possible to encourage repeat purchases. Note that it is not straightforward to tailor content for the different members of the buying unit since it is not practical to label the information under headings such as 'influencer' or 'decider', and their detailed information needs are difficult to identify!

Type of purchase

The type of purchase will vary dramatically according to scale. Companies such as the train makers referred to above will have low volume, high value orders, while others selling items such as stationery will have high-value, low-volume orders. With the low-volume, high-value purchase the Internet is not likely to be involved in the transaction itself since this will involve a special contract and financing arrangement. The high-value, low-volume orders, however, are suitable for e-commerce transactions and the Internet can offer several benefits over traditional methods of purchase such as mail and fax:

1. Easy for purchaser to assess whether item is in stock.
2. Order can be completed at any time of day or night.
3. Re-buys or repeat orders are easy to specify.
4. Delivery can be tracked online.
5. Purchasing history can be reviewed.

The design of the site should provide facilities such as the modified rebuy or allow the buyer to return to complete a partially complete order. The RS Components web site (www.rswww.com) which focuses on the B2B market highlights these types of facilities (*Figure 9.8*).

Type of buying decision

The buying decision for technical business-to-business products and services will typically be more complicated and lengthy than that for consumer products. There

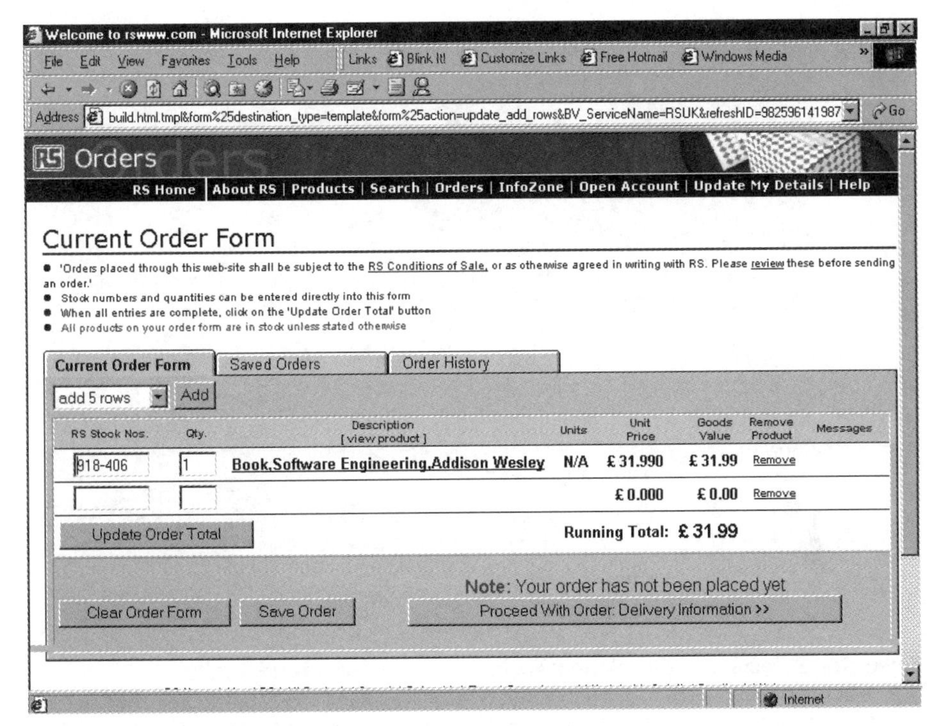

Figure 9.8 RS Components web site (www.rswww.com)

may be a lengthy period of supplier selection and product evaluation. To assist in this, business-to-business exchanges as described in *Chapter 7* (*p. 272*) have been created.

Communication differences

Fill (1999) summarizes the differences between B2B and B2C sites:

- *Balance of the communications mix.* The most important B2B elements are not typically advertising and sales communication; these are often merely vehicles to support personal selling. The Internet will not greatly change this mix.
- *Below-the-line techniques tend to be more common than above-the-line techniques.* The Internet can support these.
- *Message content.* Business products tend to be higher involvement. The Internet can help here in providing the greater depth of information needed for a high involvement product.

Customer retention management

For an e-commerce site, customer retention has two distinct goals:

1. To retain customers of the organization (repeat customers).
2. To keep customers using the online channel (repeat visits).

These are similar to the two aims of customer acquisition as described in a previous section. Ideally marketing communications should address both aims.

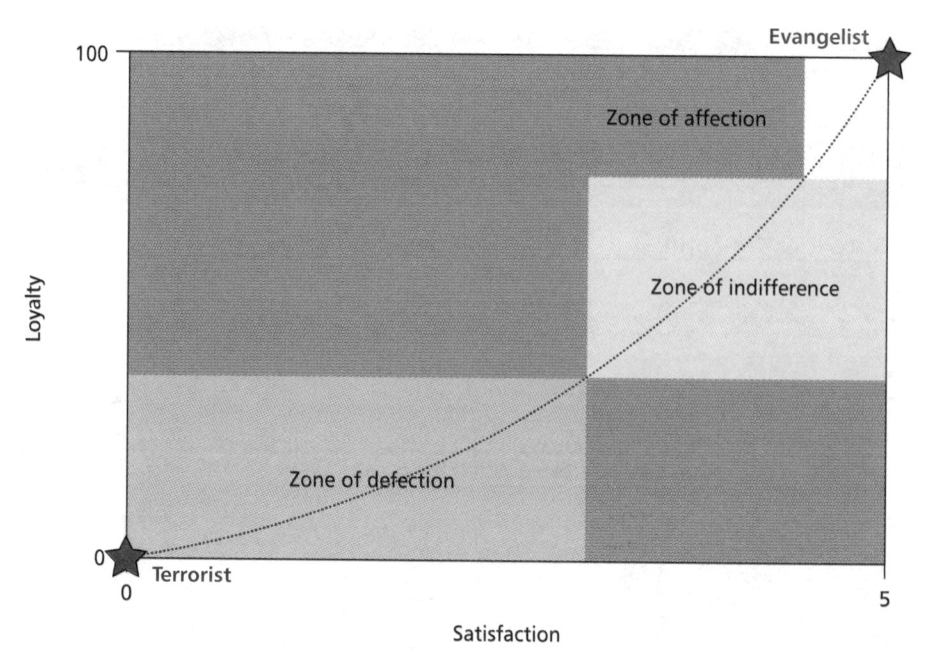

Figure 9.9 Schematic of the relationship between satisfaction and loyalty

Reprinted by permission of *Harvard Business Review*. Simplified from a graph, p. 167, from 'Putting the service–profit chain to work' by Heskett, J., Jones, T., Loveman, G., Sasser, W. and Schlesinger, L., March–April 1994. Copyright © 1994 by the Harvard Business School Publishing Corporation; all rights reserved.

Maintaining online customer relationships is difficult. Laurie Windham says:

That's what's so scary about customer retention in the online space. We've created this empowered, impatient customer who has a short attention span, a lot of choices, and a low barrier to switching.

To create long-term online customer relationships that build on acquisition, to retain and extend, we need to analyse the drivers of satisfaction amongst these e-customers, since satisfaction drives loyalty and loyalty drives profitability. The relationship is shown in *Figure 9.9*. The objective of marketers is to drive customers up the curve towards the zone of affection. However it is worth remembering that the majority are not in that zone and to achieve retention marketers must understand why customers defect or are indifferent.

It follows from *Figure 9.9* that we need to understand different factors that affect loyalty. The type of approach that can be taken is highlighted by Reicheld and Schefter (2000). They reported that Dell Computer has created a customer experience council that has researched key loyalty drivers, identified measures to track these and put in place an action plan to improve loyalty (*Table 9.5*).

Since quality of service is so crucial in determining satisfaction and loyalty, see the *Focus on excelling in e-commerce service quality* section later in this chapter.

Now let's consider key e-marketing tools that help retain customers. Repeat visits can be generated by a variety of means and brainstorming sessions can help generate these. Often it may simply be the expedient of regularly updated market and product or technical information that helps customers perform their day-to-day work or fresh content. Such information can be delivered through extranets such

Table 9.5 Relationship between loyalty drivers and measures to assess their success at Dell Computer

Loyalty drivers	*Summary metric*
1. Order fulfilment	Ship to target. % that ship on time exactly as the customer specified.
2. Product performance	Initial field incident rate – the frequency of problems experienced by customers.
3. Post sale service and support	On-time, first-time fix – the percentage of problems fixed on the first visit by a service rep who arrives at the time promised.

Source: Based on example related in Reicheld and Schefter (2000)

as Dell's Premier Pages or through personalization services such as that described for RS Components. Information to help people perform their work is the proposition of the vertical portals such as VerticalNet (www.vertical.net) that are essentially online trade papers with industry news and events. However it adds to this by providing other information such as careers and detailed product information and community. Online communities are popular for both consumer and business markets since users can discuss topical issues or ask for answers to their queries. For example, the UK Net Marketing Group at www.chinwag.com discusses the benefits of new technologies such as mobile commerce and recommends suppliers of Internet services. Many such communities work because they are independent of suppliers, so it may be difficult to introduce these types of facilities onto a corporate site. Finally, traditional sales promotion techniques translate well to the Internet. RS Components use Product of the Week or Month to discount some items and offer competitions and prize draws to encourage repeat visits. These are often publicized in offline mail-outs to encourage repeat visits.

Personalization and mass customization

The potential power of personalization is suggested by these quotes from Evans *et al.* (2000) that show the negative effects of lack of targeting of traditional direct mail:

> *Don't like unsolicited mail . . . haven't asked for it and I'm not interested.* (Female 25–34)
>
> *Most isn't wanted, its not relevant and just clutters up the table . . . you have to sort through it to get to the 'real mail'.* (Male 45–54)
>
> *It's annoying to be sent things that you are not interested in. Even more annoying when they phone you up . . . If you wanted something you would go and find out about it.* (Female 45–54)

Personalization and **mass customization** can be used to tailor information and opt-in e-mail can be used to deliver it to add value and at the same time remind the customer about a product. Personalization and mass customization are terms that are often used interchangeably. In the strict sense, personalization refers to customization of information requested by a site customer at an *individual* level. An example of personalization is given in *Figure 9.10*. Mass customization involves providing tailored content to a *group* with similar interests. An example of mass customization is when Amazon recommends similar books according to what

Personalization
Delivering individualized content through web pages or e-mail.

Mass customization
Delivering customized content to groups of users through web pages or e-mail.

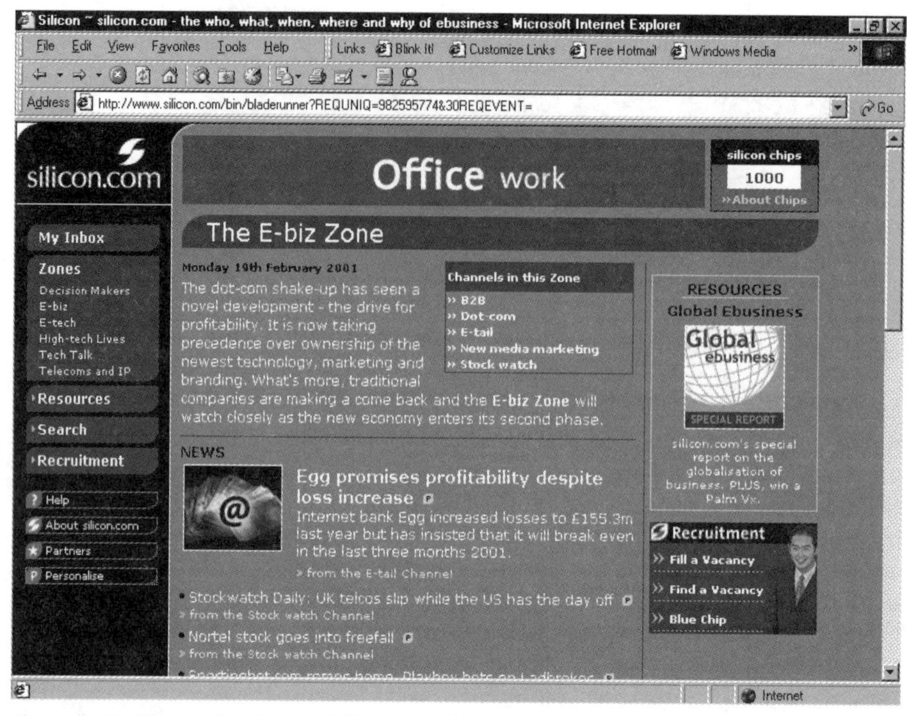

Figure 9.10 Personalization on Silicon.com (www.silicon.com) for an IT manager audience

others in a segment have offered, or if it sends a similar e-mail to customers who had an interest in a particular topic such as e-commerce. This approach is sometimes also referred to as **collaborative filtering**.

Collaborative filtering
Profiling of customer interest coupled with delivery of specific information and offers, often based on the interests of similar customers.

All these personalization techniques take advantage of the dynamic possibilities of web content. Users' preferences are stored in databases and content is taken from a database. Personalization can be achieved through several dynamic variables including:

- the customers' preferences
- the date or time
- particular events
- the location

Personalization can also be used to offer innovative services. Online bookseller BOL (www.bol.com) allows customers to choose their favourite parts from different types of travel guides, perhaps history from the Rough Guides and maps from the Lonely Planet, but excluding night clubs and restaurants. The personalized book can then be printed on demand on the customer's printer.

A more typical personalization service is that provided by the portals such as Yahoo! and Excite! These enable users to configure their home page so that it delivers the information they are most interested in. Perhaps their regional weather, the results from their soccer team and the prices of shares they have purchased.

Turning to negative aspects of personalization. There are two chief difficulties. First, cost, for the reasons explained in the next section and second, it may act as a barrier to users. For example, some personalization requires the user to log-in.

This may be a problem if a customer has mislaid a password. Equally for a new visitor to the site the need to apply for a password can be offputting and a customer may disappear, never to return. Effective personalization will still enable a new visitor to view a good deal of content even if they do not have a password. Use of *cookies* can avoid the need for the customer to log-in with this occurring automatically.

Creating personalization

Personalization of web content is much more expensive than developing static content, since it requires database integration and specialized software tools such as Broadvision and Bladerunner, which enable users to select the type of content they want, recognize them when they return and then access and display the relevant information from a database.

Extranets

Extranets were introduced in *Chapter 3*. Since they require a user to log-in they signify differential services through premium content and services. Many options are possible. A dynamic example of using an extranet is the use of the web to host online events that mirror traditional events such as seminars, trade shows and user group conferences, virtual seminars with a guest speaker by webcast, virtual trade shows where exhibitors, seminars speakers and delegates are linked by the web. Dell Computer have a special brand variant known as Premier Pages that can be used to provide value-added services for key accounts. Other traditional retention methods such as loyalty schemes and sales promotions translate well to the online environment.

The use of extranets presents a barrier to entry, particularly if users lose their passwords. To limit this effect RS Components send out password reminders to help retention. A Dutch insurer combined online and offline techniques to use an extranet to deliver mass customization. Existing customers were divided into six segments and then contacted through a direct mail campaign. Members of each segment were given one of six passwords, so that when they accessed the extranet there were six different versions of content for the web site giving product suggestions and offers consistent with the segment. Extranets provide good traceability of marketing outcomes and tagging of visitors. In this case the effectiveness of this campaign in terms of response rate from the e-mail and conversion to sales could also be monitored for different segments.

Opt-in e-mail

Opt-in e-mail is vital in communicating the retention offers either through regular e-mail communications such as a newsletter or higher impact irregular e-mail communications such as details of a product launch. Remember that e-mail has the power of traditional push communication. It enables a targeted message to be pushed out to a customer to inform and remind and they are certain to view it within their e-mail inbox; even if it is only deleted, it cannot be ignored. Contrast this with the web – a pull medium where customers will only visit your site if there is a reason or a prompt to do this.

Despite its potential, use of e-mail for marketing has negative connotations due to **SPAM**. Spam is best known as tinned meat, but a modern version of this acronym is 'Sending Persistent Annoying e-Mail'. The negative perception of e-mail derives

SPAM
Unsolicited e-mail (usually bulk mailed and untargeted).

from the many unsolicited e-mails we have all received from unscrupulous 'get rich quick merchants'. The spammers rely on sending out millions of e-mails in the hope that even if there is only a 0.01 per cent response they may make some money, if not get rich.

Many anti-spam activists have formed organizations such as CAUCE (the Coalition Against Unsolicited Commercial Email, www.cauce.org). These organizations take a dim view of commercial organizations that send unsolicited mail and prepare a list of all SPAM perpetrators. They have also been successful in creating legislation to outlaw SPAM. It is now illegal within Europe, but it is often difficult to trace the originators of SPAM since they use hijacked e-mail addresses and postal boxes to collect their money.

SPAM does not mean that e-mail cannot be used as a marketing tool. As explained in the section on *permission marketing*, opt-in is the key to successful e-mail marketing. Before starting an e-mail dialogue with customers, according to European law, companies must ask customers to provide their e-mail address and then give them the option of 'opting into' further communications. Ideally they should proactively opt-in by checking a box. E-mail lists can also be purchased where customers have opted in to receive e-mail. Review *Figure 9.11*: this suggests that opt-in e-mail is effective, but how long will this last?

Once an e-mail address has been collected, managers must plan the frequency of e-mail communications. Options include:

- *Regular newsletter type*. For example, once a day, once a week, once a month. It is best if customers are given choice about the frequency.
- *Event-related*. These tend to be less regular and are sent out perhaps every three or six months when there is news of a new product launch or an exceptional offer.
- *E-mail sequence*. Software can be purchased to send out a series of e-mails. For example, after subscription to a trial version of an online magazine, e-mails will be sent out at 3, 10, 25 and 28 days to encourage a subscription before the trial lapses.

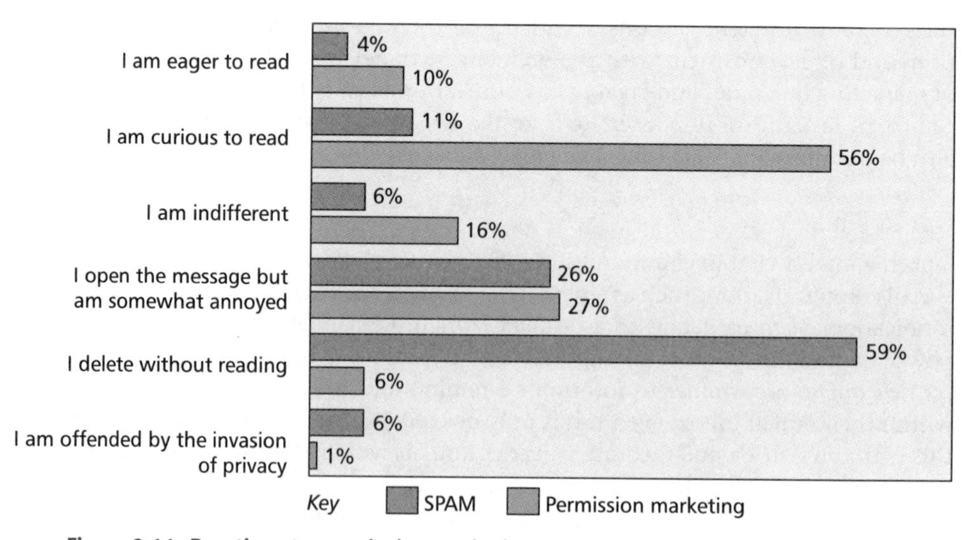

Figure 9.11 Reactions to permission marketing vs SPAM
Source: DTI (2000)

To consider the strengths and weaknesses of these techniques in more detail complete activity 9.4.

Online communities

Community is a key feature of the new interactive media that distinguishes them from traditional push media. But why is community important? Hagel and Armstrong (1997) say:

Community
A customer-to-customer interaction delivered via e-mail groups, web-based discussion forums or chat.

> *The rise of virtual communities in online networks has set in motion an unprecedented shift from vendors of goods and services to the customers who buy them. Vendors who understand this transfer of power and choose to capitalise on it by organizing virtual communities will be richly rewarded with both peerless customer loyalty and impressive economic returns.*

What is the reality behind this vision? How can companies deliver the promise of community? The key to successful community is customer-centred communication. It is a customer-to-customer (C2C) interaction. Consumers, not businesses, generate the content of the site, e-mail list or bulletin board. Its success and essential power can be gauged by the millions of customers who used Napster and Gnutella to download MP3 music files using the peer-to-peer (P2P) approach where these companies act as intermediaries to enable users to exchange files – a global swap shop. As well as these high-profile examples of successful C2C community there is also often untapped potential for applying community on any organization's web site. Remember that the C2C approach can be integrated into B2C and B2B sites.

Depending on market sector, an organization has a choice of developing different types of community for B2C, communities of purpose, position, interest and communities of profession for B2B.

1. *Purpose* – People who are going through the same process or trying to achieve a particular objective. Examples include those researching cars, such as Autotrader (www.autotrader.co.uk), or stocks online, such as the Motley Fool (www.motleyfool.co.uk). Price or product comparison services such as MySimon, Shopsmart and Kelkoo serve this community. At sites such as Bizrate (www.bizrate.com), the Egg Free Zone (www.eggfreezone.com) or Alexa (www.alexa.com), companies can share their comments on companies and their products.
2. *Position.* People who are in a certain circumstance such as a health disorder or in a certain stage of life such as communities set up specifically for young people and old people. Examples are teenage chat site Dobedo (www.dobedo.co.uk), Cennet, www.cennet.co.uk/ 'New horizons for the over 50s', www.babycenter.com and www.parentcentre.com for parents and the Pet Channel (www.thepetchannel.com).
3. Interest. This community is for people who share an interest or passion such as sport (www.football365.com), music (www.pepsi.com), leisure (www.walkingworld.com) or any other interest (www.deja.com).
4. *Profession.* They are important for companies promoting B2B services. For example Vertical Net has set up over 50 different communities to appeal to professionals in specific industries such as paints and coatings, the chemical industry or electronics. These B2B vertical portals can be thought of as 'trade papers on

steroids'. In fact, in many cases they have been created by publishers of trade papers, for example, EMAP Business Communications has created Construction Plus for the construction industry. Each has industry and company news and jobs as expected, but also offers online storefronts and auctions for buyers and sellers and community features such as discussion topics. Of course the trade papers such as Emap's *Construction Weekly* are responding by creating their own portals.

You will notice that most of these examples of community are intermediary sites that are independent of a particular manufacturer or retailer. A key question to ask before embarking on a community building programme is: *'can customer interests be best served through a company-independent community?'*.

If the answer to this question is 'yes', then it may be best to form a community that is a brand variant, differentiated from its parent. For example, Boots The Chemist has created Handbag.com as a community for its female customers. Another and less costly alternative is to promote your products through sponsorship or co-branding on an independent community site or portal or get involved in the community discussions.

What tactics can organizations use to foster community? Despite the hype and potential, many communities fail to generate activity, and a silent community isn't a community. Parker (2000) suggests eight questions organizations should ask when considering how to create a customer community:

1. What interests, needs or passions do many of your customers have in common?
2. What topics or concerns might your customers like to share with each other?
3. What information is likely to appeal to your customers' friends or colleagues?
4. What other types of business in your area appeal to buyers of your products and services?
5. How can you create packages or offers based on combining offers from two or more affinity partners?
6. What price, delivery, financing or incentives can you afford to offer to friends (or colleagues) which your current customers recommend?
7. What types of incentives or rewards can you afford to provide customers who recommend friends (or colleagues) who make a purchase?
8. How can you best track purchases resulting from word-of-mouth recommendations from friends?

A good approach to avoiding these problems is to think about the problems you may have with your community-building efforts. Typical problems are:

1. *Empty communities*. A community without any people isn't a community. The traffic-building techniques mentioned in the earlier section need to be used to communicate the proposition of the community.
2. *Silent communities*. A community may have many registered members, but community is not a community if the conversation flags. This is a tricky problem. You can encourage people to join the community, but how do you get them to participate? Here are some ideas.
   - Seed the community. Use a moderator to ask questions or have a weekly or monthly question written by the moderator or sourced from customers. Have a resident independent expert to answer questions. Visit the communities on Monster (www.monster.co.uk) to see these approaches in action and think about what distinguishes the quiet communities from the noisy ones.

- Make it select. Limit it to key account customers or set it up as an extranet service that is only offered to valued customers as a value-add. Members may be more likely to get involved.

3. *Critical communities*. Many communities on manufacturer or retailer sites can be critical of the brand, see the Egg Free Zone, for example (www.eggfreezone.com). Think about whether this is a bad thing. It could highlight weaknesses in your service offer to customers and competitors, but enlightened companies use community as a means to better understand their customers' needs and failings with their services. Community is a key market research tool. Also, it may be better to control and contain these critical comments on your site rather than them being voiced elsewhere in newsgroups where you may not notice them and can less easily counter them. The computer-oriented newsgroup on Monster shows how the moderator lets criticisms go so far and then counters them or closes them off. Particular criticisms can be removed.

Finally, remember the *lurkers* – those who read the messages but do not actively contribute. There may be ten lurkers for every active participant. The community can also positively influence these people and build brand.

Retention techniques for The B2B Company

Activity 9.4

Purpose

To develop skills of evaluating technology-led marketing options.

Activity

You have limited resources for investment in the techniques described in the section on customer retention management. Select two techniques from personalization, extranets, opt-in e-mail marketing and online communities, and explain why you have chosen them over the others. Have you chosen technology-led marketing options or marketing-led technology options?

For answers see p. 372

Focus on excelling in e-commerce service quality

F

In their article, Clemons and Row (2000) say:

> *Only differences between brands, and consumer awareness of them, can blunt pure price competition in an efficient market.*

In the virtual world customer service is a key difference between brands. Jevons and Gabbet (2000) also stress the importance of service quality in determining brand loyalty with reference to e-commerce. They say: '*the first-hand experience of the brand is a more powerful token of trust than the perception of the brand*'.

Research across industry sectors suggests that the quality of service is a key determinant of loyalty. Feinberg *et al.* (2000) report that if reasons why customers leave a company are considered, over 68 per cent leave because of 'poor service experience', with other factors such as price (10 per cent) and product issues (17 per cent) less significant. Poor service experience was broken down as:

- Poor access to the right person (41 per cent)
- Unaccommodating (26 per cent)
- Rude employees (20 per cent)
- Slow to respond (13 per cent)

This survey was conducted for traditional business contacts, but it is instructive since these reasons given for poor customer service have their equivalents online through e-mail communications and delivery of services on-site.

Delivering service quality in e-commerce can be assessed through reviewing existing frameworks for determining levels of service quality. Those most frequently used are based on the concept of a 'service-quality gap' that exists between the customers, *expected* level of service (from previous experience and word-of-mouth communication) and their perception of the *actual* level of service delivery.

Parasuraman *et al.* (1985) suggested these dimensions of service quality on which consumers judge expected and delivered service quality levels are:

- tangibles – the physical appearance and visual appeal of facilities;
- reliability – the ability to perform the service consistently and accurately;
- responsiveness – a willingness to help customers and provide prompt service;
- assurance – the knowledge and courtesy of employees and their ability to convey trust and confidence;
- empathy – providing caring, individualized attention.

Note that there has been heated dispute about the validity of this SERVQUAL instrument framework (Parasuraman *et al.*, 1985) in determining service quality, see for example Cronin and Taylor (1992). Despite this it is still instructive to apply these dimensions of service quality to customer service on the web. We will now review each dimension of SERVQUAL.

Tangibles

It can be suggested that the tangibles dimension is influenced by ease of use and visual appeal based on the structural and graphic design of the site. Design factors that influence this variable are described in *Chapter 3* in the *Focus on on user-centred design* section. The importance of these factors to consumers is indicated by a 1999 study by Forrester Research of 8600 US consumers that found that the main reason for returning to a site were high quality content (75 per cent); ease of use (66 per cent); quick to download (58 per cent) and updated frequently (54 per cent); these were the most important aspects of web site quality mentioned. Other features of the site such as coupons and incentives; favourite brands; cutting edge technology; games; purchasing capabilities and customizable content each rated less than 20 per cent.

Reliability

The reliability dimension is dependent on the availability of the web site, or in other words, how easy it is to connect to the web site as a user. *Figure 3.10* shows that many companies fail to achieve 100 per cent availability.

Reliability of e-mail response is also a key issue; Chaffey and Edgar (2000) report on a survey of 361 UK web sites across different sectors. Of those in the sample 331 (or 92 per cent) were accessible at the time of the survey and of these, 299 provided an e-mail contact point. E-mail enquiries were sent to all of these 299 web sites; of these, nine undeliverable mail messages were received. It can be seen that at the time of the survey, service availability is certainly not universal.

Responsiveness

The same survey showed that responsiveness was poor overall: of the 290 successfully delivered e-mails, a 62 per cent response rate occurred within a 28-day period. For over a third of companies there was zero response!

Of the companies that did respond, there was a difference in responsiveness (excluding immediately delivered automated responses) from eight minutes to over 19 working days! While the mean overall was 2 working days, 5 hours and 11 minutes, the median across all sectors (on the basis of the fastest 50 per cent of responses received) was 1 working day and 34 minutes. The median result suggests that response within one working day represents best practice and could form the basis for consumer expectations.

Responsiveness is also indicated by the performance of the web site; the time it takes for a page request to be delivered to the users' browser as a page impression. *Figure 3.9* indicates that there is a wide variability in the delivery of information and hence service quality from web servers hosted at ISPs and companies should be careful to monitor this and specify levels of quality with suppliers in service level agreements (SLAs). Zona Research (2000) have conducted an analysis that suggests that $4.35 billion may be lost in e-commerce revenues due to customer 'bailout' when customers are unwilling to wait for information to download. The report notes that many customers may not be prepared to wait longer than eight seconds! The advent of systematic reporting or responsiveness by monitoring agencies such as Keynote (www.keynote.com) and ActualIT (www.actualit.com) will highlight the importance of this aspect of service quality in the future.

As explained in *Chapter 7*, effective fulfilment is also an essential part of responsiveness.

Assurance

In an e-mail context, assurance can best be considered as the quality of response. In the survey reported by Chaffey and Edgar (2000), of 180 responses received, 91 per cent delivered a personalized human response with 9 per cent delivering an automated response which did not address the individual enquiry; 40 per cent of responses answered or referred to all three questions with 10 per cent answering two questions, and 22 per cent one. Overall 38 per cent did not answer any of the specific questions posed!

A further assurance concern of e-commerce web sites is the privacy and security of customer information. A company that adheres to the UK Which Web Trader (www.which.net/webtrader) or TRUSTe principles (www.truste.org) will provide better assurance than one that does not. The following actions can be suggested to achieve assurance in an e-commerce site:

1. Provide clear and effective privacy statements
2. Follow privacy and consumer protection guidelines in all local markets
3. Make security of customer data a priority
4. Leverage independent certification bodies
5. Emphasize the excellence of service quality in all communications

Empathy

Although, it might be considered that empathy requires personal human contact, this can still be achieved, to an extent, through e-mail. Chaffey and Edgar (2000) report that of the responses received, 91 per cent delivered a personalized human response, with 29 per cent passing on the enquiry within their organization. Of these 53, 23 further responses were received within the 28-day period and 30 (or 57 per cent) of passed-on queries were not responded to further.

Provision of personalization facilities is also an indication of the empathy provided by the web site, but more research is needed as to customers' perception of the value of web pages that are dynamically created to meet a customer's information needs.

An alternative approach for considering how service quality can be delivered through e-commerce is to consider how the site provides customer service at the different stages of the buying decision shown in *Figure 9.7*. Thus quality service is not only dependent on how well the purchase itself is facilitated, but also how easy it is for customers to selects products and after-sales service, including fulfilment quality. The Epson UK site (www.epson.co.uk) illustrates how the site can be used to help in all stages of the buying process. Interactive tools are available to help users select a particular printer, diagnose and solve faults and technical brochures can be downloaded. Feedback is solicited on how well these services meet customers' needs.

It can be suggested that for managers wishing to apply a framework such as SERVQUAL in an e-commerce context there are three stages appropriate to managing the process.

1. *Understanding expectations*. Customer expectations for the e-commerce environment in a particular market sector must be understood. The SERVQUAL framework can be used with market research and benchmarking of other sites as described in *Chapter 12* to understand requirements such as responsiveness and empathy. Scenarios can also be used to identify the customer expectations of using services on a site.
2. *Setting and communicating the service promise*. Once expectations are understood, marketing communications can be used to inform the customers of the level of service. This can be achieved through customer service guarantees or promises. It is better to under-promise than over-promise. A book retailer that delivers the book in two days when three days were promised will earn the customer's loyalty better than the retailer who promises one day, but delivers in two! The enlightened company may also explain what it will do if it doesn't meet its promises – will the customer be recompensed? The service promise must also be communicated internally and combined with training to ensure that the service is delivered.
3. *Delivering the service promise*. Finally, commitments must be delivered through on-site service, support from employees and physical fulfilment. If not, online credibility is destroyed and a customer may never return.

For a summary of this section refer to *Table 9.6* which is presented as requirements from an e-commerce site that must be met for excellent customer service.

As a conclusion to this section review *activity 9.5* to gain an appreciation of solutions that e-commerce sites are using to provide service quality.

Table 9.6 Summary of factors required for online service quality

E-mail response requirements	*Website requirements*
1. Defined response times and named individual responsible for replies. 2. Use of autoresponders to confirm query is being processed. 3. Personalized e-mail where appropriate. 4. Accurate response to inbound e-mail by *customer-preferred channel*: outbound e-mail or phone call-back. 5. Opt-in and opt-out options must be provided for promotional e-mail with a suitable offer in exchange for a customer providing their information. 6. Clear layout, named individual and privacy statements in e-mail.	7. Support for customer-preferred channel of communication in response to enquiries (e-mail, phone, postal mail or in person). 8. Clearly indicated contact points for enquiries via e-mail mailto: *and* forms 9. Company internal targets for site availability and performance. 10. Testing of site usability and efficiency of links, HTML, plug-ins and browsers to maximize availability. 11. Appropriate graphic and structural site design to achieve ease of use and relevant content with visual appeal. 12. Personalization option for customers. Specific tools to help a user answer specific queries such as interactive support databases and frequently asked questions (FAQ).

Source: Chaffey and Edgar, 2000

Delivering customer support on an e-commerce site

Activity 9.6

Purpose

To review how on-site facilities are used to deliver customer service excellence.

Activity

Visit the web site of an airline and e-tailer within your country, for example British Airways (www.britishairways.com) and Lands End (www.landsend.com). Review how the site content and in particular the customer support area delivers in the SERVQUAL areas of tangibles, reliability, responsiveness, assurance and empathy. The Landsend live area of the Lands End site provides a good example of state of the art features such as online chat for customer support.

Customer extension

Customer extension has the aim of increasing the **lifetime value** of the customer to the company by encouraging cross-sales, for example, an Egg credit card customer may be offered the option of a loan or a deposit account. When a customer returns to a web site this is an opportunity for cross-selling and such offers can be communicated. Direct e-mail is also an excellent way for informing a customer about other company products and it is also useful in encouraging repeat visits by publicizing new content or promotions. E-mail is vitally important to achieving online CRM since the web site is a pull medium which the customer will only be exposed to if they decide to visit the web site and they are unlikely to do this unless there is some stimulus for this. However, e-mail is a push medium where the customer can be reminded about current promotions and offers and

Lifetime value (LTV)
The combined revenue attributable to a customer during their relationship with a company.

Customer extension
Deepening the relationship with the customer through increased interaction and product transactions.

why they should visit the web site. This is why it is so important to capture the customer's e-mail address at the acquisition stage. The use of direct e-mail to communicate promotions to customers prevents a dilemma to the online marketer since although it is potentially powerful in achieving new orders, as explained in the section on *retention*, if it is used too frequently or e-mail is unsolicited then it may achieve the opposite to the desired effect and the customer will be lost.

Many companies are now only proactively marketing to favoured customers. Seth Godin says '*Focus on share of customer, not market share – fire 70 per cent of your customers and watch your profits go up!*' One UK financial services provider has analysed characteristics of high churn rate customers, and when a new prospect fitting this profile contacts the call centre they are actively discouraged. Using these techniques it is possible to increase **share of customer**.

Share of wallet or share of customer
The proportion of customer expenditure in a particular category that belongs to a single customer.

Product evaluation and feedback

The Internet has great potential for gaining feedback from customers about use of products and customer service on the site. However, this opportunity does not seem to have been seized since, as with this chapter, the emphasis of the CRM efforts often seems to be on techniques for customer acquisition and retention. An example of detailed feedback is the Cisco site (*Figure 9.12*). Cisco also uses extranets to preview new products that are being finalized before release to market.

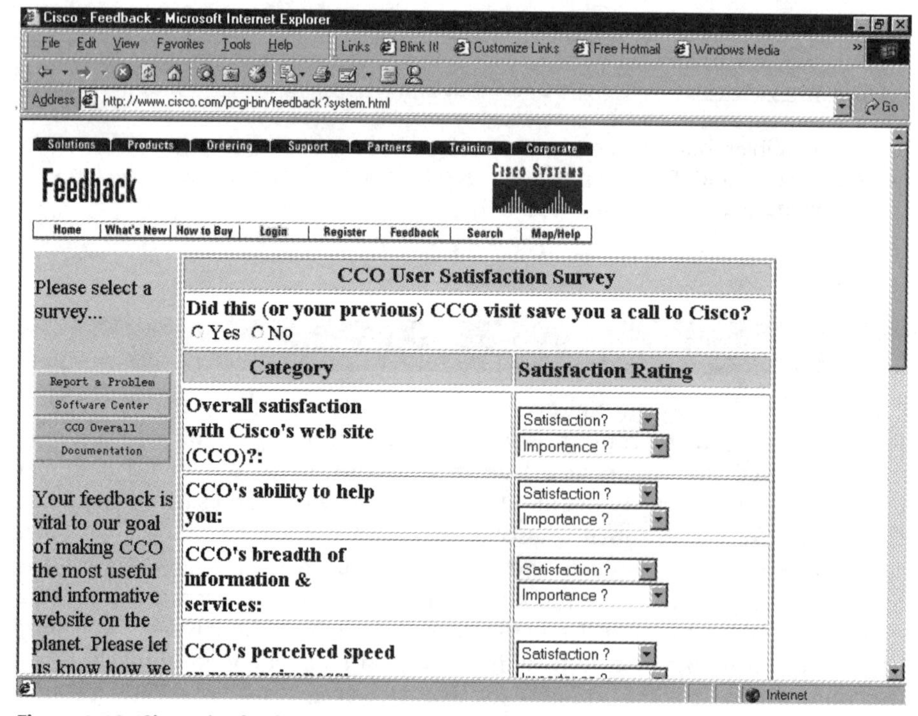

Figure 9.12 Cisco site feedback options (www.cisco.com)

Technology solutions for CRM

Case study 9.2 shows the significant expenditure on CRM solutions. In this section, we look at the options available to managers wishing to invest in CRM. The article identifies three key issues managers have to face when selecting CRM solutions and we shall review each in this section. These are:

1. Type of applications, the article identifies customer support (call centre), marketing automation and sales automation.
2. Integration with back office systems.
3. The choice of single-vendor solutions or a more fragmented choice.

CASE STUDY 9.2

Worldwide demand for CRM applications

Organizations are increasingly thinking in terms of IT systems that are linked right across an enterprise – and beyond. From the flashy web page advertising the latest range of products, through order processing, customer accounting and after-sales support, to raw material purchasing, businesses need integrated IT systems as never before.

The scramble to cope with the demands of electronic commerce (e-commerce) is one of the main driving forces. In the emerging world of e-commerce, businesses must be able to present a consistent image both to their customers and to their business partners. Inevitably, this means that IT applications must be accessible – either to users who want to use them directly or to other applications that need to invoke business processes.

Installation of a customer relationship management (CRM) system is central to most organizations' plans for electronic commerce. Industry forecasters are agreed that the markets for CRM software and services will grow rapidly in the next few years. US researcher AMR Research, for example, predicts a worldwide market for CRM of $16.8 bn by 2003 – up from $3.7 bn last year and representing a compound annual growth rate of 49 per cent.

Frost and Sullivan is less bullish but still puts worldwide annual growth at 30 per cent now, rising to 43 per cent by 2005.

The market in Europe is especially buoyant. Researcher International Data Corporation (IDC) says that from 1997 to 1998 the European market for CRM grew by 47 per cent and expects this trend to continue through 2003. It says that front-end applications – such as sales, marketing and customer support – and help desk applications are the fastest-growing segment in the applications market.

IDC expects further integration of front and back-office applications to increase demand for CRM products even more. Bill Crothers, managing partner for CRM systems in the EMEA (Europe, Middle East and Africa) region at Andersen Consulting, says the stunning growth figures are the result of a marked change in business strategy: 'A survey we conducted last year with the Economist Intelligence Unit found that there is a shift in business strategy from cost-saving management to growing the top line. With e-commerce you need insight into what your customers are doing and what they want.'

He goes on to say that often the IT systems needed to gain this insight already exist. But they must be brought together: 'You need to draw together the different strands that give you insight into the customer – data warehousing and data mining, for example – and feed those back to customer support in the call centre.'

CRM demands close integration of a wide range of applications. Indeed, the scope of CRM starts to blur the traditional distinction between 'back office' applications such as production control, distribution and accounting and 'front office' applications such as order processing, sales force automation and call centre support.

The CRM products currently on the market fall into three categories – customer support (call centre), marketing automation and sales automation. They all require links to applications such as order processing and data stores such as product and customer databases. They also need links to the web.

▶

▶ CASE STUDY *continued*

Two clear 'integration' strategies have emerged. Businesses can use one of the many so-called 'middleware' solutions – IBM's MQSeries or Microsoft's DCOM, for example – and tie their existing applications together.

Alternatively, they can buy in one of the growing number of integrated packages – many of which have emerged from the enterprise resource planning (ERP) market that grew so rapidly at the end of the 1990s.

Leading suppliers such as SAP, PeopleSoft and Baan have all planted a flag in the CRM market with extensions to their existing ERP packages.

Smaller ERP software suppliers have opted to offer links to market-leading CRM products such as Siebel and Oracle. In both cases, the creation of a seamless technology environment that can provide effective customer support is likely to be costly and time consuming – but businesses will have to bite the bullet and make their choice soon.

Technology is not the only area where integration is important, however. Mr Crothers from Andersen Consulting sees technology as only one of many changes that companies need to make to cope with the new business environment. He says: 'The technology is not really the challenge. Much more difficult is bringing the business processes together. You have to break down the barriers between the "silos". You have to get sales and marketing working with customer support. The real challenge is to get these people to work together to meet the same objectives.'

Businesses worldwide will have to face this challenge in the next two years, or find themselves isolated. There are undoubted benefits that will come from meeting the challenge successfully.

According to a survey of the CRM market, published in January 2000 by Granville Equity Research, there is every reason, despite the cost, to rate CRM as bringing a massive return on investment. It cites examples of Novell increasing quarterly revenues by $20–$30 m and Boeing cutting help desk costs by 20 per cent.

The survey also notes, however, that the failure of CRM projects is high – between 55 and 75 per cent – and the cost can be daunting. An unnamed bank is reported to have spent $100 m on CRM software with no result.

Source: 'Integration: Scramble to cope with the demands of e-commerce', by Philip Manchester, *Financial Times*, 2 February 2000

Questions

1. Why is installation of a CRM system central to most organizations' plans for electronic commerce?
2. Summarize the different types of CRM applications that are being developed in the e-business world and different approaches for introducing these types of applications.
3. The article is very positive about CRM applications. What can you identify as weaknesses of the CRM approach from the article or your own experience?

Type of CRM applications

Figure 9.13 is intended to convey the complexity of providing CRM solutions. The aim of CRM technology is to provide an interface between the customer and the employee that replaces or facilitates direct interaction. From both a customer and employee perspective, the ultimate aim of CRM systems is to enable contact regardless of the communications channel that the customer wants to use, whether this is traditional methods such as phone or fax or newer digital technologies. Thus the ideal CRM system will support multi-channel communication or the customer-preferred channel. Regardless of channel, the customer will have different needs depending on their stage in the buying process (see section on *buyer behaviour*). In the figure, we identify three core needs for the customer – to find out more information about a product, to place an order or to receive post-sales support. Applications must be provided to support each of these needs. Likewise, the

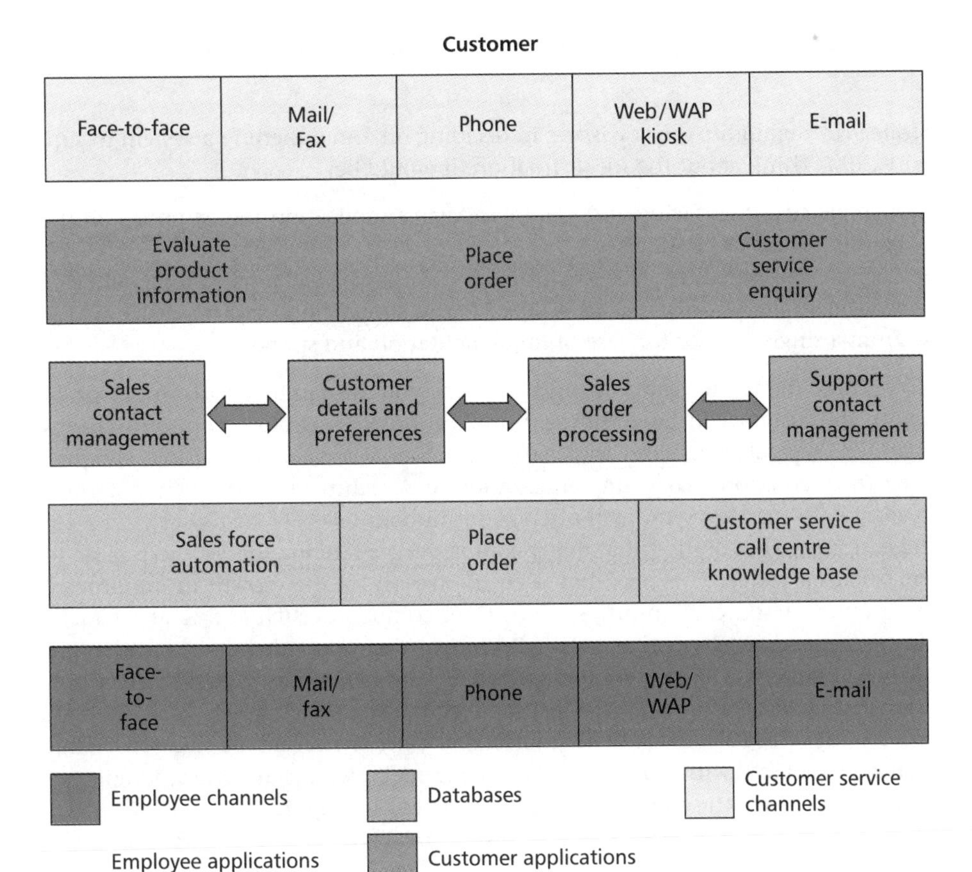

Figure 9.13 An overview of the components of CRM technologies

employee will have applications requirements to support the customer and the sales and marketing objectives of the organization; in the figure these are sales force automation, to place an order received by phone, fax or in-person and to answer customers' questions via a support system and knowledge base. At the heart of the system is the database storage needed to support these applications. The IT infrastructure described in *Chapter 3* such as servers, middleware and networking is not shown in the figure.

Integration with back office systems

When introducing a CRM system to an organization, a company will have previously invested in systems for other key business functions such as sales order processing or customer support. These existing, legacy systems appear at both the applications and database level in *Figure 9.13*. It will not be financially viable to discard these applications, but integration with them is vital to give visibility of the customer information to everyone in the organization and provide excellent customer support. Thus integration of legacy systems is a vital part of deciding on and implementing CRM systems.

The choice of single-vendor solutions or a more fragmented choice

Figure 9.13 highlights the key issues in deciding on and designing a system to support CRM. Think about the ideal situation, it would be:

- A single customer-facing and employee-facing application that supports all the communications channels
- A single integrated database such that any employee has total visibility about a customer – they can access all visit, sales and support histories
- From a single vendor for ease of implementation and support

Now think about the reality in organizations you are familiar with: in all probability the system will have different applications for different communications channels, separate databases in different functional areas and multiple vendors. Such fragmentation makes implementation and maintenance of such systems a headache for managers and will often result in poor levels of customer service for the customer. The solution that many companies are looking to move to is close to the situation above. This need has been the reason for the growth in importance of enterprise resource planning systems from companies such as SAP and Oracle. However, the difficulty is that no single company can provide best-of-breed applications in all areas. To gain competitive edge, companies may need to turn to solutions from innovators who, for example, support new channels such as WAP, provide knowledge management solutions or sales management solutions. Thus managers are faced with a precarious balancing act between standardization or core product and integrating innovative systems where applicable.

Summary

1. The objective of customer relationship management (CRM) is to increase customer loyalty in order to increase profitability. CRM is aimed at improving all aspects of the level of customer service.

2. CRM tactics can be based around the acquisition, retention, extension model of the ideal relationship between a company and customer.

3. In an e-commerce context, acquisition refers to gaining new customers to a company and converting existing customers to online services. To enable an online relationship it is important to profile customers to find out their needs and expectations and obtain an opt-in e-mail agreement to continue the dialogue.

4. Marketing communications techniques to achieve acquisition, retention and extension include traditional online mass-media techniques and specialized online techniques such as search engine registration, link building, e-mail marketing and banner advertising.

5. Techniques for customer retention include the use of extranets, online communities, online sales promotions and e-mail marketing.

6. Customer extension involves better understanding of the customer through

feedback on new product development and encouraging customers to increase the depth of their relationship by offering complementary products for purchase or increasing purchase frequency.

7. Knowledge of online buyer behaviour, and in particular, the differing needs of the customer through the different stages of the buying decision can be used to improve CRM management.
8. Customer service quality is important in achieving loyalty and the SERVQUAL framework can be used to consider how to use the Internet to achieve this.
9. Technology solutions for CRM are aimed at providing interaction between employees and customers across multiple communications channels with all customer information stored in a single database to provide complete visibility of the customer by employees. Managers look to minimize the number of solutions partners they work with to achieve these goals.
10. Specific technology application requirements for CRM are sales force automation (contact management) and call centre applications which integrate workflow to manage queries and a knowledge base from which queries can be reviewed.

ACTIVITY ANSWERS

9.1 Customer acquisition for B2B and B2C companies

Your answer should refer to:

1. Incentivization.
2. Information capture or profiling.
3. Confirmation and follow-up.

9.3 Differences in Internet usage in different countries

The following points are apparent for each measure:

- Number of sessions per month – this seems to be higher in countries such as the US and Singapore where the Internet is better established.
- Unique sites visited – this is lowest in the US; we can speculate that there is more directed information seeking to known sites rather than exploratory 'surfing'.
- Page views per month – this broadly increases with sessions per month.
- Time spent per month – this broadly increases with sessions per month. Lower connection costs in the US reflect the relatively high figure here.
- Duration of page viewed – similar, not much can be read into these figures.
- The number of active Internet users against those who could potentially use the Internet is similar in most countries, running at about 50 per cent. This suggests that actual usage is much lower than predicted by generalizations about those with access to the Internet.

The overall similarities are the relatively small number of sessions and amount of time on average spent online each month compared with other media such as TV. This report also showed that search engines and portals were the most popular categories for users in all five non-US countries. However, shopping was the most popular category in the US. This perhaps also illustrates the evolving usage of the medium.

9.4 Retention techniques for The B2B Company

Any of the answers are suitable provided the cost/benefit can be justified. For the SME, opt-in e-mail and online communities are probably the most cost-effective solution.

EXERCISES

Self-assessment questions

1. What are the goals of acquisition and retention in an online context?
2. Outline the differences between permission marketing and interruption marketing including reference to the terms opt-in and opt-out.
3. Summarize the main types of online marketing communications for traffic building.
4. Explain why mixed-mode buying needs to be understood by those managing an e-commerce site.
5. Explain a range of techniques for attracting repeat visits to a web site.
6. What is the difference between personalization and mass customization?
7. How can an e-commerce site be used to achieve extension in CRM?
8. What are the management issues in managing data and applications integration in CRM?

Essay and discussion questions

1. On what basis should marketing managers decide on the communications mix for an e-commerce site?
2. Evaluate the current communications mix for an online e-tailer and make recommendations for future communications to achieve customer acquisition and retention.
3. Show how an understanding of the online buying process can be used to revise marketing communications.
4. Explain, using examples, typical differences between a traffic building campaign for a B2B and a B2C company.
5. Examine the relationship between customer satisfaction, loyalty and sales in relation to a pure-play e-commerce site.
6. Examine the benefits and disadvantages of personalization, community building and direct e-mail. For an organization of your choice recommend a suitable balance between these e-marketing tools.
7. Assess whether a multi-vendor or single (limited number) vendor strategy is best for the implementation of eCRM systems.
8. Recommend a CRM data and application architecture for the B2C company that provides integration with related legacy systems.

Examination questions

1. Explain the concept of mixed mode buying with reference to a pure-play e-commerce bookseller.
2. You are the e-commerce manager for a B2C site. Write an explanation to be included in a report to the managing director of why a permission marketing approach is required.
3. What different types of searching behaviour are exhibited by online users and what are the implications for someone responsible for traffic building on a site?
4. With reference to customer acquisition and retention, explain two goals for each required by an e-commerce site manager.
5. Outline four different methods of building web site traffic.
6. Explain three factors that will influence the balance of online and offline web site promotion for an organization.
7. How can an e-commerce site be used to inform new product development?
8. What is a legacy system and what is its relevance to CRM?

REFERENCES

Cartellieri, C., Parsons, A., Rao, V. and Zeisser, M. (1997) The real impact of Internet advertising. *The Mckinsey Quarterly* 3, 44–63

Chaffey, D. and Edgar, M. (2000) Measuring online service quality. *Journal of Targeting, Analysis and Measurement for Marketing*, 8(4), 363–78.

Chaston, I. (2000) *E-marketing Strategy*. McGraw-Hill, UK.

Clemons, E. and Row, M. (2000) Behaviour is key to web retailing strategy. *Financial Times*, Mastering Management Supplement, 13 November.

Cronin, J. and Taylor, S. (1992) Measuring service quality: a reexamination and extension. *Journal of Marketing*, 56, 55–63.

DTI (2000) *Business In The Information Age – International Benchmarking Study 2000*. UK Department of Trade and Industry. Based on 6000 phone interviews across businesses of all sizes in eight countries. Statistics update available online at: www.ukonlineforbusiness.gov.uk.

Evans, M., Patterson, M. and O'Malley, L. (2000) Bridging the direct marketing–direct consumer gap: some solutions from qualitative research. *Proceedings of the Academy of Marketing Annual Conference*, Derby, UK.

Feinberg, R., Trotter, M. and Anton, J. (2000) At any time – from anywhere – in any form. In Renner, D. (ed.) *Defying the Limits, Reaching New Heights in Customer Relationship Management*. Report from Montgomery Research Inc, San Francisco, CA. Http://feinberg.crmproject.com.

Fill, Chris (1999) *Marketing Communications, Contexts, Contents and Strategies*, 2nd edn. Prentice Hall Europe.

Fisk, R., Grove, S. and John, J. (2000) *Interactive Services Marketing*. Houghton Mifflin, Boston, MA.

Forrester Research (1999) Strong content means a loyal audience, Forrester Research report. 27 January.

Godin, S. (1999) *Permission Marketing*. Simon and Schuster, New York.

Hagel, J. and Armstrong, A. (1997) *Net Gain: Expanding Markets through Virtual Communities*. Harvard Business Press.

Hoffman, D.L., and Novak, T.P. (2000) How to acquire customers on the web. *Harvard Business Review*, May–June, 179–88. Available online at: http://ecommerce.vanderbilt.edu/papers.html.

Jevons, C. and Gabbet, M. (2000) Trust, brand equity and brand reality in Internet business relationships: an interdisciplinary approach. *Journal of Marketing Management*, 16(6), 619–34.

Kotler, P. (1997) *Marketing Management – Analysis, Planning, Implementation and Control*. Prentice Hall, Englewood Cliffs, NJ.

Levine, R., Locke, C., Searls, D. and Weinberger, D. (2000) *The Cluetrain Manifesto*. Perseus Books, Cambridge, MA.

Lewis, H. and Lewis, R. (1997) Give your customers what they want. *Selling on the Net. Executive book summaries*, (3).

Nielsen, J. (2000) Web Research: Believe the Data. *Jakob Nielsen's Alertbox, July 11, 1999*: www.useit.com/alertbox/990711.html.

O'Malley, L. and Tynan, C. (2001) Reframing relationship marketing for consumer markets, *Interactive Marketing*, 2(3), 240–46.

Parasuraman, A., Zeithaml, V. and Berry, L. (1985) A conceptual model of service quality and its implications for future research. *Journal of Marketing*, 49, Fall, 41–50.

Parker, R (2000) *Relationship Marketing on the Web*. Adams Streetwise publication.

Peppers, B. and Rogers, P. (1999) *One-to-one Field Book*. Currency/Doubleday, NY.

Reicheld, F. and Schefter, P. (2000) E-loyalty, Your secret weapon on the web. *Harvard Business Review*, July–August, 105–13.

Smith, P.R. (1999) *Marketing Communications*, 3rd edn. Kogan Page.

Webster, F. and Wind, Y. (1972) *Organisational Buying Behaviour*. Prentice Hall, Englewood Cliffs, NJ.

Windham, L. (2001) *The Soul of the New Consumer. The Attitudes, Behaviours and Preferences of e-customers*. Allworth Press, New York, NY.

Zona Research (1999) The Economic impacts of unacceptable web-site download speeds. White paper, April 1999 (www.zonaresearch.com).

WEB LINKS

Advertising About.com (advertising.about.com): portal about advertising.

Adrelevance (www.adrelevance.com): surveys about advertising online.

AdKnowledge (www.adknowledge.com): surveys about advertising online.

Nielsen Netrating (www.nielsennetratings.com): data about global use of advertising.

Internet Advertising Bureau (www.iab.net): some articles, not updated recently.

CRMProject (www.crmproject.com): excellent collection of articles coordinated by Accenture and Montgomery research.

Customers.com (www.customers.com): supports Patricia Seybold's customers.com book, but contains many excerpts of practical strategies. Free 10-page guide worth downloading since it summarizes key concepts.

Permission marketing (www.permission.com): site supporting book by Seth Godin of Yahoo! on permission marketing. No content, but four sample chapters.

Websearch about (websearch.about.com): portal about web searching.

Searchenginewatch.com (www.searchenginewatch.com) advice on search engines from point of view of organizations hosting sites and end users.

Database Marketing (www.dbmarketing.com/articles): good source of articles, some of which refer to e-CRM.

Direct Marketing Association UK (www.dma.org.uk): source of up-to-date data protection advice and how-to guides about online direct marketing.

Personalization.com (www.personalization.com): information and analysis on web personalization.

What's New in Marketing (www.wnim.com): contains detailed monthly features on developments in C-marketing and CRM.

Part 3

IMPLEMENTATION

Management of e-business implementation is described in Part 3 of the book in which we examine practical management issues involved with creating and maintaining e-business solutions.

Chapter 10

Change management

CHAPTER AT A GLANCE

Main topics

Focus on . . .

Case studies

LEARNING OBJECTIVES

After completing this chapter the reader should be able to:

- Identify the different types of change that need to managed for e-commerce;
- Develop an outline plan for implementing e-commerce change;
- Describe alternative approaches to organization structure resulting from organizational change.

MANAGEMENT ISSUES

The issues for managers raised in this chapter include:

- Should we change organizational structure in response to e-business? If so, what are the options?
- How do we manage the human aspects of the implementation of organizational change?
- How do we share knowledge between staff in the light of high staff turnover and rapid changes in market conditions?

Links to other chapters

The main related chapters are:

- Chapters in Part 2 on strategy development should be read before this chapter since they explain the reasons for change. *Chapter 5* describes structural change for e-business.
- *Chapters 11 and 12* on strategy implementation that follow this chapter describe how the change management approach is implemented through analysis, design and implementation.

Introduction

What we anticipate seldom occurs: what we least expect generally happens.

Benjamin Disraeli

Disraeli's quote, referring to changes that need to be responded to in government, could equally be applied to the responses that are necessary by an organization venturing into e-business. However, for managing e-business within a particular organization it is possible to anticipate many of the changes that will be required by learning lessons from the pioneers of e-business. Through applying best practice and adopting risk management, it is possible to be proactive and manage change successfully.

In the chapters of Part 2 it was noted that significant changes to a company will usually be required to implement e-business successfully. In this chapter we examine the different aspects of change that may need to occur, from changes in the roles of individuals through to changes in the structure of the company.

This chapter also acts as an introduction to Part 3 of this book since it outlines the different stages of implementing change that occur as part of implementing e-business, whether it be the creation or enhancement of a web site for sell-side e-commerce, or implementation of a supply chain management or e-procurement system. Note that Part 3 concerns broad use of the term 'implementation' to describe **strategy implementation**. In *Chapter 12*, the narrower use of implementation refers to implementing the system design through coding and testing.

Strategy implementation
Execution of strategy through project planning and creation of a system through analysis, design, implementation of design and maintenance.

We start by considering the different aspects of **change management** and the chapter is then structured around the different aspects of change we need to plan for; these include:

Change management
Managing process, structural, technical, staff and culture change within an organization.

- *Schedule* – what are the suitable stages for introducing change?
- *Budget* – how do we cost e-business?
- *Resources needed* – what type of resources do we need, what are their responsibilities and where do we obtain them?
- *Organizational structures* – do we need to revise organizational structure?
- *Managing the human impact of change* – what is the best way to introduce large-scale e-business change to employees?
- *Technologies to support e-business change* – the role of knowledge management, groupware and intranets are explored.

- Finally, we summarize the aspects of change management through looking at risk management approaches to e-business led change.

Different perspectives on e-business change

Perhaps the biggest problem that is faced by both B2B and B2C companies is how to manage the change that is necessitated by e-business. *Figure 10.1* shows key aspects or levers of change that need to be assessed in order to maximize the benefits of e-business. The main change levers required are:

1. Market and business model (described in *Chapter 2*).
2. Business process (described in *Chapter 4*).
3. Organization structure, culture and staff responsibilities (described in this chapter).
4. Technology infrastructure changes (described in *Chapters 3, 9 and 11*).

These are all major changes that are required in order for an organization to be agile enough to respond to marketplaces changes and deliver competitive customer service. To help achieve these different aspects of change, a series of success factors seem to be required. These include

- management buy-in and ownership;
- effective project management;
- action to attract and keep the right staff to achieve change;
- employee ownership of change.

This chapter focuses on how to best achieve these success factors. *Activity 10.1* introduces some of the changes required by e-business.

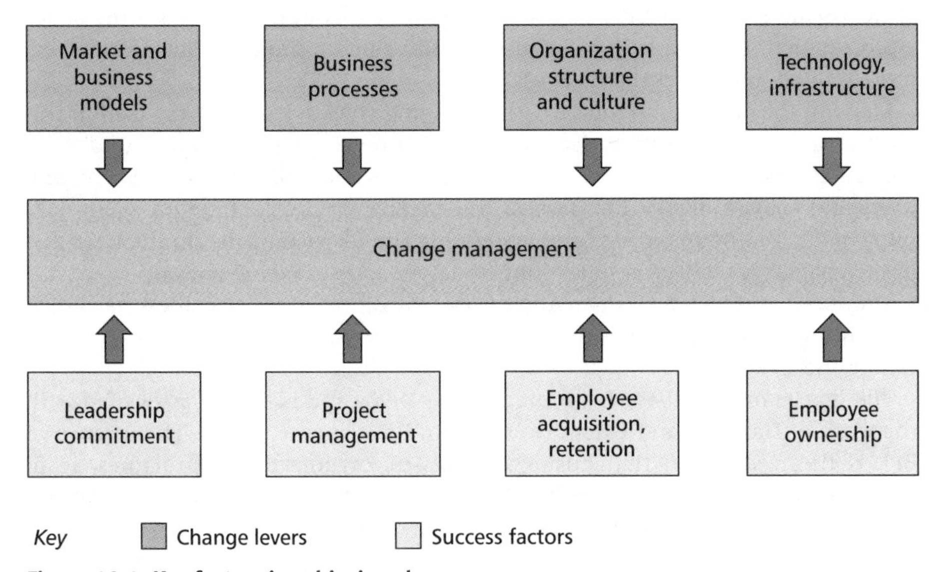

Figure 10.1 Key factors in achieving change

Activity 10.1 Managing change at The B2C Company

Purpose

To investigate the impacts of change on employees associated with e-business.

Activity

Speculate how the introduction of changes by a CEO or managing director such as those illustrated by the top four boxes of *Figure 10.1* would be affect different employees at The B2C Company. Imagine you are each of the following people: what would your reaction be on a professional and a personal level; what would be your role in affecting change?

- Marketing Manager
- Warehouse Manager
- HR Manager
- IS manager
- Employee in call-centre

For answers see p. 412

The scale of change

The change described in this chapter can be considered on two different levels. First there is a large-scale change within the business that can be characterized as e-business or business process engineering change. This change is likely to affect the whole business including functions such as marketing and fulfilment, procurement, manufacturing and the support functions of the value chain. There may be different implementation projects in each of these areas. Second, we have change on a smaller scale on a single project that has narrower objectives. Such change may be in response to an e-marketing strategy and would include a smaller-scale project to introduce a new sell-side e-commerce system, introduce e-procurement or enhance an e-commerce site. Such a project is likely to have a more limited impact on the business.

Many of the activities involved with managing change that are described in this chapter will apply equally to large-and small-scale change. Both types of change will usually be based on a project-based structure and will include planning and managing change. In the first part of the chapter we concentrate on small-scale implementation of an e-commerce system for The B2C Company, in the later part of the chapter we look at implications for larger-scale implementation.

The speed at which a company makes the transition to an e-business has much in common with approaches used to achieve **business process re-engineering (BPR)** during the 1990s.

Business process re-engineering (BPR)
Identifying radical, new ways of carrying out business operations, often enabled by new IT capabilities.

BPR has its origins at the beginning of the 1990s and is closely associated with the work of Hammer and Champy (1993) and Davenport (1993). The essence of BPR is the recognition that business processes, organizational structures, team structures and employee responsibilities can be fundamentally altered to improve business performance. Hammer and Champy (1993) defined BPR as

the fundamental rethinking and radical redesign of business processes to achieve dramatic improvements in critical, contemporary measures of performance, such as cost, quality, service, and speed.

The key words from this definition that encapsulate the BPR concept are:

- *fundamental rethinking* – re-engineering usually refers to changing of significant business processes such as customer service, sales order processing or manufacturing.
- *radical redesign* – re-engineering is not involved with minor, incremental change or automation of existing ways of working. It involves a complete rethinking about the way business processes operate.
- *dramatic improvements* – the aim of BPR is to achieve improvements measured in tens or hundreds of percent. With automation of existing processes only single figure improvements may be possible.
- *critical contemporary measures of performance* – this point refers to the importance of measuring how well the processes operate in terms of the four important measures of cost, quality, service and speed.

Similarities between BPR and the e-business concept include the extent of the change and the role of information systems; IS are central to enabling the business change. In *Re-engineering the Corporation* Hammer and Champy have a chapter giving examples of how IS can act as a catalyst for change (disruptive technologies). These technologies are familiar from applications of e-business such as those described in *Chapters 7* through *9* and include tracking technology, decision support tools, telecommunications networks, teleconferencing and shared databases. Hammer and Champy label these as 'disruptive technologies' which can force companies to reconsider their processes and find new ways of operating.

Many re-engineering projects were launched in the 1990s and failed due to their ambitious scale and the problems of managing large information systems projects. As a result BPR as a concept has fallen out of favour and more caution in achieving change is advocated. Less radical approaches are referred to as **business process improvement (BPI)** or by Davenport (1993) as business process innovation. Organizations considering e-business implementation need to agree the scale of change. In the context of *Chapter 7*, do all supply chain activities need to be revised simultaneously or can certain activities such as procurement or outbound logistics be targeted? Modern thinking would suggest that the latter approach is preferable.

Business process improvement (BPI)
Optimizing existing processes typically coupled with enhancements in information technology.

If a less radical approach is adopted, care should be taken not to fall into the trap of simply using technology to automate existing processes which are sub-optimal –

Table 10.1 Alternative terms for using IS to enhance company performance

Term	*Involves*	*Intention*	*Risk of failure*
Business process re-engineering	Fundamental redesign of all main company processes	Large gains in performance (>100%?)	Highest
Business process improvement	Targets key processes in sequence for redesign	(<50%)	Medium
Business process automation	Automating existing process	(<20%)	Lowest

Business process automation (BPA)
Automating existing ways of working manually through information technology.

in plain words, using information technology 'to do bad things faster'. Although benefits can be achieved through this approach, the improvements may not be sufficient to generate a return on investment.

A staged approach to the introduction of BPR has been suggested by Davenport (1993). This can also be applied to e-business change. He suggests the following stages that can be applied to e-business as follows:

- *Identify the process for innovation* – these are the major business processes from the organization's value chain which add most to the value for the customer or achieve the largest efficiency benefits for the company. Examples include customer relationship management, logistics and procurement.
- *Identify the change levers* – these can encourage and help achieve change. The main change levers are innovative technology and, as we have seen, the organization's culture and structure.
- *Develop the process vision* – this involves communication of the reasons for changes and what can be achieved in order to help achieve buy-in throughout the organization.
- *Understand the existing processes* – current business processes are documented. This allows the performance of existing business processes to be benchmarked and so provide a means for measuring the extent to which a re-engineered process have improved business performance.
- *Design and prototype the new process* – the vision is translated into practical new processes which the organization is able to operate. Prototyping the new process operates on two levels. First, simulation and modelling tools can be used to check the logical operation of the process. Second, assuming that the simulation model shows no significant problems, the new process can be given an full operational trial. Needless to say, the implementation must be handled sensitively if it is to be accepted by all parties.

Planning change

Our starting point for managing change is when the objectives, strategy and tactics for introducing e-business change have already been specified as outlined in Part 2. Here, we are concerned with how to implement the strategy to achieve the objectives through the activities performed by the project management team as part of project planning.

For effective project management the following elements need to be incorporated as part of the project management process as described, for example, by Bocij *et al.* (1999):

- *Estimation* – identifying the activities involved in the project, sometimes referred to as a work breakdown structure (WBS). The main tasks for an e-business system are shown in *Figure 10.2*.
- *Resource allocation* – after the initial WBS, appropriate resources can be allocated to the tasks.
- *Schedule/plan* – after resource allocation, the amount of time for each task can be determined according to the availability and skills of the people assigned to the tasks. There are two different concepts. Effort time is the total amount of work that needs to occur to complete a task. Elapsed time indicates how long in time

(such as calendar days) the task will take and is dependent on the number of people working on a task, and their skills.

- *Monitoring and control* – monitoring involves ensuring the project is working to plan once it has started. Control is taking corrective action if the project deviates from the plan. In particular the project manager will want to hit **milestones**, events that need to happen on a particular date are defined for which performance against objectives can be measured (e.g. end of analysis, production of first prototype).

Milestone
Key deadline to be achieved during project, usually with defined deliverable

The project plan and schedule for an e-business system

The project plan for an e-business system will involve all of the stages shown in *Figure 10.2*. This diagram also shows how the final part of the book is structured.

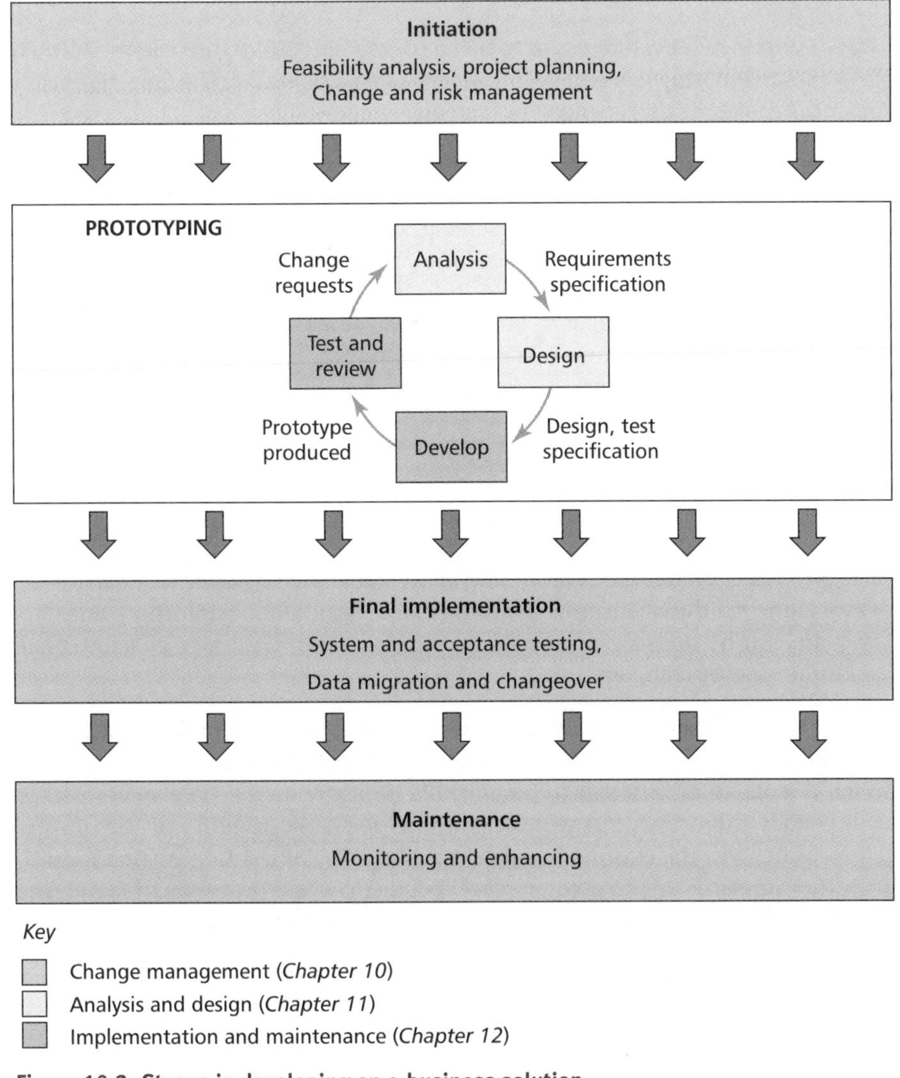

Figure 10.2 Stages in developing an e-business solution

Initiation
The start-up phase of the project.

- In *Chapter 10* we review the activities needed during the **initiation** phase of a project that involves the creation of a change management programme including project planning, managing organizational change and risk management. In this chapter we do not consider feasibility analysis since assessment of the costs and benefits of the e-business system has already been considered as an aspect of strategy as described in Part 2.
- In *Chapter 11* the analysis and design phases are described. In these the requirements of the organization and users of the system are defined and translated into a design from which the system can be built. Analysis and design occur in an iterative fashion through prototyping as described in the section that follows.
- In *Chapter 12* the final stages of developing the e-business system are described. These include writing the programme code, building the databases, migrating data, testing the system and managing the changeover to the live system. *Chapter 12* also describes the maintenance of the system once it is live. This is monitoring the system and enhancing it as bugs and opportunities arise.

Systems development lifecycle
The sequence in which a system is created from initiation, analysis, design, implementation, build and maintenance.

These stages in developing an e-business system build on well-established approaches to building IS based on the **systems development lifecycle**. But significant differences project managers need to take into account are:

- The timescales for delivery of the system are compressed compared to traditional applications – the system needs to be developed in 'Internet time'. Prototyping and making activities such as analysis, design and testing occur in parallel are used to achieve tight deadlines, as is the use of off-the-shelf systems perhaps hosted with an ASP (*Chapter 3, p. 105*).
- The e-commerce system may be hosted outside of an organization so we need to consider the constraints imposed by hosting the site externally with an ISP and integrating external components of the system with data stored and processes occurring inside an organization.
- The focus of the project is on content and services rather than an application; this means that delivery of information is the key.
- Analysis and design are arguably more closely related in an e-commerce implementation since the usability of the site is critically dependent on the needs of the user and the prototyping approach is used to achieve users' needs.
- Once launched the site is more dynamic than a traditional application: an effective site will be updated continuously in response to customer demands. The solution is never complete.

With the use of tailored off-the-shelf packages such as Siebel's CRM solutions or SAP's supply chain solutions to implement e-business, the analysis, design stages and build tends to be different to bespoke BIS implementation. The analysis stage is still equally important, but will focus on mapping the facilities of the off-the-shelf software with the existing business practices. A vital decision is the extent to which the company will change or adapt its practices and processes to match the software or the extent it will be possible to tailor the software to match the processes. With a tailored off-the-shelf approach it is inevitable that a move away from the existing business processes and practices will be required.

The design phase will require much less input than for a bespoke system. It will focus on issues of how to tailor the user interface, database structures and security of the off-the-shelf package to the needs of the e-business solution. The build and implementation phases will still be involved and as for any implementation the project manager will have to schedule software and database configuration, data migration, testing and training.

An illustration of a typical project schedule for a sell-side e-commerce system is illustrated in the box *A task breakdown and schedule for The B2C Company.* A further example is given in *Figure 12.1.*

A task breakdown and schedule for The B2C Company

Purpose

This case illustrates the different tasks that need to be performed as part of a sell-side e-commerce implementation for a company that does not have a web site presence.

The schedule can be structured as followed:

1. *Pre-development tasks.* These include domain name registration and deciding on the company to host the web site. It is important to register the domain name for the site as early as possible – there is then less risk of another company adopting the same name first. It also includes preparing a brief of the aims and objectives of the site, then if intending to outsource, presenting this to rival companies to bid.
2. *Content planning.* This is the detailed analysis and design of the site including prototyping.
3. *Content development and testing.* Writing the HTML pages, producing the graphics and testing.
4. *Publishing the site.* This is a relatively short stage.

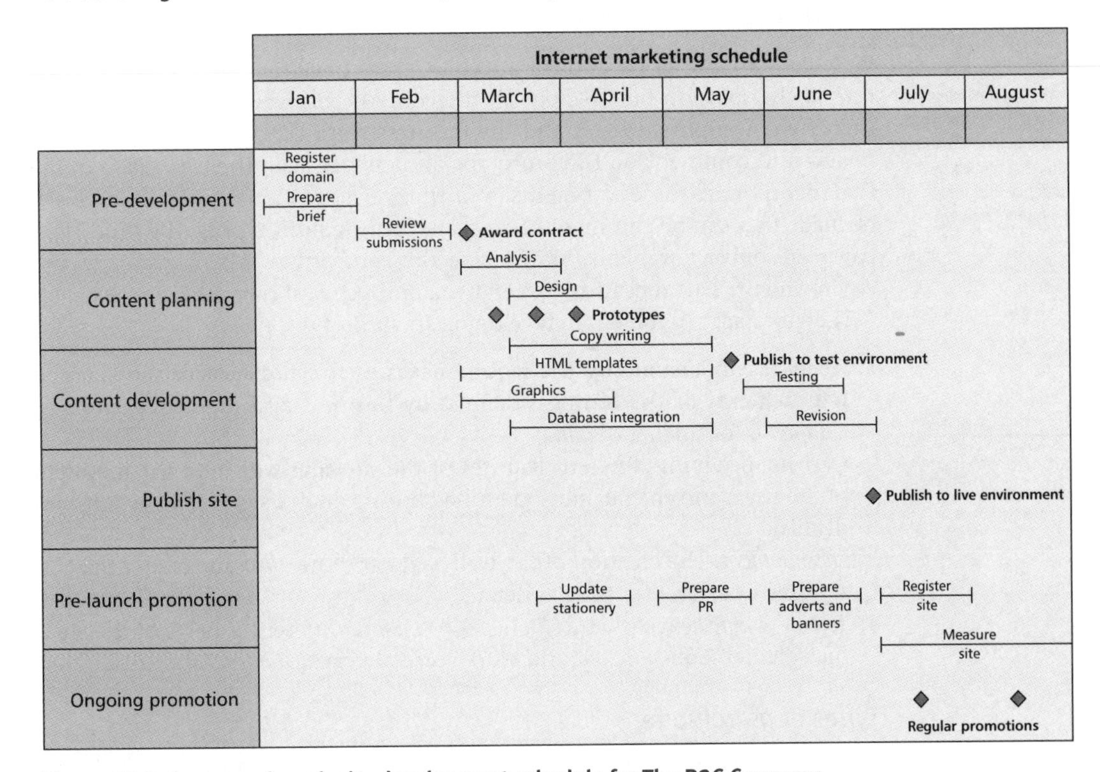

Figure 10.3 An example web site development schedule for The B2C Company

5. *Pre-launch promotion*. These are the marketing communications techniques described in *Chapter 9*.
6. *Ongoing promotion*. The schedule should also allow for periodic promotion which might involve discount promotions on the site or competitions. These are often reused each month.

Figure 10.3 gives an indication of the relationship between these tasks, and how long they may take for a typical initial e-commerce site.

Prototyping

Prototyping
Prototyping is an iterative process by which web site users suggest modifications before further prototypes and the live version of the site are developed.

Prototyping is now a popular approach to developing all kinds of BIS. It is also essential to developing e-business and e-commerce solutions. The prototyping approach has the following benefits in the context of a sell-side e-commerce site:

- It prevents major design or functional errors being made during the construction of the 'web site' that may be costly and time consuming to fix once the site becomes live and may also damage the brand. Such errors will hopefully be identified early on and then corrected.
- It involves the team responsible for the web site and ideally the potential audience of the web site in proactively shaping the 'web site'. This should result in a site that more closely meets the needs of the users.
- The iterative approach is intended to be rapid and a site can be produced in a period of months or weeks.

Prototypes
A prototype is a preliminary version of part or a framework of all of an e-business solution which can be reviewed by its target audience and the business project team.

Prototypes are initial versions of a web site that have the basic features and structure of the solution but without all the content and services in place. The idea is that the development team and the business team commissioning the work can review and comment on the prototype and changes can then be made to the site that incorporates these comments. A further version or iteration of the web site can be made that can be commented on again. During prototyping, the prototype web pages are only viewable by staff inside the company – this is known as the test environment. This repeating or iterative approach is shown in *Figure 10.2*.

The key stages involved in developing the prototype are:

1. *Analysis*. Understanding the requirements of the audience of the site and the requirements of the business defined by business and marketing strategy (see *Chapter 8* for further details).
2. *Design*. Specifying different features of the site that will fulfil the requirements of the users and the business identified during analysis (see *Chapter 8* for further details).
3. *Development*. The creation of the web pages and the dynamic content of the web site (see *Chapter 9* for further details).
4. *Testing and review*. Structured checks to ensure different aspects of the site meet the original requirements and work correctly (see *Chapter 9* for further details).

Types of prototyping

Preece *et al*. (1994) identify three different types of prototyping:

- *Throwaway prototyping*. This is self-explanatory; the prototype is not kept as the basis for the final system. Paper prototyping and storyboarding that often occur at the start of the development of e-commerce systems are throwaway prototyping techniques.

- *Evolutionary prototyping.* Here the prototype is not discarded, but acts as the basis for the next iteration of the system. This situation is common within the development of e-business systems.
- *Incremental prototyping.* This can be combined with evolutionary prototyping. It is where modules of the system are prototyped until each is complete, until eventually the whole system becomes complete.

When using the prototyping approach for an e-commerce site, a company sometimes has to decide whether to implement the complete version of the solution before making it available to its target audience or to make available a more limited version of the site. If it is necessary to establish a presence rapidly, to gain a presence in the market or as a response to new entrants the second approach could be used. This also has the benefit that feedback can be solicited from users and incorporated into later versions. Many companies will, however, prefer the security of the first approach in which the web site can be revised and market tested before making a professional and complete version of the site available. This approach is less likely to cause damage to the brand or corporate image. It will still be possible to make subsequent changes to the site based on feedback from users. An example of this approach is indicated by *case study 10.1*.

CASE STUDY 10.1

Orange evolves customer services to achieve 12,000 visitors to site each week

Orange first started using the Internet as a business tool in 1995. In this time, the site has been updated continually to reflect the needs of its customers. According to Nigel Shardlow, the new media manager at Orange (Shardlow, 1999), the site started off targeting a relatively limited audience. This was thought to be a lower risk than setting up a major site when the medium was relatively new. The initial audience was thought to be technical, consisting of students, academics and IT staff at organizations with Internet access. The initial content reflected this audience, with a tool for finding out the Orange coverage area and another for asking technical queries.

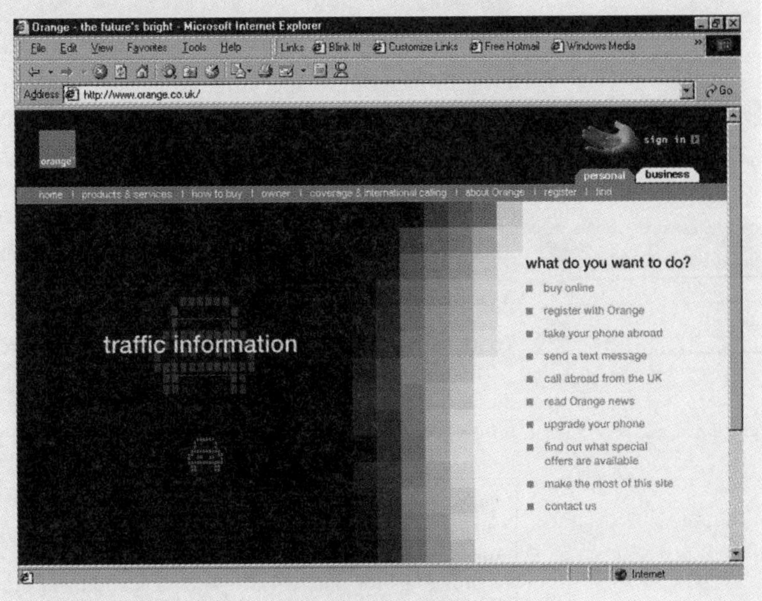

Figure 10.4 Orange web site (www.orange.co.uk)

▶ CASE STUDY *continued*

In June 1996, the company decided to broaden the scope of the site with more information on products and services such as a Talk Plan calculator that suggests to potential users which tariff is most suitable for them and a mechanism to look up the nearest Orange dealership according to postcode. News and press releases and an interactive coverage map followed later in the year.

By the beginning of 1997 the amount of content on the site had made it difficult for customers to find the information they needed, so in June 1997 a complete restructuring of the site was necessary to make it easier for customers to find information. Further information on products was added, but this time broken down into those looking for a phone for the first time, existing phone owners and business users. The buying guide leads each of these types of people through a series of choices available on onscreen forms to put together a suitable package.

Today the site is seen as a useful tool not only by customers, but also dealers, journalists, investors and potential employees. For dealers, it is a central place where up-to-date product and service information can be found; journalists use the site for researching and downloading press releases, and for investors corporate information such as interim and annual reports are available. Many employees have now joined the company following applications made online. As a result of visits from all these different types of site customer, the Orange site now receives 12,000 visitors each week. So that it can keep customers informed without them having to remember to access the web site, Orange has registered 20,000 people whom it keeps informed through regular e-mail bulletins.

The web site is today used as just one element of new media activity. To drive visitors two additional sites have been created such as that for the Orange Prize for Fiction.

Source: Adapted from Shardlow (1999)

Web link: www.orange.co.uk

Questions

1. Why was the site not initially developed for a wide audience?
2. Reading the extract above and through visiting the site, identify tools on the site that give users a service not readily available from other media.
3. Produce a table of the different types of customer the web site receives and the types of information and services oriented to these users.
4. What are the main benefits of registering at the site (for both Orange and its customers)?

Human resource requirements

E-business requires specialist skills that may not be present within an organization. E-business project managers have a choice of building a new skills set within their organization or outsourcing and partnering with other organizations. Refer to *activity 10.2* to look at some of the different skills required.

Activity 10.2 Building an e-commerce team for the B2C Company

Purpose

To identify skills requires for a sell-side e-commerce team.

The e-commerce team needs to build up the skills necessary to operate its e-commerce site. The e-commerce manager is reviewing some recruitment profiles from a new media magazine. These are the adverts they have marked as being appropriate:

Web designer
Skilled and experienced web designers with a proven track record required to join dynamic sports media organization. To be successful in this role you will have outstanding design skills, a strong feel for web structure and navigation and you will have closely worked with Internet programmers on the design of high-quality contemporary web sites. Excellent Photoshop, Flash, Director and knowledge of HTML with an awareness of the constraints of web graphics.

Web developer
A new and exciting long-term contract requires us to appoint a highly skilled web developer on a permanent basis to initiate the project. You should be a confident self-starter with at least 1–2 years' commercial experience. Your skills will include Visual Basic, SQL Programming, database to web site integration, excellent working knowledge of the Internet, HTML, Windows NT and VB Script.

Webmaster
Fantastic opportunity to join a newly formed team who will be responsible for the launch of an exciting and dynamic e-commerce web site. Based in luxury offices in the West End, you will be a 'key pin' in managing the site and updating it on a regular basis. Your skills set should include a broad understanding of web technology to include HTML and DHTML, Javascript, Perl and Director.

Online marketer
This job involves far more than just copywriting or coordinating promotions. Your day-to-day activities will be to manage online marketing campaigns, maintaining relationships with external partners including portal sites, ISPs and online promotional agencies. You will also be required to support the marcomms team on wider campaigns where required, write product descriptions and marketing materials. You must have between one and three years' experience in sales, advertising, or other marketing related areas. Agency experience is a plus. Strong copywriting skills are a requirement and you must also have a strong interest and knowledge of the web. Direct web experience is preferred, but web surfing experience is a must. Fluency in French or German is a plus.

Project manager
You will be responsible for a team of 3–4 designers/programmers, working with the production manager, account director and client. You should have excellent communication skills, as the position is client facing.

Activity

The e-commerce manager has an additional budget for three new staff. Create a summary profile (thumbnail sketch) of the skills of three different types of people required on the team, based on the adverts.

For answer see p. 413

Even more problematic than selecting the type of staff is attracting and retaining e-business staff. If we wanted effective, experienced staff then these will demand high salaries. We will be competing for these staff with dot-com companies who are trying to recruit and also other established medium-to-large companies who are looking to build an e-business capability. Smaller companies who cannot afford to recruit into each of these areas will have an even trickier problem of needing to find all of these skills rolled into one person!

Staff retention

The difficulties in staff resourcing for e-business do not end with the recruitment of staff. As Crush (2000) says, 'Getting good staff is difficult, keeping them is a nightmare'! Since there is a highly competitive marketplace for e-business staff, many staff will want to move on to further their career. This will often be after the company has spent some time training them. The Job Characteristics model developed by Hackman and Oldman (1980) provides a useful framework for designing jobs that provide a good experience to improve staff motivation and so help retention. The five intrinsic characteristics of a job are:

1. Skill variety.
2. Task identity, how well the work is defined relative to other tasks or whether an employee sees a job through from 'start to finish'.
3. Task significance or the importance of the work.
4. Autonomy or freedom in completing work.
5. Feedback from employer.

To enhance these psychological characteristics Hackman and Oldham (1980) suggest the following approaches can be used:

- *Task combination* – by combining tasks employees see more of the whole task.
- *Natural work groups* – this also helps in task combination through creating a team to complete task.
- *Establish customer relations* – this helps in task significance.
- *Vertical loading* – employees take responsibility for tasks completed by supervisors.
- *Opening feedback channel* – from internal or external customers, via managers where necessary.

Complete *activity 10.3* and *case study 10.2* to evaluate alternatives for improving staff retention.

Activity 10.3 Staff retention at The B2C Company

Purpose

To understand the reasons for high staff-turnover and identify solutions to this problem.

Activity

The B2C company has recruited the staff for their e-business initative referred to above, but finds that after 12 months they only have one of the three staff they originally recruited. They now need to recruit more staff and need to put in place a strategy to try and ensure they stay. Identify techniques that could be employed to reduce the risk of losing staff.

For answer see p. 413

CASE STUDY 10.2

Staff acquisition and retention at Netdecisions

Netdecisions is an e-services company. HR Manager Ivan Mildenhall is charged with growing the company by 60 people per month. Any shortfall in this target will result in difficulties in delivering services to customers. At the same time, other staff may be attracted to other companies. Mildenhall is

▶ CASE STUDY *continued*

quoted as saying 'We're going like a train and it's a situation that can't allow for any slack'.

'Dotcoms must realize that people are still people. Whether they bake bread or design the web site for McDonalds, they still need a better reason for working than pay.' The approach of Netdecisions to staff can be outlined thus:

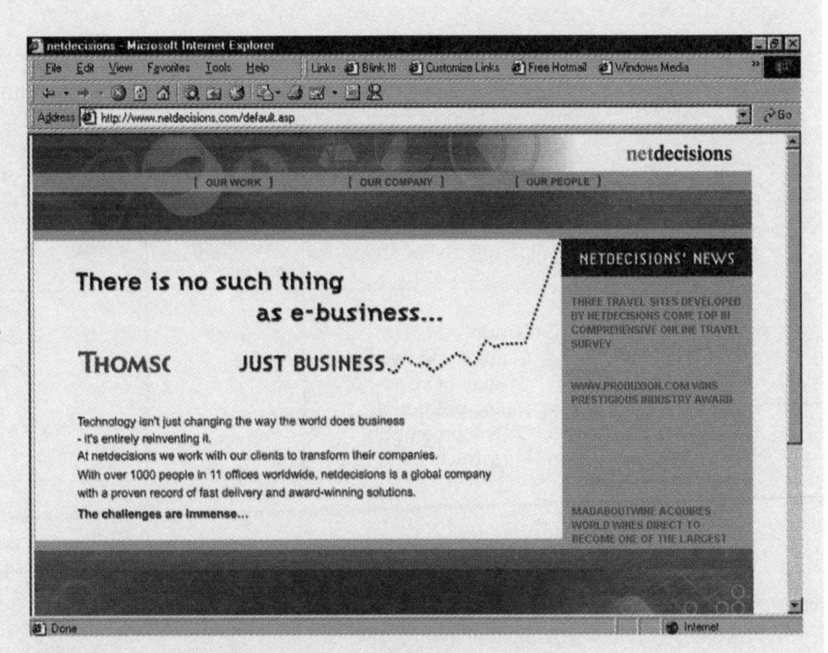

Figure 10.5 Netdecisions (www.netdecisions.com)

- First, pay is identified as important, but not the only factor. In fact, Netdecisions consciously pay less than some competitors.
- Share options are offered to staff, but this is not the only motivator as at many dot-coms.
- There is an ongoing career development programme.
- It is part of the company's ethos to make staff valued and recognize that employees do have a life beyond work and sometimes there will be conflict between the two. Flexible working arrangements are a response to this.
- New staff have a mentor for the first two weeks – that is, an existing member of staff who is given the responsibility of looking after the initial development of the new member of staff.
- There is face-to-face communication every week between HR and the staff.
- Dan Perrett, head of human assets describes the structure of the company as follows: 'working hierarchies are non-existent, which means that if someone new has a better way of doing things, that is fine'.
- Pensions are offered as is the case with other UK dot-coms such as Virgin Net (www.virgin.net) and Amazon (www.amazon.co.uk).
- Staff are encouraged to move within the company to try out new techniques and help build their skills.

Source: Based on Crush, 2000.

Questions

1. Imagine you were looking for a job with a dot-com company. How would you assess the benefits listed above as a potential employee?
2. As a manager in the company, which of the above would you believe to be most cost-effective to implement to retain staff?

Outsourcing

Given the difficulties of recruiting new business staff referred to above, many companies turn to third parties to help in their e-business efforts. However, there is a bewildering series of supplier choices. Complete *activity 10.4* to help understand the choices required.

Activity 10.4 Options for outsourcing different e-business activities

Purpose

To highlight the outsourcing available for e-business implementation and to gain an appreciation of how to choose suppliers.

Table 10.2 Options for outsourcing different e-business activities

E-marketing function	*Traditional marketing agency*	*New media agency*	*ISP or traditional IT supplier*	*Management consultants*
1. Strategy 2. Design 3. Content and service development 4. Online promotion 5. Offline promotion 6. Infrastructure				

Activity

Select a single supplier (by ticking one column) who you think can best deliver each of these services indicated in *Table 10.2*. Justify your decision.

For answer see p. 414

We are seeing a gradual blurring between these types of supplier as they recruit expertise so as to deliver a 'one-stop shop' service, but they still tend to be strongest in particular areas. Companies need to decide whether to partner with the best of breed in each, or to compromise and choose the one-stop shop that gives the best balance; this would arguably be the new media agency or perhaps a traditional marketing agency that has an established new media division. Which approach do you think is best?

Observation of the practice of outsourcing suggests that two conflicting patterns are evident:

1. *Outside-in.* Company starts an e-business initiative by outsourcing some activities where there is insufficient in-house expertise. These may be areas such as strategy or online promotion. The company then builds up skills internally to manage these areas as e-business becomes an important contributor to the business. The easyjet case referred to in *Chapter 8* is an example of this approach. The company initially partnered with a new media agency to offer online services, but once the online contribution to sales exceeded 20 per cent the management of e-commerce was taken inside. The new media agency was, however, retained for strategy guidance. An outside-in approach will probably be driven by the need to reduce the costs of outsourcing, poor delivery of services by the supplier or simply a need to concentrate a strategic core resource in-house as is the case with easyJet.
2. *Inside-out.* Company starts to implement e-business using existing resources within the IT department and marketing department in conjunction with recruitment of new media staff. They may then find that there are problems in

developing a site that meets customers' needs or in building traffic to the site. At this point they may turn to outsourcing to solve the problems.

These approaches are not mutually exclusive, and an outside-in approach may be used for some e-business functions such as content development, while an inside-out approach is used for other functions such as site promotion. It can also be suggested that these approaches are not planned; they are simply a response to prevailing conditions. However, in order to cost e-business and manage it as a strategic asset it can be argued that the e-business manager should have a long-term picture of which functions to outsource and when to bring them in-house.

The increased use of outsourcing marks a move towards the virtual organization (*Chapter 6, p. 229*). With the introduction of electronic networks such as the Internet it becomes easier to outsource aspects of the production and distribution of goods to third parties. Employees may work in any time zone and customers are able to purchase tailored products from any location. For example, new media design agency e-xcentric, based in London, used programmers based in Hyderabad, India to develop web-based solutions for clients. Through doing this, they are able to increase the number of hours worked on projects per 24-hour period and also enjoy lower staff costs, even though the Indian employees are well-paid in local terms.

Revising organizational structures

When a company first embarks on e-business, perhaps through creating a new web site to promote its products, it will normally operate within the existing company structure, perhaps using outsourcing to make good a resource deficit. However, as the contribution of the web site to the company increases, the work involved increases and more staff from different parts of the organization are involved in e-business, it may be necessary to adopt new organizational structures and working practices. This issue has been considered by Parsons *et al.* (1996) from a sell-side e-commerce perspective. They recognize four stages in the growth of what they refer to as the digital marketing organization. These are:

1. *Ad-hoc activity*. At this stage there is no formal organization related to e-commerce and the skills are dispersed around the organization. At this stage it is likely that there is poor integration between online and offline marketing communications. The web site may not reflect the offline brand, and the web site services may not be featured in the offline marketing communications. A further problem with ad-hoc activity is that the maintenance of the web site will be informal and errors may occur as information becomes out of date.
2. *Focusing the effort*. At this stage, efforts are made to introduce a controlling mechanism for Internet marketing. Parsons *et al.* (1996) suggest that this is often achieved through a senior executive setting up a steering group which may include interested parties from marketing, IT and legal experts. At this stage the efforts to control the site will be experimental with different approaches being tried to build, promote and manage the site.
3. *Formalization*. At this stage the authors suggest that Internet marketing will have reached a critical mass and there will be a defined group or separate business unit within the company which manages all digital marketing.

4. *Institutionalizing capability*. This stage also involves a formal grouping within the organization, but is distinguished from the previous stage in that there are formal links created between digital marketing and a company's core activities. Baker (1998) argues that a separate e-commerce department may be needed as the company may need to be restructured in order to provide the necessary levels of customer service over the Internet if existing processes and structures do not do this.

Although this is presented as a stage model with evolution implying all companies will move from one stage to the next, many companies will find that true formalization with the creation of a separate e-commerce or e-business department is unnecessary. For small and medium companies with a marketing department numbering a few people and an IT department perhaps consisting of two people, it will not be practical to have a separate group. Even large companies may find it is sufficient to have a single person or small team responsible for e-commerce with their role being to coordinate the different activities within the company using a matrix management approach. That many companies are not ready to move to a separate digital marketing department was indicated by the KPMG report (Baker, 1998). Here it was found that over three-quarters of respondents were against establishing a separate e-commerce department.

Activity 10.5 reviews different types of organizational structures for e-commerce. *Table 10.3* reviews some of the advantages and disadvantages of each.

Activity 10.5

Which is the best organization structure for e-commerce?

Purpose

To review alternative organizational structures for e-commerce.

Activity

1. Match the four types of companies and situations to the structures (a) to (d) in *Figure 10.6*.

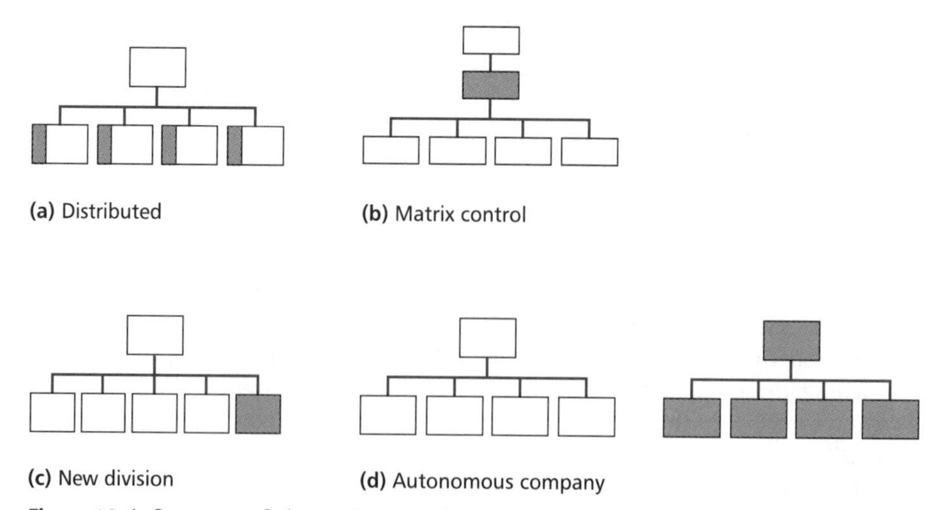

Figure 10.6 Summary of alternative organizational structures for e-commerce suggested in Parsons *et al.* (1996)

   (a) A separate operating company. Examples: Prudential and Egg (www.egg.com).
   (b) A separate business unit with independent budgets. Examples: RS Components Internet Trading Company (www.rswww.com).
   (c) A separate committee or department manages and coordinates e-commerce. Example: Derbyshire Building Society (www.derbyshire.co.uk).
   (d) No formal structure for e-commerce. Examples: many small businesses and the Retail and Engineering Company.
2. Under which circumstances would each structure be appropriate?
3. Summarize the advantages and disadvantages of each approach.

For answer see p. 414

Table 10.3 Advantages and disadvantages of the organizational structures shown in Figure 10.6

Organizational structure	*Circumstances*	*Advantages*	*Disadvantages*
(a) No formal structure for e-commerce	Initial response to e-commerce or poor leadership with no identification of need for change.	Can achieve rapid response to e-commerce service responses (e-mail, phone). Priorities not decided logically. Insufficient resources	Poor quality site in terms of content quality and customer
(b) A separate committee or department manages and coordinates e-commerce	Identification of problem and response in (a)	Coordination and budgeting and resource allocation possible.	May be difficult to get different departments to deliver their input due to other commitments
(c) A separate business unit with independent budgets	Internet contribution (*Chapter 6*) is sizeable (>20%)	As for (b), but can set own targets and not be constrained by resources. Lower risk option than (d)	Has to respond to corporate strategy. Conflict of interests between department and traditional business
(d) A separate operating company	Major revenue potential or flotation. Need to differentiate from parent	As for (c), but can set strategy independently. Can maximize market potential	High risk if market potential is overestimated due to start-up costs

The changes to organizational structure described above have mainly been reviewed from the point of view of change required to introduce sell-side e-commerce. Changes necessary for e-business may require different types of organizational change. For instance a supply chain management perspective (*Chapter 7*) may require an e-business committee that manages the resource inputs for both buy-side and sell-side e-commerce.

It can also be suggested than in addition to the type of structural changes highlighted in *Figure 10.6*, it is also necessary to modify hierarchical structures – shallow structures may increase the likelihood of success since they may improve communication, help achieve process orientation and indicate less bureaucratic management. This is covered further in the section on *cultural change*. The box *Organizational change at Oticon* illustrates one example of change.

Organizational change at Oticon

Figure 10.7 Oticon (www.oticon.com)

An example of a company that implemented BPR with major organizational change is Oticon (www.oticon.com), a Danish hearing aid company that is described by Boddy *et al.* (2001) on the basis of a study conducted by Bjorn-Anderson and Turner (1994). In early 1990s the company was rapidly losing market share, and its profitability was declining. The board appointed a new chief executive, Lars Kolind and he took a radical approach to the problem by trying to create an organization that could respond better to customer needs. Some of the changes he made were:

- Creation of a project-centred approach where senior management appointed project leaders rather than projects being run within a department. Project leaders then recruit from within the company using electronic advertising.
- Elimination of traditional departments – staff worked on projects rather than in a department – this is a process-oriented approach.
- Introduction of staff mobility. Staff would typically contribute to several projects.
- Use of hot-desking or mobile caddies, each with a PC.
- Elimination of paper through the use of electronic document management systems for project documents and resulting meetings.

It can be seen that this company was forward-thinking and implemented in 1994 many of the concepts that we today refer to as e-business.

Managing the human dimension of change

For a manager seeking to introduce e-business led change, it is important to define how staff will be positively influenced to facilitate change. To achieve this an oft-quoted prerequisite is to have real backing for e-business change from the senior management team. This should not simply be 'lip-service'; management should be seen by their actions to be involved in, and supportive of, e-business change. Jack Welch, CEO of General Electric instituted 'management boot camps' to increase managerial participation in e-business and also created a system of mentoring where younger, technically literate staff pass on their knowledge to 600 more senior managers. Equally self-evident is that the need for and consequences of change must be communicated to everyone throughout the organization. The overall picture of different e-business implementation projects needs to be explained in the context of how it affects an individual's main activities. Using these basic approaches, which we will now consider in more detail, can help develop the staff commitment that is needed to achieve the rapid and significant changes that are part of e-business.

Achieving management commitment

Support from the senior managers is one of the key factors in achieving success in introducing e-business, as for other strategy initiatives. Schein (1992), one of the leading thinkers on organizational change management, concluded that three variables are critical to the success of any organizational change:

1. The degree to which the leaders can break from previous ways of working.
2. The significance and comprehensiveness of change.
3. The extent to which the head of the organization is actively involved with the change process.

Note that points 1 and 3 both involve the roles of senior management. In the context of point 2, e-business is a significant and comprehensive change that suggests that active senior management involvement is essential. One of the difficulties is that senior management may be at best unfamiliar with use of the Internet and information technology, or at worst, technophobic.

If the senior management team has the vision to realize the impact of the Internet and related technologies, they are more likely to commit the resources and sponsor the changes required for success. Note also Schein's point that the head of organization needs to be actively involved. It is not a matter of simply communicating change at the start, but seeing it through and actively monitoring change by talking to staff and communicating progress on the e-business project. It will also become a major element of corporate strategy rather than 'something to be left to the IT department'. If managers are cynical, treating technology as a support function rather than a major change lever, then not only will they be unlikely to invest sufficiently in e-business, but they will not drive the initiative with sufficient enthusiasm and this will be apparent to staff. A KPMG survey reported by Baker (1998) showed that having board level support for the initiative was one of the key success factors for 'leaders' – companies in Europe achieving profitable e-commerce. The survey also showed that there was a higher level of investment in such companies (e-commerce budgets averaging $222,000 compared to $130,000). In addition, the successful companies had implemented integration of e-commerce into their supply chain.

Often the roles of the e-commerce manager within a business may be to lobby more senior managers within a company, explaining the benefits of investing in a web site, highlighting the consequence of not investing sufficiently and explaining their role in the success of e-commerce.

Achieving staff commitment

The strategic significance of e-business needs to be clearly communicated to staff. Why? E-business will have a significant impact on individuals' work. There may be disruption to staff as new working practices and information systems are introduced. The change involved with the introduction of the new system needs management such that staff motivation and productivity are not adversely affected. Some resistance to all types of change is inevitable, but this is particularly true with the introduction of systems associated with e-business since the way work is performed and peoples' job functions will be changed. If the rationale behind the change is not explained then all the classic symptoms of resistance to change will be apparent. Resistance to change usually follows a set pattern. For example Adams *et al.* (1976) have used the transition curve (*Figure 10.8*) to describe the change from when staff first hear about a system to the change becoming accepted.

While outright hostility manifesting itself as sabotage of the system is not unheard of, what is more common is that users will try to project blame onto the system and will identify major faults where only minor bugs exist. This will obviously damage the reputation of the system and senior managers will want to know what went wrong with the project. Arguably a more significant problem is *avoidance* of the system. Here workers will work around the system to continue their previous ways of working. Careful management is necessary to ensure that this does not happen. A number of techniques can be used. Try to think of techniques that can be used by completing *activity 10.6*.

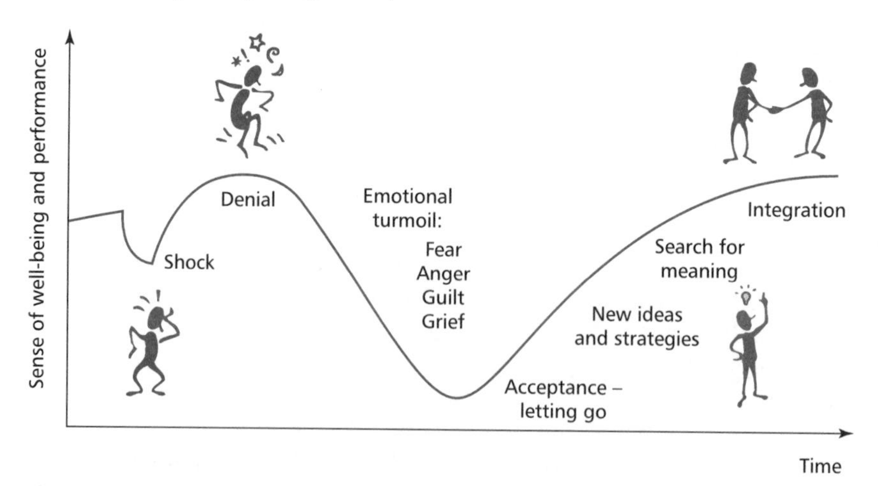

Figure 10.8 Transition curve indicating the reaction of staff through time from when change is first suggested

Source: Bocij *et al.* (1999)

Achieving staff commitment to e-business

Activity 10.6

Purpose

To highlight the practical techniques that can be used to counter change through the stages of denial, acceptance through to integration as shown in Figure 10.8.

Activity

For the retail company, suggest actions managers can take to reduce resistance to change.

For answer see p. 414

An example of an approach to communicating change to employees is provided by RS Components who, when first introducing an e-commerce site, set aside an area of their staff canteen and set up a stand staffed by members of the electronic commerce team. Other staff were then encouraged to learn about using the Internet and the services that the web site would provide. By doing this all staff understood the purpose of using the Internet and were more supportive of it. Additionally, it helped support the adoption of an in-company intranet. More formal education and training which explains the purpose of the Internet marketing strategy and provides practical training for those involved was also necessary.

Lewin and Schein suggested a model for achieving organizational change that involves three stages:

1. Unfreeze the present position by creating a climate of change by education, training and motivation of future participants.
2. Quickly move from the present position by developing and implementing the new system.
3. Refreeze by making the system an accepted part of the way the organization works.

To achieve the unfreeze stages different staff can be identified for different roles by the project manager:

- *System sponsors* are senior managers or board members who have bought into the e-business initiative, are committed to major change and want to achieve success. The sponsors will try to fire up staff with their enthusiasm and stress why introducing the system is important to the business and its workers.
- *System owners* are managers in the organization of key processes such as a procurement manager or marketing manager who will use the e-business system to achieve benefits in their area.
- *System users*. These are staff in the different areas of the business who are actively involved in making the process happen. This could be a buyer in procurement or a brand manager within the marketing department.

Special types of system users can be identified, and it is important for the change manager to try to influence these staff to help achieve commitment among other staff. The three main types of system users that should be influenced are:

- *Stakeholders* should be identified for each of the process areas where change will be introduced. These will be staff who are respected by their co-workers and will again act as a source of enthusiasm for the system. The user representatives used in specification, testing and sign-off are key stakeholders.
- The *legitimizer* protects the norms and values of the system; they are experienced in their job and regarded as the experts by fellow workers; they may be initially resistant to change and therefore need to be involved early.
- *Opinion leaders* are people whom others watch to see whether they accept new ideas and changes. They usually have little formal power, but are regarded as good ideas people who are receptive to change and again need to be involved early in the project.

For e-business implementation these roles will need to be identified for each implementation project as well as the overall change.

Organizational culture

Culture

This concept includes shared values, unwritten rules and assumptions within the organization as well as the practices that all groups share. Corporate cultures are created when a group of employees interact over time and are relatively successful in what they undertake.

Bocij *et al.* (1999) suggest that social relationships in an organization, that are part of its **culture** are important. They say '*the efficiency of any organization is dependent on the complex formal and informal relationships that exist within it*'. Formal relationships include the hierarchical work relationships within and between functional business areas. Informal relationships are created through people working and socializing with each other on a regular basis and will cut across functional boundaries. E-business led change has the capacity to alter both types of relationships as it brings about change within and between functional business areas.

Boddy *et al.* (2001) summarize four different types of cultural orientation that may be identified in different companies. These vary according to the extent to which the company is inward looking or outward looking, in other words to what extent it is affected by its environment. They also reflect whether the company is structured and/or formal or whether it has a more flexible, dynamic, informal character. The four cultural types of cultural orientation are:

1. *Survival (outward-looking, flexible)* – the external environment plays a significant role (an open system) in governing company strategy. The company will likely be driven by customer demands and will be an innovator. It may have a relatively flat structure.
2. *Productivity (outward-looking, ordered)* – interfaces with the external environment are well structured and the company is typically sales-driven and is likely to have a hierarchical structure.
3. *Human relations (inward-looking, flexible)* – this is the organization as family, with interpersonal relations more important than reporting channels, a flatter structure and staff development and empowerment is thought of important by managers.
4. *Stability (inward-looking, ordered)* – the environment is essentially ignored with managers concentrating on internal efficiency and again managed through a hierarchical stucture.

Now complete *activity 10.7* to investigate how companies may need to re-align their culture to succeed in e-business.

Changing the culture for e-business

Activity 10.7

Purpose

To identify appropriate cultural changes that may be necessary for e-business success

Activity

Review the four general categories of organizational cultural orientation summarized by Boddy *et al.* (2001) and take each as characterizing four different companies and then suggest which is most appropriate for e-business. State whether you think they are most likely to occur in a small organization or a larger organization.

For answer see p. 414

Focus on knowledge management

Knowledge management has an important role within e-business since business success is critically dependent on staff knowledge about all aspects of the micro-environment such as customers, suppliers, intermediaries, competitors and how to shape internal processes to best deliver customer service. With the move towards globalization and responding more rapidly to changing market conditions knowledge transfer is a key to competitiveness. Knowledge management is also a change management response to the problems of staff retention referred to earlier. As Saunders (2000) puts it

> *Every day, knowledge essential to your business walks out of your door, and much of it never comes back. Employees leave, customers come and go and their knowledge leaves with them. This information drain costs you time, money and customers.*

What is knowledge?

The concept of **knowledge** is more difficult to state than that of data or information. However, knowledge can be regarded as the next level of sophistication or business value in the cycle from data through information to knowledge. Consider a retail manager analysing their sales figures. Raw data on sales figures will simply consist of the figures in each individual store for a given month. We can use an information system to present this data within the context of sales compared to previous months as information. This information might include trends from previous years, sales against budget and maps of sales for different regions. However, this information is of little value if the manager does not know how to act in response to it. Managers apply their knowledge to decide how to respond if the sales in one region are much lower than others, or if one store is underperforming against budget. Thus knowledge is the processing of information and is a skill based on previous understanding, procedures and experience. **Knowledge management** seeks to share this experience within a company.

Knowledge
Applying experience to problem solving.

Knowledge management
Techniques and tools disseminating knowledge within an organization.

Theorists have identified two different types of knowledge and different approaches can be used to disseminate this type of knowledge within an organization:

Explicit knowledge
Knowledge that can be readily expressed and recorded within information systems.

Tacit knowledge
Mainly intangible knowledge that is typically intuitive and not recorded since it is part of the human mind.

1. **Explicit** – details of processes and procedures. Explicit knowledge can be readily detailed in procedural manuals and databases. Examples include records of meetings between sales representatives and key customers, procedures for dealing with customer service queries and management reporting processes.
2. **Tacit** – less tangible than explicit knowledge, this is experience on how to react to a situation when many different variables are involved. It is more difficult to encapsulate this knowledge, which often resides in the heads of employees. Techniques for sharing this knowledge include learning stories and histories. Examples include knowing how to react when changes occur in the marketplace, such as a competitor launching a new product or a major customer looking to defect. Knowing how to analyse and respond to information in management reports depends on tacit knowledge. To acquire tacit knowledge may rely on sharing knowledge with partners outside a company or others in different sectors. So knowledge management should not be considered solely as confining corporate knowledge within the firewalls.

It follows that one goal of knowledge management is to turn tacit knowledge into explicit knowledge which can then be shared between employees and used to train new employees.

Sveiby (1997/2000) suggests that one of the best ways to understand knowledge management is by looking at how people use the term knowledge management. This includes both academic researchers, consultants and industry practitioners. The two different views of knowledge management are:

- IT-based view of knowledge management. In this view, knowledge can be stored as objects within databases and information systems.
- People-track view of knowledge management. In this view, knowledge management is about trying to improve individual skills and behaviour.

Objectives of knowledge management

The reasons for moving to knowledge management are highlighted by a 1999 IDC survey. The main reasons given by 355 US IS manager respondents were:

- Improving profit/growing revenue (67 per cent)
- Retaining key talent/expertise (54 per cent)
- Increasing customer retention and/or satisfaction (52 per cent)
- Defending market share against new entrants (44 per cent)
- Gaining faster time to market with products (39 per cent)
- Penetrating new market segments (39 per cent)
- Reducing costs (38 per cent)
- Developing new products/services (35 per cent)

It is evident that although employee retention is important, knowledge management is also seen as a competitive force for acquiring and retaining customers. Unlike other e-business initiative cost reduction is relatively unimportant.

Sveiby (1997/2000) identifies an evolution of knowledge management objectives through time starting with a realization around 1992 that many companies were reinventing the wheel by not applying the experience acquired through previous, similar projects. Sharing knowledge was achieved by using best practice databases using groupware such as Lotus Notes. Later the database was again the focus as companies aimed to learn more about their customers through data warehousing and data mining. The third phase is, he says, associated with sell-side e-commerce and learning more about *interactions* with customers through web-based forms and online purchases.

Sveiby (1997/2000), based on his analysis of over 40 companies implementing knowledge management, suggests that knowledge management can focused at three general types of initiative:

1. *External structure initiatives*, for example to gain knowledge from customers or offer customers additional knowledge.
2. *Internal structure initiatives* such as building a knowledge-sharing culture; creating new revenues from existing knowledge; capturing individuals' tacit knowledge then storing and spreading it and measuring knowledge creating and/or intangible assets.
3. *Competence initiatives* such as creating careers based on knowledge management; create micro-environment for knowledge transfer and learning from simulations and pilot installations.

Implementing knowledge management

The reasons for difficulties in moving to knowledge management (KM) are also highlighted by the 1999 IDC survey. The main problems noted were:

- Lack of understanding of KM and its benefits (55 per cent)
- Lack of employee time for KM (45 per cent)
- Lack of skill in KM techniques (40 per cent)
- Lack of encouragement in the current culture for sharing (35 per cent)
- Lack of incentives/rewards to share (30 per cent)
- Lack of funding for KM initiatives (24 per cent)
- Lack of appropriate technology (18 per cent)
- Lack of commitment from senior management (15 per cent)

Note that lack of the appropriate technology is not a major issue, although selecting the right technology may be more important. All the main barriers relate to organizational structure and culture. A key finding seems to be the need to explain the benefits of knowledge management, develop skills and encourage sharing. A quote from Marianne Hedin, Research Manager at IDC Research (IDC, 2000) highlights this. She says:

> *It is impossible to achieve full benefits from knowledge management unless individuals are willing and motivated to share their knowledge or unless organizations lose their structural rigidity to permit information and knowledge flow.*

Hansen *et al.* (1999) suggest that incentives are required to encourage staff to share knowledge such as making knowledge sharing a factor in the employees' performance review, assessed by recording of knowledge electronically or transferring it person-to-person. See the box *Implementing knowledge management at Chevron* for a review of how these problems in implementing knowledge management can be overcome.

Implementing knowledge management at Chevron

Saunders (2000) suggests that for Chevron, the approach to knowledge management can be summarized as 'connection'. This is the term described by Jeff Stemke, an internal consultant on the knowledgement management programme, who refers to himself as 'an evangelist for knowledge management'. The connections Stemke refer to are:

1. Connection to the explicit knowledge via an intranet with a portal with search tools and a directory of information.
2. Connection of people to people with specialized knowledge through an expertise locator; a type of phone directory with people in different expertise categories, again also accessed via search tools.
3. Connection to communities of practice which can help sharing and learning between people.
4. Connection of knowledge and people with processes, products and services.

Further recommendations from Stemke include, again, the need for senior management buy-in; focus on achieving key objectives on Chevron's case cost-effectiveness; teach and train employees how to share knowledge and put in place a measurement programme. At Chevron, a $2 billion saving in operating costs has occurred. These savings are not all attributable to knowledge management, but development and sharing of best practices has contributed to this. A 50 per cent reduction in incidents and injuries amongst refinery workers has also occurred as a result of the programme.

Technologies for implementing knowledge management

Hansen *et al.* (1999) estimate that during the late 1990s consulting companies such as Andersen and Ernst & Young each spent more than $500 million on knowledge management. This is a significant investment – 6 per cent of Ernst and Young's revenue in one year. US companies seem to have been more convinced by the benefits of knowledge management. IDC (2000) estimate that by 2003, US companies will spend $5 billion on knowledge management products and services while in the remainder of the world the figure will be $3 billion.

Alternative tools for managing knowledge include:

- Intranets and document databases or knowledgebases such as Lotus Notes/Domino
- Communications techniques such as chat, discussion groups and video-conferencing
- Electronic Document Management Systems such as Interleaf publisher
- Expert systems

We will now look at some examples of how these different tools have been combined with different strategies for sharing knowledge in organizations. *Figure 10.9* gives an example of a knowledge management tool, Livelink, that can also be used for project collaboration.

Hansen *et al.* (1999) identify two contrasting approaches for implementing knowledge management which they illustrate through case studies of management consultancies. They refer to these approaches as codification and personalization. They found that companies tend to focus on one approach or the other, although

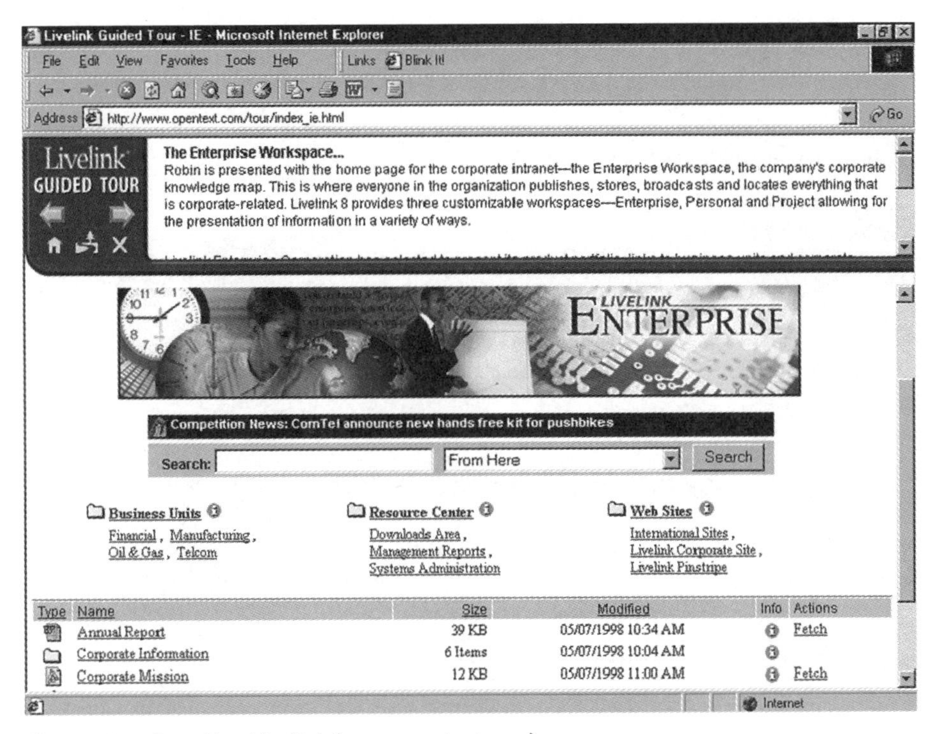

Figure 10.9 OpenText Livelink (www.opentext.com)

there was some overlap. In the codification approach, that used by Andersen Consulting and Ernst & Young, knowledge is codified or translated into a form suitable for searching using a database. Hansen *et al.* (1999) give the example of a partner in the Los Angeles office of Ernst & Young who needed assistance in creating a bid for implementation of an ERP system. Since he did not have this type of implementation he tapped into the knowledge management repository to find similar bids completed by others in the past. The re-use of a previous bid made it possible to complete the bid in half the normal period of four to six weeks, even though the partner was relatively inexperienced in this area. The codification process has been a major initiative at Ernst & Young with over 250 employed at the Centre for Business Knowledge to codify information and help others perform searches. In addition each of Ernst & Young's forty practice areas has a specialist in codifying documents.

The personalization approach has been adopted more by strategy consulting firms such as Bain and McKinsey. Hansen *et al.* (1999) relate the case of a partner in the London office of Bain who had to advise a UK financial institution how to solve a particular strategy dilemma. This assignment required knowledge of different market and geographical sectors and creative input. She used the Bain people-finder system to find those with suitable information then convened a meeting in Europe that involved videoconferencing with others in Singapore and Sydney. Over the next four months, the partner then consulted regularly through e-mail, videoconferencing and by phone. As well as using these technological approaches, McKinsey also fosters knowledge transfer by moving staff between offices, by having directories of experts and a culture that encourages prompt return of calls.

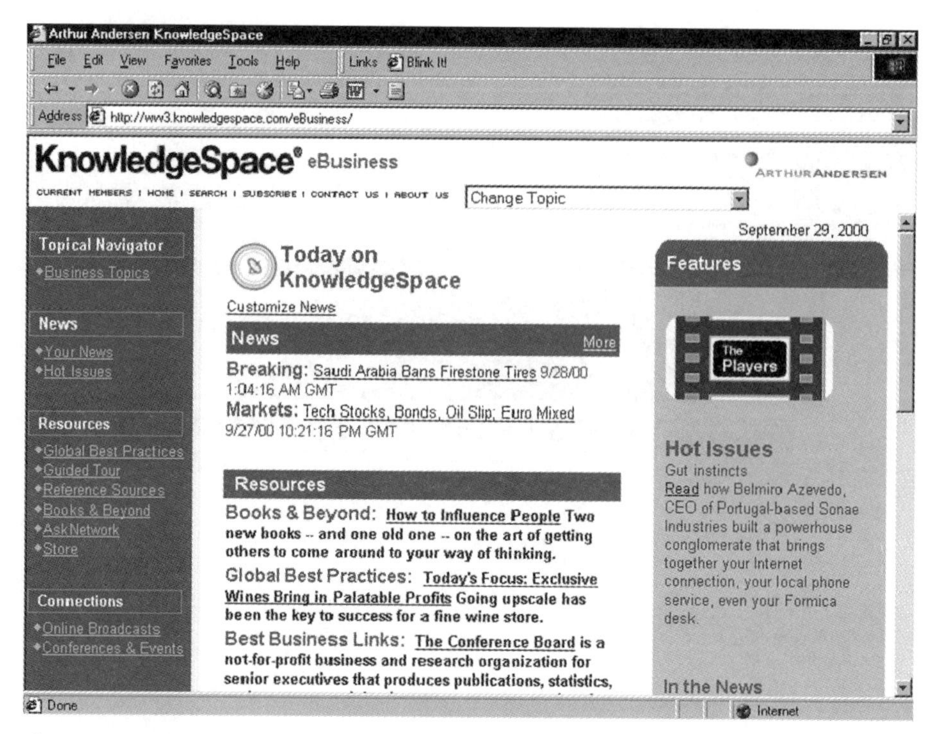

Figure 10.10 KnowledgeSpace (www.knowledgespace.com)

The Arthur Andersen global best practices database (*Chapter 11, p. 423*) has been extended beyond the company as a knowledge base for its customers; this is a subscription-based service known as KnowledgeSpace (*Figure 10.10*). It gives an indication of the portal structure many companies use for their intranet knowledgebases. This approach of paying for knowledge from external experts is a possible future trend and similar portals may be created for different sectors.

To summarize this section, the stages for achieving knowledge management are:

1. Capturing knowledge.
2. Interpreting knowledge.
3. Deploying knowledge through intranets or knowledge portals.
4. Staff training.
5. Measurement of the impact of knowledge management programme.

Risk management

Risk management
Evaluating potential risks, developing strategies to reduce risks and learning about future risks.

To conclude this chapter and act as a bridge to the two final chapters we review the problems associated with change when managing an e-business implementation. **Risk management** is intended to identify potential risks in a range of situations and then take actions to minimize the risks. We all unconsciously perform risk management throughout our lives. For example, when crossing a country road we will assess the likely risk of a car approaching, or a silent cyclist approaching around the blind bend and perhaps increase our pace accordingly. The activity e-business risk management is intended to illustrate these risks. Risk management involves these stages:

1. Identify risks including their probabilities and impacts.
2. Identify possible solutions to these risks.
3. Implement the solutions targeting the highest impact, most likely risks.
4. Monitor the risks to learn for future risk assessment.

Activity 10.8 illustrates typical risks identified during this process.

E-business risk management for The B2C Company

Activity 10.8

Purpose

To highlight risks that are part of an e-business implementation and suggest solutions. This activity acts as a summary of many of the change management concepts reviewed in this chapter.

Activity

Review this chapter with reference to *Chapters 4 and 5* and produce a grid with four columns describing the risk for a company with which you are familiar, or for The B2C Company, assessing its probability on a scale of 0 (no risk) to 10 (very high risk), its impact from a scale of 0 (no impact) to 10 (catastrophic) and possible solutions.

For answer see p. 415

As an alternative view of risks with a wider organization context, Simons (1999) presents a simple risk calculator based on different types of risks faced at a company level (*Table 10.3*). This calculator can be usefully applied to e-business change or a high growth dot-com company since significant change may accentuate these risks.

Table 10.4 Organizational risk exposure factors (from Simon, 1999)

Growth risks	*Culture risks*	*Information management risks*
Pressures for performance (overambitious targets due to external demands)	Rewards for entrepreneurial risk taking (Nick Leeson syndrome)	Transaction complexity and velocity (a particularly high risk for companies having to purchase or sell raw materials in bulk)
Rate of expansion (expansion difficult to control and recruit new employees)	Executive resistance to bad news (. . . and lack of action)	Gaps in diagnostic performance measures (poor reporting capabilities)
Inexperience of key employees	Levels of internal competition (is the culture cooperative or too competitive)	Degree of decentralized decision making (lack of central control and management of other risks)

As a summary to this chapter we consider the approaches to changed involved in Guinness, a large multinational organization. See *case study 10.3*.

CASE STUDY 10.3

Managing global change at Guinness

Programme aims

In 1997 Guinness embarked on a three-year programme of business transformation referred to as the Integrated Business Programme (IBP). This change would impact on 10,000 employees in five areas of the £2.2 billion business – Ireland, the UK, Europe, the US and the Global Support division – and across product lines including the largest, Guinness, and Harp lager, Kilkenny ale and Irish cider.

The IBP was intended to support the company's strategic aim to grow the business following the merger with Grand Metropolitan in 1991. It was also combined with rectifying the millennium bug. The IBP involved redesigning common business processes and the information systems that supported them. To achieve an integrated international supply chain and to replace inefficient activities was the main aim. Reducing stock levels would enable it to reduce costs and make better use of its assets. Global reporting on its activities would also become possible.

Reduced costs are possible from rationalizing the supply chain and reducing the number of suppliers, and moving to guided sourcing, especially over the Internet, where things like electronic catalogues and global negotiation become feasible. Guided sourcing, which 'everyone has to use', according to Roy Jakes, Guinness finance director, saves money by cutting out expensive, off-contract maverick purchasing, and is one example of the kind of tighter rigour that now applies across the company. Such is the way the new system works that no supplier can deliver if they can't quote an order number. This number has to be entered into the system in an authorized fashion.

According to Roy Jakes, who was sponsor of IBP, both cultural and organizational changes were needed since the businesses operating globally were very different in character. Each Guinness site had been working as a separate business unit.

Julia Vowler, the author of the case study, notes that there is great difficulty in successfully implementing global change. She puts the failure rate as being as high as 75 per cent. This failure rate is not usually due to the processes, but rather problems with the implementation of the underlying system. Lack of communication with the staff about what is occurring is also a common error. The impact of the change programme on the business as a whole is also underestimated.

Programme structure and organizational changes

A project team was drawn out of all parts of the global business, with some of the best people in each area selected. This enabled important decisions about the programme to be taken quickly. According to Jakes, 'Communication was key during this period and, indeed, it still is. It was essential to get buy-in from everyone across the organization for a project like this right from the start. Leadership from the top was excellent and really helped in building awareness of what was going on at a time of great cultural change and nervousness.'

The toughest challenge was breaking down local cultures, according to Jakes: 'wading through politics and inter-regional suspicion required positive leadership from the managing director. It wasn't painless.' On the approach used he says: 'We had to sufficiently educate and communicate what was coming. People don't believe change is happening until it arrives. Internal public relations has been very important throughout the project, and we used lots of different ways to communicate what we were doing. We generally tried to make it fun – you've got to use all the levers you can to make a project like this work.'

The organizational architecture Guinness has selected is a shared-services model, whereby core functions, most notably finance, are carried out by a dedicated department that services all the separate business divisions. The processes within the shared-services centres, based in London and Dublin, include consolidation of financial accounting and reporting, online access to up-to-date information, as well as the centralized operation of accounts payable and accounts receivable. The IS department has also become more centralized with a single department operating out of London and Dublin.

IS implementation

Like the processes, the IS within Guinness were also different in the existing business units. Each of

▶ CASE STUDY *continued*

the five divisions had its own IT department. However, before the programme there had been some standardization of applications with Microsoft Office applications and e-mail. Other applications were quite mixed. In Ireland, for example, there were legacy applications, including an in-house sales order-processing system and packages for finance and human resources, and Europe had locally purchased packages. Guinness in the UK had implemented SAP R/3 over the two years prior to the IBP, and this was now selected as the core enterprise resource planning (ERP) platform for the globalized company. Jakes says: 'It was excellent to have had the UK as a prototype for R/3 because you do get hurt putting in ERP. So we'd already got the scars and learned the lessons.' Of course the downside of having used SAP in the UK was that other divisions might regard the extension of R/3 out of the UK with suspicion. This problem was reduced since the UK system was not rolled out without changes; it was upgraded in line with the agreed business process transformation. The implementer for SAP R/3 was Druid. The supplier centred on five processes: finance, sales and operations planning, procurement, customer order fulfilment and product supply. In terms of different types of IS applications, the solution included workflow, data warehousing and advanced supply chain planning solutions and integration of some legacy systems as well. Jakes says: 'around 80 per cent of the corporate back office goes on R/3 – all the finances, all order processing, all the production ordering, stores and logistics. We use Manugistics for production planning, which we were already using. It takes the data out of R/3, produces the work plan and feeds it back to R/3.' It has not been possible to use SAP as a single supplier. Jakes says 'our MIS is still being built: SAP R/3 is feeding our SQL Server data warehouse, which has both Brio and Essbase front-ends to give us a consistent picture of production, finance and sales reporting.'

A benefit of this integrated approach for customers is integration of order-processing activities across Guinness's businesses. The new process enables greater control over its assets such as kegs of beer – to ensure better traceability of products and ultimately improve customer satisfaction and quality management.

Some 2500 people (out of 10,000) now use the system, but there are some difficulties with use of the system. Jakes says: 'not everyone has found the system user-friendly. For occasional users it's not the most friendly. For them, using workflow or, increasingly, new Internet front-ends, is more palatable.'

The IBP doctrine has not been applied regardless. Some regional differences or localization also make sense. At this stage the Far East and African operations have remained separate. Since, in Ireland, most pubs are still owner-managed rather than owned by big chains, a different sales order-processing system is used from the UK one, where the brewer just takes in orders from the major wholesalers and then distributes the beer to their pubs.

Project history

1997

- Guinness merges with Grand Metropolitan to form Diageo

1998

- February: IBP launched

1999

- January: First go-live of base line SAP R/3 across Guinness in the UK
- May: Roll-out of IBP within the UK
- July: IBP extended to sites in Ireland
- November: Customer Order Fulfilment (Cof) went live in both the UK and Ireland. IBP rolled out in Northern Ireland

2000

- Further roll-out of Cof in the US and Guinness Ireland Group.

Source: Feature by Julia Vowler, *Computer Weekly*, 27 July 2000, 20–21

Questions

1. Outline the main cultural and organizational problems associated with change that are described in the case.
2. What actions were taken to overcome resistance to organizational change at Guinness?
3. Outline the technical solution adopted by Guinness. To what extent was it possible to source from a single supplier?

Summary

1. Change as a result of e-business needs to be managed on two levels. First the change that needs to be managed as part of projects to introduce e-business. Second, organization-wide change is required for e-business. We focus on this change in this chapter.
2. Sound project management is required to achieve change. Traditional project management activities such as estimation, resource allocation, scheduling, planning and monitoring are all important here. A project manager also needs to facilitate change by communicating the need for change.
3. Traditional lifecycle stages analysis, design, build can be used to estimate the tasks required for an e-business implementation. Since most e-business solutions will be based on tailoring off-the-shelf packages, there will be a change in balance between the analysis, design, build and implementation phases in comparison with a bespoke solution. Prototyping is essential to achieve the fast timescales required by e-business.
4. Building a team for e-business will require technical, marketing and project management skills. This will be difficult in the face of a competitive marketplace for these scales and high staff turnover. Tactics should be developed to help retain staff in this environment.
5. To implement e-business, a company will need to partner with a variety of companies. The e-business manager will need to decide whether to outsource activities such as strategy, content development and site promotion at the outset of an e-business project and whether it may be necessary to bring these activities back in-house at a later stage.
6. Changes to organizational structures are likely to be required to build the e-business. Coordination of e-business related activities can be achieved through a working party, e-business manager or a separate department. Companies may also spin-off sell-side e-commerce to a completely separate business.
7. Managing staff responses to change is an important aspect of change. Managers will need to consider how to achieve commitment and action from senior managers and also how to gain staff acceptance of the new system and new working practices. Techniques that may be used are user education, user involvement and achieving support from respected staff. Companies with an outward-looking cultural orientation will be predisposed to e-business led change while others that have an inward-facing, inflexible cultural orientation may have to consider changes in culture.

ACTIVITY ANSWERS

10.1 Managing change at The B2C Company

- Marketing Manager – marketing managers are likely to welcome e-business led change in a professional capacity since it potentially gives them the opportunity to develop a new channel to market which could help increase turnover. On a personal level, they may be worried about whether they have time to manage change and whether they or their staff have the appropriate skills. They may also be concerned as to whether the senior managers are prepared to 'walk the talk' as well as 'talking the talk'. They are also uncertain where the responsibility for e-business lies – is it with the CEO, the IS manager or themselves?

- Warehouse Manager – the warehouse manager may imagine that this change will not have much effect on him or her and that it is 'business as usual'.
- HR Manager – the HR manager will be worried about recruiting staff and educating staff about the change; it is going to mean a lot more work.
- IS manager – the IS manager may see the purpose of e-business as increasing power and budget, but like the marketing manager, may be concerned as to whether the CEO will 'put the money where its mouth is'. They will also be concerned with re-skilling, but this may be a way of helping to retain staff, some of who have recently left for dot-com companies.
- Employee in call centre –the employees in the call centre may feel unaffected by this change, but in fact their role could change since they may have to field e-mail and phone queries related to the web site about which they may have limited knowledge.

10.2 Building an e-commerce team for The B2C Company

Confusing, isn't it? We can see we need a blend of traditional marketing skills and new technical skills in the three roles:

- The online marketer needs to able to perform traditional marketing functions such as copywriting and coordinating promotions, but also needs to be web literate to know how best to promote the site. The need to work with different partners to raise the site's profile is also important.
- The web designer or web master needs to be versed in technical tools for site design such as Photoshop, Flash, Director, HTML, have database experience and know how to manage the site content. In a larger company, these roles would be occupied by more than two people.
- The project manager will need established skills to deliver the web enhancement on time and within budget, but will also need good knowledge of marketing and technical concepts. It could be argued that the project management could be part of the online marketer or e-commerce manager's role and then we could recruit a webmaster with database management skills in addition to our webmaster.

10.3 Staff retention at The B2C Company

You may have mentioned the following:

- Assessing the likelihood of a recruit to move on during the interview process (whether they have a history of short stays at companies).
- Create some sort of lock-in by offering a recruitment package or 'golden-hello' such as relocation that is tied to them staying with the company for two years.
- Develop a clear career path in conjunction with training that suggests to the employee it will be easier to advance within the company than by moving elsewhere.
- Improve job design using the techniques of Hackman and Oldham (1980), such as providing a balance of increasing the variety of tasks, empowering employees to complete more tasks and giving feedback on design.

And finally the obvious, but most difficult solutions:

- Don't make them work too hard, i.e. produce an environment in the company or a company ethos that means they don't want to move.
- Pay more or offer share options, again tied in with length of time at company or performance.

10.4 Options for outsourcing different e-business activities

1. Strategy – management consultant. These organizations have an established reputation in strategic consultancy and many are thought leaders in implementing e-business.
2. Design – new media agency. These are start-up companies who specialize in e-commerce and e-business design. They tend to offer all the skills in *Table 10.1* other than infrastructure.
3. Content development – new media agency. This is the 'bread and butter' of the media agency.
4. Online promotion – new media agency. Also the 'bread and butter' of the media agency.
5. Offline promotion – traditional marketing agency. New media agencies tend to have less experience in traditional communications channels, so an established company may be best here.
6. Infrastructure – ISP or traditional IT supplier. This is the clear choice for this activity, although larger companies may want to retain this facility in-house.

10.5 Which is the best organization structure for e-commerce?

1. The organization structures match as follows:
   (a) iv. No formal structure for e-commerce.
   (b) iii. A separate committee or department manages and coordinates e-commerce.
   (c) ii. A separate business unit with independent budgets.
   (d) i. A separate operating company.

2 and 3. Some of the main advantages and disadvantages are summarized in *Table 10.3*. You will identify many more!

10.6 Achieving staff commitment to e-business

The best approach to managing this change is to use education to communicate the purpose of the new approach to the staff, in other words, sell it to them. This education should target all employees in the organization who will be affected by the change. It can include:

- Sponsorship by senior staff from the beginning in explaining why the system is being implemented and how staff will be affected. Realistic goals must be set.
- Active participation by senior managers in talking to staff about the problems of change and reassuring where necessary.
- Early and active involvement of users in specification, testing and review or sign-off; treat them as customers and make key staff members of the project team.
- Training users in use of the software ('hands-on' training).
- Above all listening to staff and acting on what they say.
- Developing a system that is an improvement in terms of reliability and efficiency will help final acceptance.

10.7 Changing the culture for e-business

- *Survival (outward-looking, flexible)* – this organization is likely to be responsive and will have a 'thriving on chaos' mentality that will fit in well with the dynamic e-business environment. There could be problems in efficient updating of web content and services and there could also be problems with the efficiency of customer service such as through responding to e-mail enquiries. Small-medium start-up. Staff responsive to change.
- *Productivity (outward-looking, ordered)* – this company is arguably best placed to meet e-business. Existing interfaces with the environment such as links with suppliers and customers can perhaps be most readily transferred into electronic links. The only problem

may be that a hierarchical structure makes decision making and implementation slow with lack of creativity in response to customer needs. The company may not be as responsive as some of its competitors. Established medium to large company. Staff less responsive to change.

- *Human relations (inward-looking, flexible)* – this company is well placed to communicate well with customers and understand their needs from e-business. The lack of well-defined control structures may cause problems for implementation as for the *Survival* orientation. Small to medium company. Staff responsive to change.
- *Stability (inward-looking, ordered)* – it is difficult to imagine how this company has survived pre e-business. It will be slow to respond to the e-business challenge, perhaps waiting for others in its sector to 'test the water'. Once it does decide to react it should be able to implement e-business quite well, in a similar manner to the *productivity* orientation. Medium to large company. Staff very unresponsive to change.

10.8 E-business risk management for The B2C Company

Table 10.5 provides a model answer for risk assessment.

Table 10.5 Risk assessment for an e-business implementation project

Risk	*Probability*	*Impact*	*Solution*
Insufficient senior management commitment	5	7	Education/training/lobbying by e-business manager to achieve buy-in
High staff turnover/key staff leave	6	5	Use monetary incentives and improve working environment
Project milestones not met, overrun budget	8	6	Appoint experienced project manager and provide support and resources needed. Manager will perform risk management such as this
Problems with new technology delaying implementation (bugs, speed, compatibility)	8	8	Allow sufficient time for volume, performance testing
Staff resistance to change	4	4	Education, training identification of change facilitators amongst staff
Problem with integrating with partner's systems (e.g. customers or suppliers)	6	8	Tackle these issues early on, identify one contact point/manager for each of partnerships
New system fails after changeover (too slow or too many crashes)		9	See solution to delayed implementation

EXERCISES

Self-assessment questions

1. Summarize the main types of change that need to be managed during introduction of e-business.
2. What approaches must managers take to achieve change management successfully?
3. Outline the main stages of a sell-side e-commerce implementation.
4. Explain the role of prototyping in developing a sell-side e-commerce solution.

5. Describe four different approaches to retain staff.
6. What alternative approaches are there to structuring e-commerce within an organization?
7. Which type of organizational culture is most amenable to e-business related change?
8. What are some of the risks of e-business change, and how can they be managed?

Essay and discussion questions

1. Write an essay on approaches to managing e-business change.
2. 'Total outsourcing of e-business operations is the best method to overcome the skills shortage.' Discuss.
3. Contrast the project management stages involved with a sell-side and buy-side e-commerce implementation (referring to *Chapters 11 and 12* will help with this question).
4. 'High turnover of technical staff is a fact of life in a buoyant job market and there is little that can be done to reduce turnover.' Discuss.
5. Develop a change management plan for a company you are familiar with.
6. You are the HR Manager at a new media design agency and are evaluating the use of overseas contract workers to help on projects. Write a report summarizing the feasibility of this approach.
7. Write a report on how the knowledge within a company can be better managed. Refer to particular technologies and procedures for managing explicit and tacit knowledge.
8. Assess the merits of virtualization in an organization of your choice.

Examination questions

1. Explain what prototyping is and why it may be used on an e-commerce implementation.
2. Summarize the main human resource requirements for an e-commerce implementation.
3. A company has implemented a brochureware site without any changes to managerial or organizational structure. They are now seeking to achieve one third of their revenues via the web site. What changes to managerial and organizational structure would you suggest?
4. Explain how knowledge management differs from information management.
5. Explain the concept of the virtual organization. What are the advantages over a traditional organization?
6. Name four approaches a company can take to increase retention of technical staff.
7. Prioritize, with justification, your recommendations for outsourcing these functions: e-commerce strategy, e-commerce hosting, e-commerce content updating.
8. You are project manager of an e-procurement implementation. How would you maximize acceptance of the new system among staff?

REFERENCES

Adams, J., Hayes, J. and Hopson, B. (1976) *Transitions: Understanding and Managing Personal Change*. Martin Robertson, London.

Baker, P. (1998) *Electronic Commerce. Research Report 1998*. KPMG Management Consulting.

Bjorn-Anderson, N. and Turner, J. (1994) Creating the twenty-first century organization: the metamorphosis of Oticon, in Baskerville *et al.* (eds) *Transforming the Organisations with Information Technology.* Elsevier Science, Holland.

Bocij, P., Chaffey, D., Greasley, A. and Hickie, S. (1999) *Business Information Systems. Technology, Development and Management*. FT Management, London.

Boddy, D., Boonstra, A. and Kennedy, G. (2001) *Managing the Information Revolution*. Pearson Education, Harlow, UK.

Chaffey, D., Mayer, R., Johnston, K. and Ellis-Chadwick, F. (2000) *Internet Marketing: Strategy, Implementation and Practice*. Financial Times Prentice Hall, Harlow, UK.

Crush, P. (2000) What's my motivation? *Revolution*, 2 August, 34–6.

Davenport, T.H. (1993) *Process Innovation: Re-engineering Work through Information Technology*. Harvard Business School Press, Boston.

Davidow, W.H. and Malone, M.S. (1992) *The Virtual Corporation. Structuring and revitalizing the Corporation for the 21st Century*. HarperCollins.

Hackman, J. and Oldham, G. (1980) *Work Redesign*. Addison-Wesley, Reading, MA.

Hammer, M. and Champy, J. (1993) *Re-engineering the Corporation: A Manifesto for Business Revolution*. HarperCollins, New York.

Hansen, M., Nohria, N. and Tierney, T. (1999) What's your strategy for measuring knowledge? *Harvard Business Review*. May–June, 106–16.

IDC (1999) Knowledge Management Survey. IDC Research. (www.idcresearch.com).

IDC (2000) Capitalizing on Knowledge Management. IDC Research Report. (www.idcresearch.com #W18864).

Kraut, R., Chan, A., Butler, B. and Hong, A. (1998) Coordination and virtualisation: the role of electronic networks and personal relationships. *Journal of Computer Mediated Communications*. 3(4). Online-only, no page numbers.

Magretta, J. (1998) The power of virtual integration. An interview with Michael Dell. *Harvard Business Review*, March–April, 72–84.

Malone, T., Yates, J. and Benjamin, R. (1987) Electronic markets and electronic hierarchies: effects of information technology on market structure and corporate strategies. *Communications of the ACM*, 30(6), 484–91.

Parsons, A., Zeisser, M. and Waitman, R. (1996) Organising for digital marketing. *McKinsey Quarterly*, 4, 183–92.

Preece, J. (1994) *Human–Computer Interaction*. Addison-Wesley, Wokingham, UK.

Saunders, R. (2000) Managing Knowledge. *Harvard Management Communication Letter*, June, 3–5.

Schein, E. (1992) *Organisational Culture and Leadership*. Jossey Bass, San Francisco, CA.

Shardlow, N. (1999) Web blossoms for Orange. *Computing*, 14 January.

Simons, R. (1999) How risky is your company? *Harvard Business Review*, May–June, 85–94.

Sveiby, K.E. (1997–2000) *The New Organizational Wealth: Managing and Measuring Knowledge-Based Assets*. Berrett-Koehler. Updated on author's web site (www.sveiby.com.au/KnowledgeManagement.html)

Venkatraman, N. and Henderson, J. (1998) Real strategies for virtual organising. *Sloan Management Review*, Fall, 33–48.

FURTHER READING

Bocij, P., Chaffey, D., Greasley, A. and Hickie, S. (1999) *Business Information Systems. Technology, Development and Management*. FT Management, London. Chapter 7 introduces traditional lifecycle models for the implementation of BIS. Chapter 9 introduces the elements of project management. Chapter 13 considers elements of change management. Chapter 14 has a *Focus on* topic on outsourcing.

Boddy, D., Boonstra, A. and Kennedy, G. (2001) *Managing the Information Revolution*. Pearson Education, Harlow, UK. Chapter 5, Information and people, and Chapter 6, Information and structure, are relevant to this chapter and contain good examples.

WEB LINKS

BRINT.com (www.brint.com): a Business Researcher's Interests. Extensive portal with articles on e-business, e-commerce, knowledge management, change management and IS strategy.

Karl-Erik Sveiby has a regularly updated definition of different views of knowledge management. The FAQ, 'What is Knowledge Management', is recommended. (www.sveiby.com.au/KnowledgeManagement.html).

Andersen Knowledgespace (www.knowledgespace.com) is an external initiative to enable customers to access a wide range of market information for different sectors. A test drive will highlight some of the available features.

Knowledge Management Central (www.kmcentral.com): KM Central provides practical advice and support for business professionals working on knowledge management issues and projects.

Managing Change (www.managingchange.com): introductory articles by book authors.

Chapter 11

Analysis and design

CHAPTER AT A GLANCE

Main topics

Focus on . . .

Case studies

LEARNING OBJECTIVES

After completing this chapter the reader should be able to:

- Summarize approaches for analyzing requirements for e-business systems
- Identify key elements of approaches to improve the interface design and security design of e-commerce systems

MANAGEMENT ISSUES

Analysis and design of e-business systems raises these issues for management:

- What is the balance between requirements for usable and secure systems and the costs of designing them in this manner?
- What are the best approaches for incorporating new IS solutions with legacy systems into the architectural design of the e-business?

Links to other chapters

The main related chapters are:

- *Chapter 10* places analysis and design into the context of the change management for e-business as shown in *Figure 10.2*.
- *Chapter 12* – the sections on measurement and marketing research shows how the effectiveness of analysis and design are evaluated.

Introduction

Analysis and design
Analysis of system requirements and design for creation of a system.

In the context of strategy implementation, **analysis and design** activities are required to specify the business and user needs for a system and to develop a plan for building it (*Figure 10.2*).

This chapter reviews new approaches to analysis and design required for e-business systems. It does not aim to explain how to follow well-established techniques for analysis and design such as data flow diagramming, information flow diagrams and entity relationship diagramming. These have been described many times before, for example in Bocji *et al.* (1999).

The chapter is intended to provide managers with an appreciation of some analysis and design techniques for e-business, to provide familiarity with techniques such as process analysis, data modelling and use-case design. This familiarity should aid collaboration when the managers are involved in discussing the requirements of the system with technical staff.

It is in two main parts. In the first part we review analysis techniques and in particular process analysis for re-engineering which is important in many e-business implementations. We also touch on data modelling, looking at an example from The B2C Company. Data modelling is not described in detail since this is a very well-established technique.

The second part looks at the design of e-business systems. The techniques described are aimed at improving the information quality of end-users of e-business systems – ensuring information is timely, secure, has the correct content in terms of accuracy, relevance, completeness and is in a form that is easy to interpret. The section on architectural design looks at how systems are integrated to improve flow of information and also to achieve timely delivery of information. Focus on user-centred design demonstrates how using use-case analysis and interface design guidelines can be applied to produce usable sell-side or buy-side e-commerce systems with good information quality. Focus on security design reviews security requirements for the e-business, reviews generic approaches to security and finally looks at the current usage of e-commerce security techniques.

The importance of analysis and design is such that even if an effective strategy has been developed, its execution can be destroyed by ineffectual analysis and design. Complete *activity 11.1* to review some of the consequences of poor analysis and design.

The consequences of poor analysis and design

Activity 11.1

Purpose

To highlight the impact of poor analysis and design on customer satisfaction and business performance.

Activity

Form a focus group and discuss your own experiences of online purchasing. What have been your problems and frustrations? Refer to a particular example such as purchasing a book – what are your expectations?

For answer see p. 463

Analysis for e-business

Analysis for e-business is concerned with understanding the business and user requirements for a new system. Typical analysis activity can be broken down into: understanding the current process and then reviewing possible alternatives for implementing the e-business solution. In the following sections we will review different techniques that enable us to summarize the operation of current processes and proposed e-business processes. In this section we focus on using diagrams to demonstrate the business processes. User requirements capture techniques are described in the *Focus on user-centred design* section.

Analysis for e-business
Using analytical techniques to capture and summarize business and user requirements.

Analysts recognize that delivering quality information to employees and partners, or exchanging it between processes, is the key to building information systems that improve efficiency and customer service. Pant and Ravichandran (2001) say:

> *Information is an agent of coordination and control and serves as a glue that holds together organisations, franchises, supply chains and distribution channels. Along with material and other resource flows, information flows must also be handled to effectively in any organisation.*

This shows that in the era of e-business analysis should be used as a tool to optimize the flow of information both inside and outside organizations. In this chapter we start by looking at how workflow management is a key to managing time-based information flows. We then review how process modelling is used to analyse information flows to optimize business processes and then look at information storage analysis through a brief review of data modelling.

Workflow management

Analyzing and revising an organization's workflow as part of **workflow management** is a concept that is integral to many e-business applications, so before we look at process analysis techniques, let's look at why workflow is integral to e-business.

Workflow management
Workflow management (WFM) is the automation of information flows and provides tools for processing the information according to a set of procedural rules.

WFM is defined by the Workflow Management Coalition (WFMC, 1996) as

> *the automation of a business process, in whole or part during which documents, information or tasks are passed from one participant to another for action, according to a set of procedural rules.*

Workflow systems automate e-business processes by providing a *structured* framework to support a process. Applications of workflow in e-business include actioning queries from external customer queries or internal support queries. These queries may arrive by e-mail, phone or letter. E-mail enquiries can be analysed and routed to the right person depending on their subject. Letters may need to be scanned before adding to the workflow queue.

Workflows helps manage business processes by ensuring that tasks are prioritized to be performed:

→ as soon as possible
→ by the right people
→ in the right order.

The workflow approach gives a consistent, uniform approach for improved efficiency and better customer service. Workflow software provides functions to:

- assign tasks to people
- remind people about their tasks which are part of a workflow queue
- allow collaboration between people sharing tasks
- retrieve information needed to complete the task such as a customer's personal details
- provide an overview for managers of the status of each task and the team's performance

What type of workflow applications will exist in a company? For The B2B Company, e-business applications of workflow might include:

1. *Administrative workflow*. These concern internal administrative tasks. Examples include managing purchase orders for procurement and booking holiday and training.
2. *Production workflow*. These are customer-facing or supplier-facing workflows. An intranet or extranet-based customer support database and stock management system integrated with a supplier's system are examples of production workflow.

Process modelling

Traditional approaches to process analysis use established systems analysis and design methods that are part of methodologies such as SSADM, like the data flow diagram technique outlined in Bocij *et al.* (1999). Such approaches often use a hierarchical method of establishing

- the processes and their constituent sub-processes
- the dependencies between processes
- the inputs (resources) needed by the processes and the outputs

Activity-based process definition methods
Analysis tools used to identify the relationship between tasks within a business process.

Process
Part of a system that has a clearly defined purpose or objective and clearly defined inputs and outputs.

The processes and sub-processes are essentially the activities or tasks that need to be performed by the business information system, so these are sometime referred to as **activity-based process definition** methods. A **process** can be defined at the business level in terms of the main activities of a business. Each process can be broken down further as explained in the section on *task analysis*. Significant business processes are elements of the value chain; they include inbound logistics (including procurement), manufacture, outbound logistics or distribution and customer relationship management or sales and marketing activity. Davenport (1993) notes that even for large multi-national organizations the number of main processes will rarely exceed ten.

Note that in addition to the approaches shown here, use-case analysis to assist in defining interface requirements is also described in the *Focus on user-centred design* section.

Analysing the efficiency of processes is key to e-business design. Fortunately companies, whether new or start-ups, can tap into existing knowledge about how to improve process efficiency. The Arthur Andersen Global Best Practices knowledge base uses standard definitions of processes. There are seven operating processes that are broken down further:

1. Understand markets and customers.
2. Develop vision and strategy.
3. Design products and services.
4. Market and sell.
5. Produce and deliver services.
6. Produce and deliver services (services organization).
7. Invoice and service customer.

There are also six support and management processes:

1. Develop and manage human resources.
2. Manage information.
3. Manage financial and physical resources.
4. Execute environmental management programme.
5. Manage external relationships.
6. Manage improvement and change.

The performance of all of these processes needs to be analysed for e-business implementation.

Process mapping

Existing business processes often overlap between different functional areas of a business. So, before detailed activities are identified the analyst needs to identify where in the organization processes occur and who is responsible for them. This procedure is often known as **process mapping**. *Table 11.1* illustrates the activities which occur across functions in a business. Such a process mapping is clearly important for identifying potential users of an e-business system. *Table 11.1* shows an outline process map that might be used for The B2B Company to prepare a proposal for a new major account.

Process mapping
Identification of location and responsibilities for processes within an organization.

Task analysis and task decomposition

Before a process such as the 'prepare proposal' can be designed and implemented, a more detailed breakdown is required. This is usually referred to as **task analysis**.

Task analysis
Identification of different tasks, their sequence and how they are broken down.

Noyes and Baber (1999) point out that a difficulty with this type of process or task decomposition is that there are no set rules for what to call the different levels of decomposition or how far to decompose the process. The number of levels and the terminology used for the different levels will vary according to the application you are using and the consultant you may be working with. Georgakoupoulos

Table 11.1 Process map for activities with process 'prepare proposal'

Process activity	*Marketing*	*Engineering*	*Finance*	*Senior management*
1. Cost estimation		M		
2. Assess financial risk		m	M	
3. Publicity presentation	M	m		
4. Review	M	M	M	m
5. Authorization			M	M

M = major role in function, m = minor role in function

et al. (1995) talk about 'task nesting' of tasks broken down into sub-tasks as part of the activity-based method for describing workflows. They give the example of a workflow process for procurement where the task 'procure materials' is broken down further into the sub-tasks of 'verify status', 'get bids' and 'place order'. Curtis *et al.* (1995) provide a useful framework, referring to *process units* or *elements* at each process level as follows:

Level 1 *business process* are decomposed into:
Level 2 *activities* which are further divided to:
Level 3 *tasks* and finally:
Level 4 *sub-tasks.*

An example of a four-level task decomposition is presented in *Figure 11.1.*

Attempts to standardize the meanings of these terms have been produced by the workflow management coalition, an industry standards body (WFMC, 1996), which describes the different process elements as follows:

1. *Business process.* A set of one or more linked procedures or activities which collectively realize a business objective or policy goal, normally within the context of an organizational structure defining functional roles and relationships.
2. *Activity.* A description of a piece of work that forms one logical step within a process. An activity may be a manual activity, which does not support computer automation, or a workflow (automated) activity. A workflow activity requires human and/or machine resource(s) to support process execution; where human resource is required an activity is allocated to a workflow participant.
3. *Work item.* The representation of the work to be processed (by a workflow participant) in the context of an activity within a process instance. An activity typically generates one or more work items which together constitute the task to be undertaken by the user (a workflow participant) within this activity.

Process dependencies

Process dependencies summarize the order in which activities occur according to the business rules that govern the processes. Normally, activities occur in a sequence and are *serial*; sometimes activities can occur simultaneously when they are known as *parallel*. Data flow diagrams and flow charts are widely used as diagramming techniques to show process dependencies. In this section we will review three techniques for showing dependencies that are more commonly applied in

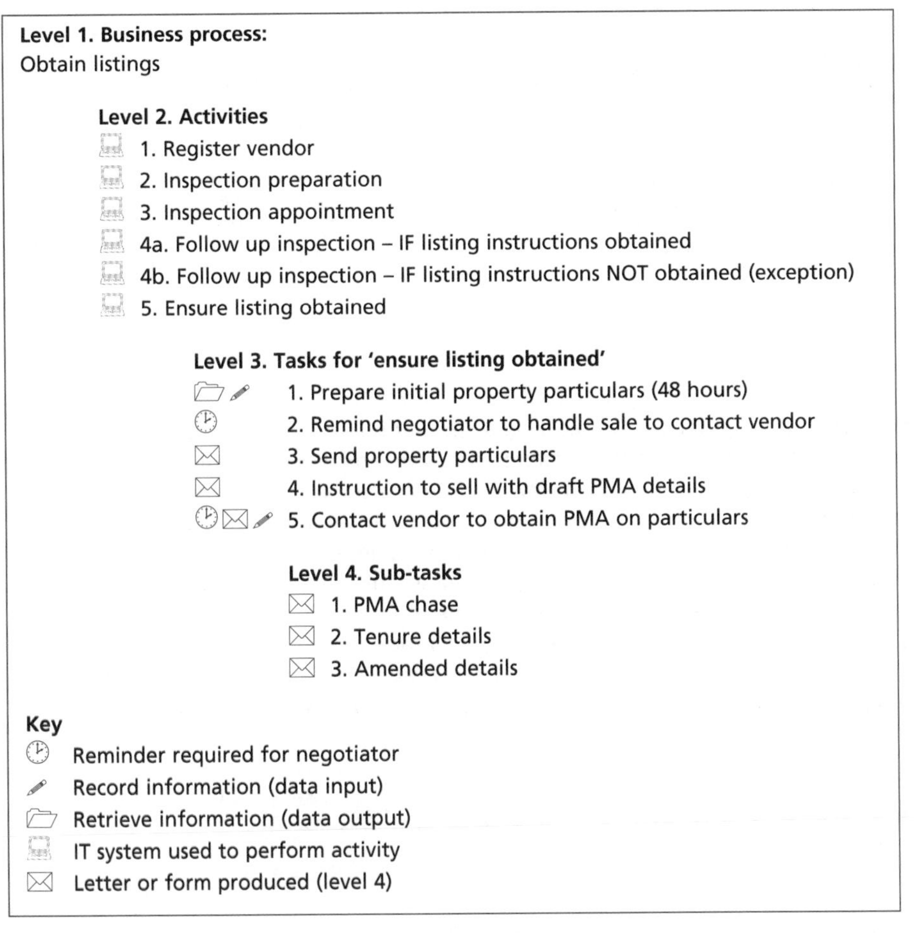

Level 1. Business process:
Obtain listings
Level 2. Activities
1. Register vendor
2. Inspection preparation
3. Inspection appointment
4a. Follow up inspection – IF listing instructions obtained
4b. Follow up inspection – IF listing instructions NOT obtained (exception)
5. Ensure listing obtained
Level 3. Tasks for 'ensure listing obtained'
1. Prepare initial property particulars (48 hours)
2. Remind negotiator to handle sale to contact vendor
3. Send property particulars
4. Instruction to sell with draft PMA details
5. Contact vendor to obtain PMA on particulars
Level 4. Sub-tasks
1. PMA chase
2. Tenure details
3. Amended details
Key
Reminder required for negotiator
Record information (data input)
Retrieve information (data output)
IT system used to perform activity
Letter or form produced (level 4)

Figure 11.1 An example task decomposition for an estate agency
Source: Chaffey (1998).

e-business analysis. These are flow process charts and network diagrams including the EPC standard used by the SAP product.

Flow process charts

A simple flow chart is a good starting point for describing the sequence of activities of a workflow that is part of an e-business process. Despite their simplicity, flow charts are effective in that they are easy to understand by non-technical staff and also highlight bottlenecks and inefficiencies. Flow process charts are used commonly when solving e-business problems, whether in the front-office or back-office. Each symbol in the chart refers to a particular operation within the overall process. An explanation of the symbols used in flow process chart analysis is shown in *Figure 11.2*. The box *Use of flow process charts for design of workflow systems* and *Figure 11.3* show one form of laying out flow process charts. Another example of how flow process charts are applied in practice using a tabular arrangement is presented in *activity 11.2*. An example of how tabular flow process charts can be applied to e-procurement analysis is also given in *Chapter 7*.

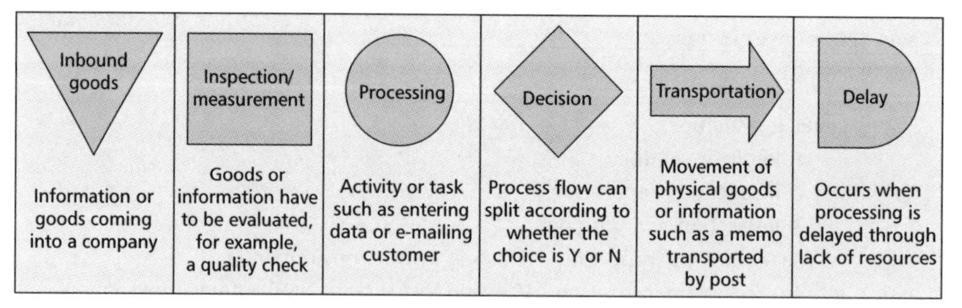

Figure 11.2 Symbols used for flow process charts

Use of flow process charts for design of workflow systems

In this example mortgage (loan) applications are received by post. It is then necessary to identify *new applications* and supporting documentation for applications already received. (This is a decision point indicated by a diamond-shaped decision box.) New applications are keyed into the workflow system as a new *case* and the original form scanned in for reference (these are processes shown as circles on the chart). Supporting material such as ID (driving licences), letters from employers are also scanned in. A team member will then assign or associate all scanned images of material which has been scanned in to a particular case. Assigning new documents (*assignment tasks*) is always the most important task so these need to be automatically placed by the software at the head of the workflow queue. Once assigned the documents will need to be actioned (*action tasks)* by the operator, so according to the type of document and when it needs to be chased the workflow

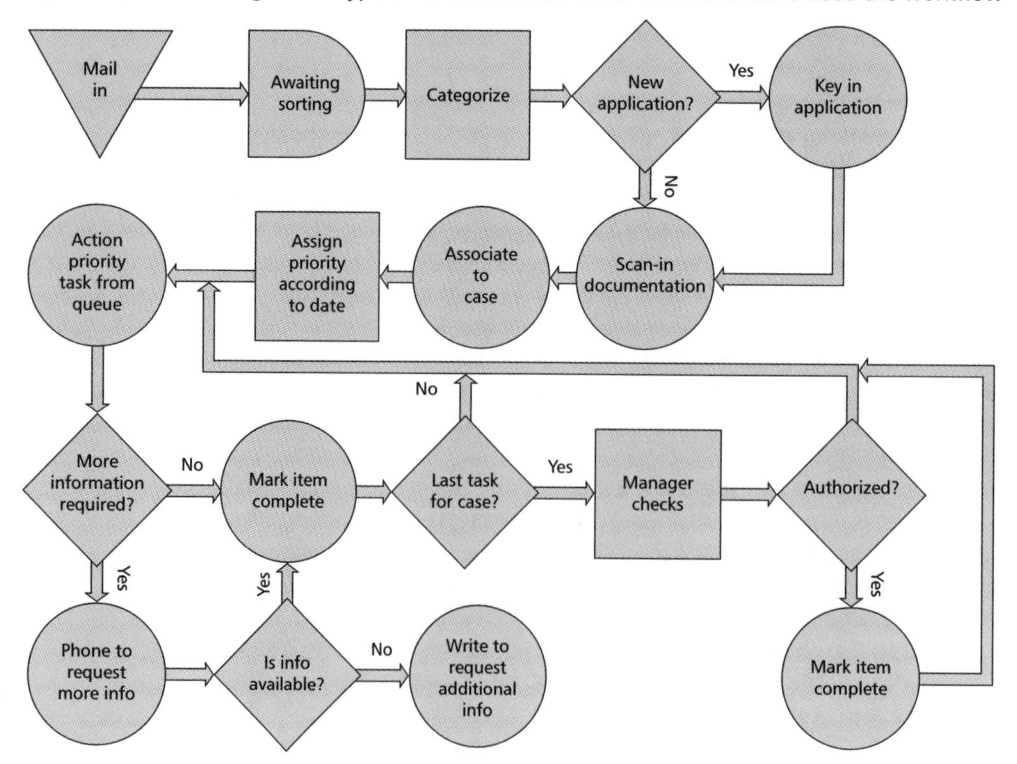

Figure 11.3 Flow process chart showing the main operations performed by users when working using workflow software

system will assign a priority to the task and place it on the workflow queue. Team members will then have to action tasks from the workflow queue which are prioritized according to date. Processing an action task will usually involve phoning the customer for clarification or writing a letter to request additional information. After this has been achieved the operator will mark the item as complete and a new workflow task will be created if necessary: for example, to follow up if a letter is not received within ten days.

This diagram is also useful for summarizing system design since it can identify different modules of a system and the hardware and software necessary to support these modules. In this case some of the modules are:

- Scan document (scanner and scanning software)
- Associate document to customer case (link to customer database)
- Prioritize document (specialized workflow module)
- Review document (link to customer database)
- Contact customer (link to phone system and letter printer)

Transforming invoice processing at The B2B Company

Activity 11.2

Purpose

To illustrate how the flow process chart can be used to simplify a business process.

Background

Table 11.2 has been drawn up following observation of tasks performed during a

Table 11.2 Flow process chart for invoice processing – original situation

No.	*Task description*	*Chart symbols*	*Distance (m)*	*Average time (hours)*
1	Receive invoice, stamp date	●⇨□D▼	–	0.1
2	To first payable clerk	○➡□D▽	50	5
3	On first payable clerk's desk	○⇨□◗▽	–	1
4	Write and attach purchase order	●⇨□D▽	–	0.1
5	To cost accountant	○➡□D▽	20	5
6	On cost accountant's desk	○⇨□◗▽	–	5
7	Code to appropriate job number	●⇨□D▽	–	0.1
8	Return to first payable clerk	○➡□D▽	20	5
9	On first payable clerk's desk	○⇨□◗▽	–	1
10	Make copies	●⇨□D▽	–	0.1
11	To Managing Director	○➡□D▽	200	5
12	On Managing Director's desk	○⇨□◗▽	–	48
13	Reviewed and approved by MD	●⇨□D▽	–	0.1
14	To second payable clerk	○➡□D▽	200	5
15	On second payable clerk's desk	○⇨□◗▽	–	1
16	Add vendor number and due date	●⇨□D▽	–	0.1
17	Write to accounts payable ledger in accounting systems	●⇨□D▽	–	0.5
18	Pay invoice – write cheque	●⇨□D▽	–	0.1
19	To file clerk	○➡□D▽	20	5
20	On file clerk's desk	○⇨□◗▽	–	1
21	File invoice	●⇨□D▽	–	0.1

systems analysis project at The B2B Company. The main problem is the delay currently occurring when the MD has to authorize an invoice of >£10,000. The company can obtain a discount of 10 per cent if payment is made in 10 days. This is not achievable currently and the MD wants to use IT to make this possible. As part of this re-engineering, restructuring may be required also – the MD believes that fewer staff are needed for invoice payment.

Activity

As business analyst you have to produce a more efficient way of working. You should restructure the workflow by filling in a blank table. You should also write down assumptions about changed roles and give details of new software needed to support the new workflow. You can assume each member of staff has access to a networked PC and the MD has access to a notebook with fax/modem that they use twice daily.

For answer see p. 464 and Table 11.3

Table 11.3 Flow process chart for invoice processing – re-engineered process

No.	*Task description*	*Chart symbols*	*Distance (m)*	*Average time (hours)*
1	Receive invoice, stamp and scan	●⇨□D▼	–	0.1
2	E-mail to first payable clerk	○➡□D▽	–	0.1
3	In worklist of first payable clerk	○⇨□◗▽	–	5
4	Fill in purchase order, code job number	●⇨□D▽	–	0.5
5	E-mail to MD	○➡□D▽	–	0.1
6	In MD's worklist	○⇨□◗▽	–	12
7	Review and approval by MD	●⇨□D▽	–	0.1
8	E-mail to second payable clerk	○➡□D▽	–	0.1
9	In worklist of second payable clerk	○⇨□◗▽	–	5
10	Add vendor number and due date	●⇨□D▽	–	0.1
11	Key into accounting system	●⇨□D▽	–	0.1
12	Pay invoice and mark task as complete	●⇨□D▽	–	0.1

Effort duration analysis

Effort duration analysis is an analytical tool that can be used to calculate the overall efficiency of a process when we have performed a detailed analysis such as that in *activity 11.2*. To do this, we sum the average time it takes workers to complete every activity making up the overall process, then divide this by the total length of time the whole process takes to occur. The total process time is often much longer since this includes time when the task is not being worked on. Here this is during transport of the forms, and when they are waiting in out-trays and in-trays. The efficiency relationship can be given as:

$$\text{Efficiency} = \frac{\Sigma\,(T_{(\text{effort on tasks})})}{T_{(\text{total process time})}}$$

If we apply effort duration analysis to the first scenario in *activity 11.2*, with delays and transport not contributing to the overall process, we can see that the efficiency of this extremely inefficient process is barely 2 per cent! This measure can be extended by noting the activities that add value to the customer rather than simply being administrative.

Network diagrams

While data flow diagrams and flow process charts may give a good indication of the sequence in which activities and tasks occur, they do often do not give a sufficiently tight, formal definition of the process sequence necessary for input into a e-business, workflow or ERP system. To do this we can use a network diagram known as a GAN (Generalized Activity Network). Here, nodes are added between the boxes representing the tasks, to define precisely the alternatives that exist following completion of a task. The most common situation is that one activity must follow another, for example a check on customer identity must be followed by a credit check. Where alternatives exist, the logic is defined at the node as follows: where a single pathway is taken from two or more alternatives, the node is defined as an OR node, and when several pathways may be followed this is an AND node. Join nodes combine previous activities, and splits determine which activities occur next. Where there are alternatives, business rules are defined as pre-conditions or post-conditions. A summary of the alternative dependencies is given in *Table 11.4*.

Table 11.4 Workflow dependencies at a node on a network diagram

Node type	*Description*	*Summary*
AND-SPLIT	Workflow splits into two or more parallel activities which all execute	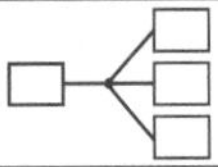
OR-SPLIT	Workflow splits into multiple branches of which only one is followed	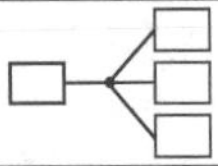
AND-JOIN	Multiple executing activities join into a single thread of control	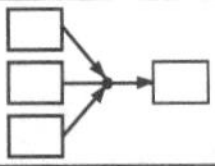
OR-JOIN	An exclusive alternative activity joins into a single thread of execution	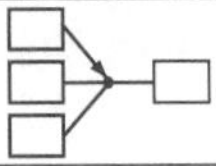
Iteration	Repetition of one or more workflow activity(ies) until a condition is met.	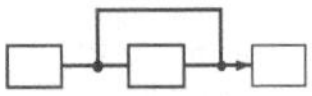
Must follow	No alternative paths exist	

Event-driven Process Chain (EPC) model

One of the most widely used methods for describing business events and processes is the Event-driven Process Chain method (EPC). This has been popularized by its application to re-engineering of enterprises performed using the SAP R/3 ERP product which accounts for worldwide sales of several billion dollars. Over 800 standard business EPCs are defined to support the SAP R/3 system; they are intended to illustrate business rules clearly for interpretation by business users before enactment in the software. The different elements of the EPC model are shown in *Table 11.5*; these include the different types of dependencies previously reviewed in *Table 11.4*.

Table 11.5 Elements of the Event-driven Process Chain (EPC) model

EPC symbol	*Description of EPC element*
Business Event	An event occurs when there is a change in the status of a process. It occurs in response to completion of a function
Business Function	A function is an activity or task that is usually completed by a person in the organizational unit responsible for the function. Alternatively it can be completed automatically through the workflow system.
xor and or Logical operation	Control flow logic between processes is denoted by joins/splits as follows: ● xor – a single activity follows the completed process(es) ● and – an and-split gives rises to multiple subsequent functions ● or – an or-split gives a multiple choice split
	control flow forming the process network
Information Object	Data needed for completion of a function and acting as input to subsequent functions (workflow relevant data in the WfMC definition). Also known as entity.
Organizational Unit	The unit responsible for the execution of a function

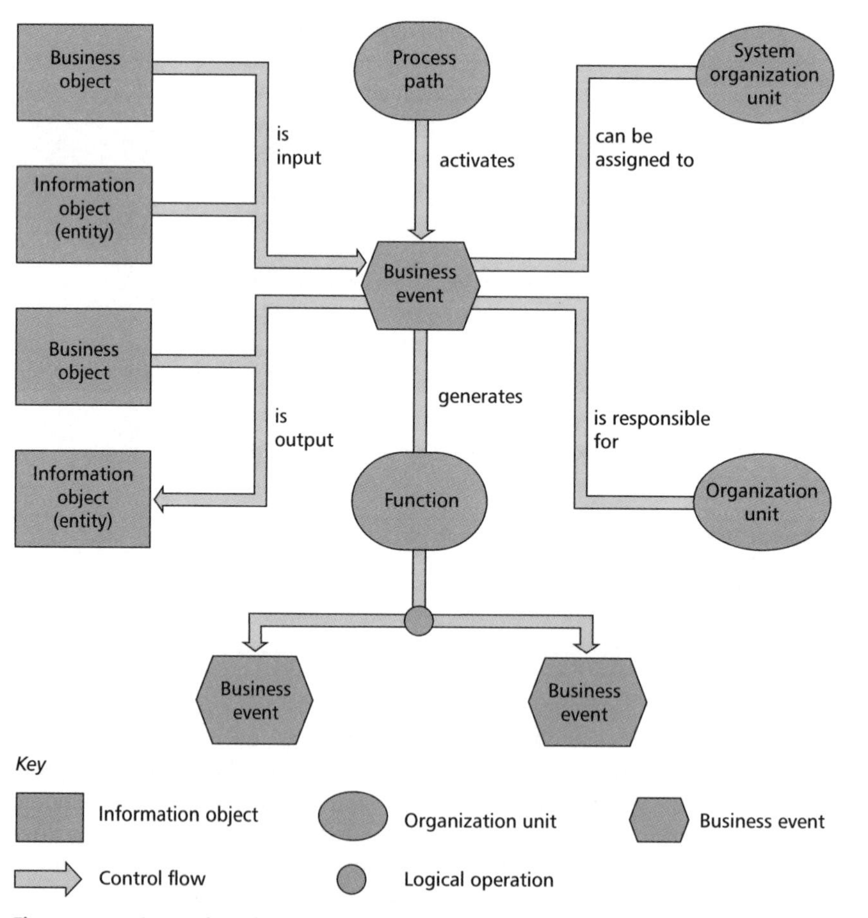

Figure 11.4 General model for the EPC process definition model

Figure 11.4 is an EPC metamodel illustrating how the different elements relate to one another. This figure shows how business functions are triggered through transactions on *business objects* which also lead to a *business event*. *Control flows* link the activities, events and logical operators. Entities or information objects are items such as sales orders or invoices.

Validating a new process model

Whichever method has been used to arrive at the process definition, we need to check that the process definition is realistic. When developing a wish list of process capabilities and corresponding business rules the stages described by David Taylor in his book on concurrent engineering (Taylor, 1995) may be useful. He suggests that once new processes have been established they are sanity checked by performing a 'talk-through, walk-through and run-through'. Here, the design team will describe the proposed business process as a model in which different business objects interact and in the talk-through stage will run through different business scenarios using cards to describe the objects and the services they provide to other business objects. Once the model has been adjusted, the walk-through stage involves more detail in the scenario and the design team will role-play the services the objects provide. The final run-through stage is a quality check in which no on-the-spot debugging occurs – just the interactions between the objects are described. Increasing use is made of simulation software to model alternative scenarios.

Data modelling

Data modelling of e-business and e-commerce systems uses well-established techniques such as normalization that are used for relational database analysis and design. As a consequence, this section is brief in comparison with that on process modelling which introduces some novel techniques. See Bocij *et al.* (1999), Chapter 12 for an introduction to normalization and relational database design. Some basic definitions are given in this section as a reminder of key terms. Before we start it is worth mentioning that the advent of data mining and object-oriented approaches has meant increasing use of non-relational database design. These are outlined further in Chapters 6 and 12 of Bocij *et al.* (1999).

The approach we use to explore data modelling for e-commerce is to use examples that identify typical elements of data modelling for a sell-side e-commerce system (The B2C Company). We will use ER (entity relationship) modelling to review typical structures for these databases. In simple ER modelling there are three main stages:

Entity
A grouping of related data, example customer entity. Implementation as table.

Database table
Each database comprises several tables.

Attribute
A property or characteristic of an entity, implementation as field.

1. Identify entities.

Entities define the broad groupings of information such as information about different people, transactions or products. Examples include customer, employee, sales orders, purchase orders. When the design is implemented each design will form a **database table**.

2. Identify attributes for entities.

Entities have different properties known as **attributes** that describe the characteristics of any single instance of an entity. For example, the customer entity has attributes such as name, phone number and e-mail address. When the design is implemented each attribute will form a **field**, and the collection of fields for one instance of the entity such as a particular customer will form a **record**.

Field
Attributes of products, example date of birth.

Record
A collection of fields for one instance of an entity, example Customer Smith.

Relationship
Describes how different tables are linked.

Primary key
The field that uniquely identifies each record in a table.

Secondary key
A field that is used to link tables, by linking to a primary key in another table.

3. Identify relationships between entities

The **relationships** between entities requires identification of which fields are used to link the tables. For example, for each order a customer places we need to know which customer has placed the order and which product they have ordered. As is evident from *Figure 11.5*, the fields customer id and product id are used to relate the order information between the three tables. The fields that are used to relate tables are referred to as key fields. A **primary key** is used to uniquely identify each instance of an entity and a **secondary key** is used to link to a primary key in another table. In *Figure 11.5* the primary key of the customer table is customer id, but the field customer id in the order table is here a secondary key that links back to the customer table. This relationship is an example of a one-to-many relationship since each customer may place many orders over the lifetime of the relationship.

Normalization is an additional stage, not covered here, used to optimize the database to minimize redundancy or duplication of information.

If you have previous experience in analysis and design for databases, complete *activity 11.3* to develop an ERD for The B2C Company. If you do not have this experience then refer to the generic answers to gain an appreciation of how databases are structured.

Activity 11.3 ER modelling for the B2C company

Purpose

To gain an understanding of the generic structure for transactional e-commerce databases.

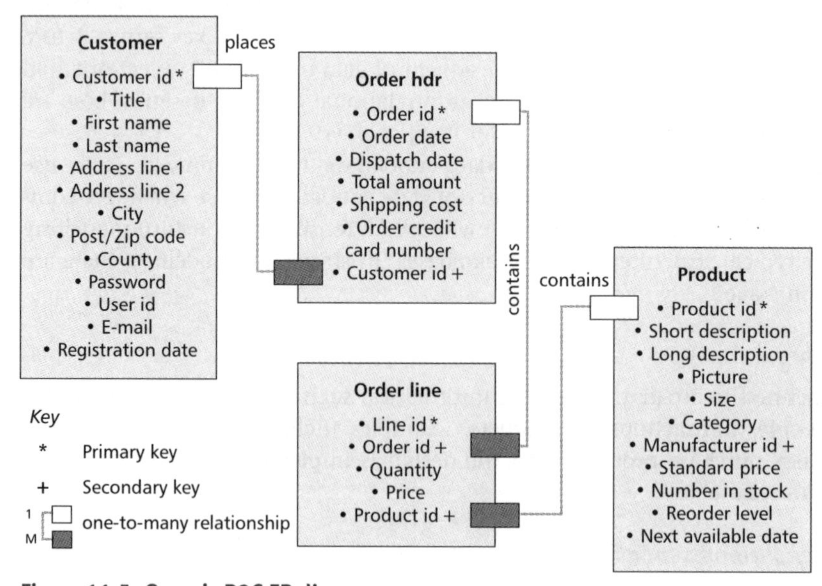

Figure 11.5 Generic B2C ER diagram

Activity

Create a normalized ER diagram for The B2C Company, or an B2C consumer transactional site.
For answers see Figure 11.5.

Comments

- Customer. May also have a separate delivery address.
- Order. Many items may be required on each order, so each order header can have many line items.
- Product. Includes catalogue information, such as description and a picture.
- Product. Informs the customer the number in stock and when they will be available from.
- There will be a separate manufacturer table not shown here.

Design for e-business

The **design** element of creating an e-business system involves specifying how the system should be structured.

In the two *Focus on* sections that follow we look at two aspects of design of that are of great importance to how e-business systems are perceived by customers – security and interface design. Before that, we consider the overall architectural design of e-business systems.

System design
Defines how an information system will operate.

Architectural design of e-business systems

The starting point for design of e-business systems is to ensure that a common architecture exists across the company in terms of hardware and software technology, applications and business processes. This goal is summarized in *Figure 3.13*.

E-business systems follow the same **client/server model** architecture of many business information systems created in the 1990s. For the e-business, the clients are typically employees, suppliers or customers' desktop PCs which give the 'front-end' access point to e-business applications. The clients are connected to a 'back-end' server computer via an intranet, extranet or Internet.

Client/server model
A system architecture in which end-user machines such as PCs known as clients run applications while accessing data and possibly programs from a server.

A key design decision in client/server systems is how different tasks involved in delivering a working application to the users are distributed between client and server. The typical situation for these tasks in an e-business system is:

- *Data storage*. Predominantly on server. Client storage is ideally limited to cookies for identification of users and session tracking. Cookie identifiers for each system user are then related to the data for the user which is stored on a database server.
- *Query processing*. Although some validation can be performed on the client.
- *Display*. This is largely a client function.
- *Application logic*. Traditionally, in early PC applications this has been a client function, but for e-business systems the design aim is to maximize the application logic processing including the business rules on the server.

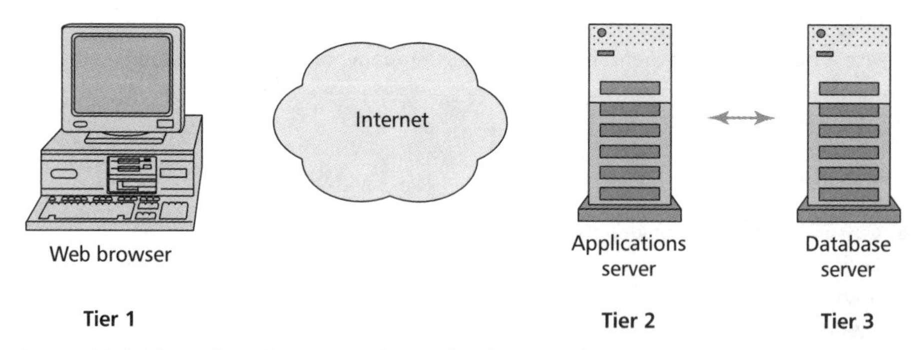

Figure 11.6 Three-tier client server in an e-business environment

Three-tier client/server
The first tier is the client that handles display, second is application logic and business rules, the third tier is database storage.

Thin client
An end-user access device (terminal) where computing requirements such as processing and storage (and so cost) are minimized.

A typical e-business architecture uses a **three-tier client/server** model where the client is mainly used for display with application logic and the business rules partitioned on a server, which is the second tier, and the database server is the third tier. Since most of the processing is executed on the servers rather than client, this architecture is sometimes referred to as a '**thin client**', because the size of the executable program is smaller. The application server provider (ASP) described in *Chapter 3* is typically based upon the three-tier model. This is shown in *Figure 11.6*.

Although the three-tier model of an e-business system suggests a relatively simple architectural design, the reality is more complex. Different servers are needed which combine applications logic and database storage for different requirements. These may be physically separate servers or combined. *Figure 11.7* shows a typical e-business architecture. The purpose of each of the servers is as follows:

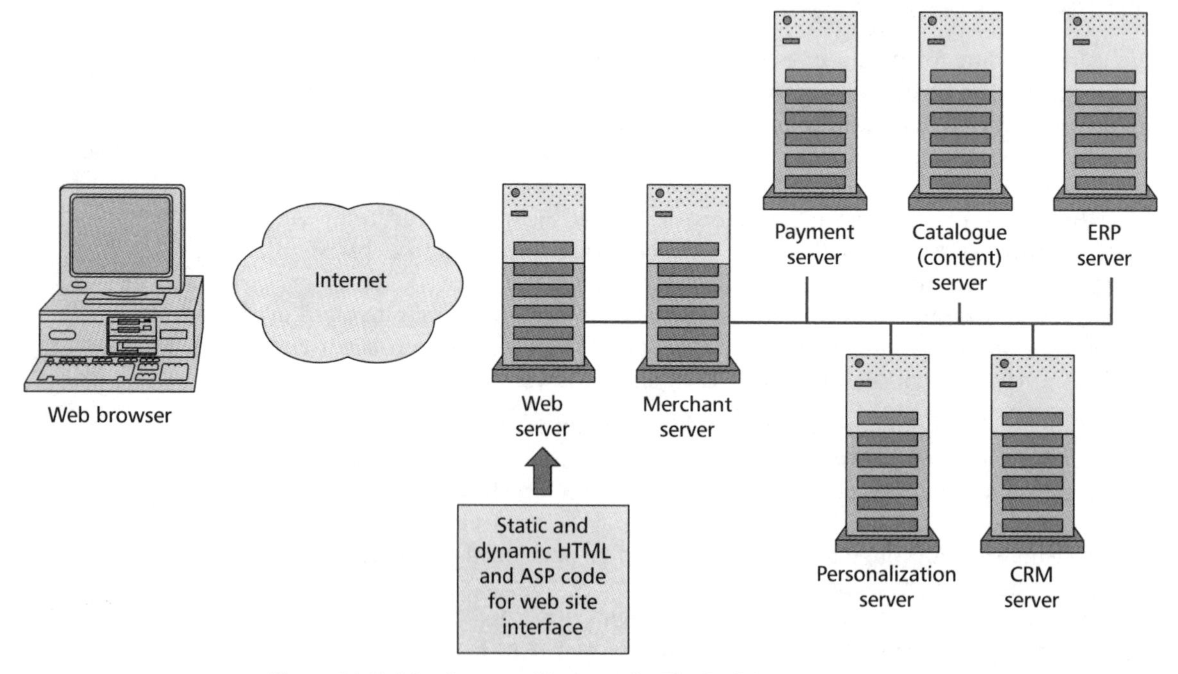

Figure 11.7 E-business architecture for The B2C Company

- *Web server.* Manages http requests from client and acts as a passive broker to other servers. Returns or serves web pages.
- *Merchant server.* This is the main location of the application logic and integrates the entire application by making requests to the other server components.
- *Personalization server.* Provides tailored content – may be part of commerce server functionality.
- *Payment commerce server.* Manages payment systems and secure transactions.
- *Catalogue server.* A document management server used to display detailed product information and technical specifications.
- *CRM server.* Stores information on all customer contacts.
- *ERP server.* Required for information on stock availability and pricing from the customer. Will also need to be accessed for sales order processing and histories. Logistics for distribution will also be arranged through the ERP server.

It is evident that designing the method of integration and between different components is not straightforward – creating a fully integrated e-business is not straightforward! As was discussed in *Chapter 9* the best approach to simplify the design is to reduce the number of suppliers of components to improve the ease of data and applications integration.

Case study 11.1 highlights some of the difficulties of integrating existing systems into new architectures.

CASE STUDY 11.1

Legacy data integration

FT

As companies embrace e-business and seek to build an extended supply chain, the challenges and costs of integrating 'legacy' data grow sharply. Data integration has been described as the dirty little secret of e-business. While companies spend millions of dollars on impressive-looking web sites, they often overlook the need to link their new e-business applications into existing back-end 'legacy' systems.

Industry experts say the challenge associated with integrating 'legacy' data from ageing financial, order entry and accounting systems into new e-commerce or customer relationship management applications is the single greatest barrier to success for most e-business initiatives.

Even within the enterprise, the complexity of integration can be overwhelming. Each type of application presents a different view of information such as customers, sales orders or stock levels. The most common way to tie applications together is for programmers to manually 'hard-code' the links.

That is acceptable for a couple of applications but, as the number grows, so too do the integration challenges. In addition, these proprietary hard-coded interfaces are inflexible and difficult to maintain.

The difficulties grow as companies embrace e-business and seek to build an extended supply chain integrating their customers, suppliers and trading partners. As the challenges soar, so too do the costs.

'For the first time in history more IT dollars are being allocated to integration projects than to the hardware that drives them,' says Bluestone Software, a US company specializing in integration software.

One of its customers is TNT Express, the European express courier, which wanted to provide a package-tracking capability on its web site. Using Bluestone's Sapphire/Web application server, TNT linked its web server to legacy applications on an IBM mainframe and to a local Informix database.

Now, by simply typing a consignment number into the web page, TNT customers can track the progress of their express documents, parcels or freight around the world, in more than 200 countries.

▶

▶ CASE STUDY *continued*

The Sapphire/Web application server provides customers with information on delivery, including date and time of delivery, who signed for the shipment and a detailed report of the shipment check-in points en route to its final destination.

Bluestone recently released a new e-business integration server based on Extensible Markup Language (XML). This product can draw data from different sources and dynamically convert it to XML, the new universal standard for electronically exchanging data, which is rapidly becoming the lingua franca for business-to-business transactions.

Many companies in the enterprise integration market see XML as a solution to the problems of incompatible data formats. But according to Charles Saunders, marketing director of Mercator Software, XML will not make integration problems go away. 'XML is going to be a useful tool but it is not the be-all and end-all.'

Mercator has developed a Commerce Broker product which, unlike web integration tools developed around XML, can work with both web-based and traditional e-commerce standards, such as EDI.

Mr Saunders gives the example of a large UK retailer which every night transfers a 4GB file containing the day's transactions. If those transactions had to be converted to XML the file size would grow enormously.

Mercator is one of a small group of software companies specializing in data integration. Others include Neon, Level 8, Active Software and Web Methods – the latter is currently acquiring Active. Initially, these companies, often called enterprise application integration (EAI) vendors, have focused on the problems of linking internal applications together.

This is done with a range of 'adapters' to connect one application to another. 'You don't need to know how to get the data out of the applications because the adaptor does that,' says Mr Saunders.

The EAI vendors have recently sought to expand into the more challenging market for linking different partners together in trading communities.

For example, Level 8 has used its Geneva Integrator technology at ABN Amro, the big Dutch bank, to integrate its back-end legacy systems with web-based applications to handle the growing number of online customer inquiries. In four months, Geneva Integrator enabled ABN Amro to use data from its legacy systems and convert it quickly to different web formats.

Now it is going further and using Geneva Integrator as a 'message broker' to link ABN Amro's core processing systems to the external infrastructure of Integrion, an international banking consortium which includes ABN Amro.

EAI is not the only way to integrate e-business applications and analysts at the Meta Group say that EAI, while good for internal applications, can be too 'invasive' to use with partner organizations.

A different approach to inter-enterprise integration is offered by companies such as Tibco, Iona and BEA, which favour using middleware to create an extra integration layer between different applications. A third alternative comes from Actional Software, which until last month was called Visual Edge.

John Orcutt, chief executive of Actional, claims his company's control broker technology is superior to other approaches. 'If you want to get inventory or shipping information from the front-end application with zero latency [no delays], EAI cannot do this. Our control broker lets you create a very direct connection from the front-end to the back-end without introducing an additional middleware layer.'

As well as allowing direct access, Actional's integration products implement the concept of "forward command and control", meaning that business services can readily be made available to any customer 'touchpoint,' such as a call centre operator, a self-service transaction on a website, or a bank teller machine.

'Companies are looking to drive more and more of their products forward to their customers,' says Mr Orcutt.

Banks, in particular, have severe integration problems as they seek to 'empower' their customers and keep track of customers' transactions and preferences across multiple channels. The wave of consolidation in the banking and other sectors adds to the integration headaches of IT managers.

But it is an ill wind that blows no good and the integration vendors have learned the best source of new business comes from reading the mergers and acquisitions stories in the newspapers.

'We now have a team of people who just look out for acquisitions,' says Mr Saunders.

Source: Article by Geoffrey Nairn, Financial Times, 5 July 2000.

Questions

1. Describe the nature of and reasons for the problems of data integration described in the article.
2. What solutions to the data integration problem are suggested?
3. Research these solutions further by visiting the web sites of the companies described. What do you think are the strengths and weaknesses of each of the approaches? Which would you select?

Focus on user-centred design

Since e-business systems are often customer or employee-facing systems, the importance of human computer interaction is high in the design of web applications. Referring to web site design, Nigel Bevan says:

> *Unless a web site meets the needs of the intended users it will not meet the needs of the organization providing the web site. Web site development should be user-centred, evaluating the evolving design against user requirements.* (Bevan, 1999a)

Case study 11.2 illustrates how, for one company, user interface enhancements translated into significant gains for the company.

CASE STUDY 11.2

User interface enhancements at Waterstone's

Waterstone's, part of the HMV Group, has 12 per cent of the UK book market with its 224 stores but has had bigger ambitions since it first went online in October 1996.

Initially, the web site was designed and hosted by the same company, Hyperlink, and offered book searching among 1.2 m books, secure ordering, diary, Waterstone's club and online chat. However, according to Andrew Hatton, project manager, the technology was holding the company back, particularly as Amazon continued to use its huge market capitalization to invest in web interface and back-end fulfilment systems.

Based on an in-house developed application and web server, the site was unable to deliver new functionality quickly or cost effectively, he says. 'Hyperlink had to perform a time-consuming software upgrade to meet our request for the site's pages to change more rapidly.'

As a result, Waterstone's decided to revamp its web site and was willing to undergo a complicated implementation process. This included numerous hardware and software vendors, as well as integration and design consultants, to develop the ideal retail site. Working with Siemens, web site designers Brainstormers and e-commerce integrator Nvision, Waterstone's developed an enhanced e-commerce site in 12 weeks.

Mr Hatton says: 'The site's increased functionality has enabled us to establish a more aggressive e-commerce marketing programme and combat increasing competition from international online-only retailers, such as Amazon.'

The star in the vendor team seems to have been Nvision which handled the back-end integration to link the new solution to Waterstone's existing business systems. The integrator performed a 'Swot' (strength, weakness, opportunities, threats) analysis to identify the market opportunities for an online bookstore, and these were then matched against Waterstone's existing capabilities, both on the web site and in the supply chain.

Books are now represented visually by book jackets, in an attempt to match the experience of browsing through titles in a book shop. The site includes a virtual 'greeter', which pops up in a window to

▶ CASE STUDY *continued*

give instructions and show customers where to go to complete orders. Members of the Waterstone's club have access to an online version of Waterstone's magazine.

The site also offers electronic gift vouchers, personalized browsing and online author events such as readings and question-and-answer sessions. Waterstone's has also developed branch pages that provide each store with its own pages and URL. Once the site is further integrated with stores, customers will be able to look at online book selections through store kiosks.

Now Waterstone's plans to introduce features that will provide greater personalization on the site. For example, customers will be able to send e-mails to request information about specific books.

In the first two weeks of the new site's operation, the amount of the average order increased by 25 per cent, says Mr Hatton. And the branch pages have enabled individual stores to operate their own sales and marketing campaigns. The system is used mainly by customers in the UK, Europe and the US, but a growing number of new customers browse and order books from Asia, Australia and Africa.

Waterstone's also regards the web site as a stepping-stone to future technologies such as digital TV and web phone shopping.

'We view it as strategic to our future business, and therefore it's in our interest to gain as much experience and exposure to the medium and methodologies now,' says Jonathan Wilson, Internet business manager.

The technology running the site comprises Sun servers running Netscape Enterprise, Intershop 3.0 Enterprise, Oracle 8.0 database and an NT server running the Alta Vista search engine. A wide area network links up with an IBM AS/400 server to run Eclipse, a web version of Waterstone's existing Phoenix order fulfilment system.

Source: Article by Christopher Field, *Financial Times*, 3 May 2000.

Questions

1. How does interface design translate into improved customer performance for Waterstone's?
2. What lessons can managers learn from the implications of how Waterstone's have managed their project?

User-centred design
Design based on optimizing the user experience according to all factors, including the user interface, which affect this.

Noyes and Baber (1999) explain that **user-centred design** involves more than user interface design. It can be conceived as centring on the human, but surrounded concentrically by factors that affect usability such as user interface, computers, workplace and the environment. Here we will be specifically looking at the user interface.

User-centred design starts with understanding the nature and variation within the user groups. According to Bevan (1999a), issues to consider include:

- Who are the important users?
- What is their purpose for accessing the site?
- How frequently will they visit the site?
- What experience and expertise do they have?
- What nationality are they? Can they read English?
- What type of information are they looking for?
- How will they want to use the information: read it on the screen, print it or download it?
- What type of browsers will they use? How fast will their communication links be?
- How large a screen/window will they use, with how many colours?

Rosenfeld and Morville (1998) suggest four stages that also have a user-centred basis:

1. Identify different audiences.

2. Rank importance of each to business.
3. List the three most important information needs of audience.
4. Ask representatives of each audience type to develop their own wishlists.

For an example of the principle of customer orientation in action visit retailer B&Q's DIY site (www.diy.com). This is targeted at a range of users of DIY products, so is designed around three zones: products, advice and inspiration. Experts who know what they want go straight to the product section and buy what they need. Less experienced users with queries on what to purchase can gain advice from an expert just as they would in-store and novices may visit the inspiration zone which includes room mock-ups with lists of the products needed to create a particular look. An alternative approach is used by Guinness (www.guinness.com) who have three site zones: like it, live it, love it.

Bevan (1999b) also notes the importance of defining key scenarios of use, which is consistent with the use-case approach described above. This stage, often known as knowledge elicitation, involves interviewing users and asking them to talk through their current or preferred way of working. Once the scenarios have been established card sorting techniques as described by Noyes and Baber (1999) can be used. They describe how after interviewing users, typical tasks or actions were written down onto cards. These were then used to identify the sequence of actions users required from a menu system. They explain that the menu system devised was quite different than that envisaged by the software engineers. Card sorting techniques can also be used to check through that no stages have been missed during the **talk-through** – a **walk-through** of the cards is performed. Talk-throughs do not require a physical setup but walk-throughs do in the form of a series of cards or use of a prototype of the system.

Talk-through
A user verbally describes their required actions.

Walk-through
A user executes their actions through using a system or mock-up.

Evaluating designs

A test of effective design for usability is, according to Bevan (1999b), dependent on three areas:

1. *Effectiveness* – can users complete their tasks correctly and completely?
2. *Productivity (efficiency)* – are tasks completed in an acceptable length of time?
3. *Satisfaction* – are users satisfied with the interaction?

See *Chapter 11* for further discussion of how the user interface can be created.

Use-case analysis

The **use-case** method of process analysis and modelling was developed in the early 1990s as part of the development of object-oriented techniques. It is part of a methodology known as **Unified Modelling Language (UML)** that attempts to unify the approaches that preceded it such as the Booch, OMT and Objectory notations. Jacobsen *et al.* (1994) gives an accessible introduction and how object modelling can be applied to workflow analysis.

The following stages are identified by Schneider and Winters (1998) for analysis using the use-case method:

Use-case modelling
A user-centred approach to modelling system requirements.

Unified Modelling Language (UML)
A language used to specify, visualize and document the artefacts of an object-oriented system.

Actors
People, software or other devices that interface with a system.

1. Identify actors.

Actors are those objects which are involved in using or interacting with a system.

They are not part of the system. The obvious actors are the users of a system. In a customer service application the actors may be a customer and the customer service person at the company. When performing process analysis to define use-cases we ask questions such as 'who are the actors for this process?', 'What services do these actors provide?', 'What are the actors' tasks?' and 'What changes do they make to the status of the overall process?'. Actors are typically application users such as customers and employers. They may add information to the system or receive it through reporting facilities. Note that an employee who has several roles such as a manager role and administrator would be represented by two different actors.

Schneider and Winters (1998) point out that other actors include software and hardware control devices that change the state of the process or external systems that interface with the system under consideration. These are effectively human actors who have been automated through other systems that interface with the current system under consideration. Actors are denoted using the straightforward approach shown in *Figure 11.8*.

2. Identify use-cases.

Use-case
The sequence of transactions between an actor and a system that support the activities of the actor.

Use-cases are the different things users of a system want it to perform. These can be described as activities or tasks that are part of a dialogue between an actor and

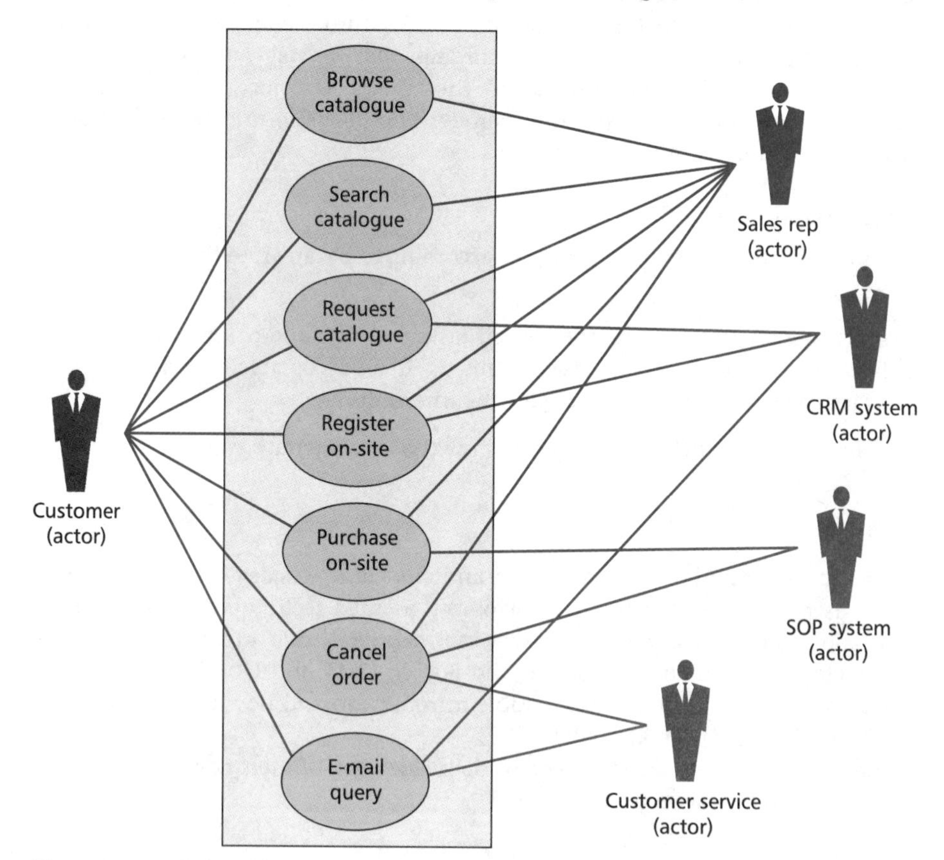

Figure 11.8 Relationship between actors and use-cases for The B2C Company, sell-side e-commerce site

system. They summarize the requirements of a system from each actor since they described the functionality that will be provided by the system. Common use-cases are:

- Starting up, shutting down or amending a system.
- Adding or amending information on a system. Examples include placing an e-commerce order or recording a complaint via e-mail.
- Using a system for reporting or decision support.

Some use-cases for The B2C Company are shown in *Figure 11.8*.

3. Relate actors to use-cases

Figure 11.8 also shows how actors relate to use-cases. It can be used to identify responsibilities and check for missing activities. For example 'Check order status' is a use-case that is missing and the company would have to discuss whether it was acceptable for a customer service rep to place an order for a customer who was complaining about a particular product. This probably would be desirable to avoid a customer being transferred from a sales person to a customer service person. One of the features of e-commerce is that the system that is used by the sales representatives will typically have common use-cases or features to that for the customer, but some may differ – for example, only a customer service representative or sales rep would be able to perform a 'give refund' use-case.

4. Develop use-case scenarios

Scenario
A particular path or flow of events or activities within a use-case.

A detailed **scenario** is then developed to detail the different paths of events and activities for each use-case. The primary scenario describes the typical case where nothing goes wrong. The use-case includes detail of activities or function, what happens when there is an alternative or decision, or if there is an error. Pre-conditions for entering and post-conditions for exiting the use-case are also specified.

Figure 11.9 shows a primary scenario for the complete e-commerce purchase cycle. A more detailed primary scenario for the particular use-case 'Register' written from the point of view of the customer actor from *Figure 11.10* is as follows.

Pre-condition: A user is active on the web site.
Scenario: Register.

Basic path:
1. Use-case starts when customer presses 'register'.
2. Customer enters name, postal address and e-mail.
3. The post/zip code and e-mail address (@ symbol) will be checked for validity after entry and the user prompted if there is an error.
4. The customer will select submit.
5. The system will check all fields are present and the customer information will be passed to the CRM system.
6. A redirect page will be displayed to thank the customer for registering and provide an option to return to the home page and the use-case ends.

Post-condition: The customer details have been saved.

Alternative paths: The customer can cancel at stages 2 to 4 before pressing 'submit' and the use-case ends.

It can be seen that by stating the use-case in this way different issues can be clarified. For instance, should the validation at stage 3 occur when the entry field loses focus (i.e. tab to next field), or should it wait until step 4 which is perhaps more

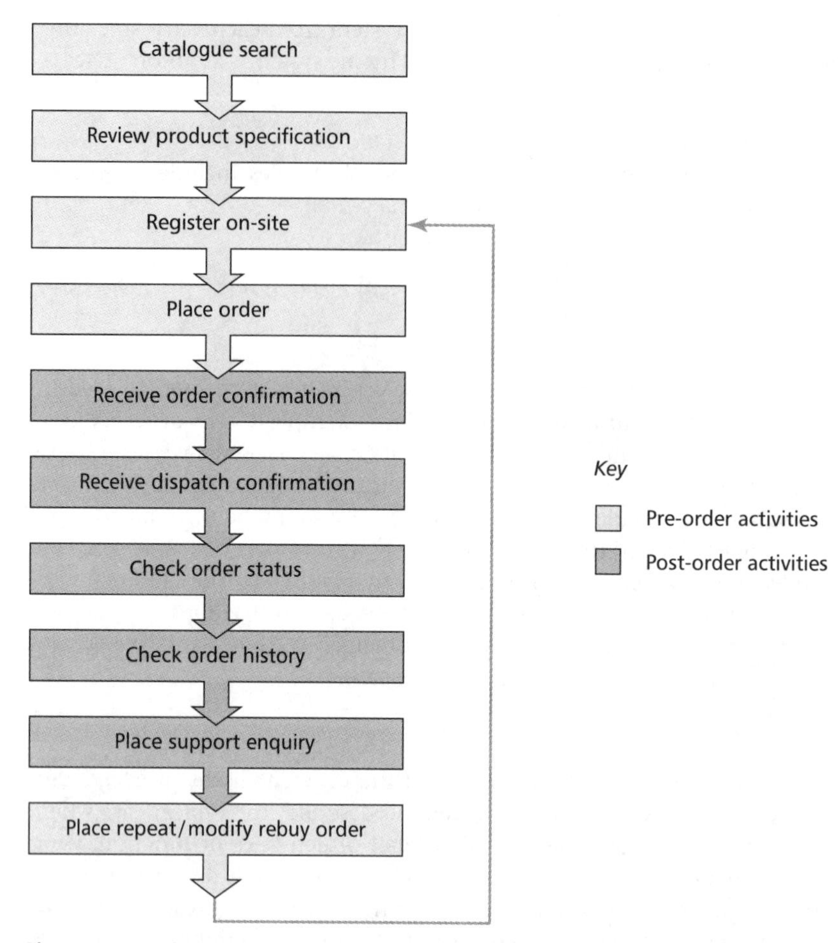

Figure 11.9 Primary use-case scenario for an entire e-commerce purchase cycle

conventional? Another issue is whether we should display the customer details at stage 6 with the option to amend them if incorrect. Discussing the options before development saves time when coding prototyping. After the primary scenario is complete, second or alternative scenarios can be developed and added to the primary scenarios as alternatives. For the register scenario, cancel is a secondary scenario, others could include error conditions such as whether the postcode isn't valid.

Figure 11.11 illustrates an e-commerce site with clear menu options which is consistent with use-case analysis.

Customer orientation

Customer orientation
Developing site content and services to appeal to different customer segments or other members of the audience.

A well-designed site will have been developed to achieve **customer orientation**. This involves the difficult task of trying to provide content and services to appeal to a wide range of audiences. For a B2B company the three main types of audience are customers, other companies and organizations and staff. The detailed breakdown of these audiences is illustrated in *Figure 11.12*. Visit the Dell web site (www.dell.com) to see how Dell segments its customer base on the home page into:

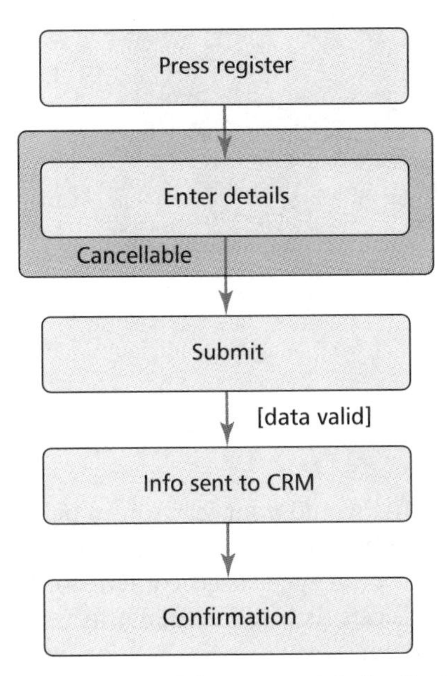

Figure 11.10 Primary scenario for the Register use-cases for The B2C Company

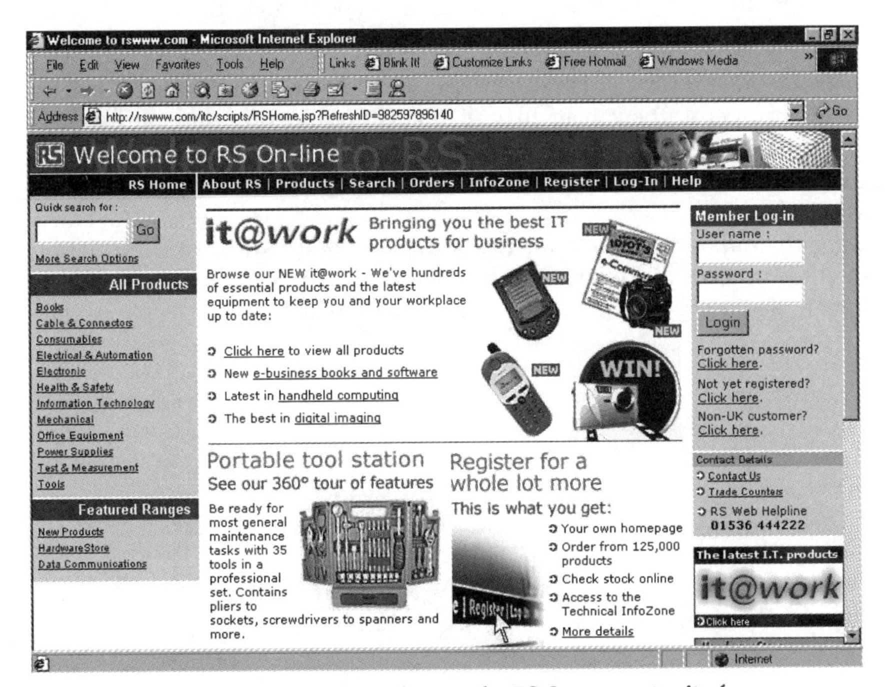

Figure 11.11 Clear user scenario options at the RS Components site (www.rswww.com)

- Small office and home users
- Small businesses
- Medium businesses
- Large businesses
- Corporates
- Government organizations

Customers
New or existing
Large, med, small
Product type
By country
Users, deciders, buyers

Third parties
Suppliers
Distributors
Investors
The media
Competitors

Staff
New or existing

Figure 11.12 Different types of audience for the web site of The B2B Company

Think about how well this approach works. What would your reaction to being classified as a mere small-business and home owner be? Do you think this is a valid approach? A similar approach, by Microsoft, is to offer specialized content for IS managers to help them in their investment decisions. Is a more straightforward product-centric structure to the web site appropriate?

As well as customer segments, designers also need to take into account variations in the backgrounds of visitors to the site. These can be thought of as four different types of familiarity:

1. *Familiarity with the Net* – are short-cuts provided for those familiar with the Net? and for novices is there help to lead them through your site? Research by Netpoll in Focus groups suggests that users pass through different stages of familiarity and confidence as shown in *Figure 11.13*. Site design should try to accommodate this.
2. *Familiarity with organization* – for customers who don't know an organization, content is needed to explain who the company is and demonstrate credibility through 'About Us' options and customer testimonials.

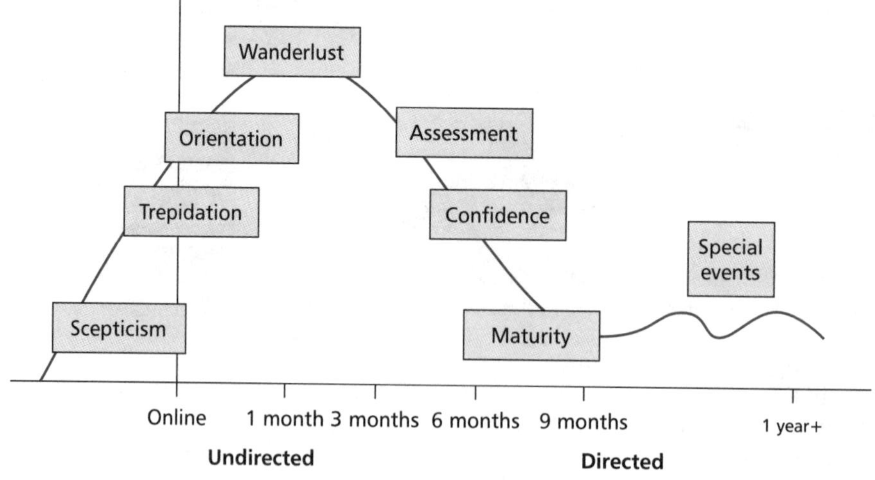

Figure 11.13 Different stages of user familiarity with the Internet.
Source: The Netpoll Internet Usage curve, www.netpoll.net.

3. *Familiarity with organizations' products* – even existing customers may not know the full range of your product offering.
4. *Familiarity with your site* – site maps, Search and Help options are not 'nice to have' options for an e-commerce site since you may lose potential customers if they cannot be helped when they are lost.

Jakob Nielsen (2000a) says this about novice users:

> *Web users are notoriously fickle: they take one look at a home page and leave after a few seconds if they can't figure it out. The abundance of choice and the ease of going elsewhere puts a huge premium on making it extremely easy to enter a site.*

But he notes that we also need to take account of experts. He says we may eventually move to interfaces where the average site visitor gets a simplified design that is easy to learn and loyal users get an advanced design that is more powerful. But for now *'in-depth content and advanced information should be added to sites to provide the depth expected by experts'*.

The principles of customer orientation can be extended from the design of the site to the tactics that are used to deliver services via a web site as explained through *activity 11.4*.

Applying Patricia Seybold's Customers.com approach to customer orientation

Activity 11.4

Purpose

To highlight how the principles of customer orientation of services offered can be applied to site design.

Activity

Read the extract of the eight success factor outlined by US industry analyst Patricia Seybold in her book, *Customers.com* (Seybold, 1999). Explain how each of these could be applied to customer-oriented site design for The B2B Company.

The eight critical success factors she suggests are:

1. *Target the right customers*. This first and most important principle suggests concentrating on either the most profitable customers, which is one of the tenets of CRM (*Chapter 9*), or those that cannot be reached so well by other media. For example, UK car insurer Swinton wished to target the young-driver market so it trialled a web site with a special 'Streetwise' brand. Alternatively the right customers in the business-to-business context could be those who make the buying decisions.
2. *Own the customer's total experience*. By managing the customer's entire experience it should be possible to increase the quality of service and hence promote loyalty. The total experience can be considered as all parts of the fulfilment cycle from product selection, purchase, delivery and setup to installation and after-sales services. Examples of how the Internet can be used to improve the customer experience taken from across this cycle are provided in the final section of this chapter. Note that since many services such as delivery are now outsourced, this requires careful selection of partners to deliver this quality service.
3. *Streamline business processes that impact on the customer*. Seybold (1999) gives the example of Federal Express as a company that has used the Internet to re-

engineer the service it delivers to customers – ordering, tracking and payment are now all available from the Fedex web site. For a financial services company such as Eagle Star selling insurance via the web, streamlining the process has meant asking underwriters to reduce the complexity of the questions that are asked before a premium is calculated.

4. *Provide a 360 degree view of the customer relationship.* This means that different parts of the company must have similar information about the customer to provide a consistent service. It implies integration of the personalization facilities of a web site with other databases holding information about the customer. If these databases are not integrated then customer trust may be lost. If, for example, the web site offers a customer a product they have already purchased offline it will appear that the company does not understand their needs. Integration of call centres with a web site are also an implication of this guideline.
5. *Let customers help themselves.* This has the benefit of reducing costs, while at the same time providing faster, more efficient customer service.
6. *Help customers do their jobs.* This guideline is similar to the previous one, but focuses more on providing them with the *information* needed to do their jobs. This is again a useful value-added facility of the web site which helps encourage loyalty.
7. *Deliver personalized service.* The importance of delivering personalized service to build a one-to-one relationship with the customer formed the basis for *Chapter 9.*
8. *Foster community.* Business web sites afford good opportunities to create communities of interest since information can be generated which helps customers in their work and again encourages returns to the web site. In the Cisco case study the community created between customers and engineers solving configuration problems is referred to as a 'self-inflating balloon of knowledge'. Independent business community sites are also important places for companies to have representation.

Elements of site design

Once the requirements of the user are established we can turn our attention to the design of the human-computer interface. Nielsen (2000b) structures his book on web usability according to three main areas, which can be interpreted as follows:

1. *Site design and structure* – the overall structure of the site.
2. *Page design* – the layout of individual pages.
3. *Content design* – how the text and graphic content on each pages is designed

Site design and structure

The structures created by designers for web sites will vary greatly according to their audience and its purpose, but we can make some general observations about design and structure. We will review the factors designers consider in designing the style, organization and navigation schemes for the site.

Site style

An effective web site design will have a style that is communicated through use of colour, images, typography and layout. This should support the way a product is positioned or its brand.

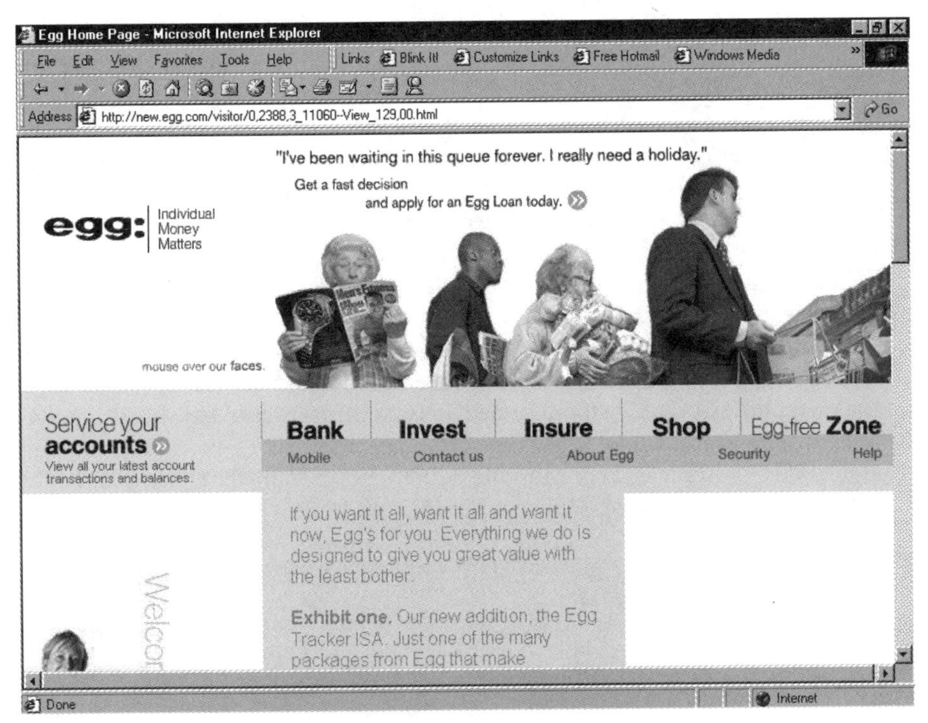

Figure 11.14 A personality that appeals to a broad audience at Egg.com

Site personality

The style elements can be combined to develop a personality for a site. We could describe site personalities in the same way we can describe people, such as 'formal' or 'fun'. This personality has to be consistent with the needs of the target audience (*Figure 11.14*). A business audience often requires detailed information and prefers an information-intensive style such as that of the Cisco site (*Figure 11.17*) (www.cisco.com). A consumer site is usually more graphically intensive. Before the designers pass on their creative designs to developers, they also need to consider the constraints on the user experience, such as screen resolution and colour depth, browser-used and download speed. The list of constraints which must be tested again is illustrated in *Chapter 12*.

Site organization

In their book on information archictectures for the web, Rosenfeld and Morville (1998) identify several different **information organization schemes**. These can be applied for different aspects of e-commerce sites, from the whole site through to different parts of the site.

Information organization schemes
The structure chosen to group and categorize information.

Rosenfeld and Morville (1998) identify the following information organization schemes:

1. *Exact*. Here information can be naturally indexed. If we take the example of books, these can alphabetical – by author or title; chronological – by date; or for travel books for example, geographical – by place. Information on an e-commerce site may be presented alphabetically, but it is not suitable for browsing.

2. *Ambiguous*. Here the information requires classification; again taking the examples of books, the Dewey Decimal system is an ambiguous classification scheme since the librarians classify books into arbitrary categories. Such an approach is common on an e-commerce site since products and services can be classified in different ways. Other ambiguous information organization schemes that are commonly used on web sites are where content is broken down by topic, by task or by audience. The use of metaphors is also common; a metaphor is where the web site corresponds to a familiar real-world situation. The Microsoft Windows Explorer, where information is grouped according to Folders, Files and Trash is an example of a real-world metaphor. The use of the shopping basket metaphor is widespread within e-commerce sites. It should be noted though that Nielsen (2000b) believes that metaphors can be confusing if the metaphor isn't understood immediately or is misinterpreted.
3. *Hybrid*. Here there will be a mixture of organization schemes, both exact and ambiguous. Rosenfeld and Morville (1998) point out that using different approaches is common on web sites but this can lead to confusion, because the user is not clear what mental model is being followed. We can say that is probably best to minimize the number of information organization schemes. To look at these complete *activity 11.5*.

Activity 11.5 **Evaluating site organization schemes**

Purpose

To assess different forms of information content on e-commerce sites.

Activity

Visit the RS Components web site (www.rswww.com) and the Dell Computer site (www.dell.com) relevant to your country. Which information organization schemes are used?

Site navigation schemes

Site navigation scheme
Tools provided to the user to move between different information on a web site.

Narrow and deep navigation
Fewer choices, more clicks to reach required content.

Broad and shallow navigation
More choices, fewer clicks to reach required content.

Devising a site that is easy to use is critically dependent on the design of the **site navigation scheme**. Hoffman and Novak (1997) stress the importance of the concept of 'flow' in governing site usability. Flow essentially describes how easy it is for the users to find the information they need as they move from one page of the site to the next, but it also includes other interactions such as filling in on-screen forms.

Most navigation systems are based upon a hierarchical site structure.When creating the structure, designers have to compromise between the two approaches shown in *Figure 11.15*. The **narrow and deep** approach has the benefit of fewer choices on each page, making it easier for the user to make their selection, but more clicks are required to reach a particular piece of information. The **broad and shallow** approach requires fewer clicks to reach the same piece of information, but the design of the screen potentially becomes cluttered. *Figure 11.15(a)* and *Figure 11.16* depict the narrow and deep approach and *Figure 11.15(b)* and *Figure 11.17* the broad and shallow approach. Note that in these case the approaches are appropriate for the non-technical and technical audiences. A rule of thumb is that site designers should ensure it only takes three clicks to reach any piece of information on a site. This

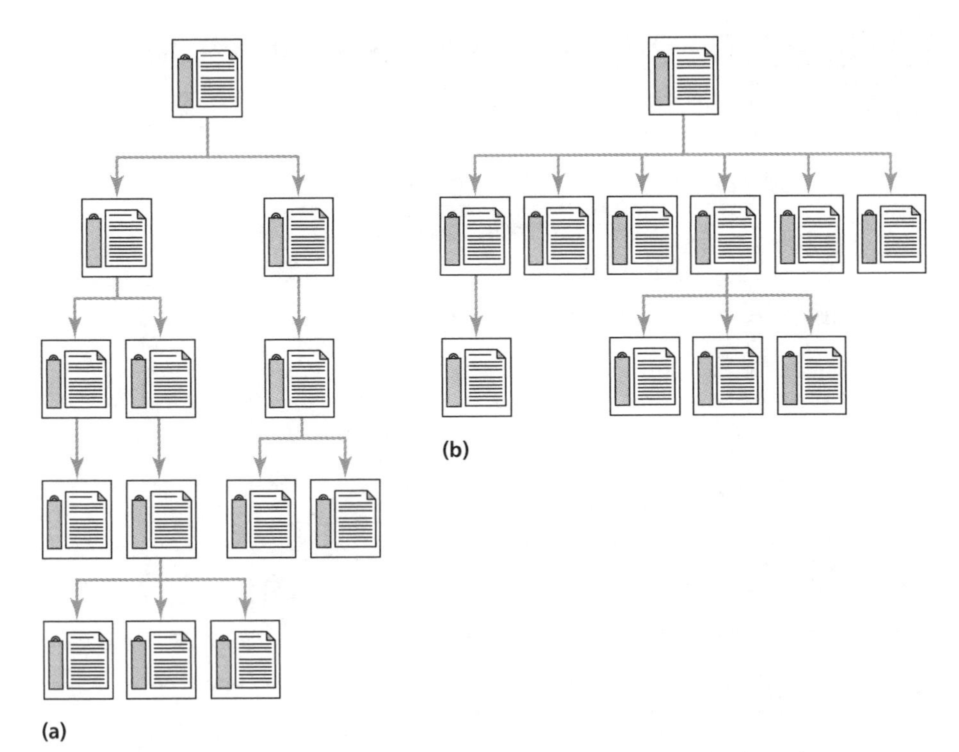

Figure 11.15(a) Narrow and deep and (b) broad and shallow organization schemes

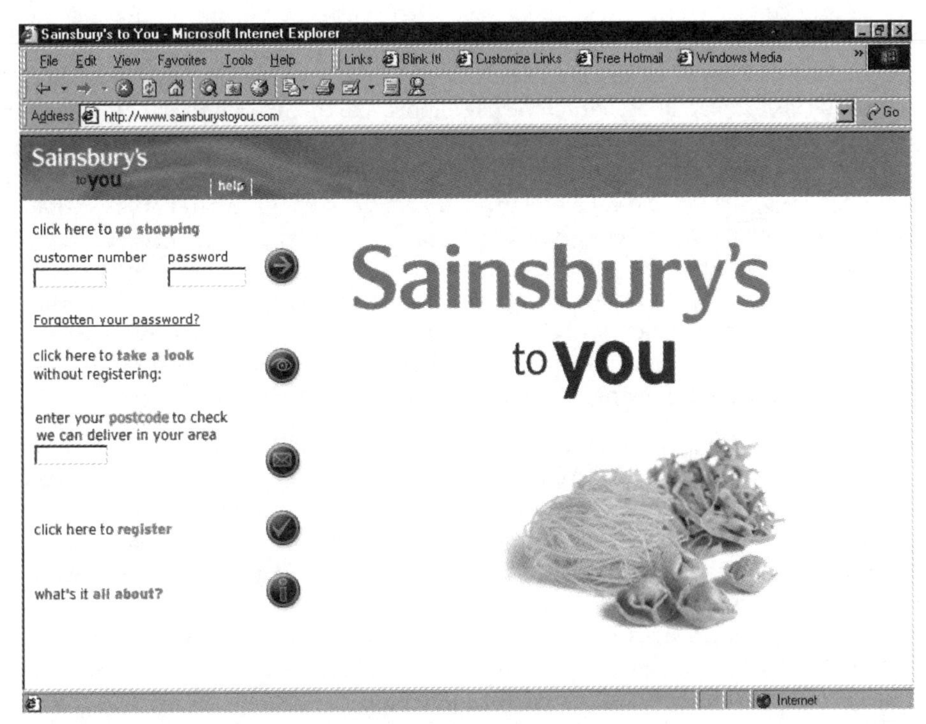

Figure 11.16 Broad and shallow organization scheme for consumers at Sainsburys to You Site (www.sainsburystoyou.co.uk)

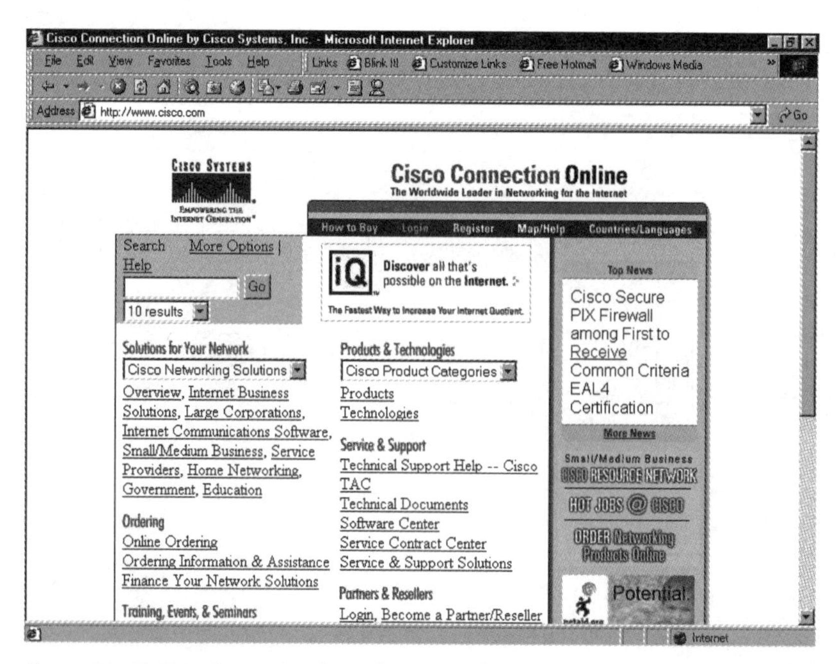

Figure 11.17 Broad organization schemes and professional style at Cisco.com

implies the use of a broad and shallow approach on most large sites. Lynch and Horton (1999) recommend a broad and shallow approach and note that designers should not conceive of a single home page where customers arrive on the site, but different home pages according to different audience types. Each of the pages in the second row of *Figure 11.15(b)* could be thought of as an example of a home page which the visitors can bookmark if the page appeals to them. Nielsen (2000b) points out that many users will not arrive on the home page, but may be referred from another site or according to a print or TV advert to a particular page such as www.b2b.com/jancomp. He calls this process **deep linking** and site designers should ensure that navigation and context are appropriate for users arriving on these pages.

Deep linking
Jakob Nielsen's term for a user arriving at a site deep within its structure.

As well as compromises on depth of links within a site it is also necessary to compromise on the amount of space devoted to menus. Nielsen (2000d) points out that some sites devote so much space to navigation bars that the space available for content is limited. Nielsen (2000d) suggests that the designer of navigation systems should consider the following information that a site user wants to know:

- *Where am I?* The user needs to know where they are on the site and this can be indicated by highlighting the current location and clear titling of pages. Chaffey *et al.* (2000) refer to this as *context*. *Consistency* of menu locations on different pages is also required to aid cognition. Users also need to know where they are on the web. This can be indicated by a logo, which by convention is at the top or top left of a site.
- *Where have I been?* This is difficult to indicate on a site, but for task-oriented activities such as purchasing a product can show the user that they are at the *n*th stage of an operation such as making a purchase.
- *Where do I want to go?* This is the main navigation system which gives options for future operations.

To answer these questions, clear succinct labelling is required. Widely used standards such as Home, Main page, Search, Find, Browse, FAQ and Help and About Us are preferable. But for other particular labels it is useful to have what Rosenfeld and Morville (1998) call scope notes – an additional explanation. These authors also argue against the use of iconic labels or pictures without corresponding text since they are open to misinterpretation and take longer to process.

Since using the navigation system may not enable the user to find the information they want rapidly, alternatives have to be provided by the site designers. These alternatives include search, advanced search, browse and site map facilities. Whatis.com (www.whatis.com) illustrates these features well.

Page design

The page design involves creating an appropriate layout for each page. The main elements of a particular page layout are the title, navigation and content. Standard content such as copyright may be added to every page as a footer. Issues in page design include:

- *Page elements*. The proportion of page devoted to content compared to all other content such as headers, footers and navigation elements. The location of these elements also needs to be considered. It is conventional for the main menu to be at the top or on the left. The use of a menu system at the top of the browser window enables more space for content below.
- *The use of frames*. This is generally discouraged for the reasons given in *Chapter 12*.
- *Resizing*. A good page layout design should allow for the user to change the size of text or work with different monitor resolutions.
- *Consistency*. Page layout should be similar for all areas of the site unless more space is required, for example for a discussion forum or product demonstration. Standards of colour and typography can be enforced through cascading style sheets.
- *Printing*. Layout should allow for printing or provide an alternative printing format.

Content design

Copywriting for the web is an evolving art form, but many of the rules for good copywriting are as for any media. Common errors we see on web sites are:

- too much knowledge assumed of the visitor about the company, its products and services;
- using internal jargon about products, services or departments – using undecipherable acronyms.

Web copywriters also need to take account of the user reading the content onscreen. Approaches to deal with the limitations imposed by the customer using a monitor include:

- writing more concisely than in brochures
- chunking or breaking text into units of 5–6 lines at most; this allows users to scan rather than read information on web pages.
- using lists with headline text in larger font

Table 11.6 A summary of information web stages described by Hofacker (2000)

Stage	*Description*	*Applications*
1. ***Exposure***	Content must be present for long enough to be processed and not obscured (i.e. off-screen).	Content on banner ads may not be onscreen long enough for processing and cognition.
2. ***Attention***	User's eyes will be drawn towards headings and content not graphics and moving items on a web page (Nielsen, 2000b).	Emphasis and accurate labelling of headings is vital to gain a user's attention. Evidence suggests that users do not notice banner adverts, suffering from 'banner blindness'.
3. ***Comprehension and perception***	The user's interpretation of content.	Designs that use common standards and metaphors and are kept simple will be more readily comprehended.
4. ***Yielding and acceptance***	Is information (copy) presented accepted by customers?	Copy should reference credible sources and present counter-arguments as necessary.
5. ***Retention***	As for traditional advertising, this describe the extent to which the information is remembered.	An unusual style or high degree of interaction leading to flow and user satisfaction is more likely to be recalled.

- never including too much on a single page, except when presenting lengthy information such as a report which may be easier to read on a single page
- using hyperlinks to decrease page sizes or help achieve flow within copy, either by linking to sections further down a page or linking to another page.

Hofacker (2001) describes five stages of human information processing when a web site is being used. These can be applied to both page design and content design to improve usability and help companies get their message across to consumers. Each of the five stage summarized in *Table 11.6* acts as a hurdle, since if the site design or content is too difficult to process, the customer cannot progress to the next stage. It is useful to consider these stages in order to minimize these difficulties.

The model of Bickerton *et al.* (2000) can be also be used to assess the different content and services offered to different audiences of a web site using intranets, extranets and the Internet. The model has three levels:

- *Presentation.* This is the delivery of static information on the web site. It can be thought of as a 'brochureware' site, but may have additional depth of information.
- *Interaction.* This stage involves methods of communicating with the customer such as the use of interactive forms and e-mail or discussion communities.
- *Representation.* Representation occurs where the Internet replaces customer services that are normally delivered by human operators. In the case of a bank this stage would involve a customer performing online money transfers between bank accounts or bill payment. IBM has referred to this concept as 'web self-service'.

Using these layers we can map content across different different access levels to produce a site which is integrated across the needs of its audiences (*Table 11.7*). This also relates to the section on security since different access levels may be given for different information.

Table 11.7 **Information and services mapping for The B2B Company**

Stage	*Intranet (employees only)*	*Extranet (favoured partners)*	*Internet (public)*
Presentation	Market research Contacts Sales reports	Technical information sheet Product/pricing information for agents	Company information Product information
Interaction	Access to sales rep reports on company visits. Data mining. E-mail briefings to staff	Key account user group Order filing	Product availability queries E-mail-based customer service
Representation	Online holiday and claims form submission and processing	Transactional e-commerce on buy-side and sell-side	Transactional e-commerce

Now complete *activity 11.6* so you can apply some of the techniques you have read about in this section.

Use case analysis for customer service desk at The B2B Company

Activity 11.6

Purpose

To develop knowledge of the use-case approach by applying it in a particular scenario.

Activity

Develop a primary use case for the situation when a customer asks a question on the online help-desk for The B2B Company. State your assumptions about the activities which would be involved. Translate this use-case into an interface design. This activity can be performed in conjunction with *activity 12.4* which describes the help-desk requirements in more detail.

Focus on security design

F

We have seen in *Chapter 6* that security fears are a major barrier to e-commerce adoption, both by businesses and consumer. On 24 August 2000, *The Financial Times* reported how a criminal gang used bogus identities to obtain credit cards and loans from online bank Egg. The bank was defrauded of approximately £10,000 through multiple applications for online banking. Once the cards and loans were granted, with spending limits of up to £2000, the gang used them to make thousands of pounds of purchases, both online and in shops. Bank spokesmen said the crime represented no threat to the bank's customers, but fraud is still a risk to the banks. The spokesman was also keen to point out that fraudulent applications for credit existed long before the Internet. Although this example suggests that customer data is not at risk, this is not the case. When a customer of an e-commerce site enters his or her credit card details, they are typically stored on servers of the merchant of the third party. Once here, they are vulnerable to downloading by hackers who can use the numbers for fraudulent purchase. Customers may lose the first £50 for which the credit card issuer does not cover them. For larger amounts the risk lies with the credit card issuer. As a result, Internet-related fraud is now the largest source of fraud affecting credit card companies such as Visa and Mastercard. To summarize we can identify the following security risks from the customer or merchant perspective.

(a) Transaction or credit card details stolen in transit.
(b) Customer's credit card details stolen from merchant's server.
(c) Merchant or customer are not who they claim to be.

In this section we assess the measures that can be taken to reduce the risk of these breaches of e-commerce security. We start by reviewing some of the theory of online security and then review the techniques used.

Principles of secure systems

Before we look at the principle of secure systems, it is worth reviewing the standard terminology for the different parties involved in the transaction:

- *Purchaser.* These are the consumers buying the goods.
- *Merchant.* These are the retailers.
- *Certification Authority (CA).* This is a body that issues digital certificates that confirm the identity of purchasers and merchants.
- *Bank.* These are traditional banks.
- *Electronic token issuer.* A virtual bank that issues digital currency.

The basic requirements for security systems from these different parties to the transaction are as follows:

1. *Authentication* – are parties to the transaction who they claim to be (Risk c above)?
2. *Privacy and confidentiality* – is transaction data protected? The consumer may want to make an anonymous purchase. Are all non-essential traces of a transaction removed from the public network and all intermediary records eliminated (Risks b and c above)?
3. *Integrity* – checks that the message sent is complete i.e. that it isn't corrupted.
4. *Non-repudiability* – ensures sender cannot deny sending message.
5. *Availability* – how can threats to the continuity and performance of the system be eliminated?

Approaches to developing secure systems

Digital certificates

Digital certificates (keys)
Consist of keys made up of large numbers that are used to uniquely identify individuals.

Symmetric encryption
Both parties to a transaction use the same key to encode and decode messages.

There are two main methods of encryption using **digital certificates**:

1. Secret-key (symmetric) encryption

This involves both parties having an identical (shared) key that is known only to them. Only this key can be used to encrypt and decrypt messages. The secret key has to be passed from one party to another before use in much the same way as a copy of a secure attaché case key would have to be sent to a receiver of information. This approach has traditionally been used to achieve security between two separate parties, such as major companies conducting EDI. Here the private key is sent out electronically or by courier to ensure it is not copied.

This method is not practical for general e-commerce, as it would not be safe for a purchaser to give a secret key to a merchant since control of it would be lost and it could not then be used for other purposes. A merchant would also have to manage many customer keys.

2. Public-key (asymmetric) encryption

Asymmetric encryption
Both parties use a related but different key to encode and decode messages.

Asymmetric encryption is so-called since the keys used by the sender and receiver of information are different. The two keys are related by a numerical code, so only the pair of keys can be used in combination to encrypt and decrypt information. *Figure 11.18* shows how public-key encryption works in an e-commerce context. A customer can place an order with a merchant by automatically looking up the public key of the merchant and then using this key to encrypt the message containing their order. The scrambled message is then sent across the Internet and on receipt by the merchant is read using the merchant's private key. In this way only the merchant who has the only copy of the private key can read the order. In the reverse case the merchant could confirm the customer's identity by reading identity information such as a digital signature encrypted with the private key of the customer using their public key.

Digital signatures

Digital signatures
A method of identifying individuals or companies using public key encryption.

Digital signatures can be used to create commercial systems by using public key encryption to achieve authentication: the merchant and purchaser can prove they are genuine. The purchaser's digital signature is encrypted before sending a message using their private key and on receipt, the public key of the purchaser is used to decrypt the digital signature. This proves the customer is genuine. Digital signatures are not widely used currently due to the difficulty of setting up transactions, but will become more widespread as the public-key infrastructure (PKI) stabilizes and use of certificate authorities increases.

The public-key infrastructure (PKI) and certificate authorities

In order for digital signatures and public-key encryption to be effective it is necessary to be sure that the public key intended for decryption of a document actually belongs to the person you believe is sending you the document. The developing solution to this problem is the issuance by a trusted third party (TTP) of a message

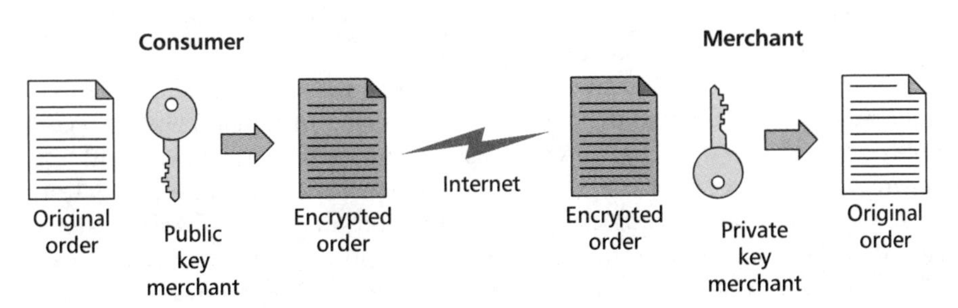

Figure 11.18 Public-key or asymmetric encryption

containing owner identification information and a copy of the public key of that person. The TTPs are usually referred to as **certificate authorities (CAs)** and various bodies such as banks and the Post Office are likely to fulfil this role. That message is called a **certificate**. In reality, as asymmetric encryption is rather slow, it is often only a sample of the message that is encrypted and used as the representative digital signature.

Certificate and certificate authorities (CAs)
A certificate is a valid copy of a public key of an individual or organization together with identification information. It is issued by a trusted third party (TTP) or certificate authority (CA). CAs make public keys available and also issue private keys.

Example certificate information could include:

- user identification data;
- issuing authority identification and digital signature;
- user's public key;
- expiry date of this certificate;
- class of certificate;
- digital identification code of this certificate.

It is proposed that different classes of certificates would exist according to the type of information contained. For example:

1. name, e-mail address
2. driver's licence, national insurance number, date of birth
3. credit check
4. organization-specific security clearance data

Virtual Private Networks

Virtual Private Network
Private networks created using the public network infrastructure of the Internet.

A **Virtual Private Network** (VPN) is a private wide area network that runs over the public network, rather than a more expensive private network. The technique by which VPN operates is sometimes referred to as tunnelling, and involves encrypting both packet headers and content using a secure form of the Internet Protocol known as IPSec. As explained in *Chapter 3* VPNs enable the global organization to conduct its business securely, but using the public Internet rather than more expensive proprietary systems.

Current approaches to e-commerce security

In this section we review the approaches used by e-commerce sites to achieve security using the techniques described above.

Secure Sockets Layer Protocol (SSL)

Secure Sockets Layer (SSL)
A commonly used encryption technique for scrambling data as it is passed across the Internet from a customer's web browser to a merchant's web server.

SSL is a security protocol, originally developed by Netscape, but now supported by all browsers such as Microsoft Internet Explorer. SSL is used in the majority of B2C e-commerce transactions since it is easy for the customer to use without the need to download additional software or a certificate.

When a customer enters a secure checkout area of an e-commerce site SSL is used and the customer is prompted that 'you are about to view information over a secure connection' and a key symbol is used to denote this security. When encryption is occurring they will see that the web address prefix in the browser changes from 'http://' to 'https://' and a padlock appears at the bottom of the browser window.

How does SSL relate to the different security concepts described above? The main facility it provides is security and confidentiality. SSL enables a private link to be set up between customer and merchant. Encryption is used to scramble the details of an e-commerce transaction as it is passed between the sender and receiver and also when the details are held on the computers at each end. It would require a determined attempt to intercept such a message and decrypt it. SSL is more widely used than the rival S-HTTP method.

The detailed stages of SSL are as follows:

1. Client browser sends request for a secure connection.
2. Server responds with a digital certificate which is sent for authentication.
3. Client and server negotiate *session keys*, which are symmetrical keys used only for the duration of the transaction.

Since, with enough computing power, time and motivation, it is possible to decrypt messages encrypted using SSL, much effort is being put into finding more secure methods of encryption such as SET. From a merchant's point of view there is also the problem that authentication of the customer is not possible without resorting to other methods such as credit checks.

Secure Electronic Transaction (SET)

Secure Electronic Transaction (SET)
A standard for public-key encryption intended to enable secure e-commerce transactions developed by Mastercard and Visa.

Secure Electronic Transactions (SET) is a significant security protocol based on digital certificates that has been developed by a consortium led by Mastercard and Visa and allows parties to a transaction to confirm each other's identity. By employing digital certificates, SET allows a purchaser to confirm that the merchant is legitimate and conversely allows the merchant to verify that the credit card is being used by its owner. It also requires that each purchase request includes a digital signature, further identifying the cardholder to the retailer. The digital signature and the merchant's digital certificate provide a certain level of trust.

Despite being launched in the late 1990s, SET is not widely used currently due to the difficulty of exchanging keys. For a customer to have their own key, they need to install a secure software wallet on their PC that contains their private key. The transaction verification process is also slower than SSL and the merchant must use special SET software on their server. SET may become more widespread as the public-key infrastructure (PKI) stabilizes and use of certificate authorities increases. There is also likely to be a move to a single online wallet for customers which means that their details will not be stored on multiple servers and entered separately for each site. The card issuers are also keen to introduce such a scheme since it will counter fraud. However, demand has not been demonstrated by customers.

A key feature of SET is that the customer's credit card number is not stored on the server, so reducing the risk of credit card fraud. Storage is not necessary since SET also involves a bank. The SET process is described by *Figure 11.19*, and operates as follows:

1. When a customer places an order, the merchant's SET software sends the order information and the merchant's digital certificate to the client's digital wallet.
2. The credit card and order information are encrypted using the merchant's *bank's* public key along with the customer's digital certificate.
3. Merchant then forwards the payment details to the bank.
4. Bank decrypts payment information since it was encrypted using bank's public key and if appropriate sends authorization to the merchant who then confirms payment with the customer.

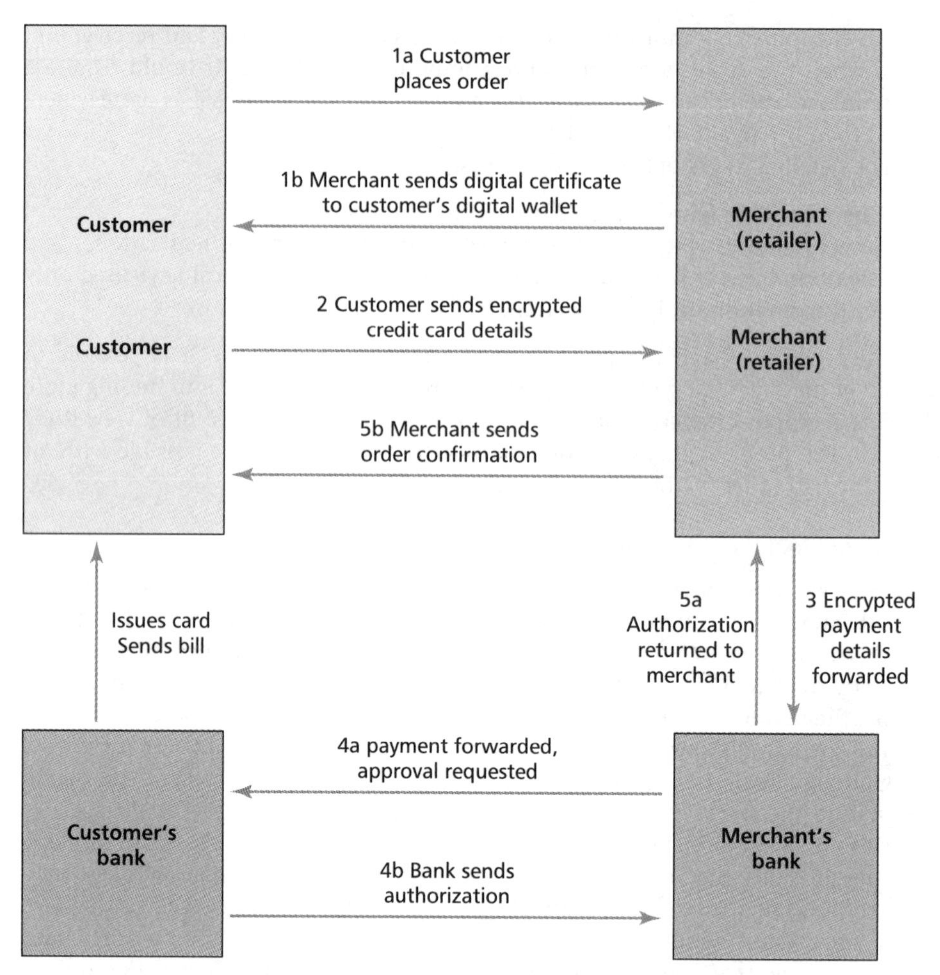

Figure 11.19 An example of the Secure Electronic Transaction (SET) standard

Certificate authorities (CAs)

For secure e-commerce, there is a requirement for the management of the vast number of public keys. This management involves procedures and protocols necesssary throughout the lifetime of a key – generation, dissemination, revocation and change – together with the administrative functions of time/date stamping and archiving. The successful establishment of a CA is an immense challenge of trust building and complex management. There are two opposing views on how that challenge should be met.

- *Decentralized*: market driven, creating brand name based 'islands of trust' such as the Consumer Association. There is a practical need for a local physical office to present certificates of attestable value e.g. passports, drivers' licences. Banks and the Post Office have a huge advantage.
- *Centralized*: In the UK, the Department of Trade and Industry (DTI) has proposed a hierarchical tree ultimately leading to the government.

The best-known commercial CA is Verisign (www.verisign.com) and this is commonly used for merchant verification. For example, the Avon site uses Verisign to prove to its customers that it is the genuine site. Post offices and telecommunications suppliers are also acting as CAs. Examples in the UK include BT (Trust Wise) and Post Office (ViaCode).

Pretty Good Privacy (PGP)

PGP is a public-key encryption system used to encrypt e-mail messages.

Hackers and viruses

Hackers can use techniques such as spoofing to hack into a system and find credit card details. Spoofing, as its name suggests, involves someone masquerading as someone else – either as individuals or an organization. Spoofing can be of two sorts.

- IP spoofing can be used to gain access to confidential information by creating false identification data such as the originating network (IP) address. The objective of this access can be espionage, theft or simply to cause mischief, generate confusion and damage corporate public image or political campaigns. **Firewalls** can be used to reduce this threat.
- Site spoofing, i.e. fooling the organization's customers, by using a similar URL such as www.amazno.com can be used to divert customers to a site which is not a bona-fide retailer.

Firewall
A specialized software application mounted on a server at the point the company is connected to the Internet. Its purpose: to prevent unauthorized access into the company from outsiders.

As explained in *Chapter 3*, firewalls can be used to minimize the risk of security breaches by hackers and viruses. Firewalls are usually created as software mounted on a separate server at the point the company is connected to the Internet. Firewall software can then be configured to accept only links from trusted domains representing other offices in the company or key account customers. A firewall has implications for marketers since staff accessing a web site from work may not be able to access some content such as graphics plug-ins.

Denial-of-service attacks

The risk to companies of these attacks was highlighted in the spring of 2000, when the top web sites were targeted. The performance of these sites such as Yahoo! (www.yahoo.com) and eBay (www.ebay.com) was severely degraded as millions of data packets flooded the site from a number of servers. This was a distributed attack where the sites were bombarded from rogue software installed on many servers, so it is difficult for the e-tailers to counter.

Alternative payment systems

The preceding discussion has focused on payment using credit card systems since this is the prevalent method for e-commerce purchases. Throughout the 1990s there were many attempts to develop alternative **payment systems** to credit cards. These focused on those for **micropayments** or electronic coinage such as downloading an online newspaper, for which the overhead and fee of using a credit card was too high.

Payment systems
Methods of transferring funds from a customer to a merchant.

Micropayments
Small denomination payments.

Electronic payment systems can be divided into two basic types, those where no-credit occurs and those where credit occurs.

Non-credit or pre-paid systems

Most of the non-credit systems operate using a pre-pay principle. In other words, before purchasing an item electronically, the purchaser must already have electronic funds available that can be immediately transferred to the merchant. These funds can exist in a variety of forms which are known as electronic tokens. **Electronic tokens** are usually purchased from various electronic token issuers using a traditional payment device such as a credit card or a transfer of cash into a personal account.

Electronic tokens
Units of digital currency in a standard electronic format.

Some examples of non-credit systems are:

1. Digital, virtual or electronic cash (e-cash).

Several companies have attempted to establish payment systems which replicate cash in that they are anonymous systems (from the retailer perspective). The names to describe these systems are confusing, particularly since some of the concepts have a limited life. DigiCash (www.digicash.com) was one of the 'early runners' in this area, but this company filed for bankruptcy in 1998 and the technology and concept is owned by eCash (www.ecash.com).

Digital cash usually follows what is known as a bearer certificate system where blank tokens are issued by the user and certified by the bank. It is very secure as the merchant must make an online real-time connection to the bank to ensure credit is available; this can make it difficult to implement for small to medium retailers. Cybercoin from CyberCash (www.cybercash.com) is a notational system using pre-paid funds that does not require inter-bank clearing. CyberCoin was terminated in 1998 and users migrated to instabuy (www.instabuy.com), a credit-card based system.

2. Microtransactions or micropayments such as Millicent

These are digital cash systems which allow very small sums of money (fractions of a pence) to be transferred, but with lower security. Such small sums do not warrant a credit card payment, because processing is too costly. The Digital Millicent scheme dating back to the mid-1990s is the best known of these, but has never been widely used in Europe. ECoin (www.ecoin.net) is a newer micropayment system that is becoming more popular. Such micropayment systems may become important for purchasing information or music to play on devices such as the Rio, a credit-card sized personal stereo, which downloads CD-quality music direct from the Internet for a small charge.

3. Debit cards.

Cards issued with standard bank accounts could theoretically be used for e-commerce purchase, but credit cards are preferred by merchants since the payment is secured by the bank. Debit cards have been used by Bank Austria to enable payments by teenagers who cannot have credit cards, but can use debit cards up to the limit of their accounts.

4. Smartcards.

These are different to the other items in the list since they are physical cards rather than virtual, so must be inserted into a smart-card reader before items can be purchased. Since such readers aren't yet a standard feature of home PCs, the use of smartcards for purchase is limited to trials in areas such as Swindon (Mondex/Mastercard) and Leeds (Visa Cash) where purchase across the Internet occurs through public kiosks in shopping centres which have smartcard readers. The Visa Cash system is a bearer certificate system (chip-card), cleared through the conventional banking system, where the issuing institution earns float. This was trialled in Leeds; 60,000 cards were in circulation and 1,400 business accepted them. *Computing* (29/10/98) reported that 'Ken Bignall, managing director of Visa UK said that the Leeds programme has shown that an electronic purse adds real convenience for cardholders'. For example, Visa Cash transactions have already replaced cash by up to 10 per cent in car parks and have also proved popular in fast food restaurants, sandwich shops and newsagents, with plans to extend coverage in these areas as well as public transport. Note that they are not commonly used for the Internet currently, because of a lack of card-reading devices, but offer this potential.

Post-paid or credit-based systems

1. Digital/electronic cheques.

These are modelled on conventional cheques except that they are authorized using digital signatures rather than handwritten signatures. An example of a digital cheque payment system operating within the UK is the BankNet service at mkn.co.uk/bank which is an online banking service between MarketNet and Secure Trust Bank plc. It offers the facility to write digitally signed cheques using public-Key/Private-key cryptographic techniques (see later section for definitions).

2. Credit cards such as Visa or Mastercard.

These are the predominant form of online payment. The reason for this is that they fulfil well the requirements for a payment system coupled with their being an existing standard.

Although credit card payment is usually made direct to the merchant, by filling in the card number and address on an online form, there may be some instances where it is more convenient for the customer to register their credit card details with a third party. In this case it is easier to make frequent purchases and the credit card details do not have to be divulged to each retailer. Such a concept is provided by Pay2See (www.Pay2See.com) which enables downloadable products such as music and reports to be paid for.

Business payment systems

There is currently no standard business payment system. Most use existing payment by account arrangements and there is not integrated transfer between merchant, bank and customer. The lack of a standard can perhaps be explained by the complexity of the transaction which must fulfil these requirements:

- The system must provide facilities for different members of the buying organization including the requisitioner, authorizer and purchasing department.
- The system must allow for repeat orders and complex orders with many items.
- The system must allow for specialized or bespoke orders.
- The system must have high levels of security for the potentially high value of the orders.

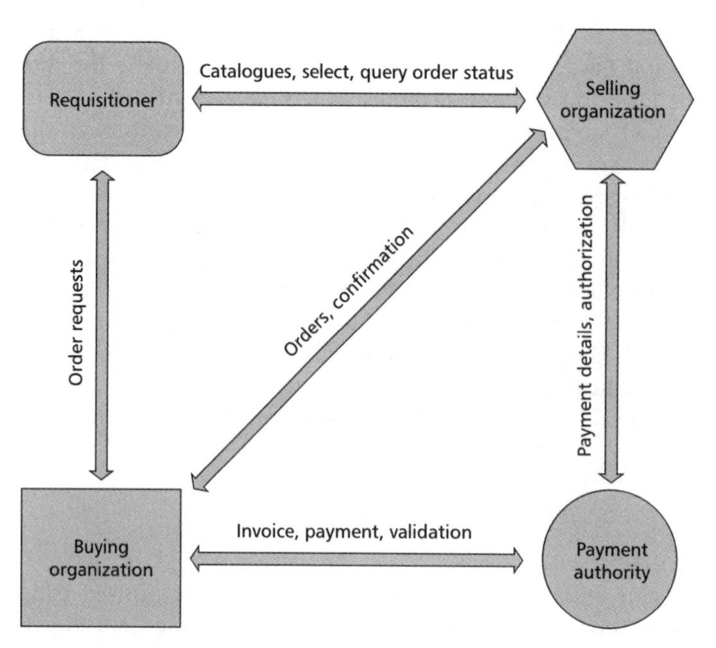

Figure 11.20 The Open Buying on the Internet model for business-to-business e-commerce transactions.

- The bank or payment authority must be fully integrated into the system.

There are currently three main standards under development:

1. **The Open Buying on the Internet (OBI)** (www.openbuy.org), created by the Internet Purchasing Roundtable, is intended to ensure that different e-commerce systems can talk to each other. It is managed by CommerceNet (www.commerce.net) and backed by, among others, 3M, Ford, Mastercard, Visa and Microsoft. *Figure 11.20* shows the model proposed by the OBI.
2. **The Open Trading Protocol (OTP)** (www.otp.org) is intended to standardize a variety of payment-related activities including purchase agreements, receipts for purchases and payments. It is backed by, among others, AT&T, Cybercash, Hitachi, IBM, Sun and BT. Despite this impressive lineup the web site has not featured any updated press releases since 1998 and seems set to be eclipsed by OBI.
3. **Internet-based EDI.** Traditional EDI standards have also been extended for use on the Internet, but mainly through initiatives of individual suppliers rather than a cross-industry move.

Reassuring the customer

Once the security measures are in place, content on the merchant's site can be used to reassure the customer, for example, Amazon (www.amazon.com) takes customer fears about security seriously judging by the prominence and amount of content it devotes to this issue. Some of the approaches used indicate good practice in allaying customers' fears. These include:

- use of customer guarantee to safeguard purchase;
- clear explanation of SSL security measures used;

- highlighting the rarity of fraud ('ten million customers have shopped safely without credit card fraud');
- the use of alternative ordering mechanisms such as phone or fax;
- the prominence of information to allay fears – the guarantee is one of the main menu options.

Companies can use also use independent third parties who set guidelines for online privacy and security. The best known international bodies are TRUSTe (www.truste.org) and Verisign for payment authentification (www.verisign.com). Within particular companies there may be other bodies such as, in the UK, Which Web Trader (www.which.net/webtrader), TrustUK (www.trustuk.org) and ChambersOnline (www.chambersonline.co.uk).

For B2B transactions and B2C transactions, SGS, the Swiss certification agency (www.sgsonline.com), has developed a Gold Seal standard to authenticate e-commerce quality. Founded in 1878 to monitor grain shipments, Société Generale de Surveillance today oversees a vast spectrum of traditional trading activities, ranging from toys to textiles and carbon steel to crude oil.

Summary

1. Analysis of business and user requirements for e-business systems is important in delivering usable and relevant systems.
2. Process modelling is used to assess existing business processes and suggest revised processes. Techniques such as task analysis and flow process charts from workflow design are useful in understanding tasks required by the system and current weakness.
3. Data modelling for e-business systems mainly involves traditional entity relationship approaches.
4. Architectural designs involve assessing appropriate integration between legacy systems and new e-commerce systems. Such designs are based on the client/server approach.
5. User interface design can be improved through using structured approaches such as use-case and following evolving standards for site structure, page structure and content.
6. Security design is important to maintain trust amongst the customer base. Security solutions target protecting servers from attack and preventing interception of messages when they are in transit.

ACTIVITY ANSWERS

Activity 11.1 The consequences of poor analysis and design

Let's take the approach of looking at expectations for buying a book online. Those where analysis and design are important are marked with (A&D). It can be seen that analysis and design are important for most of these requirements:

1. Easy to find what you're looking for by searching or browsing. (A&D)
2. Site easy to use, pages fast to download with no bugs. (A&D)

3. Price, product specification and availability information on site to be correct (A&D)
4. Specification of date, time and delivery to be possible. (A&D)
5. E-mail notification when order placed and then dispatched. (A&D)
6. Personal data remains personal and private and security is not compromised. (A&D)
7. Verification of address for high value orders.
8. Delivery on time.
9. Returns policy enabling straightforward return or replacement.
10. Effective e-mail or phone-based customer support for when any of the expectations above aren't met! This means traceability through databases, someone who knows your order status and can solve your problems. (A&D)

11.2 Transforming invoice processing at The B2B Company

It is apparent from *Table 11.2* that there are many inefficiencies in the company. These include separate people performing tasks that could be performed by one individual and unnecessary steps. Another problem is that the Managing Director is often out of the office, so authorization by him takes as long as two days on average. It can be seen that each time a new person is involved there is a delay while the item is transported via the manual mail system and then waits in their in-tray; the process chart symbols for processing, transportation and delay repeat again and again. Such is the extent of this problem that the total time for the whole process is nearly 90 hours, but with staff working nine through five this would stretch to over ten working days.

A suggestion for improving the workflow is shown in *Table 11.3*. An important change is in the role of the clerks; they have been empowered by giving them the responsibility to perform tasks such as assigning an invoice to an account number – this was originally the job of the cost accountant. Steps such as returning the invoice to the first payable clerk and that of the file clerk are then removed.

Software needed

For such an application a full functioned workflow system is probably unnecessary, rather, a forms-enabled e-mail system can be used to route information from one person to the next. So, the first payable clerk will pass a scanned copy of the invoice onto the Managing Director as an e-mail attachment which can be accessed remotely via modem when the MD is mobile. Using forms-enabled workflow has two key benefits: first it will drastically reduce the time for the transportation stages and second it will reduce the time while the item is waiting in the in-tray – an item that needs prompt action can be notified as urgent immediately. Through making all these changes the total time has been reduced from nearly 90 hours to just over 20 hours although the efficiency is still low due to time awaiting processing when an item is in the worklist.

EXERCISES

Self-assessment questions

1. What are the risks if analysis and design are not completed adequately?
2. Distinguish between process analysis and data analysis.
3. What are workflow analysis and workflow management systems?

4. What is legacy data and what are the options for incorporation into an e-commerce system?
5. What are the four requirements of a secure e-commerce site?
6. Explain the concepts of digital keys and digital signatures and how they relate.
7. Explain the notation used for use-case analysis.
8. Summarize the characteristics of a usable web site according to Jakob Nielsen (www.useit.com).

Essay and discussion questions

1. Write a plan for the analysis and design of an e-commerce site recommending which aspects of process and data analysis should be conducted and explaining how they should be integrated.
2. Write an essay on the significance of workflow systems to e-business illustrating your answer with examples of organizations of your choice.
3. Write a report summarizing the characteristics of a web site with good usability.
4. How can the concept of customer orientation be translated into e-commerce site design?
5. Assess the success of e-tailers in designing secure e-commerce systems.

Examination questions

1. Summarize the purpose of process analysis.
2. What is meant by 'user-centred design'?
3. Explain the concept of task analysis with reference to a customer placing an order online.
4. Explain the stages involved in use-case analysis with reference to a customer placing an order online.
5. Describe the stages of data modelling with reference to a database for an e-procurement system.
6. Outline the different types of services that need to be provided by different servers on an e-commerce site based on the three-tier client server system.
7. How do the attributes of a secure e-commerce site differ from customer and company viewpoints?
8. Explain the relationship between analysis, design and implementation for an e-commerce site.

REFERENCES

Bevan, N. (1999a) Usability issues in web site design. *Proceedings of the 6th Interactive Publishing Conference*, November 1999. Available online at www.usability.serco.com.

Bevan, N. (1999b) Common industry format usability tests. *Proceedings of UPA '98*, Usability Professionals Association, Scottsdale, Arizona, 29 June–2 July, 1999. Available online at www.usability.serco.com.

Bickerton, P., Bickerton, M. and Pardesi, U. (2000) *CyberMarketing*, 2nd edn. Butterworth-Heinemann, Oxford. Chartered Institute of Marketing series.

Bocij, P., Chaffey, D., Greasley, A. and Hickie, S. (1999) *Business Information Systems. Technology, Development and Management*. FT Management, London.

Burdman, J. (1999) *Collaborative Web Development: Strategies and Best Practices for Web Teams*. Addison-Wesley, Reading, MA.

Chaffey, D.J. (1998) *Groupware, Workflow and Intranets – Re-engineering the Enterprise with Collaborative Software*. Digital Press, Woburn, MA.

Curtis, B., Kellner, M. and Over, J. (1995) Process modeling. *Communications of the ACM*, 35(9).

Davenport, T.H. 1993 *Process Innovation: Re-engineering Work through Information Technology*. Harvard Business School Press, Boston.

Georgakoupoulos, D., Hornick, M. and Sheth, A. (1995) An overview of workflow management: from process modeling to workflow automation infrastructure. *Distributed and Parallel Databases*, 3, 119–53.

Hofacker, C. (2001) *Internet Marketing*. John Wiley and Sons, Inc., New York.

Hoffman, D.L. and Novak, T.P. (1997) A new marketing paradigm for electronic commerce. *The Information Society*, Special issue on electronic commerce, 13 (Jan–Mar), 43–54.

Jacobsen, I., Ericsson, M. and Jacobsen, A. (1994) *The Object Advantage. Business Process Re-engineering with object technology*. Addison-Wesley, Wokingham, UK.

Lynch, P. and Horton, S. (1999) *Web Style Guide. Basic Design Principles for Creating Web Sites*. Yale University Press. Available online at: info.med.yale.edu/caim/manual/contents.html.

Nielsen, J. (2000a) *Novice vs. Expert Users*. Jakob Nielsen's Alertbox, 6 February. www.useit.com/alertbox/20000206.html

Nielsen, J. (2000b) *Designing Web Usability*. New Riders Publishing, USA.

Nielsen, J. (2000c) *Eyetracking Study of Web Readers*. Jakob Nielsen's Alertbox, 14 May. www.useit.com/alertbox/20000514.html

Nielsen, J. (2000d) *Details in Study Methodology Can Give Misleading Results*. Jakob Nielsen's Alertbox, 21 February. www.useit.com/alertbox/990221.html

Noyes, J. and Baber, C. (1999) *User-Centred Design of Systems*. Springer-Verlag, Berlin.

Pant, S. and Ravichandran, T. (2001) A framework for information systems planning for e-business. *Logistics Information Management*, 14(1), 85–98.

Rosenfeld, L. and Morville, P. (1998) *Information Architecture for the World Wide Web*. O'Reilly & Associates, Sebastopol, CA.

Schneider, G. and Winters, J. (1998) *Applying Use Cases. A Practical Guide*. Addison-Wesley Longman, Reading, MA.

Seybold, P. (1999) *Customers.com*. Century Business Books, Random House, London.

Taylor, D. (1995) *Business Engineering with Object Technology*. John Wiley & Sons Inc., New York.

Workflow Management Coalition (WfMC). (1996) Reference model. Version 1. In *The Workflow Management Coalition Specification. Terminology and glossary*. Workflow Management Coalition, Avenue Marcel Thiry 204, 1200 Brussels, Belgium.

FURTHER READING

Bevan, N. (1999a) Usability issues in web site design. *Proceedings of the 6th Interactive Publishing Conference*, November 1999. Available online at www.usability.serco.com. Accessible, lists of web-design pointers.

Jakob Nielsen's UseIt (www.useit.com). Detailed guidelines (alertboxes) and summaries of research into usability of web media.

Noyes, J. and Baber, C. (1999) *User-Centred Design of Systems*. Springer-Verlag, Berlin. Details the user-centred design approach.

WEB LINKS

Jakob Nielsen's UseIt (www.useit.com): detailed guidelines (alertboxes) and summaries of research into usability of web media.

Knowledgespace (www.knowledgespace.com): the Arthur Andersen Global Best Practices knowledgebase uses standard definitions of processes to make it easier for the correct types of information to be found.

Serco usability (www.usability.serco.com): articles on design for usability.

SET – Secure Electronic Transactions (www.mastercard.com/set/): large volume of information.

Security About.com (security.about.com): portal about security.

Web Style Guide (info.med.yale.edu/caim/manual/contents.html): supporting site for the style guide book of Lynch and Horton of Yale Medical School. Complete text online.

Chapter 12

Implementation and maintenance

CHAPTER AT A GLANCE

Main topics

Focus on . . .

Case studies

LEARNING OBJECTIVES

After completing this chapter the reader should be able to:

- Produce a plan to minimize the risks involved with the launch phase of an e-business application
- Define a process for the effective maintenance of an e-business system
- Produce a simple web page with links to other pages
- Create a plan to measure the effectiveness of an e-business application

MANAGEMENT ISSUES

Implementation and maintenance of e-business systems raises these issues for management:

- What actions can we take to minimize the risks of implementation?
- How do we transition from previous systems to a new e-business system?
- What techniques are available to measure the success of our implementation?

Links to other chapters

This chapter follows naturally from *Chapters 10 and 11*. The context is given in *Figure 10.2*. The change management plan defined in *Chapter 10* will be enacted in the implementation phase. The coding, testing and changeover aspects of implementation will be based on the analysis and design documentation produced using the techniques described in *Chapter 11*.

Introduction

Implementation
The creation of a system based on analysis and design documentation.

Implementation activities
The creation of the system modules by coding and scripting, module integration and testing and changeover to the live system.

We started *Chapter 11* by considering the typical problems that confront users of e-commerce systems. It was shown that careful analysis and design can help minimize the risks of problems such as difficulties in navigation and slow site response. With good analysis and design, the **implementation** stage can be relatively straightforward: simply implementing the design. However, even with the best design, it is still necessary to follow **implementation activities** that test the system thoroughly and manage the transition or changeover from the old system to the new system or the launch of the site. Note that there is also a broader use of the term 'implementation' which is used to describe the implementation of strategy, this includes all aspects of Part 3: change management, analysis, design, implementation and maintenance.

Complete *activity 12.1* to review some of the risks that can occur in the implementation phase.

Activity 12.1 **Risks of e-business implementation**

Purpose

To highlight the risks of implementation and actions necessary to control them.

Activity

Refer back to *activity 11.1*. For all the problems of an e-commerce site you identified, which ones may also have occurred due to failings at the implementation phase of the system?

For answer see p. 523

Maintenance phase
Commences after the system is live.

The dynamic e-business application
The application is continuously updated in response to competitive forces.

Once an e-business application or e-commerce site is live, the **maintenance phase** is arguably of more significance than in traditional business application development since a successful application is dynamic. A **dynamic e-business application** means that content and services will be continuously updated in response to the environmental scanning described in *Chapters 4, 5 and 6*. As competitors introduce new services and offers, and as marketing research reveals problems with the site from a customer perspective, or new opportunities, rapid modifications will be required for the e-business to remain competitive.

The relationship between analysis, design, implementation and maintenance

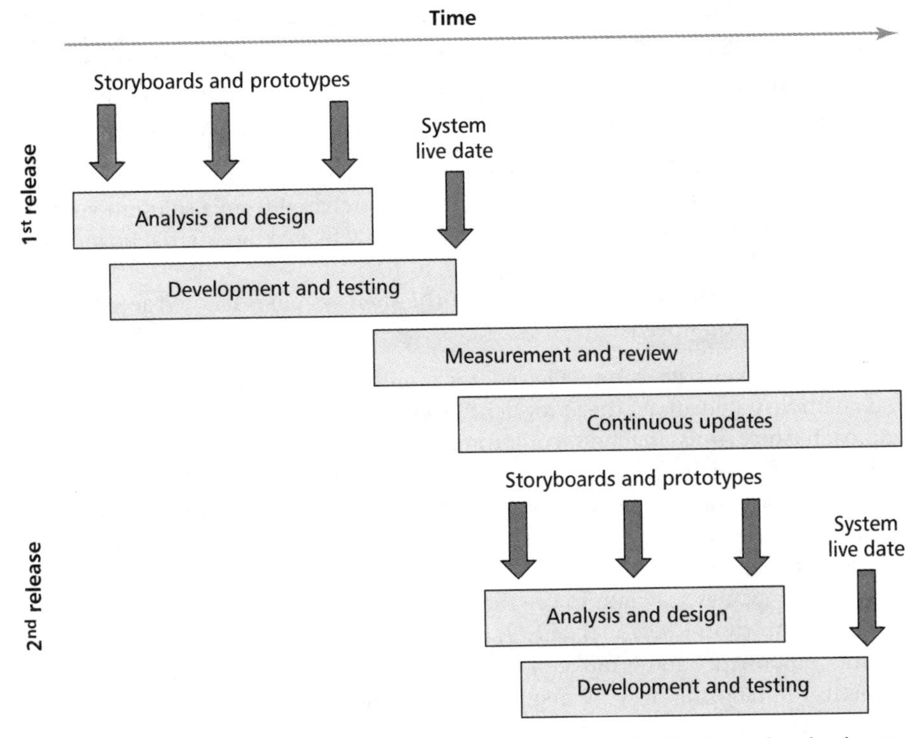

Figure 12.1 Sequencing of implementation and maintenance for the dynamic e-business application

was illustrated in *Figure 10.2*. It is evident that implementation activities such as testing and review follow analysis and design during prototyping. These activities also occur before the system becomes live in a final implementation phase. *Figure 12.1* summarizes the sequence of activities in the form of a Gantt chart. It is evident that although analysis and design, implementation and **maintenance activities** were traditionally conceived as separate in the systems development lifecycle model, in reality there is a great degree of overlap between these phases and all occur simultaneously as part of the evolutionary prototyping approach (*Chapter 10, p. 389*). While analysis of requirements is occurring, design and implementation will be occurring simultaneously in order to produce storyboards and prototypes. This prototyping may occur in timeboxes of a certain duration, perhaps 30 days or 60 days, with a prototype produced at the end of each timebox.

Maintenance activities
Involve measurement of system effectiveness and updating in response to maintain competitiveness.

Once the system is live, measurement and review will commence. Measurement of the load and user activity affecting servers can be considered as an extension of pre-launch testing. As soon as the system is live it will be necessary to make minor updates continuously to the content and services. For each update, a small-scale prototyping process involving analysis, design and testing will occur. For more major updates that perhaps may occur every 6, 12 or 18 months another full cycle of analysis and design, development and testing will be required. This is shown at the base of *Figure 12.1* and is completed by the second version of the system going live and the cycle repeating.

Alternatives for acquiring e-business systems

The basic alternatives for how e-business systems are acquired during implementation are similar to traditional business information systems. These are:

1. *Bespoke development*. The e-commerce system is developed from scratch.
2. *Off-the-shelf (packaged)*. An existing system is purchased from a solution vendor. In the e-business context this approach is often achieved by external hosting via an *applications service provider* (*Chapter 3, p. 105*).
3. *Tailored off-the shelf development*. The off-the-shelf system is tailored according to an organization's needs.

These alternatives have been reviewed, for example, in Bocij *et al.* (1999) where it was demonstrated that the prevalent approach is the tailored off-the-shelf approach since it is the best compromise between meeting an organization's specific needs, reliability while minimizing cost and development time.

Decisions also have to be taken as to whether bespoke development or tailoring occurs in-house or using a consultant who is familiar with the latest e-commerce development tools.

Acquisition method
Defines whether the system is purchased outright or developed from scratch.

While companies may aim to use the tailored off-the-shelf approach, the reality is that, as shown in *Chapters 3 and 11*, an e-commerce system will consist of a variety of components and a range of **acquisition methods** may be used and differing amounts of tailoring will be required. Referring to *Figure 11.7* the following approaches may be used for The B2C Company:

- Web server – this is standard systems software that is acquired off the shelf and will only require minor configuration.
- Merchant server – this will require limited configuration,
- Web site user interface – will need substantial bespoke work since this will need to be unique to each company. Techniques to achieve this are covered in the sections on dynamic and static web page generation in this chapter. Typically this coding will use one of the development tools described later in this chapter.
- Personalization, CRM, catalogue server and ERP servers and applications – these are standard packages, but all will require tailoring for a specific business's requirements and often will have different development tools or languages used to configure them. We do not consider how this type of tailoring occurs in a business since it depends on the toolkit used.

In this chapter we concentrate on the web site user interface since this will be the aspect of e-commerce site development that managers are most directly involved with. It should be remembered though that in a sense this is the only the tip of the systems development iceberg. In addition much configuration and coding of ERP, CRM, catalogue systems and their underlying databases will be required.

Development of web-based content and services

The delivery of e-business services via a web interface may initially appear straightforward. Everyone has heard apocryphal tales such as a 12-year-old relation creating a web site to sell used cars. Indeed the creation of **static web content** is straightforward. In this example, simple HTML code is used for layout and formatting of information to create a simple catalogue of perhaps 10 cars, with a web page for each that is accessed from a home page or simple menu. But imagine the situation for a real car dealership where a customer will want to select from a range of hundreds or thousands of cars with different specifications from different manufacturers. Here, it is impractical for the user to select from a menu of hundreds of cars. At the very least, they will expect the cars to be grouped into categories by manufacturer and perhaps sorted by age. But finding the right car through browsing these categories could take a long time and most users will demand a basic search facility by which they type in, or select, the make of car or an advanced search facility by which they choose the make, plus the specification such as engine size and year of registration. In this case the page delivered to the user will depend on their preferences and will be **dynamic web content**. Here, it is apparent that more than simple formatting and presentation is required – the site is interactive, that is to say it must accept text input from the user and respond to the request with the appropriate information. The development process will involve coding to accept the user's preferences, passing the request to a database, performing a query, returning the results and formatting them for the user. Another type of dynamic content is when a script is run to deliver information and formatting according to the user's environment. Examples might include displaying a time and date according to the date/time on the user's computer's system clock, displaying country-specific information according to the domain of the user or formatting information for a certain version of web browser. This type of dynamic updating is not possible with simple HTML, but requires a scripting language.

Static web content
A web page view that is identical every time it is loaded

Dynamic web content
A web page view that varies according to user preferences or environment constraints.

In this section we will start by introducing how simple static web pages can be developed using HTML. We will then go on to consider in the section *Focus on HTML* how scripts and databases can be used in conjunction with HTML to produce dynamic content. For each of these we will start by considering the standards used to create the content and then look at tools that facilitate the process.

Creating static web content

HTML or hypertext markup language, which was introduced in *Chapter 3*, is the standard that is used most commonly for producing static web content. HTML is an international standard established by the World Wide Web Consortium (and published at www.w3.org) intended to ensure that any web page authored according to the definitions in the standard will appear the same in any web browser. HTML files can be authored in an ordinary text editor such as the Notepad program available with Microsoft Windows. Modern word processors also have an option to save formatted information in the HTML format. Alternatively, many software utilities are available to simplify writing HTML which are described in a later section.

HTML (Hypertext Markup Language)
HTML is a standard format used to define the text and layout of web pages. HTML files usually have the extension .HTML or .HTM.

The operation of HTML is based on a web browser interpreting **HTML tags** or codes on a web page when it is loaded into the browser. For example, the <TITLE> tag indicates what appears at the top of the web browser window. Each starting tag has a corresponding end tag usually marked by a '/', for example <TITLE>The B2C Company</TITLE>. Tags can be nested or embedded when more than one style of formatting is required. For example <B><I>highlight</B></I> instructs the browser

HTML tags
Markup codes denoted by the symbol <start code> and </end code> that instruct the browser to format information or perform a particular operation.

to display the word 'highlight' as bold and italicized text. The start tags <B> and <I> tell the browser to start formatting in all text that appears from that point and the end tags </B></I> instruct the browser to stop using the formatting. Special **HTML parameters** are used to provide more detailed instructions for some HTML tags, for example the 'width' parameter in the following code <TABLE width="95%"> instructs the browser that the table should occupy 95 per cent of the screen.

HTML parameters
These occur within the tags to specify particular characteristics of the HTML statement.

The following *Focus on HTML* section outlines the main features of HTML that are used for constructing web pages.

F *Focus on* HTML

A basic working knowledge of HTML is useful for managers for two reasons. First, there may be occasions when you need to produce a simple page, perhaps to prototype or storyboard a proposal for an enhancement to a web site or perhaps a personal home page for the intranet or at home. Second, it is useful to have an appreciation of the issues involved with creating web pages using HTML in order to be able to plan and manage projects involving creation of web pages. Through knowledge of HTML and other development techniques it will be possible to discuss estimates for page development with an internal developer or quotes for page development with an external agency without the 'wool being pulled over your eyes'. For these reasons, and perhaps because it can be fun, a basic introduction to HTML is taught on many college and university courses and for these reasons it is included here.

We will review the elements of HTML by starting with a very simple page and gradually increasing its sophistication by adding different components to the page until a realistic page is produced that could act as the home page for the B2C site. As you review the elements of HTML you can put them into practice by following *activity 12.2*, creating a web page for The B2C Company.

Activity 12.2 Creating a web page for The B2C Company

Purpose

To learn the basic elements of HTML.

Activity

For each of the examples in the following section create a web page and upload to an ISP so it is published on the web. For UK readers, Freeserve (www.freeserve.co.uk) is a good free option. For readers elsewhere, a similar facility is available through Yahoo Geocities (www.yahoo.com).

<HTML> tag
Denotes an HTML document.

<HEAD> tag
The header part of an HTML document containing titles, meta tags and scripts.

<BODY> tag
The main part of an HTML document containing content.

A simple HTML page

What are the basic elements of an HTML page? First we need tags to tell the browser this is an HTML page; this is performed by the **<HTML> tag**. Second we need tags to show the header and body of the page. This is performed by the **<HEAD>** and **<BODY> tags**. Within the <HEAD> part of the HTML document it is possible (but not essential) to add the **<TITLE> tag** to indicate the text to appear in the title bar of the browser. Within the part of the document tagged by <BODY> </BODY> any text will be displayed as shown below. Comments are denoted by the **Comment tag <!— —>**.For clarity, the <HTML>, <HEAD> and <BODY> tags will be omitted in the subsequent examples which occur within the <BODY> tags unless otherwise indicated.

<TITLE> tag
The text that appears in the browser title bar.

Comment tag <!— —>
Used to document code, text does not appear in browser.

HTML code	Browser display
<HTML> <HEAD> <TITLE>The B2C Company</TITLE> </HEAD> <BODY> <!—Main content starts here—> Welcome to the web site of The B2C Company </BODY> </HTML>	Welcome to the web site of The B2C Company

Text formatting

Text formatting in HTML is straightforward. Bold, italic and underline formatting is applied using the **<B>, <I> and <U> text formatting** tags. To denote paragraphs use the **<P>** </P> tags which cause a carriage return (blank line) after each line. To break a line without a space used the break tag **
**.

<B>, <I> and <U> text formatting
Formats text as bold, italic or underlined.

<P> and <BR> line spacing
Paragraphs are denoted by <B> and line breaks by <BR>.

HTML code	Browser display
<P> This text is <B>bold </B></P> <P>This text is <I>italic</I></P> This text is <U>underlined</U>	This text is **bold** This text is *italic* This text is underlined

Text justification

Text and images are centred by enclosing the text within the **<CENTER> alignment tag**. For more sophisticated alignment, tables are the best method.

<CENTER> tag
Centres enclosed text or other objects.

HTML code	Browser display
<CENTER> This text is centred </CENTER>	This text is centred

Text size

Text size can be crudely controlled by the use of **heading tags**. The heading style changes the text to bold and increases its size according to the heading number 1

<H1>, <H2>, <H3>, <H4> heading tags
Produces a heading in bold.

to 4. It also forces a line break following the end tag. These heading styles cannot be readily used to generate a table of contents as in Word, although most HTML editors provide a facility for this.

<FONT> tag
Used to specify font characteristics.

Greater control over text size can be achieved through using the **<FONT> tag.** Here the style of font such as Arial or Times can be specified together with its colour and relative size. The default font on most browsers is a serifed font such as Times Roman. Serifed fonts are often used for typesetting books such as this one since text is easier to digest. Sans serif fonts are conventionally used for titles.

HTML code

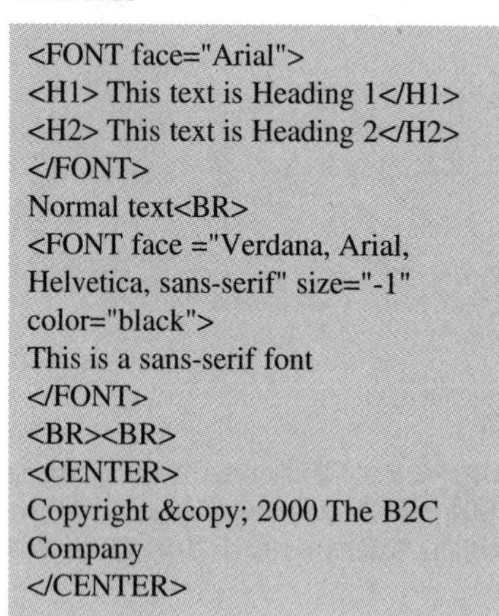

```
<FONT face="Arial">
<H1> This text is Heading 1</H1>
<H2> This text is Heading 2</H2>
</FONT>
Normal text<BR>
<FONT face ="Verdana, Arial,
Helvetica, sans-serif" size="-1"
color="black">
This is a sans-serif font
</FONT>
<BR><BR>
<CENTER>
Copyright &copy; 2000 The B2C
Company
</CENTER>
```

Browser display

This text is Heading 1

This Text is Heading 2

Normal text

This is a sans-serif font

Copyright © 2000 The B2C Company

Lists

Creating lists is straightforward. <LI> is used before each item in a list, and the basic form of the list is determined by the tag at the start and end of the list. The <UL></UL> tag is used to denote the beginning and end of an *unordered (bullet) list* and the <OL></OL>tag is used at the beginning and end of an *ordered (numbered) list.*

HTML code

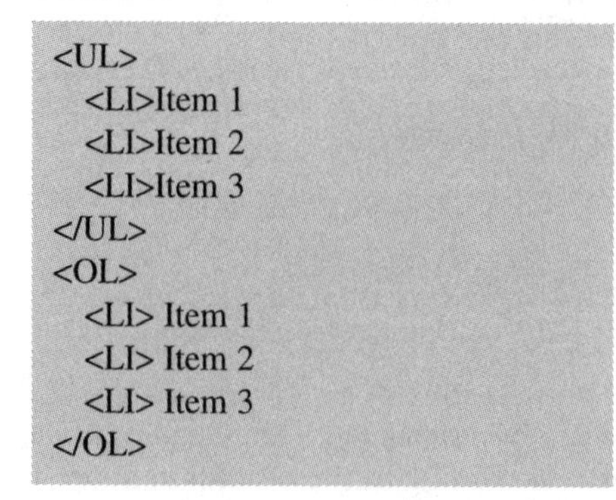

```
<UL>
  <LI>Item 1
  <LI>Item 2
  <LI>Item 3
</UL>
<OL>
  <LI> Item 1
  <LI> Item 2
  <LI> Item 3
</OL>
```

Browser display

- Item 1
- Item 2
- Item 3

1. Item 1
2. Item 2
3. Item 3

Graphics

Graphic elements are displayed using the **<IMG> tag** which refers to a graphic file which is inserted into the displayed page at that point. As explained in *Chapter 3* graphic files are usually .GIF or .JPEG images. The example below shows a .JPG graphic from a graphics subdirectory which is aligned to the right of the page. Note that the specification of width and height are not essential, but speed loading. The ALT keyword is important for two reasons. First, if the user has graphics turned off in their browser, or is viewing a page before the graphics are fully loaded, it gives a text indication of what is an image shows. Second, it is important for search engines which index the ALT keyword text, but do not know the information contained in the graphic itself. A page made entirely from graphics, but with no ALT text will not be indexed by search engines.

<IMG> tag
This is used to insert a graphic into the document by specifying a file name, size and alternative text.

HTML code	Browser display
<IMG SRC="graphics/car.jpg" WIDTH="241" HEIGHT="122" ALT ="car picture" ALIGN="RIGHT">	<Photo appears here on web page>

Links

Links or more strictly hyperlinks are essential to the function of the web since these enable a user to click on a link text, graphic or button and jump to another part of the same document, a different document on the same site, or a completely different site. The link tag is identified by **<A HEF=R" "></A>** tag and can be thought of as being in two parts as the example below shows. The first part <A HREF="index.htm"> is used to specify the target address or destination page to link to, in this case the home page of the current site. The target destination could also be a graphic, sound or plug-in, although the <EMBED> tag can also be used for this purpose. The second part specifies the form or label used for the hyperlink to link to. This can be a text, graphic or button-based hyperlink. If the hyperlink is text, the text, in this case 'Go to the home page', is specified between the <A HREF=""> tag and the closing </A> tag. If the hyperlink item is a graphic an <IMG> tag is inserted before the </A>. A form-based button (see section on *Input forms*) can be used also as the hyperlink as shown below.

HTML code

```
<A HREF="index.htm"> Go to home
page </A><BR>
<A HREF="index.htm"><IMG SRC
="home.gif"></A><BR>
<A HREF="index.htm"><INPUT
TYPE="submit"
VALUE="Home Page"></A>
```

Browser display

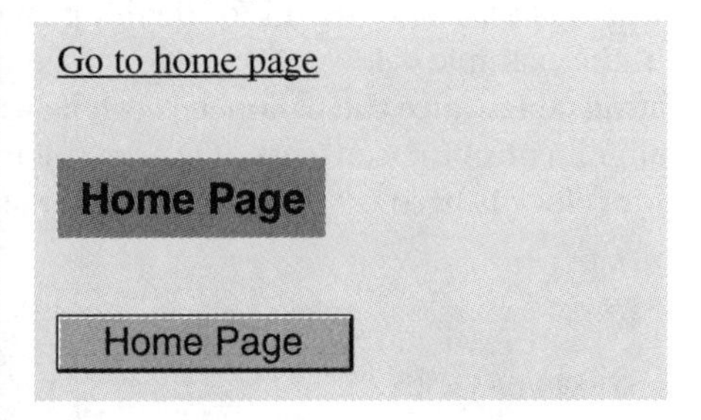

Six of the most commonly encountered options for linking to a destination document are shown in *Table 12.1*. All involve the use of the **<A HREF> tag** but specifying different information for the target address.

A HREF></A> tag
Links to a specified document.

Table 12.1 Different forms of the <A HREF> tag to link to other documents

Link to	*Approach used*	*Example*
1. Elsewhere on same page	Define a destination tag using the <A NAME> tag and then link using reference of name preceded by #	<A NAME="Top"></A> <A HREF="#top">Go to top of document</A>
2. Another document on same site, same directory	Use <A HREF> tag with the destination document name specified	<A HREF="destination.htm">Open page in sub directory</A>
3. Another document on same site, sub-directory	Use <A HREF> tag with sub folder specified followed by / and the document name	<A HREF="Sub folder/destination.htm">Open page in sub directory</A>
4. Another document on same site, parent directory	Use <A HREF> tag with sub folder specified followed by . ./ and the document name	<A HREF="destination.htm">Open page in parent directory</A>
5. A home page document on a different site	Use <A HREF> tag with full site URL of destination document. No .HTM file to open .htm	<A HREF=" http://www.marketing-online.co.uk">Marketing Online home page</A>
6. A named document on a different site	Use <A HREF> tag with full site URL of destination document including filename	<A HREF=" http:// www.marketing-online.co.uk/glossind.htm">Marketing Online glossary</A>

Tables

Tables are used commonly in web page implementation, both for formatting data in tables such as a product catalogue on an e-commerce site and also for page layout. Tables are constructed using three tags. To define a table, start with the **<TABLE> table definition tag**. As the example below shows, parameters of this tag specify the width of the browser window the table will occupy, the style of the border (use 0 for no border) and spacing. Each row in the table is denoted by the **<TR> table row tag** and the columns are defined by the **<TD> table data cell definition tag**. In the example below there are three rows, so there are three <TR> table row tag and two columns indicated by six <TD> table cell definition tags. There are six <TD> tags since the columns are defined by individual cells, two cells are nested within each row making six in total. This approach enables great flexibility in table design which is especially useful for defining layouts as described in the next section. As in the example below, <TD> table cell definition tags are frequently used when creating tables since the parameters can be used to change the background colour and alignment of the contents of the cells. For example, for the first row the parameter for colour is bgcolor="#c0c0c0" and for alignment is align="center".

<TABLE> table definition tag
Defines table parameters.

<TR> table row tag
Defines a row within a table.

<TD> table data cell definition tag
Defines the characteristics of a cell within a row of a table.

HTML code

```
< TABLE width="95% " border="1" cellspacing="0"
cellpadding="4">
<TR><!— Row 1 Column 1 —>
        <TD bgcolor="#c0c0c0" align="center">
                <B>R1C1</B>
```

Browser display

R1C1	R1C2
R2C1	R2CR
R3C1	R3C2

```
        </TD>
        <!— Row 1 Column 2 —>
        <TD bgcolor="#c0c0c0" align="center">
                <B>R1C2</B>
        </TD>
</TR>
<TR><!— Row 2 Column 1 —>
        <TD align="left">
                R2C1
        </TD>
        <!— Row 2 Column 2 —>
        <TD align="right">
                R2C2
        </TD>
</TR>
<TR>
        <!— Row 3 Column 1 —>
        <TD align="left">
                R3C1
        </TD>
        <!— Row 3 Column 2 —>
        <TD align="right">R3C2</TD>
</TR>
</TABLE>
```

R2C1	R2C2
R3C1	R3C2

Forms

Forms are used to enable interaction. In the example shown in *Figure 12.2*, and the code below, the **<Form> tag** is used to enable a customer to ask an online customer

<FORM> tag
Used to accept input from users.

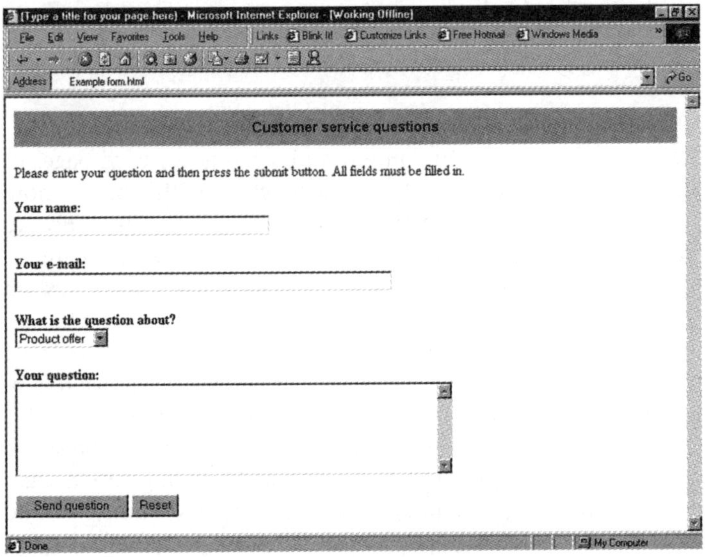

Figure 12.2 An example online customer service form

service question. The question is delivered to the customer service representative as an e-mail.

HTML code

```
<FORM ACTION="/cgi-bin/mailform.cgi" onSubmit="return validate(this.form)"
METHOD="POST" NAME="enq_form">
<P>
<B>Your name:</B>
<BR><INPUT NAME="user_name" TYPE="text" SIZE="40" VALUE="">
<BR><BR>
<B>Your e-mail:</B>
<BR><INPUT NAME="e_mail" TYPE="text" size="60" VALUE="">
<P>
<B>What is the question about?</B>
<BR>
<select name="type">
<option>Product offer</option>
<option>Product return</option>
<option>Other</option>
</select>
<P><B>Your question:</B><BR><TEXTAREA NAME="question"
TYPE="text" rows="6" cols="60" VALUE=""></TEXTAREA>
<P><P>
<INPUT NAME="forwardto" TYPE="hidden" VALUE="dc@marketing-
online.co.uk">
<P>
<INPUT NAME="nextlink" TYPE="hidden" VALUE="http://www.marketing-
online.co.uk/redirect.htm">
<P>
<INPUT TYPE="SUBMIT" Value="Send question">
<INPUT TYPE="RESET">
```

Page layout

The layout for a web page is similar in many ways to the front page of a newspaper. There will be a title area or banner, main content and a footer for each page. In addition a company logo will usually be displayed together with one or more menus. As was mentioned in *Chapter 11* on *Web interface design*, for ease of use we are usually trying to make the layout consistent between different pages. There are many permutations for laying out a page; some of the more common ones are shown in *Figure 12.3*.

There are two main options for structuring a page such that different content appears in different parts of the page. These are *frames* and *tables*. Reference to any technical discussion group will show that deciding whether to use frames for layout can arouse great passions among web designers. Managers need to be aware of the limitations and benefits of frames in order to be able to intelligently discuss the merits of frames with the design team. First, what are frames? Frames can be thought of as similar to the choice newspaper editors have for laying out front pages. *Figure 12.3* shows some common frames layouts. A common arrangement is

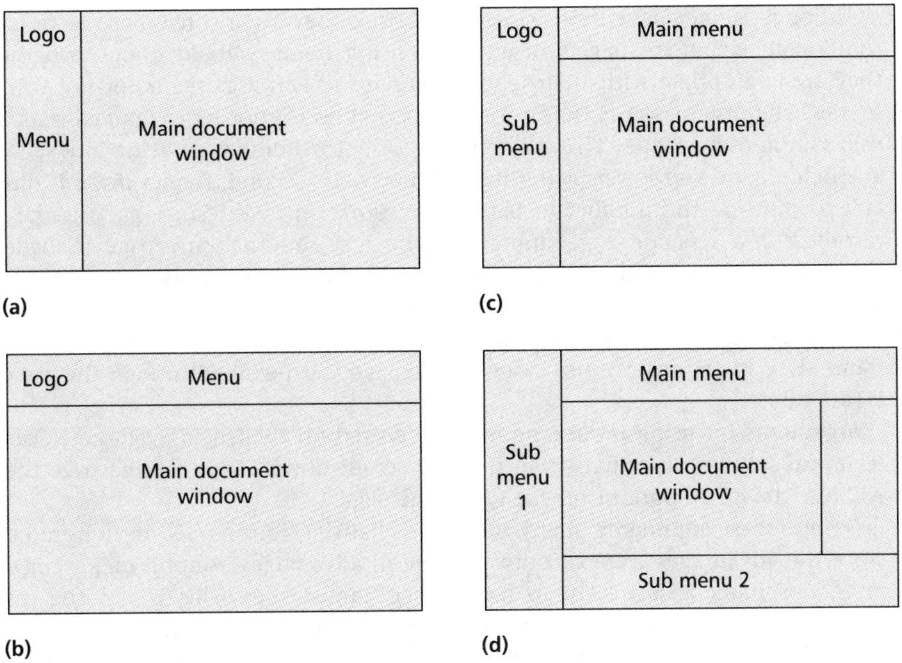

(a)

Logo

Menu

Main document window

(c)

Logo

Main menu

Sub menu

Main document window

(b)

Logo

Menu

Main document window

(d)

Main menu

Sub menu 1

Main document window

Sub menu 2

Figure 12.3 Possible web page layout options

Figure 12.3(a); here one frame on the left has fixed content used for display of company name, logo and menus. When a user selects a menu option this usually causes a new HTML page to be loaded into the main frame window to the right, so this is the only area of screen that is updated. Sometimes as in (c) and (d) one frame is used for top-level menus that remains fixed and other frames are used to give sub-menu options according to the main menu selection.

The **<FRAMESET> and <FRAME> tags** are used to produce frames.

HTML code for a two frame column arrangement such as *Figure 12.3(a)* is shown below. Here, the FRAMESET tag refers to two columns. For horizontal frames the rows parameter can be used. When code such as that below is executed in the browser it will automatically load the content of the frame source indicated by SRC="menu.htm" into the browser. Typically, the user will select a menu option by clicking on a link in the menu and this will update the frame to the right (Main_area) which is known as the target frame.

<FRAMESET> and <FRAME> tags

Frames are a technical feature of HTML that provide a straightforward means of achieving a standard page layout on screen.

HTML code

```
<HEAD>
<Frameset cols="30%,*">
<FRAME SRC="menu.htm" scrolling="yes" name="menu_area">
<FRAME SRC="main.htm" scrolling="yes" name="main_area">
</Frameset>
<Noframes>
This text is displayed if the user doesn't have frames
</Noframes>
</HEAD>
```

Although frames have been widely used since they are a convenient technical solution to layout, managers of any sites using frames should discuss whether they are appropriate with their team. There are several arguments for not using frames. The first reason is that most search engines do not index framed sites as well as non-framed sites. This may result in only the home page being indexed in a search engine and lower listing than competitors. Second, frames make it difficult to measure the number of page impressions on a site, since each frame is recorded as a separate page impression the first time a home page is loaded although the user is only viewing one page. Frames can also make it difficult for users to bookmark or print pages since it is not always clear which page is to be bookmarked or printed. Finally frames are marginally slower to load than non-frame sites. In the majority of cases, similar layout is possible through the use of HTML tables.

Arguments for using frames are mainly centred on their being a more elegant technical solution and that when the user scrolls down a non-framed page they will lose the menu options off the top of the page.

Despite these arguments, many sites have changed from framed to non-framed since the advantages seem to outweigh the disadvantages. Among major corporates, non-framed sites seem to outnumber framed sites. This is not the case amongst smaller companies since cheaper web site design tools often promote the use of frames. Now complete *activity 12.3* to consider your personal view on the merits of framed and non-framed sites.

Activity 12.3 Examples of page layout

Purpose

To experience, and evaluate the table and frame options for site layout

Activity

Visit the range of sites below and determine whether they use frames or tables. Which approach do you favour? You can tell which approach is used by scrolling down each page and seeing whether the layout remains fixed – if it does it is a frame, if not a table is used. Alternatively, in Microsoft Internet Explorer you can choose the View, Source option and see whether the <FRAME> HTML tag is included within the source code.

Sites to evaluate:

RAC (www.rac.co.uk)
Egg (www.egg.com)
easyjet (www.easyjet.com)
Orange (www.orange.co.uk)
Yahoo! (www.yahoo.com)
FirstDirect (www.firstdirect.com)
Cisco (www.cisco.com)
FT.com (www.ft.com)

For answer see p. 523

Non-framed sites are typically produced using *tables*. An example of a table-based layout for The B2C Company home page is shown in *Figure 12.4*. The code necessary to achieve this arrangement is shown below:

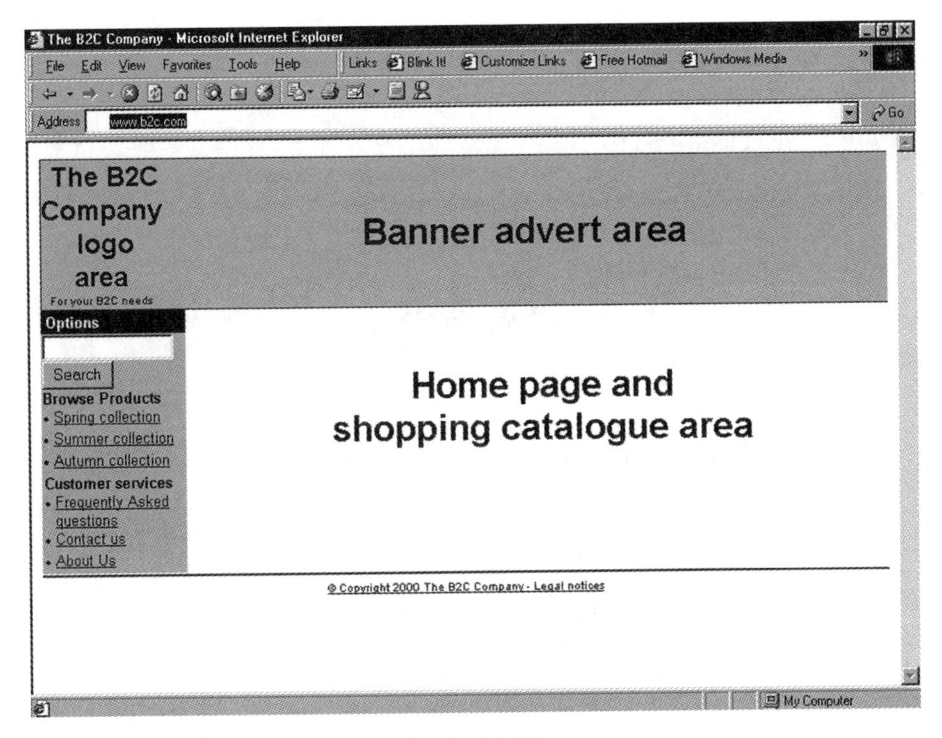

Figure 12.4 Table-based page layout for The B2C Company.

HTML code

```
<html>
<head>

<table width="100%" border=0 cellspacing=0 cellpadding=0
bgcolor="#99CCFF">
<tr>

<font face="arial" size="12" color="#000099"><b><center>
 The B2C Company<br> logo area<br></b>
<font face="arial" size="-3">
For your B2C needs</b></center></font>
</td>
<td width=100%>
<font face="arial" size="13" color="#000099"><b><center>
Banner advert area
<font face="arial" size="-3" color="#000099"><b></center>
</td>
</tr>
</table>

<table width="100%" border=0 cellspacing=0 cellpadding=0><tr valign=top>
```

```
<!— Do not need closing </table> comment here due to nesting —>
<table width=130 border=0 cellspacing=0 cellpadding=0 bgcolor="#000099">

<!— Blue menu header on left —>
<td width=130> <font face="Arial, Helvetica, sans-serif" size=-1
color="#FFFFFF"><b>Options</b></font><br>
<img src="images/singpix.gif" width=130 height=1></td></tr>

</table>

<!— Blue menu on left —>
<!— First options —>
<!— Header 1 —>
<table width=125 border=0 cellspacing=0 cellpadding=0><tr>
<td colspan=2>

<form method="get" action="http://search.atomz.com/search/">
<input size=15 name="sp-q"><br>
<input type=submit value="Search">
<input type=hidden name="sp-a" value="0005390c-sp00000000">

<font face=Arial size=-1><BR><b>Browse Products</b></font></td></tr><tr
valign=top>

<!— Suboption —>
<td>&#149; </td>
<td width="100%"><font face=Arial size=-1>
<a href="proda.htm">Spring collection</a>
</font></td></tr><tr valign=top>

<!— Suboption —>
<td>&#149; </td>
<td width="100%"><font face=Arial size=-1>
<a href="prodb.htm">Summer collection</a>
</font></td></tr><tr valign=top>

<!— Suboption —>
<td>&#149; </td>
<td width="100%"><font face=Arial size=-1>
<a href="prodc.htm">Autumn collection</a>
</font></td></tr><tr valign=top>

</table>

<!— Header 2 —>
<table width=125 border=0 cellspacing=0 cellpadding=0><tr>
<td colspan=2><font face=Arial size=-1><b>Customer
services</b></font></td></tr><tr valign=top>
```

```
<!— Suboption —>
<td>&#149; </td>
<td width="100%"><font face=Arial size=-1>
<a href="faq.htm">Frequently Asked questions</a>
</font></td></tr><tr valign=top>

<!— Suboption —>
<td>&#149; </td>
<td width="100%"><font face=Arial size=-1>
<a href="contact.htm">Contact us</a>
</font></td></tr><tr valign=top>

<!— Suboption —>
<td>&#149; </td>
<td width="100%"><font face=Arial size=-1>
<a href="about.htm">About Us</a>
</font></td></tr><tr valign=top>
</table>

</td>

<td width="100%">
<table border=0 width=100% cellspacing=0 cellpadding=2
bgcolor=#ffffff><tr><td><center></center>
</td></tr></table>


<!— Main window —>
<font face=Arial >

<table width="100%" border=0 cellspacing=1 cellpadding=0><tr>
<td height=0 colspan=3>

<td border=0>

<TITLE>The B2C Company</TITLE>
<table width="100%" border="0" cellpadding="10" cellspacing="0">
<tr><BR><BR></TR>
<tr>
<td width="100%" ><p align="center"><font size="13" face="Arial"><b>
Home page and <BR> shopping catalogue area
</b></font></td></p></tr></table>

<!— End main window —>
</td></tr>

<tr><td colspan=3 height=5></td></tr></table>
</table>
```

```
<table border=0 width=100% cellspacing=0 cellpadding=2
bgcolor=#ffffff><tr><td><center></center>
</td></tr></table>

<td></td><tr></tr>


<table width="100%" cellpadding=0 cellspacing=0 border=0><tr>
<td bgcolor="#003399"><img src="images/singpix.gif" border=0 width=0
height=2></td></tr></table>

<table width="100%" cellpadding=5 cellspacing=0 border=0><tr>
<td align=center><font size=-2 face="arial,helvetica" color="#003399">
<a href="/">&copy; Copyright 2000 The B2C Company – Legal notices</a>
</FONT>
</td></tr></table>
</body></html>
```

Menus

Sites are easier to navigate if there are limited numbers of menu options. It is usually suggested that two or possibly three levels of menus are the most that are desirable. For example, there may be main menu options at the left of the screen that take the user to the different parts of the site and at the bottom of the screen will be specific menu options that refer to that part of the site. (Sub-menus in this form are often referred to as nesting.)

Menu options

Designing and creating the menus to support navigation present several options and these are briefly described. The main options are:

1. *Text menus, buttons or images*. The site user can select menus by clicking on different objects. They can click on a basic text hyperlink, underlined in blue, by default. The use of text menus only may make a site look primitive and reduce its graphic appeal, but some professional sites such as Cisco (www.cisco.com) use this approach. Graphic images or buttons can be used to highlight menu options more distinctly. While these are graphically appealing it may not be obvious that these are menu options until the user positions the mouse over them. A combination of text menu options and either buttons or images is usually the best compromise. This way the user has the visual appeal of buttons or images, but also the faster option of text – they can select these menus if they are waiting for graphical elements to load, or if the images are turned-off in the web browser.
2. *Rollovers*. 'Rollover' is the term used to describe where the colour of the menu option changes when the user positions the mouse over the menu option and then changes again when the menu option is selected. Rollovers are useful in that they help achieve the context referred to in the previous section by highlighting the area of the site the user is in.

3. *Positioning*. Menus can be positioned at any of the edges of the screen, with left, bottom or top being conventional for western cultures. The main design aim is to keep the position consistent between different parts of the site.
4. *Number of levels*. In a hierarchical structure there could as many as ten different levels, but for simplicity it is normal to try and achieve a site structure with a nesting level of four or fewer. Even in an electronic commerce shopping site with 20,000 products it should be possible to select a product at four menu levels. For example:
   - level 1 – drink
   - level 2 – spirits
   - level 3 – whisky
   - level 4 – brand x (different size options)
5. *Number of options*. Psychologists recommend only having a limited number of choices within each menu. If you are using more than seven, then it is probably necessary to add another level to the hierarchy to accommodate the extra choices.

F *Focus on* developing dynamic web content

Scripting languages are one of the main tools for creating dynamic web content, a set of instructions intended to perform a particular task. In a web context JavaScript, for example, can be used to display today's date when it is loaded into a browser. Barron (2000) notes that the term probably originated from the use of scripts by actors in theatre and film. Scripts differ from programs in that they are usually less complex and are executed and run in a single compile and run stage. For example, when a web page is loaded, if it contains JavaScript script code it is executed or interpreted immediately. This is in contrast to traditional programming languages such as C++ where the program is compiled and checked as part of the development process before executable code is run when the user starts the program.

Scripting languages
A software standard providing a set of instructions to perform a particular task.

An early use of web scripting was for processing web forms. HTML contains some tags for accepting data inputted by a user into a form on the web browser which is then sent to the server for action. For example a user might type in a question for customer service on the e-commerce site, by typing in their details and the nature of the query. After clicking the submit button, the data is sent to the server where it can be transformed by a CGI script into an e-mail to be sent to customer service which is formatted to summarize the nature of the problem and the customer's personal details. The CGI script may then be used to produce a dynamic notification page in the browser that thanks the user for asking a question and says how and when it will be answered. The processing on the server has traditionally been performed by CGI scripts which can be written in a scripting language such as Perl. More recently the JavaScript scripting language has been used to perform some checking or validation of what the user enters within the browser before it is sent to the server. As the example in the section on JavaScript shows, we can use JavaScript in the browser to check whether a valid e-mail address has been entered. The overall process is shown in *Figure 12.5* and explained in more detail in the section on *JavaScript*. This process can be applied to many web interactions from filling in a customer service form to an electronic shopping catalogue.

We will look at one web scripting language, JavaScript, in some detail since this

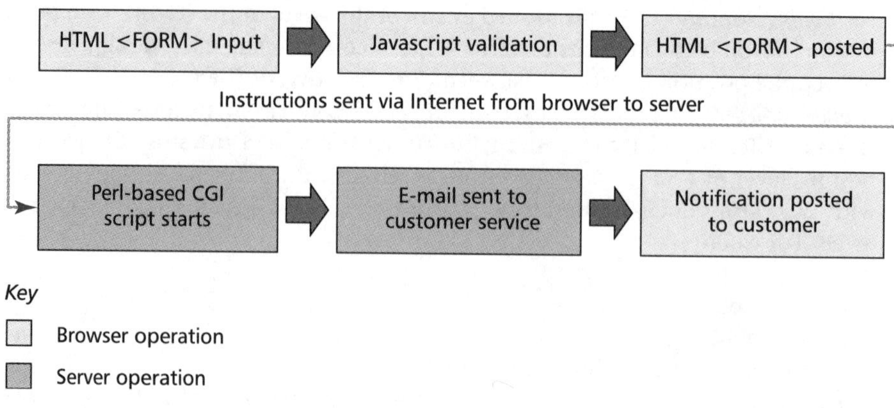

Figure 12.5 Using scripting to produce dynamic web content for form processing

is the most widely used scripting language and illustrates how dynamic web content is developed. When scripting is performed by a script which is executed by the browser, as in the form checking example above, this is referred to as **client-side scripting** while when the script is run on the server, for example a CGI script, this is referred to as **server-side scripting**.

Client-side scripting
Scripts executed on the browser.

Server-side scripting
Scripts executed on the server.

JavaScript
A web page scripting language that uses an object model.

JavaScript

JavaScript is a scripting language that was originally developed by Netscape, but is now widely used in web development and supported by all browsers. JavaScript is sometimes confused with Java, which shares some similarities, but Java is a programming rather than scripting language.

Writing JavaScript

JavaScript code is embedded directly within HTML-pages, with the <SCRIPT tag informing the browser that script code will follow. The example below shows this:

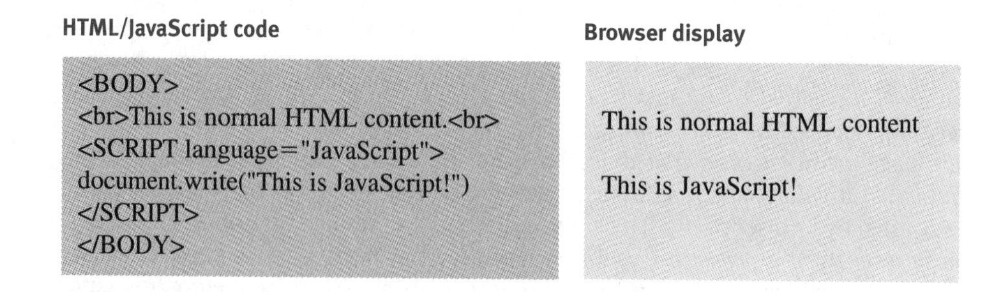

From the above example, the reason for using JavaScript may not be clear – we are simply writing a line of text which appears in the browser and we can do this with HTML. The benefits are made clear by the next example where we use JavaScript to display the current date – the page is dynamically updated according to the current date and time.

HTML/JavaScript code

```
<SCRIPT LANGUAGE="JavaScript"><!— ;


        var current_date = new Date;
        document.write("The news at " +
current_date.getHours() + ":"
        + current_date.getMinutes() + " on "
        + current_date.getDate() + "-"
        + current_date.getMonth() + "-"
        + current_date.getYear() );
// end hide —></SCRIPT>
```

Browser display

The News at 13:25 on 15-05-2001

Document object model (DOM)

JavaScript and other client-side scripting languages enable developers to access different elements of a document to update its properties. The different elements that can be accessed are referred to as the **document object model (DOM)**. The Netscape DOM enables the developer to get and change the properties of the current document and specific forms, frames and anchors. In the example above a write method is used to update the contents of the document window (document.write();).

Document object model (DOM)
Enables developers to get and set properties of different document objects such as forms and frames.

JavaScript can also perform simple calculations in response to user entry thus making the web page interactive. In the following example a user can type in the amount of loan that they require and the script is used to calculate the total repayment. The calculation is defined in a function 'calculation()' in the header section of the HTML page. This function is executed when the user presses the calculate button in the form 'MyForm'. The instruction to perform the calculation is determined by the statement within the input button: OnClick="calculation()". Note that more complex calculations in a mortgage application would probably be performed. The result is displayed for the user as an Alert box using the alert function. Alternatively the result could be written to a new page.

HTML/JavaScript code

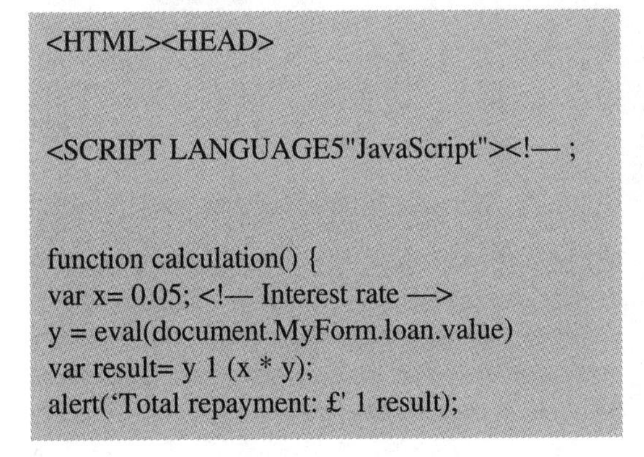

```
<HTML><HEAD>


<SCRIPT LANGUAGE5"JavaScript"><!— ;


function calculation() {
var x= 0.05; <!— Interest rate —>
y = eval(document.MyForm.loan.value)
var result= y 1 (x * y);
alert('Total repayment: £' 1 result);
```

Browser display

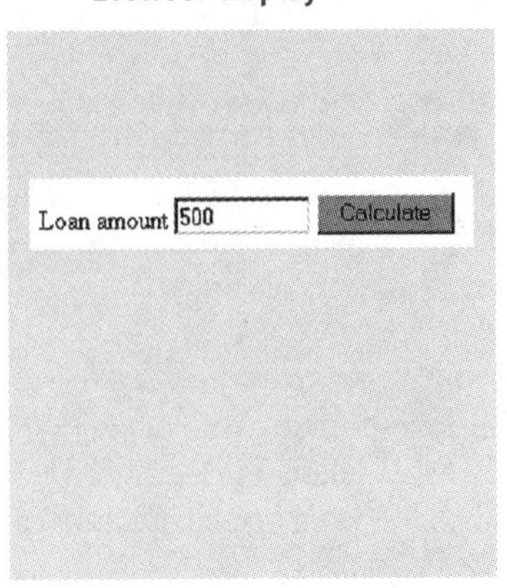

```
}
// end hide —></SCRIPT>
</HEAD>
<BODY>
<FORM name="MyForm">
Loan amount
<INPUT TYPE="number" NAME="loan"
SIZE="10" VALUE="500">
<INPUT TYPE="button"
VALUE="Calculate" OnClick="calculation()">
</FORM>
</BODY></HTML>
```

The use of the OnClick statement to execute the calculation in the above example is a common use of JavaScript to increase the interactivity of web pages. OnClick is referred to as an **event handler**.

Events and event handlers
An event handler monitors and responds to events such as a mouse click.

Examples of event handlers include the user clicking on a button (OnClick event); the mouse pointer moving across a link (OnMouseOver event) or mouse pointer moving away from a graphic (OnMouseOut event).

Validation

It is important for any input received from a form on a web site to be checked for validity. Javascript can also be used for **form validation** of data entry into a form using the document object model.

Form validation
Used to check the validity of form inputs from users.

In the *Focus on HTML* section we saw how HTML could be used to display an HTML form. In the Form statement the parameter 'onSubmit="return validate(this.form)"' is used to start a function to validate the code. The validation checks that each mandatory field is complete and checks for an e-mail address containing an '@' symbol using the JavaScript code below.

HTML/JavaScript code

```
<!—
function validate() {
var retVal=true;

if (enq_form.user_name.value == "" ) {
        alert("Please enter your name, this field is empty");
        enq_form.user_name.focus();
        enq_form.user_name.select();
        retVal=false;
        }

if (enq_form.e_mail.value == "" ) {
        alert("Please enter your e-mail address, this field is empty");
        enq_form.e_mail.focus();
```

```
            enq_form.e_mail.select();
            retVal=false;
            }
            else      {
            if (enq_form.e_mail.value.indexOf('@',0) == -1) {
                        alert("You have not entered a valid e-mail address (@
missing)");
                        enq_form.e_mail.focus();
                        enq_form.e_mail.select();
                        retVal=false;
                                    }
            }

if (enq_form.question.value == "" ) {
            alert("Please enter the nature of your query, this field is empty");
            enq_form.question.focus();
            enq_form.question.select();
            retVal=false;
            }

return retVal;
}
//—>
</SCRIPT>
```

VBScript

Like JavaScript, VBScript can be used for client-side scripting. However, it is not as widely used as Javascript since it is mainly supported by the Microsoft Internet Explorer browser. VBScript's importance is that it is most commonly used for constructing Active Server Pages (ASPs).

Perl

Perl is commonly used as a scripting language on web development projects. Its application is indicated by its full name of 'Practical Execution and Report Language'.

Perl
'Practical Execution and Report language' used mainly for server side scripting and producing CGI scripts.

Active Server Pages (ASP)

Active Server Pages are now commonly used to build dynamic content. Although originally developed for Microsoft Internet Information Server, they are increasingly supported by web server software from other manufacturers. A common application for ASPs is when a user is accessing a shopping cart on an e-commerce site. ASP is used to manage the user's requests for certain products, information about the products and their availability and add them to a shopping cart. ASP can also manage the use of cookies to recognize return visits.

Active Server Pages (ASP)
A Microsoft developed technology that can be used for dynamic web pages, often related to database query and retrieval.

When using a browser you may often see .asp at the end of the browser. When an instruction is sent via http to a web server to load an ASP page the following sequence of operations occur:

1. The parameters to the ASP statement are interpreted (these are often database query parameters such as the name of an airline, the route to be searched and to show available dates only).
2. The ASP script is executed; this may involve performing a database query, in this example to find available flights. Scripts are typically in VBScript, but other scripting languages can be used.
3. HTML pages are written dynamically to display the flight information returned from the database.

CGI (Common Gateway Interface)
CGI offers a way of providing interactivity through the web.

Active-X
A programming language standard developed by Microsoft which permits complex and graphical customer applications to be written and then accessed from a web browser. An example might be a form for calculating interest on a loan. A competitor to Java.

Java
A programming language standard supported by Sun Microsystems which permits complex and graphical customer applications to be written and then accessed from a web browser. An example might be a form for calculating interest on a loan. A competitor to Active-X.

Common Gateway Interface (CGI)

The **CGI (Common Gateway Interface)** offers a way of providing interactivity to the web since CGI provides extensions to the web server which allow server-side scripts to be run which process information submitted through web-based forms.

Other standards for dynamic content

In addition to the scripting languages described above there are now a range of competing methods which can be used to enable the user to interact with a web site by selecting menu options and entering data. The best known of these standards is the **Java** programming language. Microsoft **ActiveX** is a rival technique. Dynamic content is also increasingly developed using plug-ins from Macromedia such as Flash and Shockwave.

To put into practice some of the techniques for developing static and dynamic content described in the previous section attempt activity 12.4.

Activity 12.4 An intranet for The B2B Company

Purpose

To use HTML to develop a simple site and apply systems analysis and design skills from Chapter 11.

Activity

Develop a simple intranet web site for employees of The B2B Company.

1. First outline the requirements based on the extract below. You should include general requirements such as audience, content and services together with a use-case or scenario or storyboard of the structure of the proposed company web site.
2. Implement the web site using HTML and JavaScript. You should write your definition for the company web site based on the description given below plus any other features you feel may be useful.

Outline of requirements

This is a summary of a discussion between the marketing manager for The B2B Company and a junior member of his team who has been asked to develop the specification for the intranet site.

Q. *Who is the intranet intended for?*

A. It will be used by everyone at head office, together with regional offices and overseas distributors and agents. It will not be used directly by customers, but some of the information may be made available through an extranet.

Q. *What is the reason for the business to set up this intranet?*

A. The main aims are:
- Improved information dissemination and feedback within the company and to agents.
- Improve response to queries from customers by employees and agents.
- Improved internal exchange of information for communication and decision making.

Q. *What type of content and services will be on the intranet?*

A. The types of information that The B2B Company want to provide on the intranet include internal information about product release status, news of past and future events including meetings, trade shows and training seminars, company performance (sales figures) and social information in a monthly newsletter. Some information will be available to all employees and agents, while others such as sales figures will be restricted to certain employees at head office. Details of contact address, position, responsibility and phone numbers for company employees and agents in all countries will also be made available. Similar data will be made available for customers, and this will include their sales history and support questions related to them. Market information such as competitor addresses and market share data will also be provided.

A new database system is required as part of the intranet. Its main purpose is to provide an online question and answer forum, or virtual helpdesk. This replaces a manual system where all enquiries were entered in an Excel spreadsheet. It will enable named B2B Company employees and agents to ask a question about a particular product such as product availability, pricing, technical specifications and known problems about products and record where it applies to a particular customer. More general questions can also be asked. This virtual helpdesk will only be available to registered users who have a valid user name and password and are on the company-wide address book. They will be able to specify three levels of urgency for the reply. The question will be answered by a named support / helpdesk employee who may include reference in their answer to one or more technical info sheets. The system should record and display the date and time of each question and answer. Support and contact information will also be provided. To enable similar queries to be answered in future, the forum will build up through time to be a knowledge base. So options will be available to search the database by keyword, or a particular employee name, customer name, product name or according to the type of query. To ensure prompt responses to questions all answers will also be e-mailed to employees when answered. It will also be possible for helpdesk staff to sort / order outstanding queries in terms of priority.

Resources for web site development

It is not practical to detail fully the methods of developing content, but an indication of what is involved in developing web pages is indicated by the description and activities in the above section. Resources for readers wishing to develop these ideas further are:

- *Netskills* – Comprehensive HTML and CGI training guide at www.netskills.ac.uk.
- *Webmasters Reference.com*. Guidance and links of all aspects of development (www.webreference.com).
- *Netscape developers page*. Guidelines on development from the developers of Javascript (developer.netscape.com).

Tools for web site development and testing

A variety of software programs are available to help developers of web sites. These can save a lot of time when developing the sites and will also help in site maintenance since they will make it easier for other people not involved in the original development of the web site to be involved in web site maintenance. Tools are available with different levels of complexity and managers must decide which are most suitable to invest in. The types of tools to choose between are listed below. Although there are many rival tools, the ones here have been used for several years, are widely used and skills in these tools are often mentioned in adverts for web design staff. Part of the purpose of listing these tools is to illustrate the range of skills a web site designer will need; an advanced web site may be built using tools from each of these categories since even the most advanced tools may not have the flexibility of the basic tools.

Basic text and graphic editors.

Simple text editors can be used to edit HTML tags. Such tools are often low-cost or free including the Notepad editor included with Windows. They are flexible and all web site developers may need them to use them at some stage to develop content since more automated tools may not provide this flexibility and may not support the latest standard commands. Entire sites can be built using these tools, but it is more efficient to use the more advanced tools described below, and use the editors for 'tweaking' content.

Examples

- Microsoft Windows Notepad (www.microsoft.com)
- Program File Editor (PFE)

Graphics editors are used to create and modify GIF and JPEG pictures.

Examples

- Macromedia Fireworks (www.macromedia.com)
- Paintshop Pro (www.jasc.com)
- PhotoDraw 2000 (www.microsoft.com)
- PhotoImpact (www.ulead.com)

Specialized HTML editors

These tools provide facilities for adding HTML tags automatically. For example, adding the Bold text tag <B> </B> to the HTML document will happen when the user clicks the bold tag. Some of these editors are WYSIWYG.

Examples

There are many freeware and shareware editors in this category.

Basic tools

- Arachnoid (www.aracnoid.com) is a good, freely available (careware) tool.
- Microsoft FrontPage Express (www.microsoft.com).

- Modern versions of wordprocessors such as Microsoft Word and Lotus WordPro now have these facilities through using the Save As HTML option. These can be used to produce HTML pages, but are less good at page layout.

More advanced tools supporting JavaScript and some site management facilities

- HotDog Professional (www.sausage.com).
- HotMetal Pro (www.softquad.com).
- HomeSite (www.allaire.com).

Advanced graphics tools

- Adobe Photoshop (extensively used by graphic designers, www.adobe.com)
- Macromedia Fireworks (A web-specific graphics package, with more limited functionality compared with Photoshop, www.macromedia.com)
- Macromedia Flash and Director-Shockwave (used for graphical animations, www.macromedia.com).

Site management tools

These tools provide the advanced HTML editing facilities of the previous category, but also provide tools to help manage and test the site including graphic layouts of the structure of the site making it easy to find, modify and republish the page by sending the file to the web site using FTP (*Chapter 3*). Scripting with HTML is also possible. Style templates can be applied to produce a consistent look and feel across the site. Tools are also available to create and manage menu options. Many of the tools that started as basic HTML editors have now been developed to incorporate the site management features.

Examples

- ColdFusion (www.allaire.com)
- Dreamweaver (www.macromedia.com)
- Fusion (www.netobjects.com)
- PageMill (www.adobe.com)
- Microsoft FrontPage (www.microsoft.com)

Database management tools for interactive site development

These tools provide an automated method of updating content in a site, often by non-specialists. Lotus Notes is an example of this. Documents such as PR releases or product information sheets are stored in a Lotus Notes database and automatically published to the web using the Domino facility (). This is an efficient method of publishing content since the facility can be made available to people throughout the company.

Examples

- ColdFusion (www.allaire.com)
- Fusion (www.netobjects.com)
- Dreamweaver Ultradev which includes an ASP database interface
- Lotus Notes/Domino (www.lotus.com)

E-commerce site development tools

These include support for developing catalogue browsing and selection and creation of shopping baskets for transaction e-commerce sites. There are many examples in this category.

Examples

- Shopcreator Stall supports up to 10 products (www.shopcreator.net).
- IBM Home page creator (see mypage-products.ihost.com/uk/en_US/) supports 15–500 items.
- BT StoreFront – an online solution (www.storecentre.bt.com) – supports small–medium number of products.

Higher volume products less than £1000 are:

- Actinic Catalog (www.actinic.com)
- iShop (www.ishop.co.uk)
- Shop -assistant (www.floyd.co.uk)

Higher cost products are:

- iCat commerce Publisher (www.icat.co.uk)
- Lotus Domino Merchant Server (www.lotus.com)
- Microsoft Site Server Commerce (www.microsoft.com)
- Intershop Merchant (www.intershop.co.uk)

Testing

Testing
Aims to identify non-conformance in the requirements specification and errors.

Testing has two main objectives, first to check for non-conformance with the business and user requirements, and second to identify bugs or errors. In other words, the site does what users need and is reliable. Testing is an iterative process that occurs throughout development. As non-conformances are fixed by the development team, there is a risk that the problem may not have been fixed and that new problems have been created. Further testing is required to check solutions to problems are effective.

The testing process

Test specification
A description of the testing process and tests to be performed.

A structured testing process is necessary in order to identify and solve as many problems as possible before the system is released to users. For this testing is conducted in a structured way by using a **test specification** which is a comprehensive specification of testing in all modules of the system. If the use-case method of analysis described in *Chapter 11* is used then it will specify the different use-cases or scenarios to be tested in detailed test scripts. The comprehensive testing specification will also cover all the different types of test outlined in *Table 12.2*.

Testing in the web environment requires new constraints. Unfortunately the list of constraints is long and sometimes neglected to disastrous effect. Retailer Boo.com used a complex graphic to display clothes that was too time consuming to use for visitors to the site. If there are a thousand potential users of an e-commerce site, all of the following constraints on design may exclude a proportion:

Table 12.2 Types of testing required for an e-commerce site

Type of testing	*Description*
Developer tests	Code level tests performed by developers of modules
Feasibility testing	Tests a new approach, often near the start of a project to make sure it is acceptable in terms of user experience
Module (component) tests	Checks individual modules have the correct functionality i.e. correct outputs are produced for specified inputs (black-box testing)
Integration testing	Checks interactions between groups of modules
System testing	Checks interactions between all modules in the system
Database transaction taken	Can the user connect to the database and are transactions executed correctly
Performance/capacity testing	Tests the speed of the system under high load
Usability testing	Check that the system is easy to use and follows the conventions of user-centred design described in *Chapter 11*
Acceptance tests	Checks the system is acceptable for the party that commissioned it
Content or copy testing	Tests the acceptability of copy from a marketing view

- *Speed of access* – everyone has used sites with huge graphics that take minutes to download. Good designers will optimize graphics for speed and then test using a slow modem across phone lines. Yahoo! downloads in just one second, so this is the performance that users expect from other sites.
- *Screen resolutions* – designing for different screen resolutions is necessary since some users with laptops may be operating at low resolution such as 640 by 480 pixels, the majority at 800 by 600 pixels, a few at higher resolutions of 1064 by 768 pixels or greater. If the designers have designed the site using with PCs with high resolutions, they may be difficult to read for the majority.
- *Number of colours* – some users may have monitors capable of displaying 16 million colours giving photo-realism while other may only have the PC to set up to display 256 colours.
- *Changing font size* – choosing large fonts on some sites causes unsightly overlap between the different design elements – depends on the type of web browser used.
- *Different browsers* such as Microsoft Internet Explorer and Netscape Navigator and different versions of browsers such as version 4.0 or 5.0 may display graphics or text slightly differently or process JavaScript differently, so it is essential to test on a range of browser platforms.
- *Plug-ins such as Macromedia Flash and Shockwave* – if a site requires plug-ins that the user doesn't have, then a business will be cutting down its audience by the number of people who are unable or unprepared to download these plug-ins.

Testing environments

Testing occurs in different environments during the project. Prototypes are tested in a **development environment** which involves programmers testing data across a network on a shared server. In the implementation phase a special **test environment**

Development environment
Software and hardware used to create a system.

Test environment
Separate software and hardware used to test a system.

may be set up which simulates the final operating environment for the system. This test environment will be used for early user training and testing and for system testing. Finally the **production or live environment** is that in which the system will be used operationally. This will be used for user acceptance testing and when the system becomes live.

Production or live environment
Software and hardware used to host operational system.

Some resources for testing e-commerce sites

Validation

Validation services test for errors in HTML code which may cause a web page to be displayed incorrectly or for links to other pages that do not work.

- *Site viewer*. Enables test viewing of web pages with different browser versions (www.anybrowser.com/siteviewer.htm)
- *W3C HTML Validation Service*. Check for errors in code online (validator.w3.org)
- *CSE HTML validator*. Check for errors in HTML code – offline (www.htmlvalidator.com)

Sitemapping tools

These tools diagram the layout of the site, which is useful for site management, and can be used to assist users.

- *Elsop sitemapping tools*. SiteMap and Linkscan tools for checking site links and mapping (www.elsop.com)
- *Electrum Powermapper*. An offline tool for mapping a web site (www.electrum.co.uk)

Changeover

Migration or changeover from a previous information system to a new system is particularly important for mission-critical e-business systems where errors in management of **changeover** will result in a negative customer experience or disruption to the supply chain.

Changeover
The term used to describe moving from the old information system to the new information system.

In this section we look at significant issues involved in managing this transition from previous systems to e-business systems and transitioning from one version of an e-business system to the next. When introducing a new sell-side e-commerce system there are two basic choices. First the company can fully test the system in a controlled environment before it goes live and thus minimize the risk of adverse publicity due to problems with the site. Second, the company can perform what is known as a **soft launch**. Here, after initial testing, the site will be tested in a live environment where customers can use it. An indication of the approach used is shown in *Figure 12.6*. The approach is known as a soft launch since there is no marketing activity to promote this launch since not too many customers are wanted to visit the site. Clearly, a soft launch may have the advantage of illustrating problems which might not be highlighted by more structured testing.

Soft launch
A preliminary site launch with limited promotion to provide initial feedback and testing of an e-commerce site.

The alternatives for migrating from different versions of a system are reviewed in Bocij *et al.* (1999) and summarized in *Table 12.3*. Complete *activity 12.5* to review the relative merits of these approaches.

Welcome to the B2C Company's new website for 2001.
This site is currently a pilot which is being trialled until our official public launch scheduled for January 23rd 2001.

All aspects of the site are fully functional and you can place your orders or order a catalogue today. This pilot status gives you the perfect opportunity to use the site and make any recommendations that will enhance your experience of surfing around it. Please send any comments and suggestions to webmaster@b2c.com.

Due to unprecedented traffic on the site, we apologise for any pages which you find slow to load. This will be rectified before the public launch date.

Figure 12.6 Soft launch of a web site for The B2C Company

Table 12.3 Advantages and disadvantages of the different methods of implementation

Method	*Main advantages*	*Main disadvantages*
1. Immediate cutover. Straight from old system to new system on a single date	Rapid, lowest cost	High risk. Major disruption if serious errors with system
2. Parallel running. Old system and new system run side-by-side for a period	Lower risk than immediate cutover	Slower and higher cost than immediate cutover
3. Phased implementation. Different modules of the system are introduced sequentially	Good compromise between methods 1 and 2	Difficult to achieve technically due to interdependencies between modules
4. Pilot system. Trial implementation occurs before widespread deployment	Essential for multinational or national rollouts	Has to be used in combination with the other methods

Changeover for e-business systems

Activity 12.5

Purpose

Highlight the most suitable techniques for changeover.

Activity

1. Identify the variables which will determine the choice of changeover method.
2. What alternative would you recommend for The B2B Company as it introduces the new intranet- based virtual help desk described in *activity 12.4*?

3. Justify your answer by analysing in a table, the degree of risk, from high to low for each factor cross each approach.

For answer see p. 524

Database creation and data migration

Data migration
Transfer of data from old systems to new systems.

A final aspect of changeover that should be mentioned, and is often underestimated, is **data migration**. For an e-commerce system for a bank, for example, this would involve transferring or exporting data on existing customers and importing it to the new system. This is sometimes also referred to as populating the database. Alternatively a middleware layer may be set up such that the new system accesses customers from the original legacy database. Before migration occurs it is also necessary for a member of the development team known as the database administrator to create the e-commerce databases. This can be time consuming since it involves:

- Creating the different tables by entering the field definitions arising from the data modelling described in the previous chapter.
- Creating the different roles of users such as their security rights or access privileges. These need to be created for internal and external users.
- Creating stored procedures and triggers which is effectively server side coding to implement business rules.
- Optimizing the database for performance.

Deployment planning

Deployment plan
A deployment plan is a schedule which defines all the tasks that need to occur in order for changeover to occur successfully. This includes putting all the infrastructure in place such as cabling and hardware.

Systems integrator
A company that organizes the procurement and installation of hardware and software needed for implementation.

Site relaunch
The previous version of the web site is replaced with a new version with a new look and feel.

A **deployment plan** is needed to put in place the hardware and software infrastructure in time for user acceptance testing. This is not a trivial task since often a range of equipment will be required from a variety of manufacturers. Although the project manager is ultimately responsible for deployment planning, many companies employ **systems integrators** to coordinate these activities, particularly where there is a national rollout.

Companies are able to manage their Internet marketing-related costs better if they acknowledge that major revisions or **relaunches** of the site may be required at a frequency of every one to two years. This is highlighted by the Orange case study in *Chapter 10*. Any users of major web sites such as Dell, BA, or Amazon will be aware of the major changes that occur to the design and content of the site. These changes tend to be more frequent during the early life of the web site, and the sites stabilize with less frequent relaunches or changes being added as revisions.

A further method of estimating costs is to specify internal staff costs, capital costs such as new hardware and software and the costs paid to outside consultants. It will be possible to make this type of assessment when it has been decided which tasks to outsource as described in a previous section of this chapter.

Content management and maintenance

Sell-side e-commerce sites are continuously under development, even when they become live. The sites need to be dynamic to deal with errors reported by customers and in response to innovations by competitors. Additionally the content, such as information about different events or new product launches and price promotions, will need to be updated if the site is to generate repeat visits from customers.

Buy-side e-commerce sites are less dynamic and are more akin to traditional business information systems, so in this section we will focus on maintenance of e-commerce sites, although this description will also apply to e-business implementations of intranets and extranets.

What are the management issues involved with maintenance? We will review the following:

- Deciding on the frequency and scope of content updating
- Process for managing maintenance of the site and responsibilities for updating
- Testing and communicating changes made
- Integration with monitoring and measurement systems

Frequency and scope of content updating

The moment an e-commerce system is live it will require updates to the content and services. Different types of content updating can be identified, and a different approach will be required for each. We can apply the fault taxonomy of Jorgenson (1995) to an e-commerce site to decide on the timing of the action required according to the type of problem. We can see that the approach is quite different to that for a traditional information system or a packaged software that is distributed to thousands of customers. For example, with a mild problem such as a spelling mistake within software, it would be too costly to update and redistribute the software for a minor mistake. With the e-commerce site, a spelling mistake although trivial can be updated immediately by correcting it on the web page or in the database/content management system where it is stored. Indeed minor problems need to be corrected since they reduce the credibility of the site.

For more major errors, it is essential to fix these problems as soon as possible since revenue will be lost, both from customers who are unable to complete their current purchases, but also from users who will be unprepared to use the site in future because of their bad experience. Data from transactional e-commerce sites shows that very few have continuous availability. Problems can occur from bugs in the e-commerce software or problems with the web server hardware and software. Some are as bad as 90 per cent. If the site revenue for 24 hours, seven days a week site is £10 million per week then if availability falls to 95 per cent this is the equivalent of losing £500,000 before the loss of future revenues from disgruntled customers is taken into account. A modular or component-based approach to e-commerce systems should enable the location of the problem module or cartridge to be identified rapidly and the problem in the module fixed or possibly to revert to previous version.

As well as fixing the problems shown in *Table 12.4* companies will also wish to update the functionality of the e-commerce system in response to customer demands, sales promotions or from competitor innovations. Again a component-based approach can enable self-contained, discrete, new modules or cartridges to be plugged into the system which are designed to provide new functionality with

Table 12.4 Fault taxonomy described in Jorgenson (1995) applied to an e-commerce site

Category	*Example*	*Action–traditional BIS or packaged software*	*Action – e-commerce site*
1. Mild	Misspelled word	Ignore or when next major release occurs	Fix immediately
2. Moderate	Misleading or redundant information. Problem with font readability	Ignore or defer to next major release	Fix immediately
3. Annoying	Truncated text, failed JavaScript, but site still usable	Defer to next major release	Fix immediately
4. Disturbing	Some transactions not processed correctly, intermittent crashes in one module	Defer to next maintenance release	Urgent patch required for module
5. Serious	Lost transactions	Defer to next maintenance release. May need immediate fix and release	Urgent patch required for module
6. Very serious	Crash occurs regularly in one module	Immediate solution needed	Urgent patch required for module, revert to previous version
7. Extreme	Frequent very serious errors	Immediate solution needed	Urgent patch required for module, revert to previous version
8 Intolerable	Database corruption	Immediate solution needed	Urgent patch required for module, revert to previous version
9. Catastrophic	System crashes, cannot be restarted – system unusable	Immediate solution needed	Urgent patch required for module, revert to previous version
10. Infectious	Catastrophic problem also causes failure of other systems	Immediate solution needed	Revert to previous version

only minimal changes to existing modules. For each such update, a small-scale prototyping process involving analysis, design and testing will need to occur.

An indication of the maintenance approaches used in different countries is illustrated in *Figure 12.7*. It is apparent that in the countries which have higher levels of adoption of e-commerce there is more frequent (daily or weekly) updating and less ad-hoc updating.

Maintenance process and responsibilities

For efficient updating of an e-commerce system, it is vital to have a clearly defined process for content and service changes. Different processes will apply depending on the scope of the change as described in the previous section. We can identify two different types of changes – routine content changes such as updates to docu-

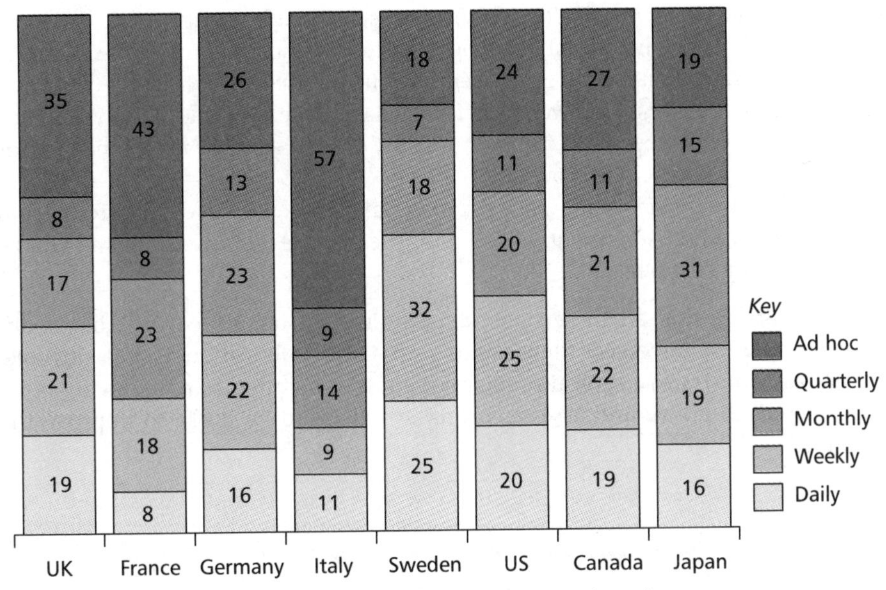

Base: All respondents with a web site weighted by number of employees
Note: e.g. in the UK 19% of businesses update their web site daily

Figure 12.7 Frequency of web site updating in different countries
Source: DTI (2000)

ments on the site or new documents and major changes where we make changes to the structure, navigation or services on the site.

Process for routine content changes

The process for routine content changes should be communicated to all staff providing content to the site, with responsibilities clearly identified in their job descriptions. The main stages involved in producing an updated web page are to design it, write it, to test it and to publish it. A more detailed process is indicated here which distinguishes between review of the content and technical testing of the completed web page. A simple model of the work involved in maintenance is shown in *Figure 12.8*. It is assumed that the needs of the users and design features of the site have already been defined when the site was originally created as described in *Chapter 8*. The model only applies to minor updates to copy, or perhaps updating product or company information.

According to Chaffey *et al.* (2000), the different tasks involved in the maintenance process for new copy are as follows:

1. *Write.* This stage involves writing copy and, if necessary, designing the layout of copy and associated images.
2. *Review.* An independent review of the copy is necessary to check for errors before a document is published. Depending on the size of organization, review may be necessary by one person or several people covering different aspects of site quality such as corporate image, marketing copy, branding and legality.
3. *Correct.* This stage is straightforward and involves updates necessary as a result of stage 2.

4. *Publish (to test environment).* The publication stage involves putting the corrected copy on a web page which can be checked further. This will be in a test environment that can only be viewed from inside a company.
5. *Test.* Before the completed web page is made available over the World Wide Web a final test will be required for technical issues such as whether the page loads successfully on different browsers.
6. *Publish (to live environment).* Once the material has been reviewed and tested and is signed off as satisfactory it will be published to the main web site and will be accessible by customers.

The difficulty is, that all these stages are required for quality control, but if different people are involved then rapid, responsive publication is not possible. *Activity 12.6* illustrates a typical problem of content maintenance, involving the 6 stages described above and assesses changes that could be made to improve the situation

Activity 12.6 Optimizing the content review process at The B2C Company

Purpose

Assess how quality control and efficiency can be balanced for revisions to web content.

Activity

The extract below and *Figure 12.8* illustrate a problem of updating encountered by The B2C Company. How can they solve this problem?

Problem description

From when the brand manager identifies a need to update copy for their product, the update might happen as follows: brand manager writes copy (1/2 day), one day later, the web manager reviews copy, three days later the marketing manager checks the copy, seven days later the legal department checks the copy, two days later the

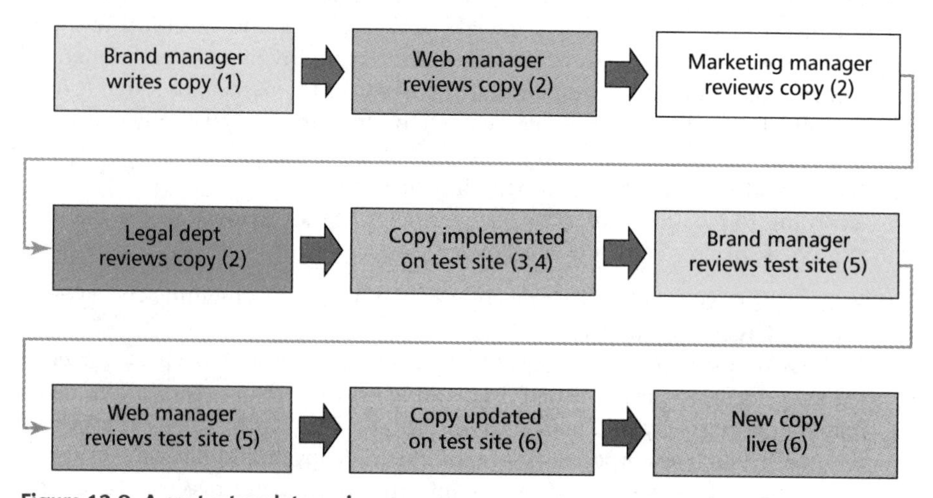

Figure 12.8 A content update review process

revised copy is implemented on the test site, two days later the brand manager reviews the test site, the next day the web manager reviews the web site followed by updating and final review before the copy is added to the live site two days later and over a fortnight from when a relatively minor change to the site was identified!

For answer see p. 524

Frequency of content updates

Since the web is perceived as a dynamic medium, customers expect new information to be posted to a site straightaway. If material is inaccurate or 'stale' then the customer may not return to the site.

As information on a web page becomes outdated and will need to be updated, it is important to have a mechanism defining what triggers this update process. Trigger procedures should be developed such that when price-changes, PR release, or product specifications are updated in promotional leaflets or catalogues, these changes are also reflected on the web site. Without procedures of this type, it is easy for there to be mismatches between online and offline content.

As part of defining a web site update process, and standards, a company may want to issue guidelines which suggest how often content is updated. This may specify that content is updated as follows:

- within two days of a factual error being identified;
- a new 'news' item is added at least once a month;
- when product information has been static for two months.

Process for major changes

For major changes to a web site, such as changing the menu structure, adding a new section of content or changing the services for users, a different process is required. Such changes will involve a larger investment and there will be limited funds for investment, so priorities for these major changes must be agreed. To achieve this there the approach that is usually used is to set up a steering committee to ratify proposed changes. Such as decision usually needs an independent chair such as the e-commerce manager or marketing manager to make the final decision. The typical structure of such a committee is shown in *Figure 12.9(a)*. It is made up of both technical and business staff and is useful for encouraging integration between these roles. Typical roles of some members of the committee who also may be involved in update of the site are shown in *Figure 12.9(b)*. *Figure 12.9(a)*, which could apply to Internet, extranet or intranet content, shows how a pyramid arrangement is used to ensure content quality on site.

Such a committee will typically have a range of responsibilities such as:

- Defining agreed update process and responsibilities for different types of changes
- Specifying site standards for structure/navigation/look and feel (*Table 12.5*)
- Specifying the tools that are used to update and manage content
- Assessing proposals for major changes to site standards, content and services
- Reviewing quality of service in terms of customer service and security

- Specifying online promotion methods for the site (e.g. search engine registration) and measurement of the site through
- Managing the budget for the site

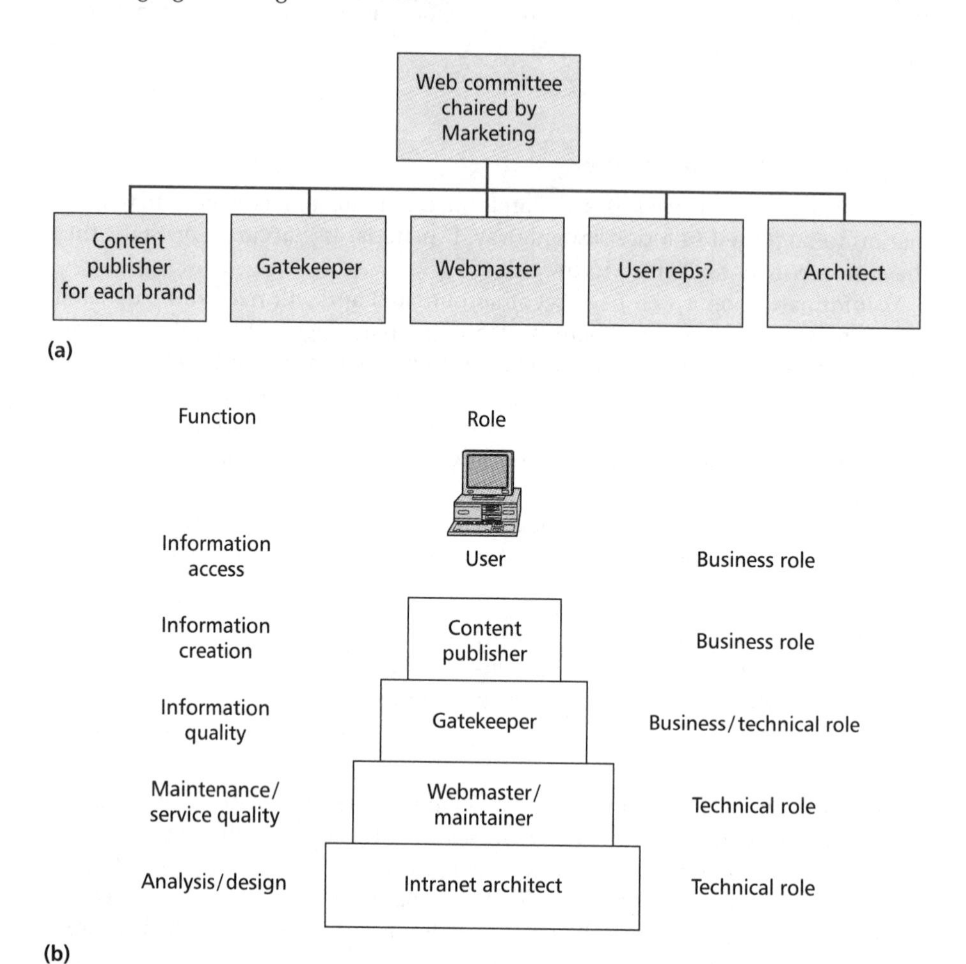

Figure 12.9 Typical structure of an e-commerce site steering group

Table 12.5 Web site standards

Standard	*Details*	*Applies to*
Site structure	Will specify the main areas of the site e.g. products, customer service, press releases, how to place content and who is responsible for each area.	Content developers
Navigation	May specify, for instance, that the main menu must always be on the left of the screen with nested (sub) menus at the foot of the screen. The home button should be accessible from every screen at the top left corner of the screen. (See Lynch and Horton (1999) for guidelines on navigation and site design).	Web site designer/ webmaster usually achieve these through site templates

Standard	Details	Applies to
Copy style	General guidelines, for example, reminding those writing copy, that copy for the web needs to be more brief than its paper equivalent. Where detail is required, perhaps with product specifications, it should be broken up into chunks that are digestible on screen.	Individual content developers
Testing standards	Check site functions for: ● different browser types and versions ● plug-ins ● invalid links ● speed of download of graphics ● spellcheck each page See *Chapter 9* for details.	Web site designer/webmaster
Corporate branding and graphic design	Specifies the appearance of company logos and the colours and typefaces used to convey the brand message.	Web site designer/webmaster
Process	The sequence of events for publishing a new web page or updating an existing page. Who is responsible for reviewing and updating?	All
Performance	Availability and download speed figures.	Webmaster and designers

Tools for managing content updates

The technology used to publish the web site is important if the power of the Internet is to be fully utilized by a company. This may not be evident when a simple brochureware site is produced which may simply require an HTML editor or Microsoft Frontpage. It becomes more significant when a company wants to make its product catalogue available for queries or to take orders online. As these facilities are added the web site changes from an isolated system to one that must be integrated with other technologies such as the customer database, stock-control and sales order processing systems. Given this integration with corporate IS, the IT department or company to which IT has been outsourced will need to be involved in the development of the site and its strategy.

A further technology issue to be addressed is to provide an infrastructure which allows the content developers throughout the company to update copy from their own desktop computer. For example, companies that have standardized on Lotus Notes can use this so that individual content developers can readily contribute their copy and the process of checking can be part-automated using workflow facilities to send messages to testers and reviewers who can then authorize or reject the content. A further issue of e-commerce site maintenance is monitoring the performance of the site against objectives. This is described in the following *Focus on* section.

F *Focus on* e-marketing measurement

Measuring the effectiveness of an e-commerce system is considered in some detail since it is a key part of managing an e-commerce initiative. Often a large investment will have been made in the site and senior managers want to ensure that the investment is delivering its objectives. They will also want to find and rectify problems with the site or exploit approaches that are working well. Effective e-business measurement requires a suitable process and structured measures in the form of a framework.

Measurement process

Measurement process
Defines the activities, sequence and responsibilities for measurement.

The **measurement process** must be repeatable and will relate to the overall strategy process model. In *Chapter 8* we studied the SOSTAC planning framework. Key elements of SOSTAC with reference to measurement are objective setting and control. *Figure 12.10* illustrates a typical measurement process. Objective setting occurs in the goal setting stage. Control is achieved through: performance measurement to collect research; performance diagnosis to compare actual performance relative to the target objectives, understand the reason for variance and corrective action to try to get closer to the objectives through taking corrective action.

Measurement framework

Measurement framework
Defines the collection of measures used to assess performance.

An integrated **measurement framework** is required for a comprehensive approach to measurement. Otherwise measurement can be haphazard with companies perhaps only measuring some elements of on-site activity such as hits or page impressions, but neglecting whether customers are happy with their experience on the site. Performance against objectives can be monitored in the categories defined by Chaffey (2000) that are shown in *Figure 12.11*. The figure is intended to be read from left to right since achieving the objectives on the left helps achieve objectives to the right. The measures should be collected for all relevant online channels whether web, mobile or digital TV and compared to performance of other channels such as mail-order, sales team or call centre. The measures can also be related to the different levels of marketing control specified by Kotler (1997); these include strategic control (question 1), profitability control (question 1), annual-plan control (question 2) and efficiency control (question 3). When identifying metrics it is useful to apply the widely used SMART mnemonic (e.g. Obolensky, 1994). SMART metrics must be:

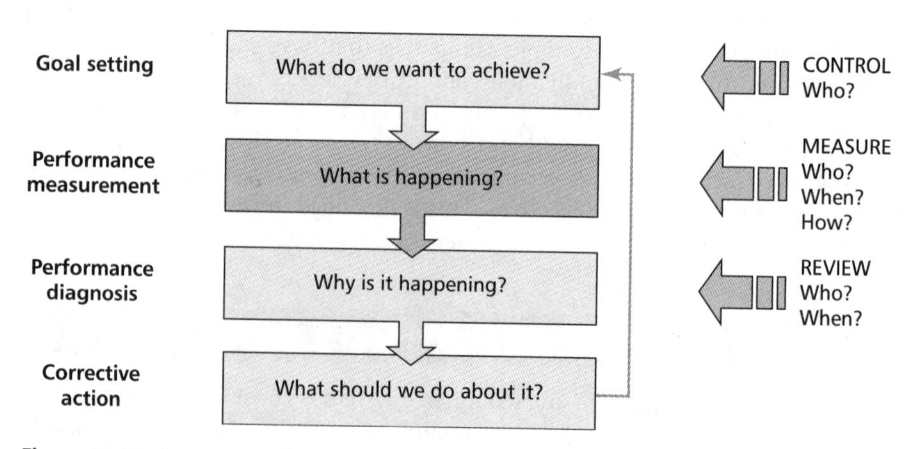

Figure 12.10 A summary of the measurement process

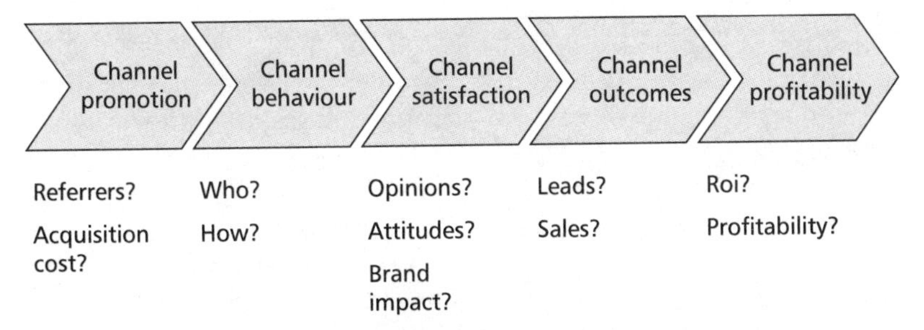

Figure 12.11 A summary of five categories for e-commerce site measurement from the framework presented by Chaffey (2000)

- Specific;
- Measurable;
- Actionable;
- Relevant;
- Timely or time-oriented, a historical analysis.

Using SMART metrics avoids the following types of problems:

1. Developing metrics for which you cannot collect accurate or complete data.
2. Developing metrics that measure the right thing, but cause people to act in a way contrary to the best interest of the business to simply 'make their numbers'.
3. Developing so many metrics that you create excessive overhead and red tape.

Before we review the measures that occur in each category in *Figure 12.11* in more detail, we will look at how the data is collected by the three main methods of primary data collection. These are the collection of site visitor activity data such as that collected in site log-files, the collection of metrics about outcomes such as online sales or e-mail enquiries and traditional marketing research techniques such as questionnaires and focus groups which collect information on the customer's experience on the web site.

Site visitor activity data
Information on content and services accessed by e-commerce site visitors.

Collecting site visitor activity data

Site visitor activity data records the number of visitors on the site and the paths or clickstreams they take through the site as they visit different content.

Hit
Recorded for each graphic or text file requested from a web server. It is not a reliable measure for the number of people viewing a page.

Traditionally this information has been collected using log file analysis. The server-based log file is added to every time a user downloads a piece of information (a **hit**) and is analyzed using a **log file analyser** as illustrated by *Figure 3.5*. Examples of transactions within the log file are:

Log file analyser
A log file analyser is a separate programme such as Webtrends that is used to summarize the information on customer activity a log file.

Yoursite.co.uk— [05/Oct/2001:00:00:49 -000] "GET /index.html HTTP/1.0" 200 33362
Yoursite.co.uk— [05/Oct/2001:00:00:49 -000] "GET /logo.gif HTTP/1.0" 200 54342

Page impression
A more reliable measure than a hit denoting one person viewing one page.

Hits are not useful measures of web site effectiveness since if a page consists of 10 graphics, plus text, this is recorded as 11 hits. **Page impressions** and site visits are better measures of site activity.

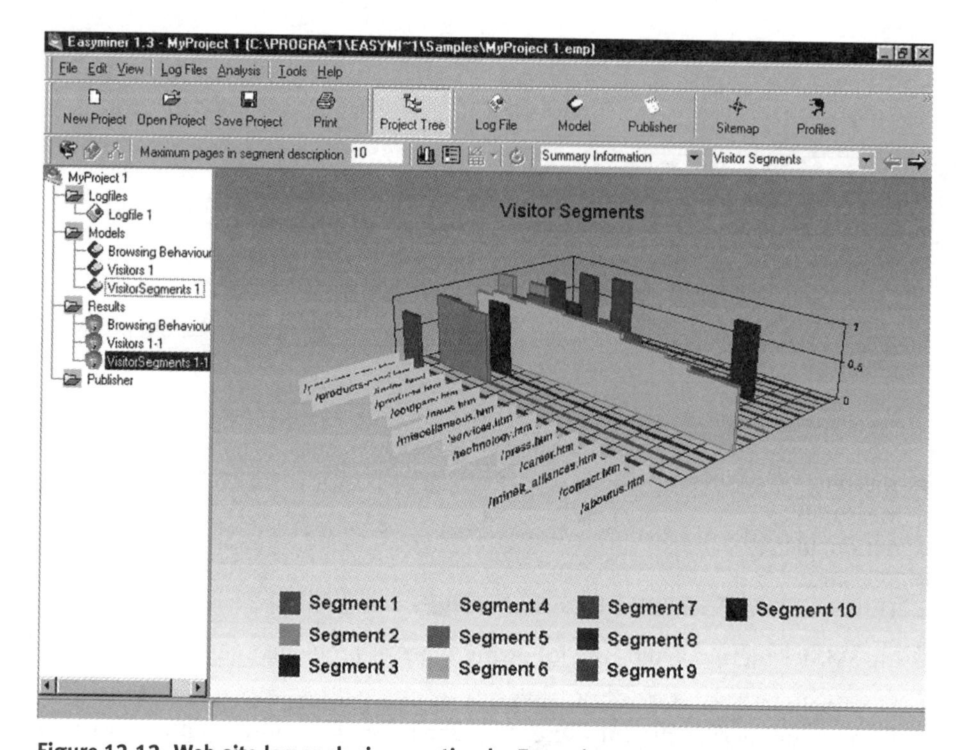

Figure 12.12 Web site log analysis reporting by Easyminer
Source: Granted by kind permission of MINEit software, © 2001 www.mineit.com

An example of the output reporting following analysis of the log file is illustrated by *Figure 12.12*. This shows how the Easyminer software can segment different types of customer behaviour on the site based on the sequence of pages visited.

Other information giving detailed knowledge of customer behaviour that can be reported by log file analysis packages of which Webtrends is the market leader by volume (www.webtrends.com) includes:

- Page impressions
- Entry and exit pages
- Path or clickstream analysis
- User (visitor) sessions
- Unique users (visitors), the number of unique visitors to a web site within a set period
- Visitor frequency report (repeat visitors)
- Session duration or the length of time a visitor spends on a site (a session ends after inactivity for a time set in the analyser preferences, e.g. 30 minutes) and page duration
- Country of origin
- Browser and operating system used
- Referring URL and domain (where the visitor came from)

Managers of e-commerce systems know that log file analysis has a number of potential weaknesses. Perhaps the worst problems are undercounting and overcounting. These are reviewed in *Table 12.6*.

A relatively new approach to the problems of undercounting and overcounting of

Table 12.6 Inaccuracies caused by server-based log-file analysis

Sources of undercounting	*Sources of overcounting*
Caching in user's web browsers (when a user accesses a previously accessed file, it is loaded from the user's cache on their PC)	Frames (a user viewing a framed page with three frames will be recorded as three page impressions on a server-based system)
Caching on proxy servers (proxy servers are used within organizations or ISPs to reduce Internet traffic by storing copies of frequently used pages)	Spiders and robots (traversing of a site by spiders from different search engines is recorded as page impressions, they can be excluded, but time consuming)
Firewalls (these do not usually exclude page impressions, but they usually assign a single IP address for the user of the page, rather than referring to an individuals PC)	Executable files (these can also be recorded as hits or page impressions unless excluded)
Dynamically generated pages, generated 'on the fly' are difficult to assess with server-based log files.	

server-based log-file analysis described in *Table 12.6* is to use a different *browser-based* measurement system that records access to web pages every time a page is loaded into a user's web browser through running a short script or program inserted into the web page. The key benefit of the browser-based approach is that potentially it is more accurate than server-based approaches. *Figure 12.13* shows how the browser-based approach works. One of the pioneers of this technique is Australian company Red Sheriff (www.redsheriff.com). Their RedMeasure approach counts pages every time they're *viewed* by customers. It does this since a small piece of JavaScript code is inserted into each web page and this is automatically run every time the page is loaded into the browser by the user. Red Sheriff refer to this as *instrumentation*. This JavaScript sends details about the page views to a remote server.

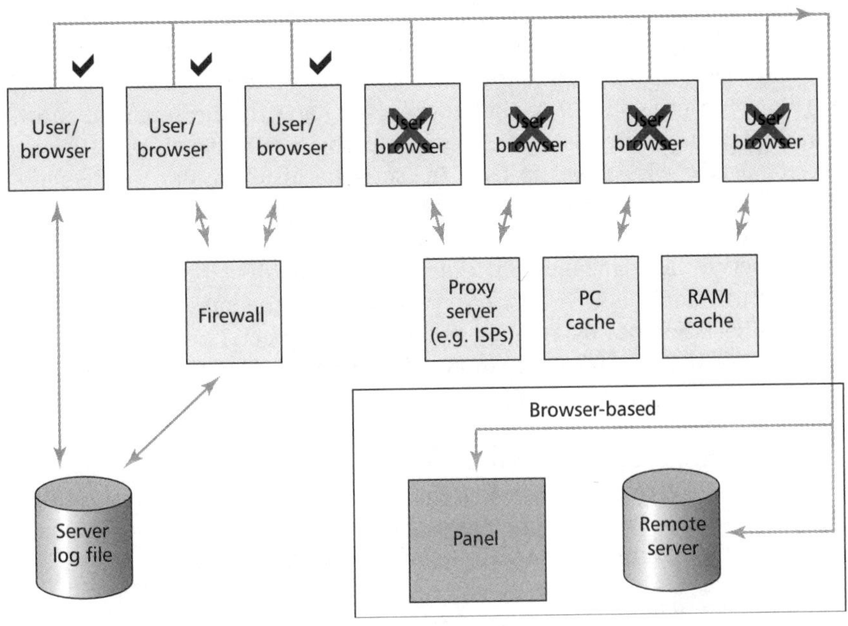

Figure 12.13 Differences between browser-based and server-based measurement systems

Collecting site outcome data

Site outcome data is about when a customer performs a significant action. This is usually a transaction that is recorded. It involves more than downloading a web page, it is a proactive act. Key marketing outcomes include:

- Registration to site or subscriptions to an e-mail newsletter.
- Request for further information such as a brochure or a request for a call-back from a customer service representative.
- Responding to a promotion such as an online competition.
- A sale influenced by a visit to the site.
- A sale on-site.

It will be apparent that to collect some of these measures we may need to integrate different information systems. Where customers provide details such as an e-mail address and name in response to an offer, these are known as leads and they may need to be passed onto a direct-sales team or recorded in a customer relationship management system. For full visibility of customer behaviour, the outcomes from these systems need to be integrated with the site visitor activity data. Analysis tools such as Accure (www.accrue.com) and NetGenesis (www.netgen.com) assist in integrating information from these different sources.

Collecting market research data

We can divide market research for e-commerce into primary research where we collect our own data and secondary data where we use published research. Market research data is intended to reveal profiles of customers and what their opinion of the e-commerce experience is. There are several different methods of collecting primary data. These are compared in *Table 12.7*. Internet panel data is collected in a similar way to home-based TV panels. Panel members agree to have software installed on their PC that sends data that is collected by the monitoring organization. This approach is similar to the browser-based activity measurement shown in *Figure 12.3*. Critics note that there may be a problem with panel accuracy since the type of person who agrees to have the software installed may not be representative of the wider population. Web site auditing is performed by independent auditing bodies who have traditionally audited print media. Analysis is based on analysis of server-based log-files. An example of an audit is that conducted by ABC Electronic's auditors (www.abc.org), who audited the site of the Periodical Publishers Association during an audit period 1–31 October 1999 and found that site activity reached 33,000 page impressions with 4425 users and 8504 user sessions. This suggests that on average the users make around two visits per month.

Despite the range of available methods evident from *Table 12.7*, care still needs to be exercised when interpreting activity data to base revenue estimates for forecasting. For example three different approaches yielded widely differing estimates for activity on the Britannica.com web site for July 2000:

Net Ratings panel data	*4 million visitors*
MediaMetrix panel data	*2.8 million*
Server-based log-file data	*2.9 million*

Table 12.7 A comparison of different online metrics collection methods

Technique	*Strengths*	*Weaknesses*
1. Server-based log-file analysis of site activity	● Directly records customer behaviour on-site plus where they were referred from ● Low cost	● Not based around marketing outcomes such as leads, sales. ● Size, even summaries may be over 50 pages long ● Doesn't directly record channel satisfaction ● Undercounting and overcounting ● Misleading unless interpreted carefully
2. Browser-based site activity data	● Greater accuracy than server-based analysis ● Counts all users cf panel approach	● Relatively expensive method ● Similar weaknesses to server-based technique apart from accuracy ● Limited demographic information
3. Panels activity and demographic data	● Provides competitor comparisons ● Gives demographic profiling ● Avoids undercounting and overcounting	● Depends on extrapolation from limited sample that may not be representative
4. Outcome data e.g. enquiries, customer service e-mails	● Records marketing outcomes	● Difficulty of integrating data with other methods of data collection when collected manually or in other information systems
5. Online questionnaires. Customers are prompted randomly – every *n*th customer or after customer activity or by e-mail	● Can record customer satisfaction and profiles ● Relatively cheap to create and analyse	● Difficulty of recruiting respondents who complete accurately ● Sample bias – tend to be advocates or disgruntled customer who complete
6. Online focus groups Synchronous recording.	● Relatively cheap to create	● Difficult to moderate and coordinate ● No visual cues as from offline focus groups
7. Mystery shoppers – example customers are recruited to evaluate the site e.g. www.emysteryshopper.com	● Structured tests give detailed feedback ● Also tests integrate with other channels such as e-mail and phone	● Relatively expensive ● Sample must be representative

Types of data collected

E-commerce site managers collect the following data which is part of the framework shown in *Figure 12.11*. The five categories of measures shown in *Figure 12.11* have differing significance to a manager according to the level of managerial decision making. Chaffey *et al.* (2000) identify three different levels of metrics.

1. *Level 1. Business effectiveness measures.*

   These types of measure assess how the Internet is affecting the performance of the whole business, in other words, what is the impact of the Internet on the business? Such measures include channel profitability measures.
2. *Level 2. Marketing effectiveness measures.*
   Marketing effectiveness measures will reflect how well the e-commerce site is fulfilling marketing objectives. These are mainly the channel satisfaction and channel outcome measures.
3. *Level 3. Internet marketing effectiveness.*
   The Internet marketing effectiveness measures involve assessing how well the particular online Internet marketing techniques required for effective Internet marketing are working. These include channel promotion, channel behaviour and satisfaction from *Figure 12.11*.

The five categories of e-commerce metrics are:

Channel promotion
Measures assess why customers visit a site – which adverts they have seen, which sites they have been referred from.

Referrer
The site that a visitor previously visited before following a link.

1. Channel promotion

These measures consider where the web site users originate – is it online and offline, what are the sites or offline media that has prompted their visit? Log file analysis can be used to assess which intermediary sites customers are **referred** from and even which keywords they type into search engines when trying to locate product information. Promotion is successful if traffic is generated that meets objectives of volume and quality. Quality will be determined by whether visitors are in the target market and have a propensity for the service offered. Overall hits or page views are not enough – inspection of log files for companies show that a high proportion of visitors get no further than the home page! Differences in cost of acquiring customers via different alternative channels can also be assessed.

Key measures:
Referral mix. For each referral source such as offline or online such as banner ads it should be possible to calculate:

- % of all referrals (or visitors)
- Cost of acquisition
- Contribution to sales or other outcomes

Channel behaviour
Describes which content is visited, time and duration.

2. Channel buyer behaviour

Once customers have been attracted to the site we can monitor content accessed, when they visit and how long they stay for and whether this interaction with content leads to satisfactory marketing outcomes such as new leads or sales. If visitors are incentivized to register on-site it is possible to build-up profiles of behaviour for different segments. It is also important to recognize return visitors for which cookies or login are used.

Key ratios are:

Home page interest	Home Page Views/all page views e.g.	20%	= (2,358/11,612)
Stickiness	Page views/visitor sessions e.g.	6	= 11,612/2,048
Repeats	Visitor sessions/visitors e.g.	2	= 2,048/970

Stickiness
An indication of how long a visitor stays on-site.

Channel satisfaction
Evaluation of the customer's opinion of the service quality on the site and supporting services such as e-mail.

3. Channel satisfaction

Customer satisfaction with the online experience is vital in achieving the desired channel outcomes, although it is difficult to set specific objectives. Online methods such as online questionnaires, focus groups and interviews can be used to assess customers' opinions of the web site content and customer service and how it has affected overall perception of brand.

Key measures are:
Customer satisfaction indices. These are discussed by Chaffey and Edgar (2000) they include ease of use, site availability and performance and e-mail response. To compare customer satisfaction with other sites, benchmarking services such as that of Gomez (www.gomez.com) can be used. Their measures of satisfaction are summarized in *Table 5.4*.

Bevan (1999) says that from a usability viewpoint, there are three key measures in determining usability for each task:

(a) The percentage of participants who completely and correctly achieved each task goal.
(b) If it is necessary to provide participants with assists, efficiency and effectiveness metrics must be determined for both unassisted and assisted conditions.
(c) The mean time taken to complete each task, together with the range and standard deviation of times across participants.

4. Channel outcomes

Channel outcomes
Records customer actions taken as a consequence to a site.

Conversion rate
Percentage of site visitors that perform a particular action such as making a purchase.

Traditional marketing objectives such as number of sales, number of leads, **conversion rates** and targets for customer acquisition and retention should be set and then compared to other channels. Dell Computer (www.dell.com) records on-site sales but also orders generated as a result of site visits, but placed by phone. This is achieved by monitoring calls to a specific phone number unique to the site.

Key measures:
Channel contribution (direct and indirect).

Attrition rate
Percentage of site visitors that are lost at each stage in making a purchase.

We need to understand the **attrition rate** or why customers do not reach the final target outcome whether it be a lead or a sale.

A widely used method of assessing channel outcomes is to review the conversion rate, which gives an indication of the percentage of site visitors who take a particular outcome. For example:

Conversion rate, visitors to purchase = 2% (10,000 visitors of which 200 make purchases)
Conversion rate, visitors to registration = 5% (10,000 visitors of which 500 register)

A related concept is the attrition rate which describes how many visitors are lost at each stage of visiting a site. *Figure 12.14* shows that for a set time period, only a proportion of site visitors will make their way to product information, a small proportion will add an item to a basket and a smaller proportion still will actually make the purchases. A key feature of e-commerce sites is that there is a high attrition rate between customer's adding an item to a basket and then subsequently making a purchase. It is surmised that this is due to fears about credit card security, and customers are merely experimenting.

5. Channel profitability

Channel profitability
The profitability of the web site taking into account revenue and cost and discounted cash flow.

A contribution to business profitability is always the ultimate aim of e-commerce. To assess this, leading companies set an Internet contribution target of achieving a certain proportion of sales via the channel. When easyjet (www.easyjet.com) launched its e-commerce facility in 1998, it set an Internet contribution target of 30 per cent by 2000. They put the resources and communications plan in place to achieve this and their target was reached in 1999. Assessing contribution is more

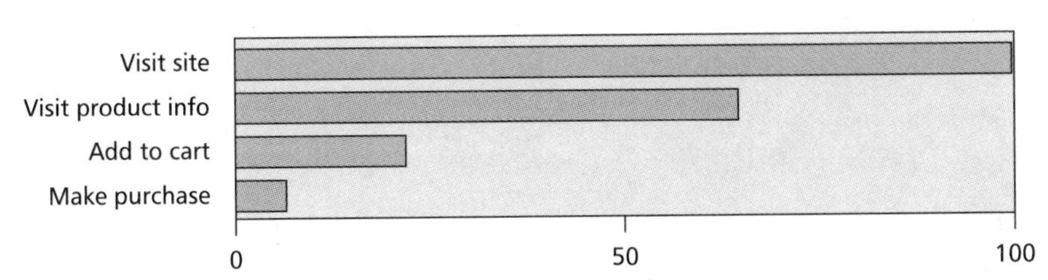

Figure 12.14 Attrition through e-commerce site activities

difficult for a company that cannot sell products online, but the role of the Internet in influencing purchase should be assessed. Discounted cash flow techniques are used to assess the rate of return over time. It was seen in *Chapter 4* that modelling of time to break-even is a key feature of e-commerce sites.

Budgeting

The channel profitability will be compared to the estimates for costs and revenue estimated during the budgeting process of feasibility or project planning. To estimate profitability and return on investment, companies need to consider both tangible and intangible costs and benefits. A suggested checklist of these is shown in the box *Suggested worksheet for calculating Return on Investment for an e-commerce site.*

Suggested worksheet for calculating Return on Investment for an e-commerce site

Tangible business benefits

1. *Reduced costs*
(a) Promotional materials, including catalogues – creative, printing, paper, distribution
(b) Product support materials – creation, printing, paper, distribution
(c) Lower infrastructure or communication costs – fewer outbound calls required
(d) Support staff savings
(e) Sales staff savings
(f) Order inaccuracies
(g) Lower cost of supporting channel

2. *Increased revenue*
(a) New sales to new geo-demographic segments
(b) Penetration / retention / repeat orders
(c) Cross-sales to existing purchasers
(d) Penetration / cross-sales to new purchasers in an organization

Intangible business benefits

3. *Faster time to market*
Reduce product introduction by *n* weeks

4. *Improved customer satisfaction / brand equity*
Also an intangible factor, how does this affect retention?

Tangible costs

1. *Physical costs*
(a) Hardware, software
(b) Network costs

2. *Planning costs*

3. *Implementation costs*
(a) Project management
(b) Software development, testing

(c) Data migration
(d) Training
(e) Promotion (online and offline)

4. *Operational costs*
(a) Hardware and software maintenance
(b) Network maintenance
(c) Technical staff costs
(d) Content maintenance staff costs
(e) Support staff costs
(f) Management staff costs
(g) Ongoing promotional costs (online and offline)

This worksheet was originally based on White Paper 'A Return on Investment Guide for Business-to-Business Internet Commerce' provided by E-commerce solution provider Openmarket (www.openmarket.com)

A similar approach can be used to calculating the ROI of enhancements to an e-commerce site. Hanson (2000) suggests an approach to this which requires identification of revenue from the site, costs from site and costs from supporting it via a call centre. These are related to profit as follows:

Operating profit = Net income from sales – e-commerce site costs – call centre costs

Net income from sales = (Product price – unit cost) × sales – fixed product costs

E-commerce site costs = Site fixed costs + ((% site support contacts) × cost site support contact*sales)

Call centre (CC) costs = CC fixed costs + ((% CC support contacts) × cost CC support contact × sales)

Different approaches for estimating costs are recommended by Bayne (1997):

- *Last year's Internet marketing budget*. This is assuming the site has been up and running for some time.
- *Percentage of company sales*. It is again difficult to establish this for the first iteration of a site.
- *Percentage of total marketing budget*. This is a common approach. Typically the percentage will start small (less than 5 per cent, or even 1 per cent), but will rise as the impact of the Internet increases.
- *Reallocation of marketing dollars*. The money for e-marketing will be often be taken by cutting back other marketing activities.
- *What other companies in your industry are spending*. This is definitely necessary in order to assess and meet competitive threats, but it may be possible that competitors are overinvesting.
- *Creating an effective online presence*. In this model of 'paying whatever it takes', a company spends sufficient money to create a web site which is intended to achieve their objectives. This may be a costly option, but for industries in which

the Internet is having a significant impact, it may be the wise option. A larger than normal marketing budget will be necessary to achieve this.

- *A graduated plan tied into measurable results*. This implies an ongoing programme in which investment each year is tied into achieving the results established in a measurement programme.
- *A combination of approaches*. Since the first budget will be based on many intangibles it is best to use several methods and present a high, medium and low expenditure option for executives with expected results related to costs.

Estimating the balance between site creation and maintenance costs

When planning an e-commerce site, an important decision is whether the correct balance has been achieved between site creation, promotion and maintenance. To consider what the appropriate approach is, complete *activity 12.7*.

Activity 12.7

Estimating e-commerce site cost elements

Purpose

To evaluate the balance between different types of expenditure for a web site.

Activity

Refer to *Figure 12.15*. Which alternative do you think is best for expenditure on creating a web site for a start-up company and a traditional company? Justify your answer.

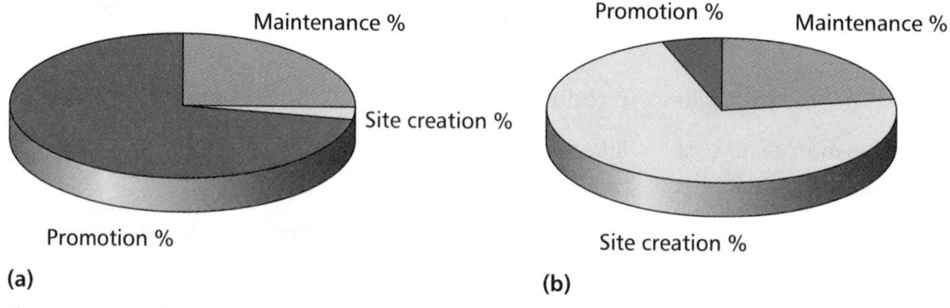

Figure 12.15 Alternatives for expenditure on an e-commerce site

For answer see p. 525

Secondary data sources

A selection of key sources of secondary data for market researchers to find out information about market characteristics is shown in the box *Secondary information sources for online marketplaces*.

Secondary information sources for the online marketplace

1 *Digests of published MR data*

Nua Strategy (Europe)	www.nua.ie/surveys
Cyberatlas (US)	www.cyberatlas.com

Oasis	www.plym.ac.uk
Market Research.com	www.marketresearch.com

2 Directories of MR companies

British Market Research Association	www.bmra.org.uk
Market Research Society	www.mra.org.uk
International MR agencies	www.greenbook.org

3 Traditional market research agencies

MORI	www.mori.com (www.e-mori.co.uk)
NOP	www.nopres.co.uk
Nielsen	www.nielsen.com

4 Government sources

OECD	www.oecd.org
European Government	www.europa.eu.int.comm/eurostat
UK Government	www.open.gov.uk, www.ons.gov.uk, www.ukbusinessoline.gov.uk
US Government	www.stat-usa.gov

5 Search engines and directories to other sources

See Searchenginewatch (www.searchenginewatch.com) for guidelines on using search engines for research. Google is currently favoured by researchers since its listing is based on the popularity of a site based on links in to that site.

Different types of search services are:

Meta search engines
Metafetcher includes country specific options (www.metafetcher.com)
WonderPort has UK specific information (www.wonderport.com)
Mamma (www.mamma.com)
WebCrawler (www.webcrawler.com)
AskJeeves contains a meta search engine component (www.ask.co.uk)

Downloadable meta search tools
Copernic.com (www.copernic.com)
WebFerret (www.ferretsoft.com)

Search engines are an unstructured searchable index of web pages.
www.altavista.com, www.fast.com, www.hotbot.com

Directories are a structured index of web sites.
www.yahoo.com, www.excite.com , www.lycos.com

Aggregators are aggregators of information on other sites.
News aggregators include:
Moreover (www.moreover.com)
Findarticles (www,findarticles.com)

As a summary to this section, complete *activity 12.8*.

Activity 12.8 Creating a measurement plan for The B2C Company

Purpose

To develop skills in selecting appropriate techniques for measuring e-business effectiveness.

Activity

This activity acts as a summary to this section on e-business measurement. Review *Table 12.8* and assess the frequency with which metrics in each of the following categories should reported for a sell-side e-commerce site and acted upon. For each column, place a R in the column for the frequency with which you think the data should be recorded.

Table 12.8 Alternative timescales for reporting e-commerce site performance

	Promotion	*Behaviour*	*Satisfaction*	*Outcomes*	*Profitability*
Hour					
Day					
Week					
Month					
Quarter					
Relaunch					

For answer see p. 525

As a summary to *Part 3* of the book, look at *case study 12.1*. This shows how an SME has used e-commerce to extend its reach and discusses some of the practical issues with creating, maintaining and monitoring the site.

CASE STUDY 12.1

E-commerce implementation at Sykes Cottages

Background

Sykes Cottages launched its web site offering holiday cottages for the UK in 1997. Expenditure was £1000 in the first year followed by £1000 investment in the second year.

Achievements

By 2000, Sykes estimated that over 70 per cent of all its business derives from customers who have visited the web site during the selection and booking of their holiday cottage. Some of these visitors were from new markets; by 1999, 5 per cent of all new business came from overseas, which represented a large increase for Sykes Cottages.

As well as increasing its reach the owner mentions other benefits included cutting costs by sending out fewer brochures since potential customers visit the site first. Summarizing the strategy, Caldwell (2000) quotes owner Clive Sykes:

> *We saw it as an opportunity to do something which our competitors weren't doing. We didn't invest a lot of money at the start. We wanted to keep control over*

▶ CASE STUDY *continued*

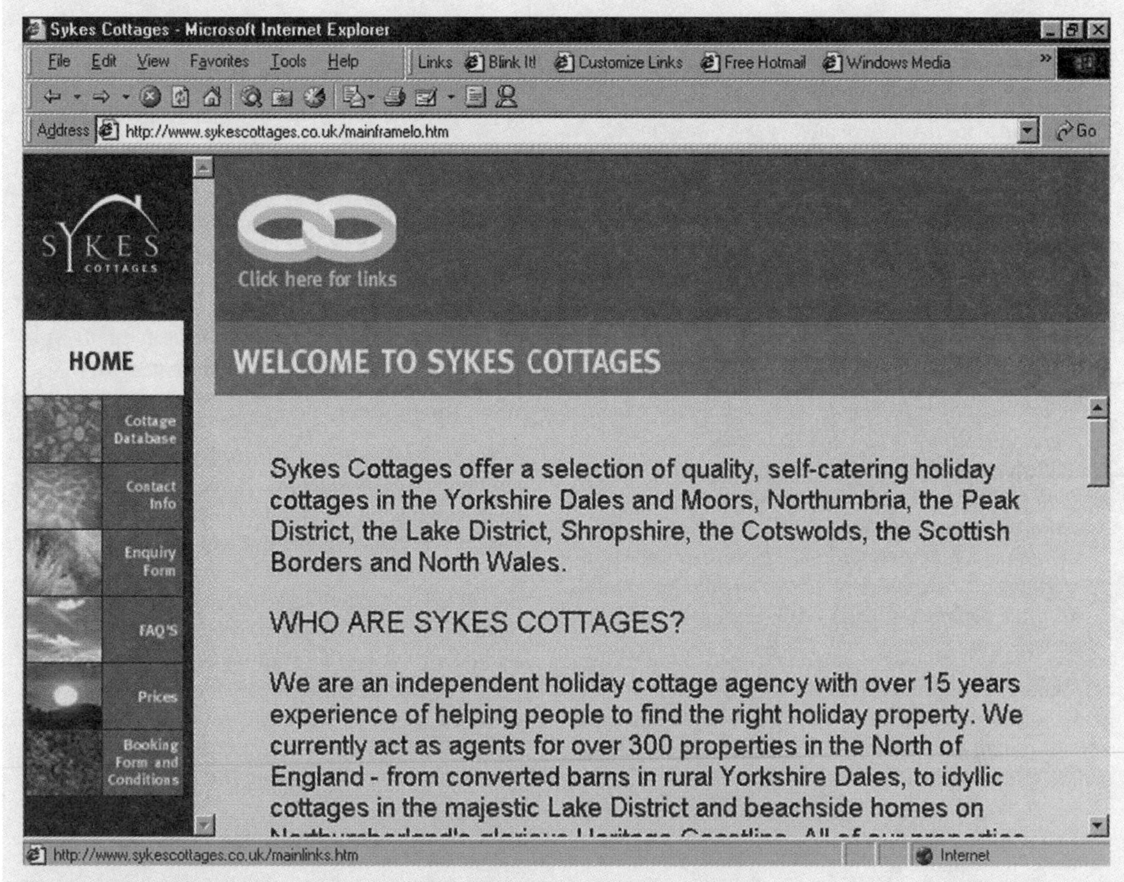

Figure 12.16 Sykes Cottages web site (www.sykescottage.co.uk)

the content and wrote all of that ourselves. We also wanted to keep the site uncluttered and easy to use.

Site maintenance

Referring to maintenance, Clive Sykes says of first attempts at using the site:

They were basically static pages and it was quite a big job to update everything. What we very quickly realised was that as soon as you publish a web site it is out of date. It's like promotional material; we publish in our brochure once a year and it's really frustrating because the day it arrives it's out of date because we have taken on two new cottages. We realised that all our internal systems were on databases and we use a piece of software called Filemaker, which had web publishing capabilities and we wanted to push forward in that direction. We decided we wanted to take control of the web development ourselves, and it was at that stage that we thought it would be great for us to be able to host our databases because then we would be able to update things ourselves very easily.

The process of setting up the web publishing facilities was described as a nightmare:

We tried contacting various people and there were lots of silly quotes about how much it would cost to do those things and it was impossible for us, so we got the help of Business Link.

When the new site went live all the cottage details were on the same database, which is copied on to a database hosted by a London-based company.

Site promotion

Caldwell (2000) reports that Sykes promotes its web site heavily within its printed brochure and gives the

▶ CASE STUDY *continued*

URL prominence in its print advertisements. The owner says:

> *If someone sees our web site advertised in the newspaper on a Sunday afternoon they don't have to phone up for the brochure and wait two days for it to arrive and the moment has gone.*

Site management

Four more extra staff have had to be recruited to deal with extra demand resulting from the staff compared to three originally. One of the main issues is e-mail management. The owner says:

> *What we need to be able to do is pick up the e-mails four or five times a day and deal with them quickly and efficiently to reflect well on our business – but we can't share a mailbox across a network. It is like a call centre in a way. A little thing like that can take months to sort out but someone has written some software to sort that out now. Until you start generating all these e-mails you don't know what your problems are going to be.*

So e-mail communications is seen as important to the success of the online venture. The conversion rate of e-mail enquiries to sales was 25.6 per cent in 2000, compared with a conversion rate of 12 per cent for enquiries generated by its adverts in *The Sunday Times*.

The future

The owner envisages a time in the future when 80 to 90 per cent of the company's business will be conducted either through web or e-mail at some point. But the company is proceeding with caution. Transactional e-commerce will require an increase in the scale of investment. At the time of writing the company does not intend to introduce transactional e-commerce in the form of online bookings in the short term, since it believes it can maintain the personal touch that gives it its competitive edge if the booking process is not entirely automated. The owner sees complications with online bookings. He believes customers might try to pay for a cottage that is not available or pay the wrong amount. About availability he says:

> *Quite a few companies are putting up availability but it doesn't always work in your favour – how would you react if you went onto our web site, looked at a new cottage we had just taken on, looked at the availability for the year and it was completely empty? You would probably wonder what was wrong with it.*

About the future he says:

> *There are a lot of things we are planning to change on our web site at the moment. What we are trying to do now is look at the big picture three or four years down the line. What we don't want to do is make a few quick fixes on our website. We are looking at all our internal systems and databases, and trying to spring clean them and get them working in a way that we could host all of those ultimately on the Internet. That will enable us to have all the info seamless, so when we take a new cottage on we can change it in the database and that changes it on our server, rather than having one that's being hosted and one on our internal systems.*

Source: Article by Tracey Caldwell, *Computing*, 7 July 2000, www.vnu.net

Questions

1. Which measures has Skyes used to assess the success of their web site that are referred to in the article? How do they relate to the framework of *Figure 12.11*? Which are missing?
2. Do you believe the owners' concerns about extending e-commerce services to availability information and online booking are valid? What would you recommend?

Summary

1. Implementation is an iterative process of managing changes involving analysis, design, testing and review as part of an evolutionary prototyping process.
2. Maintenance is a continuous process of monitoring, assessing required changes and then implanting them using evolutionary prototyping.
3. Simple web pages are developed in static HTML. Most e-business systems require

dynamic pages that are implemented using client- and server-side scripting of which the most popular are JavaScript and ASP.

4. Testing has two main objectives, first to check for non-conformance with the business and user requirements, and second to identify bugs or errors. There are many specialized techniques to test either part of the system (component testing) or all of the system (system testing).
5. Changeover has to be managed to include elements of piloting, phased implementation, immediate cutover and parallel running.
6. Content management requires a clearly defined update process and responsibilities according to different types of changes required.
7. Measurement also requires process, responsibilities and also a measurement framework. A suggested framework for sell-side e-commerce assesses channel promotion, channel behaviour, channel satisfaction, channel outcomes and channel profitability.

ACTIVITY ANSWERS

12.1 Risks of e-business implementation

Look again at the expectations for buying a book online. Those where Analysis and Design are important are marked with (A&D), those with implementation with (I). It can be seen that implementation is, of course, important for most of the same issues as A & D since we are testing adequate design:

1. Easy to find what you're looking for by searching or browsing. (A&D) (I)
2. Site easy to use, pages fast to download with no bugs. (A&D) (I)
3. Price, product specification and availability information on site to be correct. (A&D) (I)
4. Specification of date, time and delivery to be possible. (A&D) (I)
5. E-mail notification when order placed and then dispatched. (A&D)
6. Personal data remains personal and private and security is not compromised. (A&D)
7. Verification of address for high value orders
8. Delivery on time
9. Returns policy enabling straightforward return or replacement

Effective e-mail or phone-based customer support for when any of the expectations above aren't met! This means traceability through databases, someone who knows your order status and can solve your problems (A&D)

12.3 Examples of page layout

Answer (at time of writing)

Tables

Yahoo! (www.yahoo.com), Egg (www.egg.com), easyjet (www.easyjet.com), Cisco (www.cisco.com), FT.com (www.ft.com)

Frames

RAC (www.rac.co.uk), Orange (www.orange.co.uk) – since changed to tables, FirstDirect (www.firstdirect.com)

Activity 12.5 Changeover for e-business systems

1. Table 12.9 lists the main variables involved in selection of changeover methods.
2. This activity is intended to show that it is often not a clear-cut decision which changeover method to use and each of the methods may be used in the course of the whole project. For example:
   - During prototyping there is likely to be the use of piloting in one area of the company, for a single country.
   - During the project, even if it involves piloting there is going to be a phased implementation with some modules available before others. Here, the static content of the intranet, or perhaps the address book system will be implemented before the virtual helpdesk.
   - Parallel running occurs during all testing phases, since the old system will still be running with the new nearly complete, but not handling live data. Here, it is likely that initially, perhaps for a month there will be a fallback situation with parallel running of the previous manual method of answering queries.
   - At some point in all projects there is a decision to move entirely to the new system, with the parallel and phased approach this will only occur once the development team is confident in the use of the software.
3. *Table 12.9* also assigns a risk for each variable.

Table 12.9 Differences between changeover techniques

Variables	*Direct (cutover)*	*Parallel*	*Phased*	*Pilot*
1. Cost	Lowest	Highest	Medium–High	Medium
2. Time	Fastest	Slowest	Intermediate	Intermediate
3. Quality of new system after changeover	Highest risk of errors	Potentially best, since don't change to new system until satisfied with its performance	Still has elements of direct – although whole system may not fail, parts can	Better than direct, not as certain as with parallel
4. Impact on customers	Minimal unless major errors encountered	Could reduce service if staff are confused about which system	Can still have problems in new modules	Limits effect to one area until system suitable for rollout
5. Impact on employees	Lowest	More work required to run systems in parallel, but does give confidence about new system	Lower risk than direct	Helps employee buy-in since know system is tested
6. Technical issues	May be only practical method if systems are very different	May require two separate hardware platforms and operating systems to be run in parallel	Not always possible to integrate two systems	–

12.6 Optimizing the content review process at The B2C Company

In one word the answer is empowerment. The only way to increase the speed of the process is to involve fewer staff and this means training them in the skills required for update. In this case the brand manager knows their product sector best, so they have to write the copy and it is best if they have the sole responsibility for creation and review. An additional check by the legal department may be necessary for certain types of changes. Of course we need to set up different reviewing processes according to the size of the changes made.

Activity 12.7 Estimating e-commerce site cost elements

Situation A. Is typical for a start-up company. This situation is often typical for US sites where traffic building expenditure exceeds service and design (in the approximate ratios 5:2:1).
Situation B. Is typical for an existing company. Here, traffic building expenditure is less than service and design (ratio label 1:2:5). This is more typical for a traditional bricks and mortar company that already has a customer base and requires less promotion.

Note that as a rule of thumb it can be said that maintenance of the site may cost between 25 and 50 per cent of the original cost of creating the site – this is important in budgeting.

12.8 Creating a measurement plan for The B2C Company

The following are suggested, but the main issue is for a management team to agree what applies to them

- Promotion – monthly
- Behaviour – daily
- Satisfaction – monthly for customer service aspects, daily for performance aspects
- Outcomes – daily or weekly
- Profitability – weekly or monthly

EXERCISES

Self-assessment questions

1. Summarize how the activities involved with implementation and maintenance relate to analysis and design activities in previous chapters.
2. What are the risks of launching a new e-commerce site if implementation is not conducted effectively?
3. Distinguish between static and dynamic content and methods of achieving them.
4. What are the objectives of testing? How do these relate to an e-commerce site?
5. Summarize the advantages and disadvantages of the different changeover methods.
6. What are the issues for managers of content management?
7. What are the main elements of an e-commerce site measurement plan?
8. What are the elements of a budget for an e-commerce site enhancement?

Essay and discussion questions

1. Write a report to a manager recommending particular techniques that should/should not be implemented on an e-commerce site. Examples may include frames, Flash or shockwave plug-ins, JavaScript, Java and Active Server Pages.
2. Develop a plan for measuring the marketing effectiveness of an e-commerce site.
3. Discuss the balance of using a web site and traditional methods for marketing research.
4. Choose an example of a simple brochureware web site. Develop an implementation plan for this site recommending development techniques that will be used to enhance the site.

Examination questions

1. You are developing a testing plan for an e-commerce site. Outline five key aspects of the site you would test.
2. Data migration is often overlooked in implementation planning. Explain what data migration is and explain when it may need to occur for creation of an e-commerce site for an existing business.
3. Analyse the advantages and disadvantages of a soft versus hard web site launch.
4. Explain the following terms and suggest which is the most useful in measuring the effectiveness of a web site.
   (a) hit
   (b) page impression
   (c) site visit
5. Why are conversion and attrition rates important in evaluating the performance of an e-commerce site?
6. Suggest three key measures that indicate the contribution of an e-commerce site to overall business performance for a company with online and offline presence.

REFERENCES

Barron, D. (2000) *The World of Scripting Languages.* John Wiley & Sons, Chichester, UK.

Bayne, K. (1997) *The Internet Marketing Plan.* John Wiley and Sons, New York.

Bevan, N. (1999) Common Industry Format Usability Tests. *Proceedings of UPA'98, Usability Professionals Association*, Scottsdale, Arizona, 29 June–2 July 1999. Available online at www.usability.serco.com.

Bocij, P., Chaffey, D., Greasley, A. and Hickie, S. (1999) *Business Information Systems. Technology, Development and Management.* FT Management, London.

Burdman, J. (1999) *Collaborative Web Development: Strategies and Best Practices for Web Teams.* Addison-Wesley, Reading, MA.

Caldwell. T. (2000) Case study. Sykes Cottages. *Computing*, 7 July.

Chaffey, D. (2000) Achieving Internet marketing success. *The Marketing Review*, 1(1), 35–60.

Chaffey, D. and Edgar, M. (2000) Measuring online service quality. *Journal of Targeting, Analysis and Measurement for Marketing*, May.

Chaffey, D., Mayer, R., Johnston, K. and Ellis-

Chadwick, F. (2000) *Internet Marketing: Strategy, Implementation and Practice.* Financial Times Prentice Hall, Harlow, UK.

DTI (2000) *Business In The Information Age – International Benchmarking Study 2000.* UK Department of Trade and Industry. Available online at: www.ukonlineforbusiness.gov.uk.

Hanson, W. (2000) *Principles of Internet Marketing.* South Western College Publishing, Cincinnati.

Jorgenson, P. (1995) *Software Testing: a Craftsman's Approach.* CRC Press, Boca Raton, Florida.

Knight, J. (1999) *Computing for Business.* Financial Times, Harlow, UK, 2nd edn.

Kotler, P. (1997) *Marketing Management – Analysis, Planning, Implementation and Control.* Prentice Hall, Englewood Cliffs, NJ.

Lynch, P. and Horton, S. (1999) *Web Style Guide. Basic Design Principles for Creating Web Sites.* Yale University Press.

Obolensky, N. (1994) *Practical Business Re-engineering. Tools and Techniques for Achieving Effective Change.* Kogan Page, London.

FURTHER READING

Barron, D. (2000) *The World of Scripting Languages*. John Wiley & Sons, Chichester, UK. An accessible introduction to scripting languages such as Perl and Javascript.

Deitel, H., Deitel, P. and Nieto, T. (2001) *E-business and E-commerce. How to Program*. Prentice Hall, Upper Saddle River, New Jersey. An excellent guide to creating static and dynamic pages and many other issues of e-business technology also.

Knight, J. (1999) *Computing for Business*, 2nd edn. Financial Times Prentice Hall, Harlow, UK. An introduction to HTML.

WEB LINKS

Internet World news source (www.iw.com): daily news on all aspects of Internet marketing and tools.

Web Reference.com (www.webreference.com): mainly developer news but some good guidelines on e-commerce.

ASP Today (www.asptoday.com): detailed examples for ASP developers.

HTML About.com (html.about.com): portal of HTML resources.

Virgin Biznet (www.virginbiz.net): portal to enable SMEs to move online. Explains stages and tools involved in plain language.

Moonfruit (www.moonfruit.com): flash-based tool for building interactive sites.

Glossary

Archie
A tool important before the advent of the web for storing and searching documents on the Internet. Has largely been superseded by the web which provides better searching and more sophisticated document publishing.

Active Server Pages (ASPs)
A Microsoft-developed technology that can be used for dynamic web pages, often related to database query and retrieval.

Active-X
A programming language standard developed by Microsoft which permits complex and graphical customer applications to be written and then accessed from a web browser. An example might be a form for calculating interest on a loan. A competitor to **Java**.

Activity-based process definition methods
Analysis tools used to identify the relationship between tasks within a business process.

Actors
People, software or other devices that interface with a system. See **use-case**.

Affiliate networks
An e-tailer pays commission on sales referred from other sites.

Agents
Software programs that can assist humans to perform tasks.

Analysis and design
Analysis of system requirements and design for creation of a system.

Analysis for e-business
Using analytical techniques to capture and summarize business and user requirements.

Application server
An application server provides a business application on a server remote from the user.

Application server provider
A provider of business applications such as e-mail, workflow or groupware or any business application on a server remote from the user. A service often offered by ISPs.

Acquisition method
Defines whether the system is purchased outright or developed from scratch.

Asymmetric encryption
Both parties use a related but different key to encode and decode messages.

Attribute
A property or characteristic of an entity, implementation as field, see **database**.

Attrition rate
Percentage of site visitors that are lost at each stage in making a purchase.

Auction
A buying model where traders make **offers** and **bids** to sell or buy under certain conditions.

B2B electronic marketplace
Virtual locations with facilities to enable trading between buyers and sellers.

Backbones
High-speed communications links used to enable Internet communications across a country and internationally.

Balanced scorecard
A framework for setting and monitoring business performance. Metrics are structured according to customer issues, internal efficiency measures, financial measures and innovation.

Bandwidth
Indicates the speed at which data is transferred using a particular network media. It is measured in bits per second (bps).

Bid
A commitment by a trader to *purchase* under certain conditions. See **auction**.

Brand
The sum of the characteristics of a product or service perceived by a user.

Brand equity
The brand's assets (or liabilities) linked to a brand's name and symbol that add to (or subtract from) a service.

Brand identity
The totality of brand associations including name and symbols that must be communicated.

Branding
The process of creating and developing successful brands.

Bricks and mortar
A traditional organization with limited online presence.

Broad and shallow navigation
More choices, fewer clicks to reach required content.

Browser, see **web browsers**.

Burn rate
The speed at which dot-coms spend investors' money.

Business model
A summary of how a company will generate revenue identifying its product offering, value-added services, revenue sources and target customers.

Business-to-business (B2B)
Commercial transactions are between an organization and other organizations.

Business-to-consumer (B2C)
Commercial transactions are between an organization and consumers.

Business alignment IS strategy
The IS strategy is generated from the business strategy through techniques such as CSF analysis.

Business impacting IS strategy
IS strategy analyzes opportunities for new technologies and processes to favourably impact the business strategy.

Business information systems
Information systems used to support the functional areas of business. For example, an organization might use specialized information systems to support sales, marketing and human resource management activities.

Business process automation (BPA)
Automating existing ways of working manually through information technology.

Business process improvement (BPI)
Optimizing existing processes typically coupled with enhancements in information technology.

Business process reengineering (BPR)
Identifying radical, new ways of carrying out business operations, often enabled by new IT capabilities.

Business rule
A rule defines the actions that need to occur in a business when a particular situation arises. For example, a business rule may state that if a customer requests credit and they have a history of defaulting on payments, then credit will not be issued. A business rule is broken down into an event which triggers a rule with test conditions which result in defined actions.

Buy-side e-commerce
E-commerce transactions between a purchasing organization, its suppliers and partners.

Catalogues
Structured listing of registered sites in different categories.

ccTLD
There are also some 250 country code top-level **domains** (ccTLD).

Certificate and certificate authorities (CAs)
A certificate is a valid copy of a public key of an individual or organization together with identification information. It is issued by a trusted third party (TTP) or certificate authority (CA). CAs make public keys available and also issue private keys.

CGI (Common Gateway Interface)
CGI offers a way of providing interactivity through the web.

Change management
Managing process, structural, technical, staff and culture change within an organization.

Changeover
The term used to describe moving from the old information system to the new information system.

Client/server
The client/server architecture consists of **client** computers such as PCs sharing resources such as a database stored on more powerful **server** computers.

Client-side scripting
Scripts executed on the browser.

'Clicks and mortar'
A business combining an online and offline presence.

Clicks only or Internet pureplay
An organization principally with an online presence.

Client/server model
A system architecture in which end-user machines such as PCs known as clients run applications while accessing data and possibly programs from a server.

Collaborative filtering
Profiling of customer interest coupled with delivery of specific information and offers, often based on the interests of similar customers.

Community
A customer-to-customer interaction delivered via e-mail groups, web-based discussion forums or chat.

Competitor analysis for e-business
Review of e-business services offered by existing and new competitors and adoption by their customers.

Content
Content is the design, text and graphical information which forms a web page. Good content is the key to attracting customers to a web site and retaining their interest or achieving repeat visits.

Convergence
A trend in which different hardware devices such as TVs, computers and phones merge and have similar functions.

Conversion rate
Percentage of site visitors that perform a particular action such as making a purchase.

Cookies
Cookies are small text files stored on an end-user's computer to enable web sites to identity them.

Countermediation
Creation of a new intermediary by an established company.

Core competencies
Resources, including skills or technologies that provide a particular benefit to customers.

CPM
Cost for advertising is specified as CPM or cost per thousand page impressions.

Culture
This concept includes shared values, unwritten rules and assumptions within the organization as well as the practices that all groups share. Corporate cultures are created when a group of employees interact over time and are relatively successful in what they undertake.

Customer acquisition
Techniques used to gain new customers.

Customer extension
Techniques to encourage customers to increase their involvement with an organization.

Customer-to-business (C2B)
Customer is proactive in making an offer to a business, e.g. the price they are prepared to pay for an airline ticket.

Customer-to-customer (C2C)
Interactions between customers on a web site, e.g. posting/reading of topics on an electronic bulletin board.

Customer orientation
Developing site content and services to appeal to different customer segments or other members of the audience.

Customer profile
Information that can be used to segment a customer.

Customer relationship management (CRM)
An approach to building and sustaining long-term business with customers.

Customer retention
Techniques to maintain relationships with existing customers.

Customer selection
Picking the ideal customers for acquisition, retention and extension.

Customer value
Dependent on product quality, service quality, price and fulfilment time.

Data migration
Transfer of data from old systems to new systems.

Data mining
This involves searching organizational databases in order to uncover hidden patterns or relationships in groups of data. Data mining software attempts to represent information in new ways so that previously unseen patterns or trends can be identified.

Data modelling
Data modelling involves considering how to represent data objects within a system, both logically and physically. The entity relationship diagram is used to model the data.

Data warehouses
Data warehouses are large database systems (often measured in gigabytes or terabytes) containing detailed company data on sales transactions which are analysed to assist in improving the marketing and financial performance of companies.

Database
A database can be defined as a collection of related information. The information held in the database is stored in an organized way so that specific items can be selected and retrieved quickly. See **database management system**.

Database management system (DBMS)
The information held in an electronic database is accessed via a database management system. A DBMS can be defined as one or more computer programs that allow users to enter, store, organize, manipulate and retrieve data from a database. For many users, the terms *database* and *database management system* are interchangeable. A *Relational Database Management System (RDBMS)* is an extension of a DBMS and allows data to be combined from a variety of sources.

Decision support system
Decision support systems provide managers with information needed to support semi-structured or unstructured decisions.

Dedicated server
Server only contains content and applications for a single company.

Deep linking
Jakob Nielsen's term for a user arriving at a site deep within its structure.

Demand analysis for e-business
Assessment of the demand for e-commerce services amongst existing and potential customer segments.

Demographic characteristics
Variations in attributes of the populations such as age, sex and social class.

Deployment plan
A deployment plan is a schedule which defines all the tasks that need to occur in order for changeover to occur successfully. This includes putting all the infrastructure in place such as cabling and hardware.

Development environment
Software and hardware used to create a system.

Differential advantage
A desirable attribute of a product offering that is not currently matched by competitor offerings.

Digital certificates (keys)
Consist of keys made up of large numbers that are used to uniquely identify individuals.

Digital signatures
A method of identifying individuals or companies using public key encryption.

Disintermediation
The removal of intermediaries such as distributors or brokers that formerly linked a company to its customers.

Disruptive technologies
New technologies that prompt businesses to reappraise their strategic approaches.

Directories or catalogues
Structured listing of registered sites in different categories such as Yahoo! categories.

Document Object Model (DOM)
Enables developers to get and set properties of

different document (web page) objects such as forms and frames.

Downstream supply chain
Transactions between an organization and its customers and intermediaries, equivalent to sell-side e-commerce.

Domain names
The domain name refers to the name of the web server and is usually selected to be the same as the name of the company and the extension will indicate its type. The extension is known as the global top level domain (gTLD). There are also some 250 country code top-level domains (ccTLD).

Dot-coms
Businesses whose main trading presence is on the Internet.

Dynamic web page
A page that is created in real time, often with reference to a database query, in response to a user request.

Early adopter
Companies or departments that invest in new technologies and techniques.

Efficient consumer response (ECR)
A model for retail logistics to achieve rapid restocking in line with customer needs.

Electronic business (e-business)
All electronically mediated information exchanges, both within an organization and with external stakeholders supporting the range of business processes.

Electronic business (e-business) infrastructure
The hardware and software architecture necessary to achieve electronic communications within a business and with its partners.

Electronic business (e-business) strategy
Definition of the approach by which applications of internal and external electronic communications can support and influence corporate strategy.

Electronic commerce (e-commerce)
All electronically mediated information exchanges between an organization and its external stakeholders. See **sell-side** and **buy-side e-commerce**.

Electronic data interchange (EDI)
The exchange, using digital media, of structured business information, particularly for sales transactions such as purchase orders and invoices between buyers and sellers.

Electronic funds transfer (EFT)
Automated digital transmissions of money between organizations and banks.

Electronic government (e-government)
The use of Internet technologies to provide government services to citizens.

Electronic mail (e-mail)
Sending messages or documents, such as news about a new product or sales promotion between individuals. A primitive form of 'push' channel. See **inbound, outbound e-mail**.

Electronic marketing (e-marketing)
Achieving marketing objectives through use of electronic communications technology.

Electronic marketing (e-marketing) plan
A plan to achieve the marketing objectives of the e-business strategy.

Electronic marketplace
A virtual marketplace such as the Internet in which no direct contact occurs between buyers and sellers.

Electronic procurement (e-procurement)
The electronic integration and management of all procurement activities including purchase request, authorization, ordering, delivery and payment between a purchaser and a supplier.

Electronic procurement systems (EPSs)
An electronic system used to automate all or part of the procurement function by enabling the scanning, storage and retrieval of invoices and other documents; management of approvals; routing of authorization requests; interfaces to other finance systems; and matching of documents to validate transactions.

Emergent strategy
Strategic analysis, strategic development and strategy implementation are interrelated and are developed together.

Electronic tokens
Units of digital currency that is in a standard electronic format.

Encryption, see **asymmetric encryption** and **symmetric encryption.**

Enterprise resource planning applications (ERP)
Software providing integrated functions for major business functions such as production, distribution, sales, finance and human resource management.

Entity
A grouping of related data, example customer entity. Implementation as table.

Environmental scanning and analysis
The process of continuously monitoring the environment and events and responding accordingly.

Events and even handlers
An event handler monitors and responds to events such as a mouse click.

Exchange, see **B2B electronic marketplace.**

Explicit knowledge
Knowledge that can be readily expressed and recorded within information systems.

Extranet
Formed by extending the intranet beyond a company to customers, suppliers and collaborators.

Financial EDI
Aspect of electronic payment mechanism involving transfer of funds from the bank of a buyer to a seller. See **EDI**.

Field
Attributes of products, example date of birth. See **database.**

Firewall
A specialized software application mounted on a server at the point the company is connected to the Internet. Its purpose is to prevent unauthorized access into the company from outsiders.

Form validation
Used to check the validity of online form inputs from users.

FTP file transfer
The File Transfer Protocol is used as a standard for moving files across the Internet. FTP is available as a feature of web browsers that is used for marketing applications such as downloading files such as product price lists or specifications. Also used to update HTML files on web pages.

GIF (Graphics Interchange Format)
A graphics format and compression algorithm best used for simple graphics.

gTLDs are part of a domain name:
- .com represents an international or American company such as www.travelagency.com
- .co.uk represents a company based in the UK such as www.thomascook.co.uk
- ac.uk is a UK-based university (e.g.www.derby.ac.uk)
- org.uk or .org are not-for-profit organizations (e.g. www.greenpeace.org)
- .net is a network provider such as www.virgin.net

Gbps
(One gigabit per second or 1,000,000,000 bps, fibre-optic or satellite links operate at Gbsps)

Globalization
The increase of international trading and shared social and cultural values.

Gophers
A tool important before the advent of the web for storing and searching documents on the Internet. Has largely been superseded by the web which provides better searching and more sophisticated document publishing.

Governance
Control of the operation and use of the Internet.

Hacker
Hackers are often described as individuals who seek to break into systems as a test of their abilities. Few hackers attempt to cause damage to the systems they access and few are interested in gaining some sort of financial profit.

Hardware
Describes the physical components of a computer system. The hardware of a computer system can be said to consist of: input devices, memory, central processing unit, output devices and storage devices.

Hit
Recorded for each graphic or text file requested from a web server. It is not a reliable measure for the number of people viewing a page.

HTML (Hypertext Markup Language)
HTML is a standard format used to define the text and layout of web pages. HTML files usually have the extension .HTML or .HTM.

HTML parameters
These occur within the tags to specify particular characteristics of the HTML statement.

HTML tags
Markup codes denoted by the symbol <start code> and </end code> that instructs the browser to format information or perform a particular operation.

HTTP (Hypertext Transfer Protocol)
HTTP or Hypertext Transfer Protocol is a standard which defines the way information is transmitted across the Internet between web browsers and web servers.

Hub, see B2B electronic marketplace.

Hyperlink
A method of moving between one web site page and another, indicated to the user by an image or text highlighted by underlining and/or a different colour.

Implementation
The creation of a system based on analysis and design documentation.

Implementation activities
The creation of the system modules by coding and scripting, module integration and testing and changeover to the live system.

Inbound e-mail
E-mail received from outside the organization such as customer and supplier enquiries.

Inbound logistics
The management of material resources entering an organization from its suppliers and other partners.

Infomediary
A business whose main source of revenue derives from capturing consumer information and developing detailed profiles of individual customers for use by third parties.

Information
Data that has been processed so that it is meaningful.

Information organization schemes
The structure chosen to group and categorize information.

Information system
A system designed to produce information that can be used to support the activities of managers and other workers.

Initiation
The start-up phase of the project.

Intelligent agents
Software programs that can assist humans to perform tasks.

Intermediary
An organization or e-commerce site that typically brings buyers and sellers together.

Interactive digital TV (iDTV, DITV)
TV that enables interaction with viewers through handset or keyboard.

Internet
The Internet refers to the physical network that links computers across the globe. It consists of the infrastructure of network servers and communication links between them that are used to hold and transport information between the client PCs and web servers.

Internet EDI
Use of **EDI** data standards delivered across non-proprietary IP networks.

Internet pureplay
An organization principally with an online presence.

Internet Relay Chat (IRC)
This is a synchronous communications tool which allows a text-based 'chat' between different users who are logged on at the same time. Of limited use for marketing purposes.

Internet Service Provider (ISP)
A provider enabling home or business users a connection to access the Internet. They can also host web-based applications.

Interruption marketing
Marketing communications that disrupt customers' activities.

Intranet
A private network within a single company using Internet standards to enable employees to share information using e-mail and web publishing.

IP address
The unique numerical address of a computer.

Java
A programming language standard supported by Sun Microsystems which permits complex and graphical customer applications to be written and then accessed from a web browser. An example might be a form for calculating interest on a loan. A competitor to **Active-X.**

JavaScript
A web page scripting language that uses an object model.

JPEG (Joint Photographics Experts Group)
A graphics format and compression algorithm best used for photographs.

Kbps
One kilobit per second or 1,000 bps (a modem operates at up to 56.6kbps).

Key, see **primary key** and **secondary key** or **digital certificates, encryption.**

Knowledge
Applying experience to problem solving.

Knowledge management
Techniques and tools for disseminating knowledge within an organization.

Lead, see **qualified lead.**

Life time value (LTV)
The combined revenue attributable to a customer during their relationship with a company.

Log file, see **transaction log files**
A web server file that records all page requests.

Log-file analyser
A log-file analyser is a separate program such as Webtrends that is used to summarize the information on customer activity contained in a log file.

Logistics, see **inbound logistics** and **outbound logistics.**

Maintenance activities
Involve measurement of system effectiveness and updating in response to maintain competitiveness.

Maintenance phase
Commences after the system is live.

Marketing concept
The management of the range of organizational activities that impact on the customer as part of marketing.

Marketing orientation
Meeting customer requirements through the coordination of all organizational activities that impact the customer.

Marketplace, see **B2B electronic marketplace.**

Mass customization
Delivering customized content to groups of users through web pages or e-mail.

Mbps
One megabit per second or 1,000,000 bps (company networks operate at 10 or more Mbps).

Metamediaries
Third parties that provide a single point of contact and deliver a range of services between customers and suppliers.

Meta tags
Key words that are part of an HTML page that result in a higher search listing if they match the typed keyword.

Micropayments
Small denomination payments.

Middleware
Software used to facilitate communication between business applications including data transfer control.

Milestone
Key deadline to be achieved during project, usually with defined deliverable.

Mixed-mode buying
The process by which customer changes

between online and offline channels during the buying process.

MRO goods
Maintenance, repairs and operations of manufacturing facilities.

Narrow and deep navigation
Fewer choices, more clicks to reach required content.

Navigation scheme
Tools provided to the user to move between different information on a web site.

Newsgroup, see **Usenet newsgroup.**

Offer
A commitment by a trader to *see* under certain conditions. See **auction**.

Offline marketing communications
Internet-based techniques used to generate web site traffic.

Online marketing communications
Traditional techniques such as print and TV advertising used to generate web site traffic.

Online promotion contribution
An assessment of the proportion of customers (new or retained) who use the online information sources and are influenced as a result.

Online Value Proposition (OVP)
A statement of the benefits of e-commerce services that ideally should not be available in competitor offerings or offline offerings.

Online revenue contribution (ORC)
An assessment of the direct contribution of the Internet or other digital media to sales, usually expressed as a percentage of overall sales revenue.

Opt-in
A customer proactively agrees to receive further information.

Opt-out
A customer declines the offer to receive further information.

Outbound e-mail
E-mail sent from the company to other organizations.

Online or Internet revenue contribution
An assessment of the direct or indirect contribution of the Internet to sales, usually expressed as a percentage of overall sales revenue.

Outbound logistics
The management of resources supplied from an organization to its customers and intermediaries such as retailers and distributors.

Outsourcing
Contracting of functional tasks to a third party.

Packet
Each Internet message such as an e-mail or http request is broken down into smaller parts for ease of transmission.

Page impression (view)
A more reliable measure than a hit denoting one person viewing one page.

Payment systems
Methods of transferring funds from a customer to a merchant.

Perl
Practical Execution and Report language used mainly for server side scripting and producing CGI scripts.

Permission marketing
Customers agree (opt-in) to be involved in an organization's marketing activities, usually as a result of an incentive.

Personalization
Delivering individualized content through web pages or e-mail.

Positioning
Influencing the customer's perception of a product within a marketplace.

Prescriptive strategy
The three core areas of strategic analysis, strategic development and strategy implementation are linked together sequentially.

Production or live environment
Software and hardware used to host operational system.

Prototypes
A prototype is a preliminary version of part, or

a framework for all parts, of an e-business solution that can be reviewed by its target audience and the business project team.

Prototyping
Prototyping is an iterative process whereby web site users suggest modifications before further prototypes and the live version of the site are developed.

Psychographic segmentation
A breakdown of customers according to different characteristics.

Push channel
Information is broadcast over the Internet or an intranet and received using a web browser or special program for which a subscription to this channel has been set up. This technique is still used for automated software distribution, but has not proved popular as a method for accessing web content by users.

Plug-ins
An add-on program to a web browser providing extra functionality such as animation.

Portal
A web site that acts as a gateway to information and services available on the Internet by providing search engines, directories and other services such as personalized news or free e-mail.

Primary key
The field that uniquely identifies each record in a table. See **database**.

Private key, see **encryption**.

Process
Part of a system that has a clearly defined purpose or objective and clearly defined inputs and outputs.

Productivity paradox
Research results indicating a poor correlation between organizational investment in information systems and organizational performance measured by return on equity.

Public key, see **encryption**.

Pull supply chain
An emphasis on using the supply chain to deliver value to customers who are actively involved in product and service specification.

Push supply chain
A supply chain that emphasizes distribution of a product to passive customers.

Qualified lead
Contact information for a customer and an indication of their propensity to purchase different products.

Reciprocal links
An exchange of links between two site owners.

Record
A collection of fields for one instance of an entity, example Customer Smith. See **database**.

Referrer
The site that a visitor previously visited before following a link.

Reintermediation
The creation of new intermediaries between customers and suppliers providing services such as supplier search and product evaluation.

Relationship
Describes how different tables are linked. See **database**.

Resource analysis
Review of the technological, financial and human resources of an organization and how they are utilized in business processes.

Revenue models
Describe methods of generating income for an organization.

Risk management
Evaluating potential risks, developing strategies to reduce risks and learning about future risks.

Robots
Automated tools known as spiders or robots index registered sites. Users search this by typing keywords into a search engine and are presented with a list of pages.

Scenario
A particular path or flow of events or activities within a use case.

Search engines
Automated tools known as spiders or robots

index registered sites. Users use search engine by typing keywords and are presented with a list of ranked pages from the index.

Searching behaviours
Approaches to finding information vary from directed to undirected.

Scripting languages
A software standard providing a set of instructions to perform a particular task.

Secondary key
A field that is used to link tables, by linking to a primary key in another table. See **database**.

Secure Electronic Transaction (SET)
A standard for public-key encryption intended to enable secure e-commerce transactions lead-developed by Mastercard and Visa.

Secure Sockets Layer (SSL)
A commonly used encryption technique for scrambling data as it is passed across the Internet from a customer's web browser to a merchant's web server.

Segmentation
Identification of different groups within a target market in order to develop different offerings for the groups.

Sell-side e-commerce
E-commerce transactions between a supplier organization and its customers.

Server, see **web servers**.

Server-side scripting
Scripts executed on the server.

Service level agreements
A contractual specification of service standards a contractor must meet.

Share of wallet or share of customer
The proportion of customer expenditure in a particular category that belongs to a single customer.

Site navigation scheme
Tools provided to the user to move between different information on a web site.

Software (intelligent) agents
Software programs that can assist humans to perform tasks.

Soft launch
A preliminary site launch with limited promotion to provide initial feedback and testing of an e-commerce site.

Software
A series of detailed instructions that control the operation of a computer system. Software exists as programs that are developed by computer programmers.

SPAM
Unsolicited e-mail (usually bulk mailed and untargeted).

Spamming
Bulk e-mailing of unsolicited mail.

Spiders
Automated tools known as spiders or robots index registered sites. Users search by typing keywords and are presented with a list of pages.

Static web page
A page on the web server that is invariant.

Stickiness
An indication of how long a visitor stays on a site.

Strategic analysis
Collection and review of information about an organization's internal processes and resources and external marketplace factors in order to inform strategy definition.

Strategic objectives
Statement and communication of an organization's mission, vision and objectives.

Strategy
Definition of the future direction and actions of a company defined as approaches to achieve specific objectives. See **prescriptive** and **emergent**.

Strategy definition
Formulation, review and selection of strategies to achieve strategic objectives.

Strategy implementation
Planning, actions and controls needed to achieve strategic goals.

Strategy process model
A framework for approaching strategy development.

Streaming media
Sound and video that can be experienced within a web browser before the whole clip is downloaded.

Supply chain management (SCM)
The coordination of all supply activities of an organization from its suppliers and partners to its customers. See **upstream** and **downstream**.

Supply chain network
The links between an organization and all partners involved with multiple supply chains.

Supply chain visibility
Access to up-to-date, accurate, relevant information about supply chains process to different stakeholders.

Symmetric encryption
Both parties to a transaction use the same key to encode and decode messages.

System
A system can be defined as a collection of interrelated components that work together towards a collective goal.

System design
Defines how an information system will operate.

Systems development lifecycle
The sequence in which a system is created from initiation, analysis, design, implementation, build and maintenance.

Systems integrator
A company that organizes the procurement and installation of hardware and software needed for implementation.

Systems software
This form of software manages and controls the operation of the computer system as it performs tasks on behalf of the user.

Table
Each database comprises several tables. See **database**.

Tagging
Tracking of origin of site visitors and their spending patterns.

Talk-through
A user verbally describes his or her required actions.

Task analysis
Identification of different tasks, their sequence and how they are broken down.

TCP/IP
The Transmission Control Protocol is a transport layer protocol that moves data between applications. The Internet protocol is a network layer protocol that moves data (**packets**) across networks.

Telnet
This allows remote access to computer systems. For example a retailer could check to see whether an item was in stock in a warehouse using a telnet application.

Test environment
Separate software and hardware used to test a system.

Test specification
A description of the testing process and tests to be performed.

Testing
Aims to identify non-conformance in the requirements specification and errors.

Thin client
An end-user device (terminal) where computing requirements such as processing and storage (and so cost) are minimized.

Three-tier client/server
The first tier is the client that handles display, second is application logic and business rules, the third tier is database storage.

Trading hub, see **B2B electronic marketplace**.

Transaction log files
A web server file that records all page requests.

Transaction processing systems (TPS)
Transaction processing systems (TPS) manages the frequent external and internal transactions such as orders for goods and services which serve the operational level of the organization.

Uniform (universal) resource locators (URL)
A web address used to locate a web page on a web server.

Upstream supply chain
Transactions between an organization and its

suppliers and intermediaries, equivalent to buy-side e-commerce.

Use-case
The sequence of transactions between an actor and a system that support the activities of the actor.

Use-case modelling
A user-centred approach to modelling system requirements.

Unified Modelling Language (UML)
A language used to specify, visualize and document the artefacts of an object-oriented system.

Usenet newsgroups
A widely used electronic bulletin board used to discuss a particular topic such as sport, hobby or business area. Traditionally accessed by special newsreader software, can now be accessed via a web browser from www.deja.com.

User-centred design
Design based on optimizing the user experience according to all factors, including the user interface, which affects this.

Validation
This is a test of the design where we check that the design fulfils the requirements of the business users which are defined in the requirements specification.

Value chain
A model for analysis of how supply chain activities can add value to products and services delivered to the customer.

Value network
The links between an organization and its strategic and non-strategic partners that form its external value chain.

Value stream
The combination of actions required to deliver value to the customer as products and services.

Vertical integration
The extent to which supply chain activities are undertaken and controlled *within* the organization.

Viral marketing
E-mail is used to transmit a promotional message to another potential customer.

Virtual Added Network (VAN)
A secure wide-area network that uses proprietary rather than Internet technology.

Virtual integration
The majority of supply chain activities are undertaken and controlled *outside* the organization by third parties.

Virtual organization
An organization which uses information and communications technology to allow it to operate without clearly defined physical boundaries between different functions. It provides customized services by outsourcing production and other functions to third parties.

Virtualization
The process of a company developing more of the characteristics of the virtual organization.

Virtual Private Networks (VPN)
A secure, encrypted (tunnelled) connection between two points using the Internet, typically created by ISPs for organizations wanting to conduct secure Internet trading.

WAIS
A tool important before the advent of the web for storing and searching documents on the Internet. Has largely been superseded by the web which provides better searching and more sophisticated document publishing.

Walkthrough
A user executes their actions through using a system or mock-up.

Web address, see **URL**.

Web browsers
Browsers such as Microsoft Internet Explorer provide an easy method of accessing and viewing information stored as web documents on different servers.

Web page, see **static web page**, **dynamic web page** and **web server**.

Web servers
Store and present the web pages accessed by web browsers.

Wireless Application Protocol (WAP)
WAP is a technical standard for transferring

information to wireless devices, such as mobile phones.

Wireless Markup Language (WML)
Standard for displaying mobile pages such transferred by WAP.

World Wide Web (WWW)
The most common technique for publishing information on the Internet. It is accessed through web browsers which display web pages of embedded graphics and HTML/XML encoded text.

Workflow management
Workflow management (WFM) is the automation of information flows and provides tools for processing the information according to a set of procedural rules.

XML or **eXtensible Markup Language**
A standard for transferring structured data unlike HTML which is purely presentational.

Index

Note: when a phrase is best known by its acronym, this is given first.

T

U

V

W

X